74.95

W9-ALW-911

SCHOOL FINANCE

A Policy Perspective

SECOND EDITION

ALLAN R. ODDEN
University of Wisconsin—Madison

LAWRENCE O. PICUS
University of Southern California

Boston   Burr Ridge, IL   Dubuque, IA   Madison, WI   New York   San Francisco   St. Louis
Bangkok   Bogotá   Caracas   Lisbon   London   Madrid
Mexico City   Milan   New Delhi   Seoul   Singapore   Sydney   Taipei   Toronto

McGraw-Hill Higher Education

A Division of The **McGraw-Hill** *Companies*

SCHOOL FINANCE
A POLICY PERSPECTIVE, SECOND EDITION

Copyright © 2000, 1992 by The McGraw-Hill Companies, Inc. All rights reserved. Printed in the United States of America. Except as permitted under the United States Copyright Act of 1976, no part of this publication may be reproduced or distributed in any form or by any means, or stored in a data base or retrieval system, without the prior written permission of the publisher.

This book is printed on acid-free paper.

1 2 3 4 5 6 7 8 9 0 QPF/QPF 0 9 8 7 6 5 4 3 2 1 0

ISBN 0–07–228737–3

Editorial director: *Jane E. Vaicunas*
Sponsoring editor: *Beth Kaufman*
Developmental editor: *Cara Harvey*
Marketing manager: *Daniel M. Loch*
Project manager: *Jill R. Peter*
Production supervisor: *Sandy Ludovissy*
Coordinator of freelance design: *Rick Noel*
Compositor: *ElectraGraphics, Inc.*
Typeface: *10/12 Caledonia*
Printer: *Quebeor Printing Book Group/Fairfield, PA*

Cover designer: *Sean M. Sullivan*
Interior designer: *Sheilah Barrett*

Library of Congress Cataloging-in-Publication Data

Odden, Allan.
    School finance: a policy perspective / Allan R. Odden, Lawrence
O. Picus.—2nd ed.
      p.   cm.
    Includes bibliographical references (p.   ) and index.
    ISBN 0–07–228737–3
    1. Education—United States—Finance. 2. Education—United
States—Finance—Computer simulation. I. Picus, Larry, 1954– .
II. Title.
LB2825.0315   2000   99–15558
379.1′21′0973—dc21   CIP

www.mhhe.com

Contents

Preface

Public school financing in the United States is a big business; it involved over $300 billion, 47 million children, and nearly 5 million teachers, administrators, and staff in 1999. School finance has and continues to be a top-priority policy issue at the state and local levels, and one of the top issues the public identifies as needing attention at the national level as well. Further, both adequacy of funding in general and the productivity of the use of education dollars in particular are the issues that are leading school finance policy deliberations today.

In this second edition of *School Finance: A Policy Perspective,* we continue the emphasis of the first edition on the use of education dollars and the need to use current and all new dollars on more effective programs and services, in short to improve the productivity of the education system. Our goals in the second edition are to update the material in the first edition, and to provide a discussion of recent research in school finance, including how: the push for education adequacy, the need to meet high and rigorous educational standards, resource allocation and use for higher performance, site-based management of schools, and teacher compensation might impact the funding for our nation's schools in the early years of the next century. The book also includes a revised and enhanced school finance simulation that enables students, professors and researchers to use the World Wide Web (http://www.mhhe.com/schoolfinance) to simulate the effects of different school finance structures on both a 20-district sample of districts and universe state data sets. E-mail education@mhhe.com to obtain the password to the simulation.

The second edition has four major sections:

- an introduction, which provides an overview for the issues subsequently addressed,
- four chapters on equity and adequacy for districts, schools, and students, including state case studies of school finance problems and their resolution,
- three chapters on issues related to improving the productivity and effectiveness of the education system, and
- three chapters on the finance aspects of policy and management innovations designed to improve the country's public schools.

1. INTRODUCTION AND OVERVIEW

Chapter 1 serves as an introduction to the topic of school finance. It begins with information on the current status of funding for public K–12 education in the United States, showing how much is spent, the source of those funds, and how levels and sources of funding have changed over time. It shows that as a nation, we spend a great deal of money on K–12 education and that the amount we spend has grown considerably over time. Chapter 1 also discusses the manner in which school finance inequities have changed over the last 30 years. The chapter discusses the "traditional" school finance inequities in several states. In these states, districts with lower property wealth per pupil tend to have lower expenditures per pupil—even with higher school tax rates—than do districts with higher per-pupil property wealth. These high-wealth districts tend to have higher per-pupil expenditures even with lower school tax rates.

The chapter then shows that several states today have what the book terms the "new" school finance problem: higher wealth districts with higher expenditures per pupil but also higher tax rates, and lower property wealth per-pupil districts with lower expenditures per pupil but also lower school tax rates. The chapter suggests that remedying these different types of fiscal inequities might require very different school finance reform strategies. Finally the chapter discusses briefly how the issue of "adequacy" has entered the school finance policy agenda.

2. EQUITY IN SCHOOL FINANCE: PROBLEMS, ISSUES, FRAMEWORKS, AND NEW APPROACHES

Chapter 2 addresses frameworks for assessing school finance problems and challenges. It first modifies the Berne and Stiefel (1984) equity framework that was used in the first edition of the text, adding a discussion of such issues as ex ante versus ex post equity perspectives, the unit of analysis, and various elements of equity including the group, the object, and different measures of horizontal and vertical equity. The chapter includes a new horizontal equity statistic, the Verstegen Index, which measures the variation in the top half of the distribution, compared to the McLoone Index, which assesses the equity of the bottom half. The chapter also adds the concept of adequacy to the overall framework and presents an adequacy statistic, the Odden-Picus Adequacy Index.

The second half of Chapter 2 reviews the evolution of school finance court cases, from the initial *Serrano* v. *Priest* decision, through the adequacy cases in the mid- to late 1990s, to the hoped-for final, 1998 decision of the New Jersey Supreme Court in that state's 25-year-long legal battle over the equity and adequacy of its school finance system.

Chapter 3 reviews the public finance context for school finance, analyzing the base, yield, elasticity, equity, and adequacy of income, sales, and property taxes as revenue sources for public schools. It discusses mechanisms to improve the incidence of the property tax, and reviews the various property tax limitations states have enacted on this primary public school revenue source. This chapter also updates the material in Chapter 4 of the first edition, focusing on how grants from one level of government to another impact decision making in the recipient government.

Chapter 4 describes the core elements of state school finance formulas: base allocations provided through flat grant, foundation, guaranteed tax base (district power equalizing and percentage equalizing) and combination formulas, and adjustments for differences related to special needs of students, schools, and districts. The chapter describes these various elements and discusses generally how they work, using a 20-district sample in a new computer simulation program. The focus of this chapter is on how different school finance formulas work (i.e., their costs and their effects on horizontal and vertical equity, as well as adequacy). The chapter includes a discussion of three different methods for determining an "adequate" base spending level—costing out inputs, linking a spending level to a performance level, and costing out effective school designs.

Chapter 4 also discusses the rationales for and types of adjustments for three categories of special-needs children: those from low-income backgrounds, those with physical and mental disabilities, and those with limited English proficiency. The portion on disabilities draws heavily from the work conducted by the National Center on Special Education Finance. In addition, the chapter discusses various rationales for different adjustments for students at different education levels (elementary, middle, and high school) and adjustments for price differences across states and geographical regions within states (Chambers, 1995; McMahon, 1994). The chapter further discusses the issue of scale economies and describes different ways states adjust for small/large size or rural isolation.

Chapter 4 also includes a section on new economic-oriented research using the cost-function approach to determine a level of funding needed in each district/school in a state to produce a set level of outcomes, given different characteristics of students and the local community. This research provides a number that can be used as the foundation spending level, and then a global "cost adjustment" is applied to the foundation amount that accounts for differences in student need, input prices, scale, and even efficiency.

Chapter 5 uses the analytic tools identified in Chapter 4 to "solve" different kinds of school finance problems, using universe district data from three states representing different kinds of school finance situations. This chapter uses the simulation program, available on the web page of McGraw Hill (www.mhhe.com/schoolfinance), adapted for individual states. Over time, this web site should have data sets for all or nearly all of the 50 states.

The Vermont state data set discussed in Chapter 5 presents the traditional school finance problem of unequal distribution of funds due to the unequal distribution of wealth. The chapter shows how traditional school finance models can be used to increase horizontal equity, fiscal neutrality, adequacy, and adjustments for different student needs.

The Wisconsin state data set presents the "new" finance problem. In this instance, the wealthiest districts are relatively high spending but also have relatively high tax rates, while the poorest districts tend to be low spending as well as exert low tax efforts. The chapter shows how GTB programs exacerbate fiscal equity for such a state and identifies alternative school finance mechanisms to improve equity and adequacy.

The Illinois state data present a finance situation that is not only tricky to resolve but also requires substantial additional resources both on adequacy and property tax–reduction grounds.

The goal in Chapter 5 is to show how various elements of school finance structures can be used to resolve different types of school finance problems. For each state, the chapter includes both an analysis of the kind of school finance problem that the state presents and the effectiveness or ineffectiveness of different school finance formulas in resolving the problem.

One of the problems often encountered in school finance is that funding formulas are either established in a vacuum, or their parameters are the result of available dollars. In the context of the above state cases, this chapter uses policy "targets" to help remedy the school finance problems identified. For example, a state might decide that it wants to provide a certain minimum level of support for all schools equal to 90 percent of the average spending of a certain type of district. Or alternatively, policymakers may feel that all districts should have access to funds equal to the district at some fixed percentage of wealth. The simulation is used to help students understand and determine logical policy targets and to assess their impact on the school finance problems in the different states.

Over time, we will attempt to have a universe data set for each state that will include local revenues, state general aid, state categorical aid for disabled, low income, and limited English proficient students, base pupil counts, and the number of students eligible for free and reduced lunch (or some similar count of students from low-income backgrounds), the number of disabled students and the number of limited-English proficient students. The state simulations then will allow students to simulate numerous different basic school finance structures as well as different pupil weights to address these three categories of special student needs.

3. ADEQUACY, PRODUCTIVITY, AND EFFICIENCY: PROBLEMS, ISSUES, AND NEW APPROACHES

This section includes three chapters: Chapter 6 on allocation and use of educational dollars, Chapter 7 on alternative approaches to improving educational productivity, and Chapter 8 on resource reallocation at the site level.

Chapter 6 provides a detailed analysis of the way states, districts, and schools allocate and use educational resources. It summarizes research on this topic, using data on national, state, and universe district bases, and limited research on school-level databases. The conclusion of this chapter is that there are surprisingly common patterns to the uses of the education dollar. It also shows that during the past 30 years, the large bulk of new dollars has been used to provide services other than the regular, core instructional program. Finally, the chapter concludes that while these uses reflect good values—more money for many categories of special-needs students—the specific uses of those new dollars have not produced much impact on student learning. The implication of these findings is that we need to retain the values behind these extra resources but find more effective uses for all education dollars.

Chapter 6 also includes a discussion of the difficulties of collecting school-level fiscal and personnel data, while arguing that such site-level data are crucial to the task of improving the use of educational resources.

Chapter 7 summarizes several literatures concerning how to improve educational productivity (i.e., how to improve results with the current dollars in the education system):

- the economics production function literature,
- the choice, charter, and vouchers literature, and
- the high-performance management literature.

The chapter identifies the school finance implications of these three topics, which are then addressed more fully in subsequent chapters: more effective uses of education dollars that flow largely from resource use in comprehensive, whole-school designs; needs-based formula funding of school sites, which is an implication of the high performance management literature, as well as choice and charter policies; performance incentives; and teacher compensation.

Chapter 8 addresses the issue of resource reallocation to school strategies that produce higher student performance. It first uses 1994–95 Schools and Staffing Survey data to show how a 500-student elementary, a 1,000 student middle, and a 1,500 student high school are typically staffed in different regions of the country. It then describes how a series of new school models are staffed and structured, focusing on the two most expensive that were developed under the auspices of the New American Schools. It shows how the new school designs use their funds differently to provide educational services and describes the things that schools should consider in implementing these models. This chapter does not make definitive conclusions about the impact of these new school designs, but does show how these various emerging school designs have a cost structure that is different from traditional schools, and thus use dollar resources differently.

This chapter also shows that there may be sufficient resources in some regions to fund these emerging higher-performing school models, but insufficient resources in others, thus suggesting that cross-state differences in educational spending need to be considered at some point.

4. POLICY AND MANAGEMENT INNOVATIONS FOR ADDRESSING EQUITY, ADEQUACY, AND PRODUCTIVITY IN SCHOOL FINANCE

This section includes three chapters on policy and management innovations that can help improve both the equity and effectiveness of current education and school finance systems: Chapter 9 on system incentives, Chapter 10 on formula funding of schools, and Chapter 11 on new approaches to teacher compensation.

Chapter 9 describes how states and districts can create a variety of incentives for improving student performance, and identifies finance implications for many of those strategies. It identifies incentives for students, teachers, and schools, and concludes that all are needed. The primary finance implications from this chapter are that schools need more power and authority over their budget (a conclusion of the management section of Chapter 7 as well), and that teacher compensation systems also could be changed.

Implementing many of the strategies described in the previous chapters—school-based management, resource reallocation at the site, public school choice, charter school programs, and many system incentives—requires school-based funding models. Chapter 10 assesses the types of models that could be developed. The chapter first suggests that states should adopt a school-based budgeting framework that would guide each district in designing a needs-based formula funding system for resourcing its schools. The proposed framework is a modified and simplified version of the framework originally developed by Odden and Busch (1998). The framework suggests that even in a decentralized system, several functions need to remain at the district level. It also identifies several functions that would be performed by the site. And it identifies several other functions that could remain at the district or be devolved to the site over time, decisions that could vary by district. This chapter also identifies the different issues districts need to address in designing school-funding formulas, once they have decided how much of the operating budget they will provide in a lump sum to their school sites.

The single largest expenditure for all schools and school districts is teacher salaries and benefits. Since it is teachers who have the main day-to-day contact with students, new teacher compensation programs have potential for creating teacher incentives that could result in improved student achievement. Chapter 11 summarizes several proposals for changing how teachers are paid. This chapter describes how to modify the single-salary schedule to include salary increments for teacher knowledge and skills, as well as salary bonuses for all teachers and staff in schools that meet or exceed system-determined performance-improvement targets. This chapter describes programs that reflect these new approaches that already are operating around the country, and summarizes research on their impacts.

APPENDIX: THE SIMULATION

An integral part of this book is the school finance simulation designed to accompany the text. We have made a number of improvements to the simulation that accompanied the first edition of this book. The original 10-district simulation has been updated to include a total of 20 districts. Additionally, two new school finance statistics are provided: the Verstegen Index and the Odden-Picus Adequacy Index. The 20-district simulation is designed to accompany Chapter 4. We found that the previous simulation dramatically improved student understanding of the statistics used by the school finance profession, and helped them better understand the myriad complexities involved in making changes to a state's school-funding system. The 20-district simulation that accompanies this edition should continue that tradition.

The simulation is available on the World Wide Web, from McGraw-Hill's web site at http://www.mhhe.com/schoolfinance. The appendix describes the general use of the simulation, and provides information on how to access it from the World Wide Web. Additional documentation will be available on the web site.

In addition to the 20-district simulation, we are working to provide versions of the simulation for each of the 50 states. Information on what is available and the status of the current data for each state will be posted on the web site. We hope it will help students, teachers, researchers, and policymakers improve their understanding of important school finance concepts.

At the end of the preface of the first edition we said, "We hope this will help the country accomplish its goals of having all students learn to think, solve problems and communicate, graduate from high school, and be first in the world in mathematics and science." We continue this hope with this edition.

ACKNOWLEDGMENTS

Writing a book almost always is the result of activities far beyond those of the authors. To be sure, the authors are primarily responsible for the text, and responsible for errors and omissions, but without insight, assistance, support and work of others, a book might never see the light of day. We would like to thank the people who played major roles in helping us produce the second edition of this book.

First, Sarah Archibald, a researcher in the University of Wisconsin—Madison offices of the Consortium for Policy Research in Education (CPRE), and Anita Tychsen, a Ph.D. student and a CPRE research assistant, worked tirelessly on most portions of the book, but particularly Chapters 2, 4, and 7. They searched out research reports needed for the text revision, they found missing data files crucial to empirical findings, and they filled in details too numerous to mention. Both their careful assistance and continuous encouragement to complete this endeavor are greatly appreciated.

Lisa Armstrong, administrative assistant in the UW CPRE offices, and Kelley Hewitt, a secretary in those offices, were enormously helpful in the word processing needed to produce the final manuscript; they entered the editorial changes, kept track of the most recent files, and produced faultless final copy. As usual, Lisa was the pre-eminent citation sleuth, tracking down innumerable citations that either simply needed to be found or needed completion. Without their help, we would still be at the computer or in the library.

A special thank you to our reviewers David H. Monk, *Cornell University;* Leanna Stiefel, *New York University;* and Karen Hawley Miles, *Education Resources Management Strategies.*

We also would like to acknowledge the many, unnamed individuals at the national, state, district, and school level who have allowed us, as well as others, to conduct research on their use of education resources over the past eight years. Without this research, a revised edition might not have been required. But as we hope will be obvious, the landscape of school finance has changed over the past few years. What we know about the nature of these changes has depended on the cooperation of those involved in letting outside individuals intrude into their domain, research what they do, and write up the results.

Finally, we would like to thank our families, who once again have endured our working on the computer rather than engaging in family activities. Their support and sustenance knows no bounds, and we are grateful for their understanding, love, and steadfast support.

Allan R. Odden   Lawrence O. Picus
Madison, Wisconsin   Los Angeles, California

ABOUT THE AUTHORS

Allan R. Odden is a Professor of Educational Administration at the University of Wisconsin—Madison. He also is Co-Director of the Consortium for Policy Research in Education (CPRE), which is funded by the U.S. Department of Education, the director of the CPRE Education Finance Research Program, and principal investigator for the CPRE Teacher Compensation project, funded by the Pew Charitable Trusts and the Carnegie Corporation. CPRE is a consortium of the University of Wisconsin—Madison, Pennsylvania, Harvard, Michigan, and Stanford Universities. He formerly was professor of Education Policy and Administration at the University of Southern California and Director of Policy Analysis for California Education (PACE), an educational policy studies consortium of USC, Stanford University, and the University of California, Berkeley.

Odden is an international expert on education finance, school-based financing, resource allocation and use, educational policy, school-based management, teacher compensation, district and school decentralization, education incentives, and educational policy implementation. He worked with the Education Commission of the States for a decade, serving as assistant executive director, director of policy analysis and research, and director of its educational finance center. He was president of the American Educational Finance Association in 1979–80, and served as research director for special state educational finance projects in Connecticut (1974–75), Missouri (1975–77), South Dakota (1975–77), New York (1979–81), Texas (1988), New Jersey (1991), and Missouri (1992–93). In 1999, he was directing research projects on school finance redesign, resource reallocation, and teacher compensation. He was appointed Special Court Master to the Remand Judge in the New Jersey *Abbott* v. *Burke* school finance court case for 1997 and 1998. Odden has written widely, publishing over 170 journal articles, book chapters, and research reports, and 20 books and monographs. He has consulted for governors, state legislators, chief state school officers, national and local unions, The National Alliance for Business, the Business Roundtable, New American Schools, the U.S. Congress, the U.S. Secretary of Education, many local school districts, the state departments of education in Victoria and Queensland, Australia, and the Department for Education and Employment in England.

His books include *Financing Schools for High Performance: Strategies for Improving the Use of Educational Resources* (Jossey-Bass, 1998) with Carolyn Busch; *Paying Teachers for What They Know and Do: New and Smarter Compensation Strategies to Improve Schools* (Corwin Press, 1997) with Carolyn Kelley; *Educational Leadership for America's Schools* (McGraw-Hill, 1995); *Rethinking School Finance: An Agenda for the 1990s* (Jossey-Bass, 1992); *School Finance: A Policy Perspective* (McGraw-Hill, 1992) coauthored with Lawrence Picus; *Education Policy Implementation* (State University of New York Press, 1991); and *School Finance and School Improvement: Linkages for the 1980s* (Ballinger, 1983).

Odden was a mathematics teacher and curriculum developer in New York City's East Harlem for five years. He received his Ph.D. and M.A. degrees from

Columbia University, a Masters of Divinity from the Union Theological Seminary, and his B.S. from Brown University.

Lawrence O. Picus is a Professor in the Rossier School of Education at the University of Southern California. He serves as the director of the Center for Research in Education Finance (CREF), a research center in the School of Education at the University of Southern California. CREF research focuses on issues of school finance and productivity. He has also conducted research on the costs of alternative assessment programs for the Center for Research on Evaluation, Student Standards and Testing (CRESST) at UCLA.

Picus is past-president of the American Education Finance Association. He is the coauthor of *Principles of School Business Administration* (ASBO, 1995) with R. Craig Wood, David Thompson, and Don I. Tharpe. In addition, he is the senior editor of the 1995 yearbook of the American Education Finance Association, *Where Does the Money Go? Resource Allocation in Elementary and Secondary Schools* (Corwin, 1995). He has published numerous articles in professional journals as well.

Picus' teaching responsibilities include courses in school finance, educational policy, school business administration, school district budgeting, economics of education, the politics of education in the United States, and the application of computers to school district management. In his role with CREF, he is involved with studies of how educational resources are allocated and used in schools across the United States. He has also conducted studies of the impact of incentives on school district performance. Picus maintains close contact with the superintendents and chief business officers of school districts throughout California and the nation, and is a member of a number of professional organizations dedicated to improving school district management. He also serves as a consultant to the National Education Association, American Federation of Teachers, the National Center for Education Statistics, WestEd and the states of Vermont, Washington, and Arkansas.

Prior to coming to USC, Picus spent four years at the RAND Corporation, where he earned a Ph.D. in Public Policy Analysis. He holds a Masters Degree in Social Science from the University of Chicago, and a Bachelors degree in Economics from Reed College. He has a strong background in research design, statistics, and econometrics.

To my wife, Eleanor, best friend, critical colleague, and tireless supporter.

Allan Odden

For Matthew, who has reinforced my belief in the importance of this work.

Larry Picus

Chapter 1

Introduction and Overview to School Finance

School finance concerns the distribution and use of money for the purpose of providing educational services and producing student achievement. For most of the twentieth century, school finance policy has focused on equity—issues related to widely varying education expenditures per pupil across districts within a state and the uneven distribution of the property tax base that is used to raise local education dollars. In the 1990s, new attention began to focus on education adequacy and productivity—the linkages among level of funds, use of funds, and amounts of student achievement. As the 1990s end and the twenty-first century begins, policymakers increasingly want to know how much money is needed to educate students to high standards; how those dollars should be distributed effectively and fairly among districts, schools, programs and students; and how both level and use of dollars affect student performance. These policy demands are pushing school finance beyond its traditional emphasis on fiscal equity.

This book moves school finance in these new directions. It emphasizes the traditional equity issues and also discusses adequacy and productivity issues, including what is known about the linkages among dollars, educational strategies, and student performance. The 1980s and the 1990s were remarkable not only for the intensity of the school reform movement, but the duration of interest in educational reform. Today, standards-based reform elements from content standards to charter schools to new accountability structures seek to teach students to high levels. In most instances, the implications of these reforms on school finance have not been fully considered, though Odden and Clune (1998) argued that traditional school finance systems were "aging structures in need of renovation." During the 2000s, states and their respective school districts will need to rethink school finance systems to meet the productivity expectations and accountability requirements inspired by these reforms.

This book takes a policy approach to school finance analysis. It is important for graduate students in education, as well as educators and education policy makers, to understand both the finance implications of school reform policies, and equally important, to understand how decisions about the distribution of funds to local schools and school districts affect the implementation of those reforms. The book begins with a discussion of traditional school finance issues, including the legal issues surrounding school finance, analysis of general taxation systems, intergovernmental grants, and traditional school finance formulas. The analysis of school finance formulas is supplemented with a computer simulation designed to allow students the opportunity to simulate the effects of different school finance distribution decisions on a sample of school districts. By designing their own school finance formulas and simulating the effect on a sample of school districts, students will have a more realistic sense of how changes in funding formulas impact school districts across a state. The simulation will help students understand the technical and political complexities that result when one attempts to redesign school-funding programs.

The book then moves beyond this traditional approach to school finance, and in a series of chapters discusses important issues for the 2000s and how they relate to school finance. Included are chapters dealing with allocation and use of funds at the district and school levels, teacher salaries and compensation structures especially as they can be redesigned to improve productivity, site-based management, educational choice programs, fiscal incentives, and the financing of broad education programs shown by research to improve student performance. In each of these areas, current research and state activity are summarized, and the implications for school finance programs are discussed.

This introductory chapter has three sections. Section one outlines the scope of school finance within the United States; funding public schools is big business, and this section outlines its fiscal magnitude. Section two provides a quick history of school finance developments, beginning in the seventeenth century. This section shows how schools evolved from privately funded, parent- and church-run entities to the large publicly and governmentally controlled education systems of today. The last section discusses several examples of the "school finance problem" and how it has evolved from the traditional fiscal disparities across districts to the new issue of education adequacy.

1. THE SCOPE OF UNITED STATES EDUCATION FINANCING

Education is an enormous enterprise in the United States. It constitutes the largest portion of most state and local governmental budgets; engages more than 100,000 local school board members in important policy-making activities; employs millions of individuals as teachers, administrators, and support staff; and educates tens of millions of children.

Figure 1.1 provides detail on public school enrollment, including numbers of school districts and schools during most of the twentieth century. Enrollment was relatively constant during the 1930s and 1940s, but rose quickly after World

FIGURE 1.1 Historical Data on the Size of the Nation's School Systems, 1919–20 to 1994–95

Year	Public Student Enrollment (in 1,000s)	Public School Districts	Public Elementary Schools	Public Secondary Schools	Private Elementary Schools	Private Secondary Schools	Private Schools as Percent of Total
1919–20	21,578	—	—	—	—	—	—
1929–30	25,678	—	238,306	23,930	9,275	3,258	5
1939–40	25,434	117,108	—	—	11,306	3,568	—
1949–50	25,111	83,718	128,225	24,542	10,375	3,331	8
1959–60	35,182	40,520	91,853	25,784	13,574	4,061	13
1969–70	45,550	17,995[a]	65,800[a]	25,352[a]	14,372[a]	3,770[a]	17[a]
1979–80	41,651	15,912[b]	61,069[b]	24,362[b]	16,792[b]	5,678[b]	21[b]
1989–90	40,543	15,358[c,d]	61,340[d]	23,460[d]	22,223[d]	8,989[d]	21[b]
1994–95	44,111	14,881[c,e]	62,726[e]	23,379[e]	23,543[e]	10,555[e]	31[e]

Source: National Center for Educational Statistics, 1998a

[a] Data for 1970–71.

[b] Data for 1980–81.

[c] Because of expanded survey coverage, data are not directly comparable with figures for earlier years.

[d] Data for 1990–91; for private schools, these data are from sample surveys and should not be compared directly with the data for earlier years.

[e] Data for 1993–94; for private schools, these data are from sample surveys and should not be compared directly with the data for earlier years.

War II as the post-war baby boom became school-aged. After 25 years of rapid enrollment growth, public school enrollment declined during the 1970s and then began to grow again in the mid-1980s as the children of the baby boom generation began to enter schools. In 1989–90, public school enrollment was estimated to be just over 40 million students, having peaked at slightly above that level during the 1970s.

One of the major stories of this century has been the consolidation of school districts into larger entities. In 1995, there were 14,881 school districts, the lowest number during this century. In 1940, by contrast, there were 117,108 school districts. The number of school districts dropped by almost 40,000 between 1940 and 1950 (i.e., after World War II), and then dropped by another 40,000 districts between 1950 and 1960. During the 1970 school year, there were only 17,995 local school districts. The number of districts varies across the states, however, with Texas and California each having more than 1,000 districts in 1990, and Hawaii having one, statewide school district.

Interestingly, as will be discussed below, although school district consolidation entails consolidation of the local property tax base, remaining inequities in local school financing after the bulk of consolidation had occurred led courts during the late 1960s and early 1970s to declare finance structures unconstitutional (see Chapter 2).

Figure 1.1 also shows that the number of public schools has dropped over time while enrollments have risen, indicating that schools too have grown in size during the twentieth century. There were over 262,000 public schools in 1930, but that number had dropped by a factor of more than four to around 65,000 schools in 1995. On the other hand, the number of private schools has risen since 1930, from a low of about 12,500 then to around 34,000 today, almost triple the number of 1930.

Funding public schools requires large amounts of dollars. In 1995, public school revenues totaled $273.1 billion, an increase of more than $64 billion from the 1990 total of $208.5 billion (Figure 1.2). Indeed, the data show that public school revenues more than doubled during each decade from 1940 to 1990, a remarkable fiscal record.

Figure 1.2 also shows that during this century, public education consumed an increasing portion of the country's total economic activity (the gross domestic product) until 1970, then dropped a bit during the enrollment decline of the 1970s, and has recently increased almost to the 1970s' level. The same pattern is true for total public school revenues as a percent of the country's personal income. In short, the country devotes approximately 4.5 percent of its personal annual income to public schools, a considerable portion considering all the other items that individuals could purchase with annual income either themselves or through government tax revenues.

This comment is undergirded by the data in Figure 1.3. Column 2 shows that *real* expenditures per pupil (i.e., expenditures adjusted by the Consumer Price Index), have increased each decade at extraordinarily high rates: 100 percent between 1920 and 1930, 67 percent during the 1960s, and 36 percent during

FIGURE 1.2   Educational Revenues, GDP, and Personal Income (Billions), 1930–95

Year	Total Educational Revenues	Gross Domestic Product (GDP)	Revenues as Percent of GDP	Personal Income (PI)	Revenues as Percent of PI
1930	$ 2.1	$ 104	2.0	$ 85	2.5
1940	2.3	101	2.3	78	2.9
1950	5.4	295	1.8	230	2.3
1960	14.7	527	2.8	413	3.6
1970	40.3	1,036	3.9	837	4.8
1980	96.9	2,784	3.5	2,293	4.2
1990	208.5	5,744	3.6	4,804	4.3
1995	273.1	7,254	3.8	6,112	4.5

Source: National Center for Education Statistics, *Digest of Education Statistics, 1997.*

FIGURE 1.3   Educational Expenditures per Pupil and Revenues by Source, 1920–97

Year	Expenditures per Pupil Real	Expenditures per Pupil Nominal	Total Revenues (in Millions)	Percent Revenues by Source Federal	Percent Revenues by Source State	Percent Revenues by Source Local
1919–20	$ 333	$ 40	$ 970	0.3	16.5	83.2
1929–30	667	72	2,089	0.4	16.9	82.7
1939–40	868	76	2,261	1.8	30.3	68.0
1949–50	1,252	187	5,437	2.9	39.8	57.3
1959–60	1,895	350	14,747	4.4	39.1	56.5
1969–70	3,155	750	40,267	8.0	39.9	52.1
1979–80	4,275	2,089	96,881	9.8	46.8	43.4
1989–90	5,810	4,643	208,548	6.1	47.1	46.8
1994–95	5,840[a]	5,528[a]	273,138	6.8	46.8	46.4
1995–96	5,939[a]	5,774[a]	286,411[b]	7.0[b]	48.1[b]	45.0[b]
1996–97	6,060[a]	6,060[a]	299,995[b]	6.9[b]	48.9[b]	44.2[b]

Source: National Center for Education Statistics, *Digest of Education Statistics, 1997.*
[a] Data estimated.
[b] *Source:* National Education Association, *1996–97 Estimates of School Statistics.*

the 1970s. Even during the 1980s, a decade of government tax and expenditure limitations, expenditures per pupil increased by 36 percent to a total of $5,810 for current operating purposes in 1989–90. It seems that real resources for public school students have risen substantially each decade.

These facts certainly are at odds with popular perceptions that schools do not get much more money each year. Though real resources might increase only 1–3 percent each year, over a 10-year time period, that amounts to nearly a one-third increase in real resources, a substantial increase.

The last columns in Figure 1.3 show that the sources of school revenues have changed over the years. Earlier in the century, local districts provided the bulk of school revenues, and the federal role was almost nonexistent. Beginning in the 1960s, the federal government began to increase its financial role, which reached its maximum at 9.8 percent in 1980. Since then, the federal contribution has dropped by almost one-third. Today, the states are the primary providers of public school revenues, surpassing local school districts sometime in the 1970s' era of school finance reforms. During the 1996–97 school year, on average the states provided 48.9 percent of public school revenues, local districts (primarily through the local property tax) 44.2 percent, and the federal government 6.9 percent.

These national patterns, however, are very different in each of the 50 states, as shown by Figure 1.4. The national average expenditure per pupil was $5,988 in 1994–95, but expenditures ranged from a low of $3,656 in Utah to a high of $9,774 in New Jersey, a difference of almost three-to-one.

States also differ in the sources of public school revenues. In Hawaii, for example, 90 percent of revenues derive from the state, while in New Hampshire only 7.3 percent of school revenues come from state sources. States provide over 60 percent of school revenues in 11 states, while local districts provide over 60 percent of school revenues in six states. This variation reflects differences in local perceptions of appropriate state and local roles, as well as differences in school finance formula structures (Gold, Smith, and Lawton, 1995). These data document one enduring characteristic of state school finance structures: though there are some similarities, the differences are dramatic. Students of school finance need to understand both the generic similarities and the factors causing the specific differences.

2. EARLY DEVELOPMENTS IN SCHOOL FINANCE

The country has not always had a system of free, tax-supported schools. Free, public education was an idea created in the United States during the nineteenth century, and the large network of public school systems was formed in a relatively short time period, primarily during the latter part of the nineteenth and early part of the twentieth century.

American schools began as local entities, largely private and religious during the seventeenth, eighteenth, and even early nineteenth centuries. As in

FIGURE 1.4   Educational Expenditures per Pupil and Revenues by Source, by State, 1994–95

State	*Expenditures per Pupil*	Percent of Revenues by Source		
		Federal	*State*	*Local*
Alabama	$4,405	9.7	61.0	21.6
Alaska	8,963	10.8	67.5	19.4
Arizona	4,778	9.4	44.0	44.2
Arkansas	4,459	9.2	58.2	27.8
California	4,992	9.5	54.2	35.1
Colorado	5,443	5.3	42.9	48.6
Connecticut	8,817	4.0	39.5	53.6
Delaware	7,030	7.2	64.3	26.8
District of Columbia	9,335	9.5	0	90.0
Florida	5,718	7.6	49.1	39.6
Georgia	5,193	7.4	50.7	40.0
Hawaii	6,078	7.4	90.2	0.5
Idaho	4,210	7.7	61.2	29.3
Illinois	6,136	6.5	28.0	63.3
Indiana	5,826	4.8	53.3	38.9
Iowa	5,483	5.2	47.9	41.0
Kansas	5,817	5.3	57.4	34.8
Kentucky	5,217	9.3	65.8	24.1
Louisiana	4,761	11.9	52.1	33.4
Maine	6,428	5.7	47.9	45.4
Maryland	7,245	5.0	37.0	54.9
Massachusetts	7,287	5.4	36.3	56.0
Michigan	6,994	6.2	67.3	24.6
Minnesota	6,000	4.4	52.4	39.4
Mississippi	4,080	14.8	56.4	25.3
Missouri	5,383	6.5	38.7	50.7
Montana	5,692	10.0	49.6	36.3
Nebraska	5,935	5.8	32.4	55.8
Nevada	5,160	4.9	30.1	61.1
New Hampshire	5,859	3.1	7.3	87.3
New Jersey	9,774	3.3	38.0	56.0
New Mexico	4,586	11.8	74.4	11.6
New York	9,623	4.8	40.7	53.6
North Carolina	5,077	7.5	65.1	24.6
North Dakota	4,775	12.4	42.1	40.2
Ohio	6,162	6.5	40.0	49.3
Oklahoma	4,845	9.4	59.4	25.8
Oregon	6,436	6.8	46.2	43.8
Pennsylvania	7,109	5.6	40.1	52.3

FIGURE 1.4 **(Continued)**

State	Expenditures per Pupil	Percent of Revenues by Source		
		Federal	State	Local
Rhode Island	7,469	5.5	40.5	52.9
South Carolina	4,797	8.7	46.3	40.6
South Dakota	4,775	10.0	26.5	60.5
Tennessee	4,388	8.9	47.5	36.9
Texas	5,222	7.7	40.2	49.4
Utah	3,656	6.9	54.3	33.3
Vermont	6,750	4.6	29.8	63.2
Virginia	5,327	5.7	31.8	59.1
Washington	5,906	6.0	68.7	22.3
West Virginia	6,107	8.1	63.6	26.8
Wisconsin	6,930	4.4	41.1	52.5
Wyoming	6,160	6.7	48.0	43.5
United States	*5,988*	*6.8*	*46.8*	*43.8*

Source: National Center for Education Statistics, *Digest of Education Statistics 1997.*

England, educating children was considered a private rather than a public matter. Providing for education was a mandate for parents and masters, not governments. Eighteenth-century leaders of the new American republic viewed education as a means to enable citizens to participate as equals in affairs of government and thus essential to ensure the liberties guaranteed by the Constitution. Even though Thomas Jefferson proposed creation of free public elementary schools, his proposal was not adopted until the mid-1800s, largely through the efforts of Horace Mann and Henry Barnard, state superintendents of public instruction. Mann spearheaded the development of public-supported "common schools" in Massachusetts, and Barnard did the same in Connecticut.

In the nineteenth century, education began to assume significance in economic terms; that also was the time when compulsory attendance laws were passed. Even when school attendance became compulsory beginning in the mid-1800s, however, government financing of schools was not uniformly required.

In 1647, the General Court of Massachusetts passed the famous Old Deluder Satan Act. The act required every town to set up a school or pay a sum of money to a larger town to support education. It required towns with at least 50 families to appoint a teacher of reading and writing, and required towns with more than 100 families to also establish a secondary school. The Act required that these schools should be supported by masters, parents, or the inhabitants in general, thereby establishing one of the first systems of financing schools through local taxation. Pulliam (1987) states that the first tax on property for local schools was levied in Dedham, Massachusetts, in 1648. By 1693, New Hampshire also required towns to support elementary schools.

Initially, one-room elementary common schools were established in local communities, often fully supported through a small local tax. Each town functioned, moreover, as an independent school district, indeed as an independent school system, since there were no state laws or regulations providing for a statewide public education system. At the same time, several large school systems evolved in the big cities of most states. Even at this early time, these different education systems reflected differences in local ability to support them. Big cities usually were quite wealthy, while the smaller, rural one-room school districts usually were quite poor, many having great difficulty financing a one-room school.

As the number of these small rural and big-city school systems grew, however, and the importance of education as a unifying force for a developing country became increasingly realized by civic and political leaders, new initiatives were undertaken to create statewide education systems. By 1820, in fact, 13 of the then 23 states had constitutional provisions, and seventeen had statutory provisions, pertaining to public education.

In the mid-eighteenth century, several states began to completely rewrite state constitutions not only calling for creation of statewide systems of public education, but also formally establishing government responsibility for financing schools. Today, all states have constitutional provisions related to free public education.

Creation of free common schools reflected the importance of education in America. It also shifted control over education from individuals and the church to the state. Control over schools was a problematic aspect in crafting statewide, education systems. The resolution to the control issue was creation of local, lay boards of education that, it was argued, would function in the place of parents and the church.

While for the first century of common schools local boards basically controlled public schools, the strength of local control has changed substantially in recent years. In the early twentieth century, much school control was given to the new breed of educational professionals, as the Progressive Era of education sought to take politics out of education (Tyack and Hansot, 1982). Beginning in the 1960s, both the states and federal government began to exert new initiative and control affecting public schools. States continued this trend by taking the lead for education policy throughout the 1980s' education reform period (Doyle and Hartle, 1985; Odden, 1995a). Local boards were for the most part uninvolved in those reforms (Odden, 1995a). In the early 1990s, the president and the nation's governors established nationwide education goals; these were codified into law in 1994 by the U.S. Congress.

The development of the state-controlled and governmentally financed "common school" also raised many fundamental issues about school finance. The key issues concerned the level of government (local or state) that would support public education and whether new constitutional phrases such as "general and uniform," "thorough and efficient," "basic," or "adequate" meant an equal amount of dollars would be spent for every student in the state, or meant just providing a basic education program for every student, with different amounts of total dollars determined at the local level. As discussed in Chapter 2, this controversy persists today and is resolved in different ways by state legislatures and courts in the 50 states.

While major differences exist in the specific approaches taken, most states finance public schools primarily through local property taxes. Indeed, in the mid-to-late 1800s, most states required local districts to fully finance mandated public schools through local property taxation. In designing locally administered school systems, states generally gave local governments the authority to raise money for schools by levying property taxes. But when states determined school district boundaries, districts ended up with widely varying levels of property wealth per pupil, and thus large differences in the ability to raise local dollars to support public education. Districts with above-average property tax bases per pupil traditionally were able to spend at above-average levels with below-average tax rates, while districts with below-average tax bases spent at below-average levels even with above-average tax rates.

School finance policy debates throughout the twentieth century, including most school finance texts (see for example, Alexander and Salmon 1995; Guthrie, Garms, and Pierce, 1988; Odden and Picus, 1992, Chapter 1; Swanson and King, 1997) and most court cases, focused on these types of fiscal inequities. To be sure, some individuals pointed to spending differences per se, regardless of whether they were related to varying tax bases, and argued that they should be impermissible in a *state* education system (Wise, 1968). But the bulk of discussion centered on the links between spending differences and local property wealth per pupil (see also Coons, Clune, and Sugarman, 1970).

As discussed at length in Chapter 4, states began to intervene in school financing first through small per-pupil "flat grant" programs in which the state distributed an equal amount of money per pupil to each local school district. The idea was for the state to provide at least some assistance in support of a local basic education program. Over the years, these flat grants became recognized as too small.

In the early 1920s, states began to implement "minimum foundation programs," which provided a much higher level of base financial support and were financed with a combination of state and local revenues. These programs were the first in which states explicitly recognized the wide variation in the local property tax base, and designed a state aid structure to distribute larger amounts to districts with a small property tax base per pupil and smaller amounts to districts with a large property tax base per pupil.

These "equalization formulas" were designed to "equalize" differences in local fiscal capacity (i.e., the unequal ability to finance education because of the variation in the size of the local property tax base). But over time, the level of the minimum foundation programs also proved to be inadequate, and additional revenues above the foundation program were raised solely through local taxation. As a result, local educational expenditures per pupil varied widely across local districts in most states, with the differences related primarily to the size of the local property tax base.

Beginning in the late 1960s, these fiscal disparities caused by unequal distribution of the local tax base and inadequate state general equalization programs led to legal challenges to state school finance systems in which plaintiffs, usually from low-wealth and low-spending districts, argued that the disparities not only were unfair but also were unconstitutional (Coons, Clune, and Sugarman, 1970; Berke, 1974). Chapter 2 traces the course of these suits, which spawned a new political channel to improve the ways states financed public education, and which evolved in the 1990s into a strategy to link the funding structure with an education system that could teach nearly all students to high performance.

3. EVOLUTION IN THE SCHOOL FINANCE PROBLEM

This section discusses how the nature of the school finance problem has become much more complicated in the 1990s. Though many still define the core school finance problem as differences in spending across school districts caused by varying levels of property wealth per pupil, others (e.g., Odden and Clune, 1998) argue that linking finance to an adequate education is the core school finance issue today. Still others argue that educational productivity—determining how to produce higher levels of educational performance with current education resources—is the key school finance goal today (Hanushek and Associates, 1994).

Traditional Fiscal Disparities

There are many ways to depict the types of fiscal disparities among school districts created by the unequal distribution of the property tax. Figure 1.5 shows 1968–69 data that were presented in the original *Serrano* v. *Priest* court case in California; at that time, California had a typical minimum foundation program, and most districts raised additional funds to spend at a higher level. These data represent property value per child, the local school tax rate, and resulting expenditures per pupil for pairs of property-rich and property-poor districts in several counties. In each county example, the assessed valuation per pupil—the local tax base—varied substantially: by a factor of almost three-to-one in Los Angeles County and over sixteen-to-one in Alameda County. In each example, moreover, the district with the higher assessed value per child had both the higher expenditures per pupil and the lower tax rate.

These examples were selected to show that the California school finance structure produced a situation—similar to most other states at that time—in which districts with a low property tax base usually spent less than the state average even with above-average tax rates, while districts with a high property tax base usually spent above the state average with below-average tax rates. The wealthy enjoyed both the advantages of high expenditures and low tax rates, while the poor were disadvantaged by both low expenditures and high tax rates.

FIGURE 1.5   Comparison of Selected Tax Rates and Expenditure Levels in Selected California Counties, 1968–69

County	Pupils	Assessed Value per Pupil	Tax Rate	Expenditure per Pupil
Alameda				
Emery Unified	586	$100,187	$2.57	$2,223
Newark Unified	8,638	6,048	5.65	616
Fresno				
Colinga Unified	2,640	33,244	2.17	963
Clovis Unified	8,144	6,480	4.28	565
Kern				
Rio Bravo Elementary	121	136,271	1.05	1,545
Lamont Elementary	1,847	5,971	3.06	533
Los Angeles				
Beverly Hills Unified	5,542	50,885	2.38	1,232
Baldwin Park Unified	13,108	3,706	5.48	577

Source: California Supreme Court Opinion in *Serrano* v. *Priest*, August 1971.

The shortcoming of the data in Figure 1.5 is that school finance information for only a few districts is shown. While these districts statistically reflected the trends in the system, system trends should be analyzed using all of the districts in a state, not selected pairs of districts from different counties.

Another potentially misleading approach in presenting school finance data is to show the extreme cases, as indicated in Figure 1.6, which shows for Colorado the value of assessed valuation per pupil for the richest and poorest districts, districts at the 90th and 10th percentiles, and the district in the middle. These 1977 data show that the difference between the wealthiest and poorest was 77.7 to 1; at a one mill tax rate, the wealthiest district raised $326.27 per pupil, while the poorest district raised only $4.20! To raise the amount that the wealthiest district produces at one mill, the poorest district would have had to levy a 77.7 mill tax rate, which is prohibitively high. To blunt the criticism that the extreme cases might represent anomalies, the values for districts at the 90th and 10th percentiles also were presented. Those figures showed that property wealth per child still varied substantially, from a high of $57,516 to a low of $10,764, a difference of 5.3 to 1. While these differences were less than those between the very top and bottom, the data indicate that district ability to raise school funds through the local property tax varied widely.

This figure also shows the emphasis on variation in the local tax base, per se, in many early school finance analyses. What really matters, of course, is the interaction of the local tax base, state equalization aid, and local tax rates on the final per-pupil spending figure. But even in the first school finance case taken to the U.S. Supreme Court (see Chapter 2), great emphasis was given just to the

FIGURE 1.6   Assessed Valuation per Pupil in Colorado School Districts, 1977

Highest: Rio Blanco-Rangely	$326,269
90th percentile: Eagle-Eagle	57,516
Median: Mesa-Plauteau Valley	20,670
10th percentile: Montezuma-Dolores	10,764
Lowest: El Paso-Fountain	4,197
Ratio: Highest/lowest	77.7:1
Ratio: 90th/10th percentiles:	5.3:1

Source: Education Finance Center, Education Commission of the States from official data of the Colorado Department of Education.

variation in the local tax base. The data in Figure 1.6 *implied* that the Colorado school finance system would have substantial fiscal disparities.

Figure 1.7 shows the magnitude of the actual disparities by displaying statistics calculated from a sample of all Colorado school districts in 1977. At that time, Colorado had a guaranteed tax base program (see Chapter 4), but had "frozen" all local expenditures and allowed only modest increases from year to year, letting lower-spending districts increase at a somewhat faster rate than higher-spending districts. This figure organizes all data into groups (in this case five groups, or quintiles), and presents averages for each quintile.[1] Note that each quintile includes approximately an equal percentage of students, not districts.[2] Interestingly, though property wealth per pupil varied substantially, both the authorized revenue base (ARB)[3] and operating expenditures per pupil varied by a much smaller magnitude. Indeed, the ratio between the ARB of the top or wealthiest quintile and that for the bottom or poorest quintile is 1.4 to 1, much less than the 5.3 to 1 ratio of wealth at the 90th to the wealth at the 10th percentile. Further, the ratio of operating expenditures per pupil of the top quintile to that of the bottom quintile is slightly higher, at 1.5 to 1. Unfortunately, the local tax rate and state aid figures were not provided, so it is not possible to determine whether the more equal revenue and expenditure figures are produced by fiscal-capacity-equalizing state aid, or high tax rates in the low-wealth districts.

New Jersey data for two time periods—1975–76 and 1978–79—are presented by septiles (seven groups) in Figure 1.8. The purpose of these two charts is to show differences in the New Jersey school finance structure three years after

---

[1] Other studies categorize districts into seven groups (septiles) or 10 groups (deciles). The most common practice today is to use deciles.

[2] Several earlier studies grouped data into categories with equal numbers of districts, and that practice still is followed. However, the emerging practice is to have an equal number of students in each category, to assess the impact of the system on students. See Berne and Stiefel (1984) and Chapter 2 for discussion of the unit of analysis.

[3] The ARB was a Colorado-specific general fund revenue per-pupil limit that varied for each local school district. It included revenues for the regular education program.

**FIGURE 1.7   ARB and Operating Expenditures per Pupil by Quintiles
of Assessed Valuation per Pupil, Colorado, 1977**

Assessed Valuation per Pupil	Percent of Pupils	Number of Districts	Authorized Revenue Base	Operating Expenditures per Pupil
$ 4,197–12,800	19	33	1,196	$1,532
12,800–15,500	20	25	1,312	1,594
15,500–17,600	14	14	1,299	1,667
17,600–24,500	27	32	1,476	1,742
24,500–326,269	20	77	1,692	2,342

Source: Education Finance Center, Education Commission of the States from official data
of the Colorado Department of Education.

the courts, responding to a 1973 court decision overturning the school finance
structure, shut down that state's education finance system in 1976, forcing the
legislature finally to enact a major school finance reform (see Chapter 2). These
tables are somewhat difficult to read because they do not include any typical univariate or relationship statistics (see Chapter 2). Nevertheless, several characteristics of the data are clear. First, in general, expenditures per pupil increased as
property value per pupil increased; it seems that both before and after reform,
expenditures were a function of local property wealth in New Jersey. But, expen-
ditures-per-pupil in 1978–79 were nearly the same for the first four groups, suggesting that some expenditure-per-pupil equality had been produced for the bottom half by the 1976 reform.

Second, the range[4] increased for both expenditures per pupil and expenditures per weighted pupil between 1976 and 1979; even the range divided by the
statewide average increased, suggesting that overall spending disparities increased over those three years.

Third, there seems to be wider expenditure-per-pupil disparities on a
weighted pupil basis, where the weights indicate special pupil needs (see Chapter
4). Indeed, the weighted pupil count substantially reduces the expenditure-per-
pupil figure for the lowest wealth districts, indicating—correctly, it turns out for
New Jersey—that these districts have large numbers of special-need students.[5]

Finally, and quite interestingly, school property tax rates dropped in New
Jersey over these three years, and school property tax rates were almost equal
across all but the wealthiest group of districts in 1979.

It seems, therefore, that the major impact of the 1976 New Jersey reform
was to equalize school tax rates for most districts, and to increase unweighted ex-

[4] The difference between the highest and lowest value.
[5] Many of these districts are large urban districts with large numbers and percentages of poor students, physically and mentally handicapped students, and low-achieving students.

FIGURE 1.8   New Jersey School Finance

Relationship between Property Wealth, Current Expenditures, and Tax Rates, **1975–76**

Equalized Valuation per Pupil	Current Expenditures per Pupil	Current Expenditures per Weighted Pupil	Current School Tax Rate
Group 1: Less than $33,599	$1,504	$1,372	$1.79
Group 2: $33,600–$45,499	1,414	1,324	2.12
Group 3: $45,450–$58,699	1,411	1,347	2.00
Group 4: $58,700–$67,199	1,460	1,401	1.99
Group 5: $67,200–$78,499	1,604	1,543	1.89
Group 6: $78,500–$95,499	1,689	1,628	1.74
Group 7: $95,500 and over	1,752	1,681	1.17
State average	1,550	1,473	1.69

Relationship between Property Wealth, Current Expenditures, and Tax Rates, **1978–79**

Equalized Valuation per Pupil	Current Expenditures per Pupil	Current Expenditures per Weighted Pupil	Current School Tax Rate
Group 1: Less than $37,000	$1,994	$1,780	$1.67
Group 2: $37,000–$54,999	1,933	1,763	1.57
Group 3: $55,000–$73,999	1,978	1,816	1.55
Group 4: $74,000–$87,999	1,994	1,882	1.58
Group 5: $88,000–$102,999	2,200	2,061	1.69
Group 6: $103,000–$125,199	2,268	2,154	1.67
Group 7: $125,200 and over	2,390	2,262	1.11
State average	2,113	1,959	1.47

penditures per pupil in the bottom half to about the same level. On a weighted pupil basis, however, spending was not equal in the bottom half, and overall spending disparities seemed to increase. This system was overturned by a 1990 state supreme court decision, in a case filed in the mid-1980s, but not fully resolved until 1998 (again, see Chapter 2).

Texas enacted a major school finance reform as part of a comprehensive education reform during 1984 (Odden and Dougherty, 1984), but that system was challenged in state court a few years later. The 1984 law provided for a minimum foundation program with a higher expenditure-per-pupil level than before 1984, a small guaranteed yield program on top of the foundation program, weights for several different categories of pupil need, and a price adjustment to account for the varying prices Texas districts faced in purchasing education commodities. In the fall of 1987, the court ruled the school finance system unconstitutional, and the state created an Education Finance Reform Commission in early 1988.

The data in Figure 1.9 were presented to that Commission. The data are organized into groups with approximately equal numbers of children; this time, 20 different groupings are provided, thus showing the impact of the finance structure on each 5 percent of students. The numbers show that, indeed, property wealth per pupil varied substantially in Texas, from under $56,150 to over $440,987, a difference of 7.9 to 1. In fact, the difference was greater, since several districts had assessed valuation per pupil in the $800,000 and over-one-million level; moreover, these districts included several of Texas' largest cities and some very wealthy suburban districts. The bottom line in Texas was that the local property tax per pupil was distributed unequally among local school districts.

The column with local and state revenues per pupil show, however, that while there is a trend for per-pupil revenues to increase with wealth, this is a trend that exists primarily for the top 20 percent and the bottom 5 percent of the districts. For the districts in between, revenues per pupil seemed to vary by about plus or minus 10 percent from a $3,300 per-pupil figure. That was not a dramatic variation. In fact, it could be argued that such data indicate for the majority of students in the middle that revenues per pupil were basically equal, that the problem with the system was the low spending of the districts at the very bottom, and the very high spending of the districts at the top. This problem definition requires a different policy response than if disparities are spread across the entire system. Nevertheless, the Texas lower court overturned the system, and that decision moreover was upheld on appeal by a unanimous state supreme court in the fall of 1989. Thus, today (in a number of states) even modest variations in spending per pupil that are linked to local property wealth are likely to be overturned if taken to court.

We should note that at these times, the underlying school finance problem was seen as the inequity of property wealth per pupil, and many believed that the way to remedy the problem was to make the ability to raise funds for schools more equal across districts. In school finance parlance, the solution was to enact a guaranteed tax base (GTB) or "district power equalizing" program [i.e., a program that guaranteed to all or nearly all districts—rich or poor—some high level tax base (see Chapter 4)]. Such a program would allow local districts to tap the same size tax base, and, by setting a tax rate, to determine the level of spending. In this way, districts could determine for themselves the level of quality of the local education program, rather than being constrained by the circumstance of being a low-wealth district. The tax rate would be applied to the statewide GTB so the same amount of money per pupil would be raised from state and local sources for both poor and rich districts (i.e., for all districts with a local tax base

FIGURE 1.9   Selected Texas School Finance Variables, 1986–87

Number of Districts	Range of Property Wealth per Pupil	Average Property Wealth per Pupil	Local Revenue per Pupil	State Revenue per Pupil	State and Local Revenues per Pupil	Federal Revenue per Pupil
26	Under $56,150	$ 46,217	$ 508	$2,528	$3,036	$564
57	56,150–79,652	68,793	647	2,309	2,956	426
73	79,653–96,562	87,980	801	2,204	3,005	277
123	96,563–117,462	107,516	1,006	2,092	3,096	269
68	117,463–128,425	120,325	1,050	2,109	3,159	309
73	128,426–144,213	136,285	1,192	2,074	3,266	283
52	144,214–156,931	152,061	1,355	1,864	3,215	227
34	156,932–167,090	161,971	1,610	1,711	3,321	145
46	167,091–177,108	169,925	1,658	1,711	3,369	203
84	177,109–202,136	190,514	1,727	1,643	3,370	171
37	202,137–218,238	208,852	1,904	1,499	3,403	126
44	218,239–239,117	224,173	1,963	1,473	3,436	139
26	239,118–253,338	244,493	2,055	1,403	3,458	130
42	253,339–276,674	260,613	2,281	1,342	3,623	181
36	276,675–308,780	294,373	2,942	1,123	4,065	113
1	308,781–308,862	308,862	2,006	1,125	3,131	312
45	308,863–356,189	330,150	2,494	1,039	3,533	128
45	356,190–436,960	399,954	3,459	830	4,285	89
3	436,961–440,987	440,607	2,862	960	3,822	294
146	Over $440,987	799,896	4,764	418	5,182	143

Source: Texas State Board of Education.

equal to or less than the GTB). In such a program, higher spending per pupil would require a higher tax rate. Thus, differences in education spending per pupil might remain, but spending differences would result from varying tax rates, reflecting differing levels of commitment to education; these differences would not be caused by the unequal distribution of the local tax base. The expectation by many was that GTB programs would not only reduce spending differences across districts, but also would reduce the linkage between local property wealth per pupil and spending per pupil.

A Different Type of School Finance Problem

These expectations also "assumed" existence of the typical school finance problem reflected in all of the above examples—high property wealth per pupil associated with both high expenditures *and* low tax rates, together with low property wealth per pupil associated with both low expenditures *and* high tax rates. But even in the 1970s, this "typical" situation did not hold for all states. The New York school finance situation in 1978 is such an example, as the data in Figure 1.10 show. At that time, New York had a school finance system that functioned like a minimum foundation program, but was actually a low-spending level percentage equalizing formula (see Chapter 4). The data in Figure 1.10 are presented for all districts, except for New York City, divided into 10 equal groups, or deciles. Each decile has approximately an equal number of students. New York City, with an enrollment of nearly 1 million in a state with a then total of 3 million, is shown separately, since if it were included in the deciles, it alone would include over three of the deciles.

Several elements of the data should be discussed. To begin, the data are grouped by deciles of *spending* per pupil; the idea in New York was that expenditure-per-pupil disparities were the final, important variable, and analysis of correlates of that variable should be the focus of the study. Columns 1 and 8 show that revenues per pupil from local and state sources varied widely in New York during the 1977–78 school year, from a low of $1,759 in the bottom spending decile to a high of $3,443 in the highest spending decile, a difference of about 2-to-1. Note that this is a much smaller disparity than the 5.8 to 1 difference in spending between the very top ($5,752) and the very bottom ($988) spending districts.

Second, both spending per pupil and revenues per pupil from local and state sources increase with property wealth, the traditional school finance pattern. But note also that the school property tax rate also increases; in fact, the school tax rate for the top few deciles is between 50 and almost 100 percent higher than the tax rates in the lowest spending districts. This reality set New York school finance apart from the situation in most other states at that time. Indeed, one of the reasons the wealthier districts spent more per pupil was that they taxed local property at a higher rate. Yes, those districts had a larger property tax base, but they also taxed it more heavily.

It also was true that household income as measured by gross income per return on New York State income tax returns increased with property wealth, and

FIGURE 1.10 Selected New York School Finance Variables, 1977–78

Deciles of Approved Operating Expenditures per Pupil	Assessed Value per Pupil	Gross Income per Return (1977)	Property Tax Rate (mills)	Property Tax Revenue per Pupil	Other Local Revenue per Pupil	Total State Aid per Pupil	Total Local and State Revenue per Pupil	Total Federal Aid per Pupil
First decile ($988–$1,389)	$ 37,957	$12,225	13.01	$ 485	$ 54	$1,220	$1,759	$ 35
Second decile ($1,390–$1,471)	41,924	12,446	15.34	634	56	1,176	1,866	37
Third decile ($1,473–$1,542)	46,902	12,422	17.11	770	62	1,107	1,939	58
Fourth decile ($1,544–$1,640)	50,968	13,527	17.61	862	67	1,081	2,010	40
Fifth decile ($1,642–$1,789)	57,916	14,190	19.63	1,086	68	1,006	2,160	63
Sixth decile ($1,790–$1,899)	58,986	13,311	21.68	1,178	72	998	2,248	117
Seventh decile ($1,903–$2,017)	64,323	15,274	23.48	1,430	81	953	2,464	44
Eighth decile ($2,021–$2,255)	66,469	16,157	23.69	1,526	178	896	2,600	74
Ninth decile ($2,250–$2,474)	78,069	16,773	25.26	1,896	102	866	2,864	57
Tenth decile ($2,475–$5,752)	115,535	21,639	23.84	2,583	154	706	3,443	36
New York City	81,506	13,607	22.52	1,760	41	864	2,665	217
Rest of state	61,732	14,762	20.05	1,240	89	1,002	2,331	57
Statewide average	67,715	14,412	20.79	1,397	75	960	2,432	105

Source: Odden, Palaich, and Augenblick, 1979.

19

thus with spending and school tax rates. It turns out that higher-income families, not only in New York but generally, choose to levy higher tax rates for schools. Thus, while higher spending in New York was caused in part by higher local tax effort, that higher tax effort in part was aided by higher household income. Further, household income and property wealth per pupil were highly and positively correlated in New York at that time. Unlike the Texas data in the early 1970s that were not correlated but were taken to the U.S. Supreme Court, the New York data might have made a better case for using the Equal Protection Clause of the U.S. Constitution to find the fiscal disparities shown in this table to be unconstitutional (see Chapter 2 on litigation).

In short, the New York data showed that higher spending occurred in districts with higher property wealth, higher household income, and higher school tax rates, while lower spending occurred in property-poor and income-poor districts with low tax rates. These variations from the traditional pattern complicated the formulation of a school finance reform that could pass muster for both the courts and the legislature. When the state's highest court ruled that the system, while unfair, was not unconstitutional, the push for reform abated. School finance in New York was changed incrementally over time, and currently still displays these general characteristics.

But New York is not the only state today that exhibits these school finance patterns. Three quite different states—Illinois, Missouri, and Wisconsin—provide additional examples of this "new" type of school finance problem. All three states enacted different versions of school finance reforms over the 1975–95 time period. Illinois implemented a generous "reward for effort" GTB-type program in the late 1970s and early 1980s, but then changed it to a foundation-type program in the 1980s and early 1990s. Missouri implemented a combination foundation-GTB program, which was continuously enhanced over those 20 years so that in 1995, the GTB was set at the 95th percentile of property wealth per pupil, with a minimum tax rate that provided a minimum expenditure of just over $3,000 per pupil, and with the GTB providing aid up to the 95th percentile of spending. Wisconsin created and implemented a fully funded GTB-type program, with the largest element guaranteeing the property wealth per pupil of the district at the 93rd percentile, for spending up to about the 60th percentile of expenditure per pupil. To greater or lesser degrees, all three states deferred actual spending decisions to local districts, and their school finance structures represent the three major school finance systems—foundation, GTB, and combined foundation-GTB (see Chapter 4 for discussions of these structures).

Figures 1.11, 1.12, and 1.13 show the status of school finance in these three states in 1994–95, with the data organized by decile of spending from state and local sources per pupil, again excluding spending for special-needs students.[6] The

---

[6] The data show only local property tax revenues and state equalization aid for these states, and exclude other sources of revenue, which in Missouri can average $800 per student. The data also are only for K–12 districts in the three states. The tables are intended to show the final results of school finance reforms implemented over several years. The school finance structure has not changed substantively in any of the states since 1995, though in Wisconsin substantial state revenue has replaced local revenues, but because of spending controls, spending differences have not been altered much.

FIGURE 1.11   School Finance in Missouri, 1994–95, K–12 Districts

Decile	Revenues per Pupil°	Assessed Value per Pupil (at Market Value)	Local Property Tax Rate (Percent)
1	$2,987	$118,969	1.11
2	3,221	90,120	1.17
3	3,288	103,279	1.17
4	3,426	140,218	1.18
5	3,562	157,524	1.26
6	3,665	150,897	1.34
7	3,829	200,460	1.31
8	4,049	217,998	1.36
9	4,411	254,362	1.44
10	5,973	523,521	1.24

Source: Odden, 1999.

° Each district also receives an additional $648 per-pupil flat grant from a state sales tax.

Horizontal equity
Coefficient of variation: 19.5
McLoone index: 0.92

Fiscal neutrality
Correlation: 0.90
Wealth elasticity: 0.23

FIGURE 1.12   School Finance in Illinois, 1994–95, K–12 Districts

Decile	Revenues per Pupil	Assessed Value per Pupil (at Market Value)	Local Property Tax Rate (Percent)
1	$2,893	$103,238	0.60
2	3,042	126,874	0.61
3	3,130	140,313	0.63
4	3,258	157,754	0.63
5	3,400	207,211	0.67
6	3,632	220,635	0.70
7	3,922	251,595	0.83
8	4,219	280,519	0.86
9	4,687	312,488	0.89
10	5,343	386,903	1.07

Source: Odden, 1999.

Horizontal equity
Coefficient of variation: 20.4
McLoone index: 0.91

Fiscal neutrality
Correlation: 0.75
Wealth elasticity: 0.32

FIGURE 1.13   School Finance in Wisconsin, 1994–95, K–12 Districts

Decile	Revenues per Pupil	Assessed Value per Pupil (at Market Value)	Local Property Tax Rate (Percent)
1	$4,860	$164,138	1.36
2	5,188	179,004	1.45
3	5,310	147,378	1.48
4	5,350	180,601	1.50
5	5,468	172,183	1.53
6	5,569	195,932	1.55
7	5,713	196,185	1.59
8	5,962	196,601	1.73
9	6,231	222,376	1.84
10	6,828	351,184	1.74

Source: Odden, 1999.

Horizontal equity
    Coefficient of variation: 9.87
    McLoone index: 0.95

Fiscal neutrality
    Correlation: 0.59
    Wealth elasticity: 0.14

results indicate that the school finance reforms implemented in these states did not produce the equity effects that were anticipated. There are still wide spending disparities and, even with major school finance reforms, spending per pupil is still highly associated with property wealth per pupil—the higher the wealth, the higher the spending!

Further, the linkages between spending and tax rates are similar to those in New York. In all three cases, although spending per pupil increases with property wealth per pupil, so also does the local tax rate for schools. In all three states, the higher the tax rate, the higher the spending. In all three states, higher-property-wealth-per-pupil districts have higher spending per pupil but also have the highest tax rates; conversely, lower-property-wealth-per-pupil districts still have lower spending per pupil but now also have the lowest tax rates.

What happened? First, overall spending per pupil increased in real terms in all three states (122 percent, 144 percent, and 144 percent, respectively), from 1980 to 1995, using the consumer price index as the deflator. Indeed, school finance reform generally led to higher overall spending (Murray, Evans, and Schwab, 1998). But it seems that the school finance reforms, which would have allowed lower-property-wealth-per-pupil districts to increase their spending to average or higher levels while also lowering their tax rates, were not used for that purpose. Rather, lower-wealth districts appeared to use the potential of the reform programs primarily to lower their tax rates from an above-average to a below-average level. The data show that while lower-wealth districts still tend to have below-average spending levels, they have them because they also have below-average tax rates. Although the high-level GTBs in both Missouri and Wisconsin would allow these lower-wealth-per-pupil districts to spend at substantially higher levels with only modestly higher tax rates, the districts generally have chosen not to do so. They have chosen low tax rates, which in turn, have produced low expenditure levels. In short, many of the low-wealth districts did not behave as anticipated when provided a major school finance reform program.

The high-wealth districts also seemed to engage in unpredictable behavior. As these states implemented their school finance reforms over the past twenty years, it seems that the higher-wealth districts, which had enjoyed both a spending and tax rate advantage, decided to maintain their spending lead but could do so only by raising their local tax efforts for schools. Yes, some of the exceedingly wealthy districts still can spend at a high level because of their very high wealth, but with the state guaranteeing to all the tax base of the districts at the 93rd–95th percentiles, a wealth advantage exists only for a small percentage of districts, and most of these have a wealth advantage just above what the state will guarantee. For the bulk of the districts in the top third of property wealth per pupil, therefore, the higher spending is primarily produced by their higher tax rates for school purposes, reflecting the desire of their taxpayers to provide a high-quality and expensive education system.

Overall, spending disparities did drop in states that had court cases, and the states responded with school finance reforms (Murray, Evans, and Schwab, 1998). But the decreases were modest, averaging between 16 and 25 percent, depending on the statistical measure used.

In sum, the impact of the school finance changes did little to reduce fiscal inequities. Instead, the programs led to overall increases in education spending, and during that process, lower-wealth districts lowered their tax rates to below the average and settled for below-average-spending-per-pupil levels, while higher-wealth districts maintained their spending advantage by raising their tax rates and thus their spending advantages. The result was continued spending disparities, although this time driven more rationally by local tax rate differences rather than by the accident of the maldistribution of the local property tax base. The outcome was little or only modest change in these states' fiscal equity statistics—both those measuring spending disparities and those measuring the connection between spending and property wealth.

The School Finance Problem as Fiscal Adequacy

Of course, improving fiscal equity might not be the most pressing school finance issue in these states, as it was for states in the 1970s and 1980s. In fact, delineating what the school finance "problem" is for New York and the latter three states has become a major debate. Some argue that the continued existence of spending disparities and their relationship to local property wealth, whatever the cause, remains a problem. But if the "old" problem was the unequal ability to raise revenues to support public schools, and that problem is resolved by a high-level GTB or other kind of school finance reform program, others say that any remaining spending differences are a matter of local taxpayer choice and reflect neither an inherent inequity nor a school funding problem. Another group may argue that since education is a state function, spending differences per se (as a proxy for education quality) are a problem regardless of whether they are caused by the unequal distribution of the property tax base or local taxpayer choice. Still others focus on the spending of the bottom half of districts, arguing it should be higher.

The problem with all three of these arguments, however, is that they deal simply with money and largely whether base funding is equal or not, and are not related to any other substantive education goal, such as education quality or student achievement. Making this connection could be the school finance challenge of today. The driving education issue today is raising the levels of student achievement [i.e., setting high and rigorous standards and teaching students to those standards (Fuhrman, 1993; Massell, Kirst, and Hoppe, 1997; Smith and O'Day, 1991)]. Research from cognitive science suggests that we know how to produce a much higher level of learning, or at least make substantial progress towards this goal (Bruer, 1993; Siegler, 1998). Given this knowledge, Linda Darling-Hammond (1997) argues that learning to high standards should be considered a right for all children. Moreover, school finance litigation in many states has begun to stress adequacy issues over equity issues (Enrich, 1995; Heise, 1995, and Chapter 2).

Reflecting this student achievement goal and the education policy and program issues, what are the curriculum, instruction, incentive, capacity development, organization, and management strategies required to produce this higher level of student performance? The related finance issue is what level of funding is required for these programmatic strategies?

As both Odden and Clune (1998) and Reschovsky and Imazeki (1998) argue, the primary school finance problem today may be to link school finance to the strategies needed to accomplish the goal of teaching students to higher standards. In new school finance parlance, the challenge is to determine an "adequate" level of spending. The task is to identify for each district/school the level of base spending needed to teach the average student to state standards, and then to identify how much more each district/school requires to teach students with special needs—the learning disabled, those from poverty and thus educationally deficient backgrounds, and those without English proficiency—to the same high and rigorous achievement standards. As Clune (1994a, 1994b) and Odden and Clune (1998) argue, this requires a shift in school finance thinking from "equity" to "adequacy."

Interestingly, in each of the three sample states discussed earlier, educators and policymakers also began to raise the issue of school finance *adequacy* in many ways. Some questioned whether the spending levels of the bottom half of all districts (i.e., those districts with just average or mostly below-average tax rates) were a "problem" (i.e., were too low), or whether those spending levels, even though below average, were "adequate" to teach their students to acceptable standards. Others attempted to calculate a state-supported spending level that can be linked to a specified level of student performance (e.g., it will cost X dollars for 90 percent of students to meet or exceed state proficiency standards in core subjects). In a sense, this is a "back to the future" school finance objective, as many foundation programs have sought to make this linkage throughout this century. Still others explored the degree to which any "adequate" spending level should be supplemented by additional money to provide extra resources to teach students with special needs to high standards.

Chapter 4 discusses the complexities of determining an "adequate" spending level and the various methodologies that are being tapped to determine those levels. Nevertheless, for many, the focus on adequacy constitutes a shift in defining the basic school finance problem—away from the sole focus on fiscal disparities across districts and towards linking spending to what could be construed as an adequate education program (i.e., a program designed to teach students to high levels of achievement).

The School Finance Problem as Productivity

Despite disparities or any other shortcomings of current state education finance systems, many other analysts argue that the most prominent school finance problem is the low levels of system performance and student achievement produced with the relatively large levels of funding in the system (Hanushek and Associates, 1994). These analysts are convinced that, on balance, there may be a sufficient amount of revenue in the American public school system, and that the core problem is to determine how best to use those resources, particularly how to use the resources differently to support strategies that dramatically boost student performance. In one sense, the bulk of this book addresses these productivity and adequacy issues. Chapter 7 focuses solely on what is known about improving productivity in education, Chapter 8 on resource reallocation to higher performance, Chapter 9 on performance incentives for education, and Chapter 11 on restructuring teacher compensation, which consumes about 50 percent of each education dollar.

—*Chapter 2*———————————————————

Equity and Adequacy Frameworks in School Finance

Differences in educational expenditures per pupil across school districts in a state, identified as a problem as early as 1905, remains a concern in most states (Cubberly, 1905). Since then, school finance "equity" and "adequacy" have been the center of analytic attention and policy debate across the country, and became the subject of court litigation in the late 1960s. But defining and measuring school finance equity and adequacy have been difficult, complicated by different (and often unstated) definitions, different measures of the same definitions, and even different interpretations of identical measures. In the mid-1980s, Berne and Stiefel (1984) wrote a definitive book on how to conceptualize, define, and measure equity in school finance, and their work helped structure much of subsequent analysis. We borrowed heavily from their research in creating a conceptual model for analyzing school finance in the first edition of this book. Since then, new issues have emerged that are central to school finance, particularly adequacy and productivity, and thus our methods for assessing state school finance systems must also be updated.

Similarly, the topics and focus of school finance litigation have also changed. In the past, the impetus for school finance litigation was the increasing use of the federal equal protection clause to ensure rights for individuals who had been subject to discrimination. Lawyers and education finance policy analysts believed that equal protection constitutional arguments could also apply to school finance inequities and filed several suits to have traditional spending disparities among school districts—long considered unfair—declared unconstitutional as well. But in the past 10 years, litigation on school finance systems has evolved from a focus on fiscal equity to the much more complex issue of adequacy. These lawsuits raise the central question of adequacy: Are there sufficient resources in each district and each school to provide a set of programs and services sufficiently powerful to teach the vast majority of students to higher performance standards? So, litigation has become more sophisticated and has broadened its concern from equity to the issues of adequacy and productivity.

This chapter addresses these issues with the goal of presenting a framework that can be used to assess school finance equity and adequacy, including the major issues raised in the evolving legal environment. The chapter has two major sections: one addressing legal issues and one developing a comprehensive framework to assess the equity and adequacy of a state's school finance system. The legal section reviews the past 40 years of school finance litigation. It begins with the unsuccessful "educational needs" *McInnis* and *Burruss* cases in Illinois and Virginia, respectively. It then discusses the issues involved in school finance litigation based on federal and state equal protection clauses. Next, it analyzes litigation based on state education clauses, a second channel for legal action that began in the wake of the 1973 U.S. Supreme Court's ruling in the *Rodriguez* case that school finance inequities did not violate the U.S. Constitution. This portion shows how litigation based on education clauses has evolved into the topic of educational "adequacy." This section concludes with a summary of the key trends in school finance litigation.

Section two provides a framework for assessing a state's school finance structure. It is based on the original Berne and Stiefel (1984) framework and incorporates Berne and Stiefel's (1999) view of how the landscape of school finance equity has changed since then. In addition, the framework includes the new issue of educational adequacy, identifies where the key issues addressed in developing school finance litigation fit, and indicates the type of school finance structure implied by different elements of the framework.

1. SCHOOL FINANCE LITIGATION

In the late 1960s, two court cases were filed—*McInnis* v. *Shapiro*[1] in Illinois and *Burruss* v. *Wilkerson*[2] in Virginia—challenging the constitutionality of differences in educational expenditures across each state's school districts. While brought on equal protection grounds, these early cases argued that the systems were unconstitutional because education was a fundamental right and the wide differences in expenditures or revenues per pupil across school districts were not related to "educational need." The suit argued that there was no educational justification for wide disparities in per-pupil education revenues and that while differences in educational expenditures per pupil could exist, they had to be related to "educational need" and not educationally irrelevant variables such as the local tax base.

In trial, however, the court reasonably asked for a standard by which to assess and measure educational need. Plaintiffs did not have a strong response; in

---

[1] *McInnis* v. *Shapiro*, 293 F. Supp. 327 (N.O. Ill. 1968) affirmed.
[2] *Burruss* v. *Wilkerson*, 310 F. Supp. 572 Virg. (1969), aff'd., 397 U.S. 44 (1970).

fact, at that time, "educational need" was a diffuse term on which there was not even minimal agreement as to either definition or measurement. The wide variations in expenditures per pupil alone were not sufficient to move the court to find the system unconstitutional because there was no way to link expenditures to need. In both cases, therefore, the court ruled that the suits were non-justiciable because need could not be defined, measured, nor costed out; in short, the court did not have a standard by which to assess the plaintiffs' claims.

These first attempts to use the courts as a route to resolve school finance inequities, thus, were unsuccessful. In nearly all subsequent school finance cases, moreover, one of the defendants' first motions has been to declare the case non-justiciable, citing *McInnis* and *Burruss* as precedents. School finance litigants, however, continued to use equal protection as the legal route to challenge state school finance structures, but developed standards for courts to use. The next section outlines the main issues involved in equal protection litigation (see also Levin, 1977; Minorini and Sugarman, 1999a, 1999b; Sparkman, 1990; Underwood, 1995a, 1995b; Underwood and Sparkman, 1991).

Equal Protection Litigation

The U.S. Constitution was written by individuals who were strong proponents of individual rights. The founding fathers believed that everyone was entitled to life, liberty, and the pursuit of happiness. To give this broad phrase substantive meaning and to protect individuals from governmental actions that might limit life, liberty and the pursuit of happiness, the constitution's authors added the Bill of Rights as the first 10 amendments to the Constitution. These amendments specified several rights of U.S. citizens, including the right to free speech, to religion, to a free press, to bear arms, and the right of assembly. Other amendments to the U.S. Constitution also identified particular rights of citizenship, including the Thirteenth (prohibition of slavery), the Fourteenth (due process and equal protection), Fifteenth (cannot deny right to vote on basis of race), Nineteenth (women's suffrage), and Twenty-sixth (18-year old voting right). Article 1, Sections 9 and 10 of the Constitution create the rights of habeas corpus and prohibit ex post facto laws. The president also can designate fundamental rights through executive orders.

The U.S. Supreme Court has the responsibility and authority for defining the meanings of the rights identified in the U.S. Constitution, the Bill of Rights and other amendments, and also for determining whether the president, Congress, or state governors and legislatures exercise their power properly, especially as their actions might impact a right specified in the Constitution.

The equal protection clause of the Fourteenth Amendment provides that no state shall "deny to any person within its jurisdiction the equal protection of the laws." This amendment was enacted in the mid-nineteenth century during the time of slavery, and was designed to make it unconstitutional for states to treat African Americans differently from whites. But as history unfolded, new legislation was enacted that was interpreted as violating the equal protection clause, and suits were filed. Over time, the U.S. Supreme Court created mechanisms for determining whether, and how, governmental actions might violate the equal protection clause.

The equal protection clause could be read to mean that governments—local, state, and federal—could not treat individuals differently for any reason. But that is clearly not the case. Laws specify that some individuals with a particular license can drive a car or practice medicine or teach in public schools, and some cannot. In each of these cases, governments have determined that individuals need certain skills or expertise to engage in these activities, and the state provides a license only to those individuals who demonstrate that they have the requisite expertise. All states have some clause in their state constitution that has been interpreted to be the equivalent of an equal protection clause (Minorini and Sugarman, 1999a, 1999b; Underwood, 1995a). Thus, many equal protection cases today, and nearly all school finance court cases, are brought on the basis of either or both federal and state equal protection clauses.

The rational test.   How, then, does a court determine whether or not a governmental action that treats individuals differently is constitutional? When equal protection suits are brought, the court uses one of two tests to determine whether the equal protection clause has been violated. The first is the rational test. This test simply asks whether the government has a reason for the differential treatment. In the above examples, the reason for not allowing everyone who wishes to drive a car, practice medicine, or teach in the public schools is that governments feel individuals need to demonstrate that they have some expertise in these areas before engaging in these activities. Courts have accepted these explanations for treating individuals differently. Indeed, states usually can cite some reason for any action they take. Thus, if the court invokes the rational equal protection test, the state action usually is upheld because the state nearly always can identify some basis for its law.

The strict judicial scrutiny test.   The second test is "strict judicial scrutiny." When the court invokes strict judicial scrutiny, the government bears a tougher burden. It has to show that there is a "compelling state interest" for its particular action and that there is "no less discriminatory" policy for the state to carry out that compelling interest. This is an onerous test. Both parts of the test must be met. When the court invokes this test, states usually have difficulty both in identifying the compelling state interest and in claiming that no other state policies can be identified that have less discriminatory impacts. Indeed, when strict judicial scrutiny is invoked, the state usually loses the case. The strict judicial scrutiny test usually overturns the governmental action that is the basis of the suit.

Fundamental rights.   The key, then, is to identify the circumstances under which the court can invoke strict judicial scrutiny. Courts invoke strict judicial scrutiny in only two circumstances: (1) when governmental action affects a "fundamental right" or (2) when governmental action creates a "suspect classification" of individuals. Fundamental rights, as discussed above, are those identified in the Constitution or, over time, in equal protection litigation as the subject of a U.S. Supreme Court ruling. Fundamental rights today include the right to practice any religion, the right of free speech, the right of a free press, the right of assembly, and the right to due process.

Through equal protection litigation during the 1950s and 1960s, the right to vote and the right to appeal a court case also were designated as fundamental rights. Many states had required individuals to pay a poll tax in order to register to vote. Poor individuals were unable to pay the tax and thus lost the opportunity to vote. Cases challenging this governmental requirement to pay a poll tax were brought on two grounds: (1) that voting was a fundamental right of U.S. citizens and (2) that the poll tax created a suspect classification (discussed more below) of poor and nonpoor individuals. The court ruled that voting was indeed a fundamental right, and that there were less discriminatory ways for the state to collect the small amount of revenues acquired through the poll tax, and the poll tax was ruled to be unconstitutional.

During that time, some states required individuals who lost a lower court case to pay for a reproduction of the court transcript if they wanted to appeal the court decision. Individuals without the economic means to do so thus lost their opportunity to appeal. Cases challenging this governmental requirement again were brought on two grounds: (1) that the right to appeal was a fundamental right of U.S. citizens and (2) that the requirement to pay for a reproduction of the lower court transcript as a condition of appeal created a suspect classification (discussed more below) of poor and nonpoor individuals. The court ruled that the right to appeal was indeed a fundamental right, and that there were less discriminatory ways for the state to collect the small cost for reproducing the transcript (e.g., the cost could be borne by the government), and ruled unconstitutional the practice of requiring individuals to pay the cost of the transcript as a condition to appeal. In both of these cases, the U.S. Supreme Court identified new fundamental rights and overturned state actions that differentiated among individuals in their exercise of these fundamental rights.

Suspect classifications.   The second situation for invoking strict judicial scrutiny is when government action creates a "suspect classification" of individuals. The Constitution directly prohibits government actions that affect individuals differently in terms of their religion or national origin, but is silent on race. It was the 1954 U.S. Supreme Court decision in the *Brown* v. *Board of Education*[3] desegregation case that identified race as a suspect class. In this decision, the court ruled that "separate but equal" schools that had been created in many southern states violated the equal protection clause of the U.S. Constitution because it classified individuals according to race. In overturning the practice of segregating schools, the court created a new suspect class—race—that effectively overturned all state laws that treated individuals differently solely on the basis of race.

---

[3] *Brown* v. *Board of Education of Topeka,* 347 U.S. 483 (1954).

Income, while raised as a potential suspect class in both the poll tax and right to appeal cases as a suspect class, has not been recognized by the U.S. Supreme Court as a suspect class. While the decisions in both of these instances showed sympathy towards recognizing income as a suspect class, the cases turned on the fundamentality of the rights affected, not on the classification of poor and nonpoor. Thus, today individual income is not recognized as a suspect classification.

School Finance Equal Protection Litigation

In the wake of *McInnis* and *Burruss,* school finance litigation had two general challenges: to determine a strategy that would place challenges to inter-district school finance expenditure per-pupil disparities directly in the mainstream of equal protection litigation, and to identify standards that could be used by courts to decide whether school finance realities met equal protection requirements.

Arthur Wise (1968), then a doctoral student at the University of Chicago, argued that education was a fundamental right, and that the equal protection clause required that education must be provided equally across all school districts. He further argued that the variations in educational expenditures across districts in most states did not reflect uniformity of educational offerings, because the expenditure variations were not related to educational need. But as discussed above, the educational need argument was not accepted by the court.

At about the same time, John Coons, then a law professor at Northwestern University, and two law students, William Clune (now a law professor at the University of Wisconsin—Madison) and Stephen Sugarman (now a law professor at the University of California—Berkeley), began to frame another argument, namely that education funding created a suspect classification defined by district property wealth per pupil (Coons, Clune, and Sugarman, 1970). They argued that local school districts were creations of state governments and that by making school financing heavily dependent on local financing, states gave school districts unequal opportunities to raise educational revenues because the property value per child varied widely across school districts. Coons, Clune and Sugarman argued that school financing systems needed to be "fiscally neutral" (i.e., that expenditures per pupil could not be related to local district property wealth per pupil). Put differently, they argued that education could not be dependent on local wealth, but only on the wealth of the state as a whole.[4]

This argument created two major new "hooks" for school finance litigation. First, it suggested district property wealth per pupil as a suspect classification. Second, and as importantly, it created a new standard—the fiscal neutrality standard—that holds that the quality of education could only be a function of the wealth of the state as a whole, not local wealth. More concretely, the fiscal

---

[4] It should be noted that this argument would not support an adequacy argument, discussed below; adequacy could be limited by state wealth.

neutrality standard required that there be no relationship between educational spending per pupil and local district property wealth per pupil. Both of these variables were easily measured, and both were used in nearly all state school finance systems, and there were standard statistical measures to identify the magnitude of the relationship between these two variables. Thus, Coons, Clune, and Sugarman gave school finance litigation a standard that the court could use and added this new suspect class hook to the litigation arsenal. In addition, the Coons, Clune, and Sugarman strategy clearly identified aspects of a school finance system that could not exist and left wide legislative discretion to design a structure that could pass constitutional muster.[5]

School finance litigation based on either federal or state equal protection clauses makes two arguments before the court. The first is that education is a fundamental right and must be provided equally to all individuals. The second is that state school finance structures create a suspect classification based on property wealth per pupil, which makes the quality of education higher for students in districts high in property wealth per pupil, and lower for students in districts low in property wealth per pupil.

While creative from the legal perspective of equal protection litigation, this school finance litigation strategy faced several challenges. First, litigants were asking the court both to recognize a new fundamental right—education—and to recognize a new suspect classification—property wealth per pupil. Second, the suspect class not only was a new one, but a different kind of suspect class. District property wealth per pupil related to governmental entities—school districts—and not individuals, to which all previous suspect classes had pertained, and was an economic measure that had not yet been recognized as a suspect class. Again, even though the court had appeared sympathetic to individual income as a suspect class, it had not recognized it as such. But even if the court had, district property wealth per pupil would still be different, both because district property wealth related to a government entity and not an individual, and because it related to wealth—property valuation—and not income. Even though this school finance equal protection strategy was devised during a time when the U.S. Supreme Court was expanding its list of fundamental rights and suspect classifications, the Court nevertheless tends to take a conservative stance. School finance litigants knew they would need to develop a litigation strategy on a case-by-case basis that would help lead the Court to make these two new additions to equal protection litigation.

Serrano v. *Priest.*   The first case filed using the Coons, Clune, and Sugarman strategy was *Serrano* v. *Priest*[6] in California. The case was filed in 1968, and there was an immediate motion to dismiss, claiming that school finance cases were nonjusticiable, citing *McInnis* and *Burruss* as precedents. The trial court dismissed the case on that basis. The dismissal was appealed all the way to the California

---

[5] Chapter 4 details several different school finance systems, and discusses the degree to which they will create constitutional structures.

[6] *Serrano* v. *Priest,* 96 Cal. Rptr. 601, 487 P.2d 1241, 5 Cal. 3d 584 (1971).

Supreme Court, which rendered an opinion in August 1971. In that opinion, based both on the Fourteenth Amendment to the U.S. Constitution and the equal protection clause in the California constitution, the court ruled that: (1) the case was justiciable, using the fiscal neutrality standard; (2) education was a fundamental right and property wealth per pupil was a suspect class; and (3) if the facts were as alleged, the California school finance system would be unconstitutional. This was a precedent-setting opinion, gaining nationwide media, policy and legal attention, and immediately spawning a series of similar court cases in other states.[7]

It is important to understand that neither the *Serrano* opinion (nor subsequent school finance court cases) found that use of the property tax per se in financing schools was unconstitutional. Unfortunately, this policy implication was raised in several media reports on the *Serrano* opinion, but it was incorrect. As Chapter 4 indicates, there are several ways states can use the local property tax to help finance schools and still create a fiscally neutral, or constitutionally acceptable system. It is only when there is heavy reliance on local property taxes, and there is no state aid program to offset the differences in the amounts districts can raise with a given tax rate, that systems can become unconstitutional (i.e., that strong relationships evolve between expenditures or revenues per pupil and local property wealth per pupil).

Rodriguez v. *San Antonio.*   One case filed after the *Serrano* opinion was *San Antonio School District* v. *Rodriguez*[8] in Texas. This case was taken directly to a three-judge federal district court panel, with the next stage being a direct appeal to the U.S. Supreme Court.[9] The district court found for the plaintiffs, finding education to be a fundamental right, and property wealth per pupil to be a suspect classification. The decision held that the Texas school finance system violated the equal protection clause of the U.S. Constitution and ordered the legislature to devise a constitutional system.

The case was immediately appealed to the U.S. Supreme Court, even before any such school finance cases had been appealed to the state supreme court level. In March 1973, in a split 5-4 decision, the U.S. Supreme Court held that the Texas system did not violate the U.S. Constitution. The majority opinion held that as important as education was for U.S. citizens and for discharging the responsibilities of citizenship, it was not mentioned in the Constitution, and the Court was unwilling, on its own, to recognize it as a fundamental right. Further, the

[7] Arizona (*Shofstall* v. *Hollins,* 1973); Connecticut (*Horton* v. *Meskill,* 1977); Idaho (*Thompson* v. *Engleking,* 1975); *Blase* v. *Illinois,* 1973); Kansas (*Knowles* v. *Kansas,* 1981); Minnesota (*Van Dusartz* v. *Hatfield,* 1971); New Jersey (*Robinson* v. *Cahill,* 1973; Oregon (*Olsen* v. *State,* 1976); Texas (*Rodriquez* v. *San Antonio*); Washington (*North Shore School District No. 417* v. *Kinnear,* 530 P.2d 178 (Wash. 1974); Wisconsin (*Buse* v. *Smith,* 1976).

[8] *San Antonio School District* v. *Rodriguez,* 411 U.S. 45 (1973).

[9] Some have argued that the *Rodriguez* case should not have been filed so as to force an appeal to the U.S. Supreme Court so early in the process of school finance litigation, assuring that it would have been better to win several cases at the district and state level and to show that states could respond to a decision overturning the school finance system and that such decisions would not simply put a state's education system into a state of disarray.

decision held that property wealth per pupil was not a suspect class, in large part because it related to governmental entities (school districts) and not individuals, and because property wealth was so different from individual income.[10]

Thus, the Court did not invoke strict judicial scrutiny. Instead, it invoked the rational test. As was the practice then (and now) for states being sued, Texas responded that the existing method of funding education by local property taxes reflected the principle of local control. And this response, as are most responses to a rational test, was accepted as reasonable by the courts.

The *Rodriguez* decision undercut hopes that had been raised by the *Serrano* opinion about the efficacy of reforming school finance inequities through the federal courts. Just 18 months after the precedent-setting opinion in the *Serrano* case, the *Rodriguez* case eliminated the U.S. Constitution as a legal route to school finance reform. The decision threw all school finance cases out of the federal courts and back to state courts, to be argued state-by-state on the basis of state equal protection clauses,[11] as well as state education clauses.[12]

Indeed, the *Rodriguez* decision somewhat encouraged litigation at the state level. One part of the decision suggested that states could find education to be a fundamental right because, unlike the federal government, most state constitutions not only mentioned education, but had constitutional clauses explicitly creating student access to a free, public education.

Robinson v. *Cahill.*   As if responding to the U.S. Supreme Court's ruling, the New Jersey Supreme Court rendered a decision in *Robinson* v. *Cahill*[13] in April 1973, just one month after the *Rodriguez* decision. This was the first case to reach a state supreme court.[14] A loss in *Robinson,* while not eliminating litigation in other states, would have been a further blow for litigants, especially following so closely in the wake of *Rodriguez.* The New Jersey court recognized the *Rodriguez* test for finding education to be a fundamental right and acknowledged that education was mentioned in the New Jersey constitution. Nevertheless, the court held that education was not a fundamental right. Further, the court held that although rich and poor school districts had, respectively, above- and below-average spending per pupil, property wealth per pupil was not a suspect class. Thus, the *Robinson* court found that the New Jersey school finance system did not violate the New Jersey equal protection clause.

However, the court did overturn the New Jersey school finance system, citing the state constitution's education clause that required the state to create a

---

[10] In addition, the state of Texas showed that low-income children did not generally attend schools in low-wealth districts. Indeed, many low-income children attended school in districts—the big-city districts—that had quite high property value per pupil. Thus, if the court had been inclined to recognize income as a suspect class, the data did not allow plantiffs to argue that low income and low property wealth were correlated.

[11] All state constitutions have the functional equivalent of an equal protection clause.

[12] All states have some sort of education clause requiring states to create a system of public schools.

[13] *Robinson* v. *Cahill,* 303 A2d 273 (N.J. 1973).

[14] Remember that the *Serrano* ruling simply overturned a motion to dismiss the case. The California Supreme Court remanded the case back to the superior court for trial.

"thorough and efficient" public education system. The court held that a school finance structure that allowed for wide disparities in spending per pupil that were strongly linked to local property wealth per pupil was not a "thorough and efficient" system, and sent the case to the state legislature to design a new system. The court also found that the school finance system must allow schools to provide "educational opportunities that will prepare [the student] for his role as citizen and as competitor in the labor market (*Robinson* I, 1973:293)." But despite this phrase foreshadowing subsequent adequacy cases, the court went on to rule the system unconstitutional largely on the basis of spending differences, as those were the only criteria available to judge whether or not the system was thorough and efficient.

This case was important for three reasons. First, it kept school finance litigation alive just after *Rodriguez* seemed to sound its death knell. Second, it paved the way for challenging school finance systems on the basis of state education clauses, a substantively different strategy than using the equal protection clause. Third, it hinted at a new standard, which subsequently evolved into adequacy litigation.

Interestingly, the New Jersey legislature procrastinated in its response to *Robinson*. The state did not have an income tax, and each year the state budget was short of the level of funds necessary for the enhanced state fiscal role needed to finance a constitutionally permissible school finance structure. In July 1976, therefore, the New Jersey Supreme Court, in a symbolic but dramatic action, shut down the entire New Jersey school system.[15] In response, the legislature designed a new school finance structure and enacted a new tax system to fund it, as well as provide local property tax relief.

School Finance Litigation Based on State Education Clauses

Challenging state school finance structures under the state education clause entails additional legal strategies other than those used for equal protection litigation. Some cases use the education clause to frame a fiscal neutrality argument (i.e., to find that education is a fundamental interest and/or property wealth per pupil is a suspect class). Others use the education clause to buttress arguments about the fundamentality of education and wealth as a suspect class made under the equal protection clause. The cases in both Arkansas[16] and Wyoming[17] in the early 1980s were largely based on these arguments, as were the Texas[18] decisions from the late 1980s until the mid-1990s, and the Vermont[19] case in 1997.

The Texas *Edgewood* v. *Kirby* decisions entailed some fascinating interactions between the court and the legislature, and led to a legal decision and new

---

[15] Since this occurred during the summer break, only summer schools were affected. The action, however, indicated the serious posture of the New Jersey Supreme Court and was highly symbolic.

[16] *Dupree* v. *Alma School District* No. 30, 651 S.W. 2d 90 (Ark. 1983).

[17] *Washakie County School District No. 1* v. *Herschler*, 606 P.2d 310 (Wy. 1980).

[18] *Edgewood Independent School District* v. *Kirby*, 777 S.W. 2d 391 (Tex. 1989); *Edgewood* v. *Meno*, 893 S.W. 2d 450 (Tex. 1995).

[19] *Brigham* v. *State* (VT 1997).

finance structure that was unique. The Texas clause, "support and maintenance of an efficient system of public free schools," was initially overturned on fiscal neutrality grounds, but many analysts claimed that the Texas system was quite equal except for the bottom and top 50 districts. As the legislature submitted plan after plan to create a new structure for the overall system, the court kept rejecting these proposals. When the legislature then enacted a system that "recaptured" funds from the highest wealth districts, which the court decision seemed to require, the court subsequently found the system in violation of another section of the constitution prohibiting the legislature from reallocating local revenues. Finally, the legislature created a two-tiered pupil-weighted system (Picus and Toenjes, 1994) that was similar to the original system, but required the wealthiest districts to voluntarily, with voter approval, give some of their wealth or revenues to lower-wealth districts as a condition for receiving any state aid. This system, which largely focused on the top and bottom 50 districts and which the court identified as the core of the problem at the beginning of the litigation process, was finally approved. As discussed below, this was the first time that a court overturned a state's school finance system because of its impact on only a small number of districts.

Nevertheless, the use of the state education clause to make the same arguments as the fiscal neutrality cases was not successful in the courts. Courts seemed to want more than fiscal differences arguments, and wanted plaintiffs to show some "injury" rather than just a relative difference in educational offerings. Indeed, in rejecting the fiscal neutrality arguments as reasons to overturn state school finance systems, several of the court decisions of many states in the 1990s (e.g., Maine, Minnesota, Virginia, and Wyoming) suggested they might be more sympathetic to a different type of argument: namely, an adequacy argument.

The third use of the education clause is to inject substantive meaning into a state education clause, which subsequently led to the "adequacy" cases that emerged in the 1990s. The language of education clauses varies substantially across the states, with some calling for the creation of an education system, and others calling for "thorough and efficient," "thorough and uniform," or "general and uniform" school systems, yet all states have some requirement for the state to create a system of public schools. Though McUsic (1991) argued that the specific wording of the education clause could lead to stronger or weaker interpretations of the substantive meaning of the clause, both Sparkman (1994) and Underwood (1995a, 1995b) concluded that the meaning of the education clause is state specific and depends on its political history and prior interpretation. There are five aspects to challenging the school finance system on the basis of the state education clause.

Historical meaning of the education clause.   The first is to analyze the debates at the constitutional convention as they related to the phrasing of the education clause to determine how authors of the state constitution viewed education. In some states, the "general and uniform" clause appears to have been merely an attempt to create one statewide system of public schools. Prior to most states' nineteenth-century constitutional conventions, there was no *state* education system. Education systems were local entities that differed from district to district. Sometimes there were city and noncity school districts, or regional groupings of districts, but there was no statewide system. States then began to consolidate these diverse systems into one statewide system, defined primarily by state laws, rules, and regulations, especially as they pertained to school accreditation and teacher licensure. In these states, the "general and uniform" type clauses simply meant one, statewide education system. The phrase had no particular implications for school finance or differences in per-pupil education spending; indeed, in these states, the financing system usually continued to rely heavily on local property taxes, with small state contributions provided via a flat per-pupil grant (see Chapter 4).

In other states, however, such clauses meant much more than simply creating one statewide system. Records from the debates surrounding the creation of the constitution indicated that the constitutional framers envisaged a statewide uniform system, with equal spending per pupil, often fully financed with state funds. Especially in western states, there was hope that proceeds from the Northwest section lands and other land grants could provide all the funds needed for the public school system. In these states, "thorough and uniform" and "general and uniform" could reasonably be inferred to mean something close to equal spending or equal access to core educational opportunities across all school districts.

Unfortunately for school finance litigation, there is no single answer to the type of education and education finance system state constitutional framers meant to create when they wrote new state constitutions, including the education clauses. Nevertheless, one avenue both plaintiffs and defendants explore in litigation based on state education clauses is to review the constitutional history and determine whether the constitutional framers had specific ideas in mind about the nature of the state education system, the type of school finance structure that would support it, and whether those notions are relevant to current school finance legal issues.

Education clauses requiring more than just an education system.   The other three routes to school finance litigation based on state education clauses seek to inject substantive meaning into education clauses. Though state constitutional framers might or might not have implied specific school finance structures, today state supreme courts decide what state education clauses require in terms of school finance structures. Thus, the task for school finance litigants is to convince the court to accept variations of what the education clause could require.[20]

One strategy is to argue that the education clause places an "affirmative duty" on the legislature to create more than just an education system, which all states have created. This argument was used in the 1973 *Robinson* case, in which the court argued that the "thorough and efficient" clause required an education system that allowed all students equal opportunities to compete in the labor

---

[20]The next few paragraphs draw from Odden, McGuire, and Belsches-Simmons, 1983, pp. 38–39.

market. It was used again by the New Jersey court in the 1990 *Abbott* v. *Burke*[21] case (discussed below) to ensure higher educational attainment for low income and minority students in the state's property-poor and low-income central-city school districts. In both instances, the court overturned the state's education finance structure. But the Georgia Supreme Court in a 1981 case concluded that the state education clause that required state provision of an "adequate education" placed no affirmative duty on the state to equalize educational opportunities and upheld the state's school finance system. An Idaho court in 1975[22] ruled that it was the legislature's and not the court's prerogative to interpret the education clause. A 1976 Oregon court[23] ruled that their school finance system could be justified on the basis of local control. Similarly, the Colorado Supreme Court in *Lujan* v. *Colorado*[24] found that state's "thorough and uniform" clause was met when an education program was provided in each school district, even though the quality of the programs varied substantially.

Substantive demands of the education clause—adequacy arguments.   The third strategy has been to focus explicitly on the substantive demands of the education clause, and it is this strategy that led to the actual term "adequacy" and its definition in school finance litigation of the late 1980s and throughout the 1990s. The first decisions using this strategy were those in the 1978 Washington[25] and 1973 New Jersey cases. Minorini and Sugarman (1999a, 1999b) argue that these two cases actually were the precursors of the 1990s' adequacy cases, though the term "adequacy" was never used in these cases. These decisions began to expand the notion of school finance equity beyond finance to the delivery of an education program that would provide students with a fair opportunity to learn to high standards. It took New Jersey more than two decades to define what that program would be, but Washington defined that program as the staffing that the average district had been providing its schools.

It was not until the 1982 *Pauley* v. *Bailey*[26] West Virginia case that a more specific definition of such a program was developed. This definition was quite similar to later definitions of "adequacy" that emerged in the 1990s through school finance litigation and the standards-based education reform movement. On an initial motion to dismiss (again based on *McInnis* and *Burruss*), the West Virginia Supreme Court ruled that the case was justiciable, but required the trial court first to determine what a "thorough and efficient" (T & E) education system was, and then to assess the degree to which the existing system met the T & E test. The resulting trial concluded that T & E required equal programs and services across all school districts, and found that the existing finance system did not

[21] Abbott I: *Abbott* v. *Burke.* 100 N.J. 269 (1985); Abbott II: *Abbott* v. *Burke,* 119 N.J. 287 (1990).
[22] *Thompson* v. *Engelking,* 537 P.2d 635 (Idaho 1975).
[23] *Olsen* v. *State,* 554 P.2d 139 (Oregon 1976).
[24] *Lujan* v. *Colorado State Board of Education,* 649 P.2d 1005 (Colo. 1982).
[25] *Seattle School District No. 1 of King City* v. *State,* 585 P.2d 71 (Wash. 1978).
[26] *Pauley* v. *Bailey,* C.A. No. 75-126 (Cir. Ct. Kanawha Cty., W. Va. 1982), initially decided as *Pauley* v. *Kelly,* 255 S.E. 2d 859 (W. Va. 1979).

provide such equality. Even though it was only a lower court that had overturned the West Virginia school finance system, the state did not appeal. In response, the state department of education, with the support of the governor, created numerous committees around core education programs—all the core subject areas, such as mathematics, science, social studies, language arts, etc.; all categorical programs such as compensatory education, special education, and bilingual education, as well as vocational education, and all other programs—and asked them to define standards that would represent a quality, or thorough and efficient, program. An overview committee then took the reports from the various subcommittees, and compiled them into what became the state's Master Plan of standards for all operating programs, as well as for facilities. Funding this plan would have required the state to nearly double education resources in West Virginia, so the plan was only partially implemented. But in 1997, fully 15 years after the Master Plan was proposed, a court ordered the state finally to fully fund the plan.

The adequacy approach to interpreting the requirements of the state education clause matured during the 1990s. Four major cases represent what has become the adequacy approach. In 1989, the Kentucky Supreme Court not only overturned the state's school finance system, but also found the entire state education system to be unconstitutional, including its curriculum, governance, and its management. Although this case began as a fiscal neutrality case, the court decision turned it into an adequacy case. The court held that school finance equity required that all students should have access to an adequate education program, and included the following language about what such a program would include.

- sufficient oral and written communication skills to enable students to function in a complex and rapidly changing civilization,
- sufficient knowledge of economic, social, and political systems to enable the student to make informed choice,
- sufficient understanding of governmental processes to enable the student to understand the issues that affect his or her community, state, and nation,
- sufficient self-knowledge and knowledge of his or her mental and physical wellness,
- sufficient grounding in the arts to enable each student to appreciate his or her cultural and historical heritage,
- sufficient training or preparation for advanced training in either academic or vocational fields so as to enable each child to choose and pursue life work intelligently, and
- sufficient levels of academic or vocational skills to enable public school students to compete favorably with their counterparts in surrounding states, in academics or in the job market.

In response, the state completely redesigned the education system, including not only the finance structure, but also the governance, management, and curriculum programs. Moreover, the Kentucky reforms also reflected the kind of education reform that first was known as "systemic reform" (Fuhrman, 1993; Odden, 1995a; Smith & O'Day, 1991) and later evolved into standards-based education reform (Massell, Kirst, and Hoppe, 1997). They included, in addition to a new three-tiered finance system that was accompanied by a large infusion of new money, content standards for the curriculum in all major subject areas, performance standards for students including a new testing system, changes in school governance and management including much more school-based decision making, and a new accountability system with rewards and sanctions at the school-site level (Adams, 1994, 1997).

At least five aspects of the overall Kentucky policy response were and continue to be significant. First, the system focused on student performance outcomes. The primary goal was not just dollars and education inputs but to identify and produce high student achievement in a variety of educational areas. Second, school sites gained substantial discretion for allocating and using dollars with many finance decisions decentralized from the district to the school. Third, schools were rewarded financially (on an unequalized wealth basis) for meeting performance improvement goals, and sanctioned—including being taken over by the state—for consistently not meeting goals (Kelley and Protsik, 1997; Kelley, 1998a) . Fourth, preschool, which is essentially an additional grade, was provided at substantial new cost. Fifth, the finance system included a substantially increased foundation program for base expenditures across all districts. And the state limited local add-ons to an extra 50 percent, for which the first 15 percent was "equalized" by the state through a guaranteed tax base. Many of these programmatic elements became the core of standards-based education reform and the basis for a definition of adequacy.

Shortly after the 1989 Kentucky decision, the Alabama[27] and Massachusetts[28] Supreme Courts overturned state education and school finance systems on the basis of adequacy arguments. Interestingly, the decisions in both states used the same language from the Kentucky decision in defining what the court meant by an adequate education program. Massachusetts immediately enacted a comprehensive standards-based education and school finance reform, but Alabama was not able to muster the political support to enact a similarly comprehensive reform program, and by the end of 1997 had not acted in response to the court order.

In Wyoming,[29] acting on a new case, the court again overturned that state's education finance system and this time required an adequacy response by stating that "the legislature must first design the best educational system by identifying the proper education package each Wyoming student is entitled to have. . . . [T]he cost of that educational package must then be determined and the legislature must then take the necessary action to fund the package." So while not spec-

---

[27] *Alabama Coalition for Equity, Inc.* v. *Hunt,* 1993 WL 204083 (Ala. Cir.).

[28] *McDuffy* v. *Secretary of the Executive Office of Education,* 615 N.E. 2d 516 (Mass. 1993).

[29] *Campbell County School District, State of Wyoming, et al.* v. *State of Wyoming,* 907 P.2d 1238 (Wy. 1995).

ifying what an adequate education package should be, as did the courts in Kentucky, Alabama, and Massachusetts, the Wyoming court did stipulate that the legislature had to define the program and, once defined, it then had to fully fund it.

Five other state courts overturned school finance systems on the basis of adequacy arguments—Arizona,[30] Ohio,[31] New Hampshire,[32] North Carolina,[33] and Tennessee[34]—using their own rather than Kentucky's language for defining "adequacy." The courts in Florida,[35] Illinois,[36] and Rhode Island[37] rejected cases based on the adequacy argument, and four state courts—Maine, Virginia, Minnesota, and Wisconsin—suggested successful arguments could be made on the basis of educational adequacy when rejecting plaintiffs' arguments in fiscal neutrality cases.

New Jersey represents yet another twist and advance on the adequacy front. As stated earlier, though the 1973 New Jersey case foreshadowed adequacy by interpreting the T & E clause to mean an education system designed to produce students who could compete in the evolving labor market, most of the *Robinson* I decision focused largely on financial disparities. Further, the 1976 legislative response sought to address those disparities, and the first subsequent court challenge to the new school finance law actually upheld those financial elements of the new system (Minorini and Sugarman, 1999a, 1999b). But in that subsequent decision and in the multiple decisions beginning in 1989 and continuing through 1998 that systematically overturned the New Jersey system in six different *Abbott v. Burke* decisions,[38] the state supreme court focused more and more on the substantive meaning of that T & E education clause. In addition, the 1989 decision (*Abbott* I) overturned the system for just the 28 "special-needs" districts (i.e., the districts with the highest concentrations of low-income and minority students), thus joining Texas in finding the school finance system unconstitutional for just some districts in the state.

Abbott I required the state to raise the spending per pupil of the special-needs districts so that it approached the average of the wealthiest, suburban districts. The subsequent legislative response, the Quality Education Act of 1990, moved in that direction, but the state was not able to raise sufficient funds. Thus, the plaintiffs returned to the courts and were successful in obtaining two additional decisions in the early 1990s (*Abbott* II and *Abbott* III) that required a

---

[30] *Roosevelt Elementary School District* v. *Bishop*, 1994 WL 378649 (Ariz. 1994).

[31] *DeRolph, et al.* v. *State*, 677 N.E. 2d 733 (Oh. 1997).

[32] *Claremont School District* v. *Governor*, No. 92-711 (New Ham. 1993).

[33] *Leandro* v. *State*, 472 S.E. 2d 11 (NC 1996).

[34] *Tennessee Small School System* v. *McWherter*, 851 S.W. 2d 139 (Tenn. 1993); *Tennessee Small School System* v. *McWherter*, S.W. 2d 894 S.W. 2d 7374 (Tenn. 1995).

[35] *Coalition for Equity* v. *Chiles*, 680 So. 2d 400 (Fla. 1996).

[36] *Committee* v. *Edgar*, 673 N.E. 2d 1178 (Ill. 1996).

[37] *Pawtucket* v. *Sundlun*, 662 A. 2d 40 (R.I. 1994).

[38] Abbott I: *Abbott v. Burke*, 100 N.J. 269 (N.J. 1985); Abbott II: *Abbott v. Burke*, 119 N.J. 287 (N.J. 1990); Abbott III: *Abbott v. Burke*, 136 N.J. 444 (N.J. 1994); Abbott IV: *Abbott v. Burke*, 149 N.J. 149, 168 (N.J. 1997); Abbott V: *Abbott v. Burke*, 153 N.J. 480 (N.J. 1998), Appendix I; Abbott VI: *Abbott v. Burke*, 153 N.J. 480 (N.J. 1998).

revised system that could raise sufficient funds, and the court gave the state a late 1996 deadline by which to comply. In essence, the court wanted the state to define and then to fund an education program that would teach students in the 28 special-needs districts to high performance standards.

In response to both the court case and to the evolution of education reform, the state began in 1996 to create curriculum content and student performance standards in six different subject areas, and a new state testing system that would measure performance to those standards. They also designed a new finance system, called the Comprehensive Educational Improvement Finance Act (CEIFA), which was intended to be sufficient for districts and schools to implement the standards. In CEIFA, the state identified the staffing for an elementary, middle, and high school that it felt was sufficient to teach students to the new standards, and used statewide average costs to determine what that amount would provide for each of the 28 special-needs districts. The resultant figures increased funding for the special-needs districts but not to the level specified by the court. Nevertheless, the state argued in court that the proposal was sufficient to accomplish the educational goals of the new state's program, which was the ultimate intention of the school finance court case.

In early 1997, however, the court in *Abbott* v. *Burke* IV ruled that the CEIFA program was unconstitutional largely because CEIFA did not reflect a program that was specific to the needs of the special-needs districts. Indeed, the CEIFA school models were patterned after practices in districts that had very few similarities to the education challenges faced by the special-needs districts, which enrolled very large percentages of low-income and minority students. The court then ruled that the only effective schooling model they knew of was that of the highest spending districts, which were successful in teaching their students to high standards. So the court used that model as a de facto standard and mandated the state to raise the spending in each of the special-needs districts to the average level of the most advantaged districts, which was $8,664 in 1997–98, concluding that such a level of funding would be sufficient for the special-needs districts to devise a quality, core educational program. This was the "parity" standard. The court then required the state to identify the supplementary programs students in these districts would need, beyond parity, in order to offset their educational disadvantage caused by the poverty environment of their local urban neighborhoods. The court left open the possibility of adopting something different for the parity standard, but wrote that the state would have to prove the sufficiency of any new proposed standard. The court also asked a remand judge to hold hearings to identify the supplemental programs and their costs.

During those hearings, the state retained the general CEIFA structure, but replaced the staffing proposal with the staffing for a whole school model that had been specifically designed for the needs of low-income and minority students in urban locations, including language minority students—the Roots and Wings/ Success for All program (Slavin, Madden, Dolan and Wasik,1996)—and showed that this model could be funded by the dollars provided by the parity standard. After a lengthy remand hearing concerning this proposal, as well as debates about which additional programs would be required, such as preschool, summer school, and school-based youth services, which were recommended by the remand judge in *Abbott* V, the New Jersey Supreme Court ruled in *Abbott* VI in May 1998 that:

- parity funding would be retained until a different standard was proposed and accepted,
- the state proposal to use an urban specific, whole school program as the way to implement school finance reform and determine whether there was sufficient funding was now appropriate, and that the state had made the substantive case with the Roots and Wings/Success for All program,
- each school would need to offer both full-day kindergarten and a half-day preschool program to all children aged 3 and 4,
- the state was responsible for improving the physical facilities in all the Abbott districts, at a cost of billions of dollars, and
- that if schools could still demonstrate need for additional funds, they could make a request for more through the commissioner of education.

There are several important aspects of the New Jersey experience as it evolved from a fiscal equity to an educational adequacy case. First, it focused only on the most disadvantaged districts. Second, it included a new and unique approach to defining "educational adequacy," namely a comprehensive, whole school design that could be made compatible with state content and performance standards (see Stringfield, Ross, and Smith, 1996 for descriptions of additional school designs, and see Odden and Busch, 1998 for a discussion of their costs). Further, because the school design was quite specific in all of its strategies and elements, its cost could be determined and then used as the basis for calculating the amount of money a district and each school in it needed. In this way, New Jersey began a process of defining "adequacy" not only generally, as the types of standards that would need to be met, but also specifically, as the needs of a proven effective, comprehensive school design with a cost structure that could be used to determine a spending level that could be incorporated into a school finance formula. Third, the court expanded the notion of "educational adequacy" by requiring the state to provide preschool services to children who fell outside the 5–17 age bracket specifically mentioned in the education clause. Finally, New Jersey showed that rather than shy away from the complexities of defining "educational adequacy," the court wanted the state to confront those detailed issues, and their definitions helped the court resolve this 25-year-old case.

Does adequacy require equal outcomes?   Another important issue is whether adequacy cases require equal educational outcomes, or require having all students actually achieve to some high minimum standards. Legal analysts claim that they do not (Clune, 1994a, 1994b; Minorini and Sugarman, 1999a, 1999b; Underwood, 1995a). They argue that adequacy means a level of resources for a district or school that would allow it to provide the type of program that would be sufficient to teach students to high minimum standards. Compliance would require a new education system with content and performance standards; a testing system to assess performance to those standards; some set of management, governance, and incentive changes; and a finance system to fund the programs. Thus, compliance would demand some type of comprehensive reform program that was designed to teach nearly all students to high-performance standards, such as the comprehensive education reforms enacted in Kentucky, Massachusetts, and Missouri in the early 1990s.

At the same time, we suggest that it is entirely possible that some court in the future might require some uniform, minimum but high level of student achievement results. This would be a natural evolution of the adequacy issue, and the ultimate test of whether a comprehensive education program actually could deliver student achievement results.

The education clause and absolute deprivation.   Finally, courts are asked to determine whether, under the education clause, a state's school finance system functions to actually deprive plaintiffs of an education program, despite allowing fiscal and programmatic disparities across districts to exist. Such courts usually find that state education clauses require only provision of a basic education program, and that anything more than that is conditioned on local control of schools. The 1982 Court of Appeals in New York[39] (which is New York's highest state court) held that "if what is made available by this system . . . may properly be said to constitute an education, the constitutional mandate [for a system of free common schools] is met."

At the same time, we should note that the adequacy cases actually move constitutional requirements beyond provision of just some kind of an educational program. An adequacy ruling requires states to define and fund a program or plan that meets an absolute standard (i.e., adequacy, rather than just "something" versus "nothing").

Conclusion.   In short, using the education clause in school finance litigation is different from using the equal protection clause, and generally raises issues about the substance and quality of the education program required for all school districts in the state (see also Wise, 1983; Clune, 1995). Further, litigation based on state education clauses is a state-by-state strategy that is heavily dependent on the state's history, the types of arguments made by plaintiffs on what "adequacy" could mean, and the individuals who happen to be the supreme court justices at the time the case is heard and decided.

It also should be noted that courts are moving away from the traditional fiscal disparities cases and towards the more complicated educational adequacy

[39] *Board of Education, Levittown Union Free School District* v. *Nyquist,* 94 Misc. 2d 466, 408 N.Y.S. 2d 606 (1978), aff'd, 83 A.D. 2d 217, 443 N.Y.S. 2d 843 (1981), rev'd, 57 N.Y.20 27, 439 N.E. 2d 359, 453 N.Y.S. 2d 643 (1982), appeal dismissed, 459 U.S. 1139 (1983).

cases. Indeed, courts seem to prefer the more complex and more demanding issues involved in adequacy litigation, with several courts rejecting fiscal neutrality cases and inviting cases to be brought on adequacy grounds. Courts are aided in these endeavors by the evolving and increasingly sophisticated standards-based education reform movement, which through professional associations endorsed by policymakers, is creating standards that define education quality. Thus, courts can venture into the adequacy arena, draw upon standards developed by educators, and have instruments to both assess an education system and to determine the funding for it. In this way, the evolution of the adequacy litigation strategy concurrently with the standards-based education reform movement dovetailed nicely for plaintiffs and courts receptive to the adequacy argument.

Finally, as Minorini and Sugarman (1999a) conclude, the prominence of the adequacy cases does not mean courts have shifted away from the equity argument. It means only that the courts have turned from equity defined only in dollar terms to equity defined in terms of programs and services or school design, to which a dollar figure can be attached. Though this clearly is an advance, it also harkens back to the "education needs" cases at the beginning of school finance litigation. Indeed, it could be argued that the adequacy approach, together with standards-based education reform and school designs, is simply the updated version of the old education needs argument, except today it has standards and measures and has been quite successful in the courts.

A School Finance Legal Scorecard

A large table on the McGraw Hill web site (www.mhhe.com/schoolfinance) summarizes the key school finance court cases since 1968 and indicates whether the system was overturned or upheld, and the constitutional basis for court action. The chart shows that school finance cases have been decided in 42 states, and existing school finance systems were upheld in about half the cases and overturned in the other half. Thus, school finance litigants are batting about .500 in their attempts to overturn state school finance structures that allow wide variations in educational expenditures linked to local property wealth per pupil, or in education programs and services. In several states, moreover, second and third rounds of litigation have been filed, and many of these second-generation cases have been successful in making their claims. Arizona, Connecticut, Minnesota, Missouri, New Jersey, Texas, and Washington are just some of the states where second and third cases were filed that finally convinced a court to overturn the school finance system. In short, the court route to reforming state school finance systems is alive and active, and one motto could well be, "If at first you don't succeed, try and try again."

In terms of the constitutional route to overturning school finance structures, the score was about even in 1990 in terms of which strategy was the most successful in overturning systems. At that time, about half the courts had used the state education clause as the basis for their decision, and half had used equal protection, with those using equal protection holding that education was both a fundamental right and that property wealth per pupil was a suspect classification. Four states (Arkansas, Connecticut, West Virginia, and Wyoming) used both clauses. Yet only Wyoming created an equal expenditure per-pupil standard that the school finance system must meet. Though many assumed that *Serrano* required substantially equal per-pupil expenditures, the actual court decree required only that "wealth-related" per-pupil spending differ by no more than $100,[40] which suggests that spending could differ according to local tax effort, if the yield were "power equalized" by the state (see Chapter 4).[41]

Since that time, however, nearly all cases have been tried on the basis of state education clauses, and most have been successful in overturning state systems. Minorini and Sugarman (1999a) concluded that since 1973, when the state constitution became the basis for school finance litigation, the scorecard has been about even with 15–17 courts overturning systems and 15–17 upholding systems, though 11 states overturned state systems in the 1990s (Alabama, Arizona, Massachusetts, New Hampshire, New Jersey, New York, North Carolina, Ohio, Tennessee, Texas, and Wyoming).

2. A FRAMEWORK FOR ASSESSING SCHOOL FINANCE SYSTEMS

There are many ways to conceptualize how to assess a state's school finance system, and traditional frameworks have focused largely on equity. During the late 1970s and early 1980s, Berne and Stiefel (1984) proposed an equity framework that helped bring conceptual, intellectual, and technical clarity to school finance equity discussions, and we used it in our first edition. Although Berne and Stiefel were not the only scholars to outline a school finance equity framework (see also, for example, Wise, 1969 and 1983; Garms, 1979; and Alexander, 1982), theirs was the most comprehensive and was used by many analysts to conduct empirical studies of the equity of state school finance structures (see for example Adams, 1997; Goertz, 1983; Hickrod, Chaudhari, and Hubbard, 1981; Kearney, Chen, and Checkauay, 1988; Odden, 1978, 1995b; Picus and Hertert, 1993a, 1993b).

As issues in school finance evolved to include adequacy and productivity as well as equity, Berne and Stiefel (1999) modified their framework. This chapter borrows heavily from the revised Berne and Stiefel history of equity in school finance and presents a framework that can be used to assess a state's school finance structure that includes both equity and adequacy, and thus all major issues in school finance litigation. As such, the chapter expressly attempts to link the finance side of school district operations more directly to the program, curriculum, and instruction side, as well as to student achievement.

---

[40] Later court rulings have allowed this $100 "band" to be adjusted for inflation. For the 1997–98 school year, this inflation-adjusted band was $324.

[41] Such a system would also require a change in California's Proposition 13, which currently prohibits increases in the local tax rate.

The School Finance Framework in Brief

Berne and Stiefel's (1984) original framework for assessing a state's school finance structure required answers to four major questions:

1. *Who* is the group for whom school finance should be equitable? There were two major groups: (1) children who attend the public schools and (2) taxpayers who pay the costs of public education. The equity issues for each group were quite different. Equity for children was discussed largely within an educational opportunity framework. Equity for taxpayers was discussed largely in the public finance context of tax burden, as it is in Chapter 3 of this book.

2. *What* resource objects or educational services should be distributed equitably among the group of concern? The traditional answer to this question for children was dollars or revenues. But educational processes such as curriculum and instruction were also key educational resources. Outcomes such as student achievement also were possible objects to analyze. Deciding on the specific object was important to assessing the degree of school finance equity. Some objects could be distributed equitably; others inequitably.

3. *How* was equity to be defined, or what were the specific equity principles used to determine whether a distribution was equitable? There were three equity principles: (1) *horizontal equity*, in which all members of the group were considered equal; (2) *vertical equity* in which differences (for which unequal resource distributions are legitimate) among members of the group were recognized; and (3) *equal opportunity*, which identified variables such as property value per pupil that should not be related to resource distribution. Because the term "equal educational opportunity" had been used in several nonschool finance contexts and had multiple meanings, the first edition of this text used the school finance version of this term—*fiscal neutrality*. The first edition also added an equity principle, called *effectiveness*. This principle assessed the degree to which resources were used in ways that research showed was effective. While the common approach to equity was to analyze whether one student, school, or district had more or less of an object than another, the effectiveness principle shifted the perspective to whether or not resources were deployed in research-proven effective ways. The effectiveness principle suggested that a resource inequity existed both when insufficient resources were available *and/or* when resources were not *used* in ways to produce desired impacts on student performance.

4. *How much* equity was in the system, or what is the specific status of equity? This component included the specific statistics used to measure the degree of equity in the system.

As Berne and Stiefel (1984) demonstrated, different answers to the above four questions could result in different conclusions about the equity of the system. One major objective in developing and using a school finance equity framework was to help clarify how one analyst could declare a system equitable while another, using the same data, could declare it inequitable. The reason could simply be that they had different answers to these four key questions. The framework helped to sort out the issues and to show how these more complex conclusions could be made.

Solid as the framework was, it nevertheless became problematic as it was used over the subsequent 20 years. First, because wealth or fiscal neutrality was such a central issue in both litigation and school finance policy deliberations, it was difficult to establish it as just one of four different equity concepts. Second, though the framework was amenable for use with any unit of analysis—district or school—it came to be too strongly associated with the district and thus seemed out of date or inappropriate as concern moved to school-level finance (Busch and Odden, 1997a; Goertz and Odden, 1999). Third, as adequacy emerged as a preeminent issue in both school finance litigation and education policy, the framework appeared obsolete as it seemed only to address equity, and not the outcome aspect of what was popularly perceived as central to adequacy. In short, largely due to how the framework was used and defined in practice, it needed some refurbishing in order to incorporate evolving school finance issues.

Thus, in the late 1990s and as part of assessing the history of equity in school finance, Berne and Stiefel (1999) updated the framework, recasting some of its elements, and also explaining how it actually could incorporate nearly all of the salient new issues in both school finance litigation and policy deliberations. This chapter draws largely from their recent work. Berne and Stiefel suggested that school finance analysis address six topics:

1. ex ante versus ex post analysis,
2. the unit of analysis in terms of state, district, school, or student,
3. the objects of interest, whether they be input fiscal variables, educational process variables, or student achievement variables,
4. the group of concern in terms of children or taxpayers,
5. equity concepts, but now leading with equal educational opportunity and fiscal neutrality, while also incorporating horizontal and vertical equity; this chapter will include measures of equity under this general heading, and
6. the concept of adequacy, even though nearly all of its elements could be incorporated into the above five issues.

Ex Ante Versus Ex Post

Ex ante versus ex post concerns differ over whether the assessment of the school finance system is done on the basic structure, concepts, variables, and parameters prior to or before (ex ante) they are actually applied in practice, *or* on data, numbers, and results that emerge after (ex post) a system is implemented. Few analysts make this somewhat arcane but important distinction, though it is critical. Indeed, nearly all empirical analyses of state school finance systems use actual data and thus are ex post analyses.

An example might help clarify the distinction. Take the historic issue in school finance: the unequal distribution of the property tax base and the resultant linkage between spending levels and wealth levels. As Chapter 1 discussed, and as is discussed further in Chapter 4, a high-level guaranteed tax base (GTB) program, such as at the 95th percentile, would be highly equitable from an ex ante perspective. Such a program would eliminate the traditional problem of the unequal access to a school tax base, and make the tax base that could be tapped for education purposes the same, at least for 95 percent of districts or children.

At the same time, as Chapter 1 also showed, such programs tend not to reduce spending differences across districts very much nor reduce the links between spending and property wealth per pupil. Thus, from an ex post perspective, such a system would have inequity statistics only slightly better than the system before such a high-level GTB was put in place. In this example, then, the system could be deemed eminently fair from an ex ante, formula parameter analysis, but unfair from an ex post, empirical analysis. This is the dilemma that underlies assessments of the equity of the Missouri school finance system (Odden, 1995b).

A similar dilemma could arise under the emerging adequacy issues. For example, as discussed below, suppose the following definition of "adequacy" is used: sufficient funds to allow provision of a set of programs, services, and instructional efforts deemed sufficient to teach students to state performance standards. Then suppose that school districts did not translate this definition into appropriate programs and services. Such a system could correctly be characterized as adequate from an ex ante fiscal perspective but not adequate from an ex post, programs and services perspective.

The point is that beforehand (ex ante) analyses are quite different from after-the-fact empirical (ex post), analyses, and finance policy analysts should make the distinction explicit in any report or study. Particularly if an analysis is conducted using actual data after full implementation, it should be made clear that an ex post analysis is being presented; indeed, the conclusions could be compared to an ex ante analysis, even if findings about the nature of the system were different.

Unit of Analysis

There are two aspects of the discussion of the unit of analysis. The first concerns the primary unit at which measures of the object are taken (i.e., whether the measure is at the state, district, school, or student level). The second is a statistical issue of how to appropriately calculate statistical measures.

As to the first issue, historically and traditionally, measures in school finance, such as revenues and expenditures, have been taken at the district level, so the district was the unit of analysis. Moreover, usually the analysis is conducted across school districts within a state. Recently, however, analyses of school finance equity have been conducted at the district level but across the entire country without respect to state boundaries (Hertert, Busch, and Odden, 1994; Murray, Evans, and Schwab, 1998; Odden and Busch, 1998), and these analyses generally show that most fiscal disparities are due to cross-state rather than within-state differences. Since there is a virtual national goal to teach students to high standards, and since the primary issues of both equity and adequacy concern cross-state differences, this national focus might gain more attention in the future. In addition, as education policy increasingly focuses on the school site, more analysis using the school site as the primary unit will likely emerge, for such purposes as distributing revenues (e.g., Odden and Busch, 1998; Odden, 1999), analyzing fiscal equity (Hertert, 96; Odden and Busch, 1997; Clark, 1998), or assessing the efficiency and effectiveness of resource use (Speakman, et al., 1997; Miles and Darling-Hammond, 1997; Odden, 1997a; Odden and Busch, 1998).

Nevertheless, we expect most analyses of school finance issues likely will be conducted with measures taken at the district with increasing numbers of analyses at the school-site level, though gathering good school-level data is difficult (Berne, Stiefel, and Moser, 1997; Cohen, 1997; Farland, 1997, Goertz, 1997; Monk, 1997; Picus, 1997b). But whatever the unit at which measurement occurs, most analyses of school finance systems, and most of the discussion in the remainder of this chapter, are concerned with the impact of the system on students, and thus there is somewhat of a mismatch between the unit at which measurement occurs (districts or schools) and the unit of primary concern (children).

The challenge, then, is how to assess the impact on children. A statistical solution is to "weight" the district or site measure by the number of students so as to give larger districts or schools more influence on the statistical results. If this statistical weighting is not done, each district regardless of size is treated as one observation. Thus, in New York state for example, New York City with a million students and about one-third of all students in the state would affect the statistical findings exactly as much as would a small, rural district with only 100 students. That simply does not make sense, although for years analyses of school finance systems used district data without statistical weighting by the number of students.

Thus, to produce more accurate results, the usual and recommended approach is to weight each district or school measure by the number of students in it, an option provided by nearly all statistical software packages. In the above example, this procedure gives New York City more impact on the analysis than the small district with only 100 students; indeed, this procedure actually turns the number of observations into the total number of students, with New York City accounting for 1 million observations and the rural district only 100. This approach also indicates more accurately how the overall resource distribution system impacts students.

To be sure, this strategy makes the assumption that all students within a district or school receive the level of resources indicated by the district or school measure. Though this is a bold assumption, thirty-plus years of experience with federal Title I and Chapter 1 regulations requiring districts to distribute base resources equally among all schools and students makes this assumption reasonable. But since districts also legitimately distribute categorical dollars differently to schools based on variations in student need, the measures used for analysis either should exclude these additional resources, or some other adjustment should be made to ensure that these legitimate differences do not cause statistical inaccuracies (see discussion below on vertical equity).

This statistical weight should not be confused with the weight discussed below and in Chapter 4 that reflects different student need. Both the unit of analysis-statistical weight and the pupil-need weight must be considered and addressed separately in equity analyses.

Objects

Berne and Stiefel (1984) used three categories of children's equity objects: (1) inputs, such as fiscal or physical objects; (2) outputs, such as student achievement; and (3) outcomes, such as lifetime incomes. This chapter uses these three categories but combines the last two and adds an additional category: educational processes such as curriculum, instruction, and measures of teacher quality. In this way, children's school finance equity objects would include the key variables needed for determining educational adequacy.

It should be noted explicitly that equity analyses need not be confined to educational inputs, such as dollars per pupil or even the enacted curriculum. Outcome variables that include measures of student achievement could easily be the object of intense interest, to determine, for example, the distribution of average levels of achievement or the percentage of districts or schools that have taught students to new, minimum high standards. Further, because objects can include measures of educational provision (curriculum, instruction, teacher quality) as well as results in terms of student performance, this framework also can be used to assess different definitions of educational adequacy.

Fiscal and physical inputs.　There are a wide variety of fiscal and physical inputs that could be targeted for analysis as school finance equity objects. The traditional object of analysis has been some measure of educational dollars. Dollars, however, can be categorized in several ways, each of which can lead to different conclusions about the equity of the system.

First, dollars can be divided into current operating dollars and dollars for capital outlay or debt service. Analysis of current and capital dollars is usually done separately. Current dollars are analyzed on an annual basis since education services need to be provided each year. Capital and debt service dollars are usually (or should be) analyzed on a multiple-year basis because schools are built only periodically, last for decades, and are paid for incrementally over several years. Other capital items, such as buses and computers, are purchased periodically and also can be used for several years.

Second, dollars can be divided into revenues or expenditures, which are quite different. Revenues are usually identified by (1) source—local, state, and federal and (2) type—general/unrestricted aid (i.e., for any educational purpose) or categorical/restricted (i.e., for specific purposes such as special education for the handicapped or special services such as transportation). Many studies analyze current unrestricted revenues from local, state, and federal sources, and leave categorical or special-purpose dollars out of the analysis. Other studies use only state and local general revenues. These general revenues, it is argued, are the revenues that support the regular or base education program, which is one issue of concern across districts. Further, since the focus is on the equity of the state school finance system, federal dollars should be excluded from the analysis. Other studies analyze total current revenues from all sources, arguing that dollars are partially fungible, and that total dollars are what districts have to run the entire education program. Using different revenue figures can yield different conclusions about the equity of the system.

Expenditures, which usually include dollars from all three government sources, can by analyzed on a total basis (current operating expenditures per pupil), or by function (expenditures on administration, instruction, operation and maintenance, transportation, etc.) or by program (regular, special education, compensatory education, bilingual education, etc.). It also would be desirable to analyze expenditures by level of education or school-site level (i.e., elementary, middle/junior high school and high school). Though there has been much discussion of the need to collect data at the site level (Busch and Odden, 1997a), only a few states (e.g., Florida, Ohio, and Texas) provided such fiscal data. It also would be desirable to have expenditure information by curriculum content area (mathematics, science, social studies, etc.), but very few states have an accounting code that would allow expenditures to be tabulated across these categories, and no states have yet begun to collect such data.

Collecting resource data by school level and curriculum content areas is important for both state and nationwide education policy. First, if the country wants to dramatically increase student performance in mathematics and science, which is an important objective given the increasing technological nature of the economy, it would be helpful to know how much is spent for these content areas, relative to other expenditures. Such analysis likely would show small expenditures for science in elementary schools. Second, many argue that if the education system were successful in teaching all students at the elementary and middle school levels, high school and college education could be much easier. Many states, however, still spend between 25 and 33 percent more for high school students than elementary school students (see Chapter 4), and insufficient public money supports preschool services for poor children. Perhaps a shift of dollars already available toward the lower grades could improve student achievement, or perhaps higher spending in some curricular areas would be preferred. Knowing and being able to analyze educational expenditures by school site and curriculum content area could help the country, states, districts, and schools decide how to allocate scarce dollar resources to accomplish ambitious student performance goals.

Most school finance equity studies that use an expenditure figure rely on total current operating expenditures per pupil or instructional expenditures per pupil, largely because these figures commonly are available. But other, more detailed expenditure figures are preferred, especially expenditures by program, level, and content area. The latter are the key policy issues. At any rate, different choices of dollar input variables can lead to different conclusions about the equity of the system. For example, Carroll and Park (1983) found a much more equitable distribution of instructional expenditures per pupil in their study of school finance equity in six school finance reform states, than they did for either total revenues per pupil or total current operating expenditures per pupil. But Speakman, et al., (1997) often found more inequality in expenditure when the data were analyzed at the school-site level.

Physical objects traditionally include, for example, teacher/pupil ratios, administrative/teacher ratios, support staff/pupil ratios, numbers of books in the library, and square footage of instructional space or of total space. The most common figures used are teacher/pupil ratios. But care should be given to defining the ratio used. The total professional staff/pupil ratio includes several professionals who do not teach in the classroom; ratios that include these professional resources not only imply a much smaller class size than actually exists, but also that more teachers are provided for core instruction than actually may be the case. Nevertheless, the pupil/professional ratio indicates the level of professional staffing in a school, a very important overall measure of professional educational resources as discussed in Chapter 7. A more accurate indicator of class size and a good measure of core instructional services is the classroom teacher/student ratio (i.e., the average or median number of students actually in a teacher's classroom).

A new variable that will become available in the future will be the number and percentage of board-certified teachers (i.e., teachers who have earned certification from the National Board for Professional Teaching Standards) (Buday and Kelly, 1996; Rotberg, Futrell, and Liebermann, 1998). The board assesses individual teachers to high professional standards, and a board-certified teacher is an individual who has demonstrated expertise of classroom practice that reflects accomplished teaching. Such a measure would indicate the quality of the faculty in a school or district.

Educational process variables.   School finance has generally ignored measures of the resources into which dollars are transformed, except for measure of physical objects. But given the widespread standards-based education reform agenda and the legal and fiscal interest in educational adequacy that is shifting the education policy focus from fiscal inputs to programmatic inputs and student outputs, analysis of the resources more closely linked to student learning than dollars becomes more salient in order for resource equity analysis to be policy relevant. Thus, school finance analysts, particularly equity and adequacy analysts, need to gather and evaluate information on educational process variables as a further step in strengthening the substantive depth of educational resource analysis.

Porter (1991) described how district and school organizational, curriculum, and instructional variables can be conceptualized and collected for an educational indicators system. School finance analysts can draw from Porter's work to identify several education process variables, the educational resources that dollars purchase that could become part of school finance equity analyses. Three categories of variables could be used.

First are indicators of school organization, curriculum, and instruction. Specific variables on school organization could include school and class size, and school and classroom organization (multiage grouping, block scheduling, teacher teams), including indicators of site-based management (Wohlstetter, et al., 1997), all of which are current policy issues, and many are related to school effectiveness. Variables taken from the effective school literature also could be included. Indicators of overall school strategies, such as implementing a comprehensive school design (Stringfield, Ross, and Smith, 1996) also could be used. Variables for curriculum would emphasize the *intended* curriculum, such as time allocated, topics to be covered by content areas, specific areas within different topics, instructional strategies, and course-specific resources (laboratory space and equipment for science, or degree of manipulative materials for mathematics) (Porter, et al., 1993; Porter and Smithson, 1997; Schmidt, et al., 1997; Schmidt, McKnight, and Raizen, 1997). Variables for instructional quality could include measures of teacher quality such as number of college credits in subject area taught, number of hours in staff development to improve pedagogy, district-funded opportunities to engage in professional development, and in the future, number of teachers with National Board Certification (Buday and Kelly, 1996; Rotberg, Futrell, and Liebermann, 1998) or other measures of teacher knowledge and skill (Milanowski, Odden, and Youngs, 1998; Porter, Youngs, and Odden, forthcoming).

Given the importance to student learning of exposure to curriculum, measures of the *enacted* curriculum in schools and classrooms might even be more important than measures of the intended curriculum. Porter (1991) suggested that measures of the enacted curriculum would be, by content area, topics actually taught and areas within topics actually taught including, for both, length of time devoted to that instruction. Survey instruments to collect these data have been created (Porter and Smithson, 1997).

Finally, Porter suggested gathering data on actual instructional practices, arguing that there is a growing research base on good teaching (Richardson, forthcoming; Porter and Brophy, 1988; Rosenshine and Stevens, 1986). He also suggested gathering data on more general dimensions of teaching, such as the types of knowledge teachers expect students to learn (e.g., skills versus application, understanding concepts versus following rules or doing algorithms, solving routine versus novel problems, and interpreting data), and has created instruments to do so (Porter and Smithson, 1997). Several studies in the 1990s have unearthed even more comprehensive ways to measure instructional expertise of individual teachers (Dywer, 1998; Jaeger, 1998; Moss, et al., 1998; Porter, Youngs, and Odden, forthcoming).

In short, a school finance equity framework for the twenty-first century should strive to include a variety of district, school, and classroom measures of curriculum, instruction, and instructional expertise (i.e., measures of school processes that are most directly linked to student learning, and thus measures that could be used to assess educational adequacy as well).

While most of these variables are not currently measured, some are, and several others might be readily available in some states. Further, as states and professional education organizations create standards and measures of curriculum, instruction, and performance to those standards, more of these curriculum and instructional variables will be introduced, and it will be easier to include them in analyses of the equity of the distribution of educational resources.

Achievement or outcome variables.   This category includes the results of the education process, student achievement or performance in the short run, and labor market, family, and civic performance in the long run. Though Berne and Stiefel (1984) discuss longer-term outcomes such as an individual's income, job, occupational status, ability to compete in the labor market, etc., the connections between these outcomes and K–12 schooling are somewhat tenuous (Burtless, 1996); numerous other factors intervene, and will not be discussed in this book, other than in the productivity analysis in Chapter 7. In the long term, showing connections between K–12 schooling and longer-term outcomes should be a research topic. As the connections are developed, analysis of the outcomes and their link to the distribution of school resources could be included in school finance equity analyses.

Shorter-term education system outcome variables include student achievement. Variables could include student achievement in different content areas—mathematics, science, etc.—or more global achievement, such as the overall measure from a standardized, not necessarily norm-referenced, achievement test. High school graduation rates are also an important output measure. The number of academic courses taken is another outcome indicator that is closely linked to student learning (Madigan, 1997). Finally, postsecondary attendance rates are outcome measures that indicate behavior in the year immediately following high school graduation.

Several issues arise in deciding how to measure these variables. The most debated are those related to student achievement. Traditionally, norm-referenced measures of student achievement have been used. These measures can be developed at different grade levels and in different content areas, but they indicate how an individual compares to other individuals at the same age or grade. They do not indicate the degree to which a student knows a certain content area, or indicate knowledge and skills to a set standard.

Norm-referenced measures of student achievement are gradually being replaced by criterion-referenced measures, which indicate what a student knows in a certain content area. Nearly all states are creating or using new student testing systems covering numerous subject areas, and providing the data at both the district and school and sometimes even individual student level. Further, as tests expand from just multiple choice to include expanded multiple choice, short answer, writing, and actual student performance tasks, the tests will be able to indicate not only what students know but also what they can do (e.g., whether they can conduct a laboratory experience, solve multiple-step mathematics problems, or write a persuasive paragraph). As these more sophisticated measures of student achievement become available, they should be the measures used in a school finance analyses for both equity as well as adequacy purposes.

In addition to selecting specific measures of student achievement, there are additional issues of how to use those measures. Traditionally the debate has been whether to compare the actual measures and argue that, for children, resources should be allocated to produce equal achievement, or to compare gains in student achievement and argue that student ability varies so resources should be used to produce equal gains in achievement.

A new way to present achievement data has been suggested for monitoring nationwide and state progress in achieving the country's educational goals. The new way is to identify the percent of students who are performing at different levels on criterion-referenced tests, such as basic, minimal, proficient, and advanced levels. The argument is that the country needs a workforce with a certain level of skills and that the measures of student performance should indicate the degree that the educational system produces student achievement, on average, with that range of skill levels (Murnane and Levy, 1996). As states adopt this strategy, and several have moved in that direction, outcome measures for schools, districts, or states could be the percent of students performing at basic, minimal, proficient, and advanced levels on criterion-referenced assessments of what students need to know and be able to do, although the more continuous scale scores on these tests also could be used. Wide variations in such achievement could reveal economic or other variations in student performance that could lead either to additional adjustments in resource allocation to compensate for different needs (see Chapter 4) or reallocation to ensure that all schools, districts, and states meet those targets.

The Group

Children are just one, but undoubtedly the most important, group for whom the equity of a state's school finance system is an important policy issue. Children are a group of primary concern because they are the "customers" of the education system; the system is designed to educate children. Further, the ability of children to compete in the labor market and, ultimately, their incomes are determined significantly by what they learn in schools and classrooms (Odden and Odden, 1995; Murnane and Levy, 1996). Thus, school finance equity, particularly the emerging concern with adequacy, emphasizes equity for children and generally is the primary group of focus in this book.

But children also differ, so equity and adequacy analyses focused on children should make appropriate distinctions among categories of students: the "average" student, the disabled, students from low-income backgrounds, students with limited English ability, minorities versus nonminorities, gifted and talented, etc. This book will address only the first four categories of children.

However, children are not the only group for whom school finance equity can be an issue. Taxpayers—both those who have children in public schools and those who do not—pay for public education services. They clearly are another important group for whom school finance equity is an important policy issue. Chapter 3 discusses taxpayer equity, in terms of the burden various taxes place on different taxpayers, within the public finance context. But as an element of fiscal neutrality, this chapter also discusses taxpayer equity in terms of the equal yield for equal effort concept. "Yield" could include dollars or expenditures, but also programs, services, and student achievement.

Teachers increasingly are another group for whom the equity of a state's school finance system is important. The level and distribution of teacher's salaries; the state role in supporting minimum teacher salaries; the distribution of teacher quality, knowledge and skills, including the percentage of teachers certified by the National Board for Professional Teaching Standards; and other policies designed to promote teacher productivity and teacher professionalism are all policy issues (Darling-Hammond, 1997; National Commission on Teaching and America's Future, 1996; Odden and Kelley, 1997) around which to assess a state's overall school finance structure. As the next century approaches, it is likely that the equity of the school finance system as it relates to evolving teacher policy will become a more salient issue within school finance.

Parents are another group for whom school finance equity might be a policy concern. Especially as states enact interdistrict open-enrollment policies, charter schools, and even vouchers, the impact of the overall school finance system on parents may become more important. Indeed, current school finance structures may be at odds with possible new school finance structures when families can choose any school in the state for their child to attend (Odden and Busch, 1998; Odden and Kotowski, 1992).

The list could continue. Nevertheless, children are the dominant group and have received the most attention in school finance. This chapter primarily discusses issues related to school finance as they apply to children and the three subcategories of the disabled, children from low-income backgrounds, and English-language learners.

Equity Concepts

Once an object has been selected, an approach to assessing equity or adequacy needs to be determined. This entails defining and selecting an equity principle. There are four different but related children's equity principles:

- fiscal neutrality,
- horizontal equity,
- vertical equity, and
- adequacy.

This section discusses several issues surrounding each of these principles.

Fiscal neutrality for children.   This principle targets the traditional school finance problem and states that resources, or educational objects, should not vary with local fiscal capacity, such as property wealth per pupil, property value per pupil, household income, or any other measure of local fiscal capacity. This equity principle derives from the standard fiscal disparities that have plagued state school finance structures throughout the twentieth century, and directly relates to the legal standard of fiscal neutrality typically used in most school finance court cases.

Assessing the degree of fiscal neutrality entails analyzing the relationship between two variables: (1) the object chosen and (2) the variable identified as something that should not be linked to resource differences. Traditional fiscal neutrality analysis assesses the relationship between current operating expenditures per pupil and property wealth per pupil, or local and state general revenues per pupil and property wealth per pupil. But analysis of the relationship between any object discussed above and any measure of fiscal capacity, such as household income or even the sales tax base per capita, reflects analysis according to the fiscal neutrality principle. Analyzing fiscal neutrality is different from analyzing either horizontal or vertical equity, because the former requires at least two variables and is a bivariate or multivariate analysis, whereas the latter requires only one variable and is a univariate analysis.

Fiscal Neutrality Statistics.   To measure the degree of fiscal neutrality, statistics that indicate the relationship between two variables are needed. Two have become increasingly common in school finance:

- the correlation coefficient and
- the elasticity (i.e., the elasticity calculated from a simple one-variable regression).

For both statistics, measures of two variables are needed: (1) the measure of fiscal capacity, such as property value per pupil; and (2) the measure of the object of concern, such as current operating expenditures per pupil. Both fiscal neutrality statistics indicate whether the educational object is a function of some variable to which it should not be related, such as the local tax base.

The simple correlation is a statistic that indicates the degree to which there is a linear relationship between two variables [i.e., whether as one variable increases the other increases (or decreases)]. It ranges in value between −1.0 and +1.0. A value of +1.0 or close to +1.0 indicates a positive relationship (e.g., as property wealth increases so does expenditures per pupil). A negative correlation indicates that as one variable increases, the other decreases; it indicates that there is an inverse relationship between the two variables. In school finance, there is usually a negative correlation between state aid per pupil and property wealth per pupil, indicating that state aid is inversely related to wealth, that the poorer the district, the greater the state aid. A correlation coefficient of zero indicates that there is no linear relationship between the two variables.

While a correlation coefficient indicates whether or not there is a linear relationship between two variables, the elasticity indicates the magnitude or policy importance of that relationship. For example, expenditures and wealth could be strongly related, but if a tenfold increase in property wealth resulted only in a small increase in revenues, one could argue that the magnitude of the relationship was not significant or of little policy significance.

Technically, the elasticity indicates the percent change in one variable, say expenditures per pupil, relative to a 1 percent change in another variable, say property value per pupil. It is a statistic that usually ranges in value from zero to any positive number, although it also can be negative. In school finance, an elasticity that equals 1.0 or higher indicates that spending increases in percentage terms at the same or higher rate as property wealth. Elasticities below 1.0 indicate that spending does not increase at the same percentage rate as local property wealth.

The simple elasticity between a dollar object, such as expenditures per pupil and property wealth per pupil, can be calculated using the slope of the simple linear regression of expenditures on wealth; the elasticity equals the slope (the regression coefficient for wealth) times the ratio of the mean value of property wealth per pupil and the mean value of expenditures per pupil.

It often is wise to assess the correlation coefficient and elasticity jointly. If the correlation is high and the elasticity is low, there is a relationship between the two variables—fiscal neutrality does not hold—but the relationship is not of policy importance. On the other hand, if the correlation is low and the elasticity is high, even the tenuous link might have policy significance. If both the correlation coefficient and elasticity are high, then fiscal neutrality clearly does not exist—the two variables are linked, and the magnitude of the link is strong.

A correlation less than 0.5 with an elasticity less than 0.1 could function as a standard to determine whether a state system met the fiscal neutrality standard.

Berne and Stiefel (1984) discuss other relationship statistics for fiscal neutrality. Further, more complex econometric methods can be used to quantify the relationship between educational objects such as revenues per pupil and (1) property wealth, (2) the composition of the local property tax base (residential, commercial and industrial property), and (3) household income (Feldstein, 1975; Ladd, 1975; Adams and Odden, 1981).

Link to Litigation and School Finance Structural Remedies.   Fiscal neutrality also, it should be recalled, is a major focus of many school finance court cases, although this focus was more prevalent at the beginning of school finance litigation than it is today, as adequacy has taken the lead position in court cases. For both fiscal neutrality for children and fiscal neutrality for taxpayers, moreover, the implied school finance structural remedy is a guaranteed tax base (GTB), district power equalizing (DPE), or percentage equalizing program, each of which is discussed more fully in Chapter 4. These programs attempt to make the ability of districts to raise revenues at a given tax rate as close to equal as is practical.

Studies of Fiscal Neutrality.   School finance equity analyses, at least most of those focusing on within-state equity, nearly always include measures of fiscal neutrality. See the discussion of research on horizontal equity that follows.

Fiscal neutrality for taxpayers.   Fiscal neutrality for taxpayers would indicate whether the funding system allowed districts to raise equal dollars (or any object) per pupil for a given tax rate (see also Berne and Stiefel, 1979). The measure would generally be local plus state dollars per unit of tax effort, or the appropriate measure of the object per unit of tax effort. If this measure were the same across districts, it would indicate that fiscal neutrality for taxpayers would have been provided.

Since this is a single variable, the measures of dispersion discussed below under "Horizontal Equity" would be the statistics used to determine whether the system met the test of fiscal neutrality for taxpayers, using the same standards for each statistical measure.

Horizontal equity.   This principle is similar to the horizontal principle in public finance; indeed, Berne and Stiefel (1984) used traditional public finance principles and concepts initially to construct their school finance equity framework. Horizontal equity provides that students who are alike should be treated the same: "Equal treatment of equals" reflects the horizontal equity principle. Horizontal equity requires that all students receive equal shares of an object such as total local and state general revenues per pupil, total current operating expenditures per pupil, instructional expenditures per pupil, instruction in the intended curriculum, focus on thinking and problem solving, and equal minimum scores on student criterion-referenced assessments.

When horizontal equity is used, one assumes that all students are alike. While this is a crude assumption at best, it is implied when it is argued that spending should be equal across school districts or schools. Thus, horizontal equity has been widely used in school finance, despite its assumption that all students are alike.

The principle of horizontal equity is best used for subgroups of students (e.g., all elementary students in the regular program, all high school students in an academic track, or all students performing below the first quartile on a student achievement measure). For carefully selected subgroups of students, it is reasonable to require equal distribution of resources, or the object selected for equity analysis. Of course, care must be taken to create a legitimate subgroup of students, for which homogeneity claims are accurate.

Assessing the degree of horizontal equity entails measuring inequality or dispersion. Such measures, or statistics, are univariate (i.e., they measure aspects of the distribution of one variable, specifically the object chosen for analysis).

Horizontal Equity Statistics. There are numerous statistics that assess the degree of equality for one variable, such as expenditures per pupil in school finance. Berne and Stiefel (1984) identified several and analyze their various properties. Six statistics are discussed below, although many more are discussed by Berne and Stiefel.

1. The first is the *range,* which is the difference between the value of the largest and the smallest observation. The larger the range, the greater the inequality. This statistic indicates the maximum difference in the distribution of this variable among students in a state. That also is a disadvantage. It indicates the difference between only two observations, the top and the bottom. The fact is that there are a few outlying districts in every state: some very poor, low property wealth and low-income rural districts, and some very wealthy districts that might have a nuclear power plant or oil wells and few students. These districts are anomalies, and do not reflect common circumstances.

The range does not indicate the degree of equality or inequality for any of the other observations, and thus is a poor indicator for assessing the degree of equity of the *system.* Furthermore, the range increases with inflation. As inflation occurs, and all other structural variables remain the same, the range will increase. Indeed, one reason the range statistic might be used in some school finance court cases is that each year the range generally increases. An increasing range indicates a system with increasing inequality. Nevertheless, although used extensively and routinely by many school finance analysts, and showing the maximum degree of inequality in a distribution, the range has several detracting features and is not a preferred univariate statistic.

2. The second horizontal equity statistic is the *restricted range,* which is the difference between an observation close to the top and an observation close to the bottom, such as the difference between the 5th and 95th percentile, or the 10th and 90th percentile. The restricted range generally avoids the problem of outliers that afflicts the range, but the restricted range still measures the degree of inequality between just two observations, and not the overall system. Further, just as with the range, the restricted range increases (i.e., worsens with inflation), even if all other characteristics of the finance system remain the same. If a range statistic is used, the restricted range is preferred to the unrestricted range, but neither are good indicators of the equality of the distribution of the object for the entire education system.

A variation of the restricted range is the *federal range ratio,* which is the restricted range divided by the observation at the 5th percentile. Though the federal range ratio shares most of the advantages and disadvantages of the restricted range, because it is a ratio it eliminates the inflation problem (i.e., the federal range ratio does not increase with inflation). In addition, the federal range ratio has been a statistic used to determine whether states can include federal Impact Aid in calculating state equalization aid (Sherman, 1992).

3. The third horizontal equity statistic is the *coefficient of variation (CV),* which is the standard deviation divided by the mean (i.e., the average); it can be expressed in decimal or percent form. Its value usually varies between zero and

one, or in percentage terms, from zero to 100, although the values can be larger. A coefficient of variation of zero indicates that the object is distributed uniformly among all children.

The CV indicates the percent variation around the mean. For example, a coefficient of variation of 10 (or 0.1) percent indicates that two-thirds of the observations have a value within one standard deviation of the mean (i.e., 10 percent above or below the value of the average), and 95 percent of the observations have a value within two standard deviations of the average (i.e., 20 percent above or below the mean).[42] So if the average expenditure per pupil is $6,000 and the CV is 10 percent, it means that two-thirds of all districts have an expenditure per pupil between $5,400 ($6,000 minus 10 percent) and $6,600 ($6,000 plus 10 percent).

The coefficient of variation is a statistic that includes all values of a data set, unlike the range, which includes only selected values. Also, the coefficient of variation does not change with inflation, an attractive characteristic. Thus, if the structural properties of a school finance system remain constant, but all economic and dollar variables rise with inflation, the coefficient of variation would remain the same, correctly indicating that the equity of the system had not changed. The coefficient of variation is also easy to understand. Because of these attractive features, the coefficient of variation is increasingly being used by analysts.

Another issue, however, is determining the value that indicates an equitable or fair distribution of school funds. Determining a standard for the coefficient of variation is a value judgment. Berne and Stiefel (1984) suggest a variety of ways to determine what the standard should be. The key distinction is whether to use a relative standard, which would compare districts in the top, middle, and bottom quartiles, or an absolute standard, which would establish a cut-off point for determination of equity. The problem with a relative standard is that some observations are always at the bottom, no matter how small the degree of inequality. An absolute standard provides a cut-off point, which separates equitable from inequitable resource distribution patterns. It is difficult to determine an absolute standard. Nevertheless, an absolute standard of about 10 percent for the coefficient of variation is generally used throughout this text. This is a high standard, because few states have a coefficient of variation for revenue-per-pupil figures below 10 percent. It is worth remembering that standard setting is an issue of both values and politics; different states and analysts might reasonably set different levels as an acceptable coefficient of variation.

4. A fourth horizontal equity measure is the *Gini Coefficient*, a statistic taken from economists' measures of income inequality. To determine the Gini Coefficient, a graph is made by plotting the cumulative value of the measure of the object as a percent of the total value on the vertical axis and the percent increments of the number of observations on the horizontal axis. The resulting graph indicates the degree to which the object is distributed equally to children at various percentiles; put differently, the graph indicates the degree to which

---

[42] These comments assume a normal distribution.

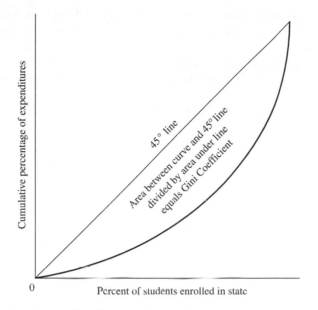

FIGURE 2.1   Example of a Graph Used to Determine a Gini Coefficient

children at different percentiles have the same amount of the object. If the object is perfectly distributed, the Gini graph would be a straight, 45 degree line. If the object is not perfectly distributed, the Gini graph would be a concave curve below that line. In school finance, the measure on the vertical axis is typically the cumulative percentage of school district expenditures, and the measure on the horizontal axis is typically percent of students enrolled in the state, as shown in Figure 2.1.

The Gini Coefficient is the area between the Gini curve and the 45 degree line divided by the area under the 45 degree line. Its value ranges from 0 to 1.0 with a completely equitable distribution occurring when the Gini index equals zero. Most values in school finance are in the 0.1 to 0.2 range. The Gini Coefficient includes all observations and is insensitive to inflation (i.e., it remains the same when inflation is the only intervening variable).

The Gini Coefficient is hard to understand conceptually. What does it mean when the area between the Gini curve and the 45 degree line—even in a system with what most would call large differences in expenditures or revenues per pupil—is 0.1 or very close to zero? A value close to zero suggests equality, but the system may, in school finance terms, be quite unequal. Nevertheless, the Gini Coefficient is a popular horizontal equity statistic in school finance. A standard for it has not been set, although a value less than 0.05 is probably desirable. The smaller the Gini Coefficient, the more equal the distribution of the object.

5. A fifth measure of horizontal equity is the *McLoone Index*, which is a statistic unique to school finance, actually created by and named after Eugene

McLoone, an economics professor at the University of Maryland. The McLoone Index was created to provide a measure of the bottom half of a distribution, to indicate the degree of equality only for observations below the 50th percentile. Since the American political culture often shows more interest in the condition of those at the bottom, the McLoone Index is a statistic that reflects that perspective.

Technically, the McLoone Index is the ratio of the sum of the values of all observations below the 50th percentile (or median) to the sum of all observations if they all had the value of the median. It ranges in value from zero to one, with a one indicating perfect equality.[43] The value of the McLoone Index for most school finance data sets is generally in the 0.7 to 0.9 range. Again, a standard has not been set for a "good" McLoone index, but higher than 0.95 is desirable.

Though Berne and Stiefel (1984) analyzed other standard statistics that are sensitive to changes in the bottom half of the distribution, the complex statistics are difficult for policymakers to understand. Because the McLoone Index is a measure of the equity of the distribution for the bottom half and is more straightforward, it has become popular in school finance and is included in many school finance equity analyses.

6. A new horizontal equity statistic is the *Verstegen Index,* which is the opposite of the McLoone Index, in that it is a measure of disparity in the top half of the distribution. Nearly all analyses of school finance assess either characteristics of the entire distribution, or characteristics of the bottom half of the distribution. But as discussed in Chapter 1, an issue that is gaining more attention is the behavior of the districts in the top half of the distribution. It seems that in some states, the differences in fiscal resources among these districts have increased over time, even while the disparities for those in the bottom half have diminished (Verstegen, 1996). The result is a McLoone Index closer to zero but a larger CV. Since the CV has become such a popular school finance equity statistic, a rising CV could be interpreted to indicate that fiscal disparities are increasing, but such an interpretation would not indicate the differences in the nature of the distribution among the top and bottom half.

The Verstegen Index helps to show this phenomenon; it is the ratio of the sum of the values of all observations above the median to the sum of all observations if they were all at the median. It has a value of 1.0 or greater, and, as the McLoone and CV, does not increase with inflation. It would increase as disparities in the top half increase. A careful analyst would calculate all three statistics: the CV, the McLoone, and the Verstegen Indices, and determine whether overall disparities have improved (a lower CV), whether differences below the median have improved (a higher McLoone), and whether differences in the top half have improved (a lower Verstegen).

---

[43] A value of 1.0 for the McLoone Index indicates that per-pupil expenditures in the lowest-spending districts containing 50 percent of the state's children is equal. A value of less than one implies that among the low-spending districts with that 50 percent of school children, expenditures vary. The smaller the McLoone Index, the larger the spending differential among the low-spending districts.

Link to Litigation and School Finance Structural Remedies. Horizontal equity is most closely associated with two legal issues: the equal protection argument that education is a fundamental interest, and the adequacy argument as the intended meaning of a state's education clause. The general legal thrust is that the core or regular education program should be provided equally to all students, or that all students should have access at least to an "adequate" education program.

School finance structures that respond to these arguments are full-state funding, a very high foundation program, and even a broader federal role to ensure adequacy across all states. Full-state funding is the primary implication of the legal finding that education is a fundamental right because if it is, it should be provided equally to all students and there would be no (or only an extraordinary) reason for allowing some students to have a better education than others. A high foundation is the primary implication of the adequacy argument, in that all students should have, at the minimum, a basic education sufficient to teach the average student to high standards. As Odden and Busch (1998) show, if the adequacy issue were considered nationwide, it might raise anew the need for a new federal role in education, as very preliminary analysis shows that many states are not providing, and might not be able fiscally to provide, any of their districts with sufficient resources to fund an adequate school program.

Studies of Horizontal Equity. There have been dozens of studies of the degree of horizontal equity within a state. Several studies have analyzed the status of school finance equity within the 50 states (Brown, et al., 1977; Evans, Murray, and Schwab, 1997; Murray, Evans, and Schwab, 1998; Odden and Augenblick, 1981; Odden, Berne, and Stiefel, 1979; Schwartz and Moskowitz, 1988). Brown (1977) was one of the first studies that used a 50-state sample. It found that expenditure disparities actually increased nationwide from 1970 to 1975, a time of intensive school finance reform. Further analysis, however, showed that for states that underwent school finance reform in the early 1970s, expenditure disparities might have increased more than they did had the states not changed their school finance systems. The Odden, Berne, and Stiefel study, using data from only 35 states, showed that several school finance reform states improved both horizontal and fiscal neutrality over a multiple-year time period during the mid-1970s. The Odden and Augenblick study used 1977 NCES data for all 50 states and found that state school finance equity ratings changed depending both on the equity object selected and statistic used. The Schwartz and Moskowitz study compared data from all 50 states for the years 1976–77 and 1984–85 and concluded that school finance fiscal equity had stayed, on average, about the same, for both horizontal and fiscal neutrality principles and for several different statistics (primarily the ones discussed above). Wyckoff (1992) then found that although fiscal neutrality was stable, horizontal equity improved modestly between 1980 and 1987. The 1997 General Accounting Office study (1997) identified bigger improvements in fiscal equity, but Hertert, Busch, and Odden (1994) showed that substantial disparities remain.

The most comprehensive study of school finance disparities analyzed 20 years of data and concluded that fiscal disparities had been reduced over this time period but only 16–25 percent and largely in those states with court cases (Evans, Murray, and Schwab, 1997; Murray, Evans, and Schwab, 1998). This study together with others (Odden and Busch, 1998) make a further advance in adjusting all dollar variables by a geographic price factor (Chambers, 1995; McMahon, 1994) to better compare differences in "real" resources across districts. Finally, Murray, Evans, and Schwab (1998) show that the majority of fiscal differences, after adjusting for cost differences, are caused by inter- rather than intrastate disparities, so that even if all within-state disparities are eliminated, two-thirds of the disparities will remain, which supports Odden and Busch's (1998) conclusion that disparities across states exceed those within states.

Numerous authors have used the Berne and Stiefel (1984) framework, or variations of the framework, to study the equity of the school finance structure within states (see for example, Hirth, 1994; Johnson and Pillianayagam, 1991; Porter, 1991; Prince, 1997; Sample and Harman, 1990; Verstegen and Salmon, 1991; Wood, Honeyman, and Bryers, 1990). These studies generally use a fiscal object, such as state and local revenues per pupil. They also typically use two or three measures for horizontal equity, including the coefficient of variation, the McLoone Index, and the Gini coefficient, as well as two measures of fiscal neutrality, the correlation coefficient and the wealth elasticity.

Vertical equity.   Vertical equity specifically recognizes differences among children and addresses the education imperative that some students deserve or need more services than others.[44] "Unequal treatment of unequals" has been a traditional public finance way to express the vertical equity principal. What this phrase means is that in some circumstances or for some reasons, it is acceptable to treat students differently, or to provide more services to some students (or districts) than others. A key step in vertical equity is to identify the characteristics that legitimately can be used as a basis for distributing more resources, or more of the specific object selected. Three categories of characteristics have been identified: (1) characteristics of children; (2) characteristics of districts; and (3) characteristics of programs.

Characteristics of children that could lead to the provision of more resources include physical or mental disabilities, low achievement perhaps caused by educational disadvantage in a low-income background, and limited English proficiency. It is generally accepted in this country, and around the world, that students with these characteristics need additional educational services in order to perform better in school. More controversy surrounds the characteristic of gifted and talented. Some argue that these students learn more from regular in-

---

[44] Chapter 4 discusses how adjustments can be made in school finance formulas to recognize vertical equity issues.

struction and do not need additional resources; others argue that the best and brightest should be given some measure of extra services.

District characteristics that could lead to provision of more resources include issues such as price, scale economies, transportation, energy costs, and enrollment growth. As Chapter 4 shows, some districts face higher prices than others, and they need more money simply to purchase the same level of resources as other districts. Some districts also face higher costs either because of factors caused by very small size, such as a one-room school in a sparsely populated rural area, or factors caused by large size, such as most large-city school districts. While size adjustments can be controversial—some argue that small districts should be consolidated or that large districts should be divided into smaller entities—differential size can be a legitimate basis for allocating some districts more resources than others. Finally, transportation costs vary widely across most districts. Sparsely populated districts must transport students long distances and face higher per-pupil transportation costs, and big-city districts often must bus for racial desegregation. States often recognize these different district circumstances by allocating additional funds, usually to be used only for a specified purpose.

Some programs also cost more than others. For example, vocational education; laboratory sciences; small classes in specialized, advanced topics; and magnet schools tend to cost more than "regular" programs. State and district decisions to provide these programs can be a legitimate reason for allocating more resources for some students than others.

Although there is general agreement that additional funds should be provided in most of the above circumstances, controversy surrounds other school and student distinctions. For example, differential treatment on the basis of race or sex is generally viewed as illegitimate. However, the question remains as to whether additional funds should be provided on the basis of race to foster desegregation (such as more money for magnet schools) or on the basis of sex to foster greater female participation in school athletics and in mathematics and science. Also controversial are issues about whether cost differences due to grade level (see Chapter 4) should be continued.

In school finance, it is generally agreed that additional resources should not be available because of fiscal capacity, such as property value per pupil, household income, or other local economic factors. On the other hand, there is more controversy surrounding tax rates as a legitimate reason for resource variation. Those who support local control argue that higher local tax rates are a legitimate reason for having more resources; others argue that from the perspective of what is best for children, educational resources should not vary because of local taxpayer preference for education.

In short, vertical equity, though simple on the surface, is difficult to implement. There is substantial agreement on some of the reasons for providing more resources to some students or districts than to others, but disagreement remains on several variables or factors. Thus, implementing or not implementing vertical equity entails making significant value and political judgments, many of which have no widespread consensus as to what is deemed "right."

Measuring and Assessing Vertical Equity.   There are two major ways to assess vertical equity. The first is to weight all students who need extra services (see Chapter 4) and then to conduct a horizontal equity analysis using the number of weighted pupils as the pupil measure. This approach combines vertical and horizontal equity in a joint analysis. Vertical equity is reflected in the weights; having recognized factors that can lead to different resource levels and made appropriate adjustments, equality of resources per weighted child indicates the degree of resource equality.

This approach can be used only when there are good data to quantify the degree to which students with different needs require different levels of resources. This approach is strengthened if some independent analysis is made of the weights themselves, to assess whether they accurately represent the degree of extra services needed. It is more valid when the different weights have been calculated relative to the statewide average expenditure per pupil. The 1997 GAO study and the National Center for Education Statistics (1997) studies used this approach, weighting each handicapped student an extra 1.3, and each low-income student an extra 0.2.

Alternatively, categorical revenues for extra services and programs can be eliminated from the object, and analysis conducted for just general revenues, or educational expenditures for the regular instructional program. This approach assesses the degree of equality of the base program for all students, but essentially skirts analysis of vertical equity.

If price differences are part of the state aid formula, the equity analysis should be conducted with price-adjusted dollars, not with nominal dollars, which is the usual approach (Barro, 1989; Chambers, 1995; McMahon, 1994). Furthermore, all dollars should be price-adjusted, not just those that might be adjusted by a state formula price factor. This approach was taken by GAO (1997), Odden and Busch (1998) and Murray, Evans, and Schwab (1998).

Link to Litigation and School Finance Structural Remedies.   Vertical adjustments are integrally embedded in the adequacy approach to school finance litigation; in fact, Underwood (1995b) argued that vertical equity was educational adequacy. Although we would not limit educational adequacy to vertical equity, we certainly would agree that any comprehensive definition of educational adequacy would include some degree of vertical equity adjustments, to ensure that students who could learn to high standards, but needed additional resources to do so, would be provided those resources.

It is not clear that vertical equity is an integral part of fiscal neutrality. The legal arguments about education as a fundamental right, have not been the arguments that have led to the legal right to appropriate education programs for the disabled [that is provided by the federal Individuals with Disabilities in Education Act (IDEA)] nor has vertical equity created a right to extra educational services for students from low-income backgrounds or students with limited English proficiency (again, provided by federal law and regulatory requirements).

As Chapter 4 shows, there are two primary ways to address vertical equity in school finance structures. The first is to weight different categories of students in a way that quantifies, relative to the base level of expenditure, the additional resources that are needed. The second is to provide a separate program, like a categorical program, that provides revenues specifically for such services.

Studies of Vertical Equity.   Chapter 4 discusses the studies that pertain to vertical equity adjustments for students, districts or programs, including the issues and controversies that surround them.

Adequacy.   This principle was not included in Berne and Stiefel's (1984) equity framework and thus is an additional principle with which to judge a state's school finance system. Indeed, if used, this principle could almost function as a way to assess the equity (and effectiveness) of the state's overall education system, but discussion here will focus on what it is and its school finance implications. At the same time, it should be clear that nearly all aspects of adequacy could be included in the above principles, as a combination of horizontal and vertical equity. Nevertheless, because it has taken on a meaning of its own, we discuss adequacy as a separate principle.

As we have suggested, the notion of adequacy is the provision of a set of strategies, programs, curriculum, and instruction, with appropriate adjustments for special-needs students, districts, and schools, and their full financing, that is sufficient to teach students to high standards. As Berne and Stiefel (1999) suggest, the notion of adequacy has its roots in the 1983 *Nation at Risk* report (National Commission on Excellence and Equity in Education), which added excellence to what had been a 20-year focus on equity. Adequacy could be viewed as having both an inputs orientation as well as an outputs orientation (I.e., the inputs being the programs, curriculum, and instruction that are sufficient to teach students to high standards, and the outputs being the measurement of the achievement that results). Indeed, as the education excellence reforms of the 1980s transformed into systemic- and standards-based education reform of the 1990s (Elmore, 1990; Fuhrman, 1993; Massell, Kirst, and Hoppe, 1997), the concept of educational adequacy matured.

Link to Litigation and School Finance Formulas.   A definition of "adequacy" as a high level of inputs—programs, services, curriculum, instruction, classroom, and school organization—certainly can be justified as part of a definition of "adequacy." This definition evolves not only from education reform but also from the education excellence movement, which was primarily concerned with making education inputs more rigorous (National Commission on Excellence and Equity in Education, 1983). Further, standards-based education reform enhances the rigor of these inputs through curriculum content, student performance standards, and changes in school management, organization, finance, and accountability. These latter dimensions of educational adequacy appeared explicitly in most of the 1990s' adequacy cases as discussed in the first part of this chapter. Moreover, Minorini and Sugarman (1999a, 1999b) argue that from the legal perspective, adequacy pertains only to inputs. They claim that the courts are neither requiring equal outcomes nor outcomes for all students who are at or above some high, minimum level.

An input definition of "adequacy" would also include a range of appropriate adjustments for special-needs students, schools, and districts. Indeed, "adequacy" in the legal context certainly requires adjustments for low-wealth and low-spending districts. Further, since the cases include the phrase or notion of "all students" achieving to high standards, adjustments for special-needs students are required.

Once a set of programs and services and other adequate educational elements are identified, it is straightforward to price them and calculate a dollar amount that could be used for each district or school as the foundation, or "adequate" base spending amount per pupil. In this way, the foundation school finance formula and educational adequacy seem to fit well with each other.

At the same time, the notion of adequacy as outputs can also be argued. Nearly all written discussion of adequacy includes the notion of students achieving to some set of performance standards, implying that "adequacy" also could be defined as a set of educational strategies and their funding that are successful in teaching students to some set of achievement standards. Odden and Clune (1998) argue that this means the school finance system needs some adequate high foundation base, with appropriate supplements for special-needs students, as well as some performance-improvement mechanisms, such as more school authority over the use of resources to allow for site reallocation to higher performance programs, changes in teacher compensation towards providing salary increases for more knowledge and skills, and school-based performance incentives to reward schools for improving student achievement results. Economic analysts (e.g., Duncombe, Ruggiero, and Yinger, 1996; Reschovsky and Imazeki, 1998, and see Chapter 4) suggest that this means moving to a "performance-based funding system" that formally links spending levels and adjustments for special needs to a specified level of output of the system.

An adequacy approach can be applied to all districts and schools, as has been done in Kentucky, Massachusetts, and Wyoming, but also could be more focused on selected populations or places, such as low-income students (Clune, 1995) or the special-needs districts in New Jersey.

One major difference between equity and adequacy is that equity implies something about a relative difference, while adequacy implies something about an absolute level. For example, a state system could have base resources distributed quite equally, such as in California and Alabama, but still not be an adequate system. Similarly, one could conceive of a state or education system (perhaps New Jersey when its response to the most recent court case is fully implemented) with substantial differences in resources, but with the lowest-spending districts still spending above some adequacy level.

Finally, given all these issues, adequacy requires some link between inputs and outputs, a set of inputs that should lead to certain outputs, or some level of spending that should be sufficient to produce some level of student achievement. This highlights the need to know and learn more about the input-output linkages. These are discussed in Chapter 7.

Measuring Adequacy.   There has been little if any work on developing measures of educational adequacy in a statistical context. Thus, we propose an approach that we will call the Odden-Picus Adequacy Index (OPAI). Arithmetically, it draws from the McLoone Index but uses an "adequate" spending level rather than the median. The idea behind the OPAI is to calculate an index that roughly indicates the percentage of students in schools or districts spending at an "adequate" level. If the calculation is conducted on the basis of weighted students, or if all expenditures are adjusted by an overall "cost function" index (see Chapter 4), then the OPAI includes vertical equity as well.

The OPAI would be calculated as follows:

1. identification of an "adequate" spending level,
2. identification of the percent of students/district spending above that level,
3. calculation of a McLoone-type ratio for those below that level, but using the "adequate" expenditure level rather than median, therefore calculating the ratio of all those spending below the adequate level to what it would be if they were spending at the adequate level; this ratio would then be multiplied by the percent of students/districts below the adequacy level, and
4. calculating the sum of these two numbers.

Assume that an adequate expenditure level has been determined. Next, assume that 60 percent of students/districts are spending above that level. So, variable #2 above is 0.60. Assume that the McLoone-type calculation would produce a ratio of 0.8, which would mean the students/schools/districts below the adequacy level would have 80 percent of the revenues needed for full adequacy. This would then be multiplied by 40 percent, the percentage below adequacy, and would equal 0.32 in this example. Then the OPAI would be 0.92 (i.e., 0.6 plus 0.32). It would indicate how close the system was to providing an adequate level of funding for all students.

Actually, the OPAI would show that if revenues would be increased by 8 percent of the adequacy level, and given just to those students, schools, or districts spending below the adequate level, everyone could be raised to the adequate level. So it could be used in a very specific way to show how close the finance system is to providing an adequate base for all students. If a weighted-pupil count were used, it would include vertical equity as well. The OPAI is about the same size as the McLoone but covers the entire distribution. It also is not subject to inflation, a positive characteristic of the CV and McLoone, as well.

Studies of Adequacy.   There have been both conceptual and empirical research on educational adequacy. Clune (1994a, 1995) has produced some of the most thoughtful conceptual analysis of how educational adequacy and school finance can be linked. Although his work has emphasized the importance of adequacy for low-income students, conceptually his work addresses the adequacy issue for all children as well.

But there also has been a segment within school finance that always has been concerned with adequacy (i.e., how high the foundation expenditure level should be, whether at a minimum, basic level, as was discussed years ago, or at an adequate level, as is discussed today). There are three major ways policymakers and policy analysts have attempted to determine an adequate spending level: (1) identifying a set of inputs and pricing them; (2) linking a spending amount per pupil to a level of student outcomes; and (3) building a total amount from the bottom up by identifying the cost of each schoolwide program that produces desired outcomes.

The input approach began nearly two decades ago when the Washington school finance system was declared unconstitutional, and that state's top court required the state to identify and fund a "general and uniform" education program. In response, the state essentially identified the average staffing (teachers, professional support staff, administration, etc.) in a typical district and, using statewide average costs, determined a spending level. To a substantial degree, Washington still uses this approach.

A more sophisticated input approach was the Resource Cost Model (RCM), created by Jay Chambers and Thomas Parrish (1994). Using groups of professional educators, the RCM first identified base staffing levels for the regular education program, and then identified effective program practices and their staffing and resource needs for compensatory, special, and bilingual education. All ingredients were priced using average price figures, but in determining the foundation base dollar amount for each district, the totals were adjusted by an education price index. This method was used to propose a foundation spending level for both Illinois and Alaska, but the proposals were never implemented. This method is very similar to what has been termed "activity-led staffing" in England, which is an English version of the RCM approach to school financing (Levacic, 1999).

Most recently, Guthrie and Rothstein (1999) made a further advance on the professional input approach as part of a response to a Wyoming Supreme Court's finding that the state's finance system is unconstitutional. Guthrie and colleagues also used a panel of professional education experts. In identifying the base staffing level for typical elementary, middle, and high schools, however, they relied on the findings of the Tennessee STAR class size reduction study results to set a class size of 15 in elementary schools (Finn, 1996; Finn and Achilles, 1990), and then used the panel to determine additional resources for compensatory, special, and bilingual education. They, too, adjusted the dollar figures by a constructed price factor.

The advantage of all of these input approaches is that they identify a set of elements that an amount of dollars would be able to purchase in each school district, including additional resources for three categories of special-needs students, all adjusted by a price factor. The disadvantage is that the resource levels are connected to student achievement results only indirectly through professional judgment and not directly to actual measures of student performance.

The second approach to determining an adequate spending level attempts to remedy this key deficiency of the input approach by seeking to link a spending level directly to a specified level of student performance. Two procedures have been used. The first determines a desired level of performance using state tests of student performance, identifies districts that produce that level of performance, from that group selects those districts with characteristics comparable or close to the state average, and then calculates their average spending per pupil. Such studies have been conducted in Illinois (Hinrichs and Laine, 1996) and Ohio (Alexander, Augenblick, Driscoll, Guthrie, and Levin 1995; Augenblick, 1997). Interestingly, in all three studies, the level of spending identified was approximately the median spending per pupil in the state.

The other procedure uses the economic cost-function approach. This approach seeks to identify a per-pupil spending level that is sufficient to produce a given level of performance, adjusting for characteristics of students and other SES characteristics of districts. This method, as discussed below, also can be used to calculate how much more money is required to produce the specified level of performance by factors such as special needs of students, scale economies or diseconomies, input prices, and even efficiency. In CPRE research using Wisconsin data, Reschovsky and Imazeki (1998) identified an expenditure level that was also close to the median of spending per pupil. Similar cost-function research has been conducted by others (e.g., Duncombe, Ruggiero, and Yinger, 1996).

To be sure, these studies used different methodologies and had different definitions of "adequate" performance levels—in Wisconsin, it was teaching students to the average on state tests, and in the other two states it was teaching at least 70 percent of students to state proficiency standards. But all studies sought to identify a spending level that was associated with a desired, substantive education result—student achievement to a specified standard, and in general that spending level was close to the respective state's median spending level.

The third approach to adequacy has been to identify the costs of a "high-performance" school model, which is a schoolwide design crafted specifically to produce desired levels of student academic achievement, and to determine a spending level that would be sufficient to fund such a model. A current example of such new school finance thinking is the situation in New Jersey. For nearly a quarter of a century, the driving issue in the New Jersey school finance case was about money, and whether all districts, not just the 28 special-needs urban districts, would have the same level of dollar resources as the high-wealth, high-spending suburban districts, plus additional dollars for the special needs of their urban students. For 1997–98, the supreme court ordered the state to provide that level of spending equality, which ensured $8,664 per pupil for every child. The supreme court also asked a remand court to work with the state and plaintiffs to identify supplemental programs for the extra needs of low-income urban students, and to identify the costs of those programs. When the state proposed that the education problem of the special-needs districts' students could be resolved by using the $8,664 to fund a proven effective schoolwide program that included supplemental programs—specifically, the Success for All/Roots and Wings program—rather than provide more money, they were accused of trying to provide education reform "on the cheap." That level of money more than covered the requirements of that school design, which was specifically designed for low-income minority students in urban school systems. In fact, the state not only picked one of the most expensive whole school models (King, 1994; Odden, 1997a), but because of the high level of funding, they also expanded every element of the model.

Although New Jersey is providing a base spending level that is above the median, its approach to re-engineering school finance to some adequate level is to start with a schoolwide program that has been proven effective. There are several other schoolwide models being developed across the country, all with costs about equal to or less than Success for All/Roots and Wings (Odden and Busch, 1998). Early results suggest that they show promise for accomplishing the goal of teaching students to higher standards (Edison Project, 1997; Slavin and Fashola, 1998; Stringfield, Ross, and Smith, 1996). To determine a spending level more affordable to most states than the high level in New Jersey, Odden and Busch (1998) analyzed the costs of two such models—the Modern Red Schoolhouse and Success for All/Roots and Wings. Both had similar overall costs and could be funded using the national median expenditure per pupil.

To be sure, additional work is needed to identify "adequate" expenditure levels. Each approach discussed above has strengths and weaknesses, and none has been perfected. Any state could begin by selecting one of the above approaches, or some other approach, to determine what their level of adequacy would be. But at their core, these new approaches to school finance seek to link spending with student achievement results, which is an increasingly important policy issue.

CONCLUSION

Figure 2.2 summarizes the equity/adequacy framework in chart form, and Figure 2.3 provides a summary of the statistics used to measure the degree of equity/adequacy. Both charts portray the key aspects of the framework and important statistics, but there are several related issues, many of which this chapter has discussed and some of which are discussed further in subsequent chapters.

FIGURE 2.2 School Finance Equity Framework—Summary and Examples of Variables

Factors	Components	Variables and Statistics
Group (who)	Children Taxpayers Teachers Parents	district value weighted by the number of students
Objects (what)	Inputs–Fiscal (per pupil)	* total revenues from local, state, and federal sources * total revenues from local and state sources * total general revenues from local and state sources * total current operating expenditures * total instructional expenditures * total expenditures for the regular programs * average student/classroom teacher ratio
	–Physical	
	Educational processes	* instructional strategies * types of knowledge emphasized, content standards * subject topics taught including length of time * areas within subject topics including length of time
	Outcome (student achievement)	* high school graduation rate * postsecondary attendance rate * % correct on criterion-referenced measures * % scoring at basic, proficient and advanced levels by content area

(Continued)

FIGURE 2.2 School Finance Equity Framework—Summary and Examples of Variables (Continued)

Factors	Components	Variables and Statistics
Principles (how)	Horizontal equity	* Equal treatment of equals –equal distribution of resources
	Vertical equity	* Unequal treatment of unequals –legitimate needs for children (handicaps, low achievement, limited English) districts (price, size, transportation, enrollment growth) programs (voc ed, lab science, advanced topics)
	Fiscal neutrality	* linear relationship between object and fiscal capacity variable * magnitude of the relationship
Statistics (how much)	Horizontal equity	* Range * Restricted range * Federal range ratio * Coefficient of variation * Gini coefficient * McLoone index * Verstegen index
	Vertical equity	* Weighted pupils for needs * Elimination of categorical revenues in the analysis * Price adjusted dollars
	Fiscal neutrality	* Correlation coefficient * Elasticity
	Adequacy	* Odden-Picus adequacy index

FIGURE 2.3 Assessing Equity Statistics

Statistic	Calculation	Value	Other Attributes	Overall Evaluation
Range	Subtract value of highest observation from that of lowest observation.	Maximum difference in observations. The larger the range, the greater the inequity.	Based on only two observations—highest and lowest. Can reflect anamolies. Sensitive to inflation.	Poor.
Federal range ratio	Difference between observation of 95th and 5th percentile, divided by value of 5th percentile.	Ratio of the range between 95th and 5th observation. Ranges from 0 to any positive number.	Based on only two observations. Not sensitive to inflation.	A good range statistic.
Coefficient of variation	Standard deviation divided by the mean.	Ranges from 0 to 1.0, or 0% to 100%. Zero indicates equal distribution. Equitable if Cv less than 0.1.	Includes all values; does not change with inflation.	Good.
McLoone index	Ratio of sum of all observations below median (50th percentile) to sum if all observations had value of median.	Ranges from 0 to 1. One indicates perfect equality. Most school finance data sets are between .7 and .95; .9 desirable.	Compares bottom half of the districts to the median (50th percentile).	Good, sensitive to bottom half of distribution.
Verstegen index	Ratio of sum of all observations above median (50th percentile) to sum if all observations had value of median.	Ranges from 1 and higher. One indicates perfect equality. Most school finance data sets are between 1.2 and 1.5.	Compares top half of the districts to the median (50th percentile).	Good at indicating variation in top half of distribution.

(Continued)

FIGURE 2.3 **Assessing Equity Statistics (Continued)**

Statistic	Calculation	Value	Other Attributes	Overall Evaluation
Gini coefficient	Area of the graph between Gini curve and 45 degree line divided by area under 45 degree line.	Ranges from 0 to 1.0; value close to 0 suggests equality, but in school finance values usually greater than 0.6.	Indicates degree to which children at different percentiles have same amount of the object. Includes all observations. Insensitive to inflation.	Complicated but a good statistic.
Correlation coefficient	Measure of linear relationship between two variables.	Ranges from −1.0 to +1.0. Values close to 0 indicate no relationship; values closer to −1 or +1 indicate a strong positive or negative relationship.	Includes all observations. Insensitive to inflation.	Not good for indicating a nonlinear relationship. Good for indicating existence of relationship, but not magnitude of relationship.
Elasticity	Ratio of percent increase in one variable to percent increase in another.	Ranges from 0 to a number above that; can exceed 1.0. Numbers greater than or equal to 1.0 indicates an elastic relationship.	Includes all observations. Insensitive to inflation.	Good for indicating the magnitude of the relationship. If correlation is low and elasticity is high, there is an important link between the two variables.
Odden-Picus adequacy index	Percentage of sum of all observations below adequacy level to sum of all observations at adequacy level.	Ranges from 1.0 or 100 percent to a percentage less than 100. Numbers close to 100 indicate a more adequate system.	Virtually includes all observations, but focuses on those below adequacy. Insensitive to inflation.	Good for indicating how close or far the system is to providing an adequate spending level for all districts.

Chapter 3

The Public Finance Context

Public K–12 education in the United States is a big business. As was shown in Table 1.2, revenue raised by all levels of government for K–12 education in 1994–95 amounted to more than $273 billion (NCES, Digest of Education Statistics, 1997a). This is approximately the same amount spent by the federal government for defense in fiscal year 1994–95 (Moody, 1998). These revenues are raised as part of the larger federal fiscal system in the United States. Under our federal system, governments at the local (city, school district, etc.), state, and federal levels all raise and spend public tax dollars. In calendar year 1995, total governmental receipts from all levels of government amounted to nearly $2.27 trillion (Moody, 1998). As this shows, revenues for K–12 education constitute only 12 percent of total governmental revenue.

Although responsibility for the education of our children almost always rests with the nearly 15,000 local school districts across the nation, nearly half of the money spent on K–12 education is now provided by the governments of the 50 states. It is only in the last 30 or so years that the state has become an equal partner with local school districts in financing education.

States have taken a more significant role in the finances of schools for a number of reasons. In response to lawsuits across the nation, states have either been forced, or have voluntarily agreed, to use their financial resources to equalize differences in the property tax–raising capacity of their school districts. As local taxpayers have grown more reluctant to increase property taxes to finance local services, including education, states have filled in, either providing additional funds for schools or using their resources to provide property tax relief. Often these two efforts work hand-in-hand, with increases in state revenues being used partially to reduce local property tax burdens and partially to increase educational spending. In addition, movements for educational reform and increased educational accountability have led to a growing state role in the provision of school services. In many instances, this growing state role is supported with additional funds.

Local school districts have traditionally financed almost all of their share of educational revenues through property taxes. This is because property is fixed in location, and values tend to change slowly, giving relatively small units of government—like school districts—a stable source of revenue (see Monk and Brent, 1997). States, which have a larger base upon which taxes can be levied, have been able to use other taxes, in particular sales and income taxes, to finance their operations. Moreover, these broad-based statewide taxes make it possible for the state to more efficiently ensure that educational spending in individual districts is more a function of the wealth of the entire state and not of the individual school district.

The purpose of this chapter is to set the context within which revenues for education are raised. The major reason for studying how governments raise revenue is that taxes are the primary source of dollars for public schools. While the focus of the chapter is on raising tax revenues, taxes can be used for other purposes as well. Taxes can be a means to redistribute income from the wealthy to the poor. Taxes also can be used as a regulatory tool. For example, rather than regulate manufacturing plant emissions, pollution could be controlled by taxing those emissions, or alternatively, providing tax breaks for companies that take steps to minimize pollution. In other words, taxes can be used for a variety of purposes. However, this chapter focuses on taxes as a source of revenues for public schools.

This chapter has four sections. The first provides an overview of trends in federal, state, and local taxes from 1957 to 1997. This section also summarizes the major structural changes in federal and state taxes over this same period. The second section presents the public finance criteria commonly used to evaluate specific taxes, while the third section uses those criteria to assess the individual income tax, sales taxes, and property taxes. The third section also contains a discussion of state lotteries, which are increasingly popular mechanisms for raising governmental revenues. Section three will also consider current trends in earmarking revenues for education and provide a discussion of potential new sources of revenue for education. Because public schools receive funds from all three levels of government—federal, state, and local—the fourth section of this chapter summarizes the economic literature on the impact that transfers of funds from one level to another (also known as intergovernmental grants) have on both the receiving and sending government.

1. TAXATION OVERVIEW

Trends in Federal, State, and Local Taxation

During the past 40 years, there have been significant changes in the tax revenues raised by different governmental levels. Table 3.1 exhibits tax revenues by type of tax for all levels of government, including school districts, from 1957 to 1995. Several trends in this table are worth noting. First, total tax revenues for all levels of government more than doubled in each of the first three decades presented in the table, and increased dramatically in the last eight years depicted in Table 3.1.

TABLE 3.1   Tax Revenue by Source and Level of Government, 1957–95

Year	Total—All Governments (in Billions)	Federal Government (in Billions)	State Governments Own Source (in Billions)	Local Governments Own Source (in Billions)	School Districts[c] (in Billions)
			Total Tax Revenue		
1957[a]	$ 98.6	$ 69.8	$ 14.5	$ 14.3	$ 4.5
1967[a]	176.1	115.1	31.9	29.1	10.8
1977[a]	419.8	243.8	101.1	74.9	27.1
1987[a]	944.5	539.4	246.9	158.2	51.8
1995[b]	1,440.7	780.2	399.1	261.4	85.6
			Property Taxes		
1957[a]	$ 12.9	—	$0.5	$ 12.4	$ 4.4
1967[a]	26.0	—	0.9	25.2	10.6
1977[a]	62.5	—	2.3	60.3	26.4
1987[a]	121.2	—	4.6	116.6	50.5
1995[b]	203.4	—	9.5	193.9	82.5
			Sales, Gross Receipts, and Customs		
1957[a]	$ 20.6	$11.1	$ 8.4	$ 1.0	—
1967[a]	36.3	15.8	18.6	2.0	—
1977[a]	83.8	23.2	52.4	8.3	$0.2
1987[a]	192.7	48.4	119.9	24.5	0.5
1995[b]	311.8	74.6	196.8	40.4	d
			Individual and Corporate Income Taxes		
1957[a]	$ 59.5	$ 56.8	$ 2.5	$ 0.2	—
1967[a]	103.5	95.5	7.1	0.1	—
1977[a]	250.0	211.6	34.7	3.8	0.2
1987[a]	582.8	476.5	96.7	9.7	0.4
1995[b]	852.7	683.4	154.7	14.6	d
			Other Sources of Revenue		
1957[a]	$ 5.6	$ 1.9	$ 3.1	$ 0.7	$0.1
1967[a]	10.3	3.8	5.3	1.8	0.2
1977[a]	23.5	9.0	11.7	2.5	0.3
1987[a]	47.8	14.5	25.7	7.4	0.4
1995[b]	72.8	22.2	38.1	12.5	3.1

[a] *Source:* Advisory Commission on Intergovernmental Relations (1988). Significant Features of Fiscal Federalism, vol II. Washington, DC: ACIR, p. 64; and U.S. Bureau of the Census, Government Finance in 1986–87. Washington, DC: U.S. Bureau of the Census. P. 7.

[b] *Source:* U.S. Bureau of the Census. (1998a). State and Local Government Finance Estimates, by State: 1994–95. *http://www.census.gov/ftp/pub/govs/www/esti95.html/*; U.S. Bureau of the Census. (1998b). Statistical Tables Public Elementary-Secondary Education Finances: 1994–95. *http://www.census.gov/ftp/pub/govs/school/95tables.pdf/*

[c] Figures for school districts are included in the state and local government totals. "Total—All Governments" column represents the sum of federal, state and local columns and includes school districts.

[d] Data for all other tax sources are included in "Other Sources of Revenue" for 1995.

These figures reflect government growth over that time period. Second, nominal (not adjusted for inflation) state government revenues have increased at a faster rate than revenues for either the federal or local governments, increasing by over 2,600 percent between 1957 and 1995.

Another trend in this table is that property taxes are the primary source of tax revenues for local governments. The federal government does not collect any property taxes, and state governments collect a small amount of property taxes. Further, just over 40 percent all property taxes are collected by school districts.

The numbers also show that most sales and gross receipt taxes are raised by state governments. Local sales taxes, though, have grown in importance as a revenue source between 1977 and 1995. Sales taxes comprise the largest single source of tax revenues for state governments. School districts raise very little revenue through sales taxes.

Finally, individual income taxes raise the largest amount of governmental tax revenues, and the bulk of income taxes are raised by the federal government. But income taxes are rising at both state and local levels. Federal individual and corporate income taxes approximately doubled between 1967 and 1977, more than doubled again between 1977 and 1987, and increased by another $207 billion by 1995. Between 1967 and 1995, state and local income taxes increased nearly fivefold. Income taxes comprise a minuscule amount of local school district revenues.

In short, sources of tax revenues have been changing over the past 40 years, and by 1995 total tax collections exceeded $1.4 trillion. Despite the changes, the individual income tax is the primary tax source for the federal government, the sales tax the primary revenue source for state governments, and the property tax the prime revenue producer for local governments, including school districts. It is important to remember these relationships as we discuss sources of revenue for schools later in this chapter.

Changes in Tax Structures

Federal, state, and local state tax structures continually experience significant structural changes over time. At the federal level, there have been shifts in the proportion of taxes paid by individuals compared to business. There have also been changes in marginal tax rates as well as the number of rate categories that are part of the tax system. The number and level of deductions, exemptions, and tax-sheltered items, as well as the treatment of capital gains, have also changed a number of times in the last 40 years. There have been a host of other modifications that alter the amount of money collected by the federal tax system and how the taxes collected impact different individuals with different levels and sources of earnings. Most of these changes have affected federal, personal and corporate income taxes, and the social security tax.

At the state level, tax structures have experienced even more changes. Over time, states have added new taxes, including on occasion a new income or sales tax. They have also changed tax rates, enacted a variety of mechanisms to alleviate tax burdens on low-income families, conformed their tax structure to the ever-changing federal tax structure, and modified their tax systems to buffer increases and decreases in federal intergovernmental grants. In addition, during recent periods of economic growth, many states have taken steps to reduce taxes and/or curtail the growth of tax revenues. Although public finance economists urge governments to create stability in the tax structure so households and the business community can make decisions in a more stable fiscal environment, political leaders have difficulty heeding this advice. Change seems to be a hallmark of state and federal tax structures and seems to be catalyzed by both economic and political variables.

At the federal level, changes in the income tax structure can be divided into two periods: pre- and post-1940. Individual income taxes were low prior to 1940, consuming only 1 percent of personal income in 1939, compared with over 23 percent in 1997 (Moody, 1998). Tax rates were increased sharply after 1940, reaching a top rate of 90 percent. Over time, federal income tax rates were significantly reduced in 1964, 1981, and 1986, and modestly reduced in 1971 and 1975. The most fundamental changes occurred in the 1980s, first in 1981 when rates were reduced to produce a long-term decrease of 23 percent, and then in 1986 when the entire federal income tax structure was overhauled. The Federal Tax Reform Act of 1986 broadened the income tax base by closing loopholes and preferences, reduced the number of rates to three, and reduced the rates themselves to 15, 28, and 33 percent. The standard deduction and earned income tax credits were raised in order to shield the working poor from paying income taxes. The intent was to keep the amount of revenues produced the same but to improve the equity of the tax itself. Most would agree that those goals were accomplished, even though the federal income tax is far from perfect.

The federal tax structure was modified again in 1990. The three rate structure was retained, but the top rate was lowered to 31 percent.[1] The earned income tax credit was increased, further sheltering the working poor from federal income taxes. The top tax rate was increased to 39 percent in 1990, and a number of important changes were enacted with the 1997 Taxpayer Relief Act. These included a tax credit for children and education costs, as well as modifications of the capital gains tax and a new form of IRA designed to encourage saving for college costs. Estate taxation regulations were also changed.

At the state and local level, changes in the tax structure divide into about three periods roughly being the 1960s, 1970s, and 1980s. State tax structures underwent significant structural change during the 1960s as the country experienced both continued economic growth and government growth, the latter spawned in large part by the War on Poverty programs. Between 1965 and 1971, for example, seven states enacted an income tax for the first time, and eight states enacted new sales taxes. The bulk of the new funds were targeted to rising state support for public elementary and secondary schools to relieve pressure on the

---

[1] Technically, the 1986 tax reform created a four-rate structure: 15, 28, 33 percent and then above a certain income level, back to 28 percent. The 1990 changes eliminated the 33 percent bubble by making it a uniform 31 percent.

local property tax that the baby boom generation had caused in the 1950s and early 1960s. While school funding had been primarily a function of local governments, and thus the local property tax, the large property tax increases that were necessary both to build school buildings and provide operating funds for the baby boom generation led in the late 1960s to a growing unpopularity of the property tax and pressures for states to relieve high property tax burdens. This new role for state school finance complemented the general growth of state and local governments into a variety of domestic policy issues that began in the mid-1960s.

During the 1970s, at least up to 1978, there was very little structural change in state taxes. Only one state—New Jersey—enacted a new income tax, and no state enacted a new sales tax. Most tax reform focused on the local property tax. This tax underwent several changes, from simple reduction in its use, to increased numbers of exemptions, to administrative reform as computer technologies allowed assessment practices to keep pace with market values, and finally to new programs, such as "circuit breakers," to protect low-income households from excessive property tax burdens. The focus on property tax changes was reinforced by the school finance reforms of the 1970s, during which nearly two-thirds of the states changed the way public elementary and secondary schools were financed, generally by increasing the state and decreasing the local (thus local property tax) role.

The period from 1978 to the present includes a variety of fast-paced state tax structure changes. First, in 1978, California's Proposition 13 inaugurated the tax limitation and tax-cutting movement. In June of that year, voters in California approved an initiative that cut the property tax rate from what then was over 2 percent on average to a constitutional limit of 1 percent of assessed value. Limits on the rate of growth of assessed value were also enacted under Proposition 13, limiting the ability of local governments to maintain and even increase spending levels based on the growth in property values over time. Several states followed with a variety of tax limitation, spending limitation, or outright tax-cutting measures. At the state level, 32 legislatures reduced income taxes between 1978 and 1980. The "tax revolt" was thus spawned.

Between 1980 and 1987, states enacted few structural changes in their tax systems, although the legacy of the late 1970s and early 1980s tax revolt left 17 states with some sort of tax or spending limitation and another 10 states with some inflation indexing feature of their individual income tax. The incremental changes that were made tended to reduce the progressivity of state tax systems, narrow the bases for the major taxes, and make the tax systems more volatile and closely linked to national economic up- and downturns.

Then tax reform fever hit states in 1987. The major factor was the 1986 federal tax reform because, without structural tax reform change, most states either would experience a major increase or decrease in their income tax receipts. Indeed, the themes involved in the 1986 federal income tax reform also became salient themes at the state level, since at both levels two decades of incremental change had produced tax systems that were perceived as overly complex, unfair, and burdensome. The following themes characterized state tax reform that began in 1987 (Gold, 1986):

- Broadening tax bases—just as the federal government had eliminated several deductions, exemptions, and special treatments, states could consider similar changes in state income and sales taxes, as well as local property taxes. Thus, complexity could be reduced, fairness enhanced, and revenue yields stabilized.

- Flattening and reducing tax rates—by broadening the base, tax rates could be reduced and revenues held constant (or increased moderately). Thus, base broadening offered the possibility of reducing the number of tax rates (the federal income tax was reduced to just three rates) and flattening the overall structure.

- Shifting burdens from individuals to the business community. Just as the federal government had, prior to 1987, increased taxes on individuals and reduced them on corporations and businesses, and then shifted some of that tax burden back onto businesses in their 1986 reform, that option also existed for state governments.

- Treating different industries more uniformly. The federal tax reform eliminated the investment tax credit, extended depreciation schedules, and cut most tax shelters, changes that placed capital intensive and goods producing industries on a more equal basis with knowledge-intensive and service-producing industries. For states, more uniform treatment of the business community would mean similar changes as well as fundamental changes in the sales tax, either eliminating it all together for businesses or further expanding exemptions. More uniform treatment of all business was especially important in the increasing interstate competition for business enterprises.

- Eliminating tax burdens on the poor. While the federal tax reform took most poor households off the federal income tax rolls and states could do the same for their income tax, the more salient state implication was to eliminate sales and property tax burdens on the poor, which exceeded state income taxes on the poor. While the 1986 and 1990 federal tax reforms tended to reduce the overall progressivity of the tax structure, it was accompanied by a complementary focus on eliminating altogether tax burdens for households falling below the poverty level.

- Imposing minimum taxes on both individuals and businesses. This feature of the new federal tax reflected the value that wealthy individuals and businesses should pay some minimum amount of tax, even though other features of a reformed structure could reduce their burden to zero.

Between 1987 and 1990, 27 states reformed their income tax system. Twenty states increased the standard deduction, and 17 states increased the personal exemption. Both of these structural changes enhanced progressivity and eliminated poor families from the income tax roles. Only five states enacted more thorough reforms.

The recession of the early 1990s led a number of states, particularly California, to increase taxes. No state enacted new taxes, but a number of states raised tax rates on either sales or income taxes to compensate for the reduced revenues resulting from the economic slowdown. By 1998 the economy had been running strongly for a number of years, and most state tax actions were focused on reducing taxes on both individuals and corporations. According to the National Conference of State Legislatures (NCSL, 1998) the robust economy kept most states in excellent fiscal condition. In fiscal year 1997–98, taxes fell in 35 states for a total reduction of $6.8 billion. Projected tax cuts for fiscal year 1998–99 equaled 1.5 percent of 1997 tax collections.

Legislatures in 21 states took significant action to reduce fiscal year 1999 taxpayer liability, cutting taxes by 1 percent or more of the previous year's collections, while 28 states did not act to lower taxes by that amount. Personal income tax reductions were the main focus of cuts, with legislatures in 30 states adopting some form of income tax reductions. Sales and use taxes were lowered in 21 states.

Excess revenues generated rebates and refunds in a few states. Among the states that refunded the largest amounts of money to taxpayers in fiscal year 1997–98 were Minnesota, Colorado, and Connecticut.

2. ASSESSING AND UNDERSTANDING TAXATION

Raising taxes is not a simple endeavor. Not only are actions to increase tax revenues—or institute new taxes—unpopular politically, new taxes often have side effects that may create economic inefficiencies (Musgrave and Musgrave, 1989). In looking at the revenue potential of any tax, policymakers consider both the tax rate and the tax base.

The rate is the level of taxation. The tax base is the entity to which the tax rate is applied. The relationship between tax rate and tax base is crucial to understanding the yield of any tax, and can be captured in a simple equation as follows:

$$\text{Tax Yield} = \text{Tax Rate} \times \text{Tax Base}$$

Policymakers seeking to increase revenue can increase either the rate or the base, or both, to garner that revenue. The decision they make will have differential impacts on individuals in different circumstances. It is important to understand what those impacts might be before recommending that changes in tax rates or tax bases be implemented. In general, economists argue that the most efficient taxes, which are those that create the fewest inefficiencies in the economy, are those with low rates and broad bases (see for example, Musgrave and Musgrave, 1989).

Public Finance Criteria for Evaluating Taxes

Public finance economists use several analytic criteria to evaluate taxes. These criteria are commonly accepted as both the economic and policy assessments needed when analyzing the goodness of any tax (see Musgrave and Musgrave, 1989, or Rosen, 1992, for an example). These criteria include:

- The tax base,
- Yield,
- Equity,
- The economic effects of the tax, and
- Administration and compliance issues.

This section discusses each of these in some detail. These criteria are used to assess income, sales and property taxes, as well as lotteries, in the next section of this chapter.

Tax base.   The tax base is the entity to which a tax rate is applied. For example, a tax could be based on the number of cars or television sets a person owned. The rate, then, could be a fixed dollar amount per car or television. Usually tax bases are related to some economic category such as income, property or consumption. Broad-based taxes, such as property, income, and sales taxes, are taxes with broad or comprehensive bases. There are four major tax bases: wealth, income, consumption, and privilege.

Wealth.   There are many forms of wealth, some typically taxed and others not taxed. In economic terms, wealth represents an accumulation of value, or a stock of value, at any one point in time. Net worth—the sum of all economic assets minus all economic liabilities at some fixed point in time—is one measure of wealth. A wealth tax could then be levied on an individual's net worth. Proposals for net worth taxes have been made over the years but have never been enacted into law.

Another common measure of wealth is property. Property can be divided into two general categories: real property and personal property. Real property includes land and buildings. For individuals, personal property includes assets with a shorter life span, such as automobiles and other vehicles, and household items, such as furniture, video equipment, computers, rugs, and appliances. For businesses, personal property includes machinery and equipment, furniture and other office supplies, and inventories. Stocks, bonds, and other financial instruments—certificates of deposit, notes, bank accounts, etc.—are other forms of wealth that could theoretically be taxed. The value of an inheritance is yet another form of wealth that often is taxed.

A pure tax on wealth would tax all of these different categories of wealth. The United States does not have and has never had a wealth tax. Financial instruments rarely have been taxed. Large portions of real property owned by the government and religious organizations are not taxed. And there has been an increasing tendency on the part of states to exempt some types of real and many forms of personal property from taxation.

The property tax comes closest to a wealth tax in this country. But the property tax generally covers only real property. The trend during the past three decades has been to eliminate both individual and business personal property from the property tax.[2] The advantages and disadvantages of taxing property and the rationale for establishing relatively narrow definitions of wealth will be discussed in the section on property taxes later in this chapter.

Income.   Income represents another tax base. Compared to wealth, which is a measure of economic worth at one point in time, income is a measure of an economic flow over time. The net value of income minus expenses over a time period represents the change in net worth over that time period. Income includes salaries, interest from financial instruments, dividends from stocks, gifts, money from the sale of an item of wealth including both property and a financial instrument, and other forms of money flow. Earned income is typically money earned through work, such as wages and salaries. Unearned income represents money received from the returns on financial assets and investments, such as stocks, bonds, and mutual funds.

While income from salaries is rather easy to identify, income from business activities is more complicated, since net income is determined by subtracting legitimate expenses from gross receipts or sales. While conceptually straightforward, defining "gross receipts," "sales," and "legitimate expenses" is technically complex, and income can vary substantially depending on the specifics of the definition.

Regardless of how "income" is defined, it is generally viewed as the measure of ability to pay. This measure of ability to pay refers to all forms of taxation, not just income taxes. For example, if the value of a person's wealth is fixed, such as the value of a home, some current income is needed to pay a tax on that element of wealth. If current income is insufficient to pay the tax, the element of wealth would need to be sold, or partially sold, to meet the tax liability. Alternatively, the individual would need to borrow funds to pay the tax or alter his/her consumption patterns to be able to pay the taxes. This would likely result in a reduced ability to purchase other goods and services. The same is true for a sales or consumption tax; that tax is paid from an individual's current income, so the greater the tax, the less of other things an individual can purchase with current income sources.

An important factor in using income as a measure of ability to pay is the time period over which income is measured. Typically income is measured in annual amounts, and most tax structures assume yearly income to be both the tax base and the measure of ability to pay. But individuals and businesses purchase capital items such as plants, factories, equipment, homes, and cars on a longer-term basis, and often on assumptions that average income will increase over a

---

[2] It should be noted that while motor vehicles are typically exempted from property taxation, they are generally subject to a variety of vehicle registration and use taxes by each of the states.

longer time period. For example, assuming their income would rise over the next decade, a family might purchase an expensive home with a mortgage that consumes a high proportion of their current income. Their assumption that income will grow over time means that in a few years the cost of the mortgage (monthly payments) will be less burdensome, eventually being a relatively small portion of their monthly expenses. Thus, some measure of long term, or lifetime income, might be a better measure of income as it relates to ability to pay. Economists have urged the use of a lifetime income measure for years (see, for example, Musgrave and Musgrave, 1989), but current income continues to be the most politically viable and accepted measure of ability to pay.

Consumption. Theoretically, a tax on consumption would include taxation of all goods and services purchased by individuals and businesses. A consumption tax is usually called a sales tax if it applies to a broad range of items that can be purchased. Most state and local sales taxes fall into this category. A consumption tax is usually called an excise tax if it applies to specific items, such as beer, alcohol, cigarettes, furs, jewelry, etc.

A broad-based consumption tax would tax income less savings—all income spent on purchases for current consumption. The United States does not have a broad-based consumption tax at the present time although there have been a number of calls for such a tax to be implemented. While most state sales taxes come the closest to this definition, they generally exclude services that are an increasing component of current consumption, and they include both small and large products such as food, prescription medicine, and homes. Thus, sales taxes in this country are more aptly described as broad-based selective sales taxes.

Privilege. A small portion of revenues for federal, state, and local government services are raised by granting individuals or businesses a privilege and charging a fee for that privilege. A driver's license fee is paid for the privilege of driving a car; a car license plate fee is paid for the privilege of owning a car. Privilege fees are paid for a variety of other purposes such as franchise fees for running certain businesses, fees for using park facilities, fees for a permit to operate a taxi cab, and fees for using port facilities. A privilege tax is similar to an excise tax, the major difference being that the privilege tax is paid for the privilege of engaging in some activity, while an excise tax is paid for the privilege of purchasing and owning or using some product.

Yield. The yield is the amount of revenues a tax will produce. Yield is equal to the tax rate times the tax base. Rates are usually but not always given in percentage terms, such as a 5 percent sales tax, or a 10 percent gasoline tax, a 33 percent marginal federal income tax rate, or a 4 percent state income tax rate. Given a defined tax base, it is easy to determine the yield for each percent of tax rate on that tax base. Knowing generally the revenue-raising or yield potential of a tax (with a defined tax base) is important information. From the perspective of yield, the preferred situation is to be able to raise substantial revenues at low or modest rates.

Broad-based taxes by definition can produce high yields even at modest rates, whereas selective taxes, like a cigarette tax, are limited in the amount of revenue they can produce. A tax that produces a large amount of revenue, such as a property tax, is difficult to eliminate (a proposal often made for the unpopular property tax). This is because doing so would require either large cuts in governmental services or substantial increases in other tax rates. Neither option is politically popular. Consequently, once in place, a broad-based tax is difficult, if not impossible, to eliminate. Indeed, it can even be "easy" to raise new revenues with small tax rate increases in some instances.

Other aspects of tax yield include revenue stability and the elasticity of the tax. Stability is the degree to which the yield rises or falls with national or state economic cycles. Stable tax revenues decrease less in economic downturns but also increase less during economic upturns. The property tax historically has been a stable tax since property values consistently increase over time and fall only in deep, major recessions. Sales taxes on products tend to rise and fall more in line with economic cycles, as do taxes on income. Corporate income taxes follow economic cycles even more closely and thus tend to be an even more volatile revenue source.

Elasticity measures the degree to which tax revenues keep pace with change in either their base, or more commonly, the change in personal income. To measure the income elasticity of a tax, one compares the ratio of the percentage change in the tax yield to the percentage change in personal income. An elasticity less than one indicates that tax revenues do not keep pace with income growth; an elasticity equal to one indicates that tax revenues grow at the same rate as incomes; and an elasticity greater than one indicates that tax revenues increase faster than income growth. Since prices and demands for governmental (including school) services at least keep pace with income growth, an income elasticity of at least one is a highly desirable feature of any tax. Individual income taxes, especially if marginal rates are higher for higher incomes, tend to be elastic, while sales tax revenues generally track income growth. Over time, property taxes have exhibited elasticities of approximately one.

To some degree, a trade-off exists between stability and elasticity. Elastic taxes tend to be less stable since their yield falls in economic downturns when personal income also tends to fall or at least grow more slowly. Stable taxes are less elastic. As a result, their yields remain steadier during economic fluctuations.

Tax equity.   Tax equity addresses the issue of whether the tax is fair, treating individuals or businesses equitably. Although conceptually simple, it is difficult to determine with preciseness the degree to which a tax treats all fairly. There are two primary aspects of tax equity: horizontal equity and vertical equity.

Horizontal equity concerns equal tax treatment of individuals in the same, or equal, circumstance. For example, if an income tax met the horizontal equity test, individuals with the same taxable income ($40,000 for example) would pay the same amount of tax ($4,000 for example). Or, two families with a home with the same market value would pay the same amount of property tax. But as will be discussed later, these two simple examples mask a variety of technical issues. In the income tax case, the issue is determining taxable income. At both the federal and state level, there are a variety of exemptions, deductions, and adjustments made to gross income in determining taxable income. If there is disagreement about any of those modifications, the above conclusion about horizontal equity could be challenged. As a result, even horizontal tax equity is difficult to attain.

Most individuals are not equally situated. Vertical equity is the principle used to describe how a tax treats individuals in different economic situations. Determining vertical equity is more complex than estimating horizontal equity. The first issue is to decide on the criterion for differentiating tax treatment. That is, if taxes are to burden some individuals more than others, what variable should determine those differences? The degree to which the tax would vary is a value judgment. But determining on what basis a tax should vary is an important tax policy decision.

One possible criterion would be benefits received—that is, taxes should vary with the benefits received—where the greater the benefits, the higher the tax paid. A gasoline tax burdens drivers but meets the benefits-received criterion since individuals who drive benefit from use of public roads and highways. Moreover, the more they drive, the more they benefit from the roads, but the more they pay in gasoline taxes as they consume more gasoline.

By definition, a fee-for-service tax meets the benefits principle—the fee is simply the tax for the service (or benefit) received. Appealing as the benefits-received criterion is, it is difficult, if not impossible, to measure the individual benefits received for a broader array of services. For example, police and fire services generally benefit the individuals within the locality where police and fire protection are provided. But education, which is another locally provided service, provides benefits not only to individuals in the form of higher incomes but also to society in general in the form of economic growth and lower needs for social services (Cohn and Geske, 1990). Even if education benefits accrued only to individuals, today most individuals move from the city where they are educated, making it difficult to have anything other than a national tax related to those benefits.

At broader levels, the benefits principle becomes more problematic. For example, how do we measure the individual benefits from spending on national defense, public transportation systems, interstate highway systems, a statewide higher education system, or an interstate system of waterways for transit and agriculture? It would seem foolish to increase the taxes for individuals receiving public assistance (welfare) benefits since taxation of their benefits would defeat the purpose of providing the assistance in the first place. For these reasons, a benefits principle, though appealing to economists, has not been implemented as a basis for differentiated tax treatment, at least for broad-based income, sales, and property taxes.

Instead, ability to pay has been adopted in this country as the criterion for vertical tax equity. Ability to pay generally is measured by income. If taxes differ among individuals, they should differ because of differences in their ability to pay—that is, because they have different income levels.

Vertical tax equity can be measured by comparing taxes expressed as a percent of income. Vertical equity is broadly defined by the terms "progressive," "proportional," or "regressive." Progressive tax burdens increase with income—as income rises, so does the tax liability as a percent of income. Proportional tax burdens would impose the same percentage tax burden regardless of the level of income. Regressive taxes are the opposite of progressive taxes in that individuals with lower incomes pay a higher percentage of their income in taxes than do those with higher incomes. They may not pay more in total taxes, but as a portion of their income, more goes to taxes. For example, if an individual with $10,000 in income paid a 12 percent income tax and an individual with an income of $100,000 paid 10 percent income tax, the tax would be regressive. However, the total dollar tax burden would be $1,200 for the low-income individual and $10,000 for the individual with the higher income.

In this country, it is generally agreed that regressive tax burdens should be avoided. It is widely felt that the poor, or low-income individuals or households, should not pay a larger percentage of income in taxes than average or above-average individuals. It is also generally agreed that the tax system should be at least proportional, and probably progressive, although support for progressive tax burdens has waned in recent years as initiatives at both federal and state levels have reduced the degree of progressivity of many taxes. The current interest in a flat tax rate for federal income taxes is representative of this view. While a progressive tax burden has generally been sanctioned in the past, there is less consensus for that position today.

Measuring vertical tax equity entails an additional series of technical problems. First, one needs to distinguish tax impact from tax incidence or tax burden. Put differently, one needs to differentiate between who actually pays the tax to the tax collector from who actually bears the burden of the tax. For example, merchants actually submit sales tax payments to governments, but individuals who purchase products almost always bear the burden of the sales tax. Likewise, companies or organizations usually remit income tax payments to state and federal governments, but working individuals almost always bear the burden of that tax since income taxes are withheld from periodic salary payments. The issue of tax incidence or tax burden for other taxes is not as clear cut.

Tax incidence for the property tax is the most complex. Property taxes have four components: owner-occupied homes, residential rental property, business and industry property, and commercial property. The property tax on individuals who own homes is not only paid by homeowners, but they also bear the full burden of the tax. But property taxes on the other components can be shifted. For example, property taxes on rental property might be shifted to renters in the form of higher rents. Depending on competitive conditions, property taxes on industries and corporations could be shifted forward to consumers in the form of higher prices or backward to workers in the form of lower wages, or could be borne by stockholders in the form of lower dividends and stock prices.

A similar issue exists for corporate income taxes: are they shifted forward to consumers into higher prices, or backwards to stockholders and/or workers? Likewise, depending on competitive conditions, property taxes on local commercial activities could be shifted forward to consumers, or backwards to owners. It turns out that shifting assumptions and patterns produce widely varying conclusions about property tax and corporate income tax incidence, from being steeply regressive to steeply progressive.

Another issue to consider in assessing tax equity is income transfers. The federal government and many state governments have programs that transfer income from the broader group of taxpayers to the poor. Welfare programs, income tax credits, food stamps, rent subsidies, and child-care supports are just some examples of income transfer programs. Thus, a comprehensive assessment of tax equity would consider taxes as well as income transfers. This is because although the poor might pay a large percentage of their incomes in sales taxes and in assumed shifted property taxes, that regressivity could be counterbalanced by receipt of income from a variety of transfer programs. Likewise, average and above-average income individuals pay more taxes to support income transfer programs but receive none or few income transfer benefits.

Pechman (1985, 1986) conducted analyses of the overall tax equity of the country's federal, state, and local taxes for several years. His analyses describe the total tax burden under different assumptions about property tax shifting. Table 3.2 shows tax burdens by population decile (ranked by income) for several years from 1966 to 1985 under more progressive as well as under more regressive sets of assumptions about the property and corporate income taxes, but without adjustments for transfers.

Unfortunately, similar analyses have not been conducted since 1986. Table 3.3 provides an approximate comparison to Table 3.2 displaying the average tax rate in the United States by income group for federal taxes, state and local taxes, and total taxes. The chart does not make adjustments for assumptions about property tax shifting as Pechman did.

Under Pechman's more progressive assumptions, half the burden of the corporate income tax is placed on those who receive dividends, and half is from property income in general. All property taxes on improvements (houses and buildings) are allocated to recipients of property income in general. The more regressive assumptions allocate half the corporate income tax to property income and half to consumers, and allocate all property taxes to shelter (i.e., those who pay rent) and consumption.[3]

Table 3.2 shows that the country's taxes were mildly progressive under the more progressive assumption and about proportional under the more regressive assumptions. The table also shows that there was little overall shift in the pattern of total tax burdens over the two-decade period studied. Table 3.3 shows that in 1993 total taxes were slightly progressive for income levels below $100,000 and substantially more progressive above that level, mostly due to the impact of the

---

[3] See Pechman (1985), pp. 24–37 for additional explanation of incidence assumptions and allocations.

**TABLE 3.2   Total Burden of Federal, State, and Local Taxes
by Population Decile, Selected Years, 1966–85**

Population Decile	Income Paid in Taxes by Year (%)				
	1966	1970	1975	1980	1985
	More Progressive Assumptions				
First[a]	16.8	18.8	19.7	17.1	17.0
Second	18.9	19.5	17.6	17.1	15.9
Third	21.7	20.8	18.9	18.9	18.1
Fourth	22.6	23.2	21.7	20.8	21.2
Fifth	22.8	24.0	23.5	22.7	23.4
Sixth	22.7	24.1	23.9	23.4	23.8
Seventh	22.7	24.3	24.2	24.4	24.7
Eighth	23.1	24.6	24.7	25.5	25.4
Ninth	23.3	25.0	25.4	26.5	26.2
Tenth	30.1	30.7	27.8	28.5	26.4
All deciles[b]	25.2	26.1	25.0	25.3	24.5
	More Regressive Assumptions				
First[a]	27.5	25.8	27.9	25.9	24.0
Second	24.8	24.2	21.7	22.2	20.1
Third	26.0	24.2	21.0	22.5	20.7
Fourth	25.9	25.9	24.0	23.5	23.2
Fifth	25.8	26.4	25.4	24.7	24.4
Sixth	25.6	26.2	25.5	25.1	25.0
Seventh	25.5	26.2	25.8	25.8	25.5
Eighth	25.5	26.4	26.1	26.7	26.2
Ninth	25.1	26.1	26.6	27.4	26.7
Tenth	25.9	27.8	25.9	26.8	25.0
All deciles[b]	25.9	26.7	25.5	26.3	25.3

Source: Joseph Pechman, "Who Paid the Taxes in 1966–85," Revised Tables, Washington, D.C.: The Brookings Institution, 1986.

[a] Includes negative incomes not shown separately.

[b] Includes only units in the sixth to tenth deciles.

federal income tax. It should be pointed out that in Pechman's analysis of earlier years, incomes of over $100,000 represented a very small portion of the highest decile of taxpayers. Even today, tax returns with incomes above $100,000 represent approximately 5 percent (or half of a decile) of total taxpayers (Tax Foundation, 1998a).

Economic effects.   While taxes are imposed by governments and thus by definition distort the free functioning of the competitive market, some taxes and

TABLE 3.3   Average Tax Rates by Income Group, Fiscal Year 1993

Income Group	Total Taxes (%)	Federal Taxes (%)	State and Local Taxes (%)
United States	34.6	21.3	13.2
Under $15,000	27.6	17.1	10.4
$15,000 to under $22,500	28.9	16.1	11.1
$22,500 to under $30,000	28.9	17.7	11.2
$30,000 to under $35,000	30.4	19.0	11.5
$35,000 to under $45,000	31.6	19.8	11.8
$45,000 to under $60,000	32.2	20.2	12.0
$60,000 to under $75,000	33.1	20.7	12.5
$75,000 to under $115,000	34.9	21.8	13.0
$115,000 to under $150,000	36.9	22.2	14.7
$150,000 to under $300,000	39.3	23.2	16.1
$300,000 to under $750,000	44.4	27.1	17.3
$750,000 or more	49.7	30.7	19.0

Source: Moody, 1998. Table A16, page 19.

specific tax design mechanics distort economic decision making more than others. The general goal is for taxes to have neutral economic impacts. So another criterion for assessing a specific tax structure is the degree to which it has neutral economic impacts.

Most taxes have some elements that are not economically neutral. The federal income tax allows homeowners to deduct interest on home mortgages, thus encouraging housing consumption over other kinds of consumption. Since interest from savings is taxed at both the federal and state levels, consumption is encouraged over saving. Since most sales taxes cover only products, consumption of services is favored over consumption of products. Since business purchases, even of equipment and items that will be put into products for resale, are often subject to the sales tax, vertical integration[4] is somewhat encouraged if those costs are less than the costs of paying the tax. In California, property taxes are based on market value at the time of purchase rather than current market value; therefore, moving entails a high cost and is discouraged, while remaining in one's home is encouraged by that state's property tax system.

Differences in taxes across state borders also can encourage business investment and individual location. In metropolitan areas near state boundaries, individuals are economically encouraged to live in the state with the lowest sales and/or income tax rates in order to maximize their income benefits.

---

[4] Vertical integration refers to a company that owns or produces the items needed for production, the production facilities, and the sales outlet, such as is the case for many, but not all, oil companies.

In short, almost all tax structures have elements that encourage or discourage a variety of economic behaviors. The goal is to structure the tax to neutralize its economic incentives or at least to minimize its economic distortions.

Administration and compliance.   Finally, both the administration of the tax and individual or business compliance with tax requirements should be as simple and low cost as possible. Often simplicity is gained at the cost of some tax equity and vice versa. Further, the more complex the tax, the greater the costs of both administration and compliance. Mikesell (1986) identifies seven factors in tax administration and compliance:

1. Maintaining and gathering records,
2. Computing the tax liability,
3. Remittance of the tax liability,
4. Collection,
5. Audit,
6. Appeal, and
7. Enforcement.

Depending on the tax in question, responsibility for each of these steps falls on individual taxpayers or governmental agencies. Ideally, both administration and ability to comply with the tax requirements should be simple. Monk and Brent (1997) point out that the more complicated the tax system, the greater the costs of administration and compliance.

An example of a revenue source with high administration costs is a lottery, which is increasingly popular across the country. The fact is that lotteries are poor revenue sources in large part because of the high costs of administration. In order to sell lottery tickets, a wide variety of prizes are required. In most states, prizes comprise 50 percent of all lottery sales. Put differently, for every $1 raised through lottery sales, fully 50 cents is allocated to prizes. Further, most merchants who sell lottery tickets earn a commission, which takes more away from other governmental uses. Other administrative costs also add to expenses. For example, in California, prizes are required to be 50 percent of sales, and administrative costs (which include commissions to sales agents) are capped at 16 percent of lottery ticket sales. Assuming the state lottery administration costs are equal to a full 16 percent of ticket sales, only 34 percent of each lottery dollar is available for other uses.

All other broad-based taxes, such as the income, sales, and property taxes, while requiring administrative costs for both the government and individuals, provide a much higher net yield, somewhere in the high 90 percent range. To be sure, there are ways of increasing and decreasing administration costs of these taxes, but they simply are dramatically lower than that for a lottery.

States could nearly eliminate income tax administrative costs if they simply made the state income tax a fixed percent of federal tax liability. States could eliminate sales taxes altogether, and thus sales tax administrative costs, by adopting a general consumption tax that could be administered entirely through the income tax. Short of these more dramatic choices, streamlining federal and state tax administration, though, is an important objective for any specific tax structure, as well as change in tax structure.

3. ANALYSIS OF INDIVIDUAL TAXES

The Income Tax

The individual income tax is the largest revenue producer for the federal government and is also used by 41 states. Another three states apply the income tax only to interest, dividends, and/or capital gains (i.e., on income from capital assets but not on earned income). Eleven states allow local governments to levy income taxes. In 1995, individual and corporate income taxes produced $683.4 billion for the federal government, $76.0 billion for state governments, and $14.6 billion for local governments (U.S. Bureau of the Census, 1998). In combining tax revenues from all sources, income taxes raise the largest amount and percentage. State income tax structures increasingly are being conformed to the federal tax structure enacted in recent years. In the following analysis, we focus primarily on the federal income tax. This section ends with comments on trends in state income taxes and needed changes for the future.

Basis.   Income is the base for both federal and state income taxes. But defining "income" and determining taxable income is a complex activity driven by federal and state tax codes that are revised frequently and consume hundreds of pages of law. Defining "gross income" and determining taxable income requires a series of modifications, including income adjustments, deductions both standard and itemized, and exemptions. While an income tax generally meets the horizontal equity standard since individuals with the same taxable income pay the same amount of tax, horizontal equity is violated if any of the income modifications are deemed unjustified. In addition, both the federal and state governments have different tax schedules for individuals and for households (individuals generally paying higher tax rates than families under the assumption that it costs less for one individual to maintain a household than it does for a family). Since there is disagreement over what constitutes fair tax treatment of individuals versus families, horizontal equity is also violated if there is disagreement over the particular mechanism for differential treatment of individuals and families incorporated in either the federal or state income tax structures.

Income adjustments, standard and itemized deductions, and various exemptions at first blush seem reasonable modifications to make to determine taxable income. Most would agree that two families with, for example, an income of $50,000 should pay a different amount of tax if one family consists of just husband and wife with few medical expenditures and the other consists of husband

and wife, four children, a live-in parent, and high medical costs. But a reasonable deduction or adjustment for one person can seem unreasonable or unfair to another. For example, in the past, several types of investments provided large deductions for individual taxpayers, often exceeding the dollar amount of investment made. While such tax shelters encouraged investment in those activities, some having good social values like low-income housing, the proliferation of tax shelters and their use primarily by higher-income individuals gave a perception over time that they were simply unfair.

The 1986 federal income tax reform streamlined the federal income tax to a substantial degree by eliminating most income adjustments, deductions, and tax shelters. Nearly all tax shelters were eliminated. Several deductions were eliminated, including state sales taxes; the original proposal called for eliminating the deduction for all state and local taxes, including the property tax. Interest deductions, except for interest on homes with a mortgage up to $1,000,000, were phased out.[5] Even medical and other deductions were reduced when the percentage of gross income they must exceed was increased.

Several income adjustments also were eliminated. All capital gains were included in income, whereas in the past a percentage had been excluded; investments in individual retirement accounts (IRAs) were no longer exempt from determining federal taxable income; medical deductions had to exceed 3 percent of income; and other deductions were eliminated. The personal exemption was increased by more than 100 percent, rising to $2,000 per individual, and its level was indexed to inflation so it will rise in the future.

In short, the 1986 federal tax reform made several changes in determining gross and taxable income, which can be characterized as broadening the base by excluding numerous adjustments that had been allowed in the past. The changes substantially increased the horizontal equity of the tax.

From an economic perspective, though, additional changes could have been but were not made. For example, economists suggest that imputed rent for owner-occupied homes should be included as income. The rationale is that homeowners have an asset—a home—that could produce a return—rent—if it were placed on the market, and that a true economic picture of homeowners should include that potential rent. Renters not only do not have that imputed rent, but they cannot deduct mortgage interest even if it is shifted to them in higher rents. This argument never succeeds in the political arena for at least two reasons. Policymakers do not like to include unrealized economic gains—like imputed rent—when determining a base that can be taxed. Indeed, one factor behind the unpopularity of the property tax is that when property values rise faster than incomes, the tax can become less and less related to ability to pay. Secondly, encouraging home ownership is a strong American value. Both excluding imputed rent in determining income and including home mortgage interest as an allowable deduction contribute to that value, even though those policies entail economic distortions.

---

[5] The home mortgage interest deduction reflects the American value of individual home ownership.

In 1990, federal income taxes were raised. The most noticeable change was the addition of a 39 percent marginal tax bracket for those in the highest income categories. While a number of changes in the federal tax structure were implemented during the 1990s, the most substantial was the Tax Relief Act of 1997. That law was designed to provide substantial tax relief to the middle class. This was done by establishing a tax credit of $400 for each dependent child (raised to $500 per child for tax year 1999). In addition, new incentives for saving for college expenses were introduced. Finally, major cuts in the tax rate on capital gains were enacted. To help keep the tax structure progressive, the Tax Relief Act of 1997 phased out many of these tax-cut mechanisms for taxpayers with high (over $100,000) incomes. The result is that the bulk of the tax relief is initially aimed at the "middle class." However, the long-term impact of the capital gains tax-rate reductions, while hard to predict, is most likely to reduce the tax liability of those in the highest income tax brackets (Tax Foundation, 1998b).

Yield.   Individual and corporate income taxes are the largest source of revenue for the federal government and for the state governments as well. In 1994, the federal government raised $543 billion (43.15 percent of total receipts) in individual income taxes and another $140.4 billion (11.15 percent) in corporate income taxes. That same year, the 50 states raised another $128.8 billion (20.89 percent of total state tax revenue) in individual income taxes and $28.3 billion (4.53 percent) in corporate income taxes. In 1977, estimated federal income taxes totaled $672.7 billion in individual and $176.2 billion in corporate income taxes. These figures represent 44.68 and 11.70 percent of estimated total federal tax receipts respectively in 1997.

Table 3.4 shows state and federal income taxes as a percent of personal income between 1957 and 1994, and federal income taxes as a percent of personal income for 1997. The table shows that income taxes rose rapidly between 1957 and 1994. Federal income taxes continued to rise beyond that date as shown in the last row of Table 3.4, which shows that federal income taxes in 1997 exceeded total state and federal income tax collections three years prior. State income tax collections undoubtedly continued to grow as well in those three years. However at the time of publication, those data were not available. Individual income taxes showed the same growth pattern as did total income tax collections (individual and corporate).

Table 3.4 also shows that total individual and corporate income taxes as a percent of personal income declined from 16.7 percent in 1957 to 14.6 percent in 1994. However, individual income taxes as a percent of personal income grew from 10.5 percent in 1957 to 12.6 percent in 1987, and then declined slightly to 11.7 percent in 1994. The last two columns in Table 3.4 suggest that over time, corporate income taxes have declined relative to personal income taxes.

The income tax also is an elastic tax. As income rises, income tax collections generally rise faster. Table 3.5 shows that the individual income tax elasticity exceeded one (that is, tax collections grew at a faster rate than personal income grew) in each decade between 1957 and 1987. That pattern was reversed

TABLE 3.4   Income Taxes as a Percent of Personal Income, 1957–97

Fiscal Year	Total Individual and Corporate Income Taxes (in Billions)	Total Individual Income Taxes (in Billions)	Personal Income (in Billions)	Total Individual and Corporate Income Taxes as a Percentage of Personal Income (%)	Total Individual Income Taxes as a Percentage of Personal Income (%)
1957	$ 59.5	$ 37.4	$ 356.3	16.7	10.5
1967	103.5	68.3	644.5	16.1	10.6
1977	250.0	189.5	1,607.5	15.5	11.8
1987	582.8	476.5	3,780.0	15.4	12.6
1994	840.6	671.9	5,757.9	14.6	11.7
1997[a]	848.9	672.7	6,784.0	12.5	9.9

Sources: Advisory Commission on Intergovernmental Relations (1988). *Significant Features of Fiscal Federalism*, 1988 Edition, Volume II, Washington, D.C. ACIR. p. 64; Table 59; U.S. Bureau of the Census (1988). *Government Finance in 1986–87*, Washington, D.C.: U.S. Bureau of the Census, p. 7; *Economic Report of the President*, January 1989, p. 333; Moody, Scott. ed. (1998). *Facts and Figures on Government Finance*, 32nd edition. Washington, DC: Tax Foundation, tables C23 and D22; and Bureau of Economic Analysis (1998). *Survey of Current Business*. Washington, DC: U.S. Department of Commerce. *http://www.bea.doc.gov/bea/ARTICLES/NATIONAL/NIPA/1998/0898nip3.pdf/* Table 1, p. 147.

[a]Federal tax data only

TABLE 3.5   Income Tax Yield Elasticity, 1957–94

Year	Individual Income Taxes (in Billions)	Personal Income (in Billions)	Percent Change from Previous Period		Elasticity: Ratio of Percent Change in Tax Collections to Percent Change in Income
			Individual Income Taxes	Personal Income	
1957	$ 37.4	$ 356.3	—	—	—
1967	68.3	644.5	82.6	80.9	1.02
1977	189.5	1,607.5	177.5	149.4	1.19
1987	476.2	3,780.0	151.3	135.1	1.12
1994	671.9	5,757.9	41.1	52.3	0.78

Sources: Advisory Commission on Intergovernmental Relations (1988). *Significant Features of Fiscal Federalism,* 1988 Edition, Volume II, Washington, D.C. ACIR. p. 64; Table 59; U.S. Bureau of the Census. (1988). *Government Finance in 1986-87,* Washington, D.C.: U.S. Bureau of the Census, p. 7; *Economic Report of the President,* January 1989, p. 333; Moody, Scott. ed. (1998). *Facts and Figures on Government Finance,* 32nd edition. Washington, D.C.: Tax Foundation, tables C23 and D22; and Bureau of Economic Analysis (1998). *Survey of Current Business.* Washington, D.C.: U.S. Department of Commerce. *http://www.bea.doc.gov/bea/ARTICLES/NATIONAL/NIPA/1998/0898nip3.pdf/* Table 1, p. 147.

between 1987 and 1994 when the elasticity of the income tax amounted only to 0.78. This is due largely to the income tax revisions of 1986, which substantially flattened the tax brackets and left the highest bracket at 31 percent, the recession of the early 1990s, and the indexing of income tax brackets so that increased marginal tax rates impacted only taxpayers whose incomes grow at a rate faster than the rate of inflation. Despite the low elasticity between 1987 and 1994, the income tax is still thought of as an elastic tax. In other words, individual income taxes tend to be an elastic tax source.

Federal and state income tax rates have changed substantially over this 37-year time period, and new income taxes have been enacted in many states. More economically pure elasticity figures adjust for these structural changes. Research shows that these purer elasticity figures range between 1.5 and 1.6, higher than the above figures (Gold, 1986).

Income taxes, even though they are elastic, also are quite stable. Even in economic downturns, personal income does not drop tremendously across the nation.[6] As a result, individual income taxes tend to drop little, if any at all. Since corporate profits fluctuate much more in recessions and economic growth periods, corporate income taxes tend to be less stable than individual income taxes. Thus, the trend toward making individual income taxes a larger portion of the total of individual and corporate income taxes works to make the tax more stable. The price might be less popularity.

---

[6] However, in California in the early 1990s, there was a substantial drop in personal income due to the loss of nearly 1 million jobs. The result was dramatically lower state income and sales tax revenues.

Equity.   Horizontal equity was discussed above. In terms of vertical equity, the federal individual income tax is clearly progressive due to the use of marginal income tax rates that increase with income. Most state individual income tax structures are also progressive, although they tend not to be as progressive as the federal income tax. Since individuals cannot shift the income tax, tax impact and tax burden are identical (i.e., those who pay the tax also bear its burden or economic incidence).

In addition to the marginal tax rate brackets, progressivity in the federal income tax system is increased through the use of exemptions and standard deductions. In 1997, the personal exemption was $2,650 for each person in a household. Thus, for a family of four, $10,600 in income was exempt from taxation. In addition, the federal tax system provides for a standard deduction. The amount of the deduction varies depending on tax filing status, but for married individuals filing a joint return for 1997, it amounted to $6,900. Third, the maximum earned income credit was increased to $3,756 if there were two or more qualifying children in the household. As a result, a family of four potentially would not have paid any federal income tax at all if their income was $20,256 or less.

As indicated above, federal income tax rates are progressive. The rates for 1998, which increased with income, were 15, 28, 33, 36, and 39.6 percent, and cut-in at different income levels depending on filing status.

State income tax rates are not nearly as progressive overall, ranging from flat rates to top rates that equal 12 percent. However, they do remain generally progressive (Monk and Brent, 1998). Only 10 states have indexed income brackets. More importantly, the relatively low level of income subject to the highest rate of income taxation in many states reduces the progressivity of state income taxes (Gold, 1994). Gold (1994) also points out that compression or narrowing of income tax brackets in state tax systems results in less progressivity. For example, in New York, the Tax Reform and Reduction Act of 1987 narrowed that state's income tax brackets from a range of 2 percent to 9.5 percent for earned income and 2 percent to 13.5 percent for unearned income to a range of 4 percent to 7 percent for both earned and unearned income (Monk and Brent, 1997). By 1997, the lowest bracket increased to 5.5 percent. Data on state income tax rates are available from the Federation of Tax Administrators web site: *www.taxadmin.org/fta/.*

Similarly, in California, a legislatively imposed tax surcharge on those with the highest incomes was allowed to expire through a vote of the citizens in 1996. Prior to, and following the surcharge, the highest tax bracket in California is 9.3 percent. During the time of the surcharge, additional brackets of 10 and 11 percent were used. These higher brackets affected only taxpayers with joint California taxable incomes over $200,000 and individual taxable incomes above $100,000. Despite the fact that elimination of this surcharge benefited only the wealthiest 5 percent of the taxpayers in the state, the voters overwhelmingly voted to eliminate it when given the opportunity.

Another way to look at the progressivity of the federal income tax is to consider who pays the taxes. Data from the Tax Foundation (*www.taxfoundation.org*) shows the percentage of total federal individual income taxes paid by different numbers of taxpayers in both 1985 and 1995. For 1995, the table shows that the top 5 percent of taxpayers (that is, the 5 percent of tax returns with the highest incomes) paid nearly 50 percent (48.8 percent) of the total federal individual income taxes. That top 5 percent of taxpayers earned 28.8 percent of total income. This shows that the highest earners in the country pay a substantially higher portion of the taxes than their share of total income. On the other side, the bottom 50 percent of tax returns (those with the lowest incomes) paid 4.6 percent of the federal individual income tax despite earning over 14 percent of total income. This pattern suggests a strongly progressive tax structure. In fact, as Table 3.8 shows, the average tax rate on the top 1 percent of taxpayers was 28.5 percent. That figure declines steadily to a low of 4.4 percent for the bottom 50 percent of taxpayers.

State tax burden studies have not been as detailed as those at the national level in large part because gathering such data for all 50 states is very costly. Nevertheless, Phares (1980) calculated indices of progressivity for state individual income taxes for 1977 and found state individual income taxes to be the most progressive state tax. Indeed, Phares found that only state tax structures with a major individual income tax were progressive overall.

Economic effects.   To the degree that deductions and income adjustments are limited, the income tax can be quite neutral in its economic effects. Nevertheless, there are several economic impacts created by both the federal and most state income taxes. First, as stated previously, the deduction of home mortgage interest encourages home purchases more than would be the case if the deduction were eliminated. Second, including interest earned from savings as well as returns from investments in taxable income produces some deterrent to savings. While there is reasonable debate over those tax provisions, if neither were taxed, savings and investments probably would increase and arguably would help improve the productivity of the country's economic system.

Administration and compliance.   The federal income tax, while probably fairer than it was before 1986, is still complex and costly to administer for businesses and most individuals. In fact, the changes in the 1990s have only made the system more, not less, complex. Large percentages of individuals use accountants and other services to fill out income tax forms, and businesses have large accounting departments that spend considerable time keeping tax records. Often, tax requirements are different from good accounting requirements.

Major changes in the income tax structure also have led to increased compliance costs. The income tax was not only overhauled in 1986, but further modified in 1987, 1988, 1990 and again extensively in 1997. It had experienced several major changes during the early 1980s. States also continuously enact incremental changes in their individual income taxes. This stream of changes adds to compliance burdens since new rules have to be learned and then applied correctly.

Income tax trends and issues at the state level.   While state sales tax increases received the most attention during the mid-1980s, the state income tax increased

TABLE 3.6   State Income Taxes as a Percent of Personal Income and as a Percent of Total State Taxes, 1957–94

Year	State Income Taxes as a Percent of Personal Income (%)	State Income Taxes as a Percent of Total State Taxes (%)
1957	0.7	17.2
1967	1.1	22.2
1977	2.2	34.3
1987	2.6	39.2
1994	2.7	38.2

Sources: Advisory Commission on Intergovernmental Relations (1988). *Significant Features of Fiscal Federalism,* 1988 Edition, Volume II, Washington, D.C. ACIR. p. 64; Table 59; U.S. Bureau of the Census. (1988). *Government Finance in 1986–87,* Washington, D.C.: U.S. Bureau of the Census, p. 7; *Economic Report of the President,* January 1989, p. 333; Moody, Scott. ed. (1998). *Facts and Figures on Government Finance,* 32nd edition. Washington, D.C.: Tax Foundation, tables C23 and D22; and Bureau of Economic Analysis (1998). *Survey of Current Business.* Washington, D.C.: U.S. Department of Commerce. *http://www.bea.doc.gov/bea/ARTICLES/NATIONAL/NIPA/1998/0898nip3.pdf/* Table 1, p. 147.

both as a percent of personal income and as a percent of total state taxes, as shown by the data in Table 3.6. Between 1957 and 1977, state income taxes rose from 0.7 percent to 2.2 percent of personal income, and from 17.2 to 34.3 percent of total state taxes. The increases continued through 1994, rising to 2.7 percent of personal income and 38.2 percent of total state tax revenues. The latter figure is slightly lower than the same figure for 1987, but only 1 percent lower.

These trends emerged in part because few states have reformed their income tax structures. Maximum tax rates were reached in nearly half the states when taxable incomes reached only $10,000 and the value of personal exemptions was low. Thus, inflation in the late 1970s together with general wage increases pushed individuals into the top income tax brackets. These realities interacted with rate increases in the early 1980s to combat revenue losses caused by recession and federal aid cuts, and income tax revenues rose. An unanticipated result, in part also due to unchanged income tax structures, was that increasing numbers of low-income households faced income tax burdens for the first time. While a few states began to reform their income tax in 1987, the strength of the economy in the late 1990s has led to a number of state tax reductions.

Despite the changes that have occurred over time in the structure of the state income tax, the tax should continue to provide a stable source of revenue. Four themes characterize the need for state income tax reform:

1. Broaden the base to improve horizontal equity, increase political and popular perceptions about the fairness of the tax, and negate the trend to narrow the base through exclusions; also allow for rate reduction.

2. Rate reduction in both numbers and levels, which will increase public perception of the tax and help improve the business climate.
3. Increase the values of personal exemptions, standard deductions, and earned income credits to eliminate the poor from income tax rolls.
4. Index the entire structure to require political votes to increase revenues rather than have tax revenue increases occur as a byproduct of inflation.

Conclusions about the income tax.   The income tax historically has been perceived as a fair tax and is the nation's and most states' most progressive tax. During the 1970s and 1980s, it was increasingly viewed as unfair. Many viewed the income tax as proliferating exclusions; special tax shelters, inflation, and privileged treatment drove most individuals into higher tax brackets, put the poor on the income tax rolls for the first time, and allowed many rich individuals and corporations completely to avoid paying any income taxes. The 1986 and 1997 federal income tax reforms began to reverse those trends and to restore the income tax as a fair and continued high revenue-producing tax. States began to reform state income taxes in 1987. In the 1990s, the federal income tax became slightly more progressive than it was in the late 1980s. States are relying on it for more of their revenue as well.

The Sales Tax

The general or retail sales tax is the single largest source of state revenue today. In fiscal year 1995 (FY 95), states collected nearly $132.2 billion in general sales, use, and gross receipts taxes. Although combined individual and corporate income tax revenues exceeded general sales tax revenues, individually neither provided as much revenue as the general sales tax (Federation of Tax Administrators, 1997b). The sales tax is the most common state tax, currently in use by 45 states. One state, Alaska, allows for local sales tax levies (Due and Mikesell, 1994). General sales taxes represent 34 percent or $132.2 billion of state revenue, while selective state sales taxes, such as those on motor fuel, tobacco, and alcohol sales, account for another 16 percent or $64.6 billion in state revenue. According to the Federation of Tax Administrators (1997c), in fiscal year 1996, general sales taxes represented 33.3 percent of total state revenue, or $139.4 billion, while selective sales taxes represented an additional 15.8 percent of total revenue, or $66.1 billion.

Historical context.   Mississippi was the first state to enact a sales tax. In 1932, it introduced a 2 percent sales tax designed to replace a low-rate business tax (Due and Mikesell, 1994). This action introduced a new form of taxation to the United States. Initially a desperation measure designed to help states fund essential services during the Depression years, the sales tax has become the single largest source of revenue for states. At the same time, states have typically transferred authority for property taxes to local governments (Monk and Brent, 1997).

Despite protests by retailers, sales taxes spread rapidly. Between 1933 and 1938, 26 more states, plus Hawaii (which was not yet a state), imposed a state sales tax (Due and Mikesell, 1994). Five states allowed the taxes to expire after one or two years, although they eventually re-imposed them. The sales tax was particularly favored during the Depression when income tax yields fell due to declining incomes, and local governments needed the revenues from property taxes.

Following the Depression and World War II, there was a slow trend toward renewed adoption of sales taxes. By 1963, 10 additional states had imposed sales taxes, and three of the five that allowed it to expire had renewed them, bringing the total to 37. The mid-1960s was a period of growth in state use of sales taxes with eight more states either introducing or re-imposing a state sales tax. In 1969, Vermont was the 45th and last state to introduce a sales tax. Today, only Oregon, Montana, Delaware, New Hampshire, and Alaska do not have state general sales taxes, and in Alaska, there is substantial use of the sales tax at the local level. In many cases, local sales tax rates in Alaska are comparable to state sales tax rates in other states. Local sales taxes are feasible in Alaska because communities are fairly widely separated. This limits the possibility of avoiding the tax by making purchases in an adjoining no- or low–sales tax community. This is generally not the case in most of the other 49 states.

Although no state has established a general sales tax since 1969, there have been changes to existing state sales tax provisions. Many states raised their sales tax rates to finance education reforms in the 1980s. In 1994, Michigan's voters agreed to increase the sales tax by 2 percent rather than increase income taxes to fund a dramatic reduction in property taxes to support schools. California enacted a temporary sales tax surcharge following the 1987 Loma Prieta earthquake to fund repairs. Following the 1994 Northridge earthquake, voters refused to extend that surcharge to help finance the repairs needed due to that temblor. In 1998, Ohio voters rejected a 1 percent sales tax measure designed to provide more funds for schools and property tax relief for poor districts. Between 1996 and 1998, the sales tax in Arkansas was increased from 4.5 percent to 4.625 percent, while the sales tax rate in Utah decreased from 4.88 percent to 4.75 percent.

Basis and yield.   State sales tax rates and revenue levels vary considerably (see www.taxadmin.org/fta/ for current information). In 1996–97, state tax rates ranged from a low of 3 percent in Colorado to a high of 7 percent in Mississippi and Rhode Island. Table 3.7 shows the proportion of total state revenue accounted for by sales taxes, income taxes, and other taxes in individual states for the same year. Other than the five states that do not levy general sales taxes, Vermont places the least reliance on general sales taxes. Only 21.7 percent of Vermont's tax collections come from general sales taxes. At the other extreme, nearly 60 percent of Washington State's revenue is derived through the general sales tax. The average dependence on general sales taxes among the 45 states that levy them is 33.3 percent of total revenue.

All general sales taxes are not alike. Many states offer exemptions for food

TABLE 3.7   State Tax Collections by Source, Fiscal Year 1996

State	Percent of State Revenue by Source (%)				
	General Sales	Selective Sales	Individual Income	Corporate Income	Other Taxes
Alabama	27.4	25.4	30.0	4.1	13.1
Alaska	n/a	6.5	n/a	21.5	72.0
Arizona	42.4	14.6	23.3	7.0	12.6
Arkansas	37.1	15.2	31.3	6.2	10.2
California	32.9	8.9	36.0	10.1	12.2
Colorado	27.4	14.9	47.2	4.3	6.3
Connecticut	31.2	19.0	33.4	8.2	8.2
Delaware	n/a	15.0	37.4	9.8	37.8
Florida	58.0	19.3	n/a	5.1	17.5
Georgia	37.2	9.3	41.2	7.0	5.3
Hawaii	46.6	15.1	32.6	2.1	3.6
Idaho	32.3	16.8	35.3	8.2	7.4
Illinois	29.3	19.8	33.5	9.4	8.0
Indiana	34.0	10.6	41.2	10.6	3.6
Iowa	32.8	15.6	35.8	4.6	11.3
Kansas	35.3	13.3	34.6	6.4	10.4
Kentucky	27.5	19.8	32.0	4.4	16.4
Louisiana	33.1	19.1	23.6	6.7	17.5
Maine	34.7	14.6	37.4	3.7	9.5
Maryland	24.5	19.0	42.7	4.0	9.8
Massachusetts	21.0	10.3	53.9	9.9	5.1
Michigan	34.4	9.1	30.7	11.4	14.4
Minnesota	28.8	15.0	41.1	7.0	8.1
Mississippi	47.4	19.9	19.2	5.2	8.2
Missouri	33.6	12.3	39.7	5.1	9.2
Montana	n/a	21.4	30.5	6.0	42.0
Nebraska	34.4	17.3	35.5	5.4	7.5
Nevada	54.4	29.9	n/a	n/a	15.7
New Hampshire	n/a	51.2	6.2	21.5	21.1
New Jersey	30.0	21.2	32.9	8.0	7.9
New Mexico	41.9	14.8	21.0	5.3	16.9
New York	20.4	14.5	50.9	8.0	6.2
North Carolina	25.0	18.3	41.5	7.9	7.3
North Dakota	28.6	28.2	15.4	7.5	20.3
Ohio	31.9	16.7	37.7	5.2	8.5
Oklahoma	26.2	14.3	32.8	3.5	23.2
Oregon	n/a	13.4	63.9	6.8	15.9
Pennsylvania	30.7	16.4	28.8	9.1	15.0
Rhode Island	30.0	20.2	37.5	5.6	6.7

(Continued)

TABLE 3.7   (Continued)

	Percent of State Revenue by Source (%)				
State	*General Sales*	*Selective Sales*	*Individual Income*	*Corporate Income*	*Other Taxes*
South Carolina	37.5	13.4	35.5	4.9	8.7
South Dakota	52.5	25.9	n/a	5.2	16.4
Tennessee	57.2	19.5	1.9	8.6	12.8
Texas	50.9	30.2	n/a	n/a	19.0
Utah	40.2	10.3	39.1	6.1	4.4
Vermont	21.7	26.3	33.4	5.3	13.3
Virginia	22.4	17.9	48.3	4.1	7.3
Washington	58.4	15.9	n/a	n/a	25.7
West Virginia	28.8	23.6	27.1	8.5	12.0
Wisconsin	28.2	13.5	43.2	6.0	9.1
Wyoming	33.7	10.1	n/a	n/a	56.2
U.S. total	**33.0**	**15.8**	**32.1**	**7.0**	**11.8**

Source: Federation of Tax Administrators (1997c).

and prescription (and nonprescription) drugs in an effort to reduce the regressive characteristics of the sales tax. The effect of these exemptions on the regressivity of the sales tax depends on a number of factors as described below. The most common exemption is for prescription drugs. With the exception of New Mexico, all of the 44 remaining states that levy a general sales tax exempt prescription drugs. Ten states exempt nonprescription drugs as well. Food is exempt from sales taxation in 27 of the states.

In addition, all 50 states levy one or more of a variety of additional sales and excise taxes. These are not general sales taxes, but represent additional levies on specific items. The exact nature and level of the taxes vary considerably. For example, gasoline taxes range from a low of 8 cents a gallon in Alaska to a high of 38 cents a gallon in Connecticut, while cigarette taxes vary from 3 cents a pack in Kentucky to 82.5 cents a pack in Washington. Even the five states without general sales taxes—Alaska, Delaware, Montana, New Hampshire, and Oregon—tax gasoline, cigarettes, and alcohol (Moody, 1998).

Thirty-four states allow local jurisdictions to levy sales taxes as well. Local taxing authority varies substantially among the states, but cities and counties are typically granted some leeway in levying local sales taxes. In some states, other jurisdictions such as transit agencies or special districts are also allowed to levy sales taxes. There is frequently a limit on the tax rate any jurisdiction may levy, and in a number of states, there is a cap on the total local sales tax that may be levied.[7]

---

[7] Note that this discussion concerns general sales taxes and does not include sales taxes levied on specific items such as hotel rooms.

The maximum allowable local sales tax rates vary considerably among the 34 states that allow their use. For example, localities in New York are empowered to levy sales taxes as high as 4.25 percent, 0.25 percent higher than the state sales tax. Localities that elect to levy the full rate more than double the state's sales tax. Similarly, in Louisiana, local jurisdictions are empowered to levy sales taxes as high as 5 percent, 1 percent higher than the state sales tax rate of 4 percent. Alaska is unique in that local jurisdictions can levy sales taxes as high as 6 percent, but there is no statewide general sales tax currently on the books. The remaining 31 states place varying limits on local sales tax levies, but in no case is the local levy allowed to exceed the state sales tax rate. Due and Mikesell (1994) provide details on the local sales tax authority and range of tax rates in the 50 states.

The elasticity of the sales tax is considerably lower than the elasticity of the income tax (Gold, 1994). This means that as the economy of a state grows, the more dependent the state is on income taxes compared to sales taxes, the faster state revenues will grow. The actual elasticity of a sales tax depends on the composition of its tax base. If food is taxed, elasticity tends to be relatively low since food consumption is not responsive to income growth (Gold, 1994). On the other hand, if services are taxed, the sales tax will be more elastic since demand for services is increasing more rapidly (Dye and McGuire, 1991).

Table 3.8 compares the relative elasticity of the state and local general taxes of the 50 states. The table displays an elasticity index for each state. An elasticity index of 100 implies that when income increases by 10 percent, state and local tax revenues will also grow by 10 percent (Hovey, 1998). As the table shows, on average, state tax systems do not maintain revenue growth at the same rate as the growth in income. Only 11 states have elastic revenue systems. West Virginia's elasticity index is 100.0, and the rest of the states have inelastic revenue systems. Interestingly, three of the five states without a general sales tax (Oregon, Montana, and Delaware) have highly elastic revenue systems. All three are among the top five in the rankings displayed in Table 3.8. Oregon relies heavily on personal income taxes, while Montana and Delaware both rely to a large extent on other sources of revenue (see Table 3.11). Alaska and New Hampshire, the two other states without general sales taxes, rank relatively low, but in both cases, the state has neither a sales nor an income tax.

Equity. There is considerable evidence that sales taxes are regressive. Since states generally obtain more income from taxes on consumption (sales taxes) than taxes on income, most state tax systems are regressive (Gold, 1994). A Minnesota study (Minnesota Department of Revenue, 1993) found the average sales tax incidence was 1.8 percent of income, but that for the lowest decile (lowest 10 percent) of income, it amounted to 5.2 percent and for the highest, only 1.3 percent. A study of Iowa sales tax burdens reached a similar conclusion, finding that the effective sales tax rate—the percentage of income devoted to sales tax payments—on households earning less than $10,000 a year was 6.64 percent. The effective tax rate declined as income ranges increased, with the effective tax rate on households with incomes above $200,000 only 1.38 percent of income (KMPG

110

Chapter 3

TABLE 3.8   Elasticity Index for State and Local General Fund Taxes

State	Index	Rank
Alabama	93.1	38
Alaska	90.6	42
Arizona	97.2	21
Arkansas	98.9	16
California	101.5	10
Colorado	96.3	24
Connecticut	93.8	35
Delaware	102.7	5
Florida	88.4	47
Georgia	99.0	15
Hawaii	101.8	8
Idaho	103.3	2
Illinois	92.0	41
Indiana	94.2	33
Iowa	102.1	6
Kansas	96.7	23
Kentucky	103.1	4
Louisiana	94.7	30
Maine	101.7	9
Maryland	94.4	31
Massachusetts	96.9	22
Michigan	94.3	32
Minnesota	99.7	14
Mississippi	94.1	34
Missouri	93.1	37
Montana	103.2	3
Nebraska	98.6	17
Nevada	87.5	50
New Hampshire	90.3	43
New Jersey	98.5	19
New Mexico	97.4	20
New York	98.5	18
North Carolina	100.1	12
North Dakota	92.6	39
Ohio	102.0	7
Oklahoma	94.8	29
Oregon	104.4	1
Pennsylvania	92.4	40
Rhode Island	96.1	24
South Carolina	93.4	36
South Dakota	88.5	45

(Continued)

TABLE 3.8 (Continued)

State	Index	Rank
Tennessee	88.5	46
Texas	88.1	48
Utah	95.8	26
Vermont	95.6	27
Virginia	95.2	28
Washington	87.7	49
West Virginia	100.0	13
Wisconsin	100.7	11
Wyoming	88.9	44
U.S. average	**96.2**	

Source: Hovey, 1998.

Peat Marwick, 1993). Another KMPG Peat Marwick Study (1990) in Connecticut also found the sales tax to be regressive with the effective tax rate declining from 8.15 percent of income for income levels below $5,000 to 1.24 percent for incomes above $200,000.

Despite these findings, there is still some question about how regressive the sales tax really is. Due and Mikesell (1994) point out that if sales taxes are borne in relation to factor incomes and not consumption expenditures, the tax is considerably less regressive. Essentially, the argument is that sales taxes reduce demand for factor production inputs, reducing their prices. The burden of the sales tax is then borne by individuals in relation to the amount of factor income they receive. While this makes intrinsic sense, Due and Mikesell (1994) point out that the analysis requires a number of simplifying assumptions that cast doubt on the conclusions.

Browning (1985) argues that the existence of social security and welfare payments to lower-income groups, indexed to price-level changes, reduces the burden of sales taxes on the poor and makes it less regressive. However, not all poor people are covered by this indexing (Due and Mikesell, 1994).

Fullerton and Rogers (1993) estimate the lifetime sales tax burden, arguing that consumption patterns vary over an individual's lifetime. Their estimates suggest that while the sales tax remains regressive, it is less so. The problem with this line of reasoning is that the average individual pays sales taxes out of current income, and thus for most, the ratio of taxes to current income is more important.

Regardless of the analysis, the sales tax still appears to be regressive. While this regressivity may be lessened by the progressive, or less regressive, nature of other parts of the tax system, it still places a greater burden on those in low-income categories. There are two approaches that could be considered, either alone or together, in attempting to mitigate the regressive tendencies of a sales tax. One is to reduce the tax rate, the other to expand the tax base to include more items consumed by those with high incomes.

Reducing the Tax Rate.   Since individuals in low-income categories consume a higher portion of their income, and are less likely to consume items not currently subject to sales taxation (e.g., professional services), they tend to pay a higher proportion of their income in taxes. This makes the tax regressive (see Pechman, 1985 and 1986, for example). Lower tax rates would mean that a smaller percentage of household income would be devoted to sales taxes generally, reducing the regressivity of the tax overall. While this would have some impact on the vertical equity of the sales tax, it comes at the expense of lower revenues as well, unless the tax base is increased. As the discussion below shows, the tax base can also be used to moderate the potential regressivity of the sales tax.

Changing the Tax Base.   A number of tax exemptions have been implemented by states to reduce the level of sales tax regressivity over the years. The most frequently discussed, and largest in terms of revenue impact, is the exemption on food. On the other hand, efforts to tax services that are consumed in greater proportion by those with high incomes and would thus improve the vertical equity of the sales tax have generally met with little or no success. This discussion focuses first on ways to broaden the tax base through taxation on services to improve vertical equity, and then shifts to alternatives that tend to narrow the sales tax base to achieve greater vertical equity.

Taxing Services: There are a number of alternative services that can be, and often are, taxed by the states. Services that are taxed can include custom-written computer programs, the time of an accountant or lawyer, or the costs of utilities such as phone or electricity service. The Federation of Tax Administrators has conducted a number of studies of the taxation of services. They have identified 164 different services that are taxed by one or more of the states. These services are divided into eight categories (Federation of Tax Administrators, 1996):

1. Utilities
2. Personal services
3. Business services
4. Computer services
5. Admissions and amusements
6. Professional services
7. Fabrication, repair, and installation
8. Other services

As the number of services taxed increases, the tax base is broadened, leading to greater levels of revenue per penny of sales tax rate. In Florida, efforts to broaden the sales tax to include virtually all services ended in failure and repeal of the law. As Gold (1994) points out, one of the services subject to taxation was advertising. Not surprisingly, the advertisers, not wanting to see the costs of their services increase (or alternatively, their profits diminish), devoted considerable advertising resources toward defeating the tax measure. California's experience with a more limited tax on snack foods, which was also repealed in a campaign focused on the complexity of defining snack foods, shows that changes in what is and is not subject to sales taxation can be a very controversial decision. As the role of services in the economy expands, taxation of those services will yield greater revenues for states.

One problem with broadening the tax base is that it is normally regressive (Gold, 1994). Taxation of food and utilities increases regressivity. However, if the tax is expanded to include services used more often as income increases, the regressivity is reduced.

Exemptions on food: Exemptions for food are one of the most common sales tax exemptions among the 50 states. The primary argument for these exemptions is that food and medicine consume a higher percentage of income in low income groups than in high-income groups.

Other exemptions: Another exemption that could impact the regressivity of the sales tax and is reasonably common across the states is for purchases of motor fuels. These purchases are typically exempt because they are generally subject to excise taxation by both the state and federal governments separately, and it is argued that it is unfair to tax a commodity twice. It is not entirely clear to what extent low-income households consume higher portions of their financial resources in purchase of motor fuels than high-income households, but to the extent this is the case, exemptions on motor fuels would reduce the regressivity of the sales tax. Due and Mikesell (1994) argue that the exemption is so well-ingrained in tax structures that it is unlikely to be changed. Other items exempted from sales taxes in some states include (Due and Mikesell, 1994):

- **Electricity for residential use:** Exempt from sales taxes in 20 states, taxed at a lower rate in Louisiana and Utah, and exempt in winter months only in Wisconsin and Minnesota. Electricity is exempt from general sales taxes but subject to special utility taxes in six states.
- **Medicines and other health items:** Prescription medicine is exempt from sales tax in all states but New Mexico. Other drugs are exempt in 10 other states.
- **Commodities subject to excises:** Ten states levy sales tax on motor fuel subject to excise taxes. Most of the others exempt fuel subject to the excise tax. In Missouri, all motor fuel is exempt, and South Carolina exempts fuel for farm use. Most liquor and tobacco products are subject to sales taxes as well as excises. Mississippi exempts alcoholic beverages from the sales tax, and Virginia exempts sales of liquor in state stores. Only Colorado and Texas exempt cigarettes, and Minnesota taxes them at a special higher rate.
- **Telephone service:** Thirty-one states tax local services at regular sales tax rates, and 18 levy sales tax on long-distance services as well. Seventeen states exempt phone services from sales taxes, two tax it at lower rates, and three rely on a special utility tax.

- **Clothing:** Six states exempt clothing at least to some extent. Five exempt all clothing with minor exceptions, such as sports and formal wear. Massachusetts limits the exemption to clothing selling for less than $175 and taxes all sports and specialty wear. Connecticut exempts clothing selling for less than $75 and clothing for children under age 10.
- **Publications:** The general pattern is to tax periodicals and books and to exempt newspapers. Thirty-one states exempted newspapers in 1993. This is largely a holdover from when newspapers cost only 5 or 10 cents. Today, in most states, books and periodicals are subject to sales taxation if sold over-the-counter, but subscriptions are not taxed.

These are all items (with the exception of publications) that appear to potentially consume a higher portion of low-income household finances than high-income household finances. To the extent this is the case, exemptions reduce the regressivity of the sales tax.

An alternative to blanket exemptions for all taxpayers would be to provide credits against income and/or income tax refunds for sales taxes paid by those in the lowest income groups. Nine states currently have programs that offer such refunds. Each of the nine uses a slightly different system.

In this age of technology, states might want to explore the concept of an electronic exemption card. In this way, low-income consumers would not have to wait for a tax rebate. In addition, it would facilitate targeting of exemptions to those who most need them. Broad exemptions of food and drugs would no longer have to be extended universally. This change would substantially increase state sales tax collections, but at a price. Individuals would give up some privacy, retail sales outlets would have to purchase the equipment necessary to read the magnetic strip on the card, and other compliance costs associated with collection of the tax and auditing individual business returns would be dramatically complicated.

Regardless of how reliant a state is on sales tax revenues, any attempt to increase sales taxes must address the regressive tendencies of the tax. Broad exemptions for food and other items are one approach, but the downside of these alternatives is a substantial reduction in revenue. States would be better off using some form of income tax refund based on income, or in the case of states that don't have income taxes, direct payments to low-income individuals like Wyoming uses, or some form of property tax relief such as that used in Kansas.

Horizontal Equity.   Horizontal equity—the equal treatment of individuals in the same situation—is generally not a substantial problem with sales taxes since tax rates tend to be uniform across a state. Where local sales taxes are permitted, there may be differences, but they are relatively small, and they too are uniform across a taxing jurisdiction.

The discussion above shows that achieving equity in the sales tax is not a simple task. The sales tax is generally regressive, and although a number of alternatives for changing the tax base to enhance the fairness or vertical equity of the tax exist, each comes with reductions in total available revenue. These reductions in revenue must be compensated with lower expenditures or higher tax rates. Moreover, blanket exemptions are available to anyone, regardless of income level. Alternatives that focus tax relief specifically on low-income individuals might be more successful in improving the fairness of the sales tax. These include income tax refunds or electronic exemption cards.

Economic effects.   A routine argument against any tax is that it makes an area less competitive in attracting new business and thus economic growth. To the extent that sales taxes are levied on products that are highly mobile, it can make an area less attractive for new business to locate. If the item taxed is highly mobile (for example, items that can be procured via mail order), an individual can avoid paying sales tax by purchasing the item from the provider not subject to the local jurisdiction's sales tax. In this case, the local business must bear the burden of the tax to remain competitive—if the business tries to pass the sales tax on to consumers, they will purchase the item from another provider.

On the other hand, if a sales tax is levied on products that require close proximity of customers and providers, those products can be taxed with little concern the producers will relocate. However, such taxes do add to the cost of doing business in that jurisdiction, making it somewhat less attractive for the business to locate or expand in the future. Even if the seller of the product is able to shift the entire tax burden to purchasers of the product, there are still costs of collecting the sales tax and remitting the tax receipts to the state (see the next section on administrative costs).

Administrative cost.   The administrative cost of a tax is the amount of money expended by the taxing jurisdiction to collect the tax from taxpayers. Administrative costs of a sales tax are generally lower than for income and property taxes (Due and Mikesell, 1994). Income taxes require filings by all individual taxpayers, and property taxes require accurate assessments of real, and, in some states, personal property. On the other hand, many of the collection costs of a sales tax are borne by retailers, and the state has fewer tax returns to audit. Moreover, total sales are generally easier to measure than income and property value.

Few states are able to provide estimates of the cost of administration of the sales tax. When they do, the figures tend to have relatively arbitrary allocations of common costs. The most recent data available are from 1979–81, where the average administrative costs of sales taxes as a percent of total collections amounted to 0.73 percent (Due and Mikesell, 1994). What is not known is how much collections of sales tax revenues would increase if more were spent on administration, and whether or not such increased expenditures for enforcement would "pay for themselves."

According to the Federation of Tax Administrators (1998), 26 states plus the District of Columbia offer vendors discounts for collecting the local sales tax. Under these programs, the vendor remits a percentage of sales taxes collected to the state (usually something on the order of 97 or 98 percent) and keeps the remaining funds as a "payment" for collecting the taxes.

An issue faced by all 45 states that administer sales taxes is what the potential benefits of additional administrative efforts would be. In the early 1990s, Florida experimented with a number of educational outreach activities designed to help retail establishments better understand the sales tax requirements and hopefully to improve the collection of sales taxes by making sure all taxable items sold were subject to the tax. Three specific activities showed substantial benefit-to-cost ratios. A conversational-style booklet and tax fraud leaflet sent to retail stores were estimated to bring in an additional $3.1 million in revenue at a cost of just over $24,000, for a benefit-to-cost ratio of $129.30 to 1. A model using this material along with information seminars was estimated to bring in an additional $6.2 million in revenue at a cost of $36,852, for a benefit-to-cost ratio of $167.49 to 1. Increased field visits were estimated to improve revenues by $2.7 million at a cost of $103,545, for a benefit-to-cost ratio of $24.80 to 1 (Florida Department of Revenue, no date).

While these are estimates, it is clear that there may be substantial benefits that accrue to modest increases in administrative costs for state sales taxes. It should be noted that each of these Florida examples were mostly informational programs. It is not known how the use of additional audits of retailers would succeed in improving sales tax collections. Most states do some auditing of retail sales. It is not clear if additional audits, or the threat of such audits, would improve collections (Due and Mikesell, 1994).

Administration and compliance. Many studies suggest that compliance with sales tax laws is quite high due to the relatively low cost of compliance and the relative ease with which sales can be audited. Because sales tax rates are generally quite low (ranging from 3 to 7 percent), many argue there is little incentive to avoid compliance. If tax rates or the costs of compliance were to increase, avoidance activities would also likely increase. Mikesell (1997) describes both a Tennessee study that estimated voluntary compliance with that state's sales tax at 95.9 percent and a Washington study that estimated the compliance rate to be on the order of 98.3 percent. While few think sales tax compliance is a major problem, Mikesell argues this belief stems more from faith than research.

There is no doubt that retailers experience costs in complying with sales tax collection requirements. They must invest in cash registers that compute the sales tax, keep track of total sales and the associated taxes collected against those sales, and report both to the state or other taxing jurisdiction. In addition, in states where some items are exempted from sales taxation, retailers must keep track of sales of taxable and exempt items. A 1982 study of seven states by Peat Marwick, Mitchell and Company found that the compliance costs ranged from 2 to 3.75 percent of the tax due. They found that the primary element in the level of compliance costs was distinguishing between taxable and exempt items, and this occurred mostly in grocery and drug stores.

Another option available to states to enhance their tax collections is to offer amnesty programs for those who have not paid their taxes. Under most amnesty programs, taxpayers are allowed to make past-due tax payments without penalty. Proponents of tax amnesty programs argue that they collect more taxes at a lower cost than would stricter enforcement procedures. The disadvantage of such programs is that if taxpayers believe amnesty programs will be offered on a regular basis, they are likely to avoid making tax payments until the amnesty program is established again.

According to the Federation of Tax Administrators (1997e), 35 states and the District of Columbia have offered tax amnesty programs of one sort or another since 1982. With the exception of one of Florida's amnesty programs and Idaho's in 1983, all of the programs included the sales tax. Five states—Connecticut, Louisiana, New Jersey, New York, and Rhode Island—and the District of Columbia have offered amnesty on multiple occasions, while the remaining 29 have only offered amnesty once to date.

Stability. A desirable characteristic of any tax is that it produce revenue steadily without large fluctuations from year to year. If revenue is unstable, the taxing jurisdiction will have more trouble balancing its budget (Gold, 1994). Sales taxes are clearly affected by changes in the economy. In times of recession, consumers have fewer dollars to spend, and business is less likely to purchase new equipment. On the other hand, when the economy is growing, consumer purchases tend to increase as well. Consequently, it appears that sales tax revenues are probably not as stable as property tax receipts, yet are impacted less by changes in personal income than are income taxes (see Musgrave and Musgrave, 1989; Rosen, 1992).

The tax base for an individual state's sales tax also impacts how revenues respond to changes in the economy. For example, sales taxes in states that exempt food are more sensitive to economic downturns because individuals will continue to purchase food, and in many cases will shift purchases from prepared meals (e.g., restaurant meals, which are taxed) to grocery store purchases (which are not taxed). In times of economic growth, sales tax receipts may grow more slowly than income tax receipts since individuals with higher personal incomes may consume more services, which as is discussed below, are taxed less often under state sales tax systems.

Political acceptability. If additional revenue is needed for schools, policymakers need to find a way to generate support for raising those additional funds. In today's political climate, no tax is viewed as a "good" tax. Increasing taxes to generate additional state and/or local revenue continues to be a political challenge.

When faced with using income taxes or sales taxes to replace property taxes for schools in 1994, Michigan's voters elected to increase the state sales tax from 4 percent to 6 percent rather than pay higher income taxes. Although this action does not appear to be in the best interest of those with the lowest incomes, as sales taxes tend to be more regressive than income taxes (see discussion of fairness above), support for the sales tax over the income tax seems to have been widespread in Michigan. In Ohio, voters turned down a 1 cent increase in sales taxes in 1998. The tax increase was to be split—half a cent for schools and half a cent for property tax relief.

Broadening the sales tax base through the taxation of more goods, and in particular, more services, does not appear to be particularly popular with taxpayers either. California's recent effort to increase the sales tax base by subjecting snack goods to taxation resulted in failure. The problem stemmed largely from the difficulty in determining what constituted a snack food. For example, single-portion sales of pies and cupcakes were determined to be taxable, but whole cakes and pies were considered food and thus not subject to taxation. Recently, one member of California's Board of Equalization crisscrossed the state pointing out the folly of taxing so-called snack food and gained enough popularity to get elected to Congress. The sales tax on snack foods was repealed by voter initiative in California.

In Florida, efforts to broaden the sales tax to include virtually all services similarly ended in failure and repeal of the law. As Gold (1994) points out, one of the services subject to taxation was advertising. Not surprisingly, the advertisers, not wanting to see the costs of their services increase (or alternatively, their profits diminish), devoted considerable advertising resources toward defeating the tax measure.

Exportability.   Taxes are exportable to the extent that someone else has to pay them. Taxes can be exported either to the federal government, or to nonresidents of the taxing jurisdiction. Exporting a tax to the federal government is possible if they are deductible on corporate or individual income tax returns. The federal government does not actually pay the taxes; rather, the deduction reduces federal revenues, meaning it must either borrow more money, spend less, or increase other tax sources. Since the elimination of the sales tax deduction for federal income taxes, it is no longer possible to export a portion of sales taxes to the federal government.

Sales taxes are ideal for export to other individuals. Tourists, business travelers, and other visitors to an area will purchase goods and services during their visit. To the extent these goods and services are taxed, someone other than those in the taxing jurisdiction pays the tax. This same principle accounts for the popularity of hotel taxes, parking taxes, and taxes on automobile rentals. If others can be forced to pay taxes to support local services, local taxpayers will have to pay less themselves. The downside to this type of taxation is that it is more sensitive to economic fluctuations than many other sales taxes, as travel is one of the first things that is cut back in a declining economy, whether it is travel for business or leisure.

Conclusions about sales taxes.   The discussion above shows that there are a number of important issues that must be carefully considered before relying on an increase in the sales tax rate or an expansion of the base to provide additional funds for education. Moreover, as tax rates increase, issues of fairness or equity, exportability, and compliance become more difficult. States often enact politically motivated, broad-based exemptions, reducing the potential yield of the new tax. An alternative is to broaden the base subject to sales taxation. One way to do this is to establish a sales tax on services as well as on products. To the extent that there is a trend away from consumption of goods toward purchase of more services, this will also make the tax more elastic (see Dye and McGuire, 1991).

If changes in tax rates or in the size of the tax base are enacted, how much additional revenue might be available for schools? It is hard to make firm estimates of how much revenue a sales tax rate or tax base increase might generate.

The Property Tax

The property tax has been and remains today the mainstay of local government financing. In 1994, the property tax was the major own-source revenue mechanism for local governments in 48 of the 50 states plus the District of Columbia (Moody, 1998). Alabama and Louisiana rely more on sales and gross receipts tax revenues for local governments. In the District of Columbia, property, sales, and income taxes represented almost identical shares of own-source revenue in 1994 (Moody, 1998). For the entire country, the property tax accounted for 74 percent of local government own-source tax revenues in 1994. This figure excludes intergovernmental transfers between the federal and state governments and local governments as well as other nontax revenues received[8] by local taxing jurisdictions. Nontax revenue includes such things as user charges or fees, utility charges, liquor store sales, and proceeds from insurance trusts.

For years, the property tax produced the largest percentage of revenues for schools, but that role was ceded to state governments during the flurry of school finance reforms enacted in the 1970s. Nevertheless, the property tax produces large amounts of steady local revenue and, except for the few local governments that can levy sales and income taxes, it is the only broad-based tax that most local governments, including school districts, can use to raise tax dollars. This section analyzes the property tax in terms of its base, yield, equity, economic effects, and administration and compliance costs. It ends with a summary of state approaches to property tax relief for the poor and a brief discussion of the impact of California's 1978-enacted Proposition 13.

Basis. The basis of the property tax generally is wealth. Except for the inheritance tax, which is being lowered and eliminated in many states, the property tax is the closest approximation to a wealth tax in this country. But because so many elements of wealth are not included in the property tax and because the elements of wealth that are included are primarily property, the tax historically has been called a property tax.

There are three categories of wealth or property: (1) real or land, (2) tangible, and (3) intangible. Referring to land as real property derives from the

---

[8] Intergovernmental transfers and grants are discussed later in this chapter.

medieval times when all land was owned by royalty; "real" is actually a derivative of "royal." Tangible property includes improvements on land, such as buildings, homes, business establishments, factories, and office buildings, as well as personal property, such as automobiles, furniture, other household items, and business inventories. A value can be placed on all tangible property. Intangible property refers to items that represent a value but which itself has no value, such as bank deposits, certificates of deposit, stock certificates, bonds, etc. The property tax base usually includes the bulk of real property or land, portions of tangible property (primarily land improvements but usually not personal property), and little if any intangible property.

In terms of horizontal equity, the property tax does not treat all wealth holdings equally. An individual with greater amounts of financial investments as compared to real estate would pay less property tax than an individual with a portfolio mostly in real estate. Similarly, individuals with larger portions of their wealth in personal property exempt from the property tax base will likely pay less in property taxes than will those with larger portions of their holdings in land and buildings. In short, the property tax treats holders of wealth differently primarily based on the composition of their wealth across real, tangible, and intangible property.

These generalizations mask other aspects of the property tax. A considerable amount of real property and land improvements escapes property taxation, driving up the property tax rate for the remainder that is taxed. Property and buildings owned by the government—federal, state, or local—are exempt from the property tax, as are land and buildings owned by religious and some charitable organizations. Further, there are substantial numbers of additional exemptions. Many states provide a homestead exemption that eliminates a certain amount of a home's value from the property tax altogether. There are exemptions for certain kinds of business activities. Several localities, especially cities, have enacted property tax abatements under which new business buildings are exempt from the property tax rolls for a fixed number of years, often as long as 20 years. These exemptions or exclusions add to large totals over time. Thus, while all property that is on the tax rolls is taxed equally (except for the issues described below), the large portions of property not on the tax rolls avoid the property tax altogether, further violating horizontal equity.

The assessment process.   Additional issues enter the picture because property is taxed on the basis of what is called assessed valuation, and the assessment process is riddled with technical challenges and problems. The assessment process basically has three steps:

- First, all parcels of land across the country are identified, plotted, and recorded by local taxing jurisdictions, usually city or county government agencies.
- Second, those parcels subject to the property tax are given a value, usu-

ally a value approximating the market value;[9] both land and their improvements (buildings) are included in assigning a value.
- Third, an assessed valuation is assigned, which is some percentage of true or market value.

The sum of the assessed valuation of each parcel in a taxing jurisdiction is the local property tax base. The process seems simple, but actually determining assessed valuation is a complex technical and political process.

Determining Market or True Value.   Conceptually, determining a true value for a piece of land and its improvements is straightforward. True value is the market value; true value is what an individual would have to pay to buy the piece of property. That process is pretty straightforward for homes. The market value of a home is the value for which it would sell. Since records are kept of home sales, determining the market value of homes that sell is relatively straightforward.

But what about placing market values on homes that are not sold? The use of comparable homes that have sold in recent months provides an excellent way to estimate the value of a house in a given neighborhood and is frequently used to estimate the market value of all houses in an area. While technically this is fairly simple, as most real estate agents would attest, keeping up-to-date market values on the tax rolls requires a process that would continually update the figures. Computer programs exist to provide such updating, but political pressures frequently mitigate against full record updating. Some feel it is unfair to tax a homeowner on unrealized home value gains, as happens when updating of tax files occurs regularly. That leads to the question of how often tax rolls should be updated—every year, every other year, once a decade, or some other time frame? If annual updates do not occur, horizontal equity may be violated as homeowners who do not move pay a decreasing portion of the local property tax. But annual updating costs money and creates some public displeasure.

Valuing homes is simple compared to placing values on other properties. Consider small commercial buildings or small businesses that use land and buildings that are rarely sold. Since a market value does not exist, a process called capitalizing income or capitalizing rents is often used. If net income or profits are 10 percent, the value then becomes total sales divided by 10 percent (which would be total sales multiplied by 10). That is, the value is linked to the profits that are earned by using the land and buildings. Another somewhat different method links the value of commercial buildings to the rents that can be charged for using the building. Rents are divided by an average rate of return to determine true or market value; indeed, this process often determines the building's market price if the owner decides to sell. Capitalized values are determined by two critical variables: sales and net profit, or rents and assumed rate of return. Values can be increased or decreased by changing either of these two figures.

[9] The market value generally is the price at which a piece of property could be sold.

Determining market value for factories or plants provides more complex challenges. While capitalized valuation is one possible approach, it is difficult to allocate profits and sales just to one plant for a business with multiple plants. So an alternative process, replacement costs less depreciation, is often used. Replacement costs would be an estimate of what it would cost completely to rebuild the plant. In many respects, just replacement costs updated each year would indicate the true value of that type of property. But unlike homeowners, businesses are allowed to depreciate plants and factories in order to reinvest and improve properties over time. So true values for a plant or factory would be replacement costs minus accumulated depreciation.

Utilities, such as gas and electrical lines, represent yet an additional technical challenge. While such lines have little worth in themselves, they represent a distribution network allocated by governments to utility companies, and the distribution networks have substantial value, just as plane routes and airport gates in the airline industry have a value that far exceeds the value of the item itself. States have taken a variety of approaches to valuing utilities and often use a combination of capitalized valuation and replacement costs less depreciation.

Farmland presents another set of issues. While a market usually exists for farmland, often times the actual selling price exceeds the farming value of the land, even for farms far from growing urban areas. In addition, even if the market value of farmland equaled the farming capitalized price, a drought or other type of natural disaster could reduce a farmers income to zero in any one year, making it quite difficult to pay property taxes on farmland that still retained a value. Further, for farmland that does not turn over, if the selling price of nearby farmland is used as the basis for identifying a value, care must be taken to compare comparable types of land. Land that can only be used for grazing should not be compared to land used for agriculture; and different types of agriculture, which often depend on the specific characteristics of the soil, produce different net returns for farmers. All of these factors must be considered in valuing farmland. Several states use some type of market value, and several also use the lower of market value or actual use value.

An additional issue concerns farmland near growing urban areas, and this issue raises a broader issue for assessing land. Public finance economists argue that land should be valued according to its best and highest use; such a process prevents inefficient use of valued land, which is in fixed supply all over the world. If farmland near growing urban areas is valued at its best and highest use, the value would derive from its use in residential or commercial development for the growing urban area. That value usually is substantially higher than farm use. But if that valuation is used, the farmer essentially is driven out of business and must sell the land and therefore the farm. Economically, that might make sense, but socially and politically, it often creates dissatisfaction.

Often, states allow a farmer to choose the valuation standard, so as long as the farmer chooses to farm the land, its valuation is related to farm use. This, however, decreases the amount that can be raised from a given local property tax rate and shifts financing local government services to other taxpayers. Further, when the farmer ultimately decides to sell the farm, it is usually sold at the highest and best use value to an urban developer, and the farmer reaps a substantial financial reward. The solution is to allow the farmer to use the farm-use valuation as long as the land is used for farming, but when the farm is sold, to collect back taxes on the basis of highest and best use valuation to recoup lost property tax revenues. While economically sound, that solution also runs into social and political rejection.

Actually, the same issue exists for land in an urban area. Take a downtown parking lot, for example. If it is taxed on the basis of capitalized value on its actual use, the value is quite low, and far below its market value if it were sold to someone wanting to build a tall office building. The issue is whether to use a capitalized value on actual use, so as not to drive out the parking lot owner, thus reflecting a social and political goal. Or to use highest and best use, which would force the parking lot owner to sell to a developer or to build an office building. The latter also provides increased tax revenues for the city. Further, just as for the farmer, if valuation is based on actual use, the parking lot owner reaps a huge windfall at the time of sale. Again, there are mechanisms that could be used to recoup lost property taxes, but they are rarely invoked.

In short, determining property values is conceptually straightforward, but technically, socially, and politically complex. In many cases, there are no "right" processes; technical approaches interact with value judgements. As a result, whether horizontal equity is met is both a technical and a political/social conclusion.

Determining Assessed Valuation.　　Once a value is given to a piece of property, an assessed value must be ascribed because that is the value that officially becomes part of the tax base. In the best of all worlds, this step would be eliminated, and the determined value would be the measure that becomes part of the property tax base. But for a variety of reasons, fractional assessment practices exist across the country. That is, property is assessed at some fraction or percent of actual value; percentages can range from as low as 10 percent to as high as 100 percent, which is the actual market or true value. Public finance economists argue for 100 percent valuations, and that should be the goal for most state property tax systems.

Fractional assessments have no inherent economic justification; they are simply a complicating factor and often a factor fraught with substantial inequities. Fractional assessments have been used primarily to hide some of the realities of the property tax since most individuals are not aware of the details of the local assessment process. For example, if the practice is to assess property at 25 percent of market value, a homeowner with a $100,000 home receives a tax notice showing the assessed value to be just $25,000. Most homeowners think their house is undervalued since it is assessed so far below market value, when in fact the home is assessed at the correct level. While the tax rate applied to assessed valuation to raise a fixed amount of revenue would need to be four times the rate if it were applied to full or market value, the homeowner usually takes more comfort in a perceived valuation below market levels than the actual level of the tax rate. In addition, tax rates are often limited to some maximum level. So if assessment levels are artificially low, the government reaches the maximum tax rate more quickly, and thus local taxes are kept artificially low. But this gives political decision making to the local assessor and not the local policymaking bodies, where tax rate decisions should be made.

This problem is clear in California, where Proposition 13 limits assessed value to the value of the property in 1975–76, with increases limited to no more than 2 percent a year. Property can only be reassessed at market value when it is sold. As a result, the assessed value of most property is substantially below its market value. Since property taxes are limited to 1 percent of assessed value, there is a substantial difference between the taxes actually collected and the potential tax collections if all property were assessed at its true market value. Since homes and other property sell at different times, it is possible for individuals living in identical houses next door to each other to pay substantially different amounts of property taxes based on the length of time they have owned the house. Additionally, since residential property is sold more frequently than commercial and industrial property, and thus reassessed more frequently, a growing proportion of the property tax base in California is shifting to residential property. This means that a greater share of the property taxes paid by California's citizens are paid by homeowners.

Fractional valuations can mask a host of related inequities. If the popular assumption is that most homes are assessed far below market value, two individuals with the same $100,000 home, one with an assessed value of $25,000 and another with an assessed value of $20,000, might both feel that they are being given a "deal," when in fact the latter is being unfairly assessed 20 percent less than legal requirements. This situation often happens as homes grow older and families do not move, and these kinds of differences often are popularly accepted as fair.

Differences in such valuation practices lead to what is called intraclass assessment dispersions, which show differences in actual assessments within a class of property, such as owner-occupied homes. Different assessment practices across classes of property, such as between business property and homes, are measured by interclass assessment dispersions, and differences across areas within a local assessing jurisdiction are measured by interarea assessment dispersions. Each of these provides measures of the degree to which actual assessments of property differ. High coefficients of dispersion indicate low levels of horizontal equity (i.e., that similarly situated property owners are being treated differently).

Differential assessment practices create significant problems for state school finance systems that are designed to provide relatively more state education aid to districts low in assessed value of property per pupil versus districts with average or above-average levels of local property tax wealth per pupil. If two districts are alike in all characteristics, the district that assessed at the lowest fraction of market value would look poorer and thus be eligible for more state aid. That would be unfair, and state school finance systems need to adjust for such inequitable differences.

Consider two districts, A and B, with assessed valuations of $34,500,000 and $50,000,000, respectively. Just looking at these numbers would suggest that district B is wealthier in terms of total valuation. But further assume that district A assesses property at 25 percent of true value, and district B assesses at 50 percent. To determine the real true or market value, or adjusted or equalized assessed value as it is called in school finance, the assessed valuation figures must be divided by the assessment ratios. Thus, the true valuation in district A is $138,000,000 ($34,500,000 ÷ 0.25), and the true valuation in district B is $100,000,000 ($50,000,000 ÷ 0.50), which shows that district A actually has more wealth than district B. In other words, the unadjusted assessed valuations did not give an accurate picture of relative total wealth between these two districts.

For school finance purposes, the property tax base is divided by the number of students to determine relative ability to raise property tax dollars for school purposes. Assume that district A has 2,500 students, and district B has 1,500 students. If the state used just assessed valuation per pupil, district A would have a value of $13,800 ($34,500,000 ÷ 2,500), and district B would have a value of $33,333 ($50,000,000 ÷ 1,500). District B would appear nearly three times as wealthy as district A. But if equalized or adjusted assessed valuations are used, as they should be, district B would appear just slightly more wealthy than district A, at $66,667 (district B) compared to $55,200 (district A).

Thus, it is important for the state to recognize that local assessing practices can vary from required state practice, to collect data to identify the variations, and to make adjustments in school finance formulas to adjust for the differences. Usually this adjustment is accomplished through what is commonly called a State Equalization Board, which monitors local assessing performance. The monitoring usually consists of gathering sales data and comparing them to assessed valuations and calculating assessment/sales ratios to determine the degree to which local assessment practices reflect state requirements. Since assessment/sales ratios are available, the state legislature can and usually does use them to adjust local assessed valuations in determining state aid calculations.

In summary, there are numerous issues associated with determining the local property tax base. The property tax base is primarily land and improvements on the land, although government, religious, and charitable organization-owned land is exempt. Further, tax abatements and homestead exemptions further erode the local property tax base. Determining true or market value of many types of property is a technically complex undertaking, and raises social and political issues as well. Fractional assessments are widely practiced but serve only to mask the actual functioning of the property tax. Actual property assessments tend to differ within classes of property, across classes of property, as well as across areas within local taxing jurisdictions, leading to horizontal inequities. And differential fractional assessments across local taxing jurisdictions require state adjustments in order to allocate state education aid in an equitable manner.

Yield. The property tax is a stalwart revenue producer, providing $193.9 billion of revenues for state and local governments in 1995 (Moody, 1998). Table 3.9

TABLE 3.9   Property Taxes as a Percent of Personal Income, 1957–95

Fiscal Year	Total Property Taxes (in billions)	Personal Income (in billions)	Property Taxes as a Percent of Personal Income (%)
1957	$ 12.9	$ 356.3	3.6
1967	26.0	644.5	4.0
1977	62.5	1,607.5	3.9
1987	121.2	3,780.0	3.2
1995	193.9	6,072.1	3.2

Sources: Advisory Commission on Intergovernmental Relations (1988). *Significant Features of Fiscal Federalism,* 1988 Edition, Volume II, Washington, D.C. ACIR. p. 64; Table 59; U.S. Bureau of the Census. (1988). *Government Finance in 1986–87,* Washington, D.C.: U.S. Bureau of the Census, p. 7; *Economic Report of the President,* January 1989, p. 333; Moody, Scott. ed. (1998). *Facts and Figures on Government Finance,* 32nd edition. Washington, D.C.: Tax Foundation, tables C23 and D22; and Bureau of Economic Analysis (1998). *Survey of Current Business.* Washington, D.C.: U.S. Department of Commerce. *http://www.bea.doc.gov/bea/ARTICLES/NATIONAL/NIPA/1998/0898nip3.pdf/* Table 1, p. 147.

shows total property taxes and property taxes as a percent of personal income between 1957 and 1995. Property tax yields rose from $12.9 billion in 1957 to $193.9 billion in 1995. Between 1957 and 1967, property tax revenues doubled. They more than doubled between 1967 and 1977, and doubled yet again between 1977 and 1987. Between 1987 and 1995 (less than a full decade), they increased by 60 percent.

Interestingly, property taxes represent a lower portion of personal income today than they did 30 years ago. While property taxes as a percent of personal income rose from 3.6 percent in 1957 to 4 percent in 1967, during the next decade when property taxes more than doubled, they dropped slightly to 3.9 percent. By 1987, property taxes consumed only 3.2 percent of personal income, and that figure remained the same in 1995. The drop since 1977 probably reflects the tax and expenditure-limitation fever after 1978.

Property Tax Rates.   Expressed as a percent, a property tax rate is easy to use to determine the property tax yield. If the tax rate were 1.5 percent, and assessed valuation were $50,000, the yield would be 1.5 percent times $50,000, or expressing a percent as a decimal, 0.015 times $50,000, or $750.

Unfortunately, the property tax rate is not always given as a percent of assessed valuation. Property tax rates are usually stated in "mills" and "dollars per hundred" dollars of assessed valuation. These rate units further add to the complexity surrounding the property tax. A tax rate in mills indicates the rate applied to each $1,000 of assessed valuation. Thus, if the tax rate is 15 mills, and assessed valuation is $50,000, the yield is 15 times $50, or $750. In many respects, the mill rate is useful because the mill rate can be multiplied by the assessed valuation with a decimal point replacing the comma that indicates the thousands. Technically, a mill is "one-thousandth," so a tax rate in mills, say 15 mills, expressed as a decimal would be $15 \times 1/1,000$ or $15/1,000$ or 0.015 (note this is the same as the decimal expression for 1.5 percent). If that representation of the rate is used, the yield would be just the rate times the base, or $0.015 \times \$50,000$ or still $750.

The same tax rate given in units of dollars per hundred would be $1.50. Thus, the yield would be the rate, $1.50, times the number of hundreds of dollars of assessed valuation ($50,000 ÷ 100 or $500) or again, $750. Notice that this rate is similar to the rate given as a percent; for both, the number 1.5 is used.

This may seem confusing, even though the end result is the same regardless of which method is used. Table 3.10 is designed to help clarify matters by showing how tax rates are expressed in different formats. The first column of Table 3.10 displays the tax rate expressed as a percentage of assessed value. The next three columns display the same tax rate in mills, dollars per hundred dollars of assessed value, and dollars per thousand dollars of assessed value. The fifth column of Table 3.10 shows the decimal value to use when multiplying the tax rate times the assessed value to determine the property tax yield or revenue.

Mills and dollars per hundred were used in part because assessed valuation figures were so large. Such a rate helped reduce the number of figures needed to calculate results. But these two rates are confusing, especially in comparing rates across jurisdictions and across states. If it were possible, shifting to a simple percentage rate, as was done in California, would simplify matters. Then all tax rates—income, sales, and property—would be given in the same units that could be compared.

Property tax elasticity. One of the major criticisms of the property tax has been that it is not responsive to economic growth (Mikesell, 1986). Mikesell estimated that the elasticity of the property tax is substantially less than one, meaning that as income increases, revenue from property taxes rises more slowly. This means that governments that are heavily dependent on property taxes (most school

TABLE 3.10   Tax Rate Equivalents for Determining Tax Yield

Tax Rate (%)	Mills	$/100 of Assessed Value	$/1,000 of Assessed Value	Value to Use in Calculations
1.0	10	$ 1.00	$ 10.00	0.010
1.5	15	1.50	15.00	0.015
2.0	20	2.00	20.00	0.020
2.5	25	2.50	25.00	0.025
3.0	30	3.00	30.00	0.030
100.0	1,000	100.00	1,000.00	1.000

districts) need to raise their rates to meet increases in the demand for their services, such as education (Monk and Brent, 1997).

The inelasticity of the property tax is shown in Table 3.11, which displays the simple elasticity of the property tax between 1957 and 1995. As Table 3.11 shows, the simple property tax elasticity fell between 1957 and 1987, dropping from 1.26 between 1957 and 1967 to just 0.69 between 1977 and 1987. It increased again between 1987 and 1995 to just under 1.0. These numbers show that for several reasons, property tax revenues did not keep pace with income growth after 1967. The simple elasticity does not adjust for rate changes, however, and property tax rates also fell after 1977. Beginning with the recession of 1990, many local governments were forced to increase property tax rates again, making the tax look more proportional than it did in 1987. While it is important to know the "true" property tax elasticity, the simple elasticity also has meaning because it shows just how property tax revenues track personal income. In the recent past, property tax revenues simply have increased more slowly than income.

Property tax stability.   In terms of stability, the property tax has some ideal characteristics. In times of economic slowdowns, it produces a steady revenue stream, largely because property values maintain their levels except in very deep recessions. On the other hand, in times of economic growth and/or inflation, property values rise so property tax revenues rise. In other words, property tax revenues relative to the business or economic cycle are stable on the downside and increase on the upside.

Property tax equity.   For years, the property tax was considered a regressive, actually a steeply regressive, tax (Netzer, 1966). In the 1970s, a new view of property tax incidence was developed, which concluded that it had a progressive incidence pattern (Aaron, 1975; Mieszkowski, 1972). Since the mid-1970s, analysts have essentially divided into two camps, those claiming a progressive incidence pattern and those claiming a regressive incidence pattern. This section

TABLE 3.11   Property Tax Simple Elasticity, 1957–95

	Percent Change from Previous Period (%)		
Year	*Property Taxes*	*Personal Income*	*Elasticity: Ratio of Percent Changes*
1957	—	—	—
1967	101.6	80.9	1.26
1977	140.4	149.4	0.94
1987	93.9	135.1	0.69
1995	60.0	60.6	0.99

Source: Calculated from Table 3.9.

summarizes both arguments, presents research results based on both arguments, and makes the important conclusion that property tax incidence is steeply regressive in the low-income ranges regardless of the conceptual framework used to determine incidence.

Estimating Property Tax Incidence.   To estimate property tax incidence, the tax is usually divided into four basic components:

- the land component,
- the owner-occupied residential component,
- the rented residential component, and
- the nonresidential component.

While the conventional view uses a framework that analyzes the impact of the property tax on users rather than owners, and the new view focuses on owners rather than users, both must address these different components.

First, under both views of property tax incidence, the land component is assumed to fall on landowners. Both views make the assumption that land is in fixed supply (i.e., that the amount of land is given and cannot be changed). The price of something that is fixed in supply is the same with or without the tax. There is virtually no way landowners can shift the tax to some other party. Thus, the property tax on land falls exclusively on landowners. This portion of the property tax is distributed across income classes by using data either on land ownership by income class or income from all forms of capital by income class. Since land ownership (as well as income from capital) is concentrated in the upper-income tax brackets, this component of the property tax is progressive in incidence.

Second, under both views the owner-occupied residential component is assumed to fall on homeowners. Again, at least in the short term, it is nearly impossible for a homeowner to shift the tax to some other party. Even if the homeowner moved, the price of the house would not increase or decrease because of the tax (assuming the negative effect of increased tax revenues was perfectly offset by the positive value of new services). In short, homeowners pay the property tax on owner-occupied homes. This portion of the property tax is distributed by housing consumption by income class. Since housing consumption is concentrated in the middle and upper-income ranges, this portion of the tax is proportional or mildly progressive, clearly not regressive. So essentially there is no difference in the two views about the burden of these two components of the property tax.

Property Tax Incidence under the Conventional View.   The difference occurs over the burden of the rented residential component and the nonresidential, or business, commercial and utilities component. Under the conventional view, these components of the tax are assumed to be shifted to the final consumers of the goods and services produced by the taxed structures—renters in the case of rented residences and consumers in the case of business structures.

How are these taxes shifted? Consider an increase in the property tax and take the case of a landlord who, before the tax increases, is earning what is considered an adequate rate of return on the investment in rental housing. The property tax increase causes an increase in costs and thus a decrease in profits or net rate of return. The landlord has several options: (1) to accept the lower rate of return; (2) to increase rents in the amount of the new tax (or decrease maintenance in the same amount); or (3) to shift his or her investments out of rental property.

If rents are increased or maintenance is decreased, the result is the same for the renter: a lowering of quality of rented property for a given price. This impact would encourage renters to either consume less rented property or consume the same amount but of lower-quality rented property. In both cases, the rent increase is shifted to the renter. If the landlord shifts some of the capital investment away from rental structures, in the long term, the supply of rental structures would decrease, which would in turn increase rents. As the market adjusts to this new equilibrium point, the property tax increase would again be shifted to the renter. The more inelastic the demand (i.e., the more demand for rental housing is insensitive to prices), and the more elastic the supply, the greater the extent of shifting. It is usually assumed that, in the long run, supply is quite elastic so that nearly full shifting occurs (DeLeeuw and Ekanem, 1971; Grieson, 1973; Hyman and Pasour, 1973; Orr, 1968).[10]

A similar argument is made for property tax increases on commercial, industrial, and utilities properties. Over both the long and short runs, the tax is shifted to the users of the products produced by the taxed structures (i.e., the tax is shifted to consumers).

The shifted taxes on residential rental property is distributed according to rental payments by income class. Since these tend to decrease with income, this portion of the property tax is usually regressive. The shifted property tax on non-residential property is distributed according to consumer expenditures by income class. Since these also decrease sharply with income, this portion of the property tax has a steeply regressive incidence pattern.

Empirical studies of property tax incidence under the conventional view consistently show very regressive incidence patterns (Brownlee, 1960; Musgrave and Daicoff, 1958; Netzer, 1966).

Property Tax Incidence under the New View.   The new view holds that the property tax is, at heart, a uniform tax on all property. The new view proceeds by analyzing the tax within a framework that focuses on the impact of the tax on

---

[10] Inelastic demand means that the demand for rental housing stays about the same, even if prices rise. By contrast, elastic demand would indicate that as price rose, demand would fall. Elastic supply in this case means that as taxes or costs rose (thus perhaps dropping profits), the supply of rental housing would fall. Inelastic supply would indicate that the amount of rental property provided (by investors or landlords) would stay about the same even if taxes or costs rose.

owners rather than users of capital (i.e., consumers of goods and services produced by capital).

The new view proceeds in two steps. Assuming a fixed supply of capital and a fixed level of consumption for all goods, the first step considers the property tax as a uniform tax on all property. The burden of such a tax is borne by owners of all capital, whether property or otherwise. As property taxes are increased, capital owners will move capital out of areas subject to the property tax. This will reduce the supply, increase the price, and thus decrease the consumption of goods and services produced by capital subject to the property tax. The shift of capital to other areas not subject to the property tax, however, will increase the supply of goods and services produced by this capital and thus decrease their prices. As the entire system moves to a new equilibrium point, the net rate of return on investment in both sectors shifts to a new and lower level. The final effect is a decrease in the net rate of return to capital investment in all sectors. In the long run, a uniform property tax is assumed to be borne entirely by capital owners. Since the ownership of capital is higher for upper-income groups, the burden of the property tax tends to be quite progressive in nature.

The studies based on property tax incidence under this portion of the new view show strong progressive property tax incidence patterns (Aaron, 1974; Kochin and Parks, 1982; Musgrave and Musgrave, 1989; Pechman and Okner, 1974; Pechman, 1985; Rosen, 1992.)

Step two of the new view recognizes the nonuniformity of the property tax that is caused by varying tax rates across state and local governments. These differentials tend to increase rents and prices in high-tax locations and to decrease them in low-tax locations. The precise nature of these effects is difficult to determine because they depend on the mobility of capital and the shifts in demand for goods and services caused by differential tax rates. Adherents of the new view argue, however, that the central tendency of property tax incidence, even after adjusting for these differentials, will still be progressive.

A Policy Issue Approach to Assessing Property Tax Incidence. It is difficult simply to choose a particular incidence perspective. The problem with the conventional view is that it ignores nationwide average impacts; likewise, the problem with the new view is that the tax is not a nationwide tax but a tax with varying rates across thousands of local taxing jurisdictions. If the policy question is, what is the average nationwide property tax incidence, then the new view is appropriate. If, for example, the issue were the degree to which the federal income tax offset any regressivity from the local property tax, or regressivity from all state and local taxes together, the new view would be appropriate. However, policy implications would be hard to draw for the property tax per se, since it is a local and not a national tax.

Another policy approach is to express concern for any regressive elements in any tax. Under this approach, the policy question would be whether property tax regressivity exists regardless of analytic perspective used to analyze incidence. Indeed, several studies have taken this approach and documented persistent regressivity (Musgrave and Musgrave, 1989; Odden, 1975; Odden and Vincent, 1976; Pechman, 1986; Pechman and Okner, 1974). These studies investigated property tax incidence under a variety of assumptions: from most regressive to most progressive, nationally, and for several states, including Connecticut, Minnesota, Missouri, and South Dakota. All except the Pechman (1976) study, which was a nationwide estimate, show persistent regressivity in the low-income ranges. Further, these studies document regressivity for the income ranges that include the bulk of taxpayers.

Additional studies of the vertical equity of the property tax have been performed using econometric analysis in recent years, and many of these studies also found the property tax to be highly regressive for those with low incomes. One such example is the Bell (1984) study, which uses a quadratic form to account for the nonlinearity between assessed value and sale price. Bell found a regressive inequity in the incidence of the property tax.

Indeed, these studies suggest that the major impact of the new view is to shift understanding of property tax incidence primarily for the upper-income categories, for which property tax burdens shift from regressive to progressive. In short, even accepting new understandings for analyzing property tax incidence, the property tax exhibits a regressive incidence pattern in the lower-income ranges, thus justifying policy mechanisms to stem that regressivity.

Economic and social effects.   For homeowners, the property tax is a tax on housing consumption. As such, it raises the price of housing and thus discourages housing investments. On the other hand, the property tax, which consumed 3.2 percent of personal income in 1995, is a smaller burden than the sales tax, which consumed about 5 percent of personal income, and thus a much smaller burden than if housing consumption were simply rolled into the sales tax base, a policy for which good arguments could be made. Further, property tax payments can be deducted from federal income tax payments, thus offsetting the property tax impact. At the present time, sales taxes are not deductible for federal tax purposes. In addition, states have enacted a wide-ranging array of adjustments designed to reduce the property tax impact on homeowners and to encourage housing consumption. While all of these latter mechanisms might not fully offset the regressive effect of the tax, they certainly help.

Further, the costs of property taxes are offset by the benefits in local services that they support. Indeed, both taxes and services are capitalized into the price, of property, with taxes decreasing the price, and services increasing them. Research shows that the capitalized impact of services is substantial (Wendling, 1981a).

Property taxes on the business sector raise a series of additional economic issues. A general issue is that businesses that rely more heavily on physical capital (land, buildings, equipment, machinery, including inventories) than human capital (lawyers, accountants, computer-service vendors, etc.) bear the impact of higher costs from property taxation and thus have some economic disadvantages in the market place. This reality raises the overall issue of how businesses should be taxed. During the past several years, states have generally exempted business inventories as well as machinery and equipment from the property tax rolls, thus including only land and buildings owned by the business sector.

Administration and compliance. The administration burdens of the property tax consist of recording all property parcels, maintaining a record of changing owner-ship, and assessing property, which is fraught with technical and political chal-lenges. Technically, tools exist to keep up-to-date values on just about any kind of property, and thus to maintain assessed values reasonably close to current market values. But, as noted, practice generally is otherwise. Appointed, rather than elected, local assessors with clear requirements for the skills needed to qualify for appointment; some degree of funding for the local assessment process with com-puter facilities to store, maintain, and update records; and a State Equalization Board to conduct periodic assessment-sales studies and provide equalization ra-tios for state school-aid purposes are the minimal requirements for good property tax administration.

Individual compliance is probably the most straightforward for any tax. A tax bill is submitted once a year, and property owners pay, sometimes in annual and sometimes in semiannual payments. Some homeowners have the bank col-lect property tax liabilities monthly with their mortgage payment; in these cases, the bank pays the bill annually. The annual nature of property tax bills con-tributes to the unpopularity of this tax. Individuals would rather pay taxes in little bites, as they do for the sales tax. That said, Monk and Brent (1997) point out that between 1987 and 1997, missed payments of school property taxes have in-creased dramatically in a number of states, with the number increasing by as much as 40 percent in New York state during that period.

Low-income property tax relief programs. For years, states have enacted a vari-ety of programs that ostensibly provide property tax relief for some if not all homeowners, but often only to low-income homeowners, the elderly, veterans, or the disabled. Public finance economists generally criticize these programs on a variety of grounds, but the programs remain and actually proliferate. Ebel and Ortbal (1989) summarized these programs from a detailed update by the Advi-sory Commission on Intergovernmental Relations (1989b).

Generally, property tax relief includes a variety of programs designed to re-duce reliance on the property tax to raise local revenues. As such, the programs are designed to benefit all local property taxpayers as well as to target additional relief to low-income households to reduce property tax regressivity. There are two categories of property tax relief programs: direct and indirect. Direct pro-grams include homestead exemptions or credits, circuit breakers, tax-deferral plans, and classification of the property tax base. These programs reduce property tax bills directly. Indirect programs include intergovernmental aid programs (which include school finance equalization programs at the state level), tax and spending limitations (for a review, see Gold, 1994), and local option sales and in-come taxes.

Classification of the property tax base.   The basic goal of a property tax classification program is to tax different elements of the property tax base—residential, commercial, industrial, farm, utilities, etc.—at different effective rates. Typically, the goal is to tax residential property at lower rates or, put differently, to tax non-residential (i.e., business property), at higher effective tax rates. A classification system is often called a "split roll" system. In many states, this is prohibited constitutionally. However, 19 states and the District of Columbia use some kind of classification scheme.

The usual procedure is to assess different components of the property tax base at different levels, usually assessing residential and often farm property at levels below that of other property, and to apply a uniform tax rate to total assessed valuations. West Virginia and the District of Columbia, though, assess all property at the same level and apply different tax rates to the different property classes. Though obviously less popular, the latter approach is preferred since it maintains assessment accuracy. Differential assessments add further cloudiness to what was discussed above as already a complex and difficult-to-understand set of assessment practices across the country.

The number of classifications of property varies substantially, from a low of two to what used to be a high of 34 in Minnesota. Minnesota's system was so complex that some analysts had suggested the state actually had created 70 property classifications (Bell and Bowman, 1986). In 1989, Minnesota changed its classification system, reducing the number of classes to about 10.

Homestead exemptions and credits.   Reflecting the value this country places on homeownership, 48 states have some type of homestead exemption or homestead credit that simply reduces the property tax for an individual who owns his/her home. Homestead exemptions or credits are one of the oldest property tax relief programs. For the homestead exemption, the assessed valuation is reduced by a fixed amount, often several thousand dollars. This reduces the property tax bill, and the cost is borne by local governments. Some, but not many, states reimburse local governments for these revenue losses through a homestead credit, whereby the local government reduces the homeowners property tax bill by the homestead exemption amount times the tax rate and then bills the state for the total amount for all local taxpayers. Since several of the programs are financed locally, a total cost of these programs has not been calculated.

Interestingly, a number of the states that provide this type of property tax relief do not link it to income (i.e., do not have a "needs" test—all homeowners, rich or poor, benefit from the homestead exemption or credit). Further, only 17 of the 48 states extend the program to all homesteads; others limit the program to the elderly (again rich and poor), the disabled, the poor, and/or veterans or disabled veterans (Monk and Brent, 1997).

Circuit breaker programs.   As the name suggests, a circuit breaker program of property tax relief is designed to protect homeowners from property tax overload, which could happen if current income falls in a year due to illness or unemployment or drops for several years due to retirement. Circuit breakers typically relate property tax bills to a taxpayer's income; circuit breaker relief is then some portion of the property tax bill that exceeds a given percentage of income. Such programs can help reduce regressive residential property tax burdens.

Most states link the circuit breaker program to the state income tax through a separate schedule, but several states administer the circuit breaker program separately and send cash refunds to those who qualify. Still other states have the local government provide the property tax relief, and then reimburse the local government for the total amount.

In 1994, 36 states had some type of circuit breaker program. Wisconsin enacted the first program in 1964; Michigan currently has the most comprehensive program. All 36 states make all homeowners eligible, and 21 states make renters eligible (assuming that landlords shift property tax bills to renters). Some states target relief to the elderly or disabled. Monk and Brent (1997) found that the average level of benefits granted in the states that reported such figures ranged from a high of $593 in Maryland to a low of $80 in California, with a median of $257 in Pennsylvania (Monk and Brent, 1997).

Tax deferrals. A tax-deferral program extends the time period over which property taxes can be paid. The taxpayer is given the option of paying the current tax bill or deferring the payment to some future time, usually when the property is sold. At that time, past property tax payments plus interest are due. Legally, these deferred property tax payments are liens on the property. Another way tax deferrals are used is to continue to assess property based on its current use as long as the qualifying use continues. If there is a change in use, the property owner is responsible for deferred taxes on the property. In the above examples of a farm or parking lot, if the farmer or parking lot owner sells the property for development, the taxing jurisdiction will collect back taxes, based on the highest and best use valuation of the property prior to the sale (Monk and Brent, 1997).

Tax deferrals are the most recently enacted property tax relief programs. In 1979, only nine states had such programs; the number increased to 31 by 1991 (Monk and Brent, 1997). Tax-deferral programs have the "best" economic characteristics of all the property tax relief programs because they entail minimal governmental interference in housing consumption, reflect the social goal of home-ownership and staying in one's home even when income drops, and maintain governmental revenues, at least over time. Unfortunately, as with most tax relief programs that have the best economic features, they are not so popular. Deferral programs have few participants; it seems that the negative features of placing a lien on one's home for deferred tax payments is not outweighed by the positive features of location stability and continued homeownership.

Property tax limitations. A commonly used indirect form of property tax relief is a limitation on property taxes. Many states impose a variety of limits on property taxes and taxing jurisdictions. According to the Advisory Commission on Intergovernmental Relations (1995), the most common types of limits are:

- Overall property tax rate limits that set a ceiling that cannot be exceeded without a popular vote: these limits apply to the aggregate rate of tax on all local governments.
- Specific property tax rate limits that set a ceiling that cannot be exceeded without a popular vote: these limits apply to specific types of local jurisdictions (e.g., school districts or counties).
- Property tax levy limits that constrain the total revenue that can be raised from the property tax.
- Assessment increase limits that control the ability of local governments to raise revenue by reassessment of property or through natural or administrative escalation of property values.
- Full Disclosure or Truth in Taxation provisions that require public discussion and specific legislative vote before enactment of tax rate or levy increases.

Summary of property tax relief programs.   As this discussion suggests, property tax relief programs for all homeowners, as well as programs targeted to the elderly, the poor, veterans, or disabled are popular and are increasing, rather than decreasing, in numbers. There are several major policies associated with these programs. The first is that most provide aid or relief to all homeowners—regardless of income level. Put differently, classification systems in which all residential property is taxed less than nonresidential property and general homestead exemptions and credits provide aid to the rich and poor alike. Other programs target certain groups (the elderly, veterans, and the disabled) for protection usually without needs (i.e., income tests), and exclude other groups with low property tax burdens and low incomes from assistance. On economic grounds, such programs can be challenged; these programs clearly weigh the social goals of homeownership over the economic goals of a good tax system. A public finance economist would argue that all of these programs should be linked to income (i.e., that the overall policy objective should be to reduce regressivity and thus relief should be targeted in increasing amounts to low-income property tax payers). Most public finance economists, however, go beyond this recommendation and argue that housing goals should be excluded completely from property tax adjustments and handled through other public policies (Musgrave and Musgrave, 1989).

Further, many of these programs, especially circuit breaker programs, make it easier for local governments to raise property taxes; the circuit breaker effectively cuts in for all taxpayers if residential property tax payments exceed the fixed percent of income. Thus, the programs become indirect state support for local choices either for more services or for higher-quality services.

Another example of an attempt to bring property tax relief, different from those previously discussed, is California's Proposition 13. Enacted in June 1978, Proposition 13 rolled back assessed valuations to the 1975–76 market value. Growth in assessed value was limited to 2 percent a year, with reappraisal to market value occurring only when property was sold. The tax rate was fixed at 1 percent of assessed evaluation. In passing this proposition, California shifted to an acquisition-based assessment system, under which property is assessed at market value only when it changes ownership.

Drawing on data over 10 years, Phillips (1988) analyzed the effects of this approach. Phillips' research showed that by 1981 the tax base relative to market value dropped by nearly 50 percent. By 1986, the effective tax for a long-term owner was just 0.31 percent of market value, while a recent buyer faced a burden more than three times higher at 1.0 percent. Further, assessment/market values were inversely related to property value, meaning that individuals with the higher-valued homes had lower relative assessed valuations, so that the rich benefited more than the middle or lower-income household. Therefore, the result of California's Proposition 13 or switch to an acquisition-based system of property tax assessment was to significantly lower the tax base over time and violate horizontal equity in directions that make the property tax even more regressive overall.

In sum, except for state-financed circuit breakers, most of the programs discussed in this section reduce the local property tax base. Thus, they make it more difficult to raise local tax revenues for schools as well as other functions.

Conclusions about the property tax. The property tax has never been a popular tax; for most of this century, it has been the most unpopular tax. Yet it has been and continues to be the pillar of local government and school finance. It likely will continue to play that role. It produces large amounts of revenues, maintains those revenue levels in economic downturns, and then produces revenue increases during economic growth periods. Its burden is proportional in the middle-income ranges, and its regressivity can be reduced by circuit breaker and other income tax-credit programs. While its unpopularity engendered property tax relief and reform during the 1970s, it also contributed to the tax and spending limitation in the late 1970s. But, as the federal government cut real federal aid during the 1980s, and education improvement became a national imperative, states tapped the property tax for substantial new revenues. Property taxes are crucial for funding local government services but are rarely popular taxes. They are needed even though they are not liked.

Lotteries

First introduced in 1964 in New Hampshire, lotteries have grown in popularity and importance in terms of state revenue since that time. Indeed, many lotteries earmark their receipts to education funding. Although they represent a relatively small portion of total educational revenues (generally no more than 4 percent in any given state), many think that their implementation will (or has) solved education's funding problems. This is not so.

Monk and Brent (1997) argue persuasively that lotteries are a tax. They point out that the voluntary nature of the game does not make a difference and is no different than paying the sales tax on a meal consumed in a restaurant. That is, an individual voluntarily chooses to play the game or eat the meal, but in doing so, agrees to pay the tax.

Lotteries have changed dramatically from New Hampshire's first effort, which was designed to slow down increasing property tax–rate growth in that state. In New Hampshire and New York (which was the second state to introduce a lottery in 1968), participants had to register to play, tickets were expensive, and drawings took place only a few times a year. The result was they were relatively unpopular and raised little money.

In 1971, New Jersey introduced a number of changes, which made lotteries more successful. Among the new features were lower-priced tickets, instant winners, and aggressive promotional campaigns. By 1998, 37 states and the District of Columbia had introduced lotteries. According to Monk and Brent (1997), 12 of those states earmark the proceeds of the lottery to education. The form of that earmarking varies. California, for example, provides the funds to school districts and institutions of higher education on a per-pupil basis. Georgia, on the other hand, uses the proceeds of the state lottery to provide Hope scholarships. These scholarships pay the tuition of Georgia students who attend Georgia public institutions of higher education.

Today, lottery proceeds are not derived from a single lottery, but from a variety of games each designed to attract different groups of players. Lotto games, where participants select (or have a computer randomly select for them) six numbers are the largest and most popular games. If there are no winners for several cycles of the game, in which drawings are generally held twice a week, the size of the jackpot grows. In some instances, lotto prizes have topped $100 million. A new version of lotto, called Powerball, has combined 20 states for one drawing. In 1998, one group of 13 individuals won a Powerball payout of over $250 million.

Other lottery games include instant game tickets where players scratch off numbers to see if they win an "instant" prize; numbers games where three to five numbers are drawn daily for prizes; and video lottery terminals (VLTs), which have recently been introduced. These machines allow lottery players to participate "on-line." These machines may be the fastest growing sector of the lottery industry, and it appears that the states with the largest growth in lottery proceeds between 1990 and 1994 were those with VLTs.

Americans spent $26.6 million on state-sponsored lotteries in 1994, or approximately $117 per capita (Demographics.com, 1996). Of this amount, 58 percent was paid back in prizes, and 6 percent was spent for administration. This left $10.1 billion, or 36 percent of sales, available for other services. National data shows that over time, lotteries have become less profitable, with prizes and administrative costs becoming a growing share of lottery proceeds.

Most research claims lotteries are regressive. It is generally argued that poorer individuals are more likely to play and to spend a greater portion of their income on lotteries than are wealthier individuals. Borg, et al. (1991) indicate that as lottery prizes grow, more higher-income individuals play, lessening the regressivity of the lottery. Monk and Brent (1997) suggest this makes sense intuitively since the appeal of a lottery is that if you win, you get rich. Rich people have less incentive to play than do poor people. As the size of the winnings grow, more and more individuals find the prize attractive and begin to play.

The stability of lottery proceeds is also problematic. In general, following the initial introduction when interest is high, revenues from lotteries tend to taper off. Between 1990 and 1994, state lottery revenues (adjusted for inflation) increased 24.2 percent. However the share of revenues retained as proceeds declined 1.7 percent. Total sales were down more than 15 percent in eight states. Total revenue grew by substantial amounts in Minnesota, Oregon, and South Dakota, but only 11 states saw increases in net proceeds between 1990 and 1994 (Demographics.com, 1996). In California, lottery proceeds at one time amounted to 4 percent of school district expenditures. Today, that figure is approximately 2 percent.

Lotteries are expensive to administer from the state point of view, although for individuals, there is virtually no compliance cost—you either buy a ticket or you don't. As suggested above, the lottery is very inefficient given the substantial sums of money that must be returned in the form of prizes and the high costs of administration. These administrative costs include commissions paid to vendors, usually on the order of 5 percent of sales. They also include the printing of tickets, holding drawings, and promoting the games. Combined, between 30 and 35 percent of total sales are available to the government agencies benefiting from the revenue sales.

In summary, many states have enacted lotteries to help fund public services, often earmarking funds for education. As a form of taxation, lotteries are very inefficient since over half of the revenues are used either for prizes or administrative costs. In California, only 34 cents of each dollar collected finds it way to schools. In addition, after an initial burst of excitement, most lottery sales decline somewhat. Combined with higher administrative costs for new and more complex games and higher advertising costs to attract players, the amount of revenue available for government services may decline farther. Finally, lotteries appear to be generally regressive.

4. INTERGOVERNMENTAL FISCAL RELATIONS

Chapter 1 showed that United States education financing is achieved through the efforts of all three levels of governments: local school districts, each of the 50 states, and the federal government. Indeed, the general pattern for financing public services in this country usually entails contributions from all three governments. This pattern of multiple levels of government finance is known as fiscal federalism.[11]

This section discusses several aspects of the fiscal federalism approach to school financing. It begins with a discussion of the general advantages of this approach to financing government services, specifically school districts. In a federal structure, higher levels of government can take two approaches—mandates or

[11] See also Musgrave and Musgrave (1989) for a more comprehensive discussion of fiscal federalism within the broader context of public finance.

intergovernmental grants—to influence local government behavior. Mandates are discussed in the second part of this section, while the third part analyzes intergovernmental grant theory, and its application to school financing. The fourth portion of this section discusses alternative fiscal capacity measures. This section is an important component of school finance. Because school finance formulas are a specific form of intergovernmental grants, the information in this chapter provides valuable background information. A full understanding of how school finance formulas work entails knowledge of the more general theories of public finance and intergovernmental grants.[12]

Advantages of a Federal Approach to Financing Governmental Services

Financing governmental services through the operation of multiple, specifically three, levels of government, offers four general advantages to governments in meeting public responsibilities: (1) fiscal capacity equalization; (2) equitable service distribution; (3) more economically efficient production of governmental service; and (4) decentralized decision-making authority (Musgrave and Musgrave, 1989).

Each of these advantages is discussed in terms of the state role in financing local school district operations. The discussion emphasizes the state fiscal role, but includes other roles as well. The state is the focus because the U.S. Constitution is silent on education, placing responsibility for this important function with the states. Moreover, the intergovernmental grant theory discussed below is applicable to the federal government as well.

While the state is the focus, the policy issue is the state role in a function that has been primarily financed at the local level. The problem with local financing that suggests a needed state role, as discussed in the preceding chapters, is the variation in the local ability to raise education funds (i.e., the variation in local fiscal capacity). Fiscal capacity is generally measured by a jurisdiction's tax base, which, as discussed earlier, can be income, sales, or property.

This section's initial discussion of intergovernmental fiscal issues uses property value per pupil as the measure of local school district fiscal capacity—its ability to raise local tax revenues. Property value per pupil is the fiscal capacity measure used most frequently in the 50 state school finance systems because, historically, most school districts have raised revenues by taxing property. However, other measures of fiscal capacity, such as personal income, sales, or more complex measures of fiscal capacity that include the composition of the property tax base, could be used instead of, or in addition to, property wealth per pupil. These alternatives are discussed in the last section of the chapter.

Fiscal capacity equalization.   The first, and perhaps most important, advantage of a fiscal federalism approach to financing schools is that a state, and only a state,

---

[12] This chapter refers often to various specific school finance formulas. The reader might quickly read Chapter 4 to gain some familiarity with these formulas before reading this chapter.

can equalize the fiscal capacity of its local school districts. In most states there are substantial disparities among school districts in their ability to raise revenues through local property taxes. Some districts have a large per-pupil property tax base, and others have a much smaller per-pupil property tax base. Consequently, the same tax rate produces widely varying amounts of revenue per pupil. Local districts cannot compensate for these varying dimensions of fiscal capacity; that is a role for a higher level of government, such as the state.

Indeed, school finance has a long tradition of providing state assistance to offset local disparities through what are called fiscal capacity equalization formulas (see Cubberly, 1906, and Chapter 4). Fiscal capacity equalization mitigates inequalities in the financial ability of school districts by offering relatively larger amounts of aid to districts that are less able to raise those funds from their own sources. Fiscal capacity equalization has been the major focus of school finance during the twentieth century, and it is only possible because education is financed through a system of fiscal federalism—that is, by all three levels of government.

Equity in service distribution. A second advantage of a fiscal federalism approach to school financing is that states can create mandates or provide financial assistance to school districts to promote equity in service distribution. As shown below, fiscal equalization grants do not guarantee that districts will make the same decisions regarding the level of services they offer students. In fact, different approaches to providing quantity and quality of education services (or any local government service for that matter) is one of the strengths of a fiscal federal system. However, if the state believes a minimum level of service must be provided, a federal structure offers a number of mechanisms to ensure the provision of minimum service levels.

Efficiency in service production. A third advantage for creating a multilevel school system concerns efficiency in the production of educational services. Many schools or school districts can benefit from economies of scale. That is, as the size of the school grows, the unit costs of educating each child decline; a larger school or district organization might be more efficient than a very small one. The state may be able to use its influence to encourage small school districts to consolidate and therefore promote efficiency in the local production of educational services. It is possible that if a school or school district grows beyond a certain size, it will no longer realize these efficiencies, and in fact, the unit cost of providing educational services may begin to increase. Indeed, large statewide school systems may suffer from such diseconomies of large scale. Therefore, a decentralized system of schools helps avoid the diseconomies that would exist if each state was simply one large school system. Monk (1990: Chapter 13) contains an excellent summary of current research on scale economies in education.

Decentralized Decision Making. The fourth advantage of a fiscal federal system is that decentralized decision making provides individuals choices in selecting the mix of public services that match their personal preferences. Tiebout's (1956) classic theory of local expenditures describes this phenomenon as "voting with your feet." He suggests that when there are a number of jurisdictions located within close proximity, individuals will choose to live in the area that offers a mix of public services most closely matching their preferences.

The nearly 15,000 school districts in the United States provide an example of Tiebout's theory. For example, realtors report that home buyers frequently ask about the quality of local schools. Clearly, many people make decisions about where to live, at least in part, on the basis of their perception of the quality of local educational services. One would expect young families concerned about the education of their children to move into areas identified as having good schools, even if that required higher property tax payments. By contrast, a retired couple living on a fixed income might be less directly concerned with the quality of the local schools and more interested in an area with substantial senior citizen services and generally lower property taxes. This is not to imply that people without children in schools are not concerned about the quality of education, nor that good local schools is the only item that matters to young families with school-age children. The example merely suggests how individuals can make decisions about where to live on the basis of a number of factors, the mix of governmental services—including the quality of the local schools—and resulting tax payments being only two of those factors.

In a fiscal federal system, there are two ways the central government can influence or coordinate the decisions of local governments, specifically school districts, in order to capitalize on these four advantages. The central government—states or the federal government—can mandate changes in the way local services are provided, or it can use intergovernmental grants to influence local behavior. While mandates offer the most direct way of achieving legislative goals, there are political and, in many states, financial problems with their use. Consequently, state and federal legislators frequently use grants to simulate desired local action. Central government grants provided to local government can either be general or categorical in nature, and can come with or without requirements that the recipient provide matching funds to qualify for the grant. These two approaches are discussed in the next two parts of this section. In recent years, states have begun experimenting with incentive grants to achieve educational policy goals. Incentive programs generally are discussed in Chapter 9.

Mandates and Their Use in Intergovernmental Relations

The Advisory Commission on Intergovernmental Relations (1984:16) defines mandates as "any constitutional, statutory or administrative action that either limits or places requirements on local governments." A mandate exists when costs are imposed on a local government or when its decision-making authority is restricted in some way.

A state's authority to impose mandates on local governments has long been recognized. This authority stems from "Dillon's Rule," an 1868 court ruling by

Iowa judge John F. Dillon holding that local governments owe their origin to, and derive their powers from, state legislatures (ACIR, 1984). This principle was upheld by the U.S. Supreme Court in *City of Trenton* v. *New Jersey*[13] in 1923 and state courts adhere to it today.

The Advisory Commission on Intergovernmental Relations (1984) postulates four reasons for the use of mandates.

1. Mandates are used for an activity deemed by the state to be so important that it does not want to allow local governments to decide whether or not to undertake to engage in it. Desegregating schools and serving handicapped children are two education examples.
2. Mandates are used to promote desirable social or economic goals. Many argue that K–12 education has that level of importance.
3. Mandates are used by states to shift financial responsibility for providing certain services to local governments. Local school districts often raise this issue in relation to state and federal mandates to fully serve certain groups of children.
4. Mandates sometimes are merely justified by past practice or tradition.

Arguments against mandates.   Opponents of mandates use the decentralization of decision-making authority argument; they claim that local governments are in the best position to respond in flexible and diverse ways to community problems and issues. They argue that revenue and expenditure mandates constrain the ability of local officials to respond to local circumstances. They further argue that if local and state policies are not aligned, constraints become divisive. In short, the loss of "local control" is the most frequently voiced criticism of mandates.

Another argument against mandates is that they are often enacted with little or no information about the cost burdens they place on local governments. This makes it difficult for mandate sponsors to consider the benefit-cost trade-offs of their proposals. As a result, mandates could fall short on economic efficiency goals.

Arguments for mandates.   Proponents of mandates argue they are legitimate tools to spur governmental activity that may not, but should be, fully provided by local governments, such as education generally, desegregation, or serving handicapped students. Mandates also make it possible to move in the direction of uniform levels of service across an entire state. For example, many state-mandated programs fall within areas affecting more than one local jurisdiction. Highways, education, and welfare are three examples. Proponents of mandates argue that for such programs as these, over which the state has considerable responsibility, the reordering of local priorities through the use of mandates is an appropriate state action, countering the economic efficiency arguments made by mandate opponents.

[13] 262 U.S. 182.

Another advantage of state mandates is that they make equity in service distribution feasible. By mandating a certain level of service among all school districts, for example, the state can ensure that at least a minimum level of education is offered to each student across the state. However, without state assistance to mitigate differences in the ability to pay for those services, it is possible that quality will vary depending on the local district's ability to pay and on its willingness to carry out the mandate.

Mandates also fall short of fiscal capacity equalization goals. A state-imposed mandate will require greater effort on the part of low-wealth governments or school districts than on the part of high-wealth governments or school districts, thus intensifying the school finance inequity of unequal access to local fiscal capacity. One way to mitigate this local impact of mandates is for the central government making the mandate to pay the costs associated with its implementation.

Intergovernmental Grants and Their Objectives

The most common approach taken by the states and the federal government to influence local behavior is through intergovernmental grants. For example, when the federal government decided that more attention needed to be given to low-achieving students in districts with large numbers of students living in poverty environments, it created a program—The Elementary and Secondary Education Act of 1965—which provided funds to local school districts to design and implement new compensatory education programs. Similarly, state general-education-aid grants are designed to assist local school districts in implementing overall K–12 education programs.

Different designs of state or federal grants can have quite different local fiscal impacts. Some grants simply replace local funds with state or federal funds. Other grants produce higher education expenditures than would occur if only local districts provided revenues. Still other grants both increase educational expenditures and focus the new spending on services for specific students or for specific areas within education. A key issue in establishing school finance grants is to decide on the purpose of the grant and then design it on the basis of intergovernmental grant principles to maximize those objectives.

The theoretical literature on intergovernmental grants is substantial and contains general agreement about the effects of different grant types on local expenditure decisions (Break, 1980; Musgrave and Musgrave, 1989; Oates, 1972; Wilde, 1968 and 1971). This work is based on the theory of consumer behavior that analyzes the consumption decisions of an individual on the basis of preferences, income, and the prices of the goods to be purchased.

Intergovernmental grant theory views the recipient government as the consumer, with preferences being the priorities assigned to different public goods, and to the trade-offs between public and private consumption. In general, the price of public goods is viewed as a composite of goods that are purchased for a certain tax rate or tax price. The income constraint is the portion of community income devoted to the public sector (i.e., the level of local taxes).

A local government or school district must make decisions in two areas: (1) dividing total community income between public and private consumption by setting local tax rates and (2) given this allocation, determining the combination of public and private goods that will maximize the welfare of local taxpayers—specifying within the tax revenue constraint (i.e., the local budget), the quantity and quality of education, police and fire protection, and other local services. These two decisions must be addressed simultaneously, since the division between public and private sector allocations cannot be separated from the specific quantity and quality of public and private goods actually chosen (Tsang and Levin, 1983:331).

A local government or school district chooses the mix of services it provides from its budget by attempting to maximize the satisfaction of its constituents given a set of preferences and prices for those public goods. Grant theory assumes a local government is in equilibrium—that it will allocate its local resources in a fashion to maximize its own welfare. However, the level of expenditure (i.e., the range, quantity, and quality of education services decided upon) may not be optimal from the view of the state or federal government, which may move to alter the local government's behavior (Tsang and Levin, 1983:331–32). For example, becoming first in the world in science and mathematics is a nationwide education goal. Consequently both states and the federal government will probably want local districts to spend more resources on mathematics and science education.

Altering local behavior can be accomplished in part by providing intergovernmental education grants to local governments (i.e., school districts). Intergovernmental grants from states or the federal government to local school districts can take one of two general forms: (1) general or block grants and (2) categorical aid. In addition, both of these mechanisms can include or not include requirements for matching expenditures on the part of the recipient government—the local school district. Decisions on these dimensions (i.e., the specific design of the grant or funds formula, together with programmatic requirements) affect how local districts respond to the state or federal grant initiative.

Unrestricted general aid. Unrestricted general aid or block grants increase a school district's revenue, but do not place restrictions on the use of that revenue. General-aid formulas provide additional revenues that districts can use any way they want: to reduce local revenues and thus to reduce local tax rates, to increase overall education spending and thus to increase the quantity or quality of education services, to increase education spending in specific areas such as mathematics and science, or some combination of these options. General grants are most effective when the state's goal is fiscal capacity equalization (that is, to provide districts with additional revenue to offset their varying ability to raise local education revenues). Flat grants are a school-finance mechanism that provides an equal amount of per-pupil revenue to each school district based solely on the number of students. On the other hand, foundation and guaranteed tax-base programs provide general aid to districts in inverse proportion to their property wealth per pupil.[14]

General grants are the least effective in getting school districts to change their behavior in line with state expectations, precisely because such grants carry no restrictions. Districts can use general aid to supplant local revenues and thus reduce tax rates, or to increase overall education spending and thus provide more or better educational services. Without restrictions, there likely will be no clear pattern to local district response. In particular, if the state provides general aid and hopes that the new funds will be used for specific purposes (for example, to increase spending for mathematics and science education), the likelihood of such a uniform local response is low. This is because local governments attempt to maximize their local welfare, and in the process likely will make different spending decisions than the state might like them to make.

Studies of unrestricted or general state aid grants to school districts consistently found that school districts used a portion of the grant for tax reductions and a portion for increased education spending. In reviewing numerous studies of local school district response to general aid, Tsang and Levin (1983) found that, on average, local school districts spend about half of increases in state general-aid dollars on educational programs and about half to reduce local tax rates. But, as we discussed in Chapter 1, over the past decade and a half, many lower-wealth districts in several states appeared to have used a larger portion for property tax relief.

If the state's goal for general-aid programs is fiscal capacity equalization, unrestricted grants usually succeed in meeting those goals. Since districts low in property wealth per pupil often have above-average tax rates and below-average expenditures per pupil, increases in general aid let them reduce their tax rates so they are closer to the state average while also increasing education spending.

If one accepts the notion that local districts are better able to determine the program needs of the local population (in this case, student educational needs), then unrestricted grants offer advantages in terms of economic efficiency. Unrestricted grants provide local districts with increased revenues and let each district decide how to use those revenues, drawing upon local needs and priorities. Unrestricted grants also are effective tools for maintaining an equitable but decentralized decision-making system.

Unrestricted general grants can be used to provide some equity in service distribution either to establish some kind of minimum level of service, or provide districts with at least some minimum level of funding. As Chapter 4 shows, flat grants and foundation school finance programs were designed to accomplish these objectives. However, since unrestricted grants do not place limitations on district expenditures from local sources, there is no constraint on wealthy districts to increase education spending substantially above the minimum. One way to ad-

---

[14] Chapter 4 provides a detailed description of how flat grants and foundation programs operate. It also provides the reader with examples of the effects of these programs using fiscal capacity equalization criteria.

dress these problems is to link a district's general aid to its willingness to spend local resources for education. The next section describes general grants that include a matching component in order to qualify for state funds.

Matching general grants.   The most common way to tie a district's general aid to its own willingness to spend is to use a matching grant. Matching grants link the level of state general-aid assistance at least in part to the level of effort made by the local government, as well as to its fiscal capacity. In school finance, the most common general matching grant system is the guaranteed tax base (GTB) program.[15] Many state school finance programs are called percentage equalizing, guaranteed yield, or district power equalizing. Although the specific operating details of each of these systems vary, they are all designed to achieve the same goal, namely to equalize the revenue-raising ability of each school district, at least up to some point. Chapter 4 contains a detailed discussion and simulation of the operation of a GTB program.

Intergovernmental grant theory analyzes matching grant programs differently from nonmatching grant programs. Rather than assessing the grant's impact on increasing a district's income, or total tax revenues, intergovernmental grant theory analyzes matching grants in terms of how they change the relative tax prices[16] districts pay for educational services. A GTB program, for example, lowers the tax price of educational services for districts low in property wealth per pupil, because with the GTB they are able to levy a lower tax rate, and thus pay less, for a certain level of education services. Indeed, for the level of education services supported before a GTB program, property-poor districts are able to substantially lower their tax rates to provide the same level of services. In other words, the tax price to local citizens—taxpayers—is substantially decreased. Economic theory predicts that individuals faced with choices are price-sensitive, and will purchase more of lower-priced items, all other things being equal.

As it plays out in school finance, a GTB gives a district with low property value per pupil the ability to raise as much money at a given tax rate as the wealthier district that has a per-pupil property value equal to the tax-base guarantee. Thus, with the same tax rate or tax effort, the poor district will be able to raise substantially more revenue than it could before the GTB. As predicted from the discussion above, a district would be expected to use part of this new money to increase expenditures and use part of the money to reduce its tax rate. Thus, the impact of a general matching grant is similar to that of an unrestricted general grant. Again as Chapter 1 showed, many school districts in several states have taken advantage of the property tax relief element of GTB programs at the expense of raising spending levels.

---

[15] While a foundation program also requires a local match—the local required tax effort—it functions more like a flat grant than a more open-ended matching program, such as the GTB.

[16] The tax price generally is the tax rate a district must levy to purchase a given level and quality of school services. Poor districts generally have to levy a higher tax rate and thus pay a higher tax price to purchase such a given bundle of school services than a wealthy district because, at a given tax rate, the poor district would raise less per pupil than the wealthier district.

As Chapter 4 shows, a major difference between unrestricted and matching grant programs is that under an unrestricted general grant—such as a flat grant program—even property-wealthy districts receive state aid funds, whereas under a GTB-type matching grant program, the amount of state aid a district receives is inversely related to its property wealth per pupil. In fact, depending on the level of the GTB, there may be districts that do not receive any state aid at all.

Categorical grants.   In contrast to general unrestricted grants, categorical grants have restrictions on how they can be used. Categorical grants are provided to school districts for a specific reason or purpose, and often come with strict application, use, and reporting requirements. Categorical grants are used to ensure that school districts provide services deemed important by the state or federal governments. These services are often provided more efficiently locally, but without assistance, school districts may not choose to provide them, or to provide the state or federal desired level of such services.

There are a variety of categorical grant mechanisms used by states and the federal government. Some categorical grants are used to help local school districts meet the needs of specified populations; for example, Title I assistance is provided to districts impacted by large numbers of poor children. Other categorical grant programs are designed to support specific district functions, such as pupil transportation. The manner in which a district receives categorical grant funds also varies. Many categorical grant programs are designed so that they are available to recipient districts automatically; dollars flow by formula. Others have specific application rules and procedures; districts must write proposals in order to receive funds.

States can provide school districts with categorical grants using a variety of grant formula designs. Districts might receive categorical grants on the basis of some sociodemographic characteristic, such as incidence of poverty or degree of urbanization. Alternatively, districts might be eligible for categorical grants on the basis of the number of children meeting a specific criterion, such as a handicapping condition. Finally, districts could simply be reimbursed for expenditures devoted to a specific function. District fiscal response to a categorical program will depend on the specific nature of the grant's distribution mechanism.

Like general grants, categorical grants increase the recipient's income. Funds allocated on the basis of the number of students meeting a specific criterion but with no spending requirements would be expected to create a district response similar to that of a general grant, with a portion of the funds expended for their intended purpose, and the balance either returned to the taxpayers in the form of lower property taxes, or spent on other district functions. For example, some states weight poor students in the general-aid formula but do not require that districts use the extra money to expand compensatory education services for poor students. A smaller portion of these funds is likely used for compensatory education than if they were accompanied by requirements mandating their expenditure on compensatory education.

Since one purpose of a categorical grant is to encourage specific actions on the part of local school districts, the federal government and most states that appropriate funds for categorical programs usually also promulgate rules and regulations to resolve this problem and restrict district use of these resources for their intended purpose.

A commonly used fiscal enforcement tool is the maintenance of effort provision. This provision requires districts to prove that spending on the supported program from its own funds does not decline as a result of the grant. The early Title I "supplement not supplant" requirement is an example of a maintenance-of-effort provision. Other enforcement provisions include audits and evaluations to ensure that recipient districts establish programs designed to meet the purpose or goals of the grant program. Many categorical grants have specific reporting requirements that help the contributing government monitor use of the funds. Unlike general grants, categorical grants stimulate educational expenditures by at least the level of the grant and sometimes by more than the amount of the grant. The primary explanation is that the strings and requirements attached to categorical grants make it difficult for districts to spend the funds elsewhere (Tsang and Levin, 1983) and virtually force districts to increase spending at least by the amount of the grant. Another explanation is that categorical grants are provided for specialized programs on which local districts would spend less, if anything at all, in the absence of the categorical aid (Ladd, 1975).

Categorical grants present a different trade-off between equity and efficiency than do general grants. Categorical programs encourage districts to treat needy students differently by making additional resources available to produce similar, or hopefully similar, achievement outcomes. Any time resources are devoted to a needy student, it implies a loss of what could have been produced if the resources were evenly distributed across all students (Monk, 1990). As a result, categorical grants trade economic efficiency for equity in the provision of services.

Categorical programs, by their nature, are more centralized than general grants since it is the state, or federal government, that determines what population needs extra services. Moreover, some federal programs, such as the program for handicapped children, include very specific requirements for identifying and serving eligible students. Although the final determination of what services to provide are left to local district and parental discretion, there are very specific identification and service procedures identified in the law and accompanying regulations.

Finally, since categorical grants are designed to provide assistance to groups of students or to districts on the basis of some characteristic (like expensive transportation needs in a small sparsely populated rural district), they are not generally designed to equalize fiscal capacity. Nevertheless, both special-service provision and fiscal capacity equalization can be accomplished with well-designed grant schemes. These issues are discussed in more depth in Chapter 4.

Final comments on grants.   As this discussion shows, states can use a variety of grant mechanisms to finance schools and a variety of specific educational services.

The type of grant instrument chosen, as well as its specific design features, can affect how the funds are used by local districts. General grants are most effective when the state's goal is to provide the recipient with additional revenue to meet its service obligations (a flat grant or minimum foundation to provide at least some education program), or if the goal is to equalize fiscal capacity (such as a guaranteed tax base program). These grants, however, leave all specific spending decisions to local school district discretion, and are not as effective in getting districts to provide specific services as other, targeted, categorical grant instruments.

Categorical grants can induce school districts to serve a specific population, or to get them to implement a particular program. In the first case, the district would be expected to treat the funds much like general assistance, and local spending patterns may not match the state government expectations. These grants are treated as categorical rather than general grants because they are distributed to a limited number of districts, whereas general grants are available to all districts. Categorical grants designed to meet a specific purpose frequently come with one or more mechanisms designed to ensure compliance with the grant's goals. These grants are more successful in getting the recipient district to implement state goals, but usually at a loss of efficiency.

Alternative Measures of Fiscal Capacity

School finance typically assumes that a district's fiscal capacity (i.e., its ability to raise local tax revenues) is measured by its property value per pupil. But, research has identified a number of additional factors that should be considered in measuring comprehensively a district's fiscal capacity: the mix of property types within a district, or the composition of the property tax base, and average household income within a district. Fiscal capacity should include the major economic variables that affect the school district's ability to raise revenues for educational purposes. While total property value per pupil is the major fiscal capacity component, research also shows that household income as well as the composition of the property tax base in terms of residential, commercial, and industrial property also impact local revenue raising decisions.

Consider, for example, two districts with the same property wealth per pupil, but very different property tax base composition. In district A, all of the property value is in residential housing and commercial development, while in district B, there are a number of industrial plants. Since the same tax rate will raise the same revenue per pupil, one might expect roughly similar tax effort to fund the schools. However, in district A, homeowners and local businesses pay the full property tax, whereas in district B, a large portion of the total property tax bill is paid by the industrial plants. But the plants can "export" the tax payments to individuals outside the district—either consumers through higher prices, or stockowners through lower profits. In district B, then, voters might be willing to raise higher levels of property taxes, knowing that a portion of the tax bill is financed by individuals outside the district who pay the tax on the industrial plant. Since the owner of the industrial plant has at most one vote (assuming he or she actually lives in close proximity and in the same school district), there is little the industrial plant can do to reduce its tax burden.

In her 1975 Massachusetts study, Ladd found that total property value per pupil as well as the composition of the property tax base and household income each had separate and independent impacts on school district education spending. She used her results to weight the value of commercial industrial and residential property to adjust for these factors. She found that if the weight for residential property were set at 1.0, commercial property should be weighted at 1.26 and industrial property at 0.55. The weighted property value then was a more accurate indicator of fiscal capacity as reflected in the local property tax base.

Ladd also found a major effect for household income. Her research, as well as research by several others (Adams, 1980; Adams and Odden, 1981; Feldstein, 1975; Vincent and Adams, 1978) found that the willingness to raise local taxes by local school district voters was also affected by income, even if income could not be taxed. In other words, even if total property value per pupil and the weighted property value per pupil were the same, higher-income households were willing to exert a higher tax effort for schools than were lower-income households. Intrinsically, this finding makes sense. Although property taxes are attached to a capital asset (see earlier discussion in this chapter on property taxes), homeowners pay their property taxes out of current income. As a result, the impact of a tax increase on disposable income seems likely to have an impact on school funding decisions.

This finding on household income is especially important since there is not always a strong correlation between property value and income. For example, large cities frequently contain high percentages of low-income children. Yet, because of the high value of downtown commercial property and other industrial property, the city itself may appear to have average or above-average wealth when measured in terms of property value per pupil alone. An "income factor" adjustment to the property value measure could compensate for these realities.

All studies on the effect of income on spending for education found the effect to be "multiplicative" in nature. Thus the appropriate income adjustment would be to multiply property value per pupil by an income factor, usually the ratio of the average household income in a school district to the average statewide household income. Many states simply add household income to the property value measure and property plus income per pupil as the fiscal capacity measure. Such measures have peculiar and unattractive properties (Harris, 1978) and do not reflect the research on the impact of income on school revenues.

In summary, a comprehensive measure of school district fiscal capacity would include three factors: (1) total property value; (2) a weighted total property value with different weights for the residential, commercial, and industrial components of the property tax base; and (3) a multiplicative household income adjustment. While states have considered these more comprehensive measures of fiscal capacity, only Minnesota addresses the composition of the property tax base. Further, although approximately 20 states have an income adjustment in their school aid formula, most income adjustments, unfortunately, are additive and not multiplicative.

Final Comments on Taxation and Intergovernmental Grants

This chapter shows that governmental activity in the United States represents a large share of our gross domestic product and consumes some 12 to 15 percent of personal income. This investment includes spending nearly $300 billion a year on public K–12 education. Raising the revenue to finance governmental operations is an important and complex issue.

There are five criteria on which taxes can be measured and compared. They include:

- The tax base,
- Yield,
- Equity,
- The economic effects of the tax, and
- Administration and compliance issues.

Each is important in terms of assessing the impact of taxes on individuals and on the jurisdictions that rely on the revenues they generate.

In general, the federal government relies heavily on income (corporate and individual) taxes, while state revenues are composed approximately equally of sales and income taxes.[17] Local school districts, like other local governments, are heavily dependent on the property tax.

Economists generally agree that the "best" taxes are those that have a broad base and low rate. That is, there are few exemptions to paying the tax and thus the base is relatively large, enabling the needed dollars to be collected with a low tax rate. In addition, most analysts support the notion that taxes should be progressive, consuming a larger proportion of wealthy individuals' income than of poor individuals' income. Income taxes tend to be the most progressive while sales taxes are generally the opposite, or regressive. While states have enacted many exemptions to the sales tax to make it less regressive, it remains a regressive form of taxation. Property taxes also tend to be regressive. As this chapter shows, there are two ways to think about the regressivity of the property tax. One makes the tax appear less regressive than the other, but both show substantial regressivity over most income classes.

Because different levels of government can collect different taxes more efficiently, and with fewer economic inefficiencies, a system of intergovernmental transfers, or grants, has developed in the United States. Intergovernmental grants are used by states and the federal government to provide incentives for local tax-

---

[17] The proportion of taxes collected through sales and income taxation varies dramatically across the 50 states. This statement is representative of the aggregate tax collections of all 50 states.

ing jurisdictions (including school districts) to implement programs that are a high priority for the granting government. Intergovernmental grants have also been used to reduce property tax burdens.

The major problem in school finance is the differential ability of school districts to gain equal access to property tax revenues. State and federal funding can help equalize tax burdens and ensure that a school district's spending level is based on the wealth of the state where it is located, and not on the basis of its individual property wealth. This important issue of finance equalization and the tools states use to meet district needs are the focus of the next chapter.

Chapter 4

School Finance Structures: Formula Options and Needs Adjustments

School finance is concerned with the interrelated issues of raising, distributing, allocating, and using revenues for the purpose of educating children. This chapter moves from the issues of raising revenues, discussed in the preceding chapter, to the issues involved in distributing revenues. The chapter has two sections.

Section 1 analyzes four types of formulas that states have used during the twentieth century to distribute general education aid to local school districts: (1) flat grants; (2) foundation programs; (3) guaranteed tax base[1] programs; and (4) combination foundation and guaranteed tax base programs. Full-state funding and other types of state-determined spending programs are also discussed briefly. For each formula, three issues are discussed:

- intergovernmental aid properties,
- reflection of school finance values, and
- impact on fiscal equity.

The *School Finance* computer simulation that accompanies the text should be used when reading this chapter. The text includes some printouts from that simulation, but a more in-depth understanding of the different school finance

---

[1] Guaranteed tax base programs are algebraically equivalent to district power equalization, percentage equalization, and guaranteed yield programs. These latter programs are not discussed individually in this chapter.

formulas, how they work, and what impacts they have on both the state and local districts will be developed by using the simulation to analyze variations in the funding formulas.

At this point, readers should familiarize themselves with the operation of the *School Finance* computer simulation that accompanies the book. The appendix describes how to access the simulation on the World Wide Web, download it, and use it. This chapter encourages readers to simulate and assess various versions of formulas, different from those discussed.

1. SCHOOL FINANCE EQUITY, ADEQUACY, AND POLICY GOALS

Chapter 2 developed a comprehensive equity and adequacy framework that can and should be used to assess the equity and adequacy of a state's school finance structure. If the group of concern is students, the chapter showed that distributional equity can be related to several objects, such as current operating expenditures per pupil, state plus local revenues per pupil, etc. The chapter also identified, in addition, a new focus on adequacy and equity, including four principles: (1) horizontal equity, which requires equal distribution of the object; (2) vertical equity, which allows for extra amounts of the object distributed but on the basis of special student or district need; (3) fiscal neutrality, which requires that the object not be related to local fiscal capacity such as property value per pupil; and (4) adequacy, which requires provision of an educational program adequate to teach the average student to state performance standards.

This chapter uses this framework to analyze a representative 20 district sample of school districts. The text shows how various school finance objectives can be in conflict, as well as how politics might intervene to constrain the amount of equity a state political system can produce. In general, a school finance structure is designed to: (1) compensate for the varying amounts of local tax capacity, generally property value per pupil; (2) reduce disparities in state and local revenues per pupil (indeed, some programs seek to eliminate disparities); (3) allow for local fiscal decision making, which can produce decisions to spend at different levels; (4) provide sufficient funds so all schools can teach the vast majority of its students to high academic standards; (5) keep the local and state costs within reasonable limits; (6) increase state aide to a sufficient number of districts to produce a positive majority vote in both houses of a state's legislature to enact the program; and (7) encourage efficiency, effectiveness, and greater productivity in local school operations. At times, providing property tax reduction and relief also are policy objectives. Some of these objectives may conflict (specifically, local fiscal decision making and equality of revenues per pupil), even allowing for adjustments for special needs. Thus, school finance formula design is both a substantive and political task that seeks to balance these many objectives; "perfect equity" is generally not possible (Brown and Elmore, 1982).

The discussion in Section 1 of this chapter implicitly assumes uniformity along several dimensions that, in the real world, do not hold. For example, some students have special needs and require additional educational services above those provided through state and local general fund resources. Further, some argue that it is wise to spend more on students at different education levels. Traditionally, states spend more on secondary students, although there is an increasing trend to spend more on students in kindergarten through grade three. Many states still have small schools that experience diseconomies of scale, such as those located in isolated rural areas, which incur higher costs. Finally, the price of purchasing educational goods varies across districts in a state, especially in large, diverse states such as Florida, New York, or Texas. Section 2 discusses these issues and the types of vertical equity adjustments to basic school finance formulas that reflect legitimate reasons for providing unequal resources.

2. SCHOOL FINANCE FORMULAS

This section discusses five topics: characteristics of the illustrative sample of districts included in the simulation, flat grant programs, foundation programs, guaranteed tax base (GTB) programs, combined foundation-GTB programs, and full-state funding.

In designing new school finance structures today, analysts and policymakers begin with state education finance systems that have evolved over several years. Local districts have real property tax rates, and state general aid has been distributed according to some mechanism, usually with the goal of reducing spending disparities caused by unequal distribution of the local per-pupil property tax base.

Figure 4.1 displays data for a representative sample of 20 districts that will be used throughout the chapter to demonstrate the impact of various new school finance structures. The data have been taken from a state with school finance circumstances typical of the rest of the country. The numbers indicate several characteristics of the extant school finance system in the state from which the sample was selected.

First, there are large differences in property value per pupil. The richest district has $278,052 in property value per pupil, which is almost 16 times the value ($17,456) in the poorest district. The weighted average[2] property value per student is $97,831, which is about 5.6 times the value of the poorest district, and about half the value of the second wealthiest district ($198,564).

The third column in Figure 4.1 shows that property tax rates also vary considerably, from a low of 25.5 mills to a high of 39.64 mills, a difference of over 50

---

[2] All statistics in the table and in the computer simulation are calculated in a manner that weights each district value by the number of students in the district. Thus, the values for district A, with 10,040 students, contributes more to the weighted average than the values for district J, which has only 848 students. Using student-weighted statistics has become the more prominent way to present statistics in school finance analyses. The results, thus, indicate the impact of the funding structure on students. In the past, school finance analysis treated each district value equally, giving equal weight to districts with large and small numbers of students.

Adequacy Level	$	5,350
Pupil Weights		**no**
Disabled		—
Limited English		—
Low Income		—

District	Pupils	Property Value per Pupil ($)	Property Tax Rate (Mills)	Local Revenue per Pupil ($)	State Revenue per Pupil ($)	Total Revenue per Pupil ($)
1	1,290	17,456	39.64	692	2,788	3,480
2	5,648	25,879	38.50	996	2,623	3,620
3	1,678	31,569	37.15	1,173	2,535	3,708
4	256	35,698	36.20	1,292	2,460	3,752
5	10,256	40,258	35.91	1,446	2,401	3,847
6	956	43,621	35.74	1,559	2,393	3,952
7	4,689	49,875	34.89	1,740	2,358	4,099
8	1,656	55,556	34.17	1,898	2,273	4,171
9	8,954	61,254	33.73	2,066	2,218	4,284
10	1,488	70,569	33.44	2,360	2,091	4,450
11	2,416	78,952	33.23	2,624	2,081	4,704
12	5,891	86,321	32.89	2,839	2,031	4,870
13	2,600	94,387	32.10	3,030	1,969	4,999
14	15,489	102,687	31.32	3,216	1,937	5,154
15	2,308	112,358	30.85	3,466	1,908	5,374
16	2,712	125,897	30.50	3,840	1,724	5,564
17	30,256	136,527	30.05	4,102	1,527	5,630
18	2,056	156,325	28.63	4,476	1,424	5,899
19	3,121	198,564	27.42	5,445	1,130	6,575
20	1,523	278,052	25.50	7,090	437	7,527
Weighted Average		97,831	32.34	3,028	1,925	4,953
Weighted Std. Dev.		48,514	2.91	1,209	433	841
Median		102,687	31.32	3,216	1,937	5,154

Totals		
	Amount	Percent
Local Revenue	318,727,208	61.14%
State Revenue	202,540,166	38.86%
Total Revenue	521,267,374	
Pupils	105,243	

Equity Measures	
Horizontal Equity	
Range	$4,047
Restricted Range	2,955
Federal Range Ratio	0.818
Coef. of Variation	0.170
Gini Coefficient	0.094
McLoone Index	0.810
Verstegen Index	1.086
Fiscal Neutrality	
Correlation	0.991
Elasticity	0.324
Adequacy	
Odden-Picus	0.895

FIGURE 4.1   Base Data

percent. Notably, it is the lower property-value districts that have the higher property tax rates and the higher property-value districts that have the lower property tax rates. Because of differences in the tax base, the second wealthiest district raises $199 per pupil for each mill levied and thus raises $5,445 per pupil in local revenues at its tax rate of 27.42 mills. On the other hand, the second poorest district raises only $26 for each mill levied and thus raises just $996 for its 38.5 mill tax rate. Thus, even though the poorer district exerts a higher tax effort, it produces a much lower level of revenues because its tax base is so low. On the other hand, the wealthier district raises a much higher level of local revenues per pupil even though it exerts a lower tax effort because its tax base is so much higher.

State aid is distributed in an inverse relationship to property value per pupil (i.e., the poorest districts receive the largest amount of per-pupil state aid), and state aid per pupil declines as property value per pupil rises. In fact, the poorest district receives about 6.4 times the state aid of the wealthiest district. Thus, state aid is distributed in a fiscal capacity equalizing pattern. But, even the wealthiest districts receive some level of state general aid ($437 per pupil for this sample). This distribution of state aid is characteristic of most states. All states use some type of fiscal capacity equalizing school finance formula to distribute its general aid, and all districts receive some minimum level of general aid.

But the difference in state-aid allocations, while providing higher amounts to property-poor districts, is not sufficient to offset the 16-to-one difference in property value per pupil among districts. Thus, the poorest district, receiving 6.4 times the aid of the wealthiest district and exerting 1.5 times the tax effort, still has revenues per child that total only 46 percent of total revenues in the highest spending district. The figures illustrate a consistent pattern—the lower the property value per child, the lower the total revenues per pupil, even though per-pupil state aid and property tax rates are higher.

Figure 4.1 also includes statistical measures of the fiscal equity of this school finance system. In terms of horizontal equity for students, the coefficient of variation for total revenues per pupil is 17 percent, which means that roughly two-thirds of these districts have total revenues per pupil that are within 17 percent of the weighted average ($842 in this case), and if this were a normal distribution, 95 percent of districts would have total revenues per pupil within 34 percent of the average ($1,682 in this case). The value of the coefficient of variation indicates that the fiscal-capacity-equalizing distribution of state general aid is modest, offsetting just a portion of the differences in local ability to raise property taxes. To further understand the impact of state general aid, compare Figure 4.1 with the results of a "no state-aid" situation, which can be determined by running a computer simulation and setting the "Flat Grant" equal to zero. Notice that the coefficient of variation more than doubles, showing that the state aid that was provided clearly helped to reduce but not eliminate differences in total revenues per pupil.

The McLoone Index in Figure 4.1 indicates that the average total revenue per pupil for the bottom 50 percent of students is just 81 percent of that of the student at the median, or 19 percent below the median. Again, state aid has helped push this statistic towards 1.00, which would indicate full equity for the bottom 50 percent, as compared to the McLoone Index of 0.582 in the no state-aid case (again, run a "Flat Grant" at zero from the menu in the simulation).

The Verstegen Index shows that the average total revenues per pupil in the top 50 percent is just 8.6 above the median. This figure shows that for this sample the revenue-per-pupil figures for the higher spenders are closer to the median than the revenues per pupil for the lower spenders, which are just 19 percent shy of the median.

In terms of fiscal neutrality, or the degree to which total revenues per pupil are linked to property wealth per pupil, Figure 4.1 shows a high correlation at 0.991, as well as a healthy elasticity, at 0.324. This means that revenues are strongly related to wealth, and that increases in wealth produce substantial increases in revenues—specifically, that a 10 percent increase in wealth produces a 3.2 percent increase in revenues. For example, as wealth increases about 100 percent from about $50,000 to $100,000, revenues per pupil increase about 33 percent, which is slightly more than the actual total revenue per pupil increase from $4,099 to $5,154.

We have used the figure of $5,350 as the revenue-per-pupil figure that represents an "adequate" amount in all subsequent simulations. We simply selected a figure somewhat above the median, although this was an arbitrary selection. As discussed in Chapter 2 and later in this chapter, sophisticated analysis is needed to identify an "adequate" expenditure figure. But we had to select some figure, and we use the $5,350 figure consistently in all simulations in this chapter. The Odden-Picus Adequacy Index shows that those districts spending below the "adequate level" spend on average just 89.5 percent of the "adequate" figure of $5,350.

Figure 4.2 shows graphically the relationship between revenues per pupil and property value per pupil for this sample, and Figure 4.3 shows the same data but with no state aid at all. For both, there is a linear relationship between the two variables, but the slope of the graph is much larger for the no state-aid case. Thus, state aid has reduced the magnitude but has not eliminated the role of property value per pupil in producing revenue-per-pupil disparities.

In sum, the sample of 20 districts reflects the current context of school finance in many states. There is wide disparity in the local per-pupil property tax base. State aid is distributed inversely to property wealth, and is somewhat fiscal-capacity equalizing, but not sufficiently equalizing to offset differences in property wealth, nor sufficient to produce an "adequate" spending level for all districts. As a result, the equity statistics reflect a system that needs further improvements to meet either horizontal equity, fiscal-neutrality equity, and adequacy standards. This chapter discusses how different types of school finance formulas for general school aid produce equity improvements in the distribution of fiscal resources for this sample of districts.

General-Aid School Finance Programs

All school finance general-aid programs are education block grants. They provide *unrestricted* revenues to be used by local districts and schools for any education purpose. Sometimes they require districts to spend a minimum percentage on teacher salaries or a maximum on administration, but generally they are

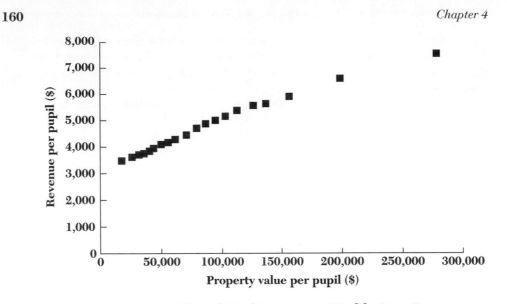

FIGURE 4.2   Scatter Plot of Total Revenue v. Wealth: Base Data

completely unrestricted. Furthermore, they rarely carry restrictions for maintaining local effort, so districts can even use large increases in general-aid revenues to help reduce local property tax rates. Indeed, as discussed in Chapter 3, on average half of each general-aid dollar is used to increase local education spending, and half is used to reduce local property tax rates.

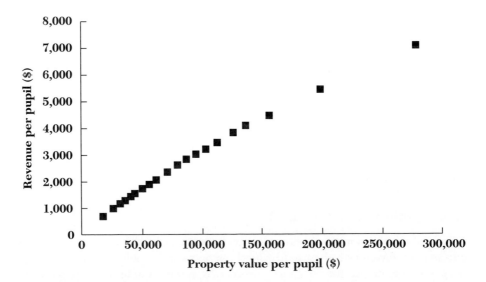

FIGURE 4.3   Scatter Plot of Revenue v. Wealth: Flat Grant

Although the history of education block grants is associated with attempts to deregulate and consolidate categorical programs for special students such as the disabled or low achievers, the idea of a block grant is attractive to local educators. Block grant funds give local school districts more autonomy since the money can be spent as the districts wish. Indeed, the history of school finance general-aid programs is a history of education block grants.

Flat Grant Programs

During the late eighteenth and early nineteenth centuries, there were few public schools in this country. Most schools were private, and churches ran many. Only a small proportion of the population attended formal schooling. As the country developed and interest emerged not only in formally educating its citizens but also in forging a common culture, local governments began to create public schools.

As discussed in Chapters 1 and 2, these schools were not part of state systems of education as exist today, but were independent creatures of local governments. Through various means, including taxation and "in kind" contributions, localities built schools (often one-room schools), hired teachers (who often lived in schools and were paid in terms of room and board rather than money), and educated increasing numbers of children.

From the beginning to at least the middle of the nineteenth century, the inequities associated with this laissez faire approach to creating and financing schools were recognized. Indeed, some localities were too poor to create any type of public school, while larger, wealthier localities were able to levy local taxes to finance them.

Recognizing these different circumstances, states began to require each locality to have at least one public elementary school and often provided a lump sum—a flat grant, usually on a per-school basis—to help support some type of local elementary school program. This approach remedied the problem of the poorest locality unable to create a school on its own; in these communities, state funds often became the only fiscal support for the school.

But the flat grant approach also provided funds to localities that had been able to create a school with their own resources, thus providing them with even more education dollars. Though the overall impact was to expand education and boost the average level of schooling, and even perhaps education quality, the flat grant program benefited poor and rich districts alike.

Over time, states increased the level of flat grants in part to reflect rising costs of education. Growing numbers of students required shifts in the formula structure from flat grants per school to flat grants per classroom or per teacher to finance schools and classrooms that had outgrown the initial one-room-school context. As the education system continued to grow, it became clear that the level of the flat grant, always quite low, would need to be increased to finance the type of education system needed for an emerging industrial society. The response to these growing needs is described in the next section on foundation programs.

Today, states do not use flat grants as the major formula to apportion state general school aid. However, as recently as 1974, Connecticut's school-aid formula was a flat grant of $250 per pupil. Nevertheless, flat grant programs have several intriguing characteristics, some of which may be quite attractive to some districts. For example, some states, such as California, have constitutional requirements to provide a minimum amount of per-pupil state aid to local districts. These minimums function as flat grant programs for the very wealthy districts. California must provide a minimum $120 per pupil in state aid for all districts even if the formula calculation would provide for no state aid.

From an intergovernmental-grant design perspective, flat grants provide general-purpose operating funds. They are based solely on some measure of local education need, such as the number of schools, classrooms, teachers, or students. Flat grants have no local matching requirements. Flat grants also flow to local districts in equal amounts per unit of educational need regardless of differences in local fiscal capacity (i.e., regardless of local property wealth per pupil or household income). As such, they are unlikely to have a major impact in improving the fiscal neutrality of a school finance system, because they are unlikely to reduce the connections between local fiscal capacity and expenditures per pupil. Moreover, flat grants are not the most effective tool for raising local education spending, since districts could use the state funds to reduce the level of local dollars and thus to reduce local property tax rates.

The flat grant formula.   However, one appealing aspect of flat grants is that they are easy to calculate. Algebraically, state aid per pupil for a flat grant is:

$$SAPP = FG$$

and, total state aid is defined as:

$$TSA = SAPP \times Pupils$$

where

> SAPP = state aid per pupil,
> FG = the amount of the flat grant,
> TSA = total state aid, and
> Pupils = the number of students in the school district.[3]

Once the unit of need is identified, which today is typically pupils, a flat grant provides an equal number of dollars for each of those units of need in all districts. Such a program is appealing because all education policy leaders, at both state and local levels can easily understand it. Furthermore, because a flat grant treats all districts equally, it seems fair on the surface. State education revenues are

[3] In this book, pupils are the unit of need. But there are other measures of local need, such as teachers, classrooms and schools, which could also be used with these formulas.

raised by taxing citizens across the state and then returning the money to localities in a what appears to be a fair manner by providing an equal number of dollars for each unit of need.

Flat grants reflect the traditional American concern with the bottom half, or poorest segment, of the population. A flat grant implements the value of providing a bare-minimum level of support for those students and districts at the bottom in terms of relative spending or fiscal capacity. As the historical discussion above indicates, education flat grants were created to ensure that even the poorest localities could offer some type of education program. And while they have been successful in doing so to some extent, the fact that flat grants were typically quite low has meant that they fall short of ensuring a minimum level of quality.

Figures 4.4 and 4.5 graphically depict the impact of a flat grant program on the ability of school districts to raise funds for education. Figure 4.4 represents the situation prior to a flat grant program. The solid lines show the revenues per pupil raised at different tax rates, 30 and 40 mills in this example, for districts with different levels of property value per pupil. For example, at 30 mills, the district with a property value per pupil of $50,000 raises just $1,500 per pupil, whereas the district with a property value of $100,000 raises $3,000. At 40 mills, the district with a property value per pupil of $50,000 raises more, $2,000 per pupil, and the district with a property value of $100,000 raises $4,000. The graph shows that revenues increase both as property value per pupil increases and as the local tax rate increases.

Figure 4.5 depicts the same districts under a flat grant program. The result

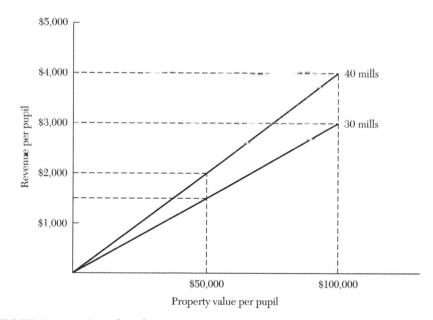

FIGURE 4.4   Graphical Representation of the Impact of No State Aid

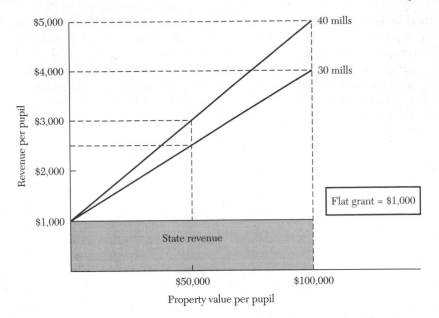

FIGURE 4.5   Graphical Representation of the Impact of a Flat Grant

is simply that the amount of the flat grant, $1,000 in this case, is added to local revenues per pupil. The slopes of the lines do not change. The district with a property value per pupil of $50,000 now has $3,000 ($2,000 of local revenues plus the $1,000 flat grant) at a 40 mill tax rate, and the district with a property value per pupil of $100,000 now has $5,000 ($4,000 of local money plus the $1,000 flat grant) at the same tax rate. Wealthier districts still raise more money, but with the flat grant all districts have at least $2,000 per pupil.

Fiscal equity impacts of flat grant programs.   Figure 4.6 shows the result of replacing the current state-aid system for the sample of districts with a flat grant of $2,000 per child. That amount is slightly higher than the average state aid in the original sample, and is about 40 percent of average total revenues per pupil, although there is no magic in the $2,000 figure. This flat grant increases state aid $7.9 million, from $521.3 million to $529.2 million.

The flat grant completely erases the fiscal capacity equalizing impact of the original state aid, actually decreasing state aid in the poorest districts and increasing it in the wealthier eight districts. All the equity statistics indicate a less equal distribution: the range increases, the coefficient of variation increases, the McLoone Index decreases, the Verstegen Index rises, and the Adequacy Index falls. Further, both fiscal neutrality statistics increase, thus showing a stronger and more significant relationship between total revenues per pupil and property value per pupil. Indeed, the graph of this flat grant (use the simulation to view the graph) is very similar to the graph of the no state-aid case (see Figure 4.3). The

Adequacy Level	$	5,350
Pupil Weights	**no**	
Disabled	—	
Limited English	—	
Low Income	—	

Amount of Flat Grant	$ 2,000.00

District	Pupils	Property Value per Pupil ($)	Property Tax Rate (Mills)	Local Revenue per Pupil ($)	State Revenue per Pupil ($)	Change In State Revenue per Pupil ($)	Total Revenue per Pupil ($)	Change in Total Revenue per Pupil ($)
1	1,290	17,456	39.64	692	2000	(788)	2,692	(788)
2	5,648	25,879	38.50	996	2000	(623)	2,996	(623)
3	1,678	31,569	37.15	1,173	2000	(535)	3,173	(535)
4	256	35,698	36.20	1,292	2000	(460)	3,292	(460)
5	10,256	40,258	35.91	1,446	2000	(401)	3,446	(401)
6	956	43,621	35.74	1,559	2000	(393)	3,559	(393)
7	4,689	49,875	34.89	1,740	2000	(358)	3,740	(358)
8	1,656	55,556	34.17	1,898	2000	(273)	3,898	(273)
9	8,954	61,254	33.73	2,066	2000	(218)	4,066	(218)
10	1,488	70,569	33.44	2,360	2000	(91)	4,360	(91)
11	2,416	78,952	33.23	2,624	2000	(81)	4,624	(81)
12	5,891	86,321	32.89	2,839	2000	(31)	4,839	(31)
13	2,600	94,387	32.10	3,030	2000	31	5,030	31
14	15,489	102,687	31.32	3,216	2000	63	5,216	63
15	2,308	112,358	30.85	3,466	2000	92	5,466	92
16	2,712	125,897	30.50	3,840	2000	276	5,840	276
17	30,256	136,527	30.05	4,102	2000	473	6,102	473
18	2,056	158,325	28.63	4,476	2000	576	6,476	576
19	3,121	198,564	27.42	5,445	2000	870	7,445	870
20	1,523	278,052	25.50	7,090	2000	1563	9,090	1,563
Weighted Average		97,831	32.34	3,028	2,000	75	5,028	75
Weighted Std. Dev.		48,514	2.91	1,269	0	433	1,269	433
Median		102,687	31.32	3,216	2,000	63	5,216	63

Totals

Category	Amount	Percent	Change from Base Amount
Local Revenue	318,727,208	60.23%	(0)
State Revenue	210,486,000	39.77%	7,945,834
Total Revenue	529,213,208		7,945,834
Pupils	105,243		

Winners and Losers

Category	Winners	Losers	No change
State Aid	8	12	0
Total Rev.	8	12	0

Equity Measures

Horizontal Equity	
Range	$6,398
Restricted Range	4,448
Federal Range Ratio	1.485
Coef. of Variation	0.252
Gini Coefficient	0.140
McLoone Index	0.742
Verstegen Index	1.149
Fiscal Neutrality	
Correlation	0.995
Elasticity	0.485
Adequacy	
Odden-Picus	0.871

FIGURE 4.6   Flat Grant from the State

difference is that revenues per pupil are about $2,000 higher with the flat grant; the graph has been shifted upward by the level of the flat grant. In short, at low levels, a flat grant is not a viable option for enhancing the fiscal equity of a state's school finance system.

As the size of the flat grant increases, though, it begins to have a positive impact on the fiscal equity of the school finance system. For example, a flat grant of $4,000 per pupil reduces the coefficient of variation from 0.252 to 0.181, and the fiscal neutrality elasticity from 0.485 to 0.347. Use the simulation to confirm these figures. A flat grant of $5,000 further improves these statistics, lowering the coefficient of variation to 0.158 and the property wealth elasticity to 0.304. Again, use the simulation to confirm these figures. Note that when the flat grant is $5,000, no district spends less than the adequacy level of $5,350, so the Adequacy Index has no meaning, indicated by "na," not applicable, in the equity measures box.

If the flat grant were increased over time to $10,000 and local tax rates and property value per pupil stayed the same, the flat grant would be the major source of school revenues. At this level, both the coefficient of variation and the wealth elasticity also would be negligible. Put a different way, though a low-level flat grant would have a deleterious impact on the fiscal equity of the sample districts, a very high flat grant would swamp the current inequities and produce a highly equalized system.[4]

Of course, as the level of the flat grant rises, so also does the total or state cost of the program. The positive impacts on fiscal equity, in other words, are achieved only at significant cost. Nevertheless, the point of this example is that while low-level flat grants are unattractive except on simplicity grounds, higher-level flat grants can improve the fiscal inequities characteristic of most state school finance structures.

Finally, reviewing the equity measures and means and standard deviations of the major variables can make a few technical statistical points. First, the standard deviation ($433) stays the same irrespective of the level of the flat grant. Thus, adding a constant amount to all variables in a sample does change the standard deviation. This phenomenon helps explain why the coefficient of variation decreases as the flat grant increases. Since the coefficient of variation is the standard deviation divided by the mean, the numerator (standard deviation) remains constant while the denominator (mean or average revenues per pupil) increases. Second, the correlation coefficient also stays the same irrespective of the level of the flat grant. Again, adding a constant amount to all variables in a sample does not change the correlation.

Flat grants were early attempts to involve the state in redressing local differences in the ability to support public schools. Flat grants are easy-to-understand intergovernmental aid programs. But they provide assistance to poor and rich districts alike. They are expensive, even at relatively low values. And at the affordable low values, they tend to worsen measures of school finance equity. For these reasons, they are not used as general-aid policy instruments today.

---

[4] Readers are encouraged to run these flat grant amounts on the computer simulation and to review the results on the computer screen as well as perhaps to print them out. In addition, the reader should view the scatter plots for each run. The scatter plot for the flat grant at $10,000 shows that the graph of total revenues per pupil versus property wealth per pupil is almost a straight, horizontal line.

Foundation Programs

As the shortcomings of flat grant programs became increasingly obvious at the turn of this century, there was a search for a new and more powerful formula. At about that time, New York State created a commission to study its school finance system with the specific charge to create a new school finance structure that went beyond the flat grant approach. George Strayer and Roger Haig, professors at Columbia University, were hired as the consultants to this commission. Their new creation was a formula that would come to dominate school finance during the rest of the century. Indeed, most states today use some variation of the Strayer-Haig foundation, or minimum foundation program as it originally was called. Indeed, in many states, the synonym for "school finance formula" is "minimum foundation program;" the state role in school finance is defined, as it were, as providing a minimum foundation program.

Strayer and Haig ingeniously incorporated several school finance issues into their new foundation program school finance formula. First, the foundation program addresses the issue of a minimum quality-education program. Though flat grants provided financial assistance for localities to provide some level of local school funding, the low level of the flat grant was rarely sufficient to finance what could be called a minimum quality-education program. A goal of the minimum foundation program, however, was to set an expenditure per pupil—the minimum foundation—at a level that would provide at least a minimum quality-education program. The idea was to put a fiscal "foundation" under every local school program that was sufficient to provide an education program that met minimum standards. Thus, the foundation program was designed to remedy the first major defect of the low-level flat grant.

But what about the cost? The reason flat grants remained low was that to raise them to higher levels required more funds than the state could afford. The foundation program resolved this dilemma by financing the foundation expenditure per-pupil level with a combination of state and local revenues. A foundation program requires a minimum local tax effort as a condition of receiving state aid. The required local tax effort is applied to the local property tax base. State aid per pupil is the difference between the foundation per-pupil expenditure level and the per-pupil revenues raised by the required local tax rate.

The foundation formula.   Algebraically, state aid per pupil for a foundation program is:

$$SAPP = FEPP - (RTR \times PVPP),$$

where

> SAPP = state aid per pupil,
> FEPP = foundation expenditure per pupil,
> RTR = the local required tax rate, and
> PVPP = local property value per pupil.

A district's total state aid would be:

$$TSA = SAPP \times Pupils$$

where

SAPP = total state aid,
SAPP = state aid per pupil, and
Pupils = the number of students in the school district.[5]

Thus, the state and local school district share the total cost of the foundation program. A state could afford to enact such a program, and therefore substantially raise the minimum expenditure per pupil, because local tax revenues financed a large portion of the increase. Indeed, the advent of foundation school-aid formulas formally underscored the joint and interrelated state and local roles in financing public elementary and secondary schools.

Foundation policy issues.   From an intergovernmental-aid design perspective, the foundation program has several attractive features. First, it links local school districts to the state in a sophisticated structure of intergovernmental fiscal relationships. Second, it continues to provide large sources of general aid to local school districts but through a mechanism by which local and state revenues are formally combined in the general-aid "pot." Third, it formally requires a local match in order to receive state aid; the district must levy the required local tax rate as a condition of receiving state foundation aid.[6]

Fourth, per-pupil state aid also is related to fiscal capacity. Since the required local tax rate produces less money in a district with low property value than in a district with high property value, state aid becomes higher in the poor district. In fact, there is nearly a linear relationship between the level of state aid and the level of local property value per pupil: as property value decreases, state aid increases. Thus, a foundation program finances a minimum base education program in each school district, provides general aid in a manner that is fiscal capacity equalizing (i.e., increases as property value per pupil decreases), and re-

[5] Again, teachers, classrooms, or schools could be used as the need measure. Several states have used a foundation program with teachers as the need measure; Texas used such a program up to 1984.

[6] Historically, states have "hedged" on this requirement. Though most districts levy a tax rate above the minimum required local tax rate, a few do not. The policy issue for most states is whether to force these districts to raise their tax rate to the minimum level. The dilemma is that most of these low-tax-effort districts are districts lowest in property wealth and household income (i.e., the poorest of the poor). States usually have not ultimately required these districts to raise their tax rates. Sometimes, as in New York State, the districts receive state aid as if they were levying that minimum tax rate. Other states, such as Texas, reduced state aid by a factor equal to the ratio of the actual local property tax rate to the foundation-required tax rate. In the school finance simulation, there is an option to force districts to levy the required minimum tax rate, or to have state aid reduced in the preceding proportionate manner. All simulations discussed in the text use the option that forced districts to levy the minimum in order to receive state general aid.

quires a local contribution as well. These are all attractive features of intergovernmental-aid formulas.

The foundation program takes one or two steps beyond the flat grant, reflecting the American concern with the less well-off, and reflects the value of providing at least a minimum quality-education program. Foundation programs were designed, in fact, to ensure that there would be sufficient revenues from state and local sources to provide a minimum quality-education program in each school district. Viewed from today's education objectives, especially educational adequacy, which seeks to have all students achieve to some high minimum level, this does not seem to be a very lofty goal. But viewed from the perspective of the beginning of the twentieth century, it was a major and bold step forward. The foundation program allowed states to implement an education finance structure that substantially upgraded the education systems in the lowest-spending schools to a level that at least passed a standard of minimum adequacy. In 1986–87, 30 states had such a foundation program or a foundation program as a component of their school-aid program (Salmon, Dawson, Lawton, and Johns, 1988); the number had changed to 40 in 1993–94 (Gold, Smith, and Lawton, 1995).

Three major shortcomings of foundation programs have emerged over the years. The first is that a foundation program typically allows districts to spend above the minimum foundation level. This fiscal leeway, or local add-on, generally is financed entirely by local revenues, though sometimes it is aided by a GTB program (see section below on combination foundation-GTB programs). Without the GTB, districts with a high property value per pupil can levy a small tax rate above the required local effort and take in large amounts of supplemental revenues, while districts with a low property value per pupil can levy a substantial extra tax rate and still see only a small amount of additional revenue per pupil. In fact, this feature of foundation programs ultimately led to the court cases discussed in Chapter 2, since over time, the local add-on component of education revenues far surpassed the foundation program revenues, producing a system that, while more equitable than a system with no state aid, still left education revenues per pupil strongly linked to local property wealth per pupil. Further, this local add-on feature is viewed by some as the "Achilles heel" of the finance structure in all states that today have a foundation program as their system for providing general school aid.

Second, though minimum foundation programs initially boosted the minimum level of local school spending, often the minimum increased slowly over time and quickly ceased being high enough to meet minimum standards. Put another way, after the initial years, minimum foundation programs often did not provide sufficient revenues per pupil even for an education program that would meet the lowest acceptable standards. The low level was maintained in part by technical problems (the law specified a specific dollar amount as the foundation expenditure and required a legislative action each year for it to increase) and in part by fiscal constraints (the state could not afford to raise it significantly). Over time, the low-level forced districts wanted to provide a higher quality-education program to expand their local add-on, which gradually moved the overall system into one based more and more on local property value per pupil.

Third, while foundation programs usually increased total education revenues in property-poor districts and thus helped them to enhance their education program, strict state-aid formula calculations for wealthier districts yielded a negative number. This result meant that these districts could raise more than the minimum foundation expenditure at the required tax rate. In a world of perfect fiscal equity, the state would have required such districts to send a check in the amount of the negative aid to the state, which the state would have put it in the general fund for redistribution to poorer districts. But states did not enact this "recapture" component. If state-aid calculations produced a negative-aid figure, the state simply provided no aid to that district.

This meant that even under a minimum foundation program, districts high in property value per pupil were able to raise more funds at the given required tax rate just with local funds than other districts had with a combination of state and local funds. The fiscal advantage for districts high in property value per pupil was further enhanced by prior receipt of flat grant state aid, which had been distributed to all districts, irrespective of their level of property wealth per pupil. For these districts, the state faced a dual-policy dilemma: whether under the foundation-aid calculation to require them to send negative-aid checks to the state, which was rarely if ever invoked, or whether to take away the flat grant aid and thereby reduce their state aid to zero. Most states took a political route to this dilemma and distributed an amount that was the larger of the new amount under the foundation formula or the previous level of aid (i.e., they did not take away the old flat grant aid). This "hold harmless" approach has typified school finance structures (as well as most other intergovernmental-aid structures) for years. So, not only were the wealthiest districts not forced to revert negative aid to the state but also they kept some minimum level of per-pupil state aid. Indeed, states often gradually increased the minimum amount over the years.

Such policy dilemmas and ultimate policy decisions substantially blunted the ability of minimum foundation programs to impact the fiscal equity of a state's school finance structure. While new minimum foundation programs clearly boosted the fiscal resources of the lowest-spending districts, which was a clear objective and definite positive feature, their shortcomings, especially over time, severely limited their role as an adequate school finance mechanism.

The base sample of districts shows the residue of these incremental approaches to school finance (see Figure 4.1); even the districts highest in property value per pupil receive state aid. Thus, the school finance policy question is what type of a foundation program can enhance the fiscal equity of the school finance condition of the sample districts? In addressing this question, there are two policy decisions that have to be made:

- the foundation expenditure level and
- the required local tax rate.

Three policy issues then have to be considered:

- the impact on the fiscal equity of the sample,
- the total costs (usually in state revenues but also considering changes in local revenues), and
- the number of "winners" and "losers" (i.e., the number of districts with increases and decreases in state aid).

Setting the Foundation Level. There are no magic solutions to setting the foundation expenditure level. Usually, states set a level that, combined with the amount raised locally by the required tax rate, equals the amount of state appropriations available. This is a politically grounded but substantively vacuous approach since it is decided on availability rather than on a needs-basis, but it is probably the norm. More recently, states simply determined a particular spending level, deemed sufficiently high enough by the appropriate cross-section of political and education leaders, and sought to fund that spending level over time. To ensure that the level stayed "current" or increased with inflation, states often legislated a mechanism that automatically increased the foundation expenditure per-pupil level each year. Inflating it by the increase in the consumer price index, or the deflator for state and local governmental services, is a common approach.

A second approach is to set a specific policy target such as 50 or 100 percent of the statewide average expenditure. The policy target could even be to bring the foundation level up to the spending in some district above the average; a late 1970s' bill in California set the expenditure of the district at the 75th percentile as the foundation expenditure target. Whatever the level, this approach provides a clear policy target as to what the foundation base spending level will be. Odden and Clune (1998) recommend the use of such policy targets in order to give the school finance system a specific and clear equalization goal.

Today, the challenge to calculating a foundation expenditure level is to determine an "adequate" level (i.e., an amount of money per pupil that would be sufficient to teach students to some high minimum standard). Odden and Clune (1998) and Odden (1999) argue that this is one of the most pressing, as well as complex, tasks for linking the school finance structure to the goals and strategies of standards- and school-based education reform.

Determining an Adequate Foundation Spending Level. There are three major ways policymakers and policy analysts have attempted and are attempting to determine an adequate spending level: (1) identifying a set of inputs and costing them out; (2) linking a spending amount per pupil to a level of student outcomes; and (3) building a number from the bottom up by identifying the cost of schoolwide programs that produce desired outcomes.

The input approach began nearly two decades ago when the Washington school finance system was declared unconstitutional, and that state's top court required the state to identify and fund an "ample" education program. In response, Washington specified a pupil/teacher ratio with an average teacher salary, an administrator/teacher ratio with an average administrator salary, and a level of funds for other instructional and school costs. The combination then translated into a foundation expenditure level per pupil. To a substantial degree, Washington still uses this approach.

A somewhat more sophisticated input approach was the Resource Cost Model (RCM), created by Jay Chambers and Thomas Parrish (1983; 1994). Using groups of professional educator experts, the RCM first identified base staffing levels for the regular education program, and then identified effective program practices and their staffing and resource needs for compensatory, special, and bilingual education. All ingredients were assessed using average price figures but, in determining the foundation base dollar amount for each district, the totals were adjusted by a geographic education price index (Chambers, 1995; McMahon, 1994). This method was used to propose a foundation spending level for both Illinois and Alaska, but the proposals were never implemented.

Guthrie and Rothstein (1999) made a further advance on the professional input approach as part of a response to a Wyoming Supreme Court's finding that that state's finance system was unconstitutional. Guthrie and colleagues also used a panel of professional education experts. They identified the base staffing level for typical elementary, middle, and high schools; however, they relied on the findings of the Tennessee STAR class-size reduction study results to set a class size of 15 in elementary schools (Finn, 1996; Finn and Achilles, 1990), and then used the panel to determine additional resources for compensatory, special, and bilingual education. They too adjusted the dollar figures by a constructed price factor.

The advantages of all of these input approaches is that they identify a set of ingredients that an amount of dollars would be able to purchase in each school district, including additional resources for three categories of special-needs students, all adjusted by a price factor. The disadvantage is that the resource levels are connected to student achievement results only through professional judgement and not to actual measures of student performance.

The second approach to determining an adequate spending level attempts to remedy this key deficiency of the input approach, by seeking directly to link a spending level to a specified level of student performance. Two procedures have been used. The first determines a desired level of performance using state tests of student performance, identifies districts that produce that level of performance, from that group selects those districts with comparable or close-to-state-average characteristics, and then calculates their average spending per pupil. Such studies have been conducted in Illinois (Hinrichs and Laine, 1996) and Ohio (Alexander, Augenblick, Driscoll, Guthrie, and Levin, 1995; Augenblick, 1997). Interestingly, in all three studies, the level of spending identified was approximately the median spending per pupil in the state.

The other procedure used the economic cost function approach (see additional discussion of the cost function approach later in this chapter in Section 2). This approach seeks to identify a spending-per-pupil level that is sufficient to produce a given level of performance, adjusting for characteristics of students and other SES characteristics of districts; this method, as discussed in

Section 2, also can be used to calculate how much more is required to produce the specified level of performance by factors such as special needs of students, scale economies or diseconomies, input prices, and even efficiency. Using Wisconsin data, Reschovsky and Imazeki (1998) identified an expenditure level that was also close to the median of spending per pupil. Similar cost function research has been conducted by others (e.g., Duncombe, Rugierrio, and Yinger, 1996).

To be sure, all of these studies used different methodologies and had different definitions of adequate performance levels. In Wisconsin, adequate performance was defined by the average, and in the other two states it was defined as having at least 70 percent of students at state proficiency standards. But all studies sought to identify a spending level that was associated with a desired, substantive education result: student achievement to a specified standard. In general, that desired level of spending was close to the respective state's median spending level.

The third approach to adequacy has been to identify the costs of a "high-performance" school model—a schoolwide design crafted specifically to produce desired levels of student academic achievement—and to determine a level of spending that would be sufficient to fund such a model. A current example of such new school finance thinking is the situation in New Jersey. For nearly a quarter of a century, the driving issue in the New Jersey school finance case was about money, and whether all districts, not just the 28 special-needs urban districts, would have the same level of dollar resources as the high-wealth, high-spending suburban districts, plus additional dollars for the special needs of their urban students. For 1997–98, the Supreme Court ordered the state to provide a level of spending equality that insured $8,664 per pupil for every child. The Supreme Court also asked a remand court to work with the state and plaintiffs to identify supplemental programs for the extra needs of low-income, urban students, and to identify the costs of those programs. The state proposed that the education problem of the special-needs districts' students could be resolved by using the $8,664 to fund a proven effective schoolwide program, specifically Success for All/Roots and Wings.

That level of money more than covered the requirements of that school design, which was specifically designed for low-income, minority students in urban school systems. In fact, the state not only picked one of the most expensive whole-school models (King, 1994; Odden, 1997a) but, because of the high level of funding, they also expanded the element of the model. For example, the standard model assumed a class size of 25, while the state proposed a class size of 21. The standard model assumed 4.0 tutors for a school of 500 with nearly all students eligible for free or reduced lunch; the state model proposed 5.5 tutors. The standard model assumed a full-day kindergarten but did not require any preschool, while the state model included a full-day kindergarten as well as a half day of preschool for four-year olds. The standard model assumed a part-time family liaison or a full-time paraprofessional parent liaison, while the state model not only proposed a certified professional as the family liaison, but went beyond that and proposed a full, five-member family, health, and social services team. The standard model assumed no technology but the state model included substantial technology. The standard model assumed a full-time, schoolwide instructional facilitator, and the state model included that position as well as a technology coordinator. The standard model assumed about $65,000 for professional development and materials, while the state proposed nearly twice that amount. So the state took the best, and one of the most expensive, research-proven effective, urban district elementary school models in the country and enhanced nearly all its key features.

Although New Jersey provided a base spending level that was substantially above the median, its approach to re-engineering school finance to some adequate level was to start with a proven effective, schoolwide program. There are several other schoolwide models being developed across the country, all with costs about equal to or less than Success for All/Roots and Wings (Odden and Busch, 1998). Early results suggest that they show promise for accomplishing the goal of teaching students to higher standards (Edison Project, 1997; Slavin and Fashola, 1998; Stringfield, Ross, and Smith, 1996). To determine a spending level more reasonable than the high level in New Jersey, Odden and Busch (1998) analyzed the costs of two such models, the Modern Red Schoolhouse and Success for All/Roots and Wings. Both had similar overall costs and would require the national median expenditure per pupil.

Much additional work is needed to identify adequate expenditure levels. Each approach discussed above has strengths and weaknesses, and none has been perfected. However, any state could select one of the above approaches, or some other approach, and determine what their level of adequacy would be.

Setting the foundation tax rate.   After the foundation expenditure level is determined, setting the required tax rate raises another set of interrelated issues. First, if the required tax rate is above the tax rate in any poor school district, it may require that district to raise its tax rate. That often is a politically difficult requirement to enact. Second, and related, the level of the required tax rate determines the state cost of the program: the higher the required local effort, the less the state cost (but the greater the local cost).

Third, the foundation expenditure level and required tax rate are connected in a way that determines which districts are eligible for at least some aid, and which districts receive zero (or actually negative) aid. The zero-aid district is defined as:

$$SAPP = FEPP - (RTR \times PVPP) = 0.$$

Solving this equation for PVPP identifies the property value per pupil below which districts will receive some foundation aid and above which they will not. The solution becomes:

$$FEPP = RTR \times PVPP,$$

or transposing and dividing by RTR,

$$\text{PVPP (the zero-aid district)} = \text{FEPP/RTR}$$

where

> FEPP = the foundation expenditure per-pupil level,
> RTR = the required tax rate, and
> PVPP = the property value of the zero-aid district in thousands of dollars
> of assessed valuation.

Thus, if the foundation level is $3,000, and the required tax rate is 30 mills, the zero-aid district has a property value per pupil of $100,000.

The zero-aid district is an important policy variable to consider. Districts with property value above this level will not be eligible for any state aid (or at best be "held harmless" with their previous level of state aid), and their legislative representatives might vote against the proposal if self-interest is the only motivating variable. Another policy aspect of the zero-aid district is that it identifies a level up to which the state provides some fiscal capacity equalization. The policy issue is the level to which the state wants to equalize fiscal capacity: to the statewide average, the 75th percentile, the 90th percentile, the property value per pupil of the wealthiest district, or any other level it chooses.

In other words, setting the foundation expenditure level and the required tax rate simultaneously determines the level of education program that becomes the base, the state and local cost, the zero-aid district, the level up to which the state seeks to equalize fiscal capacity, and the numbers of state aid gainers and losers. In short, it determines several key aspects of the political economy of the foundation program itself.

All of these characteristics of a foundation program are depicted in Figure 4.7 for a foundation program with an expenditure per pupil of $2,000 and a required tax rate of 20 mills. For the first 20 mills, all districts with a property wealth less than $100,000 (the zero-aid district) receive a total of $2,000 per child; districts with a property value per pupil above $100,000 raise more than the foundation level, as the slope of the 20 mill line shows. If districts decide to levy a tax rate above the required rate, as most districts do, the additional funds are raised solely from the local property tax base. So at 30 mills, the district with a property wealth per pupil of $50,000 would produce $2,000 per pupil for the first 20 mills and only $500 per pupil for the next 10 mills, or $2,500 per pupil in total, whereas the district with a property wealth per pupil of $100,000 also would produce $2,000 per pupil for the first 20 mills but would produce $1,000 for the next 10 mills, or $3,000 per pupil in total.

Fiscal equity impacts of foundation programs.   Setting these parameters determines how the new foundation program will impact the fiscal equity of the finance structure. Figure 4.8 shows several figures for a foundation program with

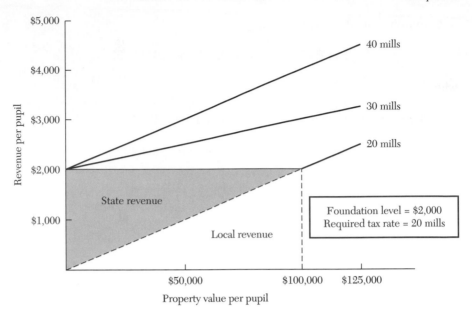

FIGURE 4.7   Graphical Representation of the Effect of a Foundation Program

the foundation expenditure level set at $5,154, the median level for the base sample, and a required tax effort of 31.32 mills (also the median).[7] This means that the zero-aid district has a property value per pupil of $164,559, which is between district 18 and 19 in the sample.

This also means that this program will provide fiscal capacity equalization for districts that enroll 95.6 percent of the students (which is the cumulative enrollment of districts 1–18). The program increases state aid by 9.7 percent—$50.6 million. It also positively impacts fiscal equity, reducing the coefficient from 17 percent for the base sample to 7.1 percent, reduces the wealth elasticity from 0.324 to 0.146, and raises the Adequacy Index from 0.895 to 0.985. It raises spending above the foundation level in the poorest and lowest-spending 13 districts. This impact can be seen by using the simulation to view the graph of the results; the left-hand portion of the graph from Figure 4.2 (the base data) has

---

[7] For the foundation, guaranteed tax base, and combination simulations, state aid has been set equal to zero if the calculation produces a negative figure, but districts are not "held harmless" (i.e., they lose state aid if the calculation produces a zero-aid figure). Further, a local tax response has been built into the simulation under which districts increase their local property tax rate to cover the lost aid. For these districts, the last column of the results show no total revenue loss, but this is a result of a loss of state aid and an equal increase in local revenues. There is also a response model for districts that have state-aid increases. These districts use half the state-aid increase to raise spending, and half to reduce local property tax rates. For the foundation part of the program, though, tax rates cannot be reduced to below the required tax rate.

Adequacy Level	$	5,350		Foundation Level	$5,154.00
				Required Tax Rate	31.32
Pupil Weights		no			
Disabled		—	—		
Limited English		—	—		
Low Income		—	—		

District	Pupils	Property Value per Pupil ($)	Old Property Tax Rate (Mills)	New Property Tax Rate (Mills)	Change in Property Tax Rate (Mills)	Old Local Revenue per Pupil ($)	New Local Revenue per Pupil ($)	Change in Local Revenue per Pupil ($)	New State Revenue per Pupil ($)	Change in State Revenue per Pupil ($)	Total Revenue per Pupil ($)	Change in Total Revenue per Pupil ($)
1	1,290	17,456	39.64	35.48	(4.16)	692	619	(73)	4,607	1,819	5,227	1,747
2	5,648	25,879	38.50	34.91	(3.59)	995	903	(93)	4,343	1,720	5,247	1,627
3	1,678	31,569	37.15	34.23	(2.91)	1,173	1,081	(92)	4,165	1,630	5,246	1,538
4	256	35,698	36.20	33.76	(2.44)	1,292	1,205	(87)	4,036	1,576	5,241	1,489
5	10,256	40,258	35.91	33.62	(2.30)	1,446	1,353	(92)	3,893	1,492	5,246	1,400
6	956	43,621	35.74	33.53	(2.21)	1,559	1,463	(96)	3,788	1,395	5,250	1,298
7	4,689	49,875	34.89	33.11	(1.79)	1,740	1,651	(89)	3,592	1,233	5,243	1,144
8	1,656	55,556	34.17	32.75	(1.43)	1,898	1,819	(79)	3,414	1,141	5,233	1,062
9	8,954	61,254	33.73	32.53	(1.21)	2,066	1,992	(74)	3,236	1,017	5,228	944
10	1,488	70,569	33.44	32.38	(1.06)	2,360	2,285	(75)	2,944	853	5,229	778
11	2,416	78,952	33.23	32.28	(0.95)	2,618	2,543	(75)	2,681	601	5,229	525
12	5,891	86,321	32.89	32.11	(0.78)	2,839	2,771	(68)	2,450	419	5,222	352
13	2,600	94,387	32.10	31.71	(0.39)	3,030	2,993	(37)	2,198	228	5,191	192
14	15,489	102,687	31.32	31.32	0.00	3,216	3,216	0	1,938	0	5,154	0
15	2,308	112,358	30.85	33.28	2.43	3,466	3,739	273	1,635	(273)	5,374	0
16	2,712	125,897	30.50	34.57	4.07	3,840	4,353	513	1,211	(513)	5,564	0
17	30,256	136,527	30.05	34.80	4.76	4,102	4,752	650	878	(650)	5,630	0
18	2,056	156,325	28.63	36.09	7.46	4,476	5,642	1,166	258	(1,166)	5,899	0
19	3,121	198,564	27.42	33.11	5.69	5,445	6,575	1,130	0	(1,130)	6,575	0
20	1,523	278,052	25.50	27.07	1.57	7,090	7,527	437	0	(437)	7,527	0
Weighted Average		97,831	32.34	33.37	1.03	3,028	3,261	232	2,173	248	5,434	481
Weighted Std. Dev.		48,514	2.91	1.56	3.17	1,269	1,598	382	1,318	907	384	610
Median		102,687	31.32	31.32	0.00	3,216	3,216	0	1,938	0	5,246	0

Totals

Category	Amount	Percent	Change from Base Amount
Local Revenue	343,155,687	60.01%	24,428,479
State Revenue	228,688,560	39.99%	26,148,394
Total Revenue	571,844,247		50,576,873
Pupils	105,243		

Winners and Losers

Category	Winners	Losers	No change
State Aid	14	6	0
Total Rev.	14	0	6

Equity Measures

Horizontal Equity	
Range	$2,373
Restricted Range	1,384
Federal Range Ratio	0.267
Coef. of Variation	0.071
Gini Coefficient	0.030
McLoone Index	0.992
Verstegen Index	1.070
Fiscal Neutrality	
Correlation	0.900
Elasticity	0.146
Adequacy	
Odden-Ficus	0.585

FIGURE 4.8 Foundation Program

been rotated up (clockwise) at about the wealth of the zero-aid district to form a horizontal line at the foundation expenditure level of $5,154. But, this foundation program also reduces aid to six districts; even districts 15–18, which receive some foundation aid, have a net loss of aid from their base context.

A foundation program with the expenditure level set at $4,000 and the required tax rate at 39 mills, which thus provides for fiscal capacity equalization up to just $102,500, the statewide average property value per pupil, produces a net drop in state aid and also a reduction of state aid for 15 of the 20 districts. (Use the simulation to assess the broader impacts of this set of parameters.) On the other hand, a foundation at $5,154 with a required tax rate of 25 mills, which provides for fiscal capacity equalization up to $206,160, provides at least some state general aid for 19 of the 20 districts, further enhances fiscal equity (the coefficient of variation drops to 5.8 percent, the wealth elasticity declines to 0.131 and the Adequacy Index becomes 1) but the state cost rises by $64 million. (Again, use the simulation to assess the broader impacts of this set of parameters.)

These results indicate that the foundation expenditure level, required tax effort, level of fiscal capacity equalization, state costs, numbers of winners and losers, and school finance fiscal equity and adequacy all are interrelated. These interrelations suggest why getting legislatures to enact complicated school finance reforms is not an easy task; several variables—educational, political, and fiscal— need to be balanced simultaneously.

As discussed in the section on how to set an adequate foundation level, a school finance system that required all districts to spend at least at the median of state spending per pupil reflects a strategy that might begin to move the system towards adequacy. Yes, research in every state would be needed to determine more explicitly what an adequate spending level would be, but ensuring that districts spent at least as much as the median would be a way for states to move immediately forward on the adequacy school finance agenda. Odden (1999) shows the results of such a school finance system for the three states with the "new" school finance problem discussed in Chapter 1: Illinois, Missouri, and Wisconsin. He simulated a foundation program set at the median spending level in each state. Not only would such a program represent progress in providing an adequate level of funding, but also the programs produce substantial improvements in fiscal equity. In all three states, both the statistical measures of spending disparities (coefficient of variation and McLoone Index) and the statistical measures of the linkage between spending and wealth (correlation and wealth elasticity) improve, as would the Adequacy Index. To work over time, the spending level would need to be inflation-adjusted each year to continue to provide an adequate spending base.

In summary, foundation programs have several attractive features. They began as programs designed to provide a minimum quality-education program but, today, can be used to guarantee a higher-quality program, perhaps one sufficient to meet the needs of an adequate education system, one in which students learn to high minimum standards. They are unique in having this base program guarantee as a critical variable. Second, they are funded by a combination of state and local funds that link states and school districts inextricably in a fiscal partnership for funding public schools. Third, they are fiscal capacity equalizing (i.e., they provide state aid in an inverse relationship to local property value per pupil), and thus also address the key structural problem of school finance—the disparity in the local property tax base. Their key defect may be that they allow local spending above the foundation program, and if the base program is low, these local fiscal add-ons—financed entirely with local property tax revenues— increase the linkages between property wealth and education spending, *the* major weakness of previous school-aid formulas and *the* issue targeted in school finance litigation.

On the other hand, it could be argued that if the state actually determined and fully funded an adequate foundation base, together with appropriate adjustments for special-student, district, and school needs, then the state's interest in education and its funding contribution would have been fulfilled. Such a position would allow districts to spend more if they wish, but only by using local money. Although this position could be criticized, a state could defend it assuming that it truly had determined an adequate spending base.

Guaranteed Tax Base Programs

Guaranteed tax base programs (GTB), surprisingly, are a relatively recent phenomenon in school finance structures. The first guaranteed tax base programs were enacted in the early 1970s after the initial rounds of school finance litigation. The late arrival of guaranteed tax base programs is perplexing because, as the name suggests, this type of school finance program addresses the traditional structural flaw in traditional approaches to local financing of public schools, namely the unequal distribution of the local property tax base. A GTB program simply erases this inequality by guaranteeing, through state-aid allocations, that each local district can function as if it had an equal property tax-base per pupil. The details of how this program works will be described below. Conceptually, it is simple, and in terms of school finance policy, it addresses a basic inequity in school finance: unequal access to a local property tax base.

This simple and straightforward program took a somewhat complicated course in evolving to its current state. The early forms of GTB programs actually were called percentage equalizing programs and were first introduced in the 1920s. They were proposed for two major reasons. First, foundation program levels remained low, and most districts enacted local add-ons that were financed entirely from their local property tax base. Local add-ons came to dominate the level of total revenues, and there was a search for a school finance mechanism that went beyond foundation programs and provided state fiscal capacity equalizing aid for the overall spending levels in local school districts.

Second, because the state fiscal role remained small as the level of the minimum foundation programs remained low, policy pressure grew to increase the state role in the financing of education. Over time, in fact, many states sought to increase the state role to some fixed target, usually 50 percent. Since most state aid was distributed in a fiscal capacity equalizing manner, the assumption was that the fiscal equity of the school finance system would improve as the state role increased towards, or even surpassed, 50 percent.

The percentage equalizing formula was designed to address both of these policy concerns. First, the state share (in percentage terms) of total costs was directly included in the formula. The formula was designed to provide a larger state role in low-property-wealth districts and a smaller state role in higher-property-wealth districts, thus providing a fiscal capacity equalizing thrust to the program. The formula calculated a state-aid ratio for each district. The ratio was higher in property-poor districts and lower in property-wealthy districts. The state role policy target, say 50 percent of total dollars spent on education, was usually set for the district with statewide average property value per pupil.[8]

To determine state aid, the state-aid ratio was applied to the local spending level, which was a local policy decision of each district. The aid ratio times the spending level produced the amount of state aid per pupil for each district. State aid, therefore, varied with both the level of wealth and the level of locally determined spending. During 1986–87, five states had percentage equalizing programs, a number that went down to four in 1993–94 (Gold et al., 1995). The percentage equalizing formula is both more complicated and algebraically equivalent to a guaranteed tax base program.

As previously stated, guaranteed tax base programs were enacted beginning in the early 1970s, at the time of the first successful school finance court cases. These court cases had directly challenged the relationship between expenditures and wealth caused by the unequal distribution of the local tax base per pupil. The book that developed the "fiscal neutrality" legal theory for these cases (Coons, Clune, and Sugarman, 1970) also discussed the design and operation of a new district power-equalizing school finance structure. Power equalizing was a system that would equalize the power of local districts to raise funds through the property tax. The mechanism was for the state to guarantee a tax base that all districts would use in deciding upon school tax rate and expenditure levels. Subsequently, these approaches became known as guaranteed tax base programs. Guaranteed tax base programs are also called guaranteed yield, or resource equalizing programs in some states.

---

[8] State aid per pupil for a percentage equalizing program is equal to:

$$\text{SAPP} = [1 - \text{LR}(\text{PVPPd}/\text{PVPPk})]\text{TREVPP},$$

where

SAPP = state aid per pupil,

LR = local role in percent terms [the state role is $(1 - \text{LR})$],

PVPPd = property value per pupil for each district,

PVPPk = property wealth per pupil in the comparative district, usually but not necessarily the statewide average, and

TREVPP = total (state and local) revenue per pupil.

The zero-aid district is PVPPk/LR. The aid ratio is $1 - \text{LR}(\text{PVPPd}/\text{PVPPk})$.

The GTB formula.　　The formula for calculating state aid for a guaranteed tax base programs is:

$$SAPP = DTR \times (GTB - PVPP)$$

where

> SAPP = state aid per pupil,
> DTR = the local district property tax rate,
> GTB = the tax rate guaranteed by the state, in thousands of dollars
>　　　of property value per pupil, and
> PVPP = the local district property value per pupil.

Total GTB state aid, therefore, is:

$$TSA = SAPP \times Pupils,$$

where

> TSA = total state aid,
> SAPP − state aid per pupil from the GTB formula, and
> Pupils = the number of students in the school district.

Several interesting features of the GTB state-aid formula should be mentioned. First, the amount of state aid a district receives varies with the size of the local tax base; the greater the local tax base (PVPP), the smaller the factor (GTB − PVPP) and thus the smaller the amount of per-pupil state aid. In other words, state aid varies inversely with property wealth per child.

A second feature is that the local expenditure (or revenues) per pupil is equal to the tax rate times the GTB. This can be shown algebraically:

> local revenue = DTR × PVPP, and
> state aid = DTR × (GTB − PVPP), so
> total revenues = local revenue + state aid,

or substituting,

$$total\ revenues = (DTR \times PVPP) + (DTR \times (GTB - PVPP)).$$

Combining terms on the right-hand side and factoring out DTR:

$$total\ revenues = DTR \times (PVPP + GTB - PVPP),$$

which is:

$$total\ revenues = DTR \times GTB.$$

In other words, the GTB operates just exactly as it is designed.[9] Districts can function as if they have the GTB as their local tax base. Once they determine their desired spending level, they divide it by the GTB to determine the local tax rate they must levy. Or conversely, by multiplying their local property tax rate by the GTB, they identify their per-pupil spending level. As a corollary, by multiplying their local property tax rate times the local property tax base, they also identify the amount of local revenues they must raise.

A final feature is that state aid is a function of the local school tax rate; the higher the tax rate, the greater the state aid. This feature has two implications. First, if local districts increase their property tax rate, they not only raise more funds locally, but they also become eligible for more state aid. This can be an attractive component for a campaign to increase the local school property tax rate. Second, and therefore related, the total amount of revenues the state needs to appropriate is, in part, determined by local action. Put differently, the state is not in complete control of the level of revenues needed to finance the general-aid school finance formula; if districts increase local tax rates more than anticipated, additional state funds are needed to fully fund the GTB formula.

This feature has been troublesome when the GTB formula has been considered by many legislatures, which themselves want to be in complete control of the level of funding needed for the general-aid program. Many states reject the GTB because of this feature. But, over time, local tax rates usually settle into fairly predictable patterns, and states can fairly easily predict the level of appropriation needed to fund the formula. Michigan, for example, had a GTB program for over a decade in the 1970s and 1980s and had no more difficulty predicting the level of appropriations needed than did other states that used different school-aid distribution mechanisms. Many other factors complicate estimation of state aid, including for example, enrollment projections, property value projections, and estimates of state tax revenues. Many factors beyond the design of the general-aid formula itself make state-aid predictions an imperfect art.

GTB policy issues.   Guaranteed tax base programs have several attractive features as an intergovernmental grant mechanism. First, a GTB requires a local match, which is equal to the district tax rate times its property value per pupil. Indeed, while GTB aid increases as the local tax rate increases, thus requiring more state funds, the local tax rate applied to the local tax base must also increase. In other words, more GTB aid does not come without a local cost; it also requires an increase in local revenues as well. Indeed, the local match feature of the GTB formula structure helps keep both local tax rates and state aid at acceptable levels over time.

Second, the GTB program equalizes fiscal capacity. As local property wealth decreases, GTB aid as a percent of local expenditure increases, and vice

[9] Strictly speaking, this holds for all districts only if the state has a total recapture plan. In the absence of such recapture, this applies only to districts with property wealth at or below the GTB level.

versa. This is generally a desired feature for school finance formulas. But, the GTB program goes further than that by directly addressing the disparity in the local property tax base per child. The GTB program simply makes the GTB tax base equal for all districts, at least for those districts with a property value per pupil less than the GTB. If the primary school finance problem is the unequal distribution of the property tax base, the GTB program is precisely the school finance structure that remedies the problem.

In terms of values, the GTB program reflects the American values of choice, local control, and equal education opportunity as defined by equal access to a tax base. For districts with a property value per pupil less than the GTB, it provides for equal dollars per pupil from state and local sources for equal school tax rates. A pure GTB program, moreover, implements the value of local control since it allows local districts to decide on the level of tax rate they want to levy for schools, and thus the level of per-pupil school spending. If localities want a higher-quality program, they are free to exert a higher school tax rate. The GTB ensures that all districts levying that tax rate will have the same spending per pupil from the general fund, and thus provides ex ante equity. If districts want a program that is funded at a level comparable to the average, they need only levy the average school tax rate.

Because a GTB program allows different local decisions on education per-pupil spending levels, equality of spending is not its focus. Indeed, without a requirement for a minimum school tax rate, GTB programs do not even require a minimum education expenditure per-pupil level. Still, in most situations where GTB programs have been enacted, they increase expenditures in all but the lowest tax-rate school districts. However, it should be emphasized that a GTB program is incompatible with the horizontal equity principle for students because it does not require equal spending per child.

Figure 4.9 indicates graphically some of these characteristics of a GTB program, for a GTB set at $100,000. The graph shows that for districts with a property value per pupil below the GTB, revenues differ according to the tax rate, but that all districts have the same revenues per pupil (from state and local sources) if they levy the same tax rate. As the 20 mill line shows, the higher a district's property wealth per pupil, the greater the share of total revenue provided from local sources. If the tax rate is raised to 30 mills, all districts get $3,000 per pupil, and the proportion of state aid is inversely related to the district's property wealth. The graph also shows that districts above the GTB raise higher revenues per pupil at any given tax rate but receive no state aid.

In implementing a GTB program, there is one primary policy issue to resolve: the tax-base level that the state wants to guarantee. While there are no absolute standards by which to assess this policy issue, there are several benchmarks. The state could seek to guarantee the tax base up to the 50th percentile of students, the statewide average, or to a higher percentile, such as the 75th, 90th, or even higher. A GTB program in response to a typical fiscal neutrality court suit would need to hit at least the 75th percentile, and probably the 90th percentile. The legal question would be: What constitutes substantial equal access to raising

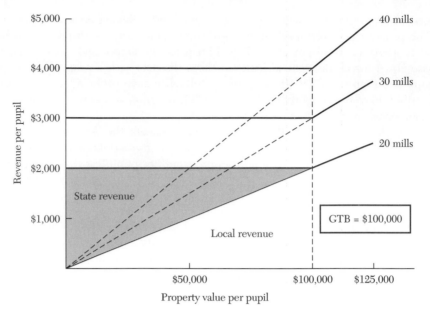

FIGURE 4.9   Graphical Representation of the Effect of a Guaranteed Tax Base Program

education dollars? The answer would be: At least the 75th percentile, and probably higher, but how much higher varies by state and court. Rather than just identifying a value for the GTB, Odden and Clune (1998) argue for selecting a specific target that provides a clear equalization goal, such as the wealth at some high level (the 90th percentile).

There are two secondary policy issues. One is whether a minimum tax rate is required. A minimum tax rate translates into a minimum expenditure per pupil (which equals the minimum tax rate times the GTB). Requiring a minimum would make a smoother transition from a minimum foundation program, for which the state policy goal includes a minimum base program, to a GTB program which in its pure form does not have a minimum expenditure requirement. Odden and Busch (1995) show that such a minimum tax rate would have eliminated all the very low spending per-pupil districts in Wisconsin, which simultaneously would have provided all districts with sufficient dollars to fund the expensive, comprehensive, high-performance Modern Red Schoolhouse school design (Odden, Archibald, and Tychsen, 1998; Odden and Busch, 1998).

A second issue is whether to cap GTB aid at some tax rate, or whether to cap local school tax rates at some level. Under the first type of cap, GTB aid would be available only up to a set tax rate. As tax rates rise above the set level, the state would no longer participate, leaving the districts with only local funds from the extra tax effort. This would give the GTB an unequalized local add-on element, as exists for all foundation programs. Over time, a tax-rate cap could turn the GTB program into a structure in which nonfiscal capacity-equalized add-ons dominate the structure and produce a system, as currently exists in most states, in which expenditures per pupil are strongly related to the level of local property value per child.

The second type of cap is an absolute cap on the local tax rate. Not only would GTB aid not be available above this tax rate, but also districts would not be allowed to levy a tax rate above the cap. This tax-rate cap would have the effect of an expenditure cap, since the maximum expenditure would be the tax-rate cap times the GTB. This type of cap certainly puts a major constraint on local control, but it also limits the variation in expenditures per pupil that would be allowed by a GTB program. The Kentucky school finance reform enacted in 1990 adopted both of these options (see discussion below in the combination foundation-GTB section).

Fiscal equity impacts of GTB programs. Figure 4.10 displays the simulation results for a GTB program where the GTB is set at $138,000, which is about the 94th percentile for the sample of districts. Interestingly, this level of GTB would require a decrease in state aid, and would leave the state role at much less than 50 percent of the total at only 29 percent ($155.8 million divided by $536.7 million).

This level of GTB has positive impacts on fiscal equity and adequacy. It reduces revenue-per-pupil disparities. In terms of horizontal equity for students, the coefficient of variation drops to 12.5 percent and the McLoone Index increases to 0.881. It also increases the Adequacy Index to 92.6.

In terms of fiscal neutrality, it reduces the correlation between total revenues per pupil and property value per pupil but more importantly reduces the wealth elasticity to 0.246. The latter is to be expected since the GTB provides equal access to a tax base for districts with 90 percent of all students. This simulation shows the impact a GTB at the 90th percentile can have on the equity of the school finance structure. Use the simulation to view the graph of the GTB results.

Although the GTB is focused on providing equal tax bases and not equal spending, it is nevertheless effective in helping to reduce overall revenue-per-pupil disparities, as the horizontal equity statistics indicate. This impact on closing spending gaps occurs because the GTB raises the effective tax base in low-wealth districts that usually have above-average tax rates. Therefore, when a GTB program is implemented, these districts qualify for substantial new amounts of state aid—due both to their low wealth and their high tax rates—and enables them to both increase their school spending (thus reducing expenditure per-pupil disparities) and reduce their tax rates to more average levels. In short, while a GTB allows for differences in spending based on tax effort, when implemented in most states, it also reduces overall revenue-per-pupil disparities.

The data in Figure 4.10 reveal several other aspects of this GTB as well as of the sample districts before application of the GTB. First, though the GTB covers 94 percent of the students, it only increases aid for 10 of the 20 districts (i.e.,

Adequacy Level	$	5,350		Guaranteed Tax Base	138,000.00
Pupil Weights		no			
Disabled		—			
Limited English		—			
Low Income		—			

District	Pupils	Property Value per Pupil ($)	Old Property Tax Rate (Mills)	New Property Tax Rate (Mills)	Change in Property Tax Rate (Mills)	Old Local Revenue per Pupil ($)	New Local Revenue per Pupil ($)	Change in Local Revenue per Pupil ($)	New State Revenue per Pupil ($)	Change in State Revenue per Pupil ($)	Total Revenue per Pupil ($)	Change in Total Revenue per Pupil ($)
1	1,290	17,456	39.64	32.43	(7.21)	692	566	(126)	3,909	1,121	4,475	995
2	5,648	25,879	38.50	32.37	(6.13)	996	838	(159)	3,629	1,005	4,466	847
3	1,678	31,569	37.15	32.01	(5.14)	1,173	1,010	(162)	3,407	871	4,417	709
4	256	35,698	36.20	31.69	(4.51)	1,292	1,131	(161)	3,242	783	4,374	622
5	10,256	40,258	35.91	31.89	(4.02)	1,446	1,284	(162)	3,117	716	4,401	554
6	956	43,621	35.74	32.19	(3.55)	1,559	1,404	(155)	3,038	645	4,442	490
7	4,689	49,875	34.89	32.29	(2.60)	1,740	1,611	(129)	2,846	488	4,457	358
8	1,656	55,556	34.17	32.20	(1.97)	1,898	1,789	(110)	2,655	382	4,443	272
9	8,954	61,254	33.73	32.39	(1.34)	2,066	1,984	(82)	2,486	267	4,470	185
10	1,488	70,569	33.44	32.84	(0.59)	2,360	2,318	(42)	2,215	124	4,532	82
11	2,416	78,952	33.23	34.09	0.86	2,624	2,691	68	2,013	(68)	4,704	0
12	5,891	86,321	32.89	35.29	2.40	2,839	3,046	207	1,824	(207)	4,870	0
13	2,600	94,387	32.10	36.23	4.13	3,030	3,419	390	1,580	(390)	4,999	0
14	15,489	102,687	31.32	37.34	6.02	3,216	3,835	619	1,319	(619)	5,154	0
15	2,308	112,358	30.85	38.94	8.09	3,466	4,375	909	999	(909)	5,374	0
16	2,712	125,897	30.50	40.32	9.82	3,840	5,076	1,236	488	(1,236)	5,564	0
17	30,256	136,527	30.05	40.79	10.75	4,102	5,570	1,467	60	(1,467)	5,630	0
18	2,056	156,325	28.63	37.74	9.11	4,476	5,899	1,424	0	(1,424)	5,899	0
19	3,121	198,564	27.42	33.11	5.69	5,445	6,575	1,130	0	(1,130)	6,575	0
20	1,523	278,052	25.50	27.07	1.57	7,090	7,527	437	0	0	7,527	0
Weighted Average		97,831	32.34	36.17	3.83	3,028	3,638	610	1,481	-444	5,119	166
Weighted Std. Dev.		48,514	2.91	3.76	6.04	1,269	1,871	674	1,279	882	638	272
Median		102,687	31.32	37.34	6.02	3,216	3,835	619	1,319	-619	5,154	0

Totals

Category	Amount	Percent	Change from Base Amount
Local Revenue	382,907,400	71.07%	64,180,192
State Revenue	155,839,458	28.93%	(46,700,708)
Total Revenue	538,746,858		17,479,484
Pupils	105,243		

Winners and Losers

Category	Winners	Losers	No change
State Aid	10	10	0
Total Rev.	10	0	10

Equity Measures

Horizontal Equity	
Range	$3,153
Restricted Range	2,173
Federal Range Ratio	0.494
Coef. Of Variation	0.125
Gini Coefficient	0.066
McLoone Index	0.866
Verstegen Index	1.086
Fiscal Neutrality	
Correlation	0.984
Elasticity	0.246
Adequacy	
Odden-Picus	0.926

FIGURE 4.10 Guaranteed Tax Base (GTB)

districts 1–10).[10] In the real world, enacting such a school finance program that at best would provide "hold harmless" aid for 50 percent of all districts would be very difficult to enact politically.

Put another way, even though 17 of the 20 districts are eligible for some state aid, only 10 districts would be eligible for greater amounts of state aid, or put differently, 7 of the districts eligible for at least some GTB aid would receive less state aid than under the old structure used by the sample state. Thus, fully half the districts would lose some or all their state aid.

These realities would reduce the political chances of having such a program legislatively enacted. Though the old school finance program arguably allocated too much aid to districts high in property wealth per pupil, and a GTB at the 94th percentile would seemingly be good enough, these actual results suggest that the politics of enactment in the sample state would be difficult at best.

These features of the simulated impact of a relatively high GTB are not dissimilar to the impact of such a GTB in many states today. The reason is that most states allocate some general state aid in sufficiently large amounts to even the wealthiest districts, so that a transition to a GTB—even at a reasonably high level—becomes problematic politically. Though a "hold harmless" provision would blunt the loss of state aid, such an overall program would mean that for most districts their general state aid would not increase in the short to medium run, an unappealing scenario. These realities also mean that unless states that want to enact a GTB program enact one soon, the transition problems of the level of state general aid provided to the highest-wealth districts could worsen over time, making it more complicated to enact a high-level GTB program.

These dilemmas for a GTB are portrayed more drastically for a GTB at $98,000, roughly the statewide average property value per pupil and just above the wealth of district 13, and the wealth of the district that includes 55 percent of the students. (Readers should run this GTB on the simulation and review the results.) Under this program, 8 of the 10 districts will lose state aid, and state aid itself will drop by almost two-thirds. This level of GTB, which is higher than the GTB component of the general aid formula in most states,[11] would not likely be politically feasible in the sample state.

A GTB of $160,000, on the other hand, which guarantees a per-pupil property value higher than nine of the 10 districts, and districts that enroll over 97 percent of the students, would push the state role to 39 percent, would lower the coefficient of variation to just 0.094 and the wealth elasticity to only 0.194, and would increase the Adequacy Index to 0.955. These are substantial impacts.

For such a high-level GTB, however, the simulation probably indicates a higher expenditure per-pupil level for the lower-wealth districts than might occur

---

[10] Recall that the fiscal response model built into the simulation increases the local property tax rate to a level where local funds replace lost state funds for state-aid "losers," and increases expenditures and reduces the tax rate each by half the amount of the state-aid increase for state aid "winners."

[11] Most state GTB programs guarantee the wealth of the district for which the cumulative percent of students is at some level below the 66th percentile.

in practice. It would be unlikely for districts to increase local spending by nearly 50 percent, as the current simulation response model assumes. With a GTB at this high a level, such districts probably would use more than half their state-aid increase to reduce property tax rates; moreover, as discussed in Chapter 1, some low-wealth districts might use most of their state-aid increases for property tax relief rather than expenditure increases. Again, readers should run this GTB using the simulation and review the results, as well as the scatter plot. Indeed, readers should run GTB programs in between $98,000 and $160,000 to find a level that reduces some of the political minuses of the former, but is less costly than the latter.

In summary, guaranteed tax base school finance formulas are relatively simple school finance structures that address a primary structural problem of local financing of schools: unequal access to a school tax base. The GTB remedies this defect by making the tax base equal to the GTB for all districts with a property value per pupil below the GTB. The primary policy question for a GTB is the level at which to set the GTB; courts likely would require the GTB to be set at a level to provide "substantial" equal access to a school property tax base. This would equal the level of the district for which the cumulative percentage of students in that district (and all districts with lower property value per pupil) is at or close to the 90th percentile.

GTB programs reflect the value of choice and local control. Thus, GTB programs allow for differences in per-pupil spending. While spending differences are allowed, they are caused not by differences in property value per pupil but by differences in tax effort. The higher the tax effort, the higher the expenditure per pupil. For policymakers and educators who hold the horizontal equity principle for students above local choice, the GTB program is not the appropriate school finance program.

Further, although GTB programs are fiscal capacity equalizing, the level of state aid is determined both by the GTB level, set by state policy, and by local property tax rates, set by local policy. Thus, the amount of state aid is not under the complete control of state policymakers. This feature has made several states skittish about enacting a GTB program, even though they may prefer it as the general-aid structure. States that have enacted GTB programs, however, have devised several phase-in mechanisms that allow them to control the level of state aid, and have found that over time, local tax rates settle into a predictable pattern that makes forecasting the level of state-aid appropriations no more difficult than for other types of formulas, all of which have variables that require both art and science for predicting and thus determining state-aid needs.

Finally, although guaranteed tax base programs are the most straightforward form of school-aid formulas designed to equalize the tax base, they often do not accomplish their objective of eliminating the link between spending and wealth, especially for the "new" type of school finance program. Because of the vagaries of local behavior, moreover, they often lead to overall rising education expenditures (because they lower the local cost of spending on education) and lead to the new type of school finance problem: high expenditures, high tax rates, and high property wealth per pupil versus low expenditures, low tax rates, and low property wealth per pupil.

It should be noted that many economists predicted these impacts (Feldstein, 1975; Ladd, 1975, and more recently, Reschovsky, 1994). GTB programs lower the local cost, or "price" of spending on education. Rather than just tapping the local tax base at a high tax rate to spend an extra $100 per pupil, the district can tap the GTB and increase that amount of spending at a much lower tax rate. When prices are lowered for desired commodities, such as education, people usually buy more of that commodity. So economic theory would predict higher overall education spending with a high-level GTB program. Secondly, research showed that the demand elasticity for education was often low in low–property wealth districts, which were also typically low in average household income, and high in higher–property wealth, higher–household income districts, such as metropolitan suburban districts. Thus, these economists predicted that lower-wealth districts would decide not to raise relative spending very much while the higher-wealth districts would decide just the opposite.

To verify these ostensibly deleterious elements of GTB programs, Odden (1999) simulated pure forms of GTB programs for the three "new" school finance problem states discussed in Chapter 1—Illinois, Missouri, and Wisconsin—by setting the GTB at the 95th percentile of property wealth per pupil and providing GTB aid for all levels of spending. All of the equity statistics worsened; spending disparities widened and the relationship between spending and property wealth strengthened. More-generous GTB programs were not what these states needed to improve fiscal equity. We discuss this issue further in Chapter 5.

Combination Foundation and Guaranteed Tax Base Programs

States also have enacted combination school finance formulas. These two-tier plans usually include two different school finance formulas in the overall approach to providing general education aid through a fiscal capacity equalizing program. One type of formula is used for the base, or tier-one program, and another type of formula is used for spending above the base, or tier-two program.

Missouri has had a two-tiered, combination foundation and guaranteed tax base program since the late 1970s. Similar to many states, Missouri had a minimum foundation program before it underwent a school finance reform in 1977. The program, which was enacted in 1977 and then updated in 1993, retained the foundation program to ensure a base spending level, a key feature of a foundation approach. The 1993 bill set the foundation expenditure level at just below the previous year's statewide average expenditure per pupil. For the second tier, the legislature put a GTB program on top, so that districts wanting to spend above the foundation level could have equal extra spending for equal extra tax rates. The 1993 bill set the GTB at the wealth of the district for which, after rank ordering all districts on the basis of property value per pupil, the cumulative percentage of students was 95 percent (i.e., the 95th percentile). The bill was technically written as a GTB at the 95th percentile, with a minimum tax rate that determined the foundation expenditure base (i.e., the GTB was also the "zero-aid" district for the foundation portion of the formula). GTB aid was provided for spending up to the 95th percentile of expenditures per pupil.

The combination approach was used for other new school finance formulas established during the early months of 1990. Both Texas and Kentucky, under court order to revise their school finance structures, enacted combination foundation and guaranteed tax base programs. In Texas, the 1989–90 foundation program provided a base spending level of $1,477, equal to about 42 percent of the statewide average expenditure per pupil. The guaranteed tax base program was set at $182,500, the wealth of the district just below the statewide average of $191,300. Texas placed a tax-rate cap on the GTB component of the formula, providing GTB aid for just an extra 3.6 mills above the foundation required tax rate, or for an extra $657 per pupil. Districts were also allowed to levy higher tax rates, for which revenues were derived solely from the local tax base.

Kentucky enacted a similar type of combination program. The 1989–90 foundation base was set at $2,305, which was about 77 percent of the statewide average. Kentucky also put a GTB on top of the foundation program, setting it at about 150 percent of the statewide average. This GTB program, however, included two tiers, each with its own type of tax-rate cap. The first tier limited the additional tax rate beyond which districts could not receive GTB aid, but it gave school boards the flexibility to increase spending (and thus the local tax rate) by 15 percent over the foundation base and still receive GTB aid. In addition, taxpayers can increase spending by a local vote (and thus the local tax rate) by another 15 percent but are not eligible for GTB aid for this second 15 percent spending boost. Thus, expenditures above the foundation base are limited to an additional 30 percent, half of which is fiscal capacity equalized by a GTB.

This combination approach merges the best features of the foundation and GTB programs and simultaneously remedies a major defect of each. The foundation portion of the combined program first ensures a base spending level, usually above what had been a minimum level. This base spending level, a key feature of foundation programs, is financed with a combination of local and state funds. The spending base remedies a possible shortcoming of pure GTB programs that do not require a minimum spending level.

The GTB portion of the combined program ensures equal education spending per pupil for equal tax rates above the foundation required tax rate. This component remedies a defect of a minimum foundation program: unequalized spending above the foundation base.

The combination foundation and GTB formula.   The formula for calculating the foundation portion of the combination program is the same as that for the regular foundation program:

$$SFAPP = FEPP - (RTR \times PVPP)$$

where

$$SFAPP = \text{state foundation aid per pupil,}$$
$$FEPP = \text{foundation expenditure per pupil,}$$
$$RTR = \text{the local required tax rate, and}$$
$$PVPP = \text{local property value per pupil.}$$

Total foundation state aid would be:

$$TFSA = SFAPP \times \text{Pupils}$$

where

$$TFSA = \text{total foundation state aid,}$$
$$SFAPP = \text{state foundation aid per pupil, and}$$
$$\text{Pupils} = \text{the number of students in the school district.}$$

For the GTB portion, state aid would be:

$$SGTBAPP = (DTR - RTR) \times (GTB - PVPP)$$

where

SGTBAPP = state guaranteed tax-base aid per pupil,
DTR = the local district property tax rate,
RTR = the required tax base for the foundation program (GTB aid is provided only for tax rates above the foundation required tax rate),
GTB = the tax rate guaranteed by the state, in thousand dollars of property value per pupil, and
PVPP = the local district property value per pupil.

Total GTB state aid, therefore, is:

$$TGTBSA = SGTBAPP \times \text{Pupils}$$

where

TGTBSA = total guaranteed tax-base state aid,
SGTBAPP = state guaranteed tax-base aid per pupil from the above formula, and
Pupils = the number of students in the school district.

Total state general aid for the combination program, therefore, would be:

$$TSA = TFSA + TGTBSA.$$

Combination foundation and GTB program policy issues.   A combination foundation and GTB program can be a fairly attractive package. Both components of
the program require local matching funds and provide for fiscal capacity equalization. A base spending level is guaranteed. The ability to spend above the base is
possible on an equal basis for rich and poor districts alike, thus providing a fiscally
neutral system, at least on an ex ante basis. And two American values—concern
for the bottom half and local choice—are tied together in a single general aid
program.

The downside of the GTB portion of the combination program is that it
allows for different spending levels and thus does not conform to the horizontal
equity principle for students. But the fact is that this value conflicts with the
value of local choice, so that both values cannot be satisfied by any one formula.
The combination foundation-GTB program is about the closest a school finance
formula can come to adhering to both of these values. There is an expenditure
equality dimension, in terms of a base program that is mandated for all students. But there is local choice to spend above this base. If a state enacted a
cap on the level of extra expenditures, such as the 30 percent cap in Kentucky,
the program might be more appealing to those who champion horizontal equity
for children.

At the same time, as discussed above, the second-tier GTB has turned out
to function as an incentive to spend more primarily in suburban, above-average-
wealth districts. As a result, the two-tier systems, just like unbridled GTB programs, create a system that generally produces the "new" school finance problem:
low-spending, low-tax-rate and low-wealth districts versus high-spending, high-
tax-rate, and high (or above-average) wealth districts, which some would not consider to be a fair system.

Figure 4.11 depicts graphically how a combination foundation-GTB program works. The lowest horizontal line shows that the minimum revenues per
pupil are the foundation expenditure level of $2,000. The upper two horizontal
lines reflect the impact of a GTB at $75,000 for total tax rates of 30 and 40 mills
(with 20 mills being the required tax rate for the foundation portion of the program). Note that the zero-aid district level for the foundation portion of the program is $100,000 and, obviously, $75,000 for the GTB portion of the program.
For each tax-rate level, the revenue-per-pupil line is initially horizontal and then
slopes upward only beyond the level of the zero-aid district, indicating that districts with a property value per pupil above this level will raise more per pupil
than is provided even by the GTB.

There are several issues that need to be addressed with a combination
foundation-GTB program. The first two are the general policy targets of:

1. The level of base spending in the foundation program and
2. The level of the GTB.

The same considerations raised above for each program individually can be applied to the combination program. States might set the base expenditure at a

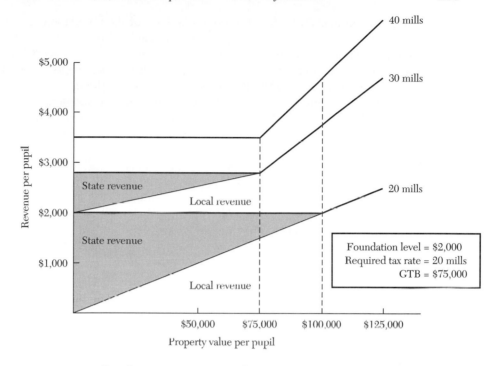

FIGURE 4.11 Graphical Representation of the Impact of a Combination Foundation and Guaranteed Tax Base Program

level sufficiently high for districts, on average, to provide an adequate education program. This type of policy target could become a new rationale for how high the base spending in state foundation programs should be in the future. Though not exactly stated in its new legislation, Kentucky sought to take this approach in its 1990 school finance reform.

For ex ante fiscal neutrality, the GTB also needs to be set at a relatively high level, such as the 90th percentile of property wealth per pupil. On the other hand, there may be some flexibility for the GTB level. For example, if the base spending level is set high enough for the average student to meet ambitious student-achievement objectives, the state might want to limit local add-ons, to 30 percent as Kentucky has done, or even to a smaller amount. At this point, since all students on average have been funded for an education program designed to meet some new high-performance level, one could argue that local add-ons are merely an element of local choice on how to spend discretionary income. Thus, a GTB at just the statewide average, or the 50th percentile, which would focus the GTB on equal access to a tax base just for the bottom half, might be viewed as sufficient. How these policy dilemmas will play out in different states remains to be seen.

The key conceptual point in the above two paragraphs is that there is potentially an implicit trade-off between the level of the foundation base spending and the level of the GTB. If the base spending level is high enough to teach most students to meet bold new achievement levels, the base level will in itself require new education funds and substantially raise school spending for all students. Fewer districts will feel they need to spend above the base. Thus, because GTB-aided spending becomes much more a matter of discretionary spending, the GTB level can be focused on districts with below-average spending. Extra spending could even be capped, since spending levels would already be at much higher levels.

On the other hand, if the base spending level is much lower, then the GTB component becomes a much larger portion of the overall program, and its level becomes much more critical to the fiscal equity impact of the system. If the base spending level is low, more districts—undoubtedly more than half the districts—would want to spend more. Thus, local add-ons become a larger part of the overall system. In order to make the system fiscally neutral, the GTB would have to be set at a high level, such as the 90th percentile.

There is a plausible rationale for having a lower foundation base spending level and a higher GTB level. The substantive argument concerns differences in educational needs and costs between metropolitan (urban and suburban) and nonmetropolitan (rural) districts. In most states, foundation expenditure per-pupil levels are too low for most districts to provide an adequate education program. But often, a modest increase in the foundation level would be sufficient to allow most nonmetropolitan school districts to provide an adequate education program.

But raising the foundation expenditure to a level that would be sufficient for metropolitan districts, which usually face educational prices that are from 10 to 20 percent higher than in nonmetropolitan districts, usually is too expensive for the state. Moreover, raising the foundation expenditure to a level that would allow metropolitan districts to provide an adequate program could, then, also allow nonmetropolitan districts to provide a higher-level quality program than they need. Indeed, it might provide so much money for rural districts that some local education leaders and their legislatures would argue that excessive funds were being allocated to schools.

Though the divergence between the resource needs of urban and rural districts should not be overstated, this is an issue that arises in nearly all states that seek to raise the foundation base to a level sufficient to provide an adequate education program. In states with the most ambitious policymakers, the level usually becomes more than rural districts need for adequacy and less than urban districts need, a compromise that is not efficient for either.

However, this dilemma could be remedied by setting the base at an adequate level for the lowest-cost districts and then adjusting it by a price index (Chambers, 1981, 1995; McMahon, 1994; Monk and Walker, 1991; Wendling, 1981b) for districts facing higher costs. But, an education price index, though technically straightforward to develop, has only been enacted in a few states, such as Texas and Ohio. Education price indices are discussed further in Section 2.

Fiscal equity impacts of combination foundation and GTB programs. Figure 4.12 shows such a combination program with the foundation set at the median, the required tax rate at the median, and the GTB add-on at about the 94th percentile. This is a fairly generous combination, two-tier school finance system.

For this simulated program, both local and state revenues increase. Local revenues increase in the wealthier districts and decrease in the poorer districts. The state role rises to nearly 41 percent. The impact on equity and adequacy is quite impressive: The coefficient of variation is below 10 percent, the McLoone Index is above 95 percent, the Verstegen Index is just 4.4 percent, and the Adequacy Index is 99 percent. These positive impacts are a result in part of the generous parameters of the program, simulated as well as the fact that the base data represent the typical school finance problem. Readers should run additional combination simulations that are somewhat less generous than the one depicted in Figure 4.12.

At the same time, combination foundation-GTB programs might not be a desired approach for states that represent the "new" school finance problem such as Illinois, Missouri, New York, and Wisconsin. Odden (1999) analyzed the results of adding a second-tier, 90/90 GTB to the adequate foundation program that was defined as the median expenditure level. The GTB was set at the 90th percentile of district wealth and provided aid to districts spending up to the 90th percentile of expenditures per pupil. He found that nearly all of the equity statistics worsen. Moreover, the extra state cost was considerable. Because these states represent the newer version of fiscal disparities (higher spending associated with higher tax rates, both attributes associated with higher wealth), the equity results are not surprising.

For states with these types of problems, the results show that GTB programs, even on top of adequate foundation spending levels, simply worsen fiscal equity. The results suggest that GTB school finance elements should probably not be a primary part of school finance systems for such states. Nevertheless, many school finance experts, including these authors in the first edition of this book (Odden and Picus, 1992) for years recommended second-tier GTB programs on top of foundation programs. Given the negative impact on fiscal equity as well as the considerable costs of such additions, such recommendations should be viewed skeptically in the future. Indeed, since a GTB simply assists districts in spending above an adequate level, one could argue that such a program, whatever its effects on fiscal equity, is beyond the state interest in school finance. The adequate spending base and the adjustments for special needs discussed below largely fulfill the state interest.

Full-State Funding and State-Determined Spending Programs

The final category of school funding programs has generally been referred to as full-state funding. A full-state funding program implements the equality value, or horizontal equity, for students by simply setting an equal expenditure per-pupil level for all districts. Districts cannot spend less than this amount nor can they

Adequacy Level	$ 5,350

Foundation Level	$5,154.00
Required Tax Rate	31.32

Pupil Weights	no
Disabled	—
Limited English	—
Low Income	—

GTB	no
GTB rate cap above	$138,000.00
foundation tax rate	99.00

District	Pupils	Property Value per Pupil ($)	Old Property Tax Rate (Mills)	New Property Tax Rate (Mills)	Change in Property Tax Rate (Mills)	Old Local Revenue per Pupil ($)	New Local Revenue per Pupil ($)	Change in Local Revenue per Pupil ($)	New State Foundation Revenue per Pupil ($)	New State GTB Revenue per Pupil ($)	Change in State Revenue per Pupil ($)	Total Revenue per Pupil ($)	Change in Total Revenue per Pupil ($)
1	1,290	17,456	39.64	35.48	(4.16)	692	619	(73)	4,607	501	2,321	5,728	2,248
2	5,648	25,879	38.50	34.91	(3.59)	996	903	(93)	4,343	403	2,123	5,649	2,030
3	1,678	31,569	37.15	34.23	(2.91)	1,173	1,081	(92)	4,165	310	1,940	5,556	1,848
4	256	35,698	36.20	33.76	(2.44)	1,292	1,205	(87)	4,036	250	1,826	5,491	1,739
5	10,256	40,258	35.91	33.62	(2.30)	1,446	1,353	(92)	3,893	224	1,716	5,471	1,624
6	956	43,621	35.74	33.53	(2.21)	1,559	1,463	(96)	3,788	209	1,603	5,459	1,507
7	4,689	49,875	34.89	33.11	(1.79)	1,740	1,651	(89)	3,592	157	1,391	5,400	1,302
8	1,656	55,556	34.17	32.75	(1.43)	1,898	1,819	(79)	3,414	118	1,259	5,351	1,179
9	8,954	61,254	33.73	32.53	(1.21)	2,066	1,992	(74)	3,236	92	1,110	5,320	1,036
10	1,488	70,569	33.44	32.38	(1.06)	2,360	2,285	(75)	2,944	71	924	5,300	850
11	2,416	78,952	33.23	32.28	(0.95)	2,624	2,548	(75)	2,681	56	657	5,286	582
12	5,891	86,321	32.89	32.11	(0.78)	2,839	2,771	(68)	2,450	41	460	5,262	392
13	2,600	94,387	32.10	31.71	(0.39)	3,030	2,993	(37)	2,198	17	245	5,208	209
14	15,489	102,687	31.32	31.32	0.00	3,216	3,216	0	1,938	0	0	5,154	0
15	2,308	112,358	30.85	32.91	2.06	3,466	3,698	232	1,635	41	(232)	5,374	0
16	2,712	125,897	30.50	34.29	3.79	3,840	4,317	477	1,211	36	(477)	5,564	0
17	30,256	136,527	30.05	34.77	4.72	4,102	4,747	644	878	5	(644)	5,630	0
18	2,056	156,325	28.63	36.09	7.46	4,476	5,641	1,166	258	0	(1,166)	5,899	0
19	3,121	198,564	27.42	33.11	5.69	5,445	6,575	1,130	0	0	(1,130)	6,575	0
20	1,523	278,052	25.50	27.07	1.57	7,090	7,527	437	0	0	(437)	7,527	0
Weighted Average		97,831	32.34	33.34	1.00	3,028	3,257	229	2,173	82	331	5,512	559
Weighted Std. Dev.		48,514	2.91	1.55	3.15	1,269	1,596	380	1,318	120	1,011	363	478
Median		102,687	31.32	31.32	0.00	3,216	3,216	0	1,938	0	0	5,471	0

Totals

Category	Amount	Percent	Change from Base Amount
Local Revenue	342,810,303	59.09%	24,083,095
State Revenue	237,324,515	40.91%	34,784,349
Total Revenue	580,134,818		58,867,444
Pupils	105,243		

Winners and Losers

Category	Winners	Losers	No change
State Aid	16	0	4
Total Rev.	20	0	0

Equity Measures

Horizontal Equity	
Range	$2,373
Restricted Range	1,367
Federal Range Ratio	0.262
Coef. of Variation	0.066
Gini Coefficient	1.000
McLoone Index	1.009
Verstegen Index	12264.273
Fiscal Neutrality	
Correlation	0.768
Elasticity	0.115
Adequacy	
Odden-Picus	0.99

FIGURE 4.12 Combination Program

spend more. For this reason, if a state wants to implement the horizontal equity principle for students (i.e., a program that provides for equal spending), a full-state funding program is the only choice.

As the name of the program connotes, in the pure form, such a program is fully funded with state revenues, which is the case in Hawaii. But that is not a necessary characteristic of such a program. The key characteristic is that a "full-state funding" program requires equal spending per pupil in all districts. The revenues, however, could be derived from a combination of state revenues and local property tax revenues. The state could require a uniform statewide property tax rate for schools and set state aid as the difference between what that would raise and the total revenues needed to provide the equal spending level. This has been the approach taken by New Mexico for years and also the approach of the 1998 school finance reform in Vermont. California has a version of full-state funding called a revenue limit program. The state sets a base spending per-pupil level for each district and finances it with a combination of state and local property tax revenues. It is conceptually equivalent to a full-state funding program.

Likewise, Florida has a different approach that makes the system function almost like a full-state funding program, financed with a combination of state and local revenues. Florida has a combination foundation and GTB program, but the GTB program has an absolute maximum tax-rate cap. Since most districts are at the cap, and since the GTB is higher than the wealth of most districts, the structure comes close to being the equivalent of a full-state funding program.

In this book, full-state funding is used to indicate a school finance program that requires equal per-pupil spending across all school districts. The program can be financed solely with state funds, but also can be financed with a combination of state and local funds, usually property tax revenues. For our purposes, the defining element of a full-state funding program is that districts cannot spend less or more than the level set by the state, thereby satisfying the horizontal equity principle.

3. ADJUSTMENTS FOR STUDENT NEEDS, EDUCATION LEVEL, SCALE ECONOMIES AND PRICE

This section discusses four types of vertical equity adjustments: special student needs, education level (elementary and secondary), scale economies/diseconomies, and geographic price indices. There are many different ways of determining just how much adjustment is necessary, as well as many different methods of providing those adjustments. The section that follows explores all of these possibilities, raising a number of policy questions in the process.

Adjustments for Different Pupil Needs

If different pupil needs that required extra educational resources were evenly distributed across all school districts in a given state, neither special adjustments to regular school finance formulas nor separate categorical programs would be needed. The extra amounts could be included in the spending levels set for the regular program. But, the distribution of different pupil needs is not distributed evenly across all school districts. Students from homes with incomes below the poverty level tend to be concentrated in large, urban districts and in small, typically rural, isolated school districts. Low-income students are much less prevalent in suburban school districts. Similarly, students for whom English is not the primary language are also not found in equal percentages in all types of school districts; these students also tend to enroll in greater percentages in urban and rural school districts. Nor are students with physical or mental disabilities found in equal concentrations in all school districts; indeed, some suburban school districts that have developed especially effective programs for disabled children see the percentage of such students rise as parents move to that district in order for their student to have access to the outstanding program.

In short, the demographics of students with different types of special educational needs vary from school district to school district. Some districts have a higher concentration of such students than others do. Indeed, some of the largest metropolitan school districts have extraordinarily high percentages of students who need supplemental educational services, approaching 50 percent in the largest districts in the country, such as Chicago, Dallas, Los Angeles, and New York City.

Furthermore, the prices districts face in providing these additional services vary considerably, further intensifying the fiscal burden caused by these special-needs students. Large central cities face the highest prices and usually have the highest concentration of special-needs students. Many rural districts, which generally have lower prices, tend to face high costs for special-needs students because the low incidence dramatically increases the per-pupil costs of the necessary services. For example, if there is only one blind student in a rural school, the cost for providing appropriate services is spread over just that one student, while in more populated areas, the incidence of blindness is typically higher, so that the costs of providing the additional services can be spread over more children.

If states required local districts to provide the necessary supplemental services solely from local funds, they would be placing an extra financial burden on districts that would vary substantially by district. Further, since the incidence of special-needs students is not necessarily related to local fiscal capacity, such a state requirement could worsen school finance inequities. In short, because of demographics and price differences, a state role is necessary to make the provision of extra services for special-needs students fair across all schools districts. This section discusses school finance programs to accommodate these vertical equity adjustments that recognize how differences among students require providing more services to meet their special needs.

Development of Special-Needs Programs

There is a rich developmental history associated with the major special-needs programs: (1) compensatory education programs for low-income students;

(2) language acquisition programs for Limited English proficient (LEP) students (Hodge, 1981); and (3) special-education programs for physical and mentally disabled students (Verstegen, 1999). Both the federal government and the states have been major actors in this history.

Compensatory education.   The federal involvement in compensatory education began in 1965 with passage of the Elementary and Secondary Education Act (ESEA); Title I provided grants to local school districts on the basis of the number of students from families with incomes below the poverty level. Within districts, schools were to use the funds to provide extra educational services for low-achieving students. While there is a long history of implementation of this federal compensatory education program, by the early 1980s the program was firmly in place across the country (Odden, 1991).

Further, while in the early years a substantial portion of Title I dollars supplanted, or replaced, local dollars, by the end of the 1970s each Title I dollar produced a minimum of an extra dollar of expenditures on compensatory education programs (Odden, 1988). A series of rules and regulations developed during the 1970s, focused primarily on funds allocation and use, helped produce these end-of-the-decade fiscal outcomes. "Comparability" required districts to allocate district and state funds equally across schools before allocating Title I dollars. "Supplement and not supplant" required districts to ensure that Title I dollars provided extra educational services and did not merely replace local funds. And "children in greatest need" requirements ensured that only the children with the lowest student achievement were eligible to receive extra educational services provided by Title I funds.

In 1981, ESEA was replaced with the Education Consolidation and Improvement Act (ECIA), and Title I was replaced by Chapter 1. In 1988, the Hawkins-Stafford School Improvement Amendments made several changes to Chapter 1 with the intent of improving compensatory education programs across the country. During the 1990–91 school year, Chapter 1 provided approximately $5.4 billion to serve close to 5 million children. In 1994, the Improving America's Schools Act was passed, which reauthorized Title I of the ESEA, and changed the name of the program back to Title I. This act represented a shift in federal aid to education, giving new responsibilities to states, districts, and the federal government to ensure quality education for low-income children.

Title I, and for a time Chapter 1, stimulated many states to enact their own compensatory education programs. Most state programs were designed to complement the federal program. California and New York were among the first states to enact compensatory education programs. A major issue for many state programs, and an issue also raised for the federal program, was whether to distribute funds on the basis of poverty, an indirect measure of student need, or student achievement, a direct measure of student need. The New York program allocates funds on the basis of student achievement criteria, while the California program uses a poverty index.

The politics surrounding the enactment of Title I (Bailey and Mosher, 1968;

Ravitch, 1983) supported poverty as the measure of need because it ensured that funds flowed disproportionately to large cities, primarily those in the Midwest and Northeast, and to rural areas, primarily in the South. Representatives of these areas were the strongest supporters of ESEA, and their districts felt they had greatest need for federal support. If compensatory education funds were instead distributed on the basis of student achievement, dollars would flow out of rural and urban areas and into suburban areas, since all districts have low-achieving students, but not as many low-income students attend suburban schools. Whatever educational argument is used to rationalize the allocation of compensatory education funds, these political dimensions affect the final compensatory education program design.

In the early 1980s, nearly 20 states had compensatory education programs in their general-aid formula, with about 10 states distributing the funds on the basis of pupil weights (McGuire, 1982). A mixture of poverty and student-achievement measures determined student eligibility. In 1993–94, the number of states with compensatory education programs and/or compensatory education pupil weights increased to 28. Figure 4.14 lists states' approaches to funding compensatory education.

It is important to keep in mind that while both federal and state compensatory programs provide opportunities for low-achieving students to receive additional educational services, the programs do not establish a legal right to such extra services. The services are available solely because of the federal and state programs.

Bilingual education.   Services for students with limited English proficiency emerged in the mid-1970s primarily after the 1974 *Lau* v. *Nicholas*[12] case in California. This case was brought in San Francisco where students who did not speak English were immersed in classes taught in English. While the case was filed as an equal protection case, it was decided on the basis of federal antidiscrimination laws. The court held that it was discriminatory to place non-English speaking students in classes where the language of instruction was English. As a result, districts created bilingual programs that provided instruction in English as a second language and instruction in subject matter classes in the student's native language until they learned enough English to be instructed in English only.

While debates have surrounded various approaches to bilingual education, the key finding of *Lau* is that the language capability of students must be considered in designing an appropriate instructional environment. Today, for example, when one class might have students with many different native languages, bilingual instruction is not possible, and a "sheltered English" instructional approach may be an acceptable option (Krashen and Biber, 1988). In all instructional approaches, lessons have dual objectives: development of English language as well as content knowledge. The *Lau* decision made access to a language-appropriate classroom environment a legal right of all LEP students.

[12] 414 U.S. 653.

In 1967, just prior to the *Lau* ruling, Title VII was added to the federal ESEA program. Title VII provided funds for districts to design and implement bilingual education programs. Funds were available on a proposal basis only; districts wrote proposals, and a review process determined which proposals received funding. In 1990, the federal government provided about $189 million for bilingual education. In 1998, the amount of federal monies allocated to bilingual education in the form of instructional services, support services, professional development, and foreign language assistance was approximately $204 million. The population of LEP students in this country continues to grow. Some estimates say that there are now 50 percent more LEP students than there were in 1990 (Pompa, 1998). Three states—New York, California, and Texas—continue to enroll the majority of LEP students, but populations are growing in Arizona, Florida, Illinois, New Mexico, Oklahoma, and Washington as well.

States began to provide bilingual education programs in part as a response to *Lau,* and many more are finding it necessary today due to the growing numbers cited above. In 1975, 13 states had bilingual education programs. By 1993–94, 30 states had bilingual education programs, many of which were allocated on the basis of pupil weights. Figure 4.15 on page 221 lists states' approaches to funding bilingual education programs.

Special education. For years, most states have supported special-education programs for physically and mentally disabled students, at least to some degree (Verstegen, 1999). But during the late 1960s and early 1970s, it became apparent that many disabled students were being prohibited from attending local public schools. Whether certain disabilities were so severe they required very costly services, or because of blatant discrimination against disabled individuals, these exclusions were challenged under equal protection litigation. One of the first court decisions occurred in the *Pennsylvania Association of Retarded Children* v. *Pennsylvania* (PARC) case in 1972, in which a Pennsylvania court held that district actions prohibiting disabled students from attending local public schools violated the equal protection clause of the U.S. Constitution. This decision spawned several other court cases as well as a spate of new federal and state policy initiatives.

In 1975, Congress enacted the federal Education for all Handicapped Children Act, P.L. 94-142, now known as the Individuals with Disabilities Education Act (IDEA). This sweeping new federal program essentially made access to a free, appropriate, public education program a legal right of all children. In order to receive any federal education dollars, states had to demonstrate that they were providing appropriate special-education services to all disabled children. The services had to meet a series of detailed new federal requirements, many of which had been written into the P.L. 94-142 law itself. While several states initially responded negatively to the detailed federal requirements, and some states refused all federal education aid for a few years, today all states comply with the mandates of this federal law.

P.L. 94-142 authorizes the federal government to fund up to 40 percent of nationwide costs for special-education services. In the year it was enacted,

Congress appropriated $300 million or about $74 per disabled student, much less than the 40 percent that had been authorized. In 1990, federal outlays for special education were $2 billion, and by 1998 that figure climbed to $3.8 billion (both in constant FY 1998 dollars), (National Center for Education Statistics, 1998b). According to the most recent data collected by the U.S. Department of Education, approximately 4.7 million children between the ages of 6 and 17 qualified for special-education services in the 1994–95 school year, representing about a tenth of the total school-age population. Of all the dollars spent on special education in this country, the most up-to-date estimate of the federal portion is 8 percent (National Research Council, 1999).

Federal funds are allocated on a per-pupil flat grant basis. The federal law requires that states identify students in the following 12 special-education categories:

1. deaf,
2. deaf and blind,
3. hard of hearing,
4. mentally retarded,
5. multihandicapped,
6. orthopedically impaired,
7. other health impaired,
8. seriously emotionally disturbed,
9. learning disabled,
10. speech impaired,
11. visually impaired, and
12. autistic.

In 1995–96, the incidence of students with disabilities comprised approximately 10 percent of the national school-age population, with individual state figures ranging from approximately 6 to 15 percent.[13] As discussed below, many states use the federal student categories to structure their state programs for the handicapped. Even though the per-pupil costs of providing services varies substantially by category, the federal program allocates the same flat grant amount for each identified student, regardless of category.

In the late 1980s, a regular-education initiative was begun by a diverse group of individuals who believed that a focus on labeling disabled students into a number of special categories and often pulling students out of regular classrooms for instruction was doing more harm than good for many of these students. This initiative reinforced the earlier views of many that labeling students was not the best approach to providing extra services for these students. Instead, many ar-

---

[13] The National Research Council estimated the national special-education student population in 1998; the state ranges given are from a 1995 Center for Special Education Finance report, which listed the percent of special-education students in each state in 1987–88, when the national figure was also 10 percent.

gued that all students had particular needs, and that schools should identify the different types of services necessary to serve their student population. The service levels needed could then determine funding. States such as Iowa and Massachusetts, in fact, structured their state programs for the disabled on this basis. Nevertheless, the federal student-labeling requirements have not changed substantively and generally are used, in some form, by most states (see also Chambers and Hartman, 1983).

In the 1990s, the regular-education initiative transformed into a more "inclusive" initiative. The goal, generally consistent with the original intent of P.L. 94-142, was to include disabled students in regular-education classrooms. Although there has been significant controversy over how best to implement inclusive practices, this remains the dominant service delivery focus for disabled students today (McDonnell, McLaughlin, and Morison, 1997).

Issues in Determining Costs of Special-Needs Programs

There are four major categories of issues that must be addressed in assessing and calculating costs for special needs programs, these categories cut across all special needs programs. They are: (1) defining student eligibility; (2) identifying appropriate services; (3) determining the appropriate placement; and (4) calculating state and local cost shares.

Student eligibility.   Since most states allocate special-needs funds on the basis of the number of eligible students, regulations on student eligibility become quite important. As mentioned above, compensatory education program guidelines define "eligibility" in two ways: (1) poverty measures such as household income, eligibility for free or reduced-price lunch, or some other measure of poverty or (2) achievement measures including the type of tests used, the content areas to be tested, and degree of divergence from the average or grade norm. States have used the number of students from families eligible for Aid to Families with Dependent Children, but with the changes in welfare policy, that practice is declining. Special-education programs need guidelines on the number of discrete handicapping categories, assessment procedures, and whether there are "caps" on eligibility in any one category, such as the federal 2 percent cap on the learning disabled (see Moore, Strang, Schwartz, and Braddock, 1988). Bilingual education programs need to identify the types of language examinations that can be used and criteria for determining partial or full English proficiency (i.e., criteria for determining the transition into "sheltered English" instruction or into the regular classroom). In each area, these issues become quite complex. Finally, there is pressure to move away from narrow categories of student eligibility to broader categories, such as simply needing a low, medium, or high level of extra services.

Further, eligible age ranges need to be identified. In many states, disabled children from birth to 21 are eligible for public education services; other states limit eligibility to conventional school age. Mainly school-age children are eligible for compensatory and bilingual education services, although for these programs most of the money is spent at the elementary level. A service and policy issue is whether secondary students should also have these extra services.

Finally, the incidence of special-needs students varies widely overall and by program. While the incidence of disabled students is about 10 percent nation-wide, some estimate that the total number of at-risk students might be as high as 25 percent (Pallas, Natriello, and McDill, 1988).

Appropriate services.   Program guidelines also need to identify the range of services on which funds can be spent. Some programs restrict spending to current operating activities, while others allow capital expenditures such as buildings and equipment as well. Within operating expenditures, some programs allow only instructional expenditures, whereas others permit spending on other functional categories, such as transportation, which is generally costly. Within instructional expenditures, some programs limit spending to certain subject areas, such as reading and mathematics, while others allow spending on all academic content areas, including art, music, and physical education.

Another issue is the degree to which program funds can be spent on administration. Because many categorical programs need special management and have reporting requirements—to ensure that only eligible students are served and that funds are spent as intended—many districts have created special categorical program administration staff to manage the program and meet reporting and compliance requirements. Many programs specify a maximum portion of program funds that can be spent on administration.

Other service issues include the diagnostic activities necessary to determine placement, class-size policies, and length of school day and year for special programs. Also at issue are the "related services" such as counseling, medical, occupational therapy, and parent counseling that may be required for special-education students. It has been difficult to determine the level of need for these services; the guideline has been that related services are required if they are related to educational need. Related services can become costly for students with multiple physical disabilities, so these guidelines can have a substantial impact on special-education costs.

Another issue is the comprehensiveness and level of quality of special services. The *Rowley* court decision held that disabled students were required to have access to an adequate educational program, but not the highest-quality educational program that would optimize their intellectual growth. In this case, a blind individual sued a district to force employment of a teacher to read materials in a one-to-one tutoring situation, arguing that such a service was needed to maximize her learning. The district refused, and the court upheld the district's action, stating that the P.L. 94-142 required provision of only adequate educational services, not services to maximize student performance. Of course, standards-based education reform has set a high bar for what cannot be considered adequate, even for disabled children (Goertz, McLaughlin, Roach, and Raber, 1999).

Educational placement.   The method by which educational services are provided to students with special needs can produce substantial cost variations for students at the same grade level and with the same special-education need. There are five basic placement categories: (1) preschool; (2) resource program; (3) self-contained classroom; (4) home or hospital program; and (5) residential care. Most compensatory education and bilingual education programs are provided through resource programs, as are special-education services for disabled students who are mainstreamed in the regular-education program. Moore et al. (1988) and Chambers and Parrish (1983) show how costs vary widely—by a factor of 2 to 1—across different educational placements. In the 1990s, individual tutoring has also become a service strategy; this clearly is the most costly service approach.

Costs. Once decisions are made about student eligibility, types of services required, eligibility for reimbursement, and educational placement, program costs are relatively easy to calculate. One of the most sophisticated mechanisms for determining special-needs program costs is the Resource Cost Model (RCM) (Chambers and Parrish, 1994; Chambers, 1999). Using groups of professional educator experts, the RCM first identified base staffing levels for the regular-education program, and then identified effective program practices and their staffing and resource needs for compensatory, special, and bilingual education. All ingredients were costed out using average price figures but, in determining the foundation base dollar amount for each district, the totals were adjusted by an education price index. Such a program could be used by a state to determine the level of cost associated with numerous local special-needs programs, but no state has yet adopted such a model. Nevertheless, it is a robust analytic tool that can be used to determine costs for special-needs programs.

Of course, after total costs have been determined, the next task is to identify the state and local shares of those costs. Those issues are discussed next.

General approaches to formula adjustments for special-needs students. States have adopted several different mechanisms to finance programs for special-needs students. These strategies can be divided into two general approaches. The first is for the state to cover the entire cost of providing the additional services. This approach certainly has strong appeal to local districts and eliminates fiscal inequities caused by requiring local districts to finance these services by raising local revenues. Under this approach, local districts document the extra costs and submit a reimbursement claim to the state each year. Alternatively, if the program costs are "forward-funded," districts submit an application for reimbursement of estimated costs. The state then needs a reconciliation mechanism to ensure that payments equal actual costs. Modifying the next year's payment by the difference between predicted and actual costs is a straightforward example of such an adjustment.

A full-state funded approach to programs for special-needs students requires rigorous state oversight or an audit mechanism to ensure that only legitimate local costs are reimbursed. With the state paying the full cost of the extra services, local districts would have a fiscal incentive to develop and implement comprehensive, high-quality programs. If the state had neither cost controls nor regulatory guidelines that monitored local programs, state costs could soar. While any state reimbursement program for special-needs students requires some regulatory and program guidelines, such mechanisms are an absolute requirement for a state program that reimburses 100 percent of local costs.

Over the long term, it is difficult for states to fully fund all special services. When service provision is mandated, as is the case for special education, a drop in state funding forces districts to encroach on the general fund for dollars to cover the full costs of the special programs (Parrish and Wolman, 1999; Murphy and Picus, 1996).

Thus, over the years, most states have devised some means of sharing the costs with local school districts, the second general approach to funding such services. States have created several types of specific financial structures for implementing the state-local sharing approach. The simplest approach has been to provide a flat grant per eligible pupil. Sometimes the flat grant is based on the number of teachers or classroom units instead of pupils. Very few states currently use this approach, but it is the mechanism the federal government uses to distribute both Title I funds and funds under P.L. 94-142 for disabled students.[14] The obvious drawback to this approach is that it provides the same per-pupil level of financial assistance to rich and poor districts alike and, if the amount does not cover all costs, districts low in property value per pupil need to levy a higher incremental tax rate to make up the difference.

A second state-local cost-sharing program is "excess cost reimbursement," in which the state reimburses a percentage (less than 100) of excess local costs. This ensures that local districts finance at least some portion of the costs of the programs they create and implement. The local match is, in part, a fiscal incentive for local districts to control costs; if program costs soar, the local match puts a direct strain on the local budget as well as the state budget. However, the fact that the local share is raised by increasing the local tax rate or encroaching on the general-fund budget may result in a disadvantage for property-poor districts, which have to exert a higher incremental local tax rate to make up the difference between full program costs and the costs shared by the state. These districts may also have less ability to use general-fund dollars to make up the difference.

A third state-local sharing strategy includes a fiscal capacity equalizing component in the state reimbursement program. For example, using this strategy, the state could turn a flat grant into a foundation grant, thereby inserting an element of need into the distribution formula. Alternatively, the state could use a separate guaranteed tax base program for the marginal tax rate to raise the extra revenues needed to finance the total costs of a special-needs program.

---

[14] However, under the 1997 amendments to the Individuals with Disabilities Act, when appropriations to states exceed $4.92 billion, a new formula will take effect. States will receive a base level of funding in the amount of the previous year, but 85 percent of the funds above that amount will be distributed based on the state's relative share of the national school-age population, and 15 percent based on the state's relative share of the national low-income school-age population (Verstegen, Parrish, and Wolman, Winter 1997–98).

The most prevalent method of state and local cost sharing that includes a fiscal capacity equalizing element emerged in the 1970s and is called pupil weighting. Under this strategy, each special-needs pupil is given an extra weight that indicates, relative to some norm expenditure (usually the statewide average), how much additional services are required. Thus, for example, if the extra weight for a compensatory education student is 0.25, that student could be counted as 1.25 students in determining state aid. The advantage of a pupil-weighting approach is its simplicity in incorporating the level of need for each student into the school-aid formula. This approach also ensures that the state share is higher in low-wealth than in high-wealth districts. Another advantage is that only one school finance formula is used to provide all state aid to local districts; in a weighted-pupil approach, the weighted-pupil count is used for all state-aid calculations.

A weighted-pupil approach also directly indicates the degree of vertical equity adjustment included in the school finance system; the weights are the vertical adjustments. The adequacy of the vertical equity adjustments turns on an evaluation of the specific pupil weights. In calculating the fiscal equity of the resultant distribution of educational resources, equity statistics are calculated using the number of weighted pupils. For this reason, pupil weights are often viewed as among the most equitable policy for distributing the additional resources needed to educate students with special needs.

Although a pupil-weighting system can be used with any type of school finance formulas, technical issues do arise in the following three ways. First, if the weight for any particular type of student is determined by comparing the excess costs required to the statewide average expenditure per pupil, this expenditure must then be included in the state-aid program in order for the weight to be accurate. However, states with foundation programs often set the foundation expenditure at a level below the statewide average expenditure per pupil, but use a pupil weight that has been calculated using the statewide average. This method inevitably leads to less additional resources provided than are required.

The second technical issue arises when a state has a guaranteed tax base program with a pupil-weighting system. In this case, districts that tax at an above-average level will have expenditures above the statewide average and thus the pupil weight might generate more additional revenues than are needed to cover excess costs.

Third, there are problems with labeling students as needing extra resources. Some argue that this practice creates a stigma, instead suggesting use of systems that identify the service levels schools need to educate the whole student body. Despite these technical concerns, pupil-weighting programs are rising in popularity (Figure 4.14).

Another approach for a state contributing to the additional resources needed for special education is census-based funding, a strategy that emerged in the 1990s. This is done through the use of a formula based on total district enrollment rather than counts of special-education students. California has approved such a system, in part because many felt the old system created too many fiscal incentives to identify students as needing special education, and in part to improve the equity of the distribution of state aid for special education. Other reasons include the desire to give the local districts more flexibility while holding them accountable, and having a system that was easy to understand. By the end of 1998, Massachusetts, Montana, North Dakota, Pennsylvania, Alabama, and Vermont all used census-based special-education funding systems as well.

As with all of the other state-local cost-sharing models, census-based funding has both advantages and disadvantages. The major advantages were all the reasons California decided to adopt it: simplicity, flexibility, equity, accountability, and built-in cost controls. The major disadvantage is that the equity depends on the distribution of special-education students across all the districts in a state; if they are concentrated in a few districts, those districts will have to make up the difference between the state aid distributed on the basis of total district enrollment and the actual count of students with special needs. This is an especially important issue with the incidence of students with severe disabilities, who are sometimes extremely expensive to educate.

Another potential disadvantage involves the potential for districts to lose funding under a census-based system. In California, the phase-in process ensures that no district will receive less aid than they received under the previous system, but the possibility exists that in the future, some districts may receive less funding under a true census-based system. While this may not result in a true loss of equity, it may be difficult politically to convince school districts if they are receiving less money than the amount to which they were accustomed.

Still another method of providing adjustments for students with special needs is the poverty adjustment. With this method, poverty is used as a proxy for special-education need in any given district based on the assumption that districts with higher percentages of students in poverty also require more special-education funds. According to the Center for Education Finance, only three states use such an adjustment: Louisiana, Oregon, and Connecticut (Parrish, 1997). One of the most compelling arguments in favor of poverty adjustments is that while it may not be a perfect proxy for special-education needs, it is the best available indicator that can be determined without district involvement, eliminating all of the complications associated with the identification of students with special needs. On the other hand, because the link between poverty and special-education need is unclear and has not been statistically significant in a number of studies, use of poverty adjustments to allocate special-education funds may be a poor way of targeting special-education dollars.

In short, there are two general approaches states can use to provide assistance for local districts to provide extra educational services for students with special-education needs: full-state funding and state-local cost sharing. For reasons already described, the more popular approach is some form of state and local cost sharing. Of the many methods of sharing the cost with localities, pupil-weighting programs have become the most popular; in 1994–95, 19 states used pupil weights in their state special-education funding system. Pupil weights provide a way to directly identify the degree of additional services the state wants to provide as well as a method of sharing the cost by allocating state aid through the general-aid formula using a weighted count of pupils. This strategy also conditions the level of extra aid received on local fiscal capacity; even if the number of special-needs students is the same, districts with a low property value per pupil will receive more money for special education than districts with a high property value per pupil.

One reason some states do not adopt a weighted-pupil approach, despite its many attractions, is because of the political difficulties created by the relative lack of state aid that is distributed to property-wealthy districts. Alternatively, using a categorical program approach, the state devises a separate program formula for distributing financial support for special-needs students, and all districts, rich or poor, become eligible for state aid. While at first blush this might seem inequitable, the politics of state-aid distribution often requires this approach. It is often the property-wealthy districts that have the stronger political voice.

The fact that pupil-weighting systems and other fiscal capacity equalizing general-aid programs distribute little or no state aid to districts high in property wealth may square with fiscal equity principles, but politics can intervene in two ways. First, many legislators feel that *all* districts should be eligible for at least *some* state aid. And, providing state support for special-needs students has surface appeal as a rationale for distributing aid to all districts, even wealthy ones. Second, it is difficult to maintain political support for strongly redistributive programs, such as robust fiscal capacity equalizing school finance formulas. Thus, providing at least some state aid for all districts, even if it is just for special-needs students, helps legislators maintain political support for a general-aid program that provides aid inversely to property value per pupil.

Unfortunately, just as with the general-aid formulas, states have used a variety of names for their method of financing additional services for students with special needs. The different terms often make the school finance programs sound like fundamentally different approaches. But just as many basic school finance formulas are algebraically equivalent, so also are many formulas for addressing special-pupil needs. Bernstein, Hartman, and Marshall (1976) show how the various approaches states use to help local districts provide extra services for special-needs students are simply variations of the general types of programs discussed above.

Finally, the interaction of the specific funding formulas and rules and regulations accompanying them provide incentives and disincentives for student identification, program placement, and dollar use. At the local level, districts sometimes identify students in higher reimbursement categories and place them in lower-cost instructional programs to increase revenues and reduce costs. While some of these interactions are desired, the limits of such flexibility need to be understood and addressed. Hartman (1980) discusses such issues for special education.

As discussed previously, census-based funding addresses the incentive problem as well. Further, after years of experience, local educators have become quite sophisticated at "pooling" dollars for special-needs students and creatively providing services (McLaughlin, 1999). And today, the push for comprehensive school reform programs (see Chapter 8) under the Obey-Porter Comprehensive School Reform legislation actively encourages schools to include special-needs students in all aspects of the regular-education program.

Costs and formulas for financing compensatory education programs.   The federal government has provided funds to local school districts for compensatory programs since the 1965 passage of the Elementary and Secondary Education Act (ESEA). Having been through a number of changes over the years, ESEA was reauthorized in 1994, and amendments were made to the Title I allocation formula through the passage of the Improving America's Schools Act (IASA).

The law postponed most of the changes it was to make until fiscal year (FY) 1996, and only slightly altered the basic and concentration grant formulas so as to allocate an amount equal to the FY 1995 appropriation. However, a few changes were to be implemented in the year following the reauthorization, including a new, targeted formula under which all appropriations above the level of the FY 95 allocation would be distributed. Also, the minimum grant level was increased, and the concentration grant formula was altered slightly in an attempt to make it more equitable. Then, beginning in FY 1996, a new formula for education finance incentive grants was put in place in an attempt to take the relationship of state average expenditure compared to income into account. This was done in response to a concern that Title I had not been sufficiently targeted to high-poverty areas.

Other changes were also made in response to concerns about the distribution of Title I. Before the amendments were passed, the federal government allocated funds to states on the basis of the number of low-income children in each county and the state's per-pupil expenditures for elementary and secondary education. The funds were then suballocated to districts. Under the reauthorized act, two major changes were to be made. The first involved the data by which the number of low-income children is counted. Previously, the number of low-income children was calculated using decennial census data. But because the numbers of children in need in each area shifted more than once every 10 years, there was concern about using census data that is only updated once a decade. Therefore, under the reauthorized act, the data on low-income children was to be updated every two years using biennial census data that was to be collected beginning in 1996. In FY 1997, these data were used for the first time.

The other change that the amendments brought involved the federal government's practice of distributing money to states on the basis of county-level poverty data. As previously described, under the old law, Title I was distributed to the state on the basis of county-level data and then suballocated to districts. If the county and school district boundaries were not coterminous (which is the case in most states), the state used a subcounty allocation formula to distribute funds to local school districts based on the number of low-income students in each district. Under the new law, allocations are to continue in this manner until FY

1999, when grants will not be determined using county-level data, but instead calculated on the basis of the poor-child population in each district.

Once the funds have been allocated to the district, they must then be distributed among the schools in that district. While districts have always had some discretion over how they distribute the money, more selection requirements have been added over the years. Today, in determining which schools will receive the money, districts must first rank all of their schools in terms of poverty levels. The poverty measure employed must be one of the five specified by Title I, including: (1) children ages 5–17 in poverty as counted by the most recent census; (2) children eligible for free and reduced-price lunches under the National Free School Lunch Act; (3) children in families receiving income assistance; (4) children eligible to receive medical assistance under the Medicaid program; and (5) a composite of any of the preceding measures.

Once all the schools in a given district are ranked according to poverty level, the district is required to serve all schools with 75 percent poverty and higher. After serving all of those areas, the district may serve the lower poverty schools using the rank that has already been determined, or by creating grade-level groupings. There are many more provisions that guide schools in determining which schools receive Title I dollars that will not be elaborated on here. Suffice it to say that while there are more rules regarding distribution than was once the case, districts still have some discretion over how Title I dollars are allocated to schools.

It is precisely because school districts have greater latitude in determining the kind of compensatory programs they offer that determining compensatory education costs is not an easy task. By contrast, programs for other special-needs students are more specified. Law requires districts, for example, to provide appropriate services to all disabled children. Once a child's disability has been identified, and an appropriate level of service agreed upon, it is relatively straightforward to determine the costs of that service. While there may be variations in costs and instructional techniques across districts, it is possible to estimate an average cost for each special service provided within a region or state.

Indeed, the problem of determining compensatory education program costs is more complex. A district receives a funding level according to the federal program requirements to provide extra services. Title I and most state compensatory programs have required that program funds be expended on low-income or low-achieving students, but specified neither how they should be served nor that all eligible children receive services. As a result, local districts have considerable flexibility in determining the breadth and intensity of services provided. This flexibility was enhanced in the 1990s by allowing schools with 50 percent or more poverty students to use Title I funds for schoolwide programs serving all students.

As a result, one district may choose to offer intensive services to a subgroup of eligible low-income students, while another district may elect to serve all of the eligible student population with a less-intense program. In fact, a number of different allocation procedures or rules are possible. Goertz (1988) found that among 17 large districts, allocation rules included:

- Uniform allocation to each eligible building,
- Allocations based on the number of low-achieving students in a building, and
- Allocations based on the relative size and/or poverty of the building's student body.

It is likely that these procedures increased in variability in the 1990s, with the trend towards more schoolwide programs.

The study also found considerable differences in instructional expenditures per pupil within and among Chapter 1 (Title I, as it was known in 1988) programs. Goertz (1988) reported these expenditure figures on the basis of the range of expenditures across schools within each district. Thus, one district had a Chapter 1 expenditure range of $300 to $2,500 per pupil, while in another district, expenditures ranged from $450 to $625. The lowest per-pupil Chapter 1 expenditures identified in the 17 districts was $175 (in a district with an expenditure range of $175 to $1,070), and the highest was the $2,500 per pupil identified above.

In 1985–86, the Texas State Board of Education (1986) reviewed the costs of compensatory education and recommended an extra weight of 0.2 for all eligible compensatory education students. Although subsequent studies suggested that many districts did not spend that much extra for compensatory education, in part because compensatory education services within the regular school day were provided in lieu of other services, the legislature retained the 0.2 extra weighting.

Another problem in identifying the costs of compensatory education programs is the fact that over 90 percent of the school districts in the United States receive Title I funds (Le Tendre, 1996). The many variations across regions, states, and districts are considerable, and the percentage of low-income children varies greatly among these districts. While it stands to reason that districts with larger concentrations of low-income students have more funds available for compensatory programs, one might expect more-intense compensatory services, but there are other mitigating factors. For example, the federal government and many state governments are now encouraging the use of Title I money to fund schoolwide programs for schools with over 50 percent of the children in poverty. This makes it extremely hard, if not impossible, to determine how much money is spent on low-income children in a school, since the compensatory education money is being used to fund a program for all children. Furthermore, because schools with high poverty levels are the ones who are eligible and therefore likely to apply their Title I allocation to schoolwide programs, it is no longer easy to discern where the more-intensive services for low-income children are offered. Nor is it clear that "intensive services" are the ones bringing the best results; hence, the move in the direction of schoolwide programs.

Given all of the complications discussed in the preceding paragraphs, finding the answer to the long-standing question of how much per pupil needs to be provided to fund those programs is difficult. The answer requires specifying the level of achievement desired, the additional programmatic strategies needed to produce this achievement, and the costs of those programmatic strategies.

A program for which this type of analysis can be approximated is the Success for All/Roots and Wings program. It is one of the most successful schoolwide strategies developed, and it includes a core curriculum designed to teach students to proficiency standards in reading, writing, mathematics, science, and social studies. There is considerable evidence of the effectiveness of this program, and it has been shown to be replicable across a wide range of schools and education systems (Slavin and Fashola, 1998). For purposes of discussion, let us assume that this program provides the types of additional services and strategies students from low-income backgrounds need to achieve to rigorous proficiency standards.

Fortunately, the 1997 costs of this program have been identified. In addition to all of the elements associated with a traditional school, the minimum elements of this program for an elementary school of 500 students, with nearly all from poverty backgrounds, are:

1. Schoolwide instructional facilitator,
2. Four reading tutors,
3. Family liaison professional,
4. $30,000 for materials, and
5. $30,000 for professional development provided by the national network associated with this school design.

These ingredients include six professional staff positions and $60,000 for training and materials. Using national average prices, this would require the school to have an additional $360,000 (6 positions times $50,000 in salary and benefits for each, plus $60,000). This would be above the core staffing of one principal, one teacher for every 25 students, appropriate additional teachers for preparation time, and art, music and physical education. The costs would be increased if the district provided only a half-day kindergarten; in fact, the program strongly recommends a full-day kindergarten program, which would require two additional teachers raising the costs to $450,000. Roots and Wings/Success for All also strongly suggests that each student receive a preschool education, which could further increase the costs. Finally, some schools find that an additional tutor or two enhances the ability of the program to teach *all* students to high-proficiency standards.

For illustrative purposes, assume a program slightly above the minimum requirements is needed, and that the additional costs of that version of the Roots and Wings/Success for All program is about $500,000. That would amount to $1,000 for every student in the school, which in this case would be every low-income student in the school. This would mean that in addition to the "adequate" foundation program, the state would need to provide an additional $1,000 for every low-income student, assuming that those extra dollars would be used to finance a strategy or set of strategies to teach *all* students to state-set proficiency standards (i.e., a schoolwide program such as Success for All/Roots and Wings). Districts should be able to pool the funds from both Title I and state compensatory education programs to provide this level of extra funding to each school.

Figure 4.13 compares the cost of this enhancement to the foundation program (i.e., providing an extra $1,000 for each student from a low-income background) to the costs of the 90/90 GTB program simulated above. The number of students eligible for free or reduced-price lunch is used to estimate the number of students from a poverty background. The data show that the cost of the extra $1,000 for each low-income student is substantial, but that in two states it is just about equal to the cost of the second-tier GTB. The numbers show that states could consider these additions to the foundation base as trade-offs. If a state has only $200–300 million more to spend above the foundation level, the question is whether it would be wiser to spend it on strategies to teach low-income students to high standards, or on strategies that allow some districts to spend above an adequate level for the average student. We would suggest the former.

In summary, compensatory education funds are distributed to school districts on the basis of the number of eligible pupils. For the federal Title I program, the number of low-income students in a district determines eligibility. Many state programs use income measures for eligibility, while others offer compensatory aid for low-achieving students. Figure 4.14 summarizes the eligibility requirements for state-operated compensatory education programs. Compensatory education programs generally include requirements to ensure that districts do not use the money to replace local funds, but do not delineate how services should be provided, or how many of the eligible students must be served. Consequently some districts attempt to provide compensatory services to all eligible schools and students, others focus their resources at specific populations, and still others use their Title I resources to fund schoolwide programs. This results in a tremendous range in the breadth and intensity of the compensatory education services provided across the United States.

Costs and formulas for financing bilingual education programs. Studies of the costs of providing bilingual education have produced widely varying results, from less than an extra 5 percent (Carpenter-Huffman and Samulon, 1981; Gonzalez, 1996) to an extra 100 percent (Chambers and Parrish, 1983). There are several reasons for these variations, and they speak to what a bilingual education program is and how it should be structured.

FIGURE 4.13   Costs above an "Adequate" Foundation Expenditure Base of a 90/90 GTB Versus an Extra $1,000 for Each Free/Reduced-Price Lunch Student

State	*Extra Costs of a 90/90 GTB*	*Extra Costs of Providing $1,000 for Each Free/Reduced-Price Lunch Student*
Illinois	$165 million	$165 million
Missouri	$ 88 million	$211 million
Wisconsin	$292 million	$281 million

FIGURE 4.14   States with Compensatory Education Programs

State	Compensatory Program Description	1993–94 Program Funding (millions of dollars)
Arkansas	Funding to provide a summer session is equally divided among all K–3 students at or below the 25th percentile on standardized tests	Remediation programs (11.4)
California	EIA funds distributed for compensatory programs on the basis of a variety of poverty measures and "gross need"	Economic Impact Aid (EIA) (297.8)
		Reading program (21.9)
		Native American and American Indian Education programs (1.9)
Delaware	Compensatory education	Unknown
Georgia	Special Instructional Assistance to K–5 pupils with developmental lags; remedial education for all pupils with low achievement test scores in reading and math	Special Instructional Assistance and Remedial Education (110.3)
Hawaii	Full-state funding for educationally disadvantaged children with limited English, alienated youth, and other targeted groups with educational problems	Compensatory Education (15.5)
Illinois	Grants provided to help fund reading programs for low-income children (K–6) as defined by the federal census count of low-income students; low-income students weighted up to 0.66 depending on poverty concentration in district	Reading Improvement (43.6) Compensatory Education Unknown
Indiana	Funding for K–12 at-risk students	Compensatory Education (14.3)
Kansas	Included in weighting system	Unknown
Kentucky	Extended school services including tutoring, counseling, and study skills reinforcement	Compensatory Education (34.1)
Louisiana	Included in basic support formula	Compensatory Education (~12)
Maryland	25% of basic-aid level per Title I eligible pupil to be used for instructional programs; a minimum portion of that amount must be devoted to Title I eligible students	Compensatory Education (85.1)
Massachusetts	Included in basic support formula	Unknown
Michigan	Aid for districts with large numbers of at-risk pupils in grades K–12	Compensatory Education (230.0)
Minnesota	Low-income pupils weighted up to 0.65 depending on poverty concentration in district	Compensatory Education (94.0)

FIGURE 4.14   (Continued)

State	*Compensatory Program Description*	*1993–94 Program Funding (millions of dollars)*
Missouri	Allocated as a portion of special-education funds to be dedicated to remedial reading; weight of 0.2 for low-income pupils	Remedial reading programs (11.0) Compensatory Education ($611/pupil)
New Jersey	Aid for at-risk pupils as determined by eligibility for free meals or free milk	Aid for At-Risk Pupils (293.0)
New York	Aid for the bottom 10 percent of school districts in terms of attendance ratios; aid for the 25 percent of districts with the greatest percentage of students scoring low on a state test; and for the reduction of class sizes for grades K–3 in the five largest urban school districts	Compensatory Education (322.9)
North Carolina	60% of remediation funds based on high school competency test failures; 40% of funds distributed on basis of number of students scoring below 35th percentile on 8th grade CAT test	Remediation (39.0) Dropout Prevention (29.5) Programs for violent children (3.7)
Ohio	Varying amount per pupil based on the percentage of low-income children in the district. Per-pupil payment increases as percentage of low-income pupils increases	Disadvantaged Pupil Impact Aid (239.2)
Oklahoma	Grants awarded to schools wishing to provide alternative education to pupils in danger of dropping out; high-challenge money available for schools with the lowest test scores	Alternative Education (1.0) High Challenge (0.65)
Oregon	Funds provided only to Portland school district	Compensatory Education (<1.0)
South Carolina	Funding for K–3 programs through a pupil weight of 0.26 for pupils eligible for free and reduced lunch; 4–12 based on both K–3 free and reduced lunch and each district's four-year average of students not meeting standards	Compensatory, Remedial, and Reading Recovery (65.0)
Texas	Pupil weight of 0.2 based on number of pupils eligible for free or reduced-price lunches	Compensatory Education (785.0)
Virginia	Funds distributed on the basis of students scoring in the bottom national quartile on achievement tests; local school divisions also receive funds on the basis of the number of pupils requiring remediation	Remedial Education (34.7)

FIGURE 4.14   (Continued)

State	Compensatory Program Description	1993–94 Program Funding (millions of dollars)
Washington	Funding provided to districts on the basis of the number of students scoring in the lowest quartile on the statewide basic skills test	Learning Assistance Program (53.0)
Wisconsin	Grants to districts on the basis of low-income and low-achieving pupils; aid provided to Milwaukee for compensatory education programs to address the academic deficiencies of low-income pupils	PK–5 Grant Program (6.7) Compensatory Aid to Milwaukee (8.0)
Wyoming	Grants available to districts with a high number of at-risk or low-achieving students	Compensatory Education (1.0)

Source: Gold, Smith, and Lawton (1995).

Five specific issues determine the costs of bilingual education programs (Nelson, 1984): (1) student eligibility; (2) minimum number of LEP students required to trigger provision of a bilingual education program; (3) instructional approach used; (4) transition into the regular program; and (5) class size.

A score on some type of English language proficiency test usually determines student eligibility. As Nelson (1984) noted, states used different tests and have selected different cut-off points for eligibility, from below the 23rd percentile in Texas, to higher levels in other states. Clearly, the higher the threshold, the more students eligible, and the fewer the number of low-incidence programs.

Most states also required a school or district to have a minimum number of students in a grade level in order to provide a bilingual education program. Minimums ranged widely, from 10 students in a grade in a school in California, to 20 students in a district in Texas (Nelson, 1984). The lower the minimum number of children and the larger the unit for that minimum, the more students will qualify.

Class size in many states also is limited, sometimes to as low as 10 students in a class. Other states do not set lower limits on class size for bilingual or English as a second language classes. Small class-size requirements boost per-pupil costs.

The instructional approach and transition policies also affect the level of services provided. Most state bilingual education policy assumes that students diagnosed as limited-English-proficient will be able to transition into regular classes, taught in English, within a three-year time period. A longer transition period (i.e., providing extra services to students who need more than three years to transition and perform well in English-only classrooms) would boost per-pupil costs.

Finally, the instructional approach used is a major determinant of program costs. A few comments on bilingual education program goals and characteristics of instructional strategies that work will help provide some background for assessing the nature of the instructional approach and thus the results of cost studies based on different instructional approaches.

Students who are eligible for bilingual education programs usually live in families where a language other than English is spoken, so that English is not the student's native language. The key issue is the degree to which the student is proficient in English as a language for learning. Literacy (i.e., the ability to read, write, do mathematics, and think) can be developed in any language; literacy is neutral with respect to language (Office of Bilingual Education, 1984). Once literacy is developed in one language, it is easily transferred to another language once the second language is learned. Students diagnosed as limited-English-proficient are students who do not have sufficient English language proficiency to learn in English. Research shows that the most effective approach for such students is to teach them regular subjects in their native language, as well as an English as a second language class (Krashen and Biber, 1988). The goal of such a program is to have the students learn English while simultaneously learning regular academic subject matter.

The same research shows that students (adults too, for that matter) learn conversational English first; this English proficiency is sufficient for conversing on the playground, playing with friends, talking about the weather, etc., but it is not sufficient for academic learning (see also Cummins, 1980). When this conversational level of English proficiency is learned, the student is ready for "sheltered English" instruction in subjects that have more language and terminology of their own, such as mathematics and science (Krashen and Biber, 1988), but still need instruction in their native language for history and language arts, and continuation of ESL classes. This intermediate approach helps the student gain the level of English proficiency needed to learn academic subjects. History/social science is the next subject for sheltered English instruction; the last such class is language arts. In other words, the most effective program is to begin instruction in the native language, transition sequentially to sheltered English instruction in mathematics, science, history/social science, and language arts, and only then transition to regular classroom instruction. ESL instruction also should continue until the full transition to the regular classroom.

The Krashen and Biber (1988) report does not make recommendations for major class-size reductions. Nor does this report recommend the common school practice of having an English-only instructor assisted by a bilingual education aid. This configuration is quite common across the country because there are insufficient numbers of bilingual teachers to teach students in their native language. In this circumstance, Krashen and Biber recommend ESL with a sheltered English instruction approach.

Thus, the major extra costs of bilingual education for the most effective instructional approach are threefold:

- An ESL teacher. If the class has a normal number of students and is used for six periods a day, the extra cost is about 1/6 (i.e., the cost of the extra period of instruction). Other related costs such as materials and space might bring the total extra cost to about 20 percent.
- Intensive staff development in sheltered English instruction. This is pro-

fessional expertise that can and should be learned by all teachers. Knowledge of a second language is not required. Sheltered English instruction is instruction mediated by a variety of mechanisms and with a conscious English-language-development component.

- Additional materials both in the native language of the student and for mediating the sheltered English instructional approach. These extras would seem to add to a maximum of an extra 25 to 35 percent. Note that regular classes are taught by either bilingual teachers, teachers using a sheltered English approach, or in a regular classroom; other than staff development, these classes entail no additional costs.[15]

Most studies of bilingual education program costs reflect these levels of costs. Garcia (1977) found the add-on costs for bilingual education in New Mexico to be about 27 percent. Three studies by the Intercultural Development Research Association found bilingual education to cost an extra 30 to 35 percent in Texas (Cardenas, Bernal, and Kean, 1976), an extra 17 to 25 percent in Utah (Guss-Zamora, Zarate, Robledo, and Cardenas, 1979), and an extra 15 to 22 percent in Colorado (Robledo, Zarate, Guss-Zamora, and Cardenas, 1978). A more recent study of such programs in California found the marginal cost of LEP services to be $361 in 1990–91 (Parrish, 1994); when compared to the total education revenues per pupil in California in the same year, the cost of LEP services amounts to an additional 8 percent. Parrish (1994) also found a broad range of costs depending on the instructional approach, which he attributes to the range in the resource teacher services needed for the different approaches. The costs in his study ranged from $131 per student in a sheltered English program to $1,066 for an ESL program, or from 3 to 22 percent above regular education costs.[16] While some of these studies analyzed program configurations quite different from that described above, the findings provide a range of cost estimates that are nevertheless comparable.

Finally, though districts have typically reported higher costs for bilingual education programs than most studies have found (Carpenter-Huffman and Samulon, 1981), there have been studies that also report considerably higher costs for bilingual education programs than those cited above. The Chambers and Parrish (1983) study in Illinois found that these additional costs ranged from $848 per pupil to $5,113 per pupil, or between 33 and 100 percent for different program structures in Illinois school districts. The highest cost figure assumed both a high incidence and a very low class size, the latter a characteristic absent from some of the other studies, including the Krashen and Biber studies of effective California programs.

[15] Some states and districts pay bilingual teachers a bonus of up to $5,000. This clearly is an extra cost. The bonus is rationalized on the basis that bilingual teachers are in short supply and have an expertise—proficiency in a second language—that other teachers do not have.

[16] If the base revenue limit ($3,331), rather than total revenues per pupil ($4,743), are used to calculate these percentages, the estimate for LEP services would be 11 percent above regular-education costs; sheltered English instruction would be 4 percent; and the more expensive ESL program would be 32 percent above regular-education costs (Gold et. al., 1992).

Bilingual education continues to be controversial. In California, Proposition 227, which took effect in the summer of 1998, sharply curtailed bilingual classes, instead encouraging immersion for LEP students. In spite of the controversy, the key ingredients for an effective program structure are an ESL program to teach English, regular teachers who either teach in the native language or in a sheltered English format, neither of which entails extra costs, supplementary materials and staff development. Moreover, as the diversity of the student's native language increases, as is increasingly the case, sheltered English instruction inevitably becomes the dominant instructional mode in addition to ESL; the many languages within each classroom preclude a bilingual teaching strategy. Additional costs for this program structure, as well as those found in several research reports, range between 25 and 35 percent.

Figure 4.15 lists states' approaches to funding bilingual education programs.

Costs and formulas for financing special-education programs. Identifying the costs of special-education programs for physically, mentally, and learning-disabled students has been a major focus of study for the past three decades. Initially, studies sought to identify different costs by disability, taking into account how that cost varied by the size of the district. Increasingly, special-education cost research has focused more on excess costs as a function of educational placement (Moore et al., 1988; Rossmiller and Frohreich, 1979).

Rossmiller conducted some of the earliest work under the auspices of the early 1970s' National Education Finance Project (NEFP) (Johns, Alexander and Jordan, 1971; Rossmiller et al., 1970). This work was probably the first analysis of special-education costs that produced results that could be used to create pupil-weighting programs. Indeed, in 1973, Florida enacted one of the first special-education pupil-weighting programs as a new approach for financing special education, a program that became a model for other states. Florida adopted the following weights for 1976–77, based in large part on the Rossmiller and NEFP analyses:

Educable mentally retarded	2.3
Trainable mentally retarded	3.0
Physically handicapped	3.5
Physical and occupational therapy, part-time	6.0
Speech and hearing therapy, part-time	10.0
Deaf	4.0
Visually handicapped, part-time	10.0
Visually handicapped	3.5
Emotionally disturbed, part-time	7.5
Emotionally disturbed	3.7
Socially maladjusted	2.3
Specific learning disability, part-time	7.5
Specific learning disability	2.3
Hospital and homebound, part-time	15.0

FIGURE 4.15   State Approaches to Funding Education for Limited English-Speaking Children

State	LEP Program Description	Program Operating Characteristics	
Alaska	Bilingual program costs included in-state support program as additional instructional units	*ADM* 1–12 13–18 19–42 43 and over	*Inst. Units* 1 2 3 3 plus 1 for each 24-weighted ADM or fraction of 24
Arizona	Weight included in block grant calculations	*Weight* 1.060	
California	Funds distributed through Economic Impact Aid program based on measures of poverty and limited English proficiency	Unknown	
Colorado	English Language Proficiency Act provides funding to build English proficiency for K–12 pupils of limited English proficiency	$2,600,000 in 1993–94	
Connecticut	State funds to help pay for the bilingual education programs that districts are required to provide in schools with 20 or more limited English proficiency pupils	$2,200,000 in 1993–94	
Florida	Pupil-weighting program	*Weights* K–3　1.600 4–8　1.617 9–12　1.454	
Georgia	Included in the basic support program as an adjustment for special factors	$7,500,000 in 1993–94	
Hawaii	Included as a component of compensatory education	Unknown	
Illinois	Excess cost for approved programs	$51,700,000 in 1993–94	
Iowa	Pupil-weighting system	LEP pupils can be weighted 1.19 for up to 3 years; state contribution was $2,100,000 in 1993–94	
Kansas	Pupil-weighting program	Bilingual program weighted 1.2	
Louisiana	Additional instructional units provided for full-time second language instructors at elementary level	Unknown	
Maryland	Annually legislated amount per pupil provided by the state	$5,900,000 or $500 per pupil in 1993–94	

FIGURE 4.15   (Continued)

State	LEP Program Description	Program Operating Characteristics
Massachusetts	Pupil-weighting program	Weight of 1.4 for Transitional Bilingual Program
Michigan	Reimbursement to districts on basis of number of LEP students	$4,200,000 in 1993–94
Minnesota	State categorical program	Lesser of 55% of salary or $15,320 for each eligible FTE teacher; districts receive 1 FTE teacher per 40 LEP students, and districts with less than 20 LEP students are eligible for 1/2 FTE teacher
New Jersey	Pupil-weighting	LEP pupils are weighted 1.18 in the state-aid formula; state contribution was $57,400,000 in 1993–94
New Mexico	Pupil-weighting	FTE LEP students weighted an additional 0.35; state contribution was $29,700,000 in 1993–94
New York	Pupil-weighting	LEP students weighted an additional 0.15; state contribution was $59,600,000 in 1993–94
Oklahoma	Pupil-weighting	Weight of an additional 0.2 in foundation program
Rhode Island	Incentive aid program for bilingual pupils	$99,000 in 1993–94
Texas	An additional 10% of adjusted allotment per pupil enrolled in a bilingual or special-language program	$75,000,000 in 1993–94
Virginia	Aid provided to local school divisions for ESL programs	$1,800,000 in 1993–94
Washington	State aid for funding a transitional bilingual program	$22,700,000 in 1993–94
Wisconsin	State reimburses a percentage of costs based on the ratio of appropriation to eligibility	State contribution was 33% or $8,300,000 in 1993–94

Source: Gold, Smith, and Lawton (1995).

In addition to the general points made above on factors that determine program costs, there are three key issues related to determining special-education program costs. The first is the level of program quality. Most of the early studies sought to identify good special-education programs and based special-education cost estimates on the expenditure patterns of those programs. Few studies set a priori standards for program quality. Thus, studies have been plagued over the years by various definitions of program quality. The second issue is identification of services included in the study. The most controversial aspect of this issue is whether to include administrative services, such as general district administration, as well as noneducational related services. A third issue, especially for determining per-pupil costs, is how the number of students is determined—whether by head count or full-time equivalents. The importance of this issue, and resultant program structures, is shown by the high weights for students receiving part-time services in the early Florida program. Kakalik (1979) provides an overview of issues in determining special-education costs. Parrish (1996) also discusses costs in his recent article on special-education finance.

Two large studies of nationwide special-education costs have been conducted, one by Kakalik, Furry, Thomas, and Carney (1981) using data from the mid-1970s and one by Moore et al. (1988) using data from the mid-1980s. Both used a representative national sample, thus providing a picture of actual special-education expenditures across all programs in the country. The results in terms of excess costs for special-education programs are quite similar. Kakalik et al. presented results as ratios of special-education expenditures to regular-education expenditures in 1977–78 for 13 categories of disabling conditions; the weights ranged from 1.37 for speech-impaired children to 5.86 for the blind. The overall weight across all categories was 2.17. Kakalik et al. also presented data comparing special-education expenditures to regular-education expenditures by 10 categories of educational placement. For the in-school program, the ratios or weights ranged from 1.37 for regular classroom plus related services to 3.24 for special all-day school. The regular classroom plus part-time special classroom arrangement had a weight of 2.85.

Moore et al. (1988) presented no pupil weights or ratios in their report, tending rather to emphasize the linkage between type of educational program or educational placement, and disabling condition. The following are summary findings of 1985–86 special-education program costs:

Handicapping Condition	Preschool	Self-Contained	Resource Room
Speech impaired	$ 3,062	$ 7,140	$ 647
Mentally retarded	3,983	4,754	2,290
Orthopedically impaired	4,702	5,248	3,999
Multihandicapped	5,400	6,674	NA
Learning disabled	3,708	3,083	1,643
Seriously emotionally disturbed	4,297	4,857	2,620
Deaf	5,771	7,988	NA
Deaf-blind	NA	20,416	NA
Hard of hearing	4,583	6,058	3,372
Other health-impaired	3,243	4,782	NA
Autistic	6,265	7,582	NA
Visually impaired	4,068	6,181	3,395

These results can be transformed into pupil weights by comparing these costs to 1985–86 expenditures per pupil for regular students, which was $2,780. Since the above figures are costs just for the special-education services, the $2,780 figure would have to be added to them in order to calculate the weight. Moore et al. found that the overall average expenditure for special education across all programs and placements was $3,649. Thus, their study produced an overall weight of 2.3 [($3,649 + $2,780)/$2,780] close to the Kakalik et al. (1981) finding of 2.17 (see also, Chaikind, Danielson, and Braven, 1993).

More recent analyses are difficult to come by because of the lack of special-education finance data from the states. Nonetheless, in a 1996 article, Parrish calls 2.3 "the generally accepted cost figure." However, caution must be applied in using this figure. Significant variation in special-education costs occur by disabling condition, educational placement, type of educational program, and size of school district. McClure (1976) and Leppert and Routh (1979) further discuss issues related to developing and implementing a state weighted-pupil approach to financing special-education services for disabled students. Parrish (1996) and Parrish and Wolman (1999) also discuss the use of pupil weights as a method of financing special education at the state level.

Unfortunately, requirements for states to report their special-education costs have not been widely enforced and therefore have not been met by many states. This lack of data makes it difficult to have accurate estimates of the current cost of special education. And, in terms of the future of special-education costs, trends such as consolidation of funding sources and inclusion will likely make it increasingly difficult to sort out the cost of educating special-needs students (Chambers, Parrish, and Guarino, 1999; National Research Council, 1999).

Simulation of Adjustments for Special-Needs Students

Adding adjustments for special-needs students to a state school finance structure clearly improves the vertical equity of the system, but also improves both horizontal equity and fiscal neutrality. However, the improvements require additional revenues. Figure 4.16 shows the base data simulated with the following weights representing additional student educational need:

- Compensatory education students (i.e., students from a family with low income usually represented by the number of students eligible for free and reduced lunch) weighted an extra 0.25,
- Limited English proficient students weighted an extra 0.2, and
- Disabled students weighted an extra 1.3.

First, a couple of explanations about the results. The simulation assumes that the state would assume the full extra cost of these pupil-need adjustments. Thus, the total revenue number in Figure 4.16 is higher than that in Figure 4.1, the base data without pupil weights. As indicated in the bottom, left-hand side of Figure 4.16, these weights produce an additional 20,250 pupil units (125,493 −

Adequacy Level	$	5,350
Pupil Weights		**yes**
Disabled		1.30
Limited English		0.20
Low Income		0.25

District	Weighted Pupils	Property Value per Weighted Pupil ($)	Property Tax Rate (Mills)	Local Revenue per Weighted Pupil ($)	State Revenue pe Weighted Pupil ($)	Total Revenue per Weighted Pupil ($)
1	1,803	12,491	39.64	495	3,173	3,668
2	7,695	18,994	38.50	731	3,145	3,877
3	2,215	23,916	37.15	888	3,091	3,979
4	329	27,781	36.20	1,006	3,014	4,019
5	12,846	32,142	35.91	1,154	2,943	4,097
6	1,185	35,178	35.74	1,257	2,946	4,203
7	5,728	40,831	34.89	1,425	2,915	4,339
8	2,002	45,952	34.17	1,570	2,834	4,405
9	10,713	51,194	33.73	1,727	2,776	4,503
10	1,780	58,980	33.44	1,972	2,728	4,700
11	2,891	65,986	33.23	2,193	2,789	4,982
12	6,963	73,030	32.89	2,402	2,703	5,105
13	3,060	80,193	32.10	2,574	2,651	5,225
14	18,037	88,181	31.32	2,762	2,560	5,322
15	2,682	96,694	30.85	2,983	2,556	5,539
16	3,131	109,049	30.50	3,326	2,364	5,690
17	34,779	118,771	30.05	3,569	2,153	5,722
18	2,353	136,588	28.63	3,911	2,041	5,951
19	3,564	173,874	27.42	4,768	1,840	6,608
20	1,735	244,012	25.50	6,222	1,308	7,530
Weighted Average		82,045	32.48	2,540	2,550	5,090
Weighted Std. Dev.		43,749	2.97	1,161	388	782
Median		80,193	32.10	2,574	2,651	5,225

Totals		
	Amount	Percent
Local Revenue	318,727,208	49.90%
State Revenue	319,972,342	50.10%
Total Revenue	638,699,550	
Weighted Pupils	125,493	

Equity Measures	
Horizontal Equity	
Range	$3,862
Restricted Range	2,731
Federal Range Ratio	0.703
Coef. of Variation	0.154
Gini Coefficient	0.085
McLoone Index	0.842
Verstegen Index	1.092
Fiscal Neutrality	
Correlation	0.989
Elasticity	0.274
Adequacy	
Odden-Picus	0.915

Additional state revenue for weighted pupil categorical programs	117,432,176

FIGURE 4.16   Base Data

105,243). The number of additional student units in each district can be determined by comparing the "Weighted Pupils" column in Figure 4.16 with those in Figure 4.1. These extra-pupil units require an additional $117.4 million in revenues, which we show as additional state revenues. This additional amount represents the full cost of the extra weights. In the state simulation that accompanies

Chapter 5, the additional amount would be the increment above what the state actually provides for special-student needs, as most states already provide some level of assistance for low-income, LEP, or disabled students. Nevertheless, the $117.4 million figure identified in Figure 4.16 is the amount required to fund the identified pupil weights.

Figure 4.17 uses these weights for the foundation program simulated above (i.e., a foundation of $5,154, the state median, at the required tax rate of 31.32 mills, also the state median. The impacts are substantial. First, the total state cost of the program increases by an additional $48.7 million, compared to the weighted-pupil base data. These increased costs should be expected because the foundation level raises spending in many districts, particularly those with large numbers of special-needs students.

Second, the bulk of the extra costs is for disabled students. Readers should run a series of simulations, each time giving a weight to just one of the three categories of special-needs students. The results will show that the incidence of bilingual students is quite low, which is the case in most states (but not California, Arizona, New Mexico, Texas, Florida, and New York). Since the extra cost for each student is just 20 percent, the total additional costs are minimal. Extra costs for compensatory education alone is higher because the incidence of low-income students is about 20 percent of all students. The incidence of disabled students is about 10 percent which, when combined with an extra cost of 130 percent for each student, produces the largest extra cost for a special-needs student category.

Third, the pupil weighting in Figure 4.17 changes the fiscal equity statistics only moderately, as compared to the unweighted scenario in Figure 4.8, which itself produced quite good equity and adequacy results. The coefficient of variation stays the same, the correlation coefficient rises, the elasticity decreases somewhat, and the McLoone Index and the Adequacy Index rise. In short, vertical adjustments for special-needs students produce equity on all fronts, with this level foundation program. Of course, costs also rise; equity gains emerge at a price.

Adjustments for Different Grade Levels

For years, the most common grade–level adjustment in school finance formulas was for secondary students, who typically were provided an additional 25 percent of resources, or weighted 1.25. The rationale for this practice was that, given current patterns of elementary and secondary school organization, costs were higher for secondary students. More specialized classes were provided, more expensive educational programs (such as vocational education) were provided, and often class sizes were smaller, at least for several types of classes.

Figure 4.18 shows the adjustments by grade level states made during the 1993–94 school year. As expected, most states provide more for secondary students, ranging from 5 to 37 percent more than is allocated to lower grades. Interestingly, several states also weight K–3 students up to an additional 25 percent. This practice began in the 1970s; the rationale was that if students learned

Adequacy Level	$	5,350

Foundation Level	$5,154.00
Required Tax Rate	31.32

Pupil Weights	yes
Disabled	1.30
Limited English	0.20
Low Income	0.25

District	Weighted Pupils	Property Value per Weighted Pupil ($)	Old Property Tax Rate (Mills)	New Property Tax Rate (Mills)	Change in Property Tax Rate (Mills)	Old Local Revenue per Weighted Pupil ($)	New Local Revenue per Weighted Pupil ($)	Change in Local Revenue per Weighted Pupil ($)	New State Revenue per Weighted Pupil ($)	Change in State Revenue per Weighted Pupil ($)	Total Revenue per Weighted Pupil ($)	Change in Total Revenue per Weighted Pupil ($)
1	1,803	12,491	39.64	35.48	(4.16)	495	443	(52)	4,763	1,590	5,206	1,538
2	7,695	18,994	38.50	34.91	(3.59)	731	663	(68)	4,559	1,414	5,222	1,346
3	2,215	23,916	37.15	34.23	(2.91)	888	819	(70)	4,405	1,314	5,224	1,244
4	329	27,781	36.20	33.76	(2.44)	1,006	938	(68)	4,284	1,270	5,222	1,203
5	12,846	32,142	35.91	33.62	(2.30)	1,154	1,080	(74)	4,147	1,204	5,228	1,130
6	1,185	35,178	35.74	33.53	(2.21)	1,257	1,180	(78)	4,052	1,106	5,232	1,028
7	5,728	40,831	34.89	33.11	(1.79)	1,425	1,352	(73)	3,875	960	5,227	887
8	2,002	45,952	34.17	32.75	(1.43)	1,570	1,505	(66)	3,715	880	5,220	815
9	10,713	51,194	33.73	32.53	(1.21)	1,727	1,665	(62)	3,551	774	5,216	713
10	1,780	58,980	33.44	32.38	(1.06)	1,972	1,910	(62)	3,307	579	5,216	516
11	2,891	65,986	33.23	32.28	(0.95)	2,193	2,130	(63)	3,037	298	5,217	235
12	6,963	73,030	32.89	32.11	(0.73)	2,402	2,345	(57)	2,857	164	5,211	106
13	3,060	80,193	32.10	32.20	0.10	2,574	2,582	8	2,642	(8)	5,225	0
14	18,037	88,181	31.32	33.22	1.90	2,762	2,930	168	2,392	(168)	5,322	0
15	2,682	96,694	30.85	35.30	4.45	2,983	3,413	430	2,126	(430)	5,539	0
16	3,131	109,049	30.50	36.23	5.73	3,326	3,951	625	1,739	(625)	5,690	0
17	34,779	118,771	30.05	36.10	6.35	3,569	4,288	719	1,434	(719)	5,722	0
18	2,353	136,588	28.63	37.16	8.53	3,911	5,075	1,165	876	(1,165)	5,951	0
19	3,564	173,874	27.42	33.00	10.58	4,758	6,608	1,840	0	(1,840)	6,608	0
20	1,735	244,012	25.50	30.86	5.36	6,222	7,530	1,308	0	(1,308)	7,530	0
Weighted Average		82,045	32.48	34.32	1.85	2,540	2,851	311	2,627	77	5,478	388
Weighted Std. Dev.		43,749	2.97	1.70	3.95	1,161	1,583	460	1,252	876	389	512
Median		80,193	32.10	32.29	0.10	2,574	2,582	8	2,642	-8	5,322	0

Totals

Category	Amount	Percent	Change from Base Amount	Change from Weighted Pupil Base Amount
Local Revenue	357,731,997	52.04%	39,004,789	39,004,790
State Revenue	329,676,325	47.96%	127,136,159	3,703,982
Total Revenue	687,408,322		163,140,948	48,708,772
Weighted Pupils	125,493			

Equity Measures

Horizontal Equity	
Range	$2,324
Restricted Range	1,396
Federal Range Ratio	0.268
Coef. of Variation	0.071
Gini Coefficient	0.031
McLoone Index	0.981
Verstegen Index	1.072
Fiscal Neutrality	
Correlation	0.930
Elasticity	0.142
Adequacy	
Odden-Picus	0.988

Winners and Losers

Category	Winners	Losers	No change
State Aid	12	8	0
Total Rev.	12	0	8

FIGURE 4.17   Foundation Program

FIGURE 4.18 States that Use a Form of Pupil Weighting for Grade-Level Differences, 1993–94

State	Pupil Weight Program Description	
Alabama	A legislative act was passed that allocates more teachers to elementary grades through FY1999–2000; details unknown	
Alaska	Secondary is weighted more heavily than elementary; 7–12 receive additional instructional units for smaller enrollment increases than do K–6	
Arizona	K–3	1.198
	4–8	1.158
	9–12	1.268
Florida	K–3	1.017
	4–8	1.000
	9–12	1.224
Georgia	K	1.34022
	1–3	1.25569
	4–5	1.01916
	6–8	1.02268
	9–12	1.00000
Illinois	Pre-K–6	1.00
	7–8	1.05
	9–12	1.25
Louisiana	K–3	1.15
	4–12	1.00
Minnesota	Half-day K	0.515
	Full-day K–6	1.0
	7–12	1.4
Montana	Higher per-pupil funding at the high school level	
Nebraska	Half-day K	0.5
	Full-day K–6	1.0
	7–8	1.2
	9–12	1.4
New Jersey	Half-day K	0.5
	Full-day K–5	1.0
	6–8	1.10
	9–12	1.33
New Mexico	K(FTE)	1.44
	1	1.2
	2–3	1.18
	4–6	1.0
	7–12	1.25
New York	Half-day K	0.5
	Full-day K–6	1.0
	7–12	1.25

FIGURE 4.18 **(Continued)**

State	Pupil Weight Program Description	
North Carolina	Grade-level weighting occurs in the formula allocating teachers, with K having the lowest pupil-teacher ratio, 1–9 the next highest, and high school the highest ratio	
North Dakota	*Elementary*	
	Preschool	1.01
	K	0.5
	One-room rural	1.28
	Graded < 100 pupils	1.09
	100–999 pupils	0.905
	1000+ pupils	0.95
	7–8	1.01
	Secondary (9–12)	
	1–74 pupils	1.625
	75–149 pupils	1.335
	150 540 pupils	1.24
	550+ pupils	1.14
Oklahoma	Pre-K	0.500
	K	1.300
	1–2	1.351
	3	1.051
	4–6	1.000
	7–12	1.200
Pennsylvania	Half-day K	0.5
	Elementary	1.0
	Secondary	1.36
South Carolina	Half-day K	0.65
	1–3	1.24
	4–8	1.00
	9–12	1.25
Tennessee	Grade-level weighting occurs in the formula allocating teachers, with K–3 having the lowest pupil-teacher ratio, followed by 4–6, 7–9 the next highest, and 10–12 the highest ratio	
Utah	K	0.55
	1–12	1.00
Vermont	Elementary	1.00
	Secondary	1.25

Source: Gold, Smith, and Lawton (1995).

successfully in the early years, compensatory or remedial programs in the later years would not be needed, at least not at current levels.

There are strong arguments for concentrating educational investments in the early years. Indeed, preschool programs provide long-term achievement and other benefits (Berrueta-Clement, Schweinhart, Barnett, Epstein, and Weikart, 1984). Further, extended-day kindergarten programs for low-income children help boost performance in later grades (Puelo, 1988). One-to-one tutoring in the early grades produces achievement gains on the order of a half to a full standard deviation (Odden, 1990; Slavin, 1989). Finally, small class sizes of about 15 also improve achievement for kindergarten and first-grade students (Folger, 1990).

Such research results firmly support investing more at the early grades, perhaps even weighting K–3 student an extra 25–30 percent. Nevertheless, current practice generally provides more at the secondary level. As educational productivity (i.e., the link between resources and student achievement) assumes greater importance in the 2000s, extra investments for the early years might also expand. In fact, as we discuss in Chapter 8, it appears that the "typical" pattern for grade-level weights varies substantially by region; the South and the West already provide more for elementary than secondary students.

Adjustments for Size

There is substantial controversy over size adjustments in state school finance formulas. There are several possible conditions that could produce higher costs that might qualify for a size adjustment in the state-aid program: (1) small school size; (2) small district size; (3) large school size; and (4) large district size. The general policy issue is whether small (or large) schools or districts experience diseconomies of scale (i.e., whether it costs more per pupil to run a small (or large) school or district). If size affects school operational costs, the policy question is whether those costs should be recognized in the state-aid formula through a special adjustment or whether the school or district should be urged or required to consolidate (or separate) into a larger (or smaller) entity, thereby reducing costs and avoiding the need to spend extra money.

The major focus for size adjustments has been on small schools and districts. The general perception in the policy-making community is that small schools or districts are inefficient and should consolidate into larger entities. Indeed, as the data in Chapter 1 showed, school and district consolidation has been a common occurrence over the past 50 years. Both districts and schools have consolidated into larger entities. Many states have incentive programs that reward small districts that consolidate into larger ones (Salmon et al., 1988).

Analysts, however, argue that the expected cost savings from the massive school and district consolidation have not been realized (Guthrie, 1979; O'Neill, 1996; Ornstein, 1990) and that consolidation might actually harm student performance in rural schools (Sher and Tompkins, 1977) as well as have broad negative effects on rural communities (Coeyman, 1998; Seal and Harmon, 1995). If small schools or districts indeed cost more, but consolidation reduces performance and disrupts communities, the better policy choice might be to resist consolidation and provide special adjustments to compensate for the higher costs.

The research on diseconomies of small and large scale generally does not support a consolidation policy. From an economic perspective, the concept of diseconomies of scale includes both costs and outputs. The issue is whether costs per unit of output are higher in small schools or districts, or put differently, whether costs can be reduced while maintaining output as size rises. In an extensive review of the literature, Fox (1981) concluded that little research had analyzed output in combination with input and size variables, and Monk (1990) concluded after assessing the meager extant research that there was little support for either school or district consolidation.

For elementary schools, research knowledge is thin, but data suggest that size economies that reduce costs by more than one dollar per pupil exist up to but not beyond 200 pupils (Riew, 1986). Thus, very small schools experience diseconomies because of small size and, except in isolated rural areas, potentially could be merged into larger ones. But the real opportunities for cost savings from school consolidation from these small sizes are not great, precisely because many such schools are located in isolated rural areas.

At the secondary level, the data are more mixed. Studies do not exist that simultaneously assess both size and output, so scale diseconomies have not been adequately studied. Riew (1986) found that there were cost savings, below one dollar per pupil, for middle schools with enrollments above 500; again, most middle schools already enroll more than this number. In analyzing whether larger secondary schools actually provided more comprehensive programs, an argument for larger size, Monk (1987) concluded in a study of New York that program comprehensiveness increased consistently in secondary schools only for size increases up to but not beyond about 400 students. In subsequent research, Haller, Monk, Spotted Bear, Griffith, and Moss (1990) found that while larger schools offered more comprehensive programs, there was wide variation among both smaller and larger schools, and there was no clear point that guarantees program comprehensiveness. Further, Hamilton (1983) shows that social development is better in small high schools.

Studies of district size generally analyze expenditures per pupil as a function of size without an output variable, such as student achievement (Fox, 1981). To document diseconomies of district size, however, expenditures, size, and output need to be analyzed simultaneously, since the goal is to determine if costs per unit of output decrease as the number of students in the district increases. Again, in reviewing the literature, Monk (1990) concluded that definitive statements could not be made about district consolidation.

In short, in most cases, there is not a strong research base for continuing to encourage school and district consolidation. As a result, states can take some comfort in continuing their various approaches to size adjustments in school-aid formulas (see Salmon et al., 1988).

Adjustments for Price Differences

An issue that gained prominence in school finance during the 1970s and 1980s was the difference in prices that school districts faced in purchasing educational resources. Districts not only purchase a different market basket of educational goods (just as individuals purchase a different market basket of goods), but they also pay different prices for the goods they purchase. Today, because some schools manage their budget on site and do all of their own purchasing, schools can also be included in this discussion. District (and/or school) expenditures determine quantity issues (numbers of different types of educational goods purchased, such as teachers, books, buildings, etc.), the level of quality of those goods, and cost of or price paid for each good. The variety, number, quality, and price of all educational goods purchases determine school district (and/or school) expenditures. While "expenditures" are often referred to as "costs" in informal school finance talk, there is a difference between these two economic terms. "Expenditure" refers to the money spent on school resources; "cost" refers to the money spent on school resources to receive a certain level of output or to provide a certain quality of service.

Costs that school districts (and/or schools) face in purchasing educational resources differ across school districts, and many states have taken an interest in trying to adjust school-aid allocations to compensate for cost or price differences. For example, a teacher of a certain quality will probably cost more in an urban area where general costs of living are higher than in nonurban areas where general costs of living are lower. But prices or cost variations that districts must pay for teachers also differ among school districts because of variations in the nature of the work required, the quality of the working environment, and the local community. Teachers might accept marginally lower salaries if, for example, they teach four rather than five periods a day, or have smaller classes. Teachers might accept marginally smaller salaries if there are numerous opportunities for staff development (McLaughlin and Yee, 1988). Or teachers might want marginally higher salaries if there are few cultural opportunities in the surrounding community. The combination of differences in general cost of living, working conditions, and the surrounding community produces differences in prices that districts must pay for teachers of a given quality.

Similarly, districts within the same state might have to allocate more or less general revenues for such noneducational activities such as transportation and heating/cooling. Districts in sparsely populated rural areas face higher-than-average transportation costs because their students are spread over a wider geographical region, and because fuel and repair costs may also be higher. Districts in especially cold or unusually warm environments must spend more for heating or air conditioning. These higher-than-average expenditures are beyond the control of the district and, holding both quality constant and assuming similar technical efficiency, impose higher costs on district budgets.

These are just a few examples of factors that constrain the ability of school districts, even those with the same total general revenue per pupil, to provide the same level and quality of educational services to their students. States have recognized these price and cost variations but only recently have begun to make adjustments for them in state-aid formulas.

While there are several different approaches that can be taken in constructing cost-of-education indices (Berne and Stiefel, 1984; Brazer, 1974; Chambers, 1981; Kenny, Denslow, and Goffmann, 1975), there is substantial correlation among price indices constructed with different methodologies (Chambers, 1981). Whatever methodology is used, price differences can vary substantially. In studies of California (Chambers, 1978, 1980), Florida (Kenny et al., 1975), Missouri (Chambers, Odden, and Vincent, 1976), New York (Wendling, 1981) and Texas (Augenblick and Adams, 1979) within-state price variations ranged from 20 percent (10 percent above and below the average) in California, to 40 percent (20 percent above and below the average) in Texas. These are substantial differences. These results mean that high-cost districts in California must pay 20 percent more for the same educational goods as low-cost districts; thus, with equal per-pupil revenues, high-cost districts are able to purchase only 75 percent of what low-cost districts can purchase. The differences in Texas are even greater. Such price differences, caused by circumstances and conditions essentially outside the control of district decision makers, qualify as a target for adjustments in some state-aid formulas.

There are two different approaches states can take in using a price or cost-of-education index. First, state aid could be multiplied by the price index, thus ensuring that equal amounts of state aid could purchase equal amounts of educational goods. But this approach leaves local revenues unadjusted by price indices. A better method would be to multiply the major elements of a school-aid formula by the price index to ensure that total education revenues could purchase the same level of resources. Thus, the price index would be applied to the foundation expenditure level in a foundation program, the tax base guaranteed by the state in a guaranteed tax base program, the state-determined spending level in a full state funding program, or total current operating expenditures for a percentage equalizing formula.

As such, including a price index in a school finance formula is relatively simple. In addition, the fact that price indices tend to remain stable over time (Chambers, 1981) suggests that states would need to develop price indices only periodically, once every three to five years, if they were used as part of a state-aid formula. Furthermore, the National Center of Education Statistics (NCES) has already developed different versions of such education price adjustments for all school districts in the country (Chambers, 1995; McMahon, 1994), which any state could use. States have been reluctant to add education price adjustments to their school-aid formulas, in part because developing them requires some complex econometric analyses and manipulations and in part because they have the potential of changing allocations considerably.

While the existence of the NCES price indices would alleviate the need for analysis, price indices do alter the distribution of state aid. In general, education price indices are higher in urban and metropolitan areas than in rural areas.

Thus, with a given amount of state aid, use of a price index would shift the shares of state aid at the margin from rural to urban school districts. This distributional characteristic injects an additional political dimension to constructing a state-aid mechanism that is politically viable.[17] Nevertheless, prices vary across school districts and affect the real levels of education goods and services that can be purchased. Including an education price index in the school aid formula is a direct way to adjust for these circumstances that are outside the control of school district policymakers.

CONCLUSION

There are many legitimate reasons for states to allocate more revenues for certain student or district characteristics. These vertical equity adjustments are not only justified, but as they become identified also become required as a matter of equity. While specific levels of adjustments can be refined and changed based on new research findings, there is strong consensus that states should share in funding services for low-achieving poor children, limited English proficient children, and children with physical and mental disabilities. There also is consensus that price adjustments are warranted, although states have been reluctant to use price indices that are developed using standard (and quite sophisticated) econometric methods. When pupil weights are used to recognize the additional costs associated with special-needs students and a price index is added to the formula, equity analyses should use both a weighted-pupil count and price-adjusted dollars.

There is less consensus surrounding adjustments for secondary and early elementary students and for small (or large) size. While many states weight high school students an extra 25 to 30 percent, this weight reflects current expenditure patterns more than productivity findings. Indeed, the research base is stronger for investing more in the K–3 grades; K–3 weightings, including extended-day kindergarten and even preschool programs for low-income four-year olds, are increasingly popular policy choices.

Controversy still surrounds the costs associated with small districts and schools. While policymakers generally support school and district consolidation, research undergirding that policy option is thin. In general, research does not support incentives to create larger schools and districts, but state policies providing extra resources for small schools and districts in isolated rural areas make sense.

States still use many different general-aid formulas and have many different methods of adjusting for the additional costs associated with students with special

---

[17] Since cost-of-education as well as cost-of-living indices also are correlated with household income, a cost index alters at the margin relative distribution of state aid towards higher-income communities. This impact is partially offset if a household income measure also is part of the fiscal capacity measure, which alters at the margin relative distribution of state aid towards lower-income communities (see Chapter 3). It could be argued that if states incorporate a cost index in their school-aid formula, they also should include income in the measure of local fiscal capacity, and vice versa (see Odden, 1979, 1980).

needs. Some of these include full-state funding, census-based funding, and pupil weights. In the years to come, policymakers will continue to grapple with the question of which of these methods is the most feasible, comprehensible, politically viable, and equitable. And while that question can be answered differently in different states, it is clear that there is no longer any question that such adjustments are needed.

A New School Finance Formula

Given all of the necessary adjustments for students with special needs, all of the other adjustments just discussed, and the push for educational adequacy rather than just educational equity, a new type of school finance formula may be in order. This new formula, one which would provide an adequate fiscal base that enables schools to deliver an education program that teaches students to high-achievement standards, would consist of six elements:

1. A base spending level that would be considered adequate for the average child, which in the short term could be approximated by the median expenditure level,
2. An extra amount of money for each child from a low-income background,
3. An extra amount for each disabled student,
4. An extra amount for each student who needs to learn English,
5. Adjustments for education level and scale diseconomies, and
6. A price adjustment for all dollar figures to ensure comparable spending power.

With such a school finance system, a state could reasonably say it had financed the state's core interests in education. And if states were allowed to pool categorical money from federal and state sources, such a school finance system could also be said to finance a large portion of the federal government's interests in education as well.

An Econometric Approach to Adjustments for Different Needs

But an even simpler type of school finance system might be possible in the future, if quite complex research is successful in quantifying how much money it takes to teach different students to standards, in different types of communities. Economists such as Reschovsky and Imazeki (1998), Downes and Pogue (1994), Duncombe, Ruggiero, and Yinger (1996), Ladd and Yinger (1994), and Ruggiero (1996) have been pursuing an approach that can simultaneously be used to determine an average, foundation spending level as well as adjustments for all of the special needs listed above, be they student needs, issues of scale, education level, or geographic price differences. The results could also be used for a somewhat simpler school finance structure. Technically, these economists are trying to construct a "cost function" for a state's education system. Simply put, a cost function would identify the level of funding needed to produce a certain level of output, such as student achievement, given different characteristics of schools and its students. In the work being conducted with Wisconsin data, Reschovsky has attempted to determine how much money a district, with the average demographic characteristics, must spend to teach students to state average-performance levels. In his analysis, he focused on average achievement levels, although he could have set the performance target at a higher level, say the 70th percentile. This amount of money would reflect the "adequate" foundation base, "adequate" being defined by the performance level that the state chooses. From the results of the cost function, he then constructs an overall cost adjustment that accounts for:

1. Different characteristics of students, specifically the percent from a low-income background (as measured by eligibility for free and reduced-price lunch), the percentage disabled, and the percentage with limited English proficiency,
2. Different prices across school districts and labor market regions, and
3. Economies and diseconomies of scale, as measured by the number of students.

Put differently, this research is trying to construct an overall cost index that adjusts for student need differences, price differences, and scale economies/diseconomies. Related work by others also attempts to adjust for efficiency differences (see for example, Duncombe, Ruggiero, and Yinger, 1996).

Although the research is state-of-the-art and uses complex econometric statistical analyses, the primary benefit of the research is that two important numbers are produced: the expenditure level needed in the average or typical district/school, and a cost adjustment that accounts for all other factors: student need, price, scale, and at some level, efficiency. Thus, the school finance formula would be a cost-adjusted foundation program. The program would provide a base spending level, which for the Wisconsin data was $6,333 using 1996–97 data. The cost factor varied widely, from a low of 0.59 percent of to a high of 2.00. The amount of money guaranteed to each district would be the foundation amount, $6,333, times the cost factor. This means that given the above characteristics of schools/students/districts, the average district required $6,333 to teach its students to average achievement levels, while the least needy districts/schools required only 59 percent of that, or $3,736 (lower than any district actually spent), and the most needy district required $12,666 (higher than the neediest district actually spent). And these amounts would be sufficient to produce the average achievement level. If Reschovsky had set the achievement level desired above the current average, the dollar figures would have been higher.

Though more research of this type is needed, the goal of the cost-function approach is very similar to the above-proposed new type of school finance structure, one that identifies an adequate base foundation level of spending which is then adjusted at least by student-need factors and price factors, and perhaps scale and efficiency factors as well. When research on this subject becomes more definitive, school finance systems can be more tightly linked to education goals. In turn, the state would know how much money is needed in each school to teach students to state-set achievement standards.

Results from the cost function research also can be disaggregated to produce different student weights, a scale-economy adjustment, an education-level adjustment, and a geographic price adjustment. When this disaggregation was conducted in a study in Kansas, the state's pupil weights for special needs were quite close to the weights calculated from the cost function analysis (Johnston and Duncombe, 1998).

CHAPTER 4 PROBLEMS

Problems 4.1, 4.2, and 4.3 should be considered as class exercises using the 20-district simulation sample after the issues developed in Chapter 4 have been covered. These problems raise the interrelated issues of school finance equity goals; state, local, and total costs; and the particular interests of districts with below-average and those with above-average property wealth per pupil.

Problem 4.1. Divide the class into groups of one, two, or three so that each group represents one of the school districts in the 20-district sample.

First, have each group design a foundation program with an increased state cost of $25 million that gives their district the greatest increase in state aid. Have each group discuss in class why their plan should be the one proposed to the legislature. Each group should argue on the basis of *the impacts of their program on school finance equity and adequacy.*

Second, have each group design a foundation program with an increased state cost of $25 million that they feel is best for their particular district *and* that they think would garner two-thirds support of their class, or of the legislature that would be deliberating such a proposed change.

Compare the different foundation programs.

Problem 4.2. Divide the class into two groups. Members of group 1 represent superintendents from districts low in property value per pupil (i.e., districts 1–10). Members of group 2 represent superintendents from districts high in property value per pupil (i.e., districts 11–20). You could vary the districts in the different groups; there does not have to be 10 districts in each group.

Ask each group to simulate a combination foundation-GTB program with total extra costs at $45 million (i.e., the sum of increased state and local revenues).

For this exercise, have each group consider school finance equity and adequacy as well as political feasibility. Have each group decide whether their interest is better served by a relatively low foundation program with a relatively high GTB or a relatively high foundation program and a modest GTB, or something in between, and have them explain why.

Compare the different designs. Some should have large increases in state aid combined with large decreases in local revenues for a total revenue increase of $45 million. Others should have increased state costs much closer to the $45 million and much less property tax relief.

Problem 4.3.   Again divide the class into groups—of two, three, or four depending on the size of the class—representing different types of districts, below-average wealth, average wealth, and above-average wealth.

Have each group design any school finance program—foundation, GTB, or combination foundation-GTB—that improves both horizontal equity and adequacy. Make sure that they identify all the key formula and policy parameters, and have clear equity goals.

Have each group argue the merits of their proposals on equity, adequacy, and cost grounds. At the end, have the class vote on the different proposals presented, reminding them that they represent taxpayers as well as the education community. The vote should be on one proposal.

Problem 4.4.   Assume that the base data for the 20-district sample on the *School Finance* simulation represents the condition of school finance in your state. A taxpayer rights group has conducted an analysis of that system, and based on that analysis, have sued in state court arguing that school spending levels are a function of district wealth. They have asked the court to invalidate the state's funding structure. You are the chief of staff of the state legislature's school finance committee. In analyzing a printout of the base data from the simulation, you see that per-pupil revenue ranges from $3,480 to $7,527, with a tax rate in the lowest revenue district of 39.64 mills and 25.5 mills in the highest revenue district. The state share of total educational revenue is under 40 percent. Moreover, you note that the correlation of revenue and wealth per pupil is 0.991, and the wealth elasticity is far above 0.10. Looking carefully at a graph of revenue versus wealth per pupil for the base data, you conclude there is substantial likelihood the court will invalidate the state finance structure.

Additionally, a number of years ago, the state's voters approved an expenditure limitation. As a result, the state is unlikely to have more than $20 million in additional funds to devote to education next year.

Using the *School Finance* simulation, design a school finance foundation program that reduces the correlation between wealth and revenue, without increasing state spending by more than $20 million. Experiment with different combinations of foundation level and required levy effort. Experiment with combinations of high and low foundation levels and high and low RLEs. Find more than one foundation level/RLE combination that costs the state $20 million or less. Identify different foundation programs at this state cost that benefit poorer districts more than wealthy districts, and then identify foundation programs that spread the additional $20 million to most districts. Once you have three or four possible options, answer each of the following questions:

1. How do each of these combinations meet the fiscal neutrality criteria that might be used in the lawsuit?
2. What impact do each of these options have on the horizontal equity of the system?
3. How does total revenue for education change under each of these options? How does the state's share of total revenue change?
4. What happens if you change the rules and base the state contribution on district tax rates rather than the RLE for districts currently levying a rate lower than the RLE?
5. Which foundation program option would you recommend to the legislature? Why?
6. How will you address legislative questions about districts that gained and lost state aid?
7. If the state suddenly found that it could devote $30 million to education next year rather than $20 million, how would you change your recommendations?

Problem 4.5.   Using the same information as presented in Problem 4.4, relax the restriction that you must use a foundation program to design a new school finance system. Experiment with the GTB option, and find a model that meets the $20 million state spending-increase limitation. How does this model compare to the foundation program you recommended to the legislature in Problem 4.4? Specifically:

1. How does total state spending change under the GTB compared to the foundation program?
2. How do local district tax rates compare?
3. Are there more winners or losers under the GTB? How does the magnitude of each district's gain or loss in state aid vary between the two options?
4. Which model, the GTB or foundation program, does a better job of minimizing the relationship between wealth and revenue?
5. Which of the two models better meets horizontal equity standards?
6. How does the state's share of total educational revenue compare between the two models?
7. Which model would you recommend to the legislature? Describe the trade-offs that policymakers will have to make in choosing one option over the other.
8. How does your analysis change if there is $30 million available for education instead of $20 million?

Problem 4.6.   A number of states have opted to use a two-tier program, relying on a foundation program to provide a base level of revenue for all districts, and a GTB to equalize district decisions to supplement that base. Using the same $20 million limitation, design a combination (two-tier) school finance system for your state. How does this model compare to the two models above? What would you now recommend to the legislature? Why? What happens if the state is willing to increase its commitment to $30 million?

Summary Tables

For all proposals, have students create summary tables to display the results of their various simulations. For foundation programs, tell students to rank them from lowest to highest foundation level (or highest to lowest). The following indicates the type of data to include:

Simulation	Flat Grant	Foundation Level	Required Tax Rate	Zero-Aid District	GTB	Adequacy Expenditure Level	Number of State-Aid Winners/Losers
Base data	—	—	—	—	—	—	—
1	$4,000	—	—	—	—	$5,350	20/0
2	—	$5,154	31.32	$164,559	—	5,350	14/6
3	—	—	—	138,000	$138,000	5,350	10/10
4	—	5,154	31.32	164,559	138,000	5,350	16/0

Simulation	Change in Local $	Change in State Dollars (in millions)	Change in Total Dollars (in millions)	Coefficient of Variation	McLoone/ Verstegen Index	Wealth Elasticity	Odden-Picus Adequacy Index
Base Data	—	—	—	0.170	0.810/1.086	0.324	0.895
1	0	$218.4	$218.4	0.181	0.814/1.107	0.347	0.994
2	$24.4	26.1	50.6	0.030	0.992/1.070	0.146	0.985
3	64.2	46.7	17.5	0.125	0.881/1.086	0.246	0.926
4	24.1	4.8	58.9	0.066	0.962/1.044	0.115	0.99

Improving State School Finance Systems

Chapter 4 described a variety of formulas and strategies for improving state school finance systems. In this chapter, we use those formulas and strategies to "fix" the school finance systems in three different states. The states present different types of school finance problems, so the chapter shows how one needs to tailor a school finance formula or structural change to the specific nature of the school finance problem being addressed. As the chapter will demonstrate, a school finance structure that improves the equity or adequacy of a school finance system in one state might exacerbate it in another, and vice versa.

The chapter has four sections. Section 1 describes the overall framework that will be used to determine the nature of the school finance problem in each state, as well as to identify the goals to be attained by any proposed improvement. Sections 2, 3, and 4 then use the framework to analyze the school finance systems in Vermont, Wisconsin, and Illinois, respectively.

1. A FRAMEWORK FOR ANALYSIS

When assessing the degree of equity or adequacy in a state's school finance system, one needs some type of framework to structure that analysis. We provided such a framework in Chapter 2. In this section of this chapter, we use the concepts developed in Chapter 2 to structure our analysis of the finance systems in each of three states.

Students are the group of concern for the following analyses. Our discussions will assess equity and adequacy from the perspective of students.

The unit of analysis will be the district, as the information in the state files on the McGraw-Hill web site (*www.mhhe.com/schoolfinance/*) includes fiscal data only on a district-by-district basis. When computing all statistics, each district's value will be statistically weighted by the number of students in the district.

241

This means the values of large districts will affect the statistical results more than the values of smaller districts. Finally, the data include information only for the K–12 districts in Wisconsin and Illinois. This excludes a small number of districts in Wisconsin, but a larger number in Illinois. In these two states, there are both elementary-only and high school–only districts, in addition to districts that serve all grades from kindergarten to grade 12. But we analyze only the data for the K–12 districts. Vermont is more complex. Many "districts" in Vermont are individual schools with locally elected boards. These schools are generally part of a Supervisory Union, which provides many district level services to the school. However, the taxing authority for the school remains in the local community, and for the purposes of this analysis, they are treated as individual districts.

In most cases, the analysis will use an ex post versus an ex ante analysis (i.e., will assess results using fiscal data on actual behavior). In some instances, though, there will be ex ante comments on the nature of the extant state formula. As the discussion will show, sometimes when systems appear highly equitable from an ex ante perspective, they produce a system that is quite inequitable from an ex post perspective.

The object of analysis will be state plus local revenues per pupil. This fiscal object essentially includes all local revenues as well as state equalization aid or state general aid. This revenue total comprises the fiscal resources essentially for the "regular" education program. Although the state data on the McGraw-Hill web site for the state simulation exercises also contain categorical program data for state compensatory education, bilingual education, and handicapped programs, we do not use those data in the analyses in this chapter. Thus, this chapter only addresses issues related to the regular-education program, and not any programs for extra student needs. In other words, the analysis here ignores the issue of vertical equity, or adjustments for special student (or district) needs.

Each analysis will assess issues of both horizontal and fiscal neutrality equity, as well as adequacy. For horizontal equity, the coefficient of variation will be the key disparity statistic, but the analyses also will incorporate the McLoone Index, to make comments on the equity of the bottom half of the distribution. The analysis will use a 0.10 standard for the coefficient of variation (CV); CVs less than or equal to 0.10 will indicate an equitable distribution. The analysis will use a 0.95 standard for the McLoone Index, labeling a distribution with a McLoone Index equal to or higher than 0.95 as providing equity for the bottom half of the distribution.

For fiscal neutrality, the analyses will focus on the wealth elasticity, using a standard of 0.10, thus concluding that a wealth elasticity less than or equal to 0.10 would indicate a negligible link between the resource variable and property wealth per pupil. The discussion will mention the correlation coefficient, particularly noting when it is below 0.5, but will use the elasticity statistic to draw conclusions about the connection between state and local revenues per pupil and property wealth per pupil.

Finally, the Odden-Picus Adequacy Index will be used to draw conclusions about the adequacy of each state's school finance system. For two states, this part of the analysis will reference studies that have suggested an adequate revenue-per-pupil figure for the regular-education program. But for the other state, the specification of the adequate amount per pupil will have less research support so we will only be able to make comments on the adequacy issue. Our standard will be an Adequacy Index of 1.0 on the assumption that there are or are not "adequate" revenues per pupil in all districts.

Following the Odden and Clune (1998) call to set "policy targets" for improving state school finance structures, we will assess the impact of two general strategies in all states for improving the equity and adequacy of their school finance structure. First, we will simulate a GTB at or above the 90th percentile, a level that provides ex ante fiscal neutrality. Second, we will simulate a foundation at least at the median, which could be a rough approximation of adequacy.

2. SCHOOL FINANCE IN VERMONT

The Vermont data are for the 1996–97 school year, the year Vermont's school finance system was declared unconstitutional in the *Brigham* v. *Vermont* court case (*Brigham* v. *State of Vermont*, No. 96-502) (VT filed Feb. 5, 1997). The data were downloaded from the Vermont Department of Education's web site and adjusted to include only public school districts that raised and spent public tax dollars. There were a total of 201 districts with some 73,000 students and regular-education expenditures of $450.2 million from state and local sources. Property wealth is equalized to 100 percent of market value.

Prior to the enactment of Act 60—the 1997 school funding law enacted in response to the Vermont Supreme Court's ruling in Brigham, the Vermont school finance system relied primarily on a foundation program. The major problem with the foundation program, as pointed out in the court decision, was that average school-funding levels substantially exceeded the foundation level. Moreover, most funds raised and spent above the foundation level were raised through unequalized property tax levies. This led to the "traditional" school finance problem identified above, low-wealth districts with high tax rates and low per-pupil revenues.

To address the problems identified by the court, the Vermont legislature passed Act 60, which established a block grant program guaranteeing each district essentially $5,000 per pupil at a uniform statewide tax rate of $1.10 per $100 of assessed valuation, or 11.1 mills. Although called a block grant, it is clearly a foundation program. A second-tier GTB was included in Act 60. However, rather than provide state funding to help districts reach their revenue goals, the second tier is funded entirely through property taxes in the districts that elect to participate in the second tier. The system, frequently referred to as the "shark tank" by the Vermont media, creates a system where districts that elect to raise revenues beyond the $5,000 level don't know what their tax rate will be until all districts have determined how much revenue they will collect through the guaranteed yield. A uniform tax rate is then established across the state. Chapter 4 pointed out that one of the potential problems with a GTB is that the cost to the state can't be predicted with certainty. In Vermont, the state has shifted the risk to school districts, with wealthy districts absorbing higher levels of risk—if they choose to participate in the second tier.

To mitigate against high property taxes, homeowner property taxes in the first tier are limited to a maximum of 2 percent of income for taxpayers with incomes below $75,000. Total property taxes including the second tier and other municipal property taxes are limited to no more than 5 percent of household income for those earning less than $75,000 a year (there is a sliding scale based on income). The impact of this is to shift more of the property tax burden to out-of-state property owners (who constitute a substantial proportion of taxpayers) and to nonresidential property. The taxation provisions of Act 60 will not be fully implemented.

The Vermont School Finance Problem

Figure 5.1 displays the base data for Vermont. The data from the 201 districts are displayed by deciles. Each decile has approximately 10 percent of the students in the state. Consequently, the number of districts in each decile (reported in the last column of the figure) varies from a low of 9 in the sixth decile to a high of 29 in the lowest revenue decile. The figure shows total state plus local spending of $450,185,325, with local districts raising over 72% of this total.

Across the deciles, average total revenue per pupil ranged from a $4,659 to $8,191, a ratio of 1.75 to 1. Property wealth generally increases as spending increases. Across the deciles, property wealth per pupil ranges from a low of $236,776 per pupil to a high of $777,284 per pupil, a factor of 3.25 to 1. State aid per pupil declines as revenues and wealth increase, while locally raised revenues climb with wealth and spending level.

The coefficient of variation is 0.147, above the 0.10 standard identified in Chapter 2. The McLoone Index is estimated at 0.90, below the 0.95 standard we also established in Chapter 2. The Verstegen Index stands at 1.016.

Determining a reasonable revenue level for the adequacy calculation was difficult. For Vermont, we have used a very low figure—the $5,000 per pupil, the block grant level established by the legislature in Act 60. With that figure, the Odden-Picus Adequacy Index is 0.994. That means that to bring those districts with revenues per pupil below $5,000 to that spending level, revenues would have to increase by 0.006 percent relative to $5,000, or only about $30 per pupil. Others might choose to set the adequacy level higher, in which case the Adequacy Index would be lower.

The adequacy calculation may be a predictor of the problems Vermont is likely to encounter as Act 60 is implemented. Recall that the second tier is equalized entirely by local property taxes levied on districts that participate in that pool. Since most districts are spending above the level of the $5,000 block grant, most would be expected to participate in the second-tier GTB. In this case, property taxes on the wealthy districts are likely to go up dramatically. The alternative

Adequacy Level	$	5,000
Pupil Weights		no
Disabled		—
Limited English		—
Low Income		—

Decile	Average Number of Pupils per District in Decile	Average Property Value per Pupil ($)	Average Property Tax Rate (Mills)	Average Local Revenue per Pupil ($)	Average State Revenue per Pupil ($)	Average Total Revenue per Pupil ($)	Number of Districts in Decile
1	252	239,362	11.51	2,719	1,940	4,659	29
2	385	242,444	12.79	3,107	2,177	5,284	18
3	368	249,748	14.02	3,475	2,056	5,531	21
4	432	236,776	14.33	3,402	2,342	5,744	17
5	371	507,437	12.86	4,392	1,536	5,928	19
6	821	317,844	13.73	4,269	1,831	6,100	9
7	391	350,994	14.60	4,805	1,540	6,345	18
8	214	432,737	14.05	5,517	1,160	6,677	27
9	466	509,522	15.09	5,699	1,436	7,136	18
10	335	777,284	13.09	7,392	800	8,191	25
Weighted Average		338,713	14.05	4,452	1,691	6,142	
Weighted Std. Dev.		223,080	2.88	1,645	1,059	905	
Median		214,200	10.91	2,337	3,699	6,037	

Totals		
	Amount	Percent
Local Revenue	326,270,231	72.48%
State Revenue	123,906,094	27.52%
Total Revenue	450,185,325	
Pupils	73,294	

Equity Measures	
Horizontal Equity	
Range	$6,712
Restricted Range	2,851
Federal Range Ratio	0.597
Coef. of Variation	0.147
Gini Coefficient	0.094
McLoone Index	0.900
Verstegen Index	1.016
Fiscal Neutrality	
Correlation	0.482
Elasticity	0.072
Adequacy	
Odden-Picus	0.994

FIGURE 5.1   Base Data (Vermont), 1996–97

is substantial declines in the level of per-pupil revenue, and hence spending. But if $5,000 is an appropriate adequate level, the argument for higher spending would be less forceful. On the other hand, if $5,000 is below an adequate expenditure level, then there could be pressures to increase the $5,000 base to a higher level, and reduce "forced" spending above the base.

In terms of fiscal neutrality, Figure 5.1 shows that the correlation between revenue and wealth is 0.482, and the elasticity is a relatively low 0.072. However, if you download the simulation from the McGraw-Hill web site and analyze the Vermont data, you will see that the graph of the base data shows the presence of a few high wealth–medium revenue-level districts. These outliers have the effect of lowering the elasticity. Eliminate those outliers from the model, and there is a very strong relationship between wealth and revenue.

Improving the Vermont School Finance System

Since the Vermont legislature has already taken steps to improve the equity of the Vermont school finance system, we will begin our analysis with the changes made in Act 60. First we will consider a simple foundation program using the parameters of the state's block grant. That will be followed by the promised GTB at the 90th percentile of wealth, and finally a combination program with similar characteristics.

First, we simulated a foundation program with a foundation level of $5,000 and a RLE of 11.1 mills, which reflects the first tier of the reform Vermont enacted. The result increased total spending by just $3.1 million, with the state share falling by just over $3.2 million, and local taxes increasing by $6.3 million. A total of 108 districts experienced a loss of state aid and were forced to make it up through increased property taxes, which occurred in all but the second and third deciles. Only districts in the two lowest revenue deciles experienced increases in revenue. Both the horizontal equity and fiscal neutrality measures showed very small improvements, while the Odden-Picus Adequacy Index improved to 1.0, meaning all of the districts received at least $5,000 per pupil in total revenue. Again, if a higher adequacy level were set, the Adequacy Index would have been less than 1.0.

Figure 5.2 shows the results of a GTB program using a per-pupil property wealth level of $510,800 representing the district at the 90th percentile of wealth. The figure shows immediately why the legislature was unwilling to fund a high-level GTB program. A GTB at this level would raise an additional $48.5 million for schools, provide taxpayers with $19.7 million in property tax relief, and cost the state an additional $68.2 million. Finding those revenues would have been difficult. Recall that additional revenues would be collected from a statewide property tax under Act 60. If this simulation is indicative of what will happen when Act 60 is implemented, at an average property wealth of $338,713, property tax rates would have to increase an average of 2.75 mills across the state, thus offsetting the modest property tax relief shown in Figure 5.2.

Interestingly, although the GTB increased spending dramatically, it did little to change the horizontal equity statistics, which remain roughly the same as in the base data. Correlation and elasticity do decline however.

Figure 5.3 displays the results of a combination program using the block grant parameters and a GTB level of $510,800. This compromise appears to be the best option of those presented, but is more generous than the program Vermont enacted. Total revenue increased by just over $30.2 million, with a drop of $4.2 million in local taxes and an increase in state funding of $34.4 million. While the horizontal equity figures show very small improvements, the elasticity declined to 0.001. The correlation is higher than under the GTB, but this is in large part due to the very low elasticity observed, and highlights the policy problem

Adequacy Level	$ 5,000
Pupil Weights	no
Disabled	—
Limited English	—
Low Income	—

Guaranteed Tax Base	510,800.00

Decile	Average No. of Pupils	Average Property Value per Pupil ($)	Average Old Property Tax Rate (Mills)	Average New Property Tax Rate (Mills)	Average Change in Property Tax Rate (Mills)	Average Old Local Revenue per Pupil ($)	Average New Local Revenue per Pupil ($)	Average Change in Local Revenue per Pupil ($)	Average New State Revenue per Pupil ($)	Average Change in State Revenue per pupil ($)	Average Total Revenue per Pupil ($)	Average Change in Total Revenue per Pupil ($)	Number of Districts in Decile
1	252	247,425	10.70	10.15	(0.55)	2,524	2,494	(30)	2,693	539	5,187	409	28
2	328	433,400	11.80	10.88	(0.92)	3,572	3,388	(184)	2,482	696	5,870	511	23
3	329	330,077	12.40	11.88	(0.52)	3,922	3,873	(49)	2,312	514	6,185	466	22
4	382	305,800	13.70	12.51	(1.19)	4,036	3,759	(213)	2,749	917	6,507	640	18
5	338	361,016	13.53	12.44	(1.08)	4,456	4,242	(285)	2,428	831	6,671	618	19
6	616	370,771	14.02	12.89	(1.12)	4,752	4,466	(285)	2,419	886	6,886	601	14
7	593	293,217	15.26	13.82	(1.44)	4,453	4,052	(402)	3,006	1,207	7,058	805	12
8	423	488,250	14.26	12.85	(1.41)	5,069	4,727	(342)	2,554	1,095	7,282	753	16
9	390	461,014	14.56	13.53	(1.03)	5,965	5,738	(226)	1,920	846	7,658	620	21
10	266	605,657	16.08	14.49	(1.59)	6,598	6,230	(368)	2,517	1,239	8,747	871	28
Weighted Average		338,713	14.05	12.90	(1.14)	4,452	4,183	(269)	2,621	931	6,804	662	
Weighted Std. Dev.		223,080	2.88	2.07	(0.23)	1,645	1,734	407	1,417	862	923	489	
Median		347,600	15.27	15.28	(0.93)	5,306	4,516	(690)	2,167	1,705	6,783	1014	

Totals

	Amount	Percent	Change From Base Amount
Local Revenue	306,579,415	61.48%	(19,699,316)
State Revenue	192,126,350	38.52%	68,220,255
Total Revenue	498,705,765		48,520,440
Pupils	73,294		

Winners and Losers

Category	Winners	Losers	No Change
State Aid	155	46	0
Total Rev.	155	0	46

Equity Measures

Horizontal Equity	
Range	$6,407
Restricted Range	3,416
Federal Range Ratio	0.639
Coef. of Variation	0.136
Gini Coefficient	0.065
McLoone Index	0.897
Verstegen Index	1.101
Fiscal Neutrality	
Correlation	0.292
Elasticity	0.029
Adequacy	
Odden-Picus	0.999

FIGURE 5.2   Guaranteed Tax Base (GTB) (Vermont)

Adequacy Level $ 5,000

Pupil Weights	no
Disabled	—
Limited English	—
Low Income	—

Foundation Level	$5,000.00
Required Tax Rate	11.10
GTB	$510,800.00
GTB rate cap above foundation tax rate	99.00

Decile	Pupils	Property Value per Pupil ($)	Old Property Tax Rate (Mills)	New Property Tax Rate (Mills)	Change In Property Tax Rate (Mills)	Old Local Revenue per Pupil ($)	New Local Revenue per Pupil ($)	Change in Local Revenue per Pupil ($)	New State Foundation Revenue per Pupil ($)	New State GTB Revenue per Pupil ($)	Change in State Revenue per Pupil ($)	Total Revenue per Pupil ($)	Change in Total Revenue per Pupil ($)	Number of Districts in Decile
1	251	235,630	10.82	11.45	0.63	2,518	2,689	170	2,385	99	210	5,173	410	27
2	408	247,653	12.87	12.18	(0.68)	3,154	3,005	(149)	2,268	285	613	5,558	458	19
3	300	446,483	11.62	12.03	0.40	3,699	3,893	194	1,676	343	18	5,912	459	24
4	377	286,265	14.21	13.47	(0.74)	4,026	3,854	(172)	1,834	511	593	6,198	552	20
5	431	336,381	13.97	13.19	(0.79)	4,400	4,254	(147)	1,627	515	612	6,395	439	16
6	461	398,325	13.36	13.18	(0.18)	4,860	4,880	19	1,247	474	208	6,600	246	16
7	590	332,077	15.23	14.18	(1.05)	4,827	4,592	(234)	1,528	627	827	6,748	389	13
8	443	392,846	14.25	14.12	(0.13)	5,119	5,119	0	1,219	598	299	6,936	311	13
9	302	515,566	14.34	13.78	(0.56)	5,848	5,773	(75)	1,069	616	480	7,458	350	29
10	315	668,483	15.62	14.62	(0.99)	6,918	6,749	(169)	1,031	850	754	8,630	376	24
Weighted Average		338,713	14.05	13.62	(0.42)	4,452	4,394	(58)	1,647	514	470	6,555	413	
Weighted Std. Dev.		223,080	2.88	2.14	1.33	1,645	1,756	447	1,080	418	781	900	398	
Median		516,700	12.24	12.60	0.37	6,324	6,513	189	-	-	(189)	6,513	-	

Totals

	Amount	Percent	Change From Base Amount
Local Revenue	322,063,154	67.04%	(4,216,076)
State Revenue	158,370,429	32.96%	34,464,335
Total Revenue	480,433,584		30,248,259
Pupils	73,294		

Winners and Losers

Category	Winners	Losers	No Change
State Aid	130	71	0
Total Rev.	106	0	95

Equity Measures

Horizontal Equity	
Range	$5,365
Restricted Range	3,182
Federal Range Ratio	0.613
Coef. of Variation	0.137
Gini Coefficient	0.076
McLoone Index	0.900
Verstegen Index	1.110
Fiscal Neutrality	
Correlation	0.371
Elasticity	0.001
Adequacy	
Odden-Picus	1.000

FIGURE 5.3   Combination Program (Vermont)

identified in Chapter 4 when using both figures. The state share of total revenue increases to almost 33 percent, and while 71 districts lose state revenue, all districts have as much total revenue or more than before. Nevertheless, the number of state-aid-loser districts represents about one-third of all districts, which diminishes the political attractiveness of even this program.

In short, the Vermont school finance system is difficult to improve without spending more state money. The reform that was enacted, Act 60, has been controversial because of its burden on out-of-state property owners and the redistributive nature of the second tier. Only time will tell how this reform will ultimately be implemented.

3. SCHOOL FINANCE IN WISCONSIN

The Wisconsin data are for the 1995–96 school year. Property wealth is equalized to 100 percent of market value.

For 1995–96, Wisconsin had a three-tiered, GTB school finance structure that was enacted in 1995, though the formula parameters changed each year. For tier one, the state guaranteed a tax base of $2 million per pupil, up to the first $1,000 of spending. Since the GTB for this tier exceeded that of all school districts, tier one provided some state aid to all 379 school districts. There were two reasons for this "generous" nature of tier one. First, this transformed what had been termed "minimum" or "hold harmless" aid for the wealthy districts into a "bona fide" state-aid allotment. To be sure, this shift was in part simply political, but it did eliminate the use of "minimum" aid, a phrase that simply indicated on the face of it an inequitable allocation of state support. Second, because this state-aid formula was enacted primarily to provide property tax relief, the provision of at least some aid ensured that even the wealthiest districts would experience some property tax relief (see discussion of cost controls below). Although many Wisconsin policymakers and education leaders criticized this element of the formula, it nevertheless was enacted as a part of the new structure.

Tier two provided the bulk of state aid. The GTB for tier two was $406,592, which covered districts that enrolled 95 percent of all students. Tier-two GTB aid was provided for spending from $1,000 up to $5,786, which was the expenditure per pupil of the district that enrolled the 56th percentile student.

Tier three had a straightforward and a unique element. The GTB was set at the statewide average. Districts with a property wealth below that level could use tier three for any amount of spending above the tier-two ceiling of $5,786. This was the straightforward element of tier two.

The unique element of tier two pertained to those districts with a property wealth per pupil above the state average, or the tier-three GTB. For these districts, there was a "negative-aid" calculation. When these districts decided to spend above the tier-two expenditure ceiling of $5,786, a negative value for tier-three aid was determined. This negative amount was then subtracted from the tier-two aid, but only until and if it reduced tier-two aid to zero. Since a previous court decision in Wisconsin had determined that it was unconstitutional for the state actually to "recapture" local property tax revenue through a negative-aid calculation, the tier-three factor never required districts to send funds to the state for redistribution to other districts. But tier-three calculations could potentially reduce tier-two aid amounts to zero. Tier-three negative calculations primarily affected higher-spending metropolitan school districts, those surrounding Milwaukee and Madison. Districts also always retained their tier-one aid which, politically, was created as an amount that all districts would receive.

Finally, when the state enacted this program, it also imposed "cost controls" on local school districts. Previously, school boards had had the power to raise local property tax rates to increase school spending. The cost controls continued that authority but only for expenditure increases, which in 1997–98 were about $211 per pupil. Districts could exceed this expenditure-per-pupil increase limit, but they needed voter approval to do so. When enacted in 1995, the $200 per-pupil cost increase limit combined with the $1,000 per pupil of aid for tier one meant that the bulk of that additional revenue, even for the wealthiest districts, had to be used for decreasing the property tax rate, absent a local vote to use it for increased spending.

The overall goal of the Wisconsin school finance structure was to set the state role in financing schools at two-thirds of all revenues.

The Wisconsin School Finance Problem

Figure 5.4 shows the base data for Wisconsin for 1997–98. The data are grouped into deciles ranked by total revenues per pupil; the simulation attempts to have approximately the same number of students in each decile. Since the data are ranked by revenues per pupil, the averages in all columns show the average of that variable for their decile of spending. So the average property wealth per pupil in the first decile is the average of property wealth per pupil for the first decile of spending, not the first decile of property wealth. Nevertheless, in our discussion, we will refer to the property wealth figure as a rough indicator of the average of the respective decile as if the data had been ranked by property wealth per pupil. But readers should know that this is a rough approximation.

The data show there is a wide variation in property wealth per pupil: the average is $218,605, but it is only $165,734 in the lowest decile and fully $331,347 in the wealthiest decile. Without substantial state equalization aid, districts would have great difficulty raising equivalent amounts of money per child at the same tax rate. Note, however, that the GTB in Wisconsin's second tier ($406,592) exceeds the average property wealth per pupil of the tenth and wealthiest decile, so it is above the 90th percentile. This shows that the second tier of the Wisconsin system provides property wealth equalization up to a very high level (i.e., provides substantial ex ante fiscal neutrality equity).

Tax rates also vary but within a small range, with an average tax rate of 12.56 mills in decile one to 17.73 mills in decile 10.

The table also shows that revenues per pupil vary, but by a much smaller

Adequacy Level	$	6,030
Pupil Weights		no
Disabled		—
Limited English		—
Low Income		—

Decile	Average Number of Pupils per District in Decile	Average Property Value per Pupil ($)	Average Property Tax Rate (Mills)	Average Local Revenue per Pupil ($)	Average State Revenue per Pupil ($)	Average Total Revenue per Pupil ($)	Number of Districts in Decile
1	1,701	165,734	12.56	2,084	3,025	5,108	47
2	1,959	168,277	13.23	2,228	3,153	5,381	41
3	2,697	186,804	13.53	2,528	2,975	5,502	30
4	1,811	167,573	13.78	2,309	3,294	5,602	32
5	34,060	151,904	13.96	2,121	3,557	5,678	3
6	2,911	183,485	14.15	2,598	3,153	5,751	28
7	1,476	169,609	14.84	2,514	3,415	5,929	54
8	1,919	188,730	15.72	2,971	3,173	6,145	38
9	1,904	204,424	17.03	3,444	3,016	6,460	47
10	1,723	331,347	17.73	5,146	2,008	7,154	47
Weighted Average		211,438	14.67	3,137	2,726	5,862	
Weighted Std. Dev.		93,728	1.85	1,487	1,154	547	
Median		218,605	13.97	3,054	2,627	5,681	

Totals		
	Amount	Percent
Local Revenue	2,527,836,576	53.50%
State Revenue	2,196,748,542	46.50%
Total Revenue	4,724,585,118	
Pupils	805,908	

Equity Measures	
Horizontal Equity	
Range	$4,694
Restricted Range	1,715
Federal Range Ratio	0.331
Coef. of Variation	0.093
Gini Coefficient	0.107
McLoone Index	0.961
Verstegen Index	1.033
Fiscal Neutrality	
Correlation	0.454
Elasticity	0.090
Adequacy	
Odden-Picus	0.947

FIGURE 5.4   Base Data (Wisconsin)

percentage than property wealth per pupil. Spending per pupil from state, general, and local sources varies from $5,108 in the lowest-spending decile, to just $5,678 in the fifth decile, and then to $7,154 in the tenth decile.

One of the most interesting features of Figure 5.4 is that it reveals a state with the "new" school finance problem. As property wealth per pupil rises, so also does spending per pupil. But local property tax rates also rise with property wealth. So Figure 5.4 shows that in Wisconsin, lower-wealth districts have lower tax rates and also lower spending levels, while higher-wealth districts have higher tax rates and thus higher spending levels. It appears that it is the link between tax rates and property wealth that drives the spending–property wealth connection in

Wisconsin. Further, recall that for a GTB, the higher the tax rate, the higher the spending-per-pupil level. In Wisconsin, most districts apply their tax rate to the GTB for spending at least up to $5,786; since the GTB is higher than the average for even the tenth decile, tax rates are more a determinant of spending levels than are property values.

Despite this phenomenon, the equity statistics show a fairly equitable distribution of education revenues. The CV is 0.093 and thus meets the equity standard for that statistic. The McLoone Index is 0.961, which also meets the standard of 0.95 for this statistic. Thus, in terms of horizontal equity, the Wisconsin school finance system in 1995–96 for K–12 districts met tough standards for an equitable distribution.

This finding is important for two reasons. First, the Wisconsin constitution requires a school finance system that is as equitable as "practical," which these statistics show has been accomplished. The distribution is not perfectly equal, and even the wealthiest districts receive some amount of state general aid. But the system nevertheless meets our horizontal equity standards. Second, though, Wisconsin uses a GTB-type school finance, which defers spending levels to local districts and thus is not focused on providing equality of spending per pupil. Nevertheless, the structure provides a high degree of spending-per-pupil equality.

In terms of fiscal neutrality, the Wisconsin system also receives good but not superlative marks. The correlation coefficient is 0.454, and the wealth elasticity is 0.090, both just meeting the equity standard for this statistic. Though some improvements could be made in reducing the linkage between spending and property wealth, the data already show a remarkable degree of fiscal neutrality equity. The problem in making improvements on this front will be the tax rate–property wealth link. Because higher-wealth districts have higher tax rates, they also have higher spending levels; the spending differences are caused mainly by tax-effort differences, not tax-base differences.

Finally, the Odden-Picus Adequacy Index is 0.947, with the adequacy expenditure level set at $6,030; this is the 1997 figure of $6,333 found by Reschovsky and Imazeki (1998) but deflated by 5 percent to a 1995–96 figure. The relatively high Adequacy Index suggests that Wisconsin may not be far from providing an "adequate" amount of money for the average child in all districts. It would need to increase the funding for those districts below the adequate level by an average of 0.053 percent relative to the adequacy level, or by an average of about $320 to produce adequacy for all K–12 districts for the average student.

Improving the Wisconsin School Finance System

A key question for Wisconsin school finance is: What needs to be improved? From an ex ante perspective, those who filed a court case in the late-1990s argued that districts with a wealth above that in the second-tier GTB should not receive any state support. They proposed eliminating tier one, which provides some aid to all districts, and either reducing state aid to zero for any district with a wealth above the tier-two GTB level or actually changing the constitution to allow for recapture. Others might take issue with that perspective, but it would produce a school finance structure with a "purer" version of ex ante fiscal equity.

A second approach is to determine whether a high-level GTB program, which provides ex ante fiscal neutrality, can in fact reduce the link between spending and property wealth per pupil. This task is difficult because of the tax rate–property wealth link. To assess the efficacy of this strategy, we ran simulations of a one-tier GTB set at $350,000, $400,000, and $500,000, all guaranteeing property wealth per pupil at more than the 90th percentile. Both the horizontal and fiscal neutrality equity statistics worsened under each one of these programs, though the simulation results portray a "rosier" picture because all state aid losses are made up with greater local taxes to insure that spending does not decline if aid is lost. And the lower of these GTB levels also produced many state-aid "losers," which diminished their political viability as well.

This result occurs because this state represents the "new" school finance situation. Since tax rates rise with property wealth per pupil, a higher GTB simply widens the spending-per-pupil difference between lower-wealth and higher-wealth districts. This result increases the coefficient of variation, reduces the McLoone Index, and increases the wealth elasticity between total revenues per pupil and property wealth per pupil. A GTB program, even a combination foundation-GTB program, with the GTB set at a high level, simply worsens fiscal equity statistics in a state like Wisconsin with the "new" school finance problem.

As an alternative, Figure 5.5 shows the results of simulating a foundation program at $6,000 per pupil with a required tax rate of 14 mills. Even though above the median, the $6,000 foundation expenditure figure was chosen because it had been suggested by many education and political leaders as an expenditure level and a school finance structure that might be more suitable for the state. The 14 mill tax rate was the median tax rate for this simulated program, and just above the median in the base data. Further, these two figures produce a "zero-aid" district of $428,571, which is slightly above the extant tier-two GTB level. Another way of interpreting this program is that it turns the extant system from a GTB at around $428,571 with local decision making on the level of a tax rate, to one with a required tax rate of 14 mills, which raises the spending in all districts now spending below $6,000 to the $6,000 per-pupil level.

As mentioned above, all Wisconsin simulations use $6,030 as the adequacy level, a figure slightly above the foundation level and the median because that was the figure determined by Reschovsky and Imazeki (1998) as sufficient for the average district to teach the average student to the average-performance level on Wisconsin standards. Actually, Reschovsky and Imazeki identified a figure of $6,333 for the 1996–97 school year; we deflated that figure by 5 percent to $6,030 for 1995–96. Although we could have set the foundation level at the adequacy level, we decided to set it just below that level simply to show it produces an Adequacy Index less than one. If adequacy were the primary goal, we would have set the foundation expenditure level at the adequacy figure.

Figure 5.5 shows that the simulated foundation programs improves equity on both fronts as well as improves the adequacy of the Wisconsin school finance

Adequacy Level	$	6,030

Pupil Weights	
Disabled	no
Limited English	—
Low Income	—

Foundation Level	$6,000.00
Required Tax Rate	14.00

Decile	Pupils	Property Value per Pupil ($)	Old Property Tax Rate (Mills)	New Property Tax Rate (Mills)	Change In Property Tax Rate (Mills)	Old Local Revenue per Pupil ($)	New Local Revenue per Pupil ($)	Change in Local Revenue per Pupil ($)	New State Revenue per Pupil ($)	Change in State Revenue per Pupil ($)	Total Revenue per Pupil ($)	Change in Total Revenue per Pupil ($)	Number of Districts in Decile
1	1,741	163,524	13.12	14.00	0.88	2,146	2,289	143	3,711	522	6,000	665	46
2	2,447	165,838	13.24	14.00	0.76	2,197	2,322	125	3,678	490	6,000	615	32
3	3,197	180,497	13.63	14.00	0.37	2,452	2,527	75	3,473	381	6,000	456	3
4	4,621	172,210	13.26	14.00	0.74	2,290	2,411	121	3,589	487	6,000	608	33
5	2,196	183,647	13.23	14.00	0.77	2,431	2,571	141	3,429	481	6,000	622	37
6	2,043	168,550	14.35	14.10	(0.25)	2,413	2,374	(39)	3,640	258	6,014	218	40
7	1,660	170,404	14.90	14.35	(0.55)	2,537	2,442	(95)	3,614	211	6,056	116	48
8	2,126	200,279	15.66	14.90	(0.76)	3,134	2,969	(166)	3,196	197	6,165	31	34
9	1,904	204,424	17.03	16.71	(0.33)	3,444	3,298	(146)	3,162	146	6,460	0	47
10	1,723	331,347	17.73	17.95	0.21	5,146	5,062	(84)	2,092	84	7,154	0	47
Weighted Average		211,438	14.67	14.61	(0.06)	3,137	3,086	(50)	3,085	359	6,171	309	
Weighted Std. Dev.		93,728	1.85	1.39	1.01	1,487	1,326	254	1,105	209	334	291	
Median		115,363	13.48	14.00	0.52	1,555	1,615	60	4,385	460	6,000	520	

Totals

	Amount	Percent	Change From Base Amount
Local Revenue	2,487,224,527	50.01%	(40,612,049)
State Revenue	2,486,126,518	49.99%	289,377,976
Total Revenue	4,973,351,045		248,765,927
Pupils	805,908		

Winners and Losers

Category	Winners	Losers	No Change
State Aid	322	32	13
Total Rev.	224	0	143

Equity Measures

Horizontal Equity	
Range	$3,032
Restricted Range	902
Federal Range Ratio	0.150
Coef. of Variation	0.054
Gini Coefficient	0.118
McLoone Index	1.000
Verstegen Index	1.057

Fiscal Neutrality	
Correlation	0.529
Elasticity	0.065

Adequacy	
Odden-Picus	0.997

FIGURE 5.5 Foundation Program (Wisconsin)

system. The coefficient of variation drops from 0.093 to 0.054, the McLoone Index increases to a perfect 1.0, the wealth elasticity drops to 0.065, and the Adequacy Index improves to 0.997.

The cost is modest, about a 13 percent increase in state funds but a decline of about 1.6 percent in local funds. At the required tax rate of 14 mills, local school districts previously levying a school tax rate below 14 mills (mostly lower-wealth districts) increased their local effort, while the middle-wealth districts previously levying above 14 mills had modest local tax-rate declines. The highest-wealth districts also had modest tax-rate drops. This foundation program could be simulated with a lower required tax rate; the equity statistics would remain about the same, and the total increased cost would be about the same, but the local portion of the increase would drop, and the state portion would rise. Where to set the required tax rate would need to be determined through the political process. At the 14 mill rate, the program increased aid to 322 districts, and not surprisingly, reduced aid to 32 districts, largely those districts that had received some aid from the first tier.

In sum, a school finance system such as that in Wisconsin, which already produces a fairly equitable school finance system but with differences in spending and wealth reflecting the "new" school finance problem, can be enhanced with high-level foundation programs. The simulations showed that GTB programs simply worsen equity measures. Further, in a state such as Wisconsin, which already spends far above the national average, the simulations show that adequacy can be approached with only modest increases in spending, however split between local districts and the state.

We should note, however, that the above results do not address the issue of providing extra funds for special-student needs, particularly those students who have disabilities, speak a native language other than English, or come from low-income families and thus need additional education supports. Busch, Kucharz, and Odden (1996) show that insufficient aid for special-needs students was a shortcoming of the Wisconsin finance system that needed enhancement. Reschovsky and Imazeki (1998) found that a 2.0 weight was needed for each low-income child (i.e., that twice as much money was required to teach a low-income child to state standards). The Wisconsin data base on the McGraw-Hill web page (*www.mcgraw-hill.com/schoolfinance/*) includes these additional data, and readers can experiment with alternative ways to address these special-education needs and assess their costs as well as their impacts on fiscal equity and adequacy.

4. SCHOOL FINANCE IN ILLINOIS

The Illinois data are for the 1994–95 school year, and again, include only the "unit districts" (i.e., the districts that serve all grades from kindergarten through grade 12). Property wealth per pupil in Illinois is equalized to only about 33 1/3 percent of market value (i.e., lower than Wisconsin). Thus, to compare the property wealth and tax rates in Illinois to those in Wisconsin, one would need to multiply the Illinois wealth figures by three and divide the tax rates by three to provide information relative to full market value.

In 1994–95, Illinois had a two-pronged school finance structure. Most districts operated under a typical foundation-type school finance formula. The foundation expenditure level was set at 2,900 with a required local property tax rate of 19 mills. Readers might conclude that the foundation level was quite low. For that year, the average expenditure per pupil for operating purposes in Illinois was $6,136 (NCES, 1998a), so the foundation expenditure level was just 47 percent of the average. The zero-aid district had a property wealth per pupil of $105,072, which was below that of many districts.

On the other hand, the state also used a weighted-pupil count to determine and allocate state aid; weights were provided by education level, counting students in kindergarten through grade 6 as 1.0, in grades 7–8 as 1.05, and grades 9–12 as 1.25. Using a weighted-pupil count as the denominator generally decreases the expenditure figure when compared to a figure without weighted-pupil counts. The data base in the simulation includes weighted pupil counts.

The data also exclude the Chicago school district; this large, urban district actually enrolls about one-third of all students in K–12 districts and thus would cover three deciles of the simulation. Such a district usually is identified separately in a school finance analysis, but the simulation data used exclude this district altogether.

The Illinois School Finance Problem

For years, Illinois struggled with proposals to enhance the state role in public school financing. As Figure 5.6 shows, the state role in 1994–95 for these K–12 districts was just 53.5 percent; when Chicago is included, the state role for K–12 districts was below 40 percent. For the decade prior to 1994–95, the state experienced school finance legal challenges, votes on constitutional changes to increase the state role, and proposals for school reform from both the governor and various members of the legislature.

Figure 5.6 shows there was a good case to be made for shortcomings in the Illinois school finance system. The data are grouped into deciles ranked by total revenues per pupil; the simulation attempts to have approximately the same number of students in each decile.

The data show there was a wide variation in property wealth per pupil: the average is $57,107, but it is close to $30,000 in the lowest deciles and fully $182,744 in the wealthiest decile. The wealthiest decile has just over six times the property wealth per pupil, and thus six times the ability to raise local revenues for public schools, than does the poorest decile. Even the average district has about twice the wealth as the poorest deciles. Without substantial state equalization aid, districts would have great difficulty raising equivalent amounts of money per child at the same tax rate. Though not shown, the property wealth per pupil in Chicago is substantially above the state average.

Tax rates also vary but within a smaller range, with an average tax rate of

Adequacy Level	$	4,500
Pupil Weights		no
Disabled		—
Limited English		—
Low Income		—

Decile	Average Number of Pupils per District in Decile	Average Property Value per Pupil ($)	Average Property Tax Rate (Mills)	Average Local Revenue per Pupil ($)	Average State Revenue per Pupil ($)	Average Total Revenue per Pupil ($)	Number of Districts in Decile
1	1,834	51,825	22.79	1,056	1,552	2,607	45
2	1,645	31,555	28.88	905	1,992	2,897	51
3	1,919	31,120	30.87	942	2,004	2,946	43
4	1,261	31,768	32.53	1,020	1,986	3,007	62
5	2,161	42,664	33.63	1,412	1,685	3,098	41
6	1,940	44,988	35.24	1,565	1,621	3,187	43
7	2,427	50,658	36.71	1,832	1,465	3,296	34
8	2,269	54,741	38.57	2,077	1,352	3,429	37
9	2,392	63,644	41.15	2,564	1,129	3,693	32
10	4,304	182,744	35.21	4,994	359	5,353	21
Weighted Average		57,107	33.45	1,881	1,450	3,330	
Weighted Std. Dev.		51,377	5.38	1,260	634	763	
Median		43,365	34.02	1,475	1,665	3,140	

Totals		
	Amount	Percent
Local Revenue	1,565,784,916	56.47%
State Revenue	1,206,982,693	43.53%
Total Revenue	2,772,767,609	
Pupils	832,553	

Equity Measures	
Horizontal Equity	
Range	$10,883
Restricted Range	1,806
Federal Range Ratio	0.646
Coef. of Variation	0.229
Gini Coefficient	0.034
McLoone Index	0.931
Verstegen Index	1.161
Fiscal Neutrality	
Correlation	0.821
Elasticity	0.190
Adequacy	
Odden-Picus	0.726

FIGURE 5.6   Base Data (Illinois)

33.45, and ranging from at or below 22.79 mills in the lowest-spending decile to 35.21 mills in the highest spending decile and 41.15 in the ninth decile.

The table also shows that revenues per pupil vary, but by a much smaller percentage than property wealth per pupil. Spending per pupil from state general and local sources varied from $2,607 in the lowest-spending decile, to just $3,098 in the fifth decile, and then to $5,353 in the tenth decile. The average was just $3,330, far below the Wisconsin average of close to $6,000, though the Wisconsin data use unweighted-pupil counts compared to the weighted counts in the Illinois data base.

The data in Figure 5.6 also show that Illinois is another state with the "new" school finance problem. As property wealth per pupil rises, so also does spending per pupil. But local property tax rates also rise with property wealth. Just as in Wisconsin, lower-wealth districts in Illinois have lower tax rates and also lower spending levels, while higher-wealth districts have higher tax rates and thus higher spending levels. It appears that it is a link between tax rates and property wealth as well as a wealth advantage that drives the spending–property wealth connection in Illinois. Although unlike in Wisconsin, where local tax rates apply to a relatively high GTB state program, for spending above the foundation in Illinois, local tax rates apply to local wealth. The result, nevertheless, is that wealth, tax rates, and spending levels all rise in tandem.

The data also show that there are anomalies in the connections among property wealth, tax rates, and spending in Illinois. For example, the lowest-spending decile actually has a wealth of $51,825, close to the state average but a very low tax rate of 22.79 mills. These are mainly rural and agricultural districts in southern Illinois. If these districts had levied just average tax rates, their expenditures per pupil would have been significantly higher. They simply have not tapped their wealth advantage. Conversely, the property wealth per pupil of the tenth decile is over double that of the nearest (ninth) decile. This dramatic wealth advantage allows these districts to enjoy very high spending with tax rates just a small bit above the state average. Thus, although there is a general, positive connection between wealth, tax rates, and spending, the bottom- and top-spending deciles represent differences from the general overall pattern.

The larger role of local wealth in driving spending disparities in Illinois is reflected in the equity and adequacy statistics, all of which are "worse" than those in Wisconsin. The coefficient of variation is 0.229, far above the standard of 0.10. The McLoone Index is below 0.95 at 0.931. The wealth elasticity is a high 0.190, and the correlation between spending per pupil and property wealth per pupil is high at 0.821. But again, since the state presents the "new" type of school finance problem, a high-level GTB, which provides ex ante fiscal neutrality equity, will unlikely improve these equity statistics by much.

Finally, the low level of spending is reflected in the Odden-Picus Adequacy Index, which is just 72.6 percent. As is indicated in the table, we set the adequate spending level at $4,500. This was a level somewhat higher than that identified by an Illinois study of the level of state and local revenues per pupil needed to have 70 percent or more of students achieve at or above state standards on the Illinois state testing system (Hinrichs and Laine, 1996).

In sum, Illinois presents several types of school finance problems. These data for 1994–95 show wide disparities in spending per pupil, a large local role in financing schools, a "new" school finance problem in which higher wealth districts have higher spending but also higher tax rates, and a system that falls far short of providing adequate revenues.

Improving the Illinois School Finance Structure

Though a state could focus on simply reducing expenditure-per-pupil disparities, or just decreasing the link between spending and wealth, or providing more adequate levels of revenues, the following analysis will assess the progress various new school finance strategies make on all three of these fronts.

We simulated a GTB program at $100,000, a figure that is at the lower-end approximation of the 90th percentile and close to the zero-aid district in the extant foundation program (Figure 5.7). We can somewhat predict the effect of this program. For a $100,000 GTB, a tax rate of 30 mills is needed to produce spending at the $3,000 per-pupil level. Higher tax rates are needed to produce higher spending levels. Because of this, even this relatively high-level GTB might require most districts to increase tax rates just to maintain former spending levels.

That is precisely what we found. A GTB of $100,000 required both local and state revenues to rise. Local revenues rose in the lower-decile districts because even this high-level GTB provided them less state aid. State revenues rose in the mid-wealth deciles because the GTB provided both more money for higher spending and for local property tax relief. Local revenues also rose for the higher-wealth districts.

Perhaps not surprisingly, this GTB did not make significant gains on equity and adequacy statistics. The coefficient of variation was still high at 0.22, the McLoone Index dropped to 0.90, the fiscal neutrality statistics improved modestly, and the Adequacy Index rose from 0.726 to 0.747. Though this program cost only an extra total of $79.5 million, it had almost no positive equity or adequacy impact on the system. The program also produced over 100 state-aid "losers," rendering the program politically problematic as well.

Thus, we ran a GTB at a much higher level—$150,000—ensuring some substantial property tax relief at the risk of not making sufficient equity gains in this state with the "new" school finance problem. Figure 5.7 presents the results. First, the state cost rose substantially, which might make such a program unaffordable. Though there was some local tax relief, which was one of the goals, it was not very high.

Though the equity and adequacy statistics improved, there is not sufficient progress to declare the system sound. The coefficient of variation at 0.178 is still far above the standard of 0.10. The McLoone Index is just 0.885. But both the fiscal neutrality and adequacy statistics are much better, with the wealth elasticity at 0.112 and adequacy at 90.2 percent.

The problem with a GTB program for a state with the "new" school finance problem is that a very high, and thus very expensive, GTB must be used, and then only modest gains on some equity and adequacy fronts are produced. Thus, we tried a foundation program to ensure that the lower-spending districts actually had to hike spending, which allowed spending above the foundation level but only with local wealth. Figure 5.8 shows a foundation program with a foundation expenditure of $4,300 and a required tax rate of 35 mills, which is one mill above the median. We simulated foundation programs at lower tax-rate levels but the costs seemed too high, though as Figure 5.8 shows, this program is not low-cost either.

Such a foundation program, which is similar to the reform enacted by Illinois in late 1997, does accomplish the goal of raising the state and lowering the

Adequacy Level	$	4,500		Guaranteed Tax Base	150,000.00
Pupil Weights		no			
Disabled		—			
Limited English		—			
Low Income		—			

Decile	Average No. Of Pupils	Average Property Value per Pupil ($)	Average Old Property Tax Rate (Mills)	Average New Property Tax Rate (Mills)	Average Change in Property Tax Rate (Mills)	Average Old Local Revenue per Pupil ($)	Average New Local Revenue per Pupil ($)	Average Change in Local Revenue per Pupil ($)	Average New State Revenue per Pupil ($)	Average Change in State Revenue per Pupil ($)	Average Total Revenue per Pupil ($)	Average Change in Total Revenue per Pupil ($)	Number of Districts in Decile
1	1,844	52,702	22.78	20.08	(2.70)	1,080	968	(112)	2,054	527	3,022	415	45
2	1,678	35,774	28.67	24.00	(4.66)	1,025	859	(166)	2,741	866	3,600	700	49
3	1,731	34,331	30.33	25.01	(5.32)	1,039	859	(180)	2,893	977	3,752	797	44
4	1,733	33,926	32.02	26.04	(5.98)	1,082	884	(198)	3,022	1,095	3,906	897	52
5	1,390	41,204	33.50	27.08	(6.42)	1,374	1,117	(257)	2,945	1,220	4,062	963	53
6	2,764	43,183	35.16	28.19	(6.97)	1,511	1,217	(294)	3,012	1,340	4,228	1,046	34
7	2,657	50,237	36.11	28.99	(7.12)	1,789	1,456	(332)	2,893	1,400	4,349	1,068	31
8	2,343	56,761	37.34	29.98	(7.37)	2,041	1,668	(373)	2,864	1,482	4,532	1,109	36
9	2,515	54,468	40.16	31.91	(8.26)	2,153	1,740	(413)	3,046	1,652	4,786	1,239	31
10	2,608	123,955	39.98	33.51	(6.47)	3,766	3,404	(361)	2,246	1,352	5,650	991	34
Weighted Average		57,107	33.45	27.66	(5.79)	1881	1599	(282)	2604	1155	4203	872	
Weighted Std. Dev.		51,377	5.38	4.18	2.06	1260	1219	165	768	408	749	298	
Median		51,477	34.22	27.79	(6.43)	1762	1431	(331)	2738	1296	4168	965	

Totals

	Amount	Percent	Change from Base Amount
Local Revenue	1,330,981,501	38.04%	(234,803,415)
State Revenue	2,168,176,978	61.96%	961,194,285
Total Revenue	3,499,158,480		726,390,871
Pupils	832,553		

Winners and Losers

Category	Winners	Losers	No Change
State Aid	398	11	0
Total Rev.	398	0	11

Equity Measures

Horizontal Equity	
Range	$10,883
Restricted Range	1,895
Federal Range Ratio	0.564
Coef. of Variation	0.178
Gini Coefficient	0.005
McLoone Index	0.885
Verstegen Index	1.125
Fiscal Neutrality	
Correlation	0.612
Elasticity	0.112
Adequacy	
Odden-Picus	0.902

FIGURE 5.7 Guaranteed Tax Base (GTB) (Illinois)

Adequacy Level	$	4,500
Pupil Weights	no	
Disabled	—	
Limited English	—	
Low Income	—	

Foundation Level	$4,300.00
Required Tax Rate	35.00

Decile	Pupils	Property Value per Pupil ($)	Old Property Tax Rate (Mills)	New Property Tax Rate (Mills)	Change in Property Tax Rate (Mills)	Old Local Revenue per Pupil ($)	New Local Revenue per Pupil ($)	Change in Local Revenue per Pupil ($)	New State Revenue per Pupil ($)	Change in State Revenue per Pupil ($)	Total Revenue per Pupil ($)	Change in Total Revenue per Pupil ($)	Number of Districts in Decile
1	1,665	38,308	25.85	34.07	8.22	869	1,176	308	3,033	1,139	4,209	1,447	49
2	1,587	28,626	29.42	35.00	5.58	824	1,002	177	3,298	1,225	4,300	1,402	53
3	1,265	36,557	30.63	35.00	4.37	1,078	1,279	201	3,021	1,160	4,300	1,361	63
4	1,941	44,736	31.52	35.00	3.48	1,372	1,566	194	2,734	1,094	4,300	1,288	45
5	2,294	57,029	31.59	35.00	3.41	1,782	1,996	214	2,304	1,013	4,300	1,226	30
6	3,355	55,841	33.92	35.04	1.12	1,879	1,956	77	2,346	1,006	4,301	1,083	29
7	2,009	43,754	36.30	35.59	(0.71)	1,585	1,552	(33)	2,769	1,095	4,321	1,063	40
8	1,951	51,579	38.18	36.55	(1.63)	1,951	1,874	(77)	2,495	1,039	4,369	963	40
9	3,384	51,440	40.32	37.66	(2.66)	2,055	1,928	(127)	2,500	1,049	4,427	922	25
10	2,591	126,140	39.30	36.53	(2.77)	3,771	3,647	(124)	1,468	601	5,115	477	35
Weighted Average		57,107	33.45	35.48	2.03	1,381	1,960	79	2,440	990	4,400	1,070	
Weighted Std. Dev.		51,377	5.33	2.53	4.14	260	1,218	233	946	342	482	424	
Median		63,337	34.00	35.00	1.00	2,153	2,227	63	2,083	968	4,300	1,032	

Totals	Amount	Percent	Change from Base Amount
Local Revenue	1,631,873,444	44.55%	66,088,528
State Revenue	2,031,483,579	55.45%	824,500,886
Total Revenue	3,663,357,023		890,589,414
Pupils	728,146		

Winners and Losers			
Category	Winners	Losers	No Change
State Aid	397	12	0
Total Rev.	393	0	16

Equity Measures	
Horizontal Equity	
Range	$10,883
Restricted Range	359
Federal Range Ratio	0.083
Coef. of Variation	0.110
Gini Coefficient	0.977
McLoone Index	0.997
Verstegen Index	1.048
Fiscal Neutrality	
Correlation	0.785
Elasticity	0.098
Adequacy	
Odden-Picus	0.964

FIGURE 5.8   Foundation Program (Illinois)

local percentage role in financing schools. And it also makes larger gains on all equity and adequacy fronts. The coefficient of variation at 0.110 is just above the 0.10 standard, the McLoone Index is 0.997, which indicates that nearly all districts are spending at the median, the wealth elasticity is below 0.10 at 0.98, and the Adequacy Index is 0.964. But the program required an extra $891 million in state revenues and $66 million more in local revenues, the latter produced by setting the required minimum local tax effort at 35 mills.

The dilemma in "fixing" the Illinois school finance system was that lower foundation levels produced less progress on equity and adequacy. Higher foundation levels could not be accompanied by a required local tax effort that exceeded 35 mills, which is still quite high, and thus required large infusions of state dollars. The bottom line was that the only way significant equity and adequacy gains could be made was by raising the foundation level, as the state ultimately did. But the "cost" of doing so was a substantially enhanced state fiscal role, close to an increase of $1 billion, which represented an 80 percent increase from the base of $1.2 billion.

The high state cost was one reason the state had struggled for years to enact a school finance reform. The only option was a much larger state role; that either required a state tax hike, which was not politically feasible, or a very healthy economy that produced increased in-state revenues that could be devoted to school finance. That was the scenario that finally prevailed. The fact that such a program also raised state aid in nearly all districts added to the political acceptability of the program.

CONCLUSION

Fixing state school finance problems is no easy task. It requires balancing equity and adequacy goals with the political economics of education—producing sufficient winners at a cost the state can afford. Though not discussed at length above, all of the final programs simulated produced many more school districts that had their state aid amounts increased than those that did not.

The above examples also show that the nature of the school finance problem varied dramatically across the three states, thus requiring different kinds of solutions. The Vermont system was somewhat easier to improve as it represented a more "traditional" school finance situation; a high GTB worked in this state, though the best structure was a two-tier system. But high GTBs did not work in either Wisconsin or Illinois, as both states represented "new" school finance problems. In these states, high-level GTBs were expensive and produced only modest equity and adequacy gains. The resolution in both states required a higher-level foundation program; such a program could be funded with quite small increases in state aid in Wisconsin but required large increases in Illinois.

Other states will require even different solutions, some perhaps requiring more of a two-tiered school finance structure as in Vermont and which we favored more in the first edition (Odden and Picus, 1992). Others will require even different mixes of state and local revenues. The bottom line in improving state school finance systems is that it requires some combination of the following:

1. Getting a clear understanding of the nature of the problems—too much local revenue, inadequate spending, wide spending disparities, significant connections between spending and wealth, or whatever.
2. Determining which type of school finance structure—GTB, foundation, or two-tiered, foundation-GTB programs—likely will work.
3. Determining a level of spending adequacy.
4. Simulating alternative forms of the formula structures that might resolve the problems and assessing the gains in equity and adequacy in light of both local and state costs as well as political impacts (state-aid winners and losers and numbers of districts that have to raise local taxes).

Judging which program might be the one to try in a state will depend on answers to these school finance, public finance, and political effects, answers that will vary by state, and probably vary with time within any individual state.

Chapter 6

Allocation and Use of Funds at the District, School, and Classroom Levels

Distributing dollars to districts in equitable ways is a first step in providing educational resources for the purposes of educating children. Interdistrict resource allocation has dominated school finance for years. But we now need to know about how to turn dollars into productive uses in districts, schools, and classrooms. Indeed, there is considerable misinformation about how schools use money. Former U.S. Secretary of Education William Bennett and many others have implied that too much money is used for administration, popularizing the term the "administrative blob."

This chapter identifies what is now known about what happens to dollars once they reach districts. The questions that require answers are:

- Where did the money go? To instruction? To regular classroom teachers? To specialist teachers working outside the regular classroom? To administration and the alleged "administration blob"? To support services? To raise teachers' salaries? To lower class size? To lengthen the school day or year? To "overhead"?
- How was it used? To increase instruction in the regular program? To boost instruction in the core academic programs? To teach more curriculum content? To improve mathematics and science, in which the country still wants to improve student performance? To provide services for special-needs students? And does resource use differ across elementary, middle, and high schools?

- What impact did it have on student achievement? How do resource allocation and use patterns relate to student performance? Have these patterns changed towards patterns that produce more learning? Are the linkages different at the elementary, middle, and high school levels?

School finance as a field of study is slowly beginning to answer these questions but as this and subsequent chapters show, there is still much more work to be done.

Since schools and classrooms are the "production units" in education, gathering data on resource allocation and use at these levels began to be the focus of research in the 1990s. For each level of schooling—elementary, middle, and high school—the following types of data are needed:

- expenditure by program—the regular instruction program; programs for special-needs students such as compensatory, bilingual, and special education; administration; staff development; and instructional materials,
- expenditures by content area—mathematics, language arts (reading in elementary schools), science, history/social science, foreign language, art, music, and physical education,
- interrelationships among these expenditure patterns, and
- relationships of these expenditure patterns to student performance.

The field of school finance is far from having this knowledge. At the present time, few states report expenditures by program area with their current accounting systems, and only Florida, Ohio, and Texas can report expenditure and staffing data by site.

Nevertheless, these data are the minimum needed to address the productivity questions that policymakers now ask. They want to know where new money goes, what resources—especially instructional and curriculum resources—it buys, and what impact those resources have on student performance. These are very reasonable questions.

As another example, the total expenditure by level for elementary, middle, and high schools across the United States and within most of the 50 states is not known. Data are not systematically collected by school level (Busch and Odden, 1997a). Yet as discussed in subsequent chapters, altering resource-use patterns at the school site might be the most promising way to improve education system productivity in the near future. Further, since early education investments seem to have high payoffs in terms of student learning, perhaps one reason that student achievement is low is because our nation underinvests in education in the early years, particularly pre-K and K–3, and overinvests in education at the secondary and postsecondary levels.

This chapter provides a brief overview of how education dollars are used. The first section describes expenditures by function and staffing patterns on a national and statewide basis. Section 2 discusses how expenditure and use patterns vary across districts within a state, especially across different spending levels. The next section describes information about expenditures at the site level. Section 4 discusses challenges associated with formally collecting resource data at the school-site level.

1. RESOURCE-USE PATTERNS AT THE NATIONAL AND STATE LEVELS

All 50 states collect some kind of fiscal data from their school districts. These data include information on district revenues and expenditures and on district employees. The revenue data generally contain information on the sources and amounts of revenue received by each school district. Expenditure data are most frequently collected by object of expenditure, divided into categories such as professional salaries, classified salaries, employee benefits, materials and supplies, and capital expenditures. States now also collect expenditure data by broad program area or function such as instruction, administration, transportation, plant operation and maintenance, and debt service.

Staffing data usually include numbers of professional staff, and within that, numbers of administrators, teachers, librarians and counselors, instructional aides, and support staff. In some states, data on teacher credentials and/or assignments are also available. Analyzing these data provide a beginning towards knowing how money is used, but the results are several steps removed from the data needed to answer important productivity issues. Nevertheless, these data provide a starting point for identifying how districts use money.

Expenditures by Function

Annually, the National Center for Educational Statistics (NCES) provides nationwide and individual state data on expenditures by function. But because definitions for functional categories differed across states, the NCES reported expenditures across only a few very broad functional categories prior to 1990.

Figure 6.1 provides data on expenditures by function at the national level from 1920 to 1980. Two points should be noted about the data in these tables. First, the distribution of expenditures by function changed over these 60 years. The data show that the percent spent on instruction declined, and that the percent spent on administration and fixed charges (benefits) increased over this time period. Second, however, the percent spent on instruction remained about the same from about 1950 onward. Since the percent figures are related to total expenditures, which include capital as well as current expenditures, the percent spent on instruction as a percentage of current expenses needs to be calculated. The figure would be 60.8 percent for 1980, a figure quite close, as we shall show, to the percent spent on instruction today.

FIGURE 6.1   Percent Distribution of Expenditures by Function, 1920–80

	1920	1930	1940	1950	1960	1970	1980
			Percentage Distribution				
Total expenditures, all schools	100.0	100.0	100.0	100.0	100.0	100.0	100.0
Current expenditures, all schools	83.4	80.0	83.4	80.9	79.8	85.7	91.2
Public elementary and secondary schools	83.1	79.6	82.8	80.3	79.0	84.1	90.6
Administration	3.5	3.4	3.9	3.8	3.4	3.9	4.4
Instruction	61.0	56.9	59.9	53.3	53.5	57.2	55.5
Plant operation	11.2	9.3	8.3	7.3	6.9	6.2	
Plant maintenance	2.9	3.4	3.1	3.7	2.7	2.4	10.2
Fixed charges	0.9	2.2	2.1	4.5	5.8	8.0	12.3
Other school services[1]	3.5	4.4	5.5	7.7	6.6	6.3	8.3
Summer schools	(2)	(2)	(2)	(2)	0.1	0.3	(4)
Adult education[2]	0.3	0.4	0.6	0.6	0.2	0.3	—
Community colleges	(2)	(2)	(2)	(2)	0.2	0.3	—
Community services	(1)	(1)	(1)	(1)	0.4	0.6	0.6
Capital outlay[3]	14.8	16.0	11.0	17.4	17.0	11.5	6.8
Interest on school debt	1.8	4.0	5.6	1.7	3.1	2.9	2.0

Source: NCES (1989), p. 151.

Note: Beginning in 1959–60, includes Alaska and Hawaii. Because of rounding, details may not add to totals.

[1] Prior to 1959–60, items included under "Other school services" were listed under "Auxiliary services," a more comprehensive classification that also included community services.

[2] Prior to 1959–60, data shown for adult education represent combined expenditures for adult education, summer schools, and community colleges.

[3] Prior to 1969–70, excludes capital outlay by state and local school-housing authorities.

[4] Less than 0.05 percent.

During the late 1980s and early 1990s, the NCES inaugurated a project to collect more detailed expenditure data that also were comparable across states. During this process, they also somewhat changed the categories of data collected. Figure 6.2 displays national data on expenditures by function for both 1990–91 and 1994–95. The data show that instructional expenditures continued to comprise about 61 percent of the operating budget, rising just a bit from 60.5 percent in 1991 to 61.7 percent in 1995. The data also show what have become typical expenditure distributional patterns: about 10 percent for student and instructional support, 3 percent for district administration, 6 percent for site administration, 10 percent for operations and maintenance, and about 10 percent for transportation, food, and other services.

Individual state patterns differ but not dramatically from this pattern.

FIGURE 6.2   Current Expenditures by Function for the United States, 1991–95

Current Expenditures	*1990–91* %	*1994–95* %
Instruction	60.5	61.7
Instructional support	4.2	4.0
Student support	6.9	6.1
District administration	2.9	2.4
School administration	5.8	5.8
Operation and maintenance	10.5	10.7
Student transportation	4.3	4.1
Food	4.2	4.2
Other	0.5	0.3

NCES, 1998a, p. 162.

Totals may not equal 100 percent due to rounding.

Figure 6.3 includes just the percent spent on instruction for several states. Hawaii, for example, with the highest state role in funding schools, spent 61.9 percent on instruction, very close to the national average of 61.7 percent. On the other hand, New Hampshire, which has the largest local and smallest state role in funding public education, spent 64.4 percent on instruction, slightly above the national average. The other states listed spent just under or just over the national average, except Utah which spent 67.390 for instruction. The data show that states quite consistently spend just over 60 percent of their current operating education budget on instruction, which are the expenditures that provide direct teaching services to students.

FIGURE 6.3   Instructional Expenditures for Selected States, 1994–95

	Instruction as Percent of Current Operating Expenses (%)
California	60.0
Hawaii	61.9
Kentucky	60.0
New Hampshire	64.4
New Jersey	60.0
Texas	61.2
Utah	67.3
Wisconsin	63.5
U.S. average	61.7

Source: NCES (1998a).

Staffing Patterns

Translating these broad expenditures into staffing patterns is the next step in analyzing what happens to the education dollar. Figure 6.4 presents national data on the distribution of school district staff by staffing category from Fall 1960 to Fall 1995. Administrators do not appear to represent a large portion of the total. District, or central office, administrators totaled just 1.7 percent of total staff in 1995 and site administrators just 2.4 percent. Combined, administrators comprised a total of just 4.1 percent of all staff, fairly small percentages given the charges that the education system spends so much on administration. Instructional staff dropped from 69.8 percent in 1960 to 67.1 percent in 1997. But this small decline masked larger changes in the composition of instructional staff. Though not shown in the table, teachers constituted 74.1 percent of total staff in 1950. The table shows that the percentage of teachers declined to 64.8 percent in 1960 and then to only 52 percent in 1995. At the same time, the percentage of instructional aides rose from almost zero in 1960 to 9.9 percent in 1995.

Similarly, the percentage of support staff also rose over this time period, from 28.1 percent in 1960 to 31.2 percent in 1995. These numbers show that about one-third of staff in the education system perform nonadministrative roles, such as secretaries, operation, maintenance, and transportation personnel. When policymakers and local taxpayers wonder why only 60 percent of expenditures are spent on instruction, one answer is that operations, maintenance, transportation, and a small amount of district administration account for nearly a third of public school expenditures.

The bottom line, though, is that the percentage of teachers has dropped nearly 33 percent in the latter half of the twentieth century. They have been "replaced" by instructional aides, pupil support staff, and as we shall show below, by specialist teachers within schools but not teaching in regular classrooms. The policy and productivity issue is whether this use of resources is the most effective.

FIGURE 6.4   Staff Employed in the Public Schools, 1960–95 (Percent Distribution)

	1960	1970	1980	1990	1995
District administrators	2.0	1.9	1.9	1.7	1.7
Instructional staff	69.8	68.0	68.6	67.9	67.1
Site administrators	3.0	2.7	2.6	2.8	2.4
Teachers	64.8	60.0	52.4	53.4	52.0
Teacher aides	—	1.7	7.8	8.8	9.9
Counselors	0.8	1.7	1.8	1.8	1.8
Librarians	0.8	1.3	1.2	1.1	1.0
Support staff	28.1	30.1	29.5	30.4	31.2

Source: NCES (1998a), p. 89.

These broad staffing categories are at best indirect indicators of how school funds are spent. Figure 6.5 disaggregates the figures a little more and shows the percentage distribution of secondary teachers by content area in 1981, 1986, and 1996. These figures give some indication of the amount spent by content area, important information in an era when improved student performance in the core academic content areas is a national priority. In 1981, 65.2 percent of secondary teachers were in the core academic areas of English, mathematics, science, social studies, and foreign language. That increased to 69.3 percent in 1986 and to 72.3 percent in 1996. The declines occurred primarily in home economics, industrial arts, and business education. The numbers suggest that academics "won" and vocational education "lost" in resource shifts reflected by secondary teachers in the years following the publication of *A Nation at Risk* (NCEE, 1983), the education report that spawned the education reform movement of the 1980s and 1990s. While not definitive, the numbers indicate that resource allocations shifted in line with reform expectations. Unfortunately, similar staff data are not available for elementary and middle schools.

In the late 1980s, NCES began a comprehensive School and Staffing Survey (SASS) to produce more detailed information on how schools and classrooms are staffed across the country. The data tapes became available in late 1990 and can be used in future analyses to identify staffing patterns by state, level of education, primary field assignment, and a variety of teacher characteristics, such as

FIGURE 6.5 Secondary Teachers by Content Area, 1981, 1986, and 1996

	Percent of Total		
Subject	*1981*	*1986*	*1996*
Agriculture	1.1	0.06	0.5
Art	3.1	1.5	3.3
Business education	6.2	6.5	4.1
English	23.8	21.8	23.9
Foreign language	2.8	3.7	5.2
Health/PE	6.5	5.6	5.9
Home economics	3.6	2.6	2.2
Industrial arts	5.2	2.2	0.5
Mathematics	15.3	19.2	17.2
Music	3.7	4.8	4.3
Science	12.1	11.0	12.6
Social studies	11.2	13.6	13.4
Special education	2.1	3.5	1.7
Other	3.3	3.4	5.2
Total	995,000	970,000	1,049,000

Source: NCES (1989), p. 73; NCES (1998a), p. 80.

sex, race, ethnic origin, age, marital status, level of education, major assignment field, and area in which licensed. Figure 6.6 indicates the distribution of teachers by primary assignment field for the overall SASS sample for both elementary and secondary schools. The data in this table show the subjects teachers actually taught, while the data in the previous table indicate the subjects for which they were licensed.

The data in Figure 6.6 show that the majority of teachers in elementary schools were elementary school generalists, with very few having content-specific assignments. Also, 13.4 percent of elementary teachers were in special education. At the secondary level, 56.9 percent of the teachers in the sample had assignments in the academic core areas of English/language arts, mathematics, social studies, science, and foreign language, somewhat below the figures in the preceding table. Indeed, though only 9 percent of secondary teachers were licensed in vocational education, close to 19 percent were actually teaching vocational education courses. These nationwide data provide the beginnings of detailed information on staffing patterns in the schools, but future analyses disaggregating the data to local and school levels would provide even more useful information on how dollars are transformed into staffing patterns.

2. RESOURCE-USE PATTERNS AT THE DISTRICT LEVEL

Since education services are organized by local education systems—school districts—and provided in schools and classrooms, statewide expenditure patterns need to be disaggregated to these lower levels. This section first analyzes several

FIGURE 6.6   Elementary and Secondary Teachers by Primary Assignment Field, 1987–88

	Percent of Total	
Primary Assignment Field	*Elementary*	*Secondary*
English/Language arts	1.3	15.5
Mathematics	1.3	13.8
Social studies	0.8	12.0
Science	0.8	11.9
General elementary, prekindergarten, and kindergarten	78.1	—
Special education	13.4	9.0
Foreign language	0.2	3.7
Art/Music	2.0	7.0
Vocational education	0.2	18.8
Physical education	2.1	8.3

Source: Bobbitt & McMillan, 1990.

studies of expenditure patterns across districts within a state and then reviews the research on how *districts* use new money.

Expenditure Patterns across Districts within a State

Research is showing that most districts follow relatively standard practices in using education resources. The major portion of the education budget is spent on instruction; but today, a large portion of instructional expenditures is spent outside the regular classroom on services for special-needs students. This strategy reflects a system characterized by good values but unimpressive results, because the typical "pull-out" strategy of providing extra services has not had much positive impact on those students' learning. Districts also provide a host of noneducation services. Districts run buses, heat and clean buildings, serve meals, and administer a complex system. The result is that only a small portion of the education dollar is spent on regular education instruction.

Figure 6.7 draws from studies of district-level expenditure patterns in three major states: Florida, California, and New York (Monk, Roellke, and Brent, 1996; Nakib, 1995; Picus, Tetreault, and Murphy, 1996). Not surprisingly, the data show that districts spend about 60 percent on instruction, which includes both regular-education instruction in mathematics, language arts, writing, history, and science, as well as instruction for students with special needs such as the disabled. The proportion of 60 percent spent on instruction is quite consistent across the states, and squares with the figure from national studies. These researchers also examined the spending patterns across a number of different district characteristics, including spending level, rural and urban location, high and low percentages of minority students, as well as students from low-income families, and the patterns

FIGURE 6.7 Current Expenditures by Function (Percent) Across the Nation and in California, Florida, and New York

Expenditure Function	Nation NCES	California*	Florida	New York
Instruction	61.2	60.8	58.4	61.8
Instructional support and student services	8.7	7.9	9.9	8.6
Total administration	8.4	11.4	8.1	10.2
District administration	2.6	3.2	4.4	5.7
School administration	5.8	8.2	6.9	4.5
Operation and maintenance	10.3	13.4	10.7	9.3
Transportation	4.2	1.5	4.2	6.3
Short-term capital		0.4	0.3	1.1
Food services	4.2	4.6	5.2	2.7

Source: Monk, Roellke & Brent, 1996; Nakib, 1995; Picus, Tetreault & Murphy, 1996; NCES, 1996a, Table 160.

* Large unified districts.

were remarkably consistent. The coefficient of variation for percent spent on instruction was just 10 percent, meaning the proportion varied from about 54 to 66 percent for two-thirds of all districts.

These figures are similar to the findings from other studies of school district expenditures, to the Odden, Palaich, and Augenblick (1979) New York study discussed in the first edition of this book, to studies of districts in Pennsylvania (Hartman 1988a, 1988b, 1994), and to studies by Cooper (1993) and Speakman, Cooper, Sampieri, May, Holsomback, and Glass (1996) in New York.

Figure 6.8 displays these data by high, medium, and low levels of operating spending levels for New York for the 1977–78 school year; the numbers include only state and local revenues. First, instructional expenditures comprised about 60 percent of state/local operating expenditures per pupil, quite close to the national average. Second, instructional expenditures per pupil as a percent of total operating expenditures *increased* with spending levels, from 58 percent for the bottom decile, to 59 percent in the middle, to 63 percent for the top-spending

FIGURE 6.8　Expenditures by Function by Level of Spending in New York, 1977–78

Component of Per Pupil Expenditures	Level of Spending*		
	High	Medium	Low
Operating expenditures	$2,863	$1,850	$1,325
Central district administration	80 (3%)	42 (2%)	48 (3%)
Central district services	329 (11%)	240 (13%)	156 (11%)
Instruction	1,822 (63%)	1,107 (59%)	800 (58%)
Employee benefits	559 (19%)	373 (20%)	271 (20%)
Transportation	114 (4%)	105 (6%)	104 (8%)
Instructional expenditures	$1,822	$1,102	$800
Curriculum development and supervision	175 (10%)	116 (10%)	55 (7%)
Teacher salaries	1,303 (72%)	807 (73%)	619 (77%)
Noninstructional salaries	28 (2%)	21 (2%)	9 (1%)
Books, materials, and equipment	58 (3%)	41 (4%)	36 (5%)
Pupil services	138 (8%)	71 (6%)	47 (6%)
Special-needs students	$220	$219	$195
Teachers			
Pupil/classroom teachers	17.2	18.9	20.4
Median teacher salary	$22,037	$16,654	$12,716
Percent with only a B.A.	9.1	20.2	33.4
Percent with M.A. and 30 points or a doctorate	35.9	15.3	6.0
Percent with more than 10 years experience	68.2	53.8	43.6

Source: Odden, Palaich & Augenblick, 1979.

* High is top-spending decile; middle is decile 6; low is lowest-spending decile.

decile. This latter pattern was different from the Pennsylvania results, as well as different from later New York studies in the 1990s, both discussed below.

Employee benefit expenditures, often called fixed costs, consumed about 20 percent of expenditures across all spending levels, higher than the national figures. Expenditures for central office administration and services also comprised about an equal percentage of expenditures across all spending levels. Transportation, on the other hand, comprised a declining percent of the budget as spending rises.

Spending for special-student needs such as for compensatory and bilingual education totaled about $200 per pupil for all three spending levels. Since the groups differed substantially in overall operating expenditures per pupil, this finding shows that spending for special-needs students constituted a much higher percentage of operating expenditures in low- as compared to middle- or high-spending districts. This finding undergirds the importance of a strong and fair state role in supporting services for special-needs students (see Chapter 4).

Though the percent spent on instruction increased from just 58 to 63 percent, the dollar amount of the increase was larger, rising from $800 per pupil in the low-spending decile, to $1,107 in the middle, and to $1,822 at the high-spending decile. These differences produced different patterns in expenditures for teachers. Low-spending districts spent 77 percent on teacher salaries, compared with only 72 percent in the high-spending districts. Nevertheless, the high-spending districts spent more than twice the per-pupil amount on teachers— $1,303 to $619. These higher expenditures were reflected primarily in different salaries; the median salaries were almost twice as high in the high-spending districts compared to the low-spending districts. Pupil-teacher ratios differed only marginally in New York, ranging from 20.4 in the lowest-spending districts to 17.2 in the higher-spending districts. In general, pupil-teacher ratios were uniformly low. Thus, differences in spending on teachers were reflected primarily in differences in teacher salary levels.

Some of these expenditure patterns had changed by 1992. As shown by the data in Figure 6.9, the major difference was that the percent spent on instruction decreased as overall expenditures increased in 1992, a pattern that was much more typical across the country in the 1970s and 1980s, and a pattern more typical today as well. The data also show that the percentage spent on some other categories then increased with overall expenditures. As expenditures per pupil rose, the percent spent on administration, pupil services, maintenance and operations, and debt service also rose. Since the absolute amount spent is the product of the percentage times the overall expenditure level, higher-spending districts not only spent more dollars on instruction (largely teacher salaries and benefits) but also on all of these other elements of the budget.

The expenditure patterns across spending levels for Pennsylvania in both 1984–85 (Hartman, 1988a, 1988b) and 1991–92 (Hartman, 1994) were similar to the latter patterns in New York. Instructional expenditures as a percent of current expenditures *decreased* as current spending increased. Though a larger portion of teacher expenditures was spent on reducing pupil-teacher ratios than on

FIGURE 6.9   New York Expenditures by Function and by Spending Level, 1991–92

Function	Quintile 1	Quintile 2	Quintile 3	Quintile 4	Quintile 5	Total
Instruction	62.5	62.2	62.0	61.9	60.0	61.8
Instructional support	5.2	5.3	5.1	4.7	5.4	5.1
Administrative District State	9.9	10.2	9.9	10.1	11.0	10.2
Pupil services	2.9	3.2	3.3	3.4	4.2	3.5
Maintenance and operation	9.0	9.2	8.8	9.4	10.2	9.3
Transportation	6.4	6.1	6.4	6.5	6.3	6.3
Food	3.5	3.3	3.1	2.5	1.8	2.7
Debt service	0.6	0.7	1.4	1.3	1.1	1.1
Total expenditures	$6,067	$6,627	$7,309	$8,786	$11,660	$8,311

Source: Monk, Roellke, & Brent, 1996, Table 3A.

Each quintile includes about one-fifth of all students, excluding the five largest districts.

increasing teacher salaries, higher-spending districts nevertheless both paid their teachers more and provided them smaller class sizes. In terms of other patterns, higher-spending districts had teachers with slightly more education and experi ence (though the differences were not as dramatic as in New York) and had more support and administrative personnel.

These studies show that higher-spending districts are able to purchase a different mix of educational services than low-spending districts. They hire more teachers, administrators, and support personnel, hire teachers with more advanced education and years of experience, pay them more (sometimes dramatically more), have smaller class sizes, provide more pupil-support services, and provide a greater variety of instructionally related support services.

In analyzing data from a larger and nationally representative sample of districts, Picus (1993a, 1993b) and Picus and Fazal (1996) found that higher-spending districts tend generally to spend the bulk of their extra funds on more staff, and only a small amount on higher salaries. Their research found that higher-spending districts spent about 50 percent of each additional dollar on more teachers and the other 50 percent on noninstructional services. Of the 50 percent spent on teachers, 40 percentage points were used to hire more teachers, and only 10 percentage points were used to provide higher salaries. Barro (1992) found similar results with state-level data; the bulk of extra revenues was used to hire more staff rather than for higher salaries.

But the schools tend not to use the additional staff for the regular instructional program, as partially hinted by the New York and Pennsylvania information above. In a fascinating analysis of 1991–92 teacher resources by core subject areas in New York secondary schools (English, mathematics, science, social studies, and foreign language), Monk, Roellke, and Brent (1996) showed that staffing in core subjects changed very little across district spending levels. Figure 6.10 shows the remarkable stability of the number of teachers per 1,000 students by five subject areas. Yes, teacher resources spiked a bit in the highest-spending quintile, but only modestly. The average spending between the highest and lowest deciles differed by almost 100 percent, but teacher resources for the core academic subjects differed by only 20 percent. Teacher resources varied by negligible amounts across the four lowest-spending quintiles, though spending varied by thousands of dollars.

However, though not systematically providing more resources for core academics, higher-spending districts did spend more on some subjects than lower-spending districts in New York. Monk, Roellke, and Brent (1996) found that higher-spending districts spent significantly more on mathematics, and somewhat more on language arts, science, and social studies. Across all spending levels, districts tended to spend the most per pupil on science and foreign language, the second most on music, and the least on health and physical education.

Though not disaggregated by spending level, the National Center for Education Statistics (1997) found that elementary teachers spend about one-third of their day on reading, half that, or one-sixth, on mathematics, and half that, or one-twelfth, on each of science and social studies. Taking the 60 percent spent on instruction, that means that approximately 20 cents of the education dollar is spent on elementary reading (60 percent times 1/3), 10 cents on mathematics, and 5 cents each on science and social studies, or about 40 cents of the dollar on teaching core academic subjects in elementary school.

In short, districts spend about 60 percent of their budget on instruction, but the percentage is a bit higher for lower-spending districts and a bit lower for higher-spending districts. But across all spending levels, instructional resources focused on the regular-education program (mathematics, science, language arts/reading/writing, history, and foreign language) might not change that much across spending levels. As spending rises, more of the dollar is spent on nonregu-

FIGURE 6.10   Instructional Staff per 1,000 Pupils by Subject Area in New York Secondary Schools (Grades 7–12), 1991–92

Subject	Quintile 1	Quintile 2	Quintile 3	Quintile 4	Quintile 5
English	5.20	5.25	5.43	5.31	6.10
Mathematics	4.46	4.51	4.67	4.54	5.00
Science	3.86	3.98	4.01	4.18	4.95
Social studies	4.04	4.05	4.06	4.09	4.65
Foreign language	2.18	2.36	2.35	2.46	3.23

Source: Monk, Roellke, & Brent, 1996, Table 7a.

Quintiles refer to spending levels, with Quintile 1 being the lowest and Quintile 5 being the highest.

lar instructional services (i.e., "supports" for the regular instructional program)—specialist teachers in resource rooms, more pupil support, etc. The end result is that less than 50 percent of the education budget is spent on regular instruction, at both secondary and elementary levels. This pattern also characterizes how the education system uses "new" money, addressed next. Though the resource deployment patterns reflect good values—putting money behind the special needs of many students—the question is whether other service strategies, and thus resource-use strategies, could be more effective with all students. The productivity question, for both the average as well as the special-needs student, is whether these expenditure behaviors provide the most "value-added." We will argue in Chapter 8 that more effective strategies could be deployed.

District Uses of New Money

These cross-sectional findings fit with longitudinal trends that have shown that rising real dollars per pupil have been accompanied by declines in the pupil-staff ratio; the average pupil-staff ratio fell from a high of 25 in 1960 to about 14 in 1990 (NCES, 1993, Table 41). But, these small pupil-staff ratios are at odds with the large, actual class sizes of 30 or more students in many districts. The resolution of this dilemma illuminates how dollars and teacher resources typically are used in schools.

Historically and largely today as well, schools reflect a bureaucratic form of organization. Jobs are defined narrowly—principals manage schools and teachers teach students often with a fairly set curriculum and assumed teaching strategies. As schools face new issues—e.g., desegregation, disabled, low-achieving, and English language learner students, emotional and psychological problems, etc.—programs are created that provide money to enable schools to hire specialist staff to deal with the problems. Teachers remain in the regular classroom and specialists are hired to teach disabled, low-achieving, and English language learner students in settings outside of the regular classrooms, or to counsel and help students with emotional/psychological needs. Earlier examples of this phenomenon were the specialists added to school staffs to teach vocational education, physical education, and even art and music. Growth by addition and specialization has characterized the education system for several decades (Odden and Massy, 1993).

Indeed, recent studies have shown that the majority of new dollars provided to schools over the past 30 years was not spent on staff for the core instructional program but on specialist teachers and other resources to provide services to special-needs students usually outside of the regular classroom (Lankford and Wyckoff, 1995; Rothstein and Miles, 1995). Unfortunately, many other studies have shown that these programs and services have produced modest if any long-lasting impacts on student achievement (Allington and Johnston, 1989; Odden, 1991). These dollars represent laudable values; low-income, disabled, and English language learning students need extra services. The values that provide the extra dollars for these extra services should be retained, but the productivity of the expenditure of these dollars needs to rise.

As a result of the increase of specialist staff and programs, regular classroom teachers—the primary service providers—comprise a declining portion of professional staff in schools. The National Commission on Teaching and America's Future (1996) found that regular classroom teachers as a proportion of all professional staff fell from 70 percent in 1950 to 52 percent in 1995, with 10 percent of the latter not engaged in classroom teaching. The fiscal implication is that a declining portion of the education dollar is being spent on the core activity in schools—teaching the regular instructional program. These findings reinforce the data discussed at the beginning of this chapter.

The findings of these more recent studies are similar to that of the few studies on this topic conducted in the 1970s (Alexander, 1974; Barro and Carroll, 1975). Generally, these studies found that districts tended to use more money to increase nonteaching aspects of the budget, and that those dollars used to increase teacher expenditures were primarily used to increase teacher-student ratios, with only a small portion used to raise average teacher salary levels.

Related research in the 1990s on the local use of new money from school finance reforms has found similar patterns of resource use. Poor districts get more money and use it for clear needs (facilities, social services, compensatory education), but little of the new money makes it to the regular-education program (Adams, 1994; Firestone, Goertz, Nagle, and Smelkinson, 1994; Picus, 1994c).

These findings in the 1990s parallel those of Kirst (1977) on the use of school finance reform dollars in California in the 1970s. He analyzed how spending changed in K–12 districts in Los Angeles county, which received a 15 percent increase in state aid from a 1972 California school finance reform in response to the *Serrano* v. *Priest* court suit. He found that salary increases were marginal, in the 5–7 percent range. His study showed that the bulk of new funds were used to hire additional instructional personnel, with some funds used to reduce class size, some to add periods to the school day, and some to hire specialists. While the specific roles of the new staff varied across districts, all exhibited a pattern of hiring more professional personnel rather than hiking salaries or salary schedules.

In an econometric analysis of local district response to increased funds from a major 1980s' education reform, Picus (1988) found that districts increased instructional expenditures more in response to fiscal incentives to increase the length of the school day and year than in response to increases in unrestricted general aid revenue.[1] In analyzing the data over a multiple time period, Picus also found that these instructional expenditure boosts dissipated when California "rolled" the incentive funds into the district's general-aid grant.

The end result is a system in which when money rises, services expand outside the regular classroom, but results in terms of student achievement stay flat or improve by only small amounts. We will return to this theme in Chapter 8 when we discuss how new school designs use site resources quite differently, with many fewer outside-of-the-regular-classroom specialists.

---

[1] This finding is consistent with predictions derived from intergovernmental grant theory discussed in Chapter 4.

3. RESOURCE-USE PATTERNS
AT THE SITE LEVEL

We are beginning to know more about how the education dollar is being spent at the school-site level. The culprit for our lack of knowledge in the past has been, in part, the accounting system. For years, school districts tracked expenditures only by objects such as salaries, benefits, books and other instructional materials, supplies, rent or operations and maintenance, and other specific objects of expenditures. Then, in the 1970s, accounting systems began to change to organize object expenditures into functional categories such as: (1) administration, sometimes divided between site and central office administration; (2) instruction, sometimes but usually not divided between direct classroom instruction and instructional support, such as staff development and curriculum development; (3) operations and maintenance; (4) transportation; (5) fixed charges, such as employed benefits (unfortunately, not linked to the different salary expenditures that induced the benefits charge); (6) capital; and (7) debt service. This grouping of expenditures represented a step forward.

In the 1980s, these changes were complemented by accounting programs that tracked expenditures by program—regular instruction, compensatory education, special education, etc. Both represented additional advances. But there are few states that use these accounting codes to indicate expenditures by function and program at the school-site level, an issue we discuss more specifically in the next section.

Expenditures by School and Classroom

Until recently, two major studies on expenditures by school and classroom formed the current information based on how funds are used below the district level. Figure 6.11 presents 1985–86 California expenditures on a *school* basis (Guthrie, Kirst, and Odden, 1990). The numbers represent a statewide average for all schools, thus merging data for elementary, middle, and high schools, for which expenditure patterns undoubtedly differ. Nevertheless, it was one of the first studies that provided information on expenditures on a school level. The figures show that 63 percent of all expenditures were spent directly on classroom services, which is close to the percent spent on instruction in the above sections. Only 50 percent was spent on classroom and specialized teachers. How was the other 13 percent spent in the classroom? Instructional aides constituted one large portion, at 5 percent; pupil personnel support such as guidance counselors constituted another 4 percent; and books, supplies, and equipment comprised the remaining 4 percent. Thus, the data indicate that about two-thirds of expenditures were on direct, classroom services.

What were the one-third noninstructional elements? First, about 31 percent was spent on other site-related items—site administration, site instructional support including curriculum support and staff development, and operations, maintenance, and transportation. Only 6 percent was spent on district, county, and state

FIGURE 6.11   California Expenditures per School, 1985–86

Category	Expenditures per School	Percent of Total (%)
Classroom expenditures	$1,286,000	63
22 classroom teachers	914,000	45
2.5 specialized instructors	102,000	5
7.0 instructional aides	94,000	5
2.0 pupil personnel support	84,000	4
Books, supplies, equipment	92,000	4
Other site expenditures	629,000	31
Operation, maintenance, and transportation	395,000	19
Instructional support	95,000	5
School-site leadership	139,000	7
District/County administration	120,000	5.5
State Department of Education	11,000	0.5
Total operating expenditures	2,046,000	100
School facilities/capital	133,000	

Source: Guthrie, Kirst & Odden, 1990.

administration. Thus, 37 percent of California 1986–87 *school-site* expenditures were spent on nonclassroom activities. Hayward (1988) shows that for many of these expenditure items, the amount spent per item (such as per meal served, per student transported, per square foot of physical plant, etc.) was below norms in the private sector, suggesting that school system expenditures were not profligate.

These figures begin to take the mystery out of how educational dollars are spent. Although only 50 percent of each dollar was spent on teachers, the other 50 percent was not simply wasted. While the efficiency of expenditures in all categories can be examined, the fact is that all categories of expenditures are needed. Students must be transported to school. Schools must be operated, heated or cooled, and maintained. Some central administration is necessary, and 6 percent is not a large figure. Book, materials, supplies, and instructional support services are needed.

In short, nonteacher expenditures are not lost in an alleged "administrative blob," though these other expenditures are noninstructional. Though a dramatically restructured school could have different spending patterns and produce more student learning, current spending patterns are not irrational. The route to improving school productivity is not in attacking administrative costs, although such costs are probably too high in many districts. The route is determining what works to boost student learning and making sure dollars support those strategies, issues addressed in Chapter 8.

National data on *classroom* expenditures generally confirm these California, subdistrict school expenditure patterns. Figure 6.12 shows nationwide classroom expenditures for 1984–85 (Fox, 1987). These numbers also reflect a merged elementary, middle, and high school classroom. The figures show that "other expen-

FIGURE 6.12   Nationwide Expenditures per Classroom, 1984–85

Item of Expenditure	Amount (Percent of Total)
Total	$78,422
Nonsite administration	5,646 (7.2)
District and state administration	3,058 (3.9)
Clerks (district and state)	2,588 (3.3)
Site administration	2,353 (3.0)
Principals	1,647 (2.1)
Assistant principals	706 (0.9)
Instruction	43,801 (55.6)
Teachers	23,546 (30.0)
Curriculum specialists and other classroom teachers	8,336 (10.4)
Other professional staff	1,490 (1.9)
Teacher aides	1,804 (2.3)
Library media specialists	549 (0.7)
Guidance and counseling	1,176 (1.5)
Instructional materials	6,430 (8.2)
Pupil support services, attendance, health	470 (0.6)
Other nonadministration and instruction	26,036 (33.2)
Maintenance	8,783 (11.2)
Transportation	3,451 (4.4)
Food service	3,137 (4.0)
Fixed charges (insurance, benefits, etc.)	10,665 (13.6)

Source: Fox, 1987.

ditures" including transportation, operation and maintenance, food services, and fixed charges constituted about one-third (33.2 percent) of total expenditures. Nonsite administration constituted another 7.2 percent.

Instruction and site administration comprised 58.6 percent of total expenditures, with classroom teachers and other specialist teachers comprising 40.4 percent of total expenditures. Indeed, these national data show that the percent of expenditures spent on teachers nationwide were lower than in California, and that the percent spent on instruction and site administration expenditures were somewhat below that spent in California.

One of the earliest attempts to look at school-level data was the work of Picus (1993a, 1993b). By merging data from the SASS with Census Bureau data on governmental expenditures, Picus was able to estimate spending patterns at the school level. Because fiscal data were not available at the school level, the analysis focused on the use of staff. What was particularly interesting in these analyses was the difference between the estimated pupil-teacher ratio and the teacher self-reported class size. He found that while the average pupil-teacher ratio reported in schools was in the vicinity of 16.5 or 17:1, self-reported class sizes ranged from 24 to 32 (Picus and Bhimani, 1993; Picus, 1994b) or from 50 to 100 percent higher than even school-level statistics indicated. Two important findings emerged from this work. First, it is clear that many individuals classified as "teachers" in our public school systems have assignments other than spending the full day in the classroom. Second, it appears that as the size of the district increases, and as its wealth declines, the disparity between the calculated pupil-teacher ratio and the actual class size grows. Further school-level analyses were not possible with the SASS and Census data.

There are several more recent studies drawing on new, national data bases. Drawing upon the Schools and Staffing Survey for 1993–94, Figure 6.13 provides more detail for the above conclusions by showing the staffing in a national average elementary, middle, and high school. Though the data do not show nonprofessional staff expenditures, the data provide additional insights into how the education dollar is spent. At the elementary level, the numbers show that the school would need 20 teachers to provide regular class sizes of 25 students. Since the school on average has 27 teachers, that means it has seven additional teachers probably used for such purposes as music, art, and physical education to provide

FIGURE 6.13   School Resources in National Average Elementary, Middle, and High Schools

Ingredient	Elementary School Grades K–5*	Middle School Grades 6–8**	High School Grades 9–12***
Average enrollment	~500	~1,000	~1,500
1. Principal	1.0	1.0	1.0
2. Assistant principals	0.0	2.0	3.0
3. Teachers	27.0	57.5	85.5
4. Librarians and media	1.5	2.0	3.0
5. Media aides			
6. Counselors and psychologists	2.5	4.0	6.0
7. Teacher aides	6.0	5.0	6.0
8. Total staff resources****	$1,690,000	$3,400,000	$5,015,000
9. Total CORE resources	1 principal; 20 teachers $1,050,000	1 principal; 40 teachers $2,050,000	1 principal; 60 teachers $3,050,000
10. Total above CORE (Line 8 minus line 9) (per 500 students)	$640,000 ($640,000)	$1,350,000 ($675,000)	$1,965,000 ($655,000)

Source: Staffing data from analysis of Schools and Staffing Survey, 1993–94.

* Enrollments from 400 to 600 students.

** Enrollments from 900 to 1,100 students.

*** Enrollments from 1,400 to 1,600 students.

**** Average professional staff cost at $50,000; average teacher aide cost at $15,000.

regular teachers "planning and preparation" time, as well as specialist teachers for special-needs programs. Schools also have a librarian and a half-time media aide, and 2.5 counselors and other pupil support personnel. The average elementary school also has 6 instructional aides. In sum, the national average school has several professional resources above the "core" of one teacher for every 25 students. Using national average figures for salaries and benefits (about $50,000 a position), the average elementary school has $640,000 over "core" resources.

Interestingly, for each grouping of 500 students, middle schools and high schools have approximately the same level of additional funds. For each level of school, these staffing resources are in addition to resources for other items such as instructional materials, books, professional development, etc.

The data confirm that schools on average had a substantial level of resources, over and above what is required to provide a regular class size of 25. Again, the productivity question is use of these resources. It is a "given" that special needs of students must be met, and some portion of the additional resources must be devoted to these needs. But the overall question is which pattern of resource use will provide the most added value for both the average student and the student with special needs. Again, this issue is addressed directly in Chapter 8.

Studies using state data.   Additional work assessing school-level spending patterns used state data bases in Florida, California, and New York. In Florida, Nakib (1995) assessed the use of resources at the school level. He concluded that when analyzed on the basis of district size, total expenditures, district wealth, percentage of minority students, and low-income students, there was little variation in spending patterns by object, function, or program at the district and school level. Nakib was not sure of the cause of these similarities, wondering if the uniform reporting requirements Florida placed on schools and districts was the cause of this consistency in findings. He wondered in his conclusion if spending patterns were similar and what other factors led to differences in school effectiveness. Additional school-level variables might lead to the answer to this question.

In California, Hertert (1996) analyzed school-level equity, finding that despite the substantial district-level equity in the distribution of general resources to education, there were substantial variations in the amount of money spent per pupil across schools within districts and among schools across districts. In addition, she found that pupil-teacher ratios were very consistent across school districts and schools, although there was substantial variation in what types of courses were offered in high schools by those teachers. Variation in the number of advanced math and science courses, for example, could be one explanation of why graduates of some schools perform better in these subjects than do graduates of other schools. In New York, Monk, Roellke, and Brent (1996) found that while spending patterns tended to be similar across districts and even schools, the use of personnel varied considerably, with some schools having substantially more resources devoted to high-level academic courses than others. Clearly the potential of these differences to impact the level of student learning is important to understanding how resources matter, even if the focus is on teacher qualifications and what they are teaching rather than how much they cost.

Sherman, Best, and Luskin (1996) conducted a study of the potential uses of school-level data sets in Ohio and Texas. Many of their findings were similar to district-level research reported above, confirming the consistency of spending patterns among schools. While Sherman, Best, and Luskin (1996) found differences in the levels of expenditures for various functions across schools, they found that there was little difference in the share of total expenditures spent on instruction, administration, and support services (p. 24).

Recently, Chambers (1998) analyzed Ohio's school-level data in an attempt to estimate the costs of special education. He was able to make a number of important estimates of the costs attributable to services provided for children with disabilities. The information he provided is highly policy-relevant in understanding how much is spent for special education and what that money buys. Its potential value in other states is very high, although it was Chamber's view that if national estimates were to be attempted, it would be necessary to collect information from each of the states individually. The analysis would be very difficult for those states that did not have state-level data like Ohio.

The collection of school-level data is a relatively new venture, and is difficult (Odden and Busch, 1997a). To date, there has been limited research use of the information collected by Florida, Ohio, and Texas (the states with the most advanced school-level data-collection systems). To a large extent, particularly in Texas, the data are used to provide citizens with a great deal of detailed information on their local schools. To date, there has been limited analysis of what those data mean, either by researchers or policymakers. Chamber's work (1998) with the Ohio data provides detailed estimates of the costs and personnel allocations for special education in Ohio. The data give a clearer picture of special-education costs than has been previously available, and enable state-level officials to compare costs of the same services across schools and school districts.

With further refinement, school-level data collections on finance, personnel, and student characteristics may make it possible to gain a better understanding of how money (and other resources) matter in improving student performance. Policymakers would be interested in these data both to better understand these links and to help develop measures of the cost-effectiveness of alternative educational strategies and their relative effectiveness with children from different backgrounds and locations.

Studies using school district specific databases.   A number of studies have been conducted using databases with school-level data constructed from individual district records. Miles' (1995) study of Boston showed that if all individuals in the district classified as teachers were placed in regular classrooms, class size could be reduced from an average of 22 to 13. While this change may not really be possible due to the need to provide special services to children with severe disabilities, Miles also provided a number of different policy options showing how the average class size would vary as some of the district's current special-education practices were continued. Her analysis provided information that a school board could use to make policy decisions on class size and the delivery of special education.

Recently, Berne and others have conducted a major study of school-level resource allocation in four urban school districts in the United States— Rochester, New York City, Chicago, and Fort Worth. In their introduction to a special issue of the *Journal of Education Finance* devoted to this work, Goertz and Stiefel (1998) focus on three things:

- Intradistrict fiscal equity,
- Decision-making processes, and
- Considerations for implementation of school-level databases.

A number of factors take on heightened importance when school-level equity is considered.

- School-level analyses can lead to public comparisons among local schools leading to potential conflicts between the goals of horizontal and vertical equity. Some schools may appear to have more resources than others due to the special needs of the children at the school. While this meets the traditional goal of vertical equity, it may appear unfair to parents of other nearby schools who see only that their school does not have as many resources available to them as the school with the children with special needs.
- Local constituents don't always understand differences between per-pupil positions and per-pupil expenditures. Differences in salaries of teachers could lead to lower teacher costs per pupil at schools with relatively more teachers, confounding analyses that rely on expenditures and pupil-teacher ratios.
- In all four of the districts studied, school-based budgeting takes place only at the margins with relatively little real discretionary authority allocated to the school sites. Moreover, it is generally the principal who has the most power in making those fiscal decisions that are possible at the school site. It is critical to be clear who is ultimately responsible for the academic and fiscal performance of the school. Where this is not clear, there have been conflicts between site councils and the principal.
- Data on dollars, positions, outcomes, and demographics should be integrated into one database. Districts typically keep these data in different databases. It is usually difficult, if not impossible, to merge the data on students, teachers, and spending into one unified database. By maintaining all of these data in one easily accessible data system, comparisons across students and schools will be facilitated.

In addition to this work, Bruce Cooper and teams of analysts from Coopers and Lybrand have collected and analyzed a great deal of data from New York City schools and other districts throughout the country. The initial "cascade" model developed by Cooper & Associates (1994) attempted to track funds starting at the central office–level as they "cascaded" down to the local schools. The model has been revised over time and is now available to school districts through Fox River Learning under the name In$ight. The model divides expenditures into 10 categories, five each at the district and school level. At each level, the same five functions are specified:

- Administration,
- Operations and facilities,
- Teacher support,
- Pupil support, and
- Instruction.

The findings from Cooper's model when applied to eight school districts across the country showed that central office expenditures consumed between 6 and 20 percent of district expenditures, leaving between 80 and 94 percent for the schools. The model forms the basis of the Ohio school-level data collection, and a form of it is in use today in South Carolina as well. B. S. Cooper (personal communication, September 24, 1998) indicates that Hawaii is looking into using the In$ight model to track expenditures in the schools that are part of that state-wide school system.

SUMMARY AND CONCLUSION

The discussion in this chapter provides an overview of how the education dollar is allocated and used. As Chapter 1 showed, the good news about education dollars is that the country provides a large number of them. But then it makes two serious errors. First, it distributes the money in highly unequal ways, and remedying these inequities has been the focus of school finance for years. Second, as this chapter shows, the education system uses the money in traditional ways, which when combined with the data on the stagnant nature of student performance in America, suggests that resource use patterns have been ineffective vis-à-vis results. These behaviors must change in order for education system performance to improve.

The substantial investment the country has made in its public educational system needs to be restructured so the investment pays off in terms of large increases in student achievement over the next few decades. First, the dollars need to be distributed more equitably; previous portions of this book have addressed how to reduce spending disparities across districts in the country.

Second, as we argue in the next chapters, the management of the education system must be redesigned to produce more results. The approach to this challenge that proposes school-site management means sending the bulk of education dollars to schools in a lump sum. Then, the long-term task is to get schools to act more like producers of high levels of student achievement rather than mere consumers of educational resources or just providers of traditional educational services. This means schools need to adopt an instructional strategy designed to teach more students to high standards, deploy all fiscal resources (current and new, general and categorical) for the purpose of teaching this curriculum effectively to all students, probably increase the proportion of the budget spent on regular-classroom teachers and less on specialists and thus reduce overall class sizes, and invest more in training and professional development. The remaining chapters show how these strategies have been implemented in a few schools around the country and could be implemented in most schools in this country.

Chapter 7

Ways to Improve Educational Productivity

Ask most teachers or school administrators if they could do a better job educating children if they had more money, and virtually every one of them will offer a resounding "yes." Ask them what they would do with that money, and their answer is less clear. Frequently, they do not have a strategic sense of how the money could be used, and more often than not the answer will conflict with what other teachers or administrators say is needed. Worse, despite the fact that there is substantial evidence our schools could be doing better, we showed in Chapter 6 that when schools or school districts receive new money, they tend to use it in patterns very similar to the way existing funds are spent.

Today's school reformers increasingly call for greater productivity in our schools. Although, as Monk (1992) shows, productivity is a difficult concept to apply to a public good like education; a straightforward working definition of "educational productivity" for the purpose of this book is the improvement of student outcomes with little or no additional financial resources, or a consistent level of student performance at a lower level of spending. Although a simple idea, improvements in student achievement without large amounts of new money have been relatively rare in public schools in the United States.

One of the difficulties in discussing educational productivity is the many different ways it can addressed. This chapter considers a number of ways the topic of productivity can be approached. The first section of this chapter reviews the literature that seeks to answer the question, "Does money matter?", largely focusing on production function research, but this section also includes a discussion of the impact of smaller class sizes on student achievement.

The second section of this chapter discusses how educational productivity can be improved through decentralized management structures. This section focuses on the literature on school-based management, decentralized decision making, and how these tools can be used to make schools better or more productive.

1. MEASURING EDUCATIONAL PRODCTIVITY

One can think of measuring educational productivity through three lenses: efficiency, effectiveness, and equity. Efficiency refers to the allocation of resources and their use in schools. Specifically, efficiency concerns revolve around how much money schools have, and how that money is used. We discussed this issue at length in Chapter 6. Effectiveness encompasses the linkage between student outcomes and the level and use of financial resources in the schools. This topic is a matter of considerable debate in educational and economic circles today and the focus of this portion of Chapter 7. The third approach to measuring productivity is equity, or the equitable distribution of funds to all children. We devoted considerable attention to this issue in Chapters 2 through 5.

This section of Chapter 7 begins with a discussion of production functions and how they are used. One part considers the use of production functions in trying to ascertain how money is related to student learning and lifetime earnings. The next part looks at two emerging approaches that show considerable promise: cost functions and data envelopment analysis. The next part reviews the literature on the impact of smaller class size on student learning. This is a special case of the production function, but important due to the more-consistent finding that smaller classes do lead to higher student outcomes, and the fact that class-size reduction has become a very popular policy option for many states. Finally, market-based alternatives to the current structure of education and their effects are discussed.

What Is a Production Function?

Understanding the effect of class size on student achievement is related to the larger question of how money impacts student performance. As Picus (1997a) points out, nearly all would agree that more money is better than less. Moreover, most would agree that the expenditure of additional funds on education should lead to improved student learning. However, there is considerable disagreement among researchers as to whether or not a statistical link can be found between student outcomes and money (or, what money buys, such as class size, teacher experience, and degrees, etc.). Chapter 6 showed that the single largest expenditure item for a school district is teacher compensation (salary and benefits). So, for example, for a district of a given size, the more money or revenue available to the system, the more teachers it can hire and the smaller the average class size will be.

Production functions are an economic tool used to measure the contribution of individual inputs to the output of some product. In simple terms, a production function takes the following form:

$$O = f(K,L)$$

where

O = some measurable output
K = capital or nonlabor inputs to the production process
L = labor

By estimating equations that include these variables, as well as other variables that control for exogenous factors known to impact the production process, it is possible to predict the impact that the application of additional units of labor and capital will have on the number of units of output produced.

This concept can be applied to education as well.[1] For example, it is possible to estimate an educational production function with the following form:

$$P = f(R,S,D)$$

where

      P = a measure of student performance
      R = a measure of resources available to students in the school or district
      S = a vector of student characteristics
      D = a vector of district and school characteristics

One possible measure of R would be the pupil-teacher ratio at a school or school district. In fact, the pupil-teacher ratio is in many ways a good choice for this particular variable as it provides a proxy for the level of resources available for children (that is, it is highly correlated with per-pupil spending), and it is a proxy for class size.

Difficulties with the educational production function research.   There are substantial methodological difficulties with estimating equations of the form presented above. First and foremost is reaching agreement on the proper measure of student performance to serve as the outcome indicator. Although there is considerable discussion about this in the education community, in recent years, the policy community—as well as most educators—have focused on the results of standardized tests as the outcome measure. The studies described below generally follow this trend.

There are a number of other methodological problems to consider. There is substantial evidence that children from minority backgrounds, children from low-income families, children who do not speak English as their first language, and children with disabilities do not do as well in school as other children. Therefore, if our model is to identify the impact that smaller classes have on student performance, it is necessary to control for differences in student characteristics. Unfortunately, it is often difficult to collect these data in ways that facilitate the estimation of a production function.

For example, it is often possible to collect data on student performance and student characteristics at the individual student level. However, other data related to school or district characteristics may only be available at the district level. This is often the case with fiscal data, such as per-pupil expenditures and even pupil-teacher ratios. The result is that regression equations contain variables with varying levels of precision. Unfortunately, the accuracy of the estimates of the impact of resources on student performance is only as good as the lowest level of

[1] For a more detailed description of production functions as they apply to education, see Monk, 1990.

precision. This is often the district-level fiscal or resource data that are of interest to the researcher. There are statistical techniques to minimize this problem, in particular, hierarchical linear modeling (HLM). However, many of the early studies on the effect of class size did not use this tool.

Another problem is that most education production function studies rely on cross-sectional data. This approach allows for a snapshot of one point in time. Yet, many of the student characteristic and schooling variables used in these equations are subject to substantial change over time. Thus, it is not clear that reliance on a one-time measure of these characteristics will adequately control for their effects on student performance. Longitudinal data sets, which would resolve many of these problems, are expensive to collect, and few are available to researchers today.

Additionally, there are substantial problems with the inputs actually measured for this research. The pupil-teacher ratio often used as a proxy for class size is an example. Picus (1994b) shows that there is considerable variation between the computed pupil-teacher ratio in a district or school, and teachers' self-reported class size. While self-reported class size averaged 50 percent larger than the computed pupil-teacher ratio, this figure ranged from one or two students more than the computed ratio to more than double that figure. Thus, if one is trying to estimate the effect of class size on student performance, the pupil-teacher ratio may not accurately reflect either the class size or the variation that exists in the number of students each teacher sees in a day.

A final problem with this research is that it is generally impossible to establish a true experimental design with both an experimental and a control group. Instead, student performance at a given grade level before class size is reduced is compared with student performance at that grade level following the implementation of the treatment, in this case, the smaller class size. This too reduces the confidence with which one can make statements about the relationship between class size and student performance.

Linking Spending to Student Outcomes: Economic Research

Despite these methodological challenges, there is considerable production function research. Such research has taken two approaches. The first focuses on defining outcomes as student achievement, usually measured through state or local assessment systems, and usually in the form of standardized tests. Other measures of student performance that are sometimes used include school attendance, dropout rates, college enrollment, and job longevity following high school.

The second approach defines outcomes as lifetime earnings. Education is viewed an investment, in that education will yield returns in the form of higher lifetime earnings. Economists term this the "human capital" approach.

Does money matter? The current debate. While interest in the question of whether or not money matters has always been high, Hedges, Laine, and Green-wald (1994a) sparked renewed debate. Prior to the publication of their article, the most-often-cited research in this field was the work of Eric Hanushek (1981, 1986, 1989). In those articles, as well as his most recent research, Hanushek (1997) argues that there does not appear to be a systematic relationship between the level of funding and student outcomes.

Hanushek has now analyzed 90 different publications, with 377 separate production function equations. He continues to argue that "These results have a simple interpretation: There is no strong or consistent relationship between school resources and student performance. In other words, there is little reason to be confident that simply adding more resources to schools as currently constituted will yield performance gains among students" (Hanushek, 1997, p. 148).

The process he uses to reach this conclusion separates the studies on the basis of the outcome measures employed by the authors, and then looks at the regression results. The regressions use a series of independent or descriptor variables to estimate the value of the dependent, or in this case outcome, variable. The regression estimates the nature of the relationship between the independent variables and the dependent variable, measures the estimated strength of that relationship, and indicates whether or not the estimate of the effect is statistically significant (whether one can say with some level of confidence that the answer is different from zero). For example, if the researcher is interested in whether or not more money leads to higher test scores, if the sign on coefficient of expenditures is positive, the implication is that higher spending leads to higher test scores. However, one needs to be sensitive to the magnitude of that relationship and to the confidence one has about that estimate (the statistical significance).

Hanushek, using the method he has used in the past, divided the results of the 377 equations into five categories as follows:

- A positive relationship that is statistically significant,
- A positive relationship that is not statistically significant,
- A negative relationship that is statistically significant,
- A negative relationship that is not statistically significant, and
- A situation where the direction of the relationship can not be determined.

In addition to school expenditures, some of the studies relied on other measures of school district resource allocation, looking at teacher-pupil ratios,[2] expenditures for central or school-site administration, teacher education, and teacher experience.

---

[2] While it is generally easier to think in terms of a pupil-teacher ratio, the advantage of reversing this ratio and considering a teacher-pupil ratio is to simplify discussion. Typically a lower pupil-teacher ratio is more expensive and considered a positive step toward improving student performance. However, if smaller classes lead to higher student performance, then the relationship between the pupil-teacher ratio and the outcome measure will be negative. If the ratio is reversed, so that it is a teacher-pupil ratio, the higher the teacher-pupil ratio, the smaller the class size. Thus if small class size leads to improved student performance, the sign on the coefficient will be positive.

Hanushek analyzes the studies and places them in one of the five categories based on the estimated effect described above. In looking across studies, at different outcome measures and different types of inputs, Hanushek argues that the variation in findings is such that systematic relationships between money and outcomes have not yet been identified. He states:

> The concern from a policy viewpoint is that nobody can describe when resources will be used effectively and when they will not. In the absence of such a description, providing these general resources to a school implies that sometimes resources might be used effectively, other times they may be applied in ways that are actually damaging, and most of the time no measurable student outcome gains should be expected (Hanushek, 1997, pp. 148–49).

He then suggests that what is needed is to change the incentive structures facing schools so that they are motivated to act in ways that use resources efficiently and that lead to improved student performance.

One of the most interesting findings in Hanushek's (1997) recent work is the impact of aggregation on the results. He finds that studies that use data aggregated to the state level are far more likely to find statistically significant and positive relationships than are studies that focus on the classroom or school level. What is not clear from his work at this point is whether the aggregation is masking much of the variance that exists (a likely occurrence), or if we simply do not yet have tools that are refined enough to adequately measure the effects of different inputs at the most disaggregated levels in the system.

Others have looked at the same studies as Hanushek and conclude that they show money does make a difference. Hedges, Laine, and Greenwald (1994a, 1994b; see also Laine, Greenwald, and Hedges, 1996; and Greenwald, Hedges, and Laine, 1996a, 1996b) conclude that in fact, money can make a difference. They argue that while in those studies only a minority of relationships indicate a positive, statistically significant relationship, the number with such a relationship exceeds what one would expect to find if the relationship were random. They also point out that one would expect the statistically insignificant studies to be evenly divided between positive and negative effects, yet as many as 70 percent of the relationships between per-pupil expenditures and student performance are positive. Relying on this and other evidence, Hedges, Laine, and Greenwald (1994a) conclude that school spending and achievement are related. In his rejoinder, Hanushek (1994b) argues that while there is evidence that the relationship exists, there is not evidence of a strong or systematic relationship.

A number of other studies have looked at this issue. Ferguson (1991, p. 485) looked at spending and the use of educational resources in Texas. He concluded that "hiring teachers with stronger literacy skills, hiring more teachers (when students-per-teacher exceed 18), retaining experienced teachers, and attracting more teachers with advanced training are all measures that produce higher test scores in exchange for more money." His findings also suggest that teachers' selection of districts in which they want to teach is affected by the education level of the adults in the community, the racial composition of that community, and the salaries in other districts and alternative occupations. This implies, according to Ferguson, that better teachers will tend to move to districts with higher socioeconomic characteristics if salaries are equal. If teacher skills and knowledge have an impact on student achievement (and Ferguson, as well as others, suggest that it does) then low socioeconomic areas may have to offer substantially higher salaries to attract and retain high-quality teachers. This would help confirm a link between expenditures and student achievement.

In a more recent study, Wenglinsky (1997) used regression analysis to analyze three large national databases to see if expenditures had an impact on student achievement of fourth and eighth graders. He found that the impact of spending was in steps or stages. For fourth graders, Weglinsky concluded that increased expenditures on instruction and on school district administration increase teacher-student ratios. Increased teacher-student ratios (smaller class sizes) in turn led to higher achievement in mathematics.

In the eighth grade, the process was more complex. Specifically, Wenglinsky found that increased expenditures on instruction and central administration increased teacher-student ratios (reduced class size). This increased teacher-student ratio led to an improved school environment or climate, and the improved climate and its lack of behavior problems resulted in higher achievement in math.

Equally interesting was Wenglinsky's (1997) finding that capital outlay (spending on facility construction and maintenance), school-level administration, and teacher education levels could not be related to improved student achievement. This is particularly intriguing in light of the fact that he found increased spending for central or district administration was associated with improved student outcomes. These findings are certain to be controversial, and to some extent conflict with the "conventional wisdom" about school administration. What makes his findings important is the point that additional spending on district administration leads to improved teacher-student ratios, where as that is not so with increased school-site administration. The reason for this is not clear, but is something that should be considered as we move to more site–managed schools.

In summary, there remains considerable disagreement over the impact of additional resources on educational outcomes of students. The complexity of the educational system, combined with the wide range of outcomes we have established for our schools, and the many alternative approaches we use to fund our schools make it difficult to come to any firm conclusions about whether or not money matters.

The human capital approach.   This approach considers education as an investment and relates the quality of education to lifetime earnings. A number of studies have attempted to do this. Card and Krueger (1996) analyzed panel data over a number of decades and compared attributes of schools and schooling to lifetime earnings, finding that more school resources are associated with higher lifetime income. Betts (1996) does not find as strong a relationship, and moreover, like Hanushek finds that as the analysis relies on smaller and smaller units (e.g., classrooms and schools as opposed to states), the link between spending and lifetime earnings becomes weaker and weaker. As this work shows, economists have the same difficulty linking educational spending at the K–12 level to lifetime earnings that production function researchers have linking spending to student outcomes.

Methodological challenges. One of the problems with both approaches is they do not take into consideration the similarity with which school districts spend the resources available to them. Research by Picus (1993a, 1993b), Picus and Fazal (1996), Cooper (1993, 1994) and Chapter 6 show resource allocation patterns across school districts to be remarkably alike, despite differences in total per-pupil spending, student characteristics, and district attributes. This does not mean that all children receive the same level of educational services. As Picus and Fazal (1996) point out, a district spending $10,000 per pupil and $6,000 per pupil for direct instruction is able to offer smaller classes; better paid, and presumably higher-quality, teachers; and higher-quality instructional materials than is a district spending $5,000 per pupil and only $3,000 per pupil for direct instruction.

What we do not know is what the impact on student performance would be if schools or school districts were to dramatically change the way they spend the resources available to them. In 1992, Odden and Picus (p. 281) suggested that the important message from the research summarized above was that, "if additional education revenues are spent in the same way as current education revenues, student performance increases are unlikely to emerge." Therefore, knowing whether or not high-performing schools use resources differently than other schools would be helpful in resolving the debate over whether or not money matters.

Nakib (1995) studied the allocation of educational resources by high-performing high schools in Florida and compared those allocation patterns with the way resources were used in the remaining high schools in that state. A total of seven different measures were used to compare student performance. In his findings, Nakib shows that per-pupil spending and per-pupil spending for instruction were not statistically significantly higher in high-performing high schools, largely because of the highly equalized school-funding formula used in Florida. On the other hand, he found the percent of expenditures devoted to instruction was lower in the high-performing high schools, implying high-performing high schools may actually spend more money on resources not directly linked to instruction than do other high schools.

Unfortunately, the results of this Florida analysis do little to clarify the debate on whether or not money matters. Comparisons of high-performing high schools with all other high schools in Florida did not show a clear distinction in either the amount of money available or in the way resources are used. As with many other studies, it was student demographic characteristics that had the greatest impact on student performance.

More recently, Odden (1997) has found that the schooling designs developed as part of the New American Schools project have generally led to increased student performance. In each of the seven models he studied, schools are required to make substantial reallocations of resources away from aides and teachers with special assignments, and focus on increasing the number of regular class-room teachers and thus lowering average class size. In addition, each of the designs require substantial investments, in both time and money, for professional development. Odden suggests that this can often be funded through elimination of a position through attrition. His optimistic assessment is that for relatively little additional money, schools can fund existing programs and organizational structures that will help them improve student learning.

Why is Educational Productivity so Elusive?

To date, economists attempting to define a production function for education have been largely unsuccessful. Much of the variation in student performance is related to student characteristics over which schools have no control. Moreover, recent research on educational resource allocation patterns shows little variation in the way school districts use the funds they have, regardless of per-pupil spending levels (see for example, Odden, Monk, Nakib, and Picus, 1995; Picus and Fazal, 1996; and Chapter 6). As a result, it has been difficult to identify productive uses of school funds. Before looking at potential ways to break these patterns and improve productivity, it is helpful to consider some possible reasons these patterns exist.

Financial organization of school districts.   School districts are typically organized in a top-down fashion, particularly with regard to their fiscal operations. There are a number of reasons for this. First, since schools spend public funds, it is essential that district administrators ensure the money is spent as budgeted and approved by the school board. Considerable expense goes into developing systems that provide this accountability, and it is easier to manage these systems centrally. Moreover, few school-site administrators have the training or desire to become financial managers. Thus, school district accounting systems have become highly centralized.

Central fiscal management has its benefits in terms of centralized purchasing and common reporting formats, but it can also reduce local creativity. Most school districts rely on allocation mechanisms to distribute resources to school sites (Hentschke, 1986). These mechanisms typically allocate resources such as teachers on a per-pupil basis, and others on either a per-pupil or dollars-per-pupil basis. Depending on the level of detail in a district's system, these allocation mechanisms often leave very little discretionary authority to the school site.

Moreover, most systems do not allow school sites the flexibility to carry-over funds if expenditures are below budgeted levels. While this pattern is changing, to the extent it still exists, schools have little incentive to create long-term plans, and find themselves better off looking for ways to be sure they have spent all the funds allocated to their site each fiscal year.

School district budgeting.   Budgeting systems also work to limit variation in school spending patterns. Wildavsky (1988) describes public budgeting systems as being incremental. He suggests that the bulk of a public organization's budget is based on the same allocation pattern as the previous year adjusted for changes in costs due to inflation, salary increases, and price increases. He argues that as a result, changes in spending patterns are unlikely, and when they occur, do so at the margin. That is, it is only after current expenditures are "covered" that new programs are considered, if more money is available.

It is not surprising that school districts have highly incremental budgets. The basic organization of a school district is to put a number of children in a classroom with a teacher. The balance of a school system is designed to support that structure. Depending on local preferences, this includes a central administrative office, school-site administrators, specialists and student support personnel, aides, and classified staff to handle clerical, custodial, transportation, and other activities. Each year the typical district budgets funds to cover the staff, materials, and fixed costs of the previous year. If funds are inadequate, then it is forced to make reductions, usually at the margin. If new programs are desired, new resources must be found.

Assuming large gains in productivity are desired, it seems that dramatic changes in the ways resources are allocated and used will be needed. Doing so requires breaking the patterns noted above.

New Ways to Assess Educational Productivity

Recently, two new approaches to assessing educational productivity have been suggested. One method, known as the cost function, attempts to estimate the resources that would be needed to have all, or most, students reach a given level of performance. The other uses data envelopment analysis to determine efficient schools and then ascertain what it would take for others to operate as efficiently. Both are described more below.

Cost functions. In economic terms, a cost function is the "dual" of a production function. Instead of using student outcomes as the dependent variable and attempting to ascertain whether or not spending has a statistically significant impact on student outcomes, the dependent variable becomes per-pupil expenditures. Student outcomes are an independent variable and set at the level of achievement desired by policymakers. The equation then controls for other exogenous variables, such as student and school characteristics, and produces the estimated cost of bringing students up to the desired level of performance (see Duncombe, Ruggiero, and Yinger, 1996; Duncombe and Yinger, 1999; Reschovsky and Imazeki, 1998).

The end result of these calculations provides a "cost index" that can be applied to the distribution of funds to school districts across a state. These differ from traditional cost indexes in that in addition to considering the costs of inputs (see Chapter 4), they also consider the differences in the cost of bringing each child to some specified level of achievement. Thus, districts with large number of children with high needs (e.g., from low-income households or from households where English is not the first language or is not spoken at all), and thus more expensive educational needs, will have a higher cost index.

In estimates of this cost function in Wisconsin (Reschovsky and Imazeki,

1998) and in New York (Duncombe, Ruggiero, and Yinger 1996; Duncome and Yinger, 1999), researchers concluded that the high educational needs of inner-city children were so great that the cost indexes needed to be dramatically higher for large-city school districts. In the case of Wisconsin, Reschovsky and Imazeki's estimates showed that Milwaukee's index would be some six times higher than the indexes for districts with between 2,500 and 10,000 students. Similarly, Duncombe and Yinger (1999) provide evidence from New York that indicates large urban poor districts might need more than $5,000 more per pupil, above Clune's (1994a) estimate of $5,000.

These studies offer valuable insight into how much it might cost to provide an educational setting that would allow all students to achieve at a high level. The problem with them at this point is that the variation in the index across any individual state is so dramatic as to make implementation of such an index very complex.

Data envelopment analysis.   Another approach, useful at both the school and district level, is data envelopment analysis (DEA). DEA is a powerful tool for measuring efficiency since it can include multiple inputs and outputs at the same time. However, DEA is technically complicated and thus difficult to explain to noneconomists (see Anderson, Walberg, and Weinstein, 1998; Rubenstein, 1997).

DEA is derived from the field of linear or mathematical programming in operations research. As applied to schools, the idea is that at any time, schools may not be operating with the same ratio of inputs per unit of output or efficiency. This is likely because in public schools, where the market does not necessarily determine price, ascertaining the most efficient ratios of inputs to outputs may be impossible. This explains the difficulty with the production function research described above, and potentially why such variances in indexes are found in cost-function methods used to date.

As Anderson, Walberg, and Weinstein (1998) point out, each school tries to use its resources economically. By finding those schools that have the lowest ratios of inputs to outputs, one can identify the most "technically efficient" schools. These schools can be compared to other schools, and the ratio of inputs adjusted so they too can be equally efficient.

The model can also be used to identify effective schools by identifying those that are doing better than might be expected given the composition of the student body and those that are doing worse than expected. This is similar to the quadraform model developed in the 1980s and early 1990s (for a recent application of the quadraform, see Anderson, 1996). In short, one could identify schools that are both efficient and effective and compare their allocation of resources to other schools identified as less effective and/or efficient.

In studying schools in Chicago over a four-year period, Anderson, et. al. (1998) found that schools were not always identified as efficient or effective. What they did find was that schools that were both effective and efficient in various years tended to have more stable student populations, greater attendance, fewer students with limited English language skills, fewer students from low-income (poverty level) households, and lower student expenditures. However, they point out that none of these results was completely consistent across years.

Rubenstein (1997) suggests that the problem with DEA is that we still do not have consensus on how to measure performance, although he did suggest that schools tend to try to maximize performance on standardized tests, making them potentially an appropriate measure for ascertaining effectiveness under DEA. The problem is that there is little evidence that schools generally seek to minimize costs, making the efficiency aspects of DEA difficult to analyze in a public school setting. As Rubenstein (1997, pp. 333–34) points out, "Until the processes by which schooling inputs are converted to outputs (test scores) for different types of students are more fully understood, the measurement of school efficiency will remain exploratory . . ."

Reducing Class Size: A Brief Synthesis of the Literature

By the late 1990s, smaller class sizes had become the most popular policy for improving school performance. Though its high costs do not make smaller class sizes a productivity-enhancing strategy, it is proposed as a performance-enhancing strategy. Even those who are not convinced there is a strong research base to show that smaller classes lead to improved student performance are willing to concede that smaller classes can lead to more individualized instruction, higher morale among teachers, and more opportunities for teachers to implement instructional programs that research shows work well.

Class-size reduction efforts become progressively more expensive as class size decreases. For example, a district with 10,000 students would need to add about 22 teachers (and classroom space) to move from 22 to 21 students per teacher (a 4.5 percent reduction). However, it would take about 42 more teachers to move from 16 to 15 students per teacher (a 6.3 percent reduction).

Although policymakers, the public, and teachers believe that smaller class size can lead to improved student performance, that view is not universally held among researchers. More importantly, research shows that there are alternative reforms that may be considerably more cost-effective in improving student performance. In particular, many have argued that investments in additional teacher training and professional development will lead to even greater gains in student performance for each dollar spent.

The policy context. Reducing class size to improve education is not a new idea. Data from the federal government show that the average pupil-teacher ratio in the United States has declined dramatically in the last 40 years (NCES, 1997).[3] The pupil-teacher ratio in the United States has declined from nearly 27:1 in

[3] Readers should note that the pupil-teacher ratio reported by the federal government is not exactly the same as class size. The pupil-teacher ratio includes a number of certificated staff members who do not have full-time teaching assignments, but are classified as teachers on district salary schedules. Consequently, it undoubtedly underestimates the number of children in an average classroom in any state. However, it is the one figure available across the 50 states, and therefore serves as both a proxy for class size and a way to compare the availability of teaching resources for children across states. For a detailed discussion of how computed pupil-teacher ratios compare to actual class size, see Picus, 1994b.

1955 to approximately 17:1 in 1997. Some of this reduction can be accounted for by the increased availability of special programs for children, which utilize very small classes or rely on "pull-out" programs, where a teacher works with children individually or in small groups (i.e., special education and Title I programs). However, changes also represent real declines in the average number of children in most classrooms across the United States.

Nationally, as per-pupil spending increases, pupil-teacher ratios have declined, a phenomenon that has occurred the years 1955 through 1997. Research by Barro (1992) found that on average, when a school district received an additional dollar of revenue, half of that dollar was spent on teachers. Of that 50 cents, 40 cents was spent on increasing the number of teachers and 10 cents on increasing salaries. Barro's findings help confirm the apparent priority educators place on more teachers and thus potentially smaller classes, and their willingness to trade increases in salary for those purposes.

The strong policy interest in smaller class size.   Despite the high costs, legislative efforts to reduce class size are common. A number of states have enacted policies to reduce class size. One of the first to do so was Texas, which began mandating limited class sizes with the educational reforms enacted in 1984. Today, K–4 programs must average no more than 22 students per classroom in a school. Table 7.1 provides a summary of class-size reduction programs across the states as of 1998. The table identifies 19 states that have some form of class-size reduction. Ten of the states rely on incentives to encourage school districts to reduce class size, while eight use mandates. Washington is unique in that it relies on both a mandate (a staffing ratio of 49 teachers per 1,000 students in grades K–3) and an incentive (an additional 5.3 certificated staff per 1,000 students if districts spend the funds on certificated staff who work with students in grades K–3).

Table 7.1 also shows that the focus of these programs is almost entirely on the primary grades, generally K–3. North Carolina's program is aimed at grades K–2, while Oklahoma's program focuses on grades K–6, and the program in Texas focuses on grades K–4. In Utah, grades K–2 are the primary focus, and funds can only be devoted to reducing class size in grades 3 and 4 if K–2 classes are all reduced to 18 or lower. Washington's program differs to some extent from the others. While the staff ratio established in the program amounts to approximately 18.4 students per certificated instructional staff member, the law does not require classes of 18 or 20 or some other number, only that the funds be spent on staff who work with children in grades K–3. Theoretically this allows for alternative staffing structures as determined by schools and their respective districts.

There is no question that class-size reductions are an important educational policy issue. They can also be very expensive, as the data above suggest. Are smaller classes effective in improving student performance? Certainly that is the general belief among most educators and policymakers. However, the investment is hardly worthwhile if student outcomes do not improve. Below, we consider the research that has been conducted on class size in the past and focus on its impact on student achievement.

TABLE 7.1 States with Class-Size Reduction Measures, 1998

State	Mandate or Incentive	Class-Size Limit	Grade Levels Affected	Year Implemented	Funding
Alaska	Mandate	18	K–3	1997	Part of foundation program
California	Incentive	20	K–3	1996	$1 billion in 1996–97 ($650/student in smaller classes plus $200 million for facilities). $1.5 billion in 1997–98 ($800 per student in smaller classes)
Florida	Incentive	20 (30 with full-time aide)	K–3	1996	$100 million for 1997–98
Illinois	Incentive	Reduce class size with reading-improvement block grants	K–3	1997	Unknown
Indiana	Incentive	18 / 20	K–1 / 2–3	1981 / 1988	$77 million through funding formula in 1995
Louisiana	Mandate	Not to exceed 20 without state superintendent authorization	K–3	1986	Unknown
Maine	Incentive	15–18	K–3	1989	Competitive Grant Program
North Carolina	Incentive	23	K–2	1993 1995 1997	Part of foundation program
Nevada	Mandate	15	K–3 Core subjects	1989	Special Revenue Fund
Oklahoma	Mandate	No more than 20 students may be assigned to a teacher	K–6	1995 1990	Part of foundation program

(continued)

TABLE 7.1   States with Class-Size Reduction Measures, 1998 (continued)

State	Mandate or Incentive	Class-Size Limit	Grade Levels Affected	Year Implemented	Funding
Rhode Island	Incentive	Encouraged to reduce class size to no more than 15	K–3	1987, 1996	Educational improvement block grants
South Carolina	Mandate	21	1–3 (math and reading classes)	1977	Through foundation program with pupil weights of 1.3 for K and 1.24 for 1–3.
South Dakota	Incentive	15	K–3	1993	Voluntary grants for up to 3 years
Tennessee	Mandate	20	K–3	1985	Part of foundation program
Texas	Mandate	22	K–4	1984	Unknown
Utah	Mandate	18	K–2 (if attained at K–2, then allocation can be used in 3–4)	1992	Weighted-pupil-funding formula distributes funds over 4 years
Virginia	Incentive	Long-term goal to reduce class size in schools with high or moderate concentrations of at-risk students	K–3	1996	State incremental funding along with local district match
Washington	Both	~18.42	K–3	1987–88	Part of basic aid formula along with incentive funding
Wisconsin	Incentive	Reduction of class size a requirement for receiving student achievement grants	K–3	1995	Funded through finance formula if part of special program

Source: Derived from ECS, 1998.

The early meta-analyses. Meta-analysis (Glass, McGaw, and Smith, 1981) is a technique for analyzing a wide variety of studies on a specific topic and determining if the results of those studies support a conclusion about that topic. The first step is to identify high-quality studies on the subject. This is done by assembling all of the studies addressing the topic and establishing decision rules as to whether or not to include the study in the meta-analysis. These decision rules usually pertain to the quality of the study (i.e., published in a refereed journal or high-quality book) and the relevance of the actual analysis to the topic of the meta-analysis.

Once identified, researchers need to compare the findings from each of the studies. This is difficult since the studies use different data sets, have different sample sizes, and analyze different variables. To compare studies, the results are standardized and the outcomes compared in terms of these standardized values.[4]

Glass and Smith (1979) conducted an early and comprehensive meta-analysis of the class-size literature. They identified more than 300 studies, going back as far as 1895 on the topic. Of those 300, 77 met their decision rules for inclusion in the meta-analysis. They calculated a total of 725 effects from the 77 studies. Based on their analysis of those studies, Glass and Smith concluded:

- There is a "clear and strong relationship between class size and student achievement." Sixty percent of the 725 effects showed higher achievement in smaller classes.
- Students learned more in small classes.
- Class size needed to be reduced to less than 20 students, preferably to 15, if strong impacts on student learning were to be found.

These are strong and important conclusions, and many have used them to support calls for reducing class size to less than 20.

Unfortunately, not everyone in the research community found this work to be convincing. Slavin (1984) criticized this meta-analysis, arguing that the technique gives equal weight to all study findings, regardless of the quality of the study design. He argued that only 14 of the 77 studies in the Glass and Smith meta-analysis were methodologically sound. He also criticized meta-analysis generally, suggesting that the technique combines studies that are on different topics while claiming to address the same topic. For example, one of the methodologically sound studies with large effects in the Glass and Smith (1979) sample had to do with learning how to play tennis.

Slavin (1989) reanalyzed the methodologically sound studies from the Glass

---

[4] The results are standardized or normalized so that each has a mean of zero and a standard deviation of one. Then, the effects of each variable on the outcome measure can be expressed in terms of standard deviations and thus compared. For example, an overall impact of half a standard deviation means that student performance would rise from the average or 50th percentile to the 69th percentile, and an impact of one standard deviation would mean average performance would rise all the way to the 83rd percentile.

and Smith work. He pointed out that there were only a small number of studies with fewer than 20 students in a class, and that there were no classes with between 4 and 14 students. He argued that the Glass and Smith findings were thus based on statistical interpolations of the findings in the 14 studies. He also concluded that the effects of reduced class size on student achievement were considerably smaller than Glass and Smith had determined.

Using these data from earlier meta-analyses, Odden (1990, p. 217) suggested that the research on class size supports "dramatic—and only dramatic—class size reductions." While he did not necessarily put a figure on what an ideal class size should be, Odden argued that reducing class size from 28 to 26, or from 24 to 22, would not be effective. He asserted that class size needed to be reduced substantially more—to something like 15 to 17 students per class—or even 1-to-1 tutoring. This line of reasoning has major implications for policymakers interested in reducing class size. States with large class sizes will need to spend substantial sums of money to make those "dramatic" class-size reductions if the policy is to succeed.

Recent studies.   In recent years, there have been a number of analyses on the impact of class size on student learning. In general, they show that smaller class size leads to greater gains in student test scores. One exception to this is the work of Eric Hanushek, who argues that we have not yet found a systematic relationship between resources and student outcomes. Hanushek (1989) reviewed 152 studies that used the pupil-teacher ratio as an independent variable in estimating the impact of spending and resources on student outcomes. Hanushek found only 27 studies with statistically significant findings, and only 14 of those found that reducing the number of pupils per teacher was positively correlated to student outcomes, while 13 found the opposite. Among the other 125 studies, Hanushek found that 34 found a positive effect, 46 a negative effect, and in the remaining 45, the direction of the effect could not be determined.

More recently, Hedges, Laine, and Greenwald (1994a) and Greenwald, Hedges, and Laine (1996a) came to the opposite conclusion after reviewing the same studies. Relying on newer and more sophisticated statistical techniques, they argued that smaller classes did indeed matter. Their analysis found that there were substantial gains in student performance when more money was spent on education, and that smaller class size was related to performance gains as well. Others have reached that conclusion also. Ferguson (1991) analyzed the effect of class size and teacher preparation on student achievement in Texas and concluded that, in elementary grades, lower pupil-teacher ratios contributed to increases in student achievement.

In a recent study in Alabama, Ferguson, and Ladd (1996) attempted to address some of the weaknesses of earlier studies in this area. They used larger samples of students, better model specification, and had access to better data than in the past. They concluded that teacher test scores, teacher education, and class size "appear to affect student learning" (Ferguson and Ladd, 1996, p. 288). They also attempted to ascertain the threshold below which further reductions in class size would no longer lead to systematic achievement gains for students. They believe that if such a threshold exists, it is in the range of 23 to 25 students per teacher. This number seems somewhat high compared to other results, but could be a result of the relatively low per-pupil spending in Alabama and the generally larger class size in that state during their study. More importantly, Ferguson and Ladd sought to measure actual class size, rather than the district or school pupil-teacher ratio. Consequently, their work may reflect a more accurate picture of the number of students in a classroom at any time.

One of the problems with this line of research has been the lack of a true experimental design. In fact, only one study with such a design has been undertaken. The Tennessee Student-Teacher Achievement Ratio Experiment (STAR) relied on an experiment in which children were randomly assigned to classes with low pupil-teacher ratios and high pupil-teacher ratios (Folger, 1992). The study design placed students into one of three groups. An experimental group where the average class size was 15.1 students, and two control groups: a regular size class with an average of 22.4 students and a regular size class with a teacher's aide and an average class size of 22.8 students. Under the study plan, each student was to stay in the original class-size assignment until the third grade. Following third grade, the experiment was concluded, and all students were assigned to regular size classrooms. Standardized tests were given each school year to measure student achievement. While there are some methodological and data problems in any study of this magnitude, two respected researchers have argued that the Tennessee STAR project is the best-designed experimental study on this topic to-date (Mosteller, 1995; Krueger, 1998). Krueger (1998) summarized the major findings of the Tennessee STAR project as follows:

- At the end of the first year of the study, the performance of students in the experimental classes exceeded that of the students in the two control groups by five to eight percentile points.
- For students who started the program in kindergarten, the relative advantage of students assigned to small classes grew between kindergarten and first grade, but beyond that, the difference is relatively small.
- For students who entered in the first or second grade, the advantage of being in a small class tended to grow in subsequent grades.
- There is little difference in the performance of students in the regular-size classrooms compared to the performance of students in regular-size classrooms with teacher aides.
- Minority students and students who qualify for free and reduced-price lunches tended to receive a larger benefit from being assigned to small classes.
- Students who were in small classes have shown lasting achievement gains through the seventh grade.

There are a number of important policy issues brought forward by the findings from Tennessee STAR. First, the results of the evaluation suggest that smaller classes do lead to improved student performance, and that those performance gains are maintained at least through the seventh grade. Moreover, the results suggest that alternative models that rely on the use of teacher aides to reduce the "effective class size" may be ineffective.

It is clear from this research that simply reducing class size without changing how teachers of smaller classes deliver instruction is unlikely to improve student performance. It is important that teachers take advantage of the smaller classes to offer material in new and challenging ways identified through research. Absent that effort and the training needed to accompany such a change, expenditures for class-size reduction may be relatively ineffective.

Alternatives to Class-Size Reduction

The research reviewed above shows that reducing class size can, and probably does, lead to improved student performance. It is, however, a very expensive option: in addition to hiring more teachers, schools need additional classroom space. Before embarking on a substantial class-size reduction program, policymakers may want to consider whether or not more cost-effective alternatives exist. Current research suggests that such alternatives are available and should be considered, either instead of—or in addition to—class-size reduction. One range of options deals with teacher knowledge and skills, while others relate to the structure of the education program offered at individual schools. Each is discussed below.

Teacher knowledge and skills.   Reducing class size gives students greater access to teacher resources. There is evidence this will help students learn. However, what the teacher knows and is able to do is at least as important in helping students learn. Darling-Hammond and Ball (1998, p. 1) argue that "teacher expertise is one of the most important factors in determining student achievement . . . ." They quote Greenwald, Hedges, and Laine's work in showing the relative impact of spending $500 more per pupil on increased teacher education, increased teacher experience, and increased teacher salaries. All three of these appear to have a greater impact on student test scores than does lowering the pupil-teacher ratio. Figure 7.1 shows the differences graphically: for an expenditure of $500, the greatest gains in student test scores (measured in standard deviation units from a range of tests in 60 studies) were found through increasing teacher knowledge. Lowering the pupil-teacher ratio was the least cost-effective of the four methods. Increasing teacher salaries and experience fell between lower pupil-teacher ratios and teacher education in terms of cost-effectiveness.

Ferguson (1991) found that the effects of teacher expertise in Texas were so great that after controlling for socioeconomic status, disparities in achievement between black and white students were virtually entirely explained by differences in teacher qualifications. He found that teacher qualifications explained 43 percent of the variation among the factors affecting math score test gains, while small classes and schools accounted for only 8 percent of the gain. Home and

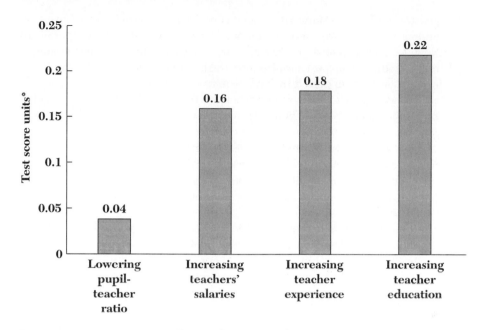

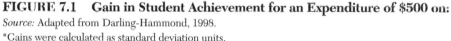

FIGURE 7.1   Gain in Student Achievement for an Expenditure of $500 on:
Source: Adapted from Darling-Hammond, 1998.
°Gains were calculated as standard deviation units.

family factors were identified as explaining the remaining 49 percent of the variance.

Darling-Hammond and Ball (1998, p. 1) summarize these findings by stating: "In other words, teachers who know a lot about teaching and learning and who work in settings that allow them to know their students well are the critical elements of successful learning." Clearly smaller classes are better in their view, but given limited funds to invest, their work suggests policymakers should at least take a close look at improving access to high-quality professional development first.

Professional development is frequently poorly funded in school districts and often the first item to be cut when finances become tight. Darling-Hammond and Balls's research (1998) suggests this may be a mistake, and in fact, more resources should be put into professional development. If class size is still reduced, professional development may be essential to help teachers maximize their skills given the reduced number of children for whom they are responsible. Certainly investments in professional development would be complementary to class-size reduction programs.

Reducing class size and providing greater training opportunities for teachers are not the only options available for improving student learning. There are many things school-site leaders themselves can do to restructure for improved learning. Some of these are discussed on the following page.

Reorganizing schools. Many of today's educational reforms restructure how educational resources are used. A number of the reform designs supported by the New American Schools (NAS) rely on using available teaching resources differently, rather than purchasing more (Stringfield, Ross, and Smith, 1996). While seven designs supported by NAS require some investment on the part of a school or school district, most are less expensive than dramatic reductions in class size or pupil-teacher ratios.[5] Most also come with substantial teacher-training components.

Ross, Sanders, and Stringfield (1998) found substantial gains in student performance at NAS design schools. These schools reach these performance levels with relatively little additional expenditures, generally averaging around $50,000 to $250,000 a year for a school of 500 students (an extra $100 to $500 per pupil each year). And Odden and Busch (1998) argued that many schools can reorganize themselves into one of the NAS designs by looking closely at their current allocation of teachers and aides and reassigning them as needed to meet the design specifications. In many instances, this calls for eliminating many of the aides and pull-out remedial specialist teachers in favor of more classroom teachers.

Another option schools can consider is restructuring the use of time. The National Commission on Time and Learning (1994) reported on a number of successful schools and school districts that had improved student performance through different ways of organizing the school day to give students more access to, and time with, teachers. Models that provide more access to learning resources, particularly teachers, may also be substantially more cost-effective than class-size reduction.

Conclusions about schooling inputs that improve results. Class-size reduction is currently one of the most popular—and most expensive—educational reforms today. At least 19 states have enacted mandatory or voluntary policies aimed at reducing class size in the primary grades, and one (California) has even created an incentive to reduce the number of students in ninth grade English and math classes.

The question facing state policymakers is, should substantial investments in smaller classes be made? The research shows that such investments will lead to improved student outcomes. However, the research also shows that attention to teacher training and expertise may have a bigger payoff per dollar spent. Moreover, as California's experience shows, states that jump into a major class-size reduction program quickly may find they have a shortage of qualified teachers. Given the importance of high-quality teaching to student learning, investment in the quality of the teaching force first might be a better way to maximize the potential of the dollars that are used to reduce class size. In short, few appear to op-

[5] The seven school designs supported by the New American Schools include: the Modern Red Schoolhouse, Expeditionary Learning-Outward Bound, National Alliance, Audrey Cohen College, Co-NECT, ATLAS, and Roots and Wings (New American Schools, 1996; Stringfield, Ross, and Smith, 1996). An eighth design, Urban Learning Center Schools, was not part of the Odden and Busch analysis.

pose class-size reduction. While there are a number of things states and school districts can do to ensure that the substantial investment made in teachers and classrooms reaps the maximum benefit possible, virtually all of them revolve around ensuring that the state has the highest quality teaching force possible.

Market Approaches

Many of today's reformers call for market-based changes in the organization of our schools. There are many ways to introduce the market into the educational arena, but most of these fall in one way or another under the heading of school choice. Public school choice can be considered as either intradistrict or interdistrict choice, and these can be broken down further into the various types of programs in each category. Two other types of choice involve the blurring of the line between public and private education: private school vouchers and privatization of former public schools. Each of these will be discussed in turn.

Intradistrict choice programs, by definition confined to one school district, grew largely out of an attempt to desegrate schools, rather than to provide competition or parent choice. The first of these programs is called controlled choice, where districts created models for assigning students to schools outside of the traditional neighborhood school model as a way of reducing segregation (Rouse and McLaughlin, 1999).

A second type of intradistrict choice program is the magnet school. Magnet schools were designed to attract white students to schools with high minority populations, often located in heavily minority communities. Magnet schools can be either entire schools with specialized education programs or specialized education programs within regular schools. Studies have shown that magnet schools are effective in reducing segregation (Blank, Levine, and Steel, 1996). And, while the desegregation was the driving force behind the development of magnet schools, such schools have introduced more choice, and competition, into the educational arena.

The newest model of intradistrict choice is the charter school. With the development of the charter school, the purpose of the choice models shifts away from desegration to a focus on providing parents with the choice to send their children to schools that may be less regulated than their traditional neighborhood school. These schools operate under a charter between those who organize the school (typically teachers and parents) and a sponsor (typically the local school board or state board of education). Charter schools may provide specialized education programs, or it may be the case that while they offer a regular-education program, the lack of regulatory constraints allows them to deliver it in innovative ways. For example, the school has more control over important issues such as hiring and budgeting, and often this control is shared with the parents as well. While the theory is that having control over hiring practices may allow these schools to hire a select staff that can positively impact student achievement, more research needs to be done to investigate whether those impacts actually exist. The same is true for the theory that charter schools stimulate creative innovations in education that positively influence student achievement. While some anecdotal evidence suggests that this is the case, more research must be done to determine the impact on student achievement.

Interdistrict choice programs allow the transfer of students between school districts. Although interdistrict choice programs also grew out of attempts to desegregate, they always had the goal of increasing parental choice as well. Many states allow interdistrict choice through open-enrollment policies, which vary from state to state; some states mandate that all districts have open enrollment, while others allow districts to choose whether they wish to be open or closed. By the 1993–94 school year, open enrollment was the most common school choice program in this country. Twenty-nine percent of school districts had open enrollment compared to only 14 percent of districts with intradistrict choice (National Center for Education Statistics, 1996). By 1997, 18 states had some form of open-enrollment legislation. However, participation in such programs is still quite low (Rouse and McLauglin, 1999).

As with intradistrict programs, many theorize that this injection of competition into education will improve its quality. This may be even more true with this type of choice because of the potential for districts to compete with each other. However, giving parents the opportunity to choose the district in which their child is enrolled may serve to weaken the link between district school quality and residents, perhaps causing a reduction in investment in the local school system. As was previously mentioned, the number of children participating in open enrollment is limited, and these potential, collateral effects have not yet been observed or studied.

Perhaps the most talked-about form of choice program is the voucher program. Voucher programs can be organized in different ways, but the basic idea is to give some children access to private schools by issuing vouchers to their families, which the families then give to the school in lieu of a tuition payment. Often these programs have the intention of allowing low-income students to go to schools they could not otherwise afford to attend, although vouchers are not necessarily limited to those in poverty. These provisions depend on the particular voucher system in place at the state or local level. While the idea of vouchers is not new, the existence of such programs is still relatively limited. In 1990, Wisconsin became the first state to implement a program that provides vouchers for low-income students to attend nonsectarian private schools in Milwaukee (Witte, Sterr, and Thorn, 1995). This program has since been changed to include parochial schools as well (Witte, 1998). Ohio adopted a similar program in 1996, one that allows students to attend both sectarian and nonsectarian private schools (Greene, Howell, and Peterson, 1997).

Since voucher programs are quite new, a limited number of them have been evaluated. However, Witte's (1998) evaluation of the Milwaukee Voucher Experiment produced mixed findings. On the one hand, parents were pleased with the choice program, especially in contrast to the schools their children attended before receiving the voucher that allowed them to transfer to another school. The fact that parents were happier with the schools their children attend also led to greater parental involvement. On the other hand, the effect on these children's test scores was not as dramatic as the program's creators might have hoped. In many cases, test score gains were similar for students in the choice program and those who were still enrolled in the Milwaukee public school system. In addition, three private schools closed midyear, creating upheaval for the families whose children attended these schools.

It is important to consider the complicated context from which these findings are taken, but Witte's conclusions do not support the argument that the competition provided by choice will positively affect student achievement. However, Green, Peterson, and Du (1997) reanalyzed Witte's data using different controls and statistical procedures and concluded that student test scores did rise in Milwaukee voucher schools. The different findings led to considerable debate. Clearly more research is needed, perhaps on larger voucher experiments. At this point, however, it is safe to say that "the verdict is still out" on the impact on student achievement of a strong voucher program.

The last market-based approach that will be discussed here is the privatization of schools that were formerly public. This is also a relatively new approach, and one that arose largely out of a demand for strategies that could save failing schools. The argument is that if public education functions like a monopoly (a firm that has control over its price and product) because it is not subject to competition, it has little incentive to function efficiently. By introducing some competition through privatization, schools would be forced to provide higher-quality education at a lower price.

Privatization in the education sector typically involves contracting out services. And while some services (such as food service) are contracted out in many public schools, the issue here is school boards and school districts who have contracted with private companies to run entire schools. Companies like The Edison Project and EAI (Education Alternatives, Inc.) form an agreement with a district whereby they receive the money that the public school would be getting for the children who attend the school, and run the school using their own methods. Ostensibly, these methods can raise student achievement even while operating at a lower cost. The Edison Project has been evaluated to determine whether these impacts indeed occur, and the results seem promising (The Edison Project, 1998). However, just as with the previous approaches that have been discussed here, not enough research has been done to know what the long-term effect will be of allowing private companies to run public institutions. There are a number of philosophical questions that must be addressed, including, if The Edison Project is successful at running the school at a lower cost than what the district (taxpayers) pays them, should private stockholders profit from this efficiency? This and other questions will have to be answered if companies like Edison continue to form such agreements with public school entities.

While there are many ways of incenting or creating competition in education, choice programs tend to be the most controversial and therefore get the most attention. Those who oppose choice programs have a number of objections. Probably the most common one is that while the introduction of market competition in education is supposed to improve the quality of education, this will only happen for a select group of children, thereby leaving the others with either the same poor-quality education or worse. They argue that the idea that competition means that the good schools will thrive and cause the bad schools to shut down may be improbable, particularly in large, overcrowded urban districts. More likely, students whose families have the resources, time, or acumen to work the system might get into the better schools, while others will not.

Picus (1994b) suggests that what is needed is market-type mechanisms within school systems. He argues that for markets to succeed, failure is an essential ingredient. Since it is unlikely schools will close (or fail), a proxy for that failure is needed. He suggests that schools be given more authority over the use of their resources and be held accountable for student outcomes, much as we argue in the next section. Schools implementing successful programs will meet their goals; those selecting inappropriate programs most likely will fall short of those goals. Providers of unsuccessful programs will go out of business—leading to the failure that is part of a market—and providers of successful programs will thrive, be they school districts, consortia of school personnel, or private companies. Picus goes on to suggest that the market for teachers within a district be made less restrictive, with principals seeking teachers who share their management style and programmatic vision.

2. IMPROVING EDUCATIONAL PERFORMANCE THROUGH DECENTRALIZED MANAGEMENT[6]

Many organizations in both the private and public sectors look to management systems and strategies as a route to improve their productivity (see for example, Lawler, 1986, 1996; Lawler, Mohrman, and Ledford, 1995; Osborne and Plastrik, 1997; Popovich, 1998). The impetus for changing management is the challenge to dramatically improve results with the same or even fewer dollars. The conclusion has been that this imperative requires a more decentralized management system, especially for organizations whose workers (like those in schools) are highly educated and produce the best results when they work collaboratively. These organizations have found that the most effective strategy for producing significant improvements in organizational performance has been to set clear performance goals at the top, flatten the organizational structure, decentralize power and authority to work teams, involve employees in making key decisions about how to organize and conduct their work, invest heavily in capacity development, and hold teams accountable for results (see also Barzelay, 1992; Katzenbach and Smith, 1993; Lawler, 1992; Mohrman, 1994a; Mohrman and Wohlstetter, 1994). In terms of school finance implications, these systems have found that a key part of this overall strategy includes providing organizations with power over their budget.

[6] This section revises and expands Odden and Busch (1998), Chapter 2.

Education today has similar performance-improvement imperatives. The dominant education reform goal is to teach all, or at least nearly all, students to high-performance standards. As indicated previously, this means increasing the percentage of students who perform at or above proficiency from the current level of 25–30 percent (National Center for Education Statistics, 1998) to 75–90 percent, a three-fold increase. Since education dollars will rise by a much smaller amount, the only way to accomplish the goal is to improve the productivity of the education system. Since teaching is intellectually challenging work (Rowan, 1994), is best done in collaborative settings (Newmann and Associates, 1996; Rosenholtz, 1989), and faces uncertainty in day-to-day work as well as an ever-changing policy environment, a decentralized management strategy also fits well with education (Mohrman, Lawler, and Mohrman, 1992; Mohrman and Lawler, 1996). Such a system would also provide a more professional work environment for teachers (see also National Commission on Teaching and America's Future, 1996).

Standards- and school-based education reform is the embodiment of this strategy in the public school system (Fuhrman, 1993; Massell, Kirst, and Hoppe, 1997; Smith and O'Day, 1991). This reform strategy seeks to educate students to high-achievement levels by setting goals, standards, testing, and accountability at the top (state or district) and decentralizing implementation to the school site by changing education management, governance, and finance.

Since, as we conclude below and elaborate on in Chapters 8 and 9, this requires substantial changes in how education dollars are distributed and used, it is important to summarize the evidence for how well decentralized management works in the education system. While the evidence to date is short of being definitive, the research on how to design an effective decentralized management strategy in education—one that improves student achievement—is rapidly expanding. This section of Chapter 7 summarizes this evidence, which includes school control over the budget as one of the critical elements.

The arguments in this chapter should not be construed to imply that standards- and school-based reform is the only way to dramatically improve the country's education system. Indeed, there may be other viable strategies, one of which could be school choice, which was discussed in the last section of this chapter. But standards- and school-based education reform is the strategy that many states and districts are trying to implement, and there is increasing evidence that—when fully designed and implemented—the strategy can produce increased results (Ross, Sanders, and Stringfield, 1998). A school-site–based finance system is a crucial element of this strategy, for it allows schools to use education dollars better; when absent, it constitutes a major obstacle to any meaningful form of school restructuring (Bodilly,1998).

To be sure, there is a substantial body of research showing that poorly designed education decentralization produces little if any effect (Malen, Ogawa, and Kranz, 1990; Murphy and Beck, 1995; Newmann and Wehlage, 1995; Summers and Johnson, 1996; Wohlstetter and Odden, 1992). These research findings indicate that the legacy of school-based management efforts in education is generally not positive. These studies also show that most failed efforts at decentralization were only partially designed and implemented or never evaluated.

Another problem with many approaches to education decentralization is that they have been conceived as ends in themselves. The belief has been that involving teachers in making decisions or democratizing schools will, in and of themselves, lead to better student performance. Evidence shows, however, that this type of decentralization produces little if any effect. Educators should know that a similar absence of impact on performance occurred in the private sector when decentralization was adopted merely to "democratize" the workplace (Mohrman, 1994a).

Another misunderstanding of school-based management (SBM) is that the composition and activities of the school council are the critical design elements (see Odden and Picus, 1992), and this misconception has often led to intense debate over the most effective composition of the council (Malen, Ogawa, and Kranz, 1990; Wohlstetter, Briggs, and Van Kirk, 1997). However, the studies discussed below show that the council is not the most important decision-making group that helps to make school-based management work.

Recently, Hannaway (1996) proposed that school decentralization needs to be combined with incentives for improved performance in order to make it work; alone, it is insufficient for making school-based management work. In short, decentralized school management itself will not improve school performance. Further, decentralized school management entails much more than just creating a school council and giving it some decision-making authority over the school and more than providing schools decision-making authority over the full-site budget. Even adding an accountability element to school-based management is not sufficient to make it successful.

Drawing on the findings from several recent research studies, this section concludes that in order for school-based management to work, the district must provide multiple organizational conditions at the school level, including school control over the allocation and use of its resources—dollars, personnel, and time. Schools then must use these conditions to work on and improve the dimension of schools that most directly impacts student achievement—the curriculum and instruction program. And, school-based management must be coupled with school-level accountability for results.

The research we cite includes several large-scale studies of fully developed school-based management and restructuring, with dozens of schools in numerous districts (Joyce and Calhoun, 1996; Newmann and Associates, 1996; Newmann and Wehlage, 1995; Odden, Wohlstetter, and Odden, 1995; Robertson, Wohlstetter, and Mohrman, 1995; Wohlstetter, 1995; Wohlstetter, Mohrman, and Robertson, 1996; Wohlstetter, Smyer, and Mohrman, 1994; Wohlstetter, Van Kirk, Robertson, and Mohrman, 1997). The literature also includes smaller studies of individual schools or districts (Beck and Murphy, 1996; Darling-Hammond, 1996; Smylie, Lazarus, and Brownlee-Conyers, 1996).

Taken as a whole, these studies show that effective school-based management must:

- use district and state goals, standards, and benchmarks to focus reform efforts on high levels of student learning and to funnel the energies of school professionals to the changes in curriculum and instruction needed to produce that level of learning,
- allow schools to recruit and select staff so they can build a cohesive faculty committed to the school's mission, vision, and culture,
- involve all of a school's teachers in decision making by establishing a network of teacher decision-making forums and work teams (i.e., creating a team-based school),
- focus on continuous improvement through ongoing, schoolwide professional development targeted to create both personal and organizational capacity,
- create a professional school culture committed to and willing to take responsibility for producing higher levels of learning for all students,
- create a well-developed system for sharing school-related information,
- develop ways to reward staff behavior that help achieve school objects and, we would add, sanction those that do not,
- select principals who can facilitate and manage change, and
- provide schools' control over the budget and the power to reallocate current resources to more productive uses.

The remainder of this section elaborates on these nine key elements of effective school-based management and the research supporting them.

1. Center change on student learning and a rigorous instructional program

The factor most strongly linked to student performance is instruction. Students basically learn what they are taught; conversely, students tend not to learn what they are not taught. Thus, in order to increase student achievement, school-improvement efforts must center on the curriculum and instructional program, on what is taught and how it is taught. Indeed, school-based management per se will not improve student learning. School-based management simply provides teachers the authority and autonomy to construct an instructional program that will improve the performance of their students, that, in the current reform parlance, will allow them to teach their students to high standards.

A central conclusion of the above studies on school-based management and restructuring is that learning must be its core focus in order for it to produce improvements in student achievement. One study termed this focus the "learning imperative" (Beck and Murphy, 1996), another "authentic learning" (Newmann and Wehlage, 1995), and a third an "instructional guidance" system (Wohlstetter, Smyer, and Mohrman, 1994). The point of all of these labels is that changes in the instructional program are what is most likely to change student performance; thus, school-based management will lead to improved student achievement only if it is used to enhance what is taught and how it is taught.

Relatedly, studies of effective school-based management found that some combination of district and state curriculum content and performance standards (see for example, Gandal [1996], National Council of Teachers of Mathematics [1989], National Research Council [1996]) helped to focus the work of the school on the curriculum and instructional program, including the notion of authentic pedagogy. An external set of such standards was one of four key elements of the supporting environment identified by the CORS study (Wehlage, Osthoff, and Porter, 1996). The standards could be state- or district-developed, but in nearly every case such a set of standards helped keep the site restructuring riveted on the instructional program. In their study of a district-created, school-based, shared-decision program, Smylie, Lazarus, and Brownlee-Conyers (1996) concluded that the district emphasis on reading and language arts helped focus the substance of site-based decision making on those elements of the curriculum and instructional program. Finally, the Consortium for Policy Research in Education's (CPRE) four-year, international study of school-based management, which researched 40 schools in 13 districts in three countries, also found that some version of district or state curriculum standards was one of eight key factors that made SBM effective (see, for example, Odden and Odden, 1996a; Robertson, Wohlstetter, and Mohrman, 1995).

The importance of the instructional focus reinforces the appropriateness of the core design element of the increasing number of school reform networks. The whole-school designs provided by these national networks [e.g., Accelerated Schools (Finnan, St. John, McCarthy, and Slovacek, 1996); Coalition of Essential Schools (Sizer, 1996); Core Knowledge Schools (Hirsch, 1996); Edison Schools (The Edison Project, 1994); and the New American Schools (NAS, 1995)] all have a rigorous curriculum and instructional program at their center. Thus, as one would hope, initial data indicate that they produce improvements in student performance relatively quickly (New American Schools, 1996; Ross, Sanders, and Stringfield, 1998; Slavin, et al., 1996; The Edison Project, 1996a, 1996b, 1996c, 1996d, 1998).

2. Allow schools to recruit and select staff

In order to build a faculty committed to the vision the school wants to implement, research also shows that schools need the authority to recruit and select staff who support that vision and want to contribute to the hard work required to put that vision into practice. Building a cohesive faculty committed to a high-standards school vision is not easy. It is hindered both by district practices that place personnel in schools with little if any school input and by contract provisions that allow teachers to transfer into and out of schools based solely on years of experience and teacher choice.

An important element of school-based management is for each school to identify a vision of what it wants to become and then work over several years to transform itself into that vision. This transformation would include implementing an entirely new, more-rigorous instructional program. Such tasks require extraordinary effort, which can only be sustained by a committed faculty. All studies of effective school-based management and restructuring found that site control over staffing was crucial to such effective school transformation (Beck and Murphy, 1996; Joyce and Calhoun, 1996; Newmann and Wehlage, 1995; Smylie, Lazarus, and Brownlee-Conyers, 1996; Wohlstetter, Van Kirk, Robertson, and Mohrman, 1997).

3. Involve all teachers in decision making

Recent studies have also shown that involving *all* teachers in school-based decision making and restructuring work groups is another key element that makes school decentralization successful. This was a particularly strong and explicit finding of the Consortium for Policy Research in Education's (CPRE) international study of school-based management, in which CPRE researchers concluded that the most effective school-based management strategies dispersed decision-making powers to all teachers through a series of horizontal and vertical teacher decision-making teams (see for example, Odden and Wohlstetter, 1995; Odden and Odden, 1996a; Wohlstetter, 1995; Wohlstetter, Van Kirk, Robertson, and Mohrman, 1997). CPRE also concluded that these types of decision-making arrangements were much more important than either school-site council subcommittees or school-site councils themselves.

This is not to devalue the need for school-site councils, for such councils were needed. Councils generally had the power to approve major school policies. Councils often were the main vehicle for directly involving parents in the processes of setting school policy. But CPRE found that councils tended to involve only a few teachers in decision-making roles. If the council became the major locus of decision-making activities, an "us" versus "them" dynamic often emerged, with "them" being those few individuals who sat on the council and made decisions, and "us" being the teachers who were in the classroom and did the job of everyday teaching. Although CPRE found that council subcommittees involved more teachers, the most effective SBM strategies devised ways to involve all teachers in multiple decision-making and restructuring activities. In this way, power and decision making were provided to *all* teachers in schools, and all worked on the core issues of restructuring. These conclusions were also reached by CORS in distinguishing between schools that "consolidated" decision-making power into a small group of school leaders versus those using school-based management to create "shared power relationships" (King, Louis, Marks, and Peterson, 1996).

4. Invest heavily in ongoing training and professional development

Training and ongoing professional development was another *sine qua non* of effective school restructuring and school-based management. All recent studies have concluded that substantial investment in ongoing professional development was key to making decentralization work (Beck and Murphy, 1996; Guskey and Peterson, 1996; Joyce and Calhoun, 1996; Newmann and Associates, 1996; Odden, Wohlstetter, and Odden, 1995; Smylie, Lazarus, and Brownlee-Conyers, 1996; Wohlstetter, Mohrman, and Robertson, 1997). The most effective professional development was structured to develop both individual and organizational capacity. Indeed, the primary intervention in the Joyce and Calhoun (1996) study was ongoing, intensive professional development. Further, broader studies of the implementation of standards-based reform conclude that capacity development is critical to effective implementation (Corcoran, 1995; Corcoran and Goertz, 1995; Goertz, Floden, and O'Day, 1995; Massell, 1998).

A comprehensive professional development strategy helps teachers acquire the new professional expertise they need to engage in successful school restructuring. Most teachers need new curriculum and instructional knowledge and skills to deploy authentic pedagogy successfully in the classroom. Because many restructuring objectives expand teacher roles, training may also be needed in counseling, advising, family outreach, and curriculum development. Most teachers also need skills to participate effectively in decision-making and work groups, such as coordinating decision-making teams, setting agendas, helping groups make decisions, ensuring that decisions are implemented, and following through on decisions made and work that needs to be done. When shifting from more hierarchically to more collegially run schools, most school personnel also need to learn collaborative skills, teamwork strategies, and leadership expertise. Additional expertise is needed for the new managerial responsibilities that accompany school-based management, such as recruiting and selecting staff, developing and monitoring budgets, supervising peers, and assessing program effectiveness. In short, substantive school restructuring requires teachers to develop an array of new professional expertise, which can only be developed through ongoing, long-term professional development.

The cost of investing in an appropriately intensive professional development program can be substantial. The professional development required to participate in national school reform networks and obtain expert assistance during the 3–4 years required for full implementation can run between 2 to 3 percent of a school site's total budget (Odden, 1997a). The level of professional development funding in New York City's Community District 2, which made extensive training a major feature of its reform strategy during the 1990s, was close to 5 percent of the budget (Elmore and Burney, 1996). The previously cited studies did not tally the actual costs of the professional development provided, but their descriptions suggest hefty programs, the costs of which could easily total $50,000–$100,000 per year in a school of 500 students, including both centrally provided (Elmore and Burney, 1996) and site-provided professional development (Odden, 1997a).

5. Create a professional school culture

The combination of allowing schools to recruit, select, and train staff; involve all teachers in decision making, particularly around creating an improved instructional program; and extensive investment in ongoing, intensive professional development leads to the creation of a "professional school culture" (Louis, Kruse, and Marks, 1996a, 1996b).

Professional community includes five key dimensions of school culture: shared norms and values, a focus on student learning (which we identify as the most important focus of school-based management), reflective dialogue about curriculum and instructional practices, deprivatization of practice, and collaboration.

Professional community includes collective responsibility for student achievement—a characteristic that helps keep school-based restructuring continuously focused on student performance. And professional communities are sustained by team-based school organizational structures.

6. Create a comprehensive, school-based information system

The CPRE school-based management study found that the most successful SBM programs were those that, through various mechanisms, had provided a vast array of information to teachers at individual schools. Moreover, the study found that the most advanced strategies automated this information and made the information system interactive through some type of relational database, similar to many "intranet" systems that now are emerging in the private and nonprofit sectors (Wohlstetter, Van Kirk, Robertson, and Mohrman, 1997).

Several states and districts are developing computer, Internet-based education information systems, all of which facilitate implementation of school-based management. Ohio and Texas have created such systems that include personnel information as well (see for example, Chambers, 1998). Oregon piloted a similar, Internet-based system in the 1998–99 school year. The Seattle public schools has placed its entire fiscal system on a Web-based computer program (http://sps.gspa.washington.edu/sps/). The system includes the school-based funding formula and the staffing for each school, and allows the principal to create the site budget on-line. It also provides ongoing information on expenditures to budget.

In addition to fiscal and personnel information, schools also need information on best practices. The Northwest Regional Educational Laboratory recently reviewed dozens of comprehensive school designs and curriculum programs in terms of their costs and impacts on student achievement. In addition to their 250-page report, the results are available on the Web (www.nwrel.org/scpd/nat-spec/catalog). Any district or state wanting to include information on best practices can simply provide a hotlink to this site and it becomes available to their schools. In other words, computer technologies make the distribution of extensive information systems to schools quite easy.

7. Provide rewards and sanctions

Accountability is another key ingredient of successful decentralized school management. Unfortunately, one of the downsides of most efforts at school-based management has been the lack of any accountability system (Hannaway, 1996; Murphy and Beck, 1995; Summers and Johnson, 1996). But accountability is important, and unless decentralized school management is held accountable for results, the probability that it will substantially improve performance is low (Hannaway, 1996). Nearly all recent studies of school-based management and school restructuring concluded that accountability was important (Joyce and Calhoun, 1996; Newmann, King, and Ringdon, 1996; Odden and Odden, 1996a; Smylie, Lazarus, and Brownlee-Conyers, 1996; Wohlstetter, Smyer, and Mohrman, 1994).

Consequences for the results of school actions help reinforce the point that the primary purpose of decentralization is to improve student achievement, and help stimulate the reflection on practice and its impacts, which are characteristic of a professional community. Consequences may include both rewards for success (i.e., meeting improvement targets) and sanctions for consistent failure.

In the 1990s, one of the most promising policies for providing rewards was the design and implementation of school-based performance awards. The details of how to design and implement such programs are discussed in Chapter 10. An additional reward that has not been considered very thoughtfully in education is the teacher salary schedule. Most past attempts to alter teacher salaries, which comprise 50 cents of each education dollar spent, have focused on merit pay, which always fail (Johnson, 1986; Murnane and Cohen, 1986). But a new form of teacher compensation, pay for knowledge and skills, is gaining in both awareness and use. Odden and Kelley (1997) show how this compensation innovation could work in education; the various issues related to new compensation schemes are discussed at greater length in Chapter 11.

The flip side of rewards is sanctions (i.e., consequences for not producing results). Here, too, the education system has been aggressively experimenting in the 1990s. One version of sanctions is state takeover of unsuccessful schools or school systems. These programs have been complicated and often never get to the curriculum and instructional reforms needed to produce higher levels of student achievement (Elmore, Abelmann, and Fuhrman, 1996; Fuhrman and Elmore, 1992). Another version of sanctions is the provision of technical assistance to struggling schools, which is the strategy used in Kentucky. Schools that consistently do not meet their improvement targets are labeled "schools in decline" and are assisted by "distinguished educators," educators identified as being highly knowledgeable and accomplished. Recent research suggests that this approach can have beneficial effects on schools: nearly all schools identified as "schools in decline" and that were provided help from distinguished educators made substantial progress in subsequent years (Kelley, 1997; Kelley and Protsik, 1997). School reconstitution constitutes a third intervention strategy. School reconstitution is a process in which consistently low-performing schools are redesigned and staffed with some combination of new management, new teachers, and new students. Although it appears to be a promising strategy, reconstitution efforts are in their infancy, and more information is needed to determine how they could work best. A variation of school reconstitution is a state or district requirement that consistently low-performing schools adopt a "high-performance" school design provided by one of the emerging numbers of school reform networks (Education Commission of the States, 1997c; Hirsch, 1996; New American Schools, 1995, 1996).

8. Select principals who can facilitate and manage change

Decentralized school management also requires a new breed of principals. Effective school restructuring needs strong, expert, and collaborative leadership. School-based restructuring to higher performance is aided by principals who can deploy the broader managerial roles that accompany more school self-management, can facilitate the work of teachers in a series of decision-making and work teams, and can manage a change process (Murphy and Louis, 1994).

Nearly all studies of school-based change find new and different, as well as more challenging, roles and functions for principals (Bryk, Easton, Kerbow, Rollow, and Sebring, 1997; Murphy and Louis, 1994; Newmann and Associates, 1996; Odden and Odden, 1996a; Wohlstetter and Briggs, 1994). Principals become responsible for more managerial tasks, such as budgeting, personnel, and local and office politics. These tasks require new skills and consume time, time a principal cannot devote to instructional leadership. Thus, the more successful principals create strategies to involve more people in providing school-level instructional leadership, which usually entails elevating teachers into instructional leadership roles, through team-based school organizations.

Principals are also charged with orchestrating the school processes of restructuring as the entire school works to transform itself into a new vision. Principals need to develop the expertise to design and manage such a large-scale school change process, which is complicated and does not proceed effectively unless consciously coordinated (Mohrman, 1994b).

9. Provide schools control over their budget

Finally, all recent studies conclude that school control over their budget was a key element of successful school-based management and restructuring.

Control over the budget is a core ingredient of decentralized management. This is true in other organizations (Lawler, 1986, 1992) and increasingly is a more explicit finding in education as well (Joyce and Calhoun, 1996; Newmann and Wehlage, 1995; Odden and Odden, 1996b; Wohlstetter, Van Kirk, Robertson, and Mohrman, 1997). Indeed, unlike the more tentative approaches in America to decentralized management that often provide only small amounts of budget authority (Hess, 1995; Wohlstetter and Odden, 1992), other countries seeking to decentralize education management to the school site take much more seriously the imperative that decentralization must include *substantial* budget control (see Odden and Busch, 1998, Chapters 4 and 5 on Victoria, Australia, and England).

Odden and Busch (1998) (and Chapter 8 of this book) show why control over the budget is so crucial. It turns out that many of the new, high-performance school visions that are part of the nearly two dozen school reform networks around the country are staffed and structured very differently from most schools in America. They have more classroom teachers and fewer nonclassroom specialists. They spend more on professional development. They group students and teachers differently, often across age levels and for multiple years. Many have full-time instructional facilitator roles rather than discipline-oriented assistant principals. Many also have more computer technologies. In sum, they use money differently. Further, in most localities, these new uses of resources can be financed with dollars already in the system.

But in order to have schools reallocate existing resources to these new—and hopefully more productive—uses, schools need control over their budget. As Lynn Olson (1997, p. 23) concluded in an article on district and school policy on budget devolution, "If teachers and principals are to call the shots at their schools, they also need control over the money. But the shift to school-based budgeting hasn't been easy . . . ," even though emerging research shows that when schools gain control over their budget, they begin to reallocate dollars to school specific purposes quite quickly (see Odden and Odden, 1996b; Odden and Busch, 1998, Chapter 5).

To be sure, the most recent programs of school-based management have found that greater portions of the budget are being devolved to schools, and that even full control of the budget is given to the select few schools that might be piloting fuller versions of school-based management within a district (Newmann and Wehlage, 1995; Wohlstetter, Van Kirk, Robertson, and Mohrman, 1997). Even though there are an increasing number of examples in the United States of large districts providing all schools with full control over their budget as part of a decentralization effort (Odden, 1998), the number is still small, and no state has moved very far on this agenda.

Chapter 9 suggests how both states and districts could devise ways to provide schools with more control over their budgets. The general notion is for the state to devise a framework within which school districts would decentralize substantial budget control to school sites.

Chapter 8

Using Education Dollars More Wisely to Improve Results[1]

As the previous chapter showed, there are several possible structural strategies for improving the performance as well as the productivity of the educational system. There is also significant debate concerning each of these approaches. But if any approach is to work, it likely will require—to greater or lesser degree—the spending of education dollars differently, and that is the focus of this chapter.

This chapter discusses several strategies some schools are already deploying that use educational dollars differently and substantially improve student performance, thus using dollars more productively. To be sure, the examples discussed are not exhaustive. In a very real sense, the nation's education system and its schools are just beginning to understand how to programmatically restructure and reallocate resources to higher performance. We expect that many other and even more powerful strategies will be identified in the future. But, the chapter analyzes some of the strategies that currently exist for using education dollars better. Our hope is that as more schools and school districts step up to the challenge of using education dollars more productively, they will discover many additional ways to use education dollars more effectively and efficiently.

We expect that more money will very likely be needed to improve student achievement by the amounts desired by many education reforms (i.e., to increase the percentage of students achieving at proficiency from 25 to 75 percent or more, or as proposed by the Consortium for Renewing Education [1998], to double education performance by 2020). Nevertheless, as this chapter will show, there are many ways to boost current levels of achievement by using extant school resources more productively.

[1] Portions of this chapter draw from Odden and Busch, 1998, Chapter 7.

Many argue, however, that because schools are labor-intensive, it is impossible for them to improve their productivity. It is true that schools are labor-intensive. But as this chapter shows, determining how educational dollars can be used more effectively requires an analysis of how school staff are used and entails using those staff resources quite differently. Using dollars more effectively in schools largely requires changing the labor mix within schools. It requires changing the number and roles of teachers and other professional resources in schools. In other words, improving the use of education dollars requires changing the labor structure of schools, which means changing how schools are staffed and thus changing the "cost structure" of schools. Although there are possibilities for using central office staff resources better (Elmore and Burney, 1996), this chapter draws from numerous research studies to identify several strategies being implemented across the country that use *school-site* resources differently to improve results, thereby improving the productivity of existing and any new education dollars.

1. EXAMPLES FROM SCHOOL RESTRUCTURING[2]

Research by Karen Hawley Miles and Linda Darling-Hammond (1997, 1998) provide good examples of the way school staff resources can be used more effectively. They studied three elementary and two high schools across the country that adopted or created a new school vision and reallocated their extant resources to the needs of their new vision. All schools were in urban districts serving large numbers of low-income and, in some cases, handicapped students. Three of the schools were "new starts," or schools created anew. Two schools restructured themselves from their previous to their new design. All schools produced large increases in student achievement and other desired results such as greater attendance, higher graduation rates, and more student engagement.

To varying degrees, the schools implemented five different resource reallocation strategies. They increased the number of regular-classroom teachers, thereby devoting more of their budget to the core education service: teaching a classroom of students. They also provided varied class sizes for different subjects, grouped students differently from the age-grade strategy of most schools, expanded common planning time for teacher teams, and increased teacher professional development. Most importantly, they strengthened their instructional program. They also produced higher levels of student performance.

None of the schools studied were given extra resources above those provided through normal district budgeting; these schools were staffed with the same total number of professional positions and resourced the same as all other schools in the district, with similar numbers and characteristics of students. But these schools used their professional teaching resources differently. They all ex-

[2] This section is from Odden and Busch, 1998.

panded the number of regular-classroom teachers. Two of the schools traded administrative positions for more teachers, and then involved more teachers in the management of the school. Most of the schools converted the bulk of their categorical specialist teacher positions, largely funded with categorical program dollars (federal Title I, state and local special education, bilingual education, etc.), to regular-classroom teacher positions, which allowed them to lower actual class sizes. Two schools, however, slightly increased class sizes (still in the mid-20's range) in order to release dollars to finance the professional reading tutors needed for the Success for All reading program they adopted (Slavin, Madden, Dolan, and Wasik, 1996).

All schools had different class sizes for different subject areas. These schools provided the lowest class sizes—sometimes as low as eight—for reading and language arts. In the Success for All schools, most teachers, including the reading tutors and sometimes even the librarians, taught a reading class during the reading period; this practice allowed schools to lower class size to 15 or less for reading. Other schools had some large lecture-style classes that were supplemented by smaller discussion groups, as well as individual student advising. Rather than have the same class size for all subjects, these schools varied class sizes. They required everyone in the school to teach at some points thus providing quite small class sizes, and then required less than half the staff to teach larger classes at other times, thus freeing those not teaching for other activities, including both common planning time and professional development.

Most of the schools also grouped students differently from the traditional age-grade approach in most schools. Several schools created multiage and multiyear student groupings, putting students of two or three different ages in the same classroom, and having the same teachers work with those students over a two- to three-year time period. This grouping strategy permitted teachers to build strong relationships and develop rapport with students, allowed them to provide a more personalized classroom atmosphere, and eliminated the need for the extended adjustment period at the beginning of each year when teachers get to know a new class of students.

The high schools created block schedules with longer class periods, which let them reduce the daily teacher-student load from over 150 to under 100, actually less than 60 in one case. This arrangement provided teachers time to get to know a smaller number of students at a deeper level and thus to provide a more individualized instructional program. The high schools also assigned small groups of students to each teacher for ongoing advising and counseling, yet another strategy that enhanced the personal, caring nature of the school environment, which research shows helps to improve achievement (Bryk, Lee, and Holland, 1993; Newmann and Associates, 1996).

All schools created more planning time for teachers, or simply rescheduled the planning time that existed to allow teams of teachers to work together during some portion of the regular school day. Many schools across the country already provide teachers with planning and preparation time. Too often, however, schools do not schedule this time for all members of a teacher team at the same time during the day. Thus, one simple, cost-free way to expand common teacher planning time is to schedule all teachers in a team for the same planning period during the normal school day. These schools tapped this uncomplicated, no-cost way to expand joint planning. But these schools also used the flexibility provided by their different class sizes for joint planning. During those times when students were in larger classes, and in the case of one high school, during those times when students were out of the school working on community service projects, the schools scheduled common teacher planning time. In this way, each school was able to provide more common planning time for their faculty by using both money and time differently.

Finally, all schools expanded professional development. The additional professional development for the teachers in these schools was an important new way of using their resources. But, none of these schools expanded professional development to the level of $50,000–$70,000 a year for a school of 500, which, as is shown later in this chapter, is about the level required for major school restructuring.

These schools traded specialist positions for regular classroom teachers, including many specialist teachers for students with mild disabilities such as the learning disabled. As a result, each school had specific strategies for instructing low-achieving or learning-disabled students within the regular classroom or as part of the core features of the school design. For example, the Success for All program not only taught reading in small classes of 15, but also tutored any student, including disabled students, not reading on grade level. A school that mainstreamed all special-education students trained the entire faculty in the expertise to instruct students in this more inclusive environment. In order to make this approach to service provision for the disabled legal, each disabled student's individual education program was modified, with parental consent, to reflect the instructional strategies of the school. The achievement data showed that these special-needs students also improved their performance, a result often not produced by pull-out, resource room programs (Allington and Johnston, 1989), the typical service identified by individualized education programs.

Schools implemented the above restructuring and resource reallocation strategies over a number of years. In no case were teachers moved precipitously; many teachers, however, assumed new roles, with training sometimes accompanying those new roles. Miles and Darling-Hammond (1997, 1998) noted that school implementation processes would have been assisted if the schools had had more authority over recruiting and selecting staff committed to the vision they were deploying, one of the key elements of effective school-based management discussed in Chapter 7.

In short, without any additional resources, these schools:

- reduced class sizes,
- created even lower class sizes for reading,
- reduced the daily student-teacher contact numbers,
- personalized the teaching-learning environment,

- provided common planning time, and
- expanded professional development.

Although all schools faced obstacles and challenges in implementing these different resource-use strategies, they nevertheless made substantial progress and engaged in substantive resource reallocation. They also improved educational results for students, including student achievement in core academic subjects. In short, all five schools improved the productivity of their existing educational dollars through programmatic and organizational restructuring, accompanied with substantial resource reallocation.

2. STAFFING IN AMERICA'S SCHOOLS

Of course, the more general question is whether the schools in the Miles-Darling-Hammond study were atypical or whether the examples of resource reallocation deployed in these schools are possible in other schools across the country. In order to begin to answer this question, we used the Schools and Staffing Survey (SASS) school-level data to determine the median staffing in elementary, middle, and high schools in each major region of the country. We calculated staffing patterns for elementary schools with between 400 to 600 students (roughly averaging 500 students), middle schools with 900 to 1,100 students (about 1,000 students, on average), and high schools with 1,400 to 1,600 students (typically averaging 1,500 students). Figure 6.13 shows the average staffing resources for the elementary, middle, and high schools of interest. In addition, Figure 6.13 indicates the dollar value associated with staffing, using the figure of $50,000 for salaries and benefits for each professional staff slot and $15,000 for each instructional aide, which reflect very roughly a national average figure in the mid-1990s.

As can be seen from Figure 6.13 on page 282, the professional staffing resources in schools of these sizes reach into the millions (line 8); if the classified staff (secretaries, maintenance), operations, utilities, discretionary resources, and other funding were included, the totals would be even higher. Line 8 indicates the total dollar value of the professional and teacher aide staff. Line 9 indicates the total dollar amount for "core" staffing; "core" staffing is defined as one principal for each 500 students and one teacher for every 25 students. Line 10 indicates the total dollar value of the staffing resources in these schools above those required for core staffing; the amount in parentheses indicates the amount for each grouping of 500 students.

The results show two important findings. First, the extra resources above the core are about the same across each level of schooling, somewhat contrary to the belief that the United States staffs secondary schools at higher levels than elementary schools. Second, the data show that there are substantial resources above core staffing, averaging about $650,000 for each level of schooling.

These resources should not be viewed as free resources, however. In some districts, a portion of these resources are spent on regular-education specialists such as art, music, physical education, library, home economics, and vocational education teachers, who have been employed over time to provide planning and preparation time for regular-classroom teachers. Assuming teachers are given one planning period a day, the number of regular-classroom teachers would need to be increased by about 20 percent to approximate the number of regular-education specialists needed to provide that time; note also that each specialist would receive a daily planning period. Thus, each group of 500 students, with 20 regular teachers in classes of 25 students, would require four additional teachers (0.2 times 20) for requisite planning and preparation time. At $50,000 each, this would reduce the additional $650,000 by $200,000, which equals $450,000.

A portion of the latter figure also would need to be devoted to special-needs students, such as students eligible for compensatory education programs, and additional services for students with disabilities, or who need to learn the English language. Indeed, the median number of Title I teachers is two, and the median for Title I aides is one at each school level. Finally, another portion of the remaining $450,000 would be spent on student support personnel, such as guidance counselors, social workers, psychologists, family outreach individuals, etc.

The Miles and Darling-Hammond studies discussed in the previous section showed how these resources above the core were used differently in the restructured schools they studied. The data in Figure 6.13 show, at the national average, the magnitude of such additional school-level resources.

But the level and types of school-level resources vary quite substantially across the country, and the national average might only be accurate for a few districts. Previous chapters have discussed the magnitude of resource disparities in fiscal terms, making the important point that the major factor causing disparities across school districts are cross-state rather than within state differences. Though the Schools and Staffing Survey sampling frame does not allow identification of school-level staffing on a state-by-state basis, it does allow it to be calculated on a regional basis. Tables 8.1 through 8.4 provide the same information as Figure 6.13, but the data are broken out into four regions of the country: the Northeast (Connecticut, Maine, Massachusetts, New Hampshire, New Jersey, New York, Pennsylvania, Rhode Island, and Vermont), the Midwest (Illinois, Indiana, Iowa, Kansas, Michigan, Minnesota, Missouri, Nebraska, North Dakota, Ohio, South Dakota, and Wisconsin), the South (Alabama, Arkansas, Delaware, District of Columbia, Florida, Georgia, Kentucky, Louisiana, Maryland, Mississippi, North Carolina, Oklahoma, South Carolina, Tennessee, Texas, Virginia, and West Virginia) and the West (Alaska, Arizona, California, Colorado, Hawaii, Idaho, Montana, Nevada, New Mexico, Oregon, Utah, Washington, and Wyoming). Though prices of staff differ by region, we provide these tables primarily to indicate the difference in staffing because again, as we show below, resource reallocation at the school site largely entails using extant staff resources differently. Thus, we used national average salary figures to calculate dollar levels, a process similar to adjusting actual dollar figures by price indices (see Chapter 4). We should note, though, that actual average salaries are quite low in the South and that one of the reasons the staffing in the South is higher than some regions is because of the

TABLE 8.1 Median School Resources in Elementary, Middle, and High Schools in the Northeast

Ingredient	Elementary School Grades K–5°	Middle School Grades 6–8°°	High School Grades 9–12°°°
Average enrollment	500	1,000	1,500
1. Principal	1.0	1.0	1.0
2. Assistant principals	0.0	1.0	3.0
3. Teachers	29.0	64.5	101.5
4. Librarians	1.0	1.0	1.0
5. Media aides	0.0	0.0	2.0
6. Counselors and psychologists	3.0	4.5	10.5
7. Teacher aides	6.0	3.0	6.0
8. Total staff resources°°°°	1,790,000	3,645,000	5,970,000
9. Total CORE resources	1 principal; 20 teachers $1,050,000	1 principal; 40 teachers $2,050,000	1 principal; 60 teachers $3,050,000
10. Total above CORE (Line 8 minus Line 9) (per 500 students)	740,000 ($640,000)	1,595,000 ($797,500)	2,920,000 ($973,000)

Source: Staffing data from analysis of Schools and Staffing Survey, 1993–94.

° Enrollments from 400 to 600 students.

°° Enrollments from 900 to 1,100 students.

°°° Enrollments from 1,400 to 1,600 students.

°°°° Average professional staff cost at $50,000; average teacher aide cost at $15,000.

very low salary levels, making their expenditures per pupil the lowest of any region.

The data in these tables show that school-level resources vary substantially across the four different regions, and that each of the four regions represent staffing patterns different from the national average. For example, line 10, total resources above the core for each group of 500 students, is about the same for elementary, middle, and high schools at the national average as depicted in Figure 6.13, but it is different in all of the four regional tables. The Northeast (Table 8.1) provides substantially more resources for its high schools than it does for either its middle or elementary schools. Indeed, the Northeast pattern is the stereotypical pattern: middle schools are resourced somewhat above elementary schools, and high schools are resourced to an even higher level above middle schools, and thus substantially above elementary schools.

In the Midwest, middle schools, surprisingly, receive the highest level of staffing resources, with elementary schools having less than the national average and high schools about the national average of resources above the core. The resourcing patterns in the South are just the opposite of those in the Northeast;

TABLE 8.2   Median School Resources in Elementary, Middle, and High Schools in the Midwest

Ingredient	*Elementary School Grades K–5**	*Middle School Grades 6–8***	*High School Grades 9–12****
Average enrollment	500	1,000	1,500
1. Principal	1.0	1.0	1.0
2. Assistant principals	0.0	1.8	2.5
3. Teachers	24.5	62.0	87.0
4. Librarians	1.0	1.0	2.0
5. Media aides	0.5	1.0	1.0
6. Counselors and psychologists	2.5	4.0	7.0
7. Teacher aides	4.0	4.0	6.0
8. Total staff resources****	1,517,500	3,565,000	5,080,000
9. Total CORE resources	1 principal; 20 teachers $1,050,000	1 principal; 40 teachers $2,050,000	1 principal; 60 teachers $3,050,000
10. Total above CORE (Line 8 minus Line 9) (per 500 students)	467,500 ($467,500)	1,515,000 ($757,500)	2,030,000 ($676,667)

Source: Staffing data from analysis of Schools and Staffing Survey, 1993–94.

* Enrollments from 400 to 600 students.

** Enrollments from 900 to 1,100 students.

*** Enrollments from 1,400 to 1,600 students.

**** Average professional staff cost at $50,000; average teacher aide cost at $15,000.

elementary schools receive the greatest level of resources, followed by middle schools, with the high schools receiving the lowest level. This pattern could reflect the predominant Southern practice of providing students in grades K–3 with a weight above one. Finally, although there are differences in resources among different school levels in the West, the predominant feature of this data is simply the lower level of resources above the core, generally less than half that of the national averages, and substantially below that in either the Midwest or the Northeast. These figures document that school-level resources are quite different in the various regions of the country, and that just using national averages to assess resource reallocation possibilities could lead to inaccurate conclusions.

3. RESOURCE REALLOCATION POSSIBILITIES

The key analytic issue is how these national and regional staffing figures relate to resource reallocation potential in the nation's schools. The following identifies

TABLE 8.3 Median School Resources in Elementary, Middle, and High Schools in the South

Ingredient	Elementary School Grades K–5*	Middle School Grades 6–8**	High School Grades 9–12***
Average Enrollment	500	1,000	1,500
1. Principal	1.0	1.0	1.0
2. Assistant principals	0.0	2.0	3.0
3. Teachers	29.0	58.0	87.0
4. Librarians	1.0	1.0	2.0
5. Media aides	0.5	1.0	1.0
6. Counselors and psychologists	2.5	4.5	6.0
7. Teacher aides	7.0	6.0	4.0
8. Total staff resources****	1,787,500	3,430,000	4,755,000
9. Total CORE resources	1 principal; 20 teachers $1,050,000	1 principal; 40 teachers $2,050,000	1 principal; 60 teachers $3,050,000
10. Total above CORE (Line 8 minus Line 9) (per 500 students)	737,500 ($737,500)	1,380,000 ($690,000)	1,705,000 ($568,333)

Source: Staffing data from analysis of Schools and Staffing Survey, 1993–94.

* Enrollments from 400 to 600 students.

** Enrollments from 900 to 1,100 students.

*** Enrollments from 1,400 to 1,600 students.

**** Average professional staff cost at $50,000; average teacher aide cost at $15,000.

some of these connections by drawing upon research on the cost structure of high-performance comprehensive school designs (e.g., Odden, 1997a, 1997b), where "high performance" is defined as maximizing achievement levels with minimum resources.

During the 1990s, many efforts were made to involve the best education talent in the country in devising higher-performance school designs. Today, several national school reform networks offer comprehensive school designs created to produce higher levels of student achievement. In fact, most designs were constructed with the goal of teaching the vast majority of students to new high-achievement standards (Education Commission of the States, 1997c, 1998). Organizations such as the New American Schools, which offers seven school designs (Stringfield, Ross, and Smith, 1996), Core Knowledge Schools (Hirsch, 1996), Accelerated Schools (Finnan, St. John, McCarthy, and Slovacek, 1996), the Coalition of Essential Schools (Sizer, 1996), The School Developmental Program (Comer, Haynes, Joyner, and Ben-Avie, 1996), The Edison Project (1994), and several others now provide comprehensive or whole-school, high-performance designs, and the technical assistance to implement them. The school designs that

TABLE 8.4 Median School Resources in Elementary, Middle, and High Schools in the West

Ingredient	Elementary School Grades K–5*	Middle School Grades 6–8**	High School Grades 9–12***
Average enrollment	500	1,000	1,500
1. Principal	1.0	1.0	1.0
2. Assistant principals	0.0	1.0	2.5
3. Teachers	23.0	41.5	67.0
4. Librarians	0.5	1.0	1.0
5. Media aides	0.5	0.5	1.0
6. Counselors and psychologists	2.0	3.5	5.5
7. Teacher aides	5.5	4.0	6.5
8. Total staff resources****	1,415,000	2,467,500	3,962,500
9. Total CORE resources	1 principal; 20 teachers $1,050,000	1 principal; 40 teachers $2,050,000	1 principal; 60 teachers $3,050,000
10. Total above CORE (Line 8 minus Line 9) (per 500 students)	365,000 ($365,000)	417,500 ($208,750)	912,500 ($304,167)

Source: Staffing data from analysis of Schools and Staffing Survey, 1993–94.

* Enrollments from 400 to 600 students.

** Enrollments from 900 to 1,100 students.

*** Enrollments from 1,400 to 1,600 students.

**** Average professional staff cost at $50,000; average teacher aide cost at $15,000.

are discussed below are those with identified cost structures, and the fiscal details needed for analyzing resource reallocation are known.

Selected High-Performance School Designs

Most comprehensive school designs were constructed to teach students to higher-achievement levels (New American Schools, 1995; Stringfield, Ross, and Smith, 1996). They were initially proffered as "break-the-mold" school designs, powerful enough to teach students to high-performance standards. The core element of each design is a high-standards curriculum, with content standards in at least mathematics, science, reading/language arts, and social studies; the Modern Red Schoolhouse design includes art and music standards as well. Some designs (e.g., Co-NECT, Expeditionary Learning-Outward Bound, Modern Red Schoolhouse, and the National Alliance) require a different teaching-learning structure than the typical school, such as multiage and/or multiyear student groupings; other designs (e.g., Audrey Cohen College and the nonreading components of Roots and Wings) function with structures more similar to current schools. Some designs have substantial computer technologies, particularly Co-NECT and the Modern Red Schoolhouse. Although all designs have been shown to work well in impoverished environments, ATLAS and Roots and Wings draw on programs designed specifically for students in urban schools in high-poverty communities.

These and other characteristics of most high-performance school designs reflect the conclusions in Chapter 7 on effective school-based management, particularly those requiring a primary focus on a rigorous curriculum and instructional program, and the involvement of teachers in school management, especially regarding the instructional program. The curricular, programmatic, and governance features of each design are described more fully in Stringfield, Ross, and Smith (1996) and their respective web sites (see http://www.naschools.org/home.htm for a way to link to each of these sites). In this chapter, we show how the costs of these designs represent seven different ways of fiscally restructuring for higher educational productivity.

Research shows that these designs are producing improvements in student performance, both educational achievement in the core subjects and other desired results, such as better attendance, more engagement in academic work, and higher satisfaction with school in general (Comer, 1993–94; New American Schools, 1996; Fashola and Slavin, 1997; Ross, Sanders, and Stringfield, 1998; Slavin, et al., 1996). Though schools and districts need to remain diligently monitoring the results of these school designs and tracking over time the degree to which each comprehensive school design boosts student learning, early results show most do improve student achievement. Because they generally can be funded with extant resources, they thus represent seven examples of how higher levels of valued educational results can be produced with current school funding levels.

Each design begins with a fairly skeletal core staffing for a school: one principal and 20 teachers for a school of 500 students with class sizes of 25. This constitutes the core that is identified in Tables 8.1–8.4. In addition to this core staffing, each design requires a set of additional ingredients (the cost figures approximate 1996–97 prices):

- *ATLAS* requires: (1) a half-time instructional facilitator, (2) a school health/family liaison team composed of various combinations of a family liaison, guidance counselor, psychologist, social worker, educational specialist, nurse, etc., (3) $4,000 for instructional materials, (4) limited technology, including a computer and Internet and e-mail connection, (5) $28,000 of team-based professional development, and (6) a week-long summer institute for the entire staff that costs $15,000 for teacher stipends. The first total-cost figure in Table 8.6 is for a school with 50 percent of its students from low-income families and a half-time health team; the second figure is for a full-time health team in a highly poverty-impacted school.
- *Audrey Cohen College* requires: (1) a full-time staff resource specialist, (2) $7,900 for instructional materials and student trip costs, (3) $36,700

of materials and team-based professional development, and (4) a week-long summer institute for the entire staff that costs $15,000 for stipends.

- *Co-NECT* requires: (1) a full-time technology coordinator/instructional facilitator, (2) substantial computer technologies that are best phased-in over a number of years at about $125,000 per year, (3) $53,500 of design team-based professional development, and (4) a week-long summer institute and other professional development activities that cost $15,000 for stipends, substitutes, and staff travel.

- *Expeditionary Learning-Outward Bound (ELOB)* requires: (1) an instructional facilitator,[3] (2) funds for instructional materials and trips (the rope course costs are one-time expenditures for the initial purchase of the items), (3) $71,000 in team-based professional development, and (4) a week-long summer institute for the entire staff that costs $15,000 for stipends.

- *Modern Red Schoolhouse* requires: (1) a full-time technology coordinator (half-time in the first year), (2) substantial computer technologies (which are shown as phased-in over many years at an annual cost of $125,000), (3) $70,000 in team-based professional development, and (4) a week-long summer institute for the entire staff as well as other training experiences that cost $29,000 for stipends and substitute teachers.

- *National Alliance* requires: (1) a school leadership team for each of the key five task areas in the National Alliance: standards and assessment, the learning environment, public engagement, community services, and high-performance management, (2) $8,000 for materials on teaching students to standards and use of the New Standards assessments, (3) participation in a national conference on standards-based teaching and leadership, and (4) work through the district with the National Alliance for ongoing professional development and training at a cost of $37,000 annually, $24,000 of which is a district-paid participation fee. In 1998, this design was renamed America's Choice (Tucker and Codding, 1998), and the design began to formally require a literacy coordinator, a design coach, and a community outreach coordinator. The table includes these additional costs.

- *Roots and Wings* requires: (1) a full- (half-) time instructional facilitator for a school with 100 (50) percent of students from low-income families, (2) a half-time family liaison, (3) four (two) tutors for a school with 100 (50) percent of students from low-income families, (4) $26,000 in instructional materials, and (5) $18,000 in team-based professional development.

---

[3] ELOB is finding that this function is best filled by several individuals in the school, working together as a team, rather than by one full-time individual. In some schools, these individuals work on the extra tasks for no extra money; in others, they are provided extra release time, which is a cost item. The high-cost figure in Table 7.1 includes this function as a cost at the equivalent of one full-time professional.

Table 8.5 summarizes and totals the above costs for these seven school designs. The cost data are based on several assumptions. First, several of the specific items of each design are grouped into major categories; the descriptive literature for each design needs to be read carefully for schools to fully understand the general nature and the specific ingredients and strategies of each design (Odden, 1997a; Stringfield, Ross, and Smith, 1996; http://www.naschools.org/home.htm). Second, for the purposes of national comparison, the table assumes that the average cost of a teacher is $50,000 for salary and benefits. Third, the data represent the first-year costs for each school design, although most designs are implemented over a three- to six-year period. Some designs cost more in the first year and taper off in the final years; other designs cost more in the middle years of implementation. But none of the design costs vary dramatically over the first three years of implementation, so the figures in the table provide a good average estimate of the ingredients and core costs that need to be financed. Fourth, since the data reflect the additional ingredients and their average extra costs for a school of 500, resource levels and costs will be higher for schools with more than 500 students and lower for schools with less than 500 students. Each school will need to determine how their specific costs will vary depending on their actual enrollment and actual salary costs.

The annual costs consist of two parts: (1) expenses paid to design teams for materials and the expert technical assistance each school needs during the 3–4 years it takes to implement the design and (2) operating costs for running the design. The design team costs range from $32,000 to $84,280, averaging about

TABLE 8.5 1996–97 First-Year Costs for NAS Designs (above the Core of a Principal and Regular-Classroom Teachers)

NAS Design	Design Team Assistance	Design Team Materials	Subtotal: Design Team Costs	Operating Costs above Core	Total Costs
ATLAS	$28,000	$ 4,000	$32,000	$150,000–$250,000	$182,000–$282,000
Audrey Cohen	$36,700	$ 7,900	$44,600	$78,000	$122,600
Co-NECT	$53,500	—	$53,500	$185,000	$238,500
ELOB	$71,000	$13,280	$84,280	$40,000–$90,000	$124,280–$174,280
Modern Red Schoolhouse	$70,000	$ 5,000	$75,000	$300,000	$375,000
National Alliance	$37,000*	$ 8,000	$45,000*	$220,000	$265,000*
Roots and Wings	$18,000	$26,000	$44,000	$250,000–$350,000	$294,000–$394,000

Source: Odden (1997a).

* $24,000 district-paid participation fee.

$45,000. However, the designs include more than technical assistance and materials: each design has a set of ingredients in addition to teachers that must be funded, such as the health team for ATLAS, technology for Co-NECT and Modern Red Schoolhouse, and tutors for Roots and Wings. Each design also requires a schoolwide instructional facilitator, performed as one individual or as a team of teachers. Schools and districts would need to finance both the design team, technical assistance/professional development costs, and the operational costs in order to fully restructure as the design prescribes.

An interesting cost element in these seven programs is the substantial professional development. This important expenditure is not found in many traditional schools, although training and capacity development is identified by many as a key ingredient for implementing standards-based reforms (Goertz, Floden, and O'Day, 1995), and is a key element of successful school restructuring (see Chapter 7). For many designs, the professional development averages about $45,000 in design-based technical assistance and training, and about $15,000 for teacher stipends, mainly for summer institutes. Assuming schools (as compared to districts) spend $6,000 per pupil on average, a 2.2 percent school set-aside would provide the $65,000 in ongoing training the average comprehensive school design requires for design-related team-based training, teacher stipends, and substitute teachers. Districts and schools would need to budget such a percentage of their dollars for ongoing professional development even after the school designs are completely implemented because teachers need to continuously upgrade and expand their professional competencies, and because effective knowledge, strategies, programs, and skills continue to be developed.

The total cost for each school design is the sum of the cost of the design team, out-of-pocket expenses, and operational costs. The total ranges from just over $100,000 to $375,000. For example, a school of 500 students would need between $100,000 and $375,000 above the core of a principal and 20 teachers in order to restructure into one of these comprehensive school designs and fund all of the necessary costs.

The fiscal goal for the development of each school design was a cost structure that would enable a school with the national average level of resources per pupil to afford it. The goal was that schools would not need extra money to fully implement the design. Instead, the idea was to have schools use extant resources differently and reallocate them to the cost structure of the selected high-performance school design.

The cost data in Table 8.5 when compared to the national average resource data in Figure 6.13 suggest that the average elementary, middle, and high school in America has sufficient resources to finance all of these school designs, even after providing planning and preparation time. Recall that after subtracting the resources needed for planning time, national average schools still had about $450,000 remaining, which is more than sufficient to finance even the most expensive school design described and costed-out at between $350,000 and $375,000.

But as the regional data show (Tables 8.1 to 8.4), this conclusion varies by region. The average school in the Northeast (Table 8.1) as well as, somewhat surprisingly, in the South (Table 8.3) would have more than sufficient resources to fund even the most expensive high-performance designs. The average elementary, middle, and high school in these two regions would be able to afford any of the high-performance school designs as well as provide planning and preparation time, with funds left over for other purposes. We should note again, however, that a major reason for the substantial staffing resources in the South is the lower teacher salaries, making expenditures per pupil much lower in the South, even after adjusting for the varying purchasing power of the education dollar.

Table 8.6 provides a specific example of a middle school in a large city in the Northeast. The numbers in the top portion of the table show that the school had large class sizes of about 31 students (1,000 students divided by 32 regular teachers), but had numerous staff above this core: nine regular-education specialists, 10 categorical program specialists, and three guidance counselors. Total resources above the core reached $1.835 million, using the district's average cost of a teacher at $65,000 for salaries and benefits and $15,000 for an instructional aide. The school's desire was to adopt the Modern Red Schoolhouse design. The lower portion shows the costs of this design above the core (the basic cost numbers are doubled to reflect the 1,000 students in the school compared to the base

TABLE 8.6   Reallocating Resources to Fund a Comprehensive School Design: An Example of an Eastern Urban Middle School

1,000 Students, High Poverty

- CORE: 1 principal, 32 teachers
- 2 APs ($130,000)
- Regular education: 2 art, 2 music, 2 home economics, 2 shop, 1 librarian ($585,000)
- Categorical education: 10 LD, 13 aides ($845,000)
- Pupil support: 3 guidance counselors ($195,000)
- Professional development ($80,000)
- Total above CORE: $1,835,000
- Teachers ($65,000); aides ($15,000)

Modern Red Schoolhouse

- 1 principal, 32 teachers
- 2 instructional facilitators ($130,000)
- 10 teachers to reduce class size ($650,000)
- 2 art and 2 music teachers ($260,000)
- Professional development ($150,000)
- Technology and materials ($250,000)
- Total design costs: $1,450,000
- Remaining: $385,000

Source: Analysis of data gathered by author.

of 500 in Table 8.5): two instructional facilitators, two art and two music teachers, $150,000 for professional development and training, and $250,00 annually to purchase the requisite computer technologies and related materials. This model also includes an additional 10 teachers to reduce actual class size to 25, the desired class size. The table shows that even after purchasing these ingredients, there would still be $385,000 left over. Some of this surplus would be needed to hire four more teachers to provide additional planning time. These additional four plus the four art and music teachers would allow the school to provide each teacher one period a day for planning and preparation. This would still leave $125,000 for extraordinary needs. We should note that this example derives from a district that spends at the lower to middle level of schools in the Northeast; other schools would have an even easier fiscal time financing this high-cost, high-performance design.

Table 8.7 provides an example from a school in a Southern state. Again, the data in the top portion of the table show the staffing and resources presently in the school and their total dollar value. Note that the cost of a teacher in this district is just $40,000 (salaries and benefits) and the cost of an instructional aide is $12,000, much lower than in the example from the Northeast. This school

TABLE 8.7   Reallocating Resources to Fund a Comprehensive School Design: An Example of a Southern Elementary School

500 Students, 60 Percent in Poverty

- 1 principal
- 20 teachers
- 1 lead teacher ($40,000)
- 1 art, 1 librarian ($80,000)
- 1.5 LD, 2 Title 1 ($140,000)
- 1 guidance counselor ($40,000)
- 12 aides (1 each K–2) ($144,000)
- Above CORE: $444,000
- Teachers ($40,000); aides ($12,000)

Roots and Wings/Success for All

- 1 principal
- 20 teachers
- 1 instructional facilitator ($40,000)
- 3 tutors ($120,000)
- 1 family liaison ($40,000)
- Professional development and materials ($70,000)
- Total design costs: $270,000
- Remaining: $126,000

Source: Analysis of data gathered by author.

wanted to adopt the Roots and Wings design, another expensive but also highly effective design, the costs of which are detailed in the lower portion. Again, this school could afford all of the design costs, in this case with $126,000 remaining. However, most if not all of this remaining funding would probably be needed to retain the art, music, and librarian teachers in order to finance the level of planning and preparation time this district typically provides. The point, nevertheless, is that this school could afford this high-performance school design, which has been dubbed the "Cadillac" design because of its use of individual tutors. Note also that this school would need to reallocate the funds for all of its instructional aides, which include one for each classroom in grades K–2.

The data in Table 8.2 show that middle and high schools in the Midwest on average would be able to afford both a high-performance school design and planning/preparation time, but that their average elementary schools would have a more difficult time financing both of these items. Table 8.8 shows an example of this situation for a Midwestern school with 540 students, 83 percent eligible for free or reduced-price lunch. The top portion of the table shows that class sizes are 32, above the typical 25 preferred by most designs, and also that the school has $560,000 above the core, where the core in this case provides for larger class

TABLE 8.8   Reallocating Resources to Fund a Comprehensive School Design: An Example of a Midwest Elementary School

540 Students, 83 Percent Low-Income

- CORE: 1 principal, 17 teachers
- No AP (540 kids—32 per class)
- Regular education: 1 each music, Tech (2), PE, reading, math, librarian ($350,000)
- Categorical education: 2 LD ($100,000)
- 4 aides ($80,000)
- Pupil support: 1 guidance counselor ($50,000) + 1 nurse
- Desegregation funds ($60,000)
- Total above CORE: $560,000 plus 1 nurse, 2 teachers for the severely disabled
- Teacher ($50,000); Aide ($20,000)

Roots and Wings/Success for All

- 1 principal, 23 teachers
- 1 instructional facilitator ($50,000)
- 4 tutors (two more than suggested) ($200,000)
- 1 family liaison ($50,000)
- Professional development ($25,000)
- Materials ($25,000)
- Total design costs: $350,000
- Remaining: $210,000

Source: Analysis of data gathered by author.

sizes. This total also leaves the two teachers for the severely disabled and the school nurse in the school. The lower portion again shows the costs of the Roots and Wings program and that the school could afford this design with $210,000 remaining. But these remaining funds would have two primary uses: one would be to lower class sizes to 25 and the other would be to provide planning and preparation time. Each of these strategies would require the full remaining amount, so the school would be able to fund only one or the other. In short, this school has the resources that would allow it to finance a very effective high-performance design, but then it would either have to have larger class sizes and planning and preparation time, or class sizes of 25 but no planning and preparation time. We should note that this example is for a school in an average spending district in an average spending state for this region.

The situation in the Western region is similarly fiscally difficult; few schools would be able to afford both a high-performance school design and planning and preparation time. Most would need to choose between these two strategies. Indeed, if they chose to finance any one of the school designs, they then would have very few remaining resources to deploy for extraordinary student needs. In short, financing a higher-performance design in the average elementary, middle, and high school in the West could be very difficult, and for most, it would require providing no planning and preparation time for teachers within the normal school day.

Table 8.9 provides an example for a middle school in a district in the Northwest (the school in this example is in a higher-spending state than many states in the West). Again the school has selected the more expensive Modern Red Schoolhouse design, a design that provides a high-quality core curriculum taught through heavy use of computer technologies. The staffing data are more global in nature for this school, reflecting the difficulty of collecting detailed school-level resource data (Busch and Odden, 1997a). Nevertheless, the top portion of the table shows this school of 1,000 students has $945,000 over the core, which exceeds the costs of financing the Modern Red Schoolhouse by $145,000. If all of these remaining funds were used to supplement the four art and music teachers, the school could almost provide one planning period a day for each teacher. But some portion of these funds might have to be used for special-needs students, so the school would fall short of the resources needed both to fund the design as well as fund full preparation time. On the other hand, the school could select a less expensive design, such as Co-NECT, another computer-intensive design, and finance all design costs and teacher planning time. The major difference is that Co-NECT does not have art and music standards.

Schools in California provide an example of a Western state context that simply has insufficient funds to reallocate to a high-performance design. For example, before the recent class-size reduction program in California, the Los Angeles Unified School District would provide an elementary school enrolling 500 students with 16 teachers (1 teacher for every 32 students), one principal, and no other staff. The district, like most districts in the state, did not have funds to provide art, music, physical education, or library-media teachers. If the school had students eligible for free and reduced-price lunches, they would have some Title

TABLE 8.9   Reallocating Resources to Fund a Comprehensive School Design: An Example of a Northwestern Middle School

1,000 Students

- CORE: 1 principal, 40 teachers
- 1 AP ($81,000)
- Other licensed professionals (11.7 positions) ($585,000)
- Instructional aides (12) ($180,000)
- Materials ($99,000)
- Total above the CORE: $945,000
- Teachers ($50,000); Aides ($15,000)

Modern Red Schoolhouse

- 1 principal, 40 teachers
- 2 schoolwide instructional facilitators ($100,000)
- 2 art and 2 music teachers ($200,000)
- Ongoing professional development ($140,000)
- Design-specific resources:
  —Materials ($10,000)
  —Technology ($250,000)
- Total Design costs: $800,000
- Leftover Funds: $145,000

Source: Analysis of data gathered by author.

I and state compensatory education funds, and if they had disabled students, they would have a small amount of special-education funding. But for schools that did not have those special needs, their staffing would be just 16 teachers. Clearly, such schools simply would have no resources to reallocate for any high-performance design; they would need extra money to fund such new programs. Though the staffing has been increased for such schools since implementation of the California class-size reduction program, the additional staff have to be used to reduce class size in kindergarten through grade 2 from 32 to 20; hence, the staff cannot be reallocated. This is only one of many such examples of insufficient funds to reallocate that can be found in schools throughout the West.

In short, the ability to reallocate school staff resources to higher-performance school strategies, at least those represented by the seven designs discussed, varies across the country. It appears to be the most feasible in the Northeast and the South. It also is feasible for middle and high schools in the Midwest. It is a fiscal tight squeeze for Midwest elementary schools, and difficult if not impossible on average in the West. In order to make it work, many schools in the West would need both to select the less-expensive, comprehensive school designs and not provide planning and preparation time.

To be sure, in the short run the restructuring and resource reallocation will be constrained by federal, state, and local rules, regulations, and contract provisions, which would need to be changed over the medium to long term. In fact, many districts and states are providing waivers for most schools and districts implementing these designs. In 1998, many schools began implementing these designs under the new federal "Comprehensive School Reform" program, and many received waivers to do so.

What about Low-Spending Districts?

As should be quite clear, the fiscal ability for schools to reallocate resources to the needs of higher-performance school designs varies by region, as well as by state and district. The above examples are clearly not exhaustive but are meant to be representative of the general ability to engage in resource reallocation on a regional basis. But because of the role of the local district in funding public schools in most states, even state average levels of school resources do not provide the full picture of resource reallocation potential. Within most states, there are high-, average-, and low-spending districts, so even though the average elementary, middle, and high school in a state could engage in resource reallocation, that ability might be severely constrained in the state's lowest-spending districts.

Odden, Archibald, and Tychsen (1998) investigated this situation for the state of Wisconsin, using data for the 1997–98 school year. They generally found that even schools in low-spending districts in Wisconsin had sufficient funds to finance the Modern Red Schoolhouse design as well as provide the requisite planning and preparation time. The fiscal ability was tight in the lowest-spending rural districts, and often was possible because those districts, just like districts in the Southern region of the country, paid teacher salaries that were significantly lower than the state average. But they found that except for a handful of districts, there were sufficient resources to finance even the highest-cost comprehensive school designs, even in the lower-spending districts.

Their conclusions pertain only to Wisconsin and perhaps other states that spend above the national average as well. Their conclusions probably would not be true in the lowest-spending districts in states spending below the national average. The point is that a state would need to analyze the ability of schools in each district to determine the fiscal ability for such schools to select higher-performing school strategies and reallocate their resources to finance those more effective strategies.

The Reason Resource Reallocation Is Possible

The reasons schools can restructure and reallocate resources to the requirements of a high-performance school design have been implicit in the above discussion and are similar to the approaches taken by the schools in the Miles and Darling-Hammond study. The bottom line concerns use and deployment of staffing resources. Both traditional schools and higher-performance schools have a principal and classroom teachers as the base of their staffing structure. But traditional schools have a staffing structure above this core that is different from most high-performance school designs.

As indicated in Table 8.10, there are three categories of this additional staffing: regular-education specialists, categorical program specialists, and pupil support specialists. Each category has become a regular part of most school programs and is assumed as necessary or expected for running schools. They are not perceived as "fat" or unnecessary positions. They have been provided to schools for many years because they have been assumed to be critical to accomplishing school goals. The reality for schools that choose to implement a new, higher-performance, comprehensive school design is that while they have these resources today, few if any of these resources are part of any of the new designs.

Regular-education specialists are teachers who generally do not have a regular class of students, such as librarians, or who teach special classes, such as art, music, physical education, vocational education, and home economics. Many elementary schools have reading and writing specialist teachers; some even have mathematics and science specialist teachers. Numerous districts also provide teachers with instructional aides who are paid from the general fund budget; for example, North Carolina provides an instructional aide for every class from kindergarten through grade two. There might be other categories of regular-education specialists in different district and school budgets.

Except for the Modern Red Schoolhouse design, which also has standards for art and music, none of these teacher resources are required in the school designs discussed above. This does not mean the new comprehensive school designs are not supportive of art, music, or other learning areas. No school design would

TABLE 8.10 Staffing in Regular- versus High-Performance Schools

Core Funding for a School of 500 Students and Class Sizes of 25 Students

1 principal
20 teachers

Additional Ingredients in Traditional Schools

Sometimes an assistant principal
Regular-education specialists
Categorical program specialists
Pupil support specialists
Little school-controlled professional development

Additional Ingredients for Comprehensive School Designs

A school-wide instructional facilitator
Teachers with multifunctional roles
$75,000 professional development
Design-specific resources—tutors, health team, computers, etc.

find the inclusion of any of these teacher specialists in a school at odds with their design. Indeed, they may include these subjects in ways that do not require a specialist teacher. However, most high-performance schools focus on mathematics, science, social studies, writing, and language arts. Specialists simply are not a core element of the design and thus would have a secondary priority for budget resources funded after the design ingredients were resourced and if additional money were still available.

Although these specialist teachers often are used to provide preparation time for teachers, each higher-performance design, just like those in the Miles/Darling-Hammond (1997) schools, has numerous alternative ways to provide for common planning time for teachers that do not depend on a school having these specialist teachers. Nevertheless, if the funds are there, schools may wish to purchase planning and preparation time. In fact, many schools might want to retain art and music teachers and other regular-education specialist teachers, both for recognizing the value of these subjects and for using them as a way to provide preparation time. As noted earlier, this adds $200,000 to the cost of the school program (for each group of 500 students), is easily afforded by schools funded at or above the national average, retains both art and music in the instructional program, and makes providing preparation and planning time much easier.

The second category of resources generally not fully required by these designs include the teachers and other ingredients typically bought with categorical funds from such sources as federal Title I, state compensatory education, desegregation, bilingual education, and a portion of the learning disabilities component of the special-education budget. Schools typically use these funds for the following three categories of services: (1) pull-out resource-room specialists who teach remedial mathematics and remedial reading to small groups of five to eight students; (2) instructional assistants; and (3) basic skills computer laboratories. Again, few if any of the comprehensive school designs require these ingredients. Indeed, nearly all school designs explicitly urge schools to trade some of these resources for the ingredients of the design.[4] At the same time, schools would be wise to preserve some of these categorical resources, both for the more severely disabled and because some students will require more attention even after being served in a more inclusive environment.

The third category of ingredients not generally found in the school designs are pupil support specialists: guidance counselors, deans, social workers, psychologists, and nurses. These staff can comprise about 10 percent of the average school district budget but, except for ATLAS, are not core ingredients of comprehensive school designs. This is largely because the designs have teachers working with a smaller number of students over more than one academic year and have moved the guidance and counseling function into teacher teams.

---

[4] Special services would need to be maintained for the severely disabled and other categories of disability that require separate, pull-out service (i.e., legal requirements under IDEA would need to be fulfilled). But a large portion of disabled students in the learning disabilities category is often not best served by these strategies.

In short, there are three categories of resources typically found in schools across America—regular-education specialists, categorical remedial specialists, and pupil support specialists—that are not generally included as core ingredients of most high-performance school designs.

To account for these functions, higher-performance school designs expand teacher jobs to include instructional as well as other specialized tasks. They require an instructional facilitator (to help teachers continually improve the instructional program) and substantial investment in ongoing professional development to develop new skills and competencies. These are key differences, with traditional schools representing a more bureaucratic approach and comprehensive school designs representing a high-performance approach to organization and management.

Indeed, the reduction in the number of specialists, the stronger emphasis on staff providing the core service of instruction, the expansion of the job of the core service provider to include multiple functions, and the emphasis on continuous training and professional development are characteristics of most evolving high-performance organizations (Lawler, 1986, 1992, 1996; Mohrman, Galbraith, and Lawler, 1996) and particularly high-involvement, high-performance schools (Darling-Hammond, 1996; National Commission on Teaching and America's Future, 1996). This is how organizations restructure and reorganize for higher performance using current or even reduced resources.

Moreover, it is for these reasons that improving efficiency is the wrong descriptor and restructuring is the correct descriptor when discussing resource reallocation to higher performance in education. The new comprehensive school reform strategies proffer schools that are staffed, structured, organized, and run differently than traditional schools. To implement such a design, a school needs to restructure itself, including the resources it purchases with its school budget; the schools do not just do what they used to do more efficiently. Instead, they fundamentally change their entire operation: their instructional program, how they group teachers and students for learning, how they govern and manage the school, and how they devise the labor cost-structure of the school.

Educators and policymakers will need to monitor the level of results produced by all of these alleged high-performance school designs to ensure that student achievement rises when the designs are fully implemented. But as stated earlier, early results are promising when the programs are completely implemented (see also, Haynes, Emmons, and Woodruff, 1998).

4. THE PROCESS OF RESOURCE REALLOCATION

Odden, Archibald, and Tychsen (1999) and Tychsen (1999) studied several schools and districts that were involved in the type of resource reallocation challenge discussed in the preceding sections. The primary purpose of their study was to investigate:

1. which potential staff resources actually were reallocated and which were not,
2. how the resource reallocation process worked,
3. the roles districts played in the resource reallocation process, and
4. the obstacles and problems districts and schools faced while engaged in significantly reallocating resources.

The results reported here concern the first stage of their research project and primarily address question 1. In this stage, they studied two major new school strategies that required resource reallocation:

- Adoption of a school design that included tutors, instructional facilitators, parent outreach, and substantially increased professional development, and
- Class-size reduction to as close to 15 as possible.

For the schools they studied, the first strategy was essentially embodied in the school's implementation of the Roots and Wings/Success for All school design (Slavin, et al., 1996). All schools studied were able to identify research that showed that this program had dramatically improved student achievement, particularly the achievement of the lowest-performing students.

This design provides for each school with 500 students:

- A full-time instructional facilitator, which is an additional resource for most schools;
- Tutors for students in grades 1–3 who need extra assistance to learn the regular Success for All reading, writing, and language arts program. Generally, one tutor is needed for every 25 percent increment of students qualifying for free or reduced lunch, so a school with most students qualifying would need four tutors. These also tend to be extra resources;
- A family outreach coordinator, which may or may not be an additional resource;
- Purchase of materials and professional development from the Roots and Wings group that totaled about $70,000 in the 1998–99 school year. Again, this usually exceeds the professional development dollars most schools control; and
- For grades 1–3, reducing the reading class size to a maximum of 15 for the 90 minutes of reading each day; this was usually produced at no extra cost by having all teachers, tutors, and staff with a teaching license teach a reading class during the 90-minute language arts period.

Thus, the extra-cost items for this strategy are the instructional facilitator, the tutors, the family outreach coordinator, and extensive professional development, which generally equated to about 7.4 additional professional positions in the school.

The second strategy was the result of schools, and in one case a district, deciding for instructional reasons that their program would be stronger if they reallocated some specialist staff to regular teaching positions to allow them to reduce class size to 15 or less. In all cases studied, the schools identified the Tennessee STAR study as the research basis for this strategy (Folger, 1992), claiming that that study showed that class-size reduction to 15 for grades K–3 was associated with higher student achievement, and that the impact was even larger for low-income and minority students. The cost of this strategy varied by district and school, depending on the regular class size and number of classes in kindergarten through third grade.

A K–6 school of about 500 students with class sizes of 25 would have about three classes of about 25 students in each of kindergarten through grade 3. They would need two additional teachers in each grade to reduce class size to 15, or a total of eight extra positions.

Thus, the costs of these two strategies were quite high and about the same. Assuming the average cost of a teacher was $50,000 for salaries and benefits, the cost of these strategies was between $350,000 and $400,000, a significant amount of money.

We provide here a short summary of Odden, Archibald, and Tychsen's (1998) resource reallocation findings by the three categories of specialist staff:

First, they generally found that the schools did not reallocate their regular-education specialists, such as their art, music, physical education, or librarian teachers. In all cases studied, schools eliminated none of these teacher positions. In two cases, the number of these staff was increased. These staffpersons were retained largely because all schools studied used these teachers to provide a daily planning and preparation period for all teachers. Schools also valued the content these teachers taught. But the primary rationale for retaining these positions was that they had historically been the way preparation periods had been provided, and that strategy was retained. At this stage of the study, the schools studied had the money to provide this resource; a daily planning and preparation period generally was also required in the union contract.

Schools did make significant change in the use of categorical-program staff. The staff primarily affected were teachers and instructional aides supported with federal and state compensatory education money, with bilingual education funds, and with the learning disabilities portion of funds for providing services to students with disabilities. The vast majority of Title I remedial reading and math teacher positions were eliminated; for the Roots and Wings program, many of the actual individuals were retrained and either became the instructional facilitator or a reading tutor. For the class-size reduction strategy, they became regular-classroom teachers. In some cases, the number of instructional aides was dramatically reduced; it took about three to four aide positions to fund a fully certified teacher tutor. But in some cases, the aides took on new roles, such as becoming reading tutors, even though some research suggests they have less of a positive impact on student achievement than professional teachers (Slavin, Karweit, and Wasik, 1994).

Nearly all schools traded a portion of their special-education teachers (in many cases learning disability [LD] teachers) either for regular-classroom teachers or for teacher tutors. But the general practice was to retain 60 percent or more of these positions. In several instances for both the Roots and Wings and the class-size reduction strategy, the LD teachers were dually certified in special education as well as regular education; when given a regular classroom, they often were given the lowest-level reading class (which tended to have the most students with a required Individual Education Program [IEP]) or the classes with the most number of IEP students. Though this was not required, school staff nevertheless thought that it provided the best educational strategy for these students.

One school that had 35 percent of students with limited English proficiency (LEP) and reduced class size to 15 traded all pull-out ESL specialists for regular-classroom teachers. In the first year, these and other teachers with dual certification in ESL had the classes with the highest percentage of LEP students, but the school also implemented a professional development strategy to dually certify all teachers as regular and ESL teachers.

Only a small number of pupil support staff at any of the schools were reallocated. Some of these staff were moved into new roles (for example, the parent outreach coordinator for the Roots and Wings design), but most were simply retained. They tended to represent staff positions that schools thought they needed to retain.

All schools studied also had access to from $25,000 to $100,000 of additional funds from a variety of sources—state reading and school-improvement grants, state compensatory education funds, federal Goals 2000 and Eisenhower training grants, federal Obey-Porter comprehensive school reform funds, etc., which they cobbled together to support their new school strategies.

All schools also rewrote every IEP for each disabled student so it conformed to the new service strategy of their restructured school. This task required extra effort in the first and second year of the school's restructuring process but was critical and absolutely necessary in the cases where schools used a portion of their disability funds to finance their new school strategy. IEPs had to be changed, or the schools would have been out of compliance with state and federal requirements. Indeed, in the state where the schools had reduced their class size, and received both state and federal waivers to do so, another school that was not part of this study implemented the same strategies but did not seek the required waivers. Its strategies were found to be out of compliance, and the school was required to reverse its resource reallocation actions.

In sum, the schools studied were able to finance quite expensive new school strategies via substantial resource reallocation. Federal Title I and state compensatory education funds were the largest sources that schools reallocated. But schools also reallocated a portion of learning disabilities staff, a small portion of pupil support staff, and a large portion of other small grants they controlled.

Nearly all regular-education specialist staff remained, as did the bulk of special-education staff and most pupil support staff. Finally, some schools propelled instructional aides into reading tutor roles rather than make the more difficult decision to redeploy these funds for more effective teacher tutors; this is often the more difficult decision because of personal and contractual issues, but some schools did eliminate instructional aide positions.

Finally, we note that districts played significant roles in helping schools implement these creative, courageous, and ambitious resource reallocation strategies. Odden, Archibald, and Tychsen (1998) describe in more detail the roles played by school districts. But in the most effective instances, districts viewed resource reallocation as part of a large-scale change process and structured consciously and directly the key elements of such a fundamental change process (see Mohrman 1994b; Odden, 1995a). As part of this process, most districts also changed leadership in many of the schools, created school-based funding formulas to provide schools with lump-sum budgets over which they had more authority, and began to create school-based information systems, particularly systems that included school revenues and expenditures.

5. RESOURCE REALLOCATION IN NEW JERSEY

The type of resource reallocation discussed in this chapter has now become a central feature of one state's school finance reform agenda. In early 1998, New Jersey became the first state in the country to join the issues of school finance equity and adequacy with comprehensive school designs and resource reallocation to higher-performing education strategies. As discussed in earlier chapters, New Jersey litigated its school finance program over the 25 years from 1973 to 1998. When in 1997 its state supreme court required the state to provide its poorest districts (called the Abbott districts and comprising largely the urban districts that enrolled 25 percent of the state's students) with the same level of dollars per pupil as spent by its wealthiest districts, it also asked a remand court to determine whether any supplemental programs were needed for the special needs of the low-income and minority students in the poorest districts. Supplemental programs were those over and above what could be funded with the existing New Jersey compensatory education programs (called Demonstrably Effective Programs) and full-day kindergarten and preschool programs (called Early Childhood Education Programs). After a lengthy trial, the remand court, supported by a subsequent supreme court decision, ruled that with the above finance provisions, there appeared to be sufficient money for schools in the Abbott districts to select a comprehensive or whole-school design that was effective in urban schools and fund it through a resource reallocation process. The "default" school design for those schools that did not wish to choose their own was the expensive Roots and Wings/Success for All, largely based on its successful track record of effectiveness with low-income and minority students in large, urban districts.

It turned out that because of the high level of resources in New Jersey, the state showed during the remand trial that the funds in a typical Abbott district could provide the following for an elementary school with 500 students:

- Half-day preschool for four-year olds,
- Full-day kindergarten for five-year olds,
- One instructional facilitator and one technology coordinator,
- 30 teachers, which was sufficient to provide class sizes of 21 students and additional teachers to provide at least one period a day for planning and development for each teacher,
- Five tutors,
- One each: social worker, counselor, nurse, and parent liaison for not just a parental outreach program but a full family health team,
- One library/media teacher,
- One security officer,
- Three preschool teacher aides and four additional teacher aides,
- Technology at about $83,000 per year, and
- Professional development at over $100,000 per year, including funds for substitute teachers.

This level of resources was substantially above those found in a typical Roots and Wings school. In fact, the New Jersey proposal in a sense expanded the Roots and Wings model in the following ways:

- Smaller classes (21 versus 25),
- Five versus four tutors in a school of 500 low-income students,
- A technology coordinator in addition to an instructional facilitator,
- Family health team rather than just one parent outreach person,
- More professional development,
- A full complement of technology (the Roots and Wings programs does not have a substantial technology program), and
- An unallocated sum of $400,000 to be used for other identified needs.

In sum, the state claimed that the level of resources already in the system would allow the typical elementary school in an Abbott district to select one of the most expensive and effective school designs in the country, one that had been called a "Cadillac" program, and stretch nearly all of its elements.

Though only time will tell whether these rather ambitious claims can be validated, during the first year of implementation in the 1998–99 school year, the initial schools seemed to be able to fund the program. We describe one example of this case for a low-income elementary school in New Jersey. It has 470 students with nearly all coming from low-income families. The average cost of a teacher in the district was about $50,000 for salaries and benefits at the beginning of the 1998–99 school year. As with many such schools, the school had a substantial level of resources, including an assistant principal, 30 teachers (many more than required for class sizes of 25 or even 21), 11 teachers and several aides for the learning disabled, and five other professional staff. These resources could finance the New Jersey version of the Roots and Wings program, with class sizes of 20, a full complement of regular-education specialists to provide planning and preparation time, the five tutors, the full family health team, and necessary professional development and materials for the program. Further, even after funding all these resources, the school would still have $400,000 remaining, in addition to its staff for the severely disabled.

Since the Roots and Wings program is one of the most expensive across the country, the numbers also implicitly show how this school, and others of which it is representative, could select any comprehensive or whole-school design and finance it through a resource reallocation process. As the New Jersey Supreme Court stated in its final decision, the state can now begin to transform the school finance debate from the historical focus on money to how the money is used to fund a program that is effective in teaching students to the New Jersey content and performance standards. Indeed, at the close of the twentieth century and the dawn of the twenty-first century, schools in New Jersey are now struggling with how to use their dollars as effectively as possible, rather than simply arguing that they need more money.

Chapter 9

Creating an Education System with Incentives

The previous chapter outlined several strategies for how schools can use the education dollar more effectively and productively. The strategies described constitute major changes in school operations. Such strategies could be reinforced with a system of incentives for students, teachers, and schools in order to stimulate engagement in these types of strategies. For the vast majority of students, there are almost no incentives to excel at academic work. Teachers face an environment with few incentives to enhance their professional practice or work hard to improve student learning; indeed, current teacher incentives—the single-salary schedule—encourage teachers to leave the classroom for nonteaching work instead of staying in the classroom to work harder to raise academic achievement. And school organizations themselves receive no incentives to engage in the restructuring and resource reallocation processes described in this textbook. In short, current education system incentives are either neutral or negative; given the ambitious and important education goals that have been set, a new array of incentives are necessary.

Incentives alone, however, will not produce the dramatic types of improvement essential to accomplish the goal of teaching all students to high standards. The elements of standards-based education reform, increasingly the focus of school finance litigation (Chapter 2) at the state and local level (Massell, Kirst, & Hoppe, 1997), or some similar set of education program elements, need to be the core of education improvement. All strategies could be enhanced with incentives. Although there may be differences of opinion about whether and how different incentives for students, teachers, and schools could or should be designed, most would agree with the general proposition that incentives aligned with and supportive of education change would be better than incentives that work in the opposite direction, and most would agree that some set of positive incentives probably would be better than no incentives at all.

This chapter discusses incentives for students, teachers, and schools that would support the current thrusts of standards- and school-based education reforms. Each set of incentives derives from a considerable amount of research suggesting that they would help the education system in its task of doubling or tripling the percentage of students achieving at high standards. Many of the incentives are nonfiscal, but the next two chapters discuss in more detail the two major fiscal incentives—providing budget authority under a strong school-based management strategy that includes needs-based formula funding of schools, and changing teacher compensation.

This chapter identifies a large array of incentives. Adding just a few new incentives that reinforce student, teacher, or school efforts to produce higher levels of student academic achievement would be better than no incentives at all, or retaining the negative incentives in the current system. States and districts may also consider adopting them all.

1. INCENTIVES FOR STUDENTS

In *Beyond the Classroom,* Larry Steinberg (1996) summarizes in crisp and provocative ways the problems related to student disengagement in school today. Drawing from numerous long-term studies, Steinberg and his colleagues found that a very large proportion of students were not engaged in school, school work, or school-related activities and as a result did not take school or academic studies seriously:

- over one-third of students said they got through the school day by goofing off with their peers,
- two-thirds of students said they have cheated on exams at some time during the past school year or copied someone else's homework, and
- a large percentage said that classes were boring, teacher expectations were low, and there was no reason to work hard.

As a result, only high school graduation is a major goal (i.e., students see educational attainment as important but do not view doing well in academic studies as important).

Steinberg and his colleagues found that one major set of reasons for student disengagement concerns their life beyond the classroom. They document how American students spend large portions of their time in out-of-school activities that do not reinforce what they are supposed to be learning in school. These activities—working at part-time jobs, watching television, hanging out with their peers, and participating in time-intensive sports such as football and basketball— compete with, rather than complement, school activities and are associated with less school engagement and lower levels of academic achievement. As a result,

- the average American high school student spent four hours a week on homework while the average child in many other countries spent four hours a day on homework,
- fewer than 15 percent of students spent five hours or more per week reading for pleasure, and
- fully two-thirds of American high school students were employed, and half held jobs that required more than 15 hours per week.

This last finding is particularly important given that Steinberg's research showed that as work time increased, school engagement and academic achievement fell, and students took easier courses.

Steinberg and his colleagues found, not surprisingly, that the peer adolescent culture in America demeans school success and reinforces academic disengagement. Finally, Steinberg found that a large percent of parents are as disengaged from their parenting roles in supporting school excellence as their children are disengaged from schools.

The result: the bulk of adolescents are disengaged from school. This disengagement, or lack of motivation to do well in school—to take hard courses, to get good grades, and to learn to high standards—is further associated with other negative behaviors of adolescents such as drug and alcohol abuse, depression, delinquency, and sexual preoccupation.

But research shows that schools as an institution play a major role in structuring the lives of teenagers and, it also turns out, play a pivotal role in remedying all of the above problems. As students become more engaged in school, Steinberg and colleagues show that the above negative social behaviors begin to diminish and academic performance begins to increase. Students engaged in schoolwork attend classes, try to do well in them, complete assigned homework, do not cheat, work less in outside jobs, participate more (but moderately) in school activities, and engage less in socially nondesirable actions. And according to recent research, the cause-and-effect relationship is from school engagement to these other desired results, not so much the other way around. Further, research shows that students do not generally approve of the low standards in school and would support making school harder by raising both standards and requirements (Public Agenda, 1997).

These arguments lead to the conclusion that in order to improve student academic achievement through the use of a set of incentives, school engagement should become a major focus. The goal is to devise a set of incentives and rewards that send a multiple set of messages—both inside and outside of school—that says it is important for students to engage in the task of learning.

We discuss three such student incentives:

- Standards for being promoted from one education level to the next,
- Standards for graduation from high school, and
- Requirements for admission into higher education,

and mention two others:

- Requirements for employment or entry into an apprenticeship program and
- Opportunities to participate in extracurricular school organized activities.

Standards for Being Promoted from One Education Level to the Next

The country is engaged in a process of developing curriculum content and student performance standards in core academic subject areas, usually mathematics, language arts/writing, science, and social studies. In most places, states are taking the lead in this process and are developing these standards at key demarcation points in the education system, usually for the end of elementary school (such as fourth or fifth grade), the end of middle schools (such as the eighth grade), and at some point in high school (often the tenth grade). The test administered in high school often allows students to match their academic work to the career path they will pursue after high school (see, for example, Education Commission of the States, 1997a, 1997b; Glidden, 1998; Massell, Kirst, and Hoppe, 1997). Although a few states are requiring students to pass some form of a test to graduate from high school, a smaller number attach any stakes to the elementary and middle school standards, such as requiring students to perform at or above the elementary standards to be promoted to middle schools, or at or above the middle school standards to be promoted into high school. In short, although states are developing rigorous curriculum content and student performance standards, they are attaching few if any stakes to them that impact students.

Therefore, at least for older middle school students and for the bulk of adolescents in high school (i.e., those not choosing to attend an elite college), there are no clear reasons to work hard or exert the effort to learn to the level of the standards. Although some students have a natural love of learning, which is certainly more the case for younger elementary school students, developmental psychologists argue that adolescents need a substantial dose of extrinsic reasons to work hard in school. If they do not get them, which largely is the case today, most adolescents would rather, and actually do, spend their time disengaged from academic studies and engaged in something else, such as holding a job, hanging out with their friends, watching television, or playing video games (Owen, 1996; Steinberg, 1996, 1997).

The education system could play a major role in remedying this disengagement by attaching consequences to the standards that are being developed. The key incentive would be to require elementary students to achieve to the fourth or fifth grade standards as a condition for promotion into middle school, and to require middle school students to achieve to the eighth grade standards as a condition for promotion into high school. If such a policy were implemented intelligently and fairly, it could have both an equity and an excellence result (Feldman, 1997).

As is becoming more widely known, most other countries through some means or another make student participation at the subsequent level of the system dependent on performance at the preceding level. The policy sends the message that students should take schooling seriously, and more students do so. It may be time for this country to adopt similar student performance incentives.

Such new student incentives would seem to contradict conventional wisdom about the negative effects of holding students back. Research reviews conclude that students who are held back in elementary school learn much less at the end of the subsequent year than similar students who are promoted (Shepard and Smith, 1989). The implication is that denying grade-to-grade promotion is not a strategy to improve learning. But two points should be made. First, the research pertains to grade-to-grade promotion, while the above recommendation concerns level-to-level promotion: elementary to middle school, and middle school to high school. Second, the typical practice for retained students is that they are exposed to the same (largely unspecified) curriculum in nearly the same pedagogical way, while similar students who are promoted are exposed to the next year's curriculum. The fact is there are many better ways to deal with slower-learning students than simply holding them back and giving them a second dose of the same material (Feldman, 1997).

Schools committed to teaching students to a set of fourth to fifth grade and eighth grade proficiency standards would need to deploy two primary strategies to be successful. First, they would need to create grade-to-grade content and performance standards, coupled with even more detailed strategies for moving from one curriculum unit to another, so that students move in a deliberate manner from what they know and can do when they enter school to the levels of the specified performance standards. These tasks would require the entire school faculty to devise the strategies needed for all students to have the best chance to learn to the standards. In other words, teachers would need to systematically expose all students to the curriculum content specified in the standards. This classroom behavior does not exist in many schools today, as many teachers are free to make their own decisions about curriculum coverage. Indeed, these strategies are rarely systematically deployed in elementary and middle schools today, but they are the type of strategies discussed in Chapter 7 on successful school-based management.

Second, schools would need to provide additional services to students who needed extra time and help to learn to the proficiency levels in the standards. For example, the tutoring that is included in the Success for All/Roots and Wings program is necessary to ensure that all students in elementary schools have a sufficient number of opportunities to become proficient readers by the third or fourth grade. The required summer school program that Chicago enacted in 1997 provided extra help for eighth grade students who had not learned to the standards for admission into high schools. Tutoring and help-with-homework programs were organized in several high schools to provide the help students needed to improve their performance. If students are required to perform to state-determined proficiency standards as a condition for promotion from one schooling level to the next, then the system is obligated to ensure that every student is taught the curriculum content and to provide additional help if needed to learn to the required levels.

Standards For Graduation from High School

The deployment of such requirements at the high school level can be somewhat more elaborate: there could be incentives for all high school students to learn to high standards, as compared to the system today where there are virtually no incentives, except for the top students who attend the most elite colleges and universities.

There are several interrelated ways to design policies that make student performance in high school count. One would be to require all students to take a large, common core of academic courses. A second would be to require students to take a similarly large number of common "end-of-course" examinations; a variation would be to construct a comprehensive high school exit examination that covers the common core academic standards specified for all high school students. The third would be to require an aggressive minimum average score on a prescribed number of end-of-course examinations or a high threshold on the comprehensive examination for graduation. These three incentives would create a system in which high school students would be required to take a core set of academic courses and to do well in them in order to graduate.

Again, if such policies were implemented, high schools would be obligated to teach the common core curriculum to all students, and to provide extra assistance to those students who need it. The former could actually simplify most high school program offerings, which often include endless lists of low-demand elective courses, while the latter would require some degree of additional resources, as discussed in Chapter 4.

There is a strong body of research that shows that such requirements would have significant, substantive, and positive impacts on high school students. In response to the 1983 *Nation at Risk* report, many states increased the number of academic courses required for high school graduation. As a result, more students took more academic courses, and the content of the courses was not substantially watered down (Clune and White, 1992; Guthrie, Kirst, and Odden, 1990). Further, several studies over more than two decades have shown that students learn more when they take more academic courses; in other words, achievement rises when students are required to take tougher, academically oriented classes (e.g., Madigan, 1997). Third, large-scale analyses of the longitudinal impacts of high school course requirements show that schools that offer a constrained curriculum (i.e., that require all students to take a large set of common academic courses), produce larger levels of overall achievement. They also indicate higher levels of achievement for low-income and other students who typically achieve at lower levels (i.e., a quality and equity benefit) (Lee, Croninger, and Smith, 1997; Smith, 1996). Further, several large cities are in the process of eliminating "general mathematics" courses, typically geared to students who have low mathematical achievement, and requiring such students to take algebra instead, sometimes offered over three rather than two semesters. An emerging body of research shows that these students learn considerably more mathematics with this approach; students not only learn more basic arithmetic skills but also learn more mathematical and algebraic concepts (White, Gamoran, Smithson, and Porter, 1996). In addition, students in economically developed countries or states that have curriculum-based external exit exams learn more than students in countries or states that do not; the effect is often more than a full grade level in mathematics and science (Bishop, 1998a, 1998b). Finally, contrary to predictions by many, requiring a larger core academic curriculum for high school graduation is not associated with a larger high school dropout rate; indeed, the research over the past decade shows that when the system requires more from students, students work harder to meet the new demands and actually drop out of school at a lower rate (Kaufman, McMillen, and Bradby, 1992).

Indeed, this finding that raising the bar induces higher levels of performance occurs outside of high school as well. For example, when the NCAA Proposition 48 raised the minimum grade point average and Scholastic Aptitude Test (SAT) scores for participation in college-level athletics, the fear was that smaller percentages of low-income and minority students would be eligible for such sport teams. The opposite occurred; greater numbers and percentages of minority students qualify for athletic teams today than when the Proposition 48 requirement was enacted (Klein and Bell, 1995). In addition, there is research that shows that when states raise the standard for passing the bar exam (required of all individuals who want to practice law), a larger percentage of students meet the higher standard than in the time periods before the new requirement (S. Klein, personal communications, 1997). In short, raising expectations sends the message that better performance is required, and the overwhelming response on the part of most students is to work harder and to perform at the higher levels.

The recent efforts of Milwaukee provide another example. About four years ago, the Milwaukee public schools required students to pass a new, rigorous mathematics course in order to graduate from high school. In the first year, the pass rate was only 35 percent. The fear was that the district would lower the standards to hike the pass rate. They did not. They maintained the standards and the requirement to pass the course. They also invested in ongoing teacher training, provided after-school tutoring for students, and offered a summer school program. In about four years, the pass rate rose to 75 percent! Their experience shows that high standards and requirements to learn combined with extra help in doing so can produce higher achievement, even in urban school districts.

The research on the positive effect of stakes for students—requirements for learning in order to move from elementary to middle to high school, and then even more specific requirements to graduate from high school—is strong. It may well be wise for the education system to design and implement such requirements quickly, so that all students have more reason to become engaged in school and do their best in their academic learning.

Requirements for Admission into Higher Education

High school performance also could be linked more closely to admission into higher education. There is ample, longitudinal research information that higher education admission policies can substantially affect both the organization of high schools and student behavior. One past and one current example help make the case. In the middle of the twentieth century, when colleges began to require high school students to take a certain number and type of "Carnegie" course units as a condition of admission, high schools very quickly modified their course offerings, and students as quickly began taking the required number of Carnegie units (Tyack and Cuban, 1996). In the 1980s, as part of the *Nation at Risk* state education reforms, state universities began to require students to take a larger number of academic courses to meet minimum qualifying requirements for admission. When they did so, the percentages of students taking such courses rose substantially within a few years, as did their grade point averages (e.g., Guthrie, Kirst, and Odden, 1990). Interestingly, the positive response was so dramatic that in states like California and Florida, both of which have large numbers of low-income, ethnic- and language-minority students, the percentage of students, including minority students, now meeting the entry requirements for state colleges and universities vastly exceeds the number of spaces available. Put a different way, raising the bar for admission into higher education dramatically changed what schools and students did: more academic courses were offered, students took them, and to a large degree students passed them. But not all states made such requirements, and few states or universities make student performance in such high school courses major determinants of admission decisions.

An incentive should be in place that specifies the types and difficulties of high school courses and student performance either on the end-of-course examinations or on the comprehensive high school exit examinations; these should also be major factors for admission into higher education, at least public higher education. This is not the case today.

To be blunt, other than grade point average, high school performance on school-based examinations, or even more specifically, on end-of-course examinations or on examinations linked to content and performance standards, is ignored and not considered in college or university admission decisions, nor in course placement once a student is admitted. Colleges and universities rely on scores from the SAT, which as the name indicates is more a general aptitude than a test of academic achievement, or the American College Testing (ACT) program, which is a test in different content domains but which is not linked to any specific content standards. Neither of these two tests is linked in any substantive way to any state high school curriculum content or student performance standards. The result is that high school students receive mixed signals about what types of performance matters. Although some performance might matter for high school graduation, it does not directly matter for college admission, except for the small percentage of students who apply to the few elite colleges and universities.

This is not the case in most other countries. In nearly all other advanced, English-speaking democracies, as well as many other countries, end-of-high school examination results are a key determinant of college and university entrance; in fact, they are one and the same examination. It may be true that such heavy reliance, sometimes down to the hundredth decimal place in some countries, might bestow too much influence on the score of a single test. But the larger point is that in those countries, performance in high school is directly linked to their postsecondary education opportunities, whereas in this country it is expressly ignored.

Of course, the difficulty in having high school performance matter is that some states do not administer tests at the high school level, and those that do have different tests and different standards for passing. One void that the SAT and ACT test scores fills is to provide a measure of student performance that is uniform across the 50 different state tests and even the 14,000 different local school district tests. Such differences are not a problem in most other countries that have national education systems. We are not arguing for a national education system, but rather simply noting that the current U.S. practice fails to create a link between high school performance and college admission decisions, providing little incentive for students to exert effort to do well on high school tests.

In addition, Kirst (1997) shows that course placement within most state colleges and universities bears no relationship to high school achievement, nor to examination scores required for admission. Instead, students take one set of tests for a high school course grade, another set of comprehensive tests for high school graduation (in some states), a third set of tests for college admission, and a fourth set of tests for course placement—with virtually no formal connections among any of the tests! Looked at from any perspective, this is a ludicrous system, and one that sends clear messages to high school students that other than for graduation, high school academic performance might not matter all that much.

The time may have come to rethink the connections between any examinations the K–12 system might require for high school graduation, and the types of test scores used for college admission. At the least, college admission requirements could be weighted heavily toward K–12 system tests of academic achievement, and shifted away (potentially completely) from general aptitude tests or tests not tied directly to a state's high school curriculum content and student performance standards. At maximum, the time might have arrived for common end of course examinations for high school students, certainly at the state level, and many would argue at the national level as well. Such a strategy would give specificity both to what the general standards mean at the high school level and to the level of academic achievement the nation needs from its adolescents. Such a strategy, combined with the promotional requirements for getting into and out of high school, would also signal to students that their academic performance matters for all levels of schooling.

Additional Incentives for Students

Not all high school students enroll in higher education after high school. Many enter the labor market. Making high school performance matter for employment opportunities is a related piece of the agenda for high school students. For many reasons today, neither the types of courses taken, nor student performance in those courses, nor results on state high school graduation tests are considered in employment or apprenticeship decisions. Thus, for the substantial portion of students who decide to enter the labor market, either through an apprenticeship or otherwise during high school, or after high school, there are no system incentives to do well. Companies and organizations hiring high school graduates rarely look at high school transcripts.

The problem with this approach is that cognitive expertise is increasingly important in many blue collar job opportunities as job requirements and job knowledge continue to change rapidly over time (Murnane and Levy, 1996). As technology impacts many arenas (e.g., automobiles, the production line, processing financial reports, etc.), it is becoming increasingly necessary to have employees who can continually adapt and learn how to use complex technologies in the workplace. In short, a high level of cognitive expertise has become a necessary ingredient for being a productive employee, even when entering the workforce immediately after high school.

The implication is that companies may want to consider the nature of high school coursework and student performance when hiring graduates for entry-level jobs. Some companies are moving in the direction of making high school performance matter. IBM is an example of one large company that recently adopted a policy requiring human resource departments to consider high school performance when deciding whether to offer jobs to high school graduates and what the beginning salary will be. Though implementing such a policy will face technical, legal, and equity challenges, in order to make high school academic performance matter for all high school students, the business community must give substantial weight to the types of courses taken, grades, and examination scores when making employment, salary, and apprenticeship decisions for students entering the world of work after high school.

Opportunities to Participate in Extracurricular School-Organized Activities

Student engagement in nonacademic school activities also matters. Research shows that students who participate more generally in school activities—clubs, intramural sports, service projects, and competitive sports—are more engaged not only at school but also in schoolwork. Involved students take more academic courses, perform at higher levels in those courses, and generally learn to higher academic standards (Steinberg, 1996).

Unfortunately, this aspect of school costs money (though not much money) and is on the decline. Although not in line with the degree of positive impact on student academic achievement, the priority for after-school activities in most school districts is competitive sports, largely football and basketball. Participation in these sports is only modestly associated with higher academic performance, and participation exceeding 15–20 hours a week (a not infrequent occurrence) can be a negative influence on academic performance. By contrast, participation in other sports—soccer, volleyball, swimming, track, baseball, etc.—usually requires fewer hours per week and is more strongly, though still only modestly, associated with academic learning. On the other hand, participation in clubs, whether academically focused (such as math, French, or debate clubs) or socially focused, is more strongly linked to high academic performance. Participation in service activities is the after-school activity most strongly associated with higher academic performance. Unfortunately, very little is known about the potential of opportunities for participation in intramural sports, but the sad fact at many high schools, especially large high schools, is that the focus of resources on competitive sports means the cutting of large numbers of students from school-organized sport activities; creating an intramural sport program could remedy this current lack of opportunity.

Given these research findings, students should be provided many more opportunities to participate in after-school clubs, school-organized service activities, and school-sponsored intramural sport activities, in addition to the current array of competitive sports. Indeed, a good argument could be made to reduce the dominance of competitive sports in favor of high-school-sponsored, after-school activities.

2. INCENTIVES FOR TEACHERS

Teachers are key to accomplishing the education goal of teaching all students to higher levels of academic achievement. What and how teachers teach constitute the primary variables that affect what and how much students learn. Therefore, the education system would be wise to provide a set of incentives that focus teacher effort on the activities that matter the most in their ability to successfully teach a more rigorous curriculum program to the diverse students who attend America's public schools. The following discusses and describes five types of teacher incentives, the first three being intrinsic and thus no- or low-cost incentives, and the last two being extrinsic, fiscal incentives:

- Goal clarification via mission, standards, and testing,
- Opportunities to engage collaboratively at the school site,
- Opportunities to improve professional practice,
- Incentives to improve knowledge and skills, and
- Incentives to improve student achievement.

Goal Clarification Via Mission, Standards, and Testing

Until quite recently, teachers worked in an education system that had unclear goals: missions were not very meaningful, there were no standards for curriculum or student performance, and few tests provided meaningful information about how students were performing. Goals covered a broad range of themes: the education system was to teach academic skills (albeit without clear directions), prepare students for citizenship and family life, and provide the skills needed to be successful in the labor market. Rarely were any of these three very broad areas given priority levels. Missions were also unclear: the typical mission was to maximize student potential in a diverse community. Although such an aspiration was admirable, it nevertheless had no clear meaning; because of time, budget, and other constraints, no state, district, school, or teacher could hope to even come close to maximizing any individual student's potential.

Indeed, until the recent advent of standards and school-based reforms, teachers were presented with multiple goals, given little if any direction about which goals mattered more than others, and had little measurement or performance data on whether any goals were being accomplished. Although there is still disagreement over their precise benefits, the emergence of mission statements that stipulate "The mission of [x district or state] is to teach students to proficiency standards in language arts/writing, mathematics, science, and history/social science," followed by creation of specific education goals, development of curriculum content and student performance standards, and deployment of assessment systems that provide solid information on student learning are rapidly bringing clarity to the goals, mission, and purposes of the public education system.

Moreover, emerging research is showing that this focus on rich academics is highly motivational for teachers (Heneman, 1998; Kelley, 1998a). For example, in states or districts that have set clear performance targets for schoolwide improvement in student achievement, teachers understand the targets, believe they are good targets, begin to channel their efforts towards those ends, and many say that for the first time in their professional life they know where to concentrate their energies. Specifying the primary objective of the education system—*to teach students to high standards in core academic subjects*—functions as a significant incentive for teachers. Few teachers resent such goal clarification; in fact, many teachers find the new focus empowering.

Teaching all students to rigorous standards is a goal long sought by educators. This agenda entails more than just teaching basic skills or teaching just *some* students to high levels. Most teachers understand that advanced cognitive expertise is the key to personal, social, and economic satisfaction in the twenty-first century for all students. Current missions, standards, and tests signal to teachers to concentrate on what they always wanted to do: teach all students to high standards.

Opportunities to Work Collaboratively to Improve the School

Another intrinsic incentive for teachers is the ability to work collaboratively with colleagues, not only on curriculum and instructional issues, but also on school restructuring, school-based management, and resource allocation. Opportunities for collaborative decision making are an important incentive for many teachers, particularly those with advanced training in and a deep commitment to the teaching profession (Conley, 1991; Hart, 1994; National Commission on Teaching and America's Future, 1996; Rosenholtz, 1989).

As an example of such an incentive, the Success for All/Roots and Wings schoolwide program is structured in such way that it intrinsically involves more teacher involvement. It requires a different type of student grouping and classroom organization for the 90-minute block of time that is devoted to reading each day. Students are regrouped in homogeneous groups according to reading level. Students are then regrouped into heterogeneous groups for mathematics, and grouped into still different settings for the afternoon, integrated science/social studies curriculum. Teachers in these schools are not only concerned with curriculum and pedagogy, they are also involved in decisions regarding school organization and student grouping, decisions that are integral to the instructional program. Such a broad range of involvement is also a feature of many other school designs (see, for example, Stringfield, Ross, and Smith, 1996).

This suggests that changes in district management from top-down bureaucratic systems to more decentralized, professional systems, together with accountability for results, can function as intrinsic incentives for teachers. When such strategies are designed well at both the district and site level, teachers become engaged in a variety of decision making activities, teacher leadership is expanded at the school level, teachers willingly spend more hours per day and week on the multiple tasks of running the school, and morale and enthusiasm rises (Odden and Kelley, 1997; Odden and Odden, 1996a; Wohlstetter, Van Kirk, Robertson, and Mohrman, 1997; Yee, 1984).

Further, as argued in Chapter 7, when properly structured, such teacher collaboration can lead to professional school cultures (Louis and Marks, 1998), which are associated with effective and fair schools.

Opportunities to Improve Professional Practice

Another highly motivating activity for teachers is involvement in activities designed to improve professional practice. A powerful teacher incentive would be to dramatically expand the number and types of opportunities for teachers to become engaged in long-term, focused, and sustained professional development, largely though not solely focused on improving their curriculum and instructional skills.

There is a large body of research showing that providing opportunities to improve knowledge, skills, and professional expertise is motivating for teachers. Indeed, the more general research on worker motivation shows that opportunities to engage in training and to enhance knowledge and skills needed in the workplace is motivating to all types of workers, and especially highly educated workers (which would include teachers). Within education, research has shown that most teachers, and particularly teachers who are more committed to the profession, view engagement in good professional development opportunities as one of the most worthwhile and motivating activities in which they participate (Odden and Kelley, 1997; Rosenholtz, 1989; Yee, 1984).

Research shows that capacity development (i.e., training to develop new skills that are needed) is critical to effective implementation of standards- and school-based research (Corcoran and Goertz, 1995; Goertz, Floden, and O'Day, 1995; Little, 1993). Substantial ongoing professional development is needed not only for the more difficult curriculum and instruction program, but also for the broader roles teachers are assuming in schools today. These include advising and counseling students, developing curriculum, training colleagues, and the leadership, management, financial, and school-improvement skills needed for involvement in school management. Put another way, research shows both that teachers need to be involved in a broader set of professional development activities, and that participation in such activities functions as a strong, positive incentive.

Research also shows that the best professional development is embedded in the curriculum to be taught, sustained over a long time period, and includes substantial opportunities for classroom practice and feedback. Such training not only is successful in enhancing teacher classroom expertise, but also in improving student achievement (Cohen and Hill, 1997, 1998; Corcoran, 1995; Darling-Hammond and McLaughlin, 1995; Joyce and Calhoun, 1996; Loucks-Horsley, et. al., 1997).

Finally, there is the cost of capacity development activities. The cost can range from 2 to 5 percent of the operating budget (Elmore and Burney, 1996; Odden and Busch, 1998). In many cases, some resources can be found by reallocating current revenues. But states, districts, and schools could also target capacity development as the recipient of new money; if funds rose 2 percent in real terms, that might be the time to set aside that amount of the budget for ongoing training and professional development. Such an investment of new money could produce handsome returns.

Incentives to Improve Knowledge and Skills

Teacher salary structures have been static for decades. The single-salary schedule that provides for pay increments based on years of experience and education units and degrees was created in the early twentieth century to root out practices that only paid different salaries to elementary and secondary teachers, men and women teachers, and minority and nonminority teachers. The single-salary schedule also eliminated the administrative whim that often determined annual salary changes when each teacher had an individual contract that was negotiated privately between the teacher (who had little power) and the administrator (who had virtually all the power). The single-salary schedule has remained in the system for nearly the entire century because it is fair, predictable, and easy to administer (Odden and Kelley, 1997).

However, as currently structured, this salary schedule is either neutral to or only mildly supportive of the need for teachers to fundamentally enhance their professional knowledge and skills. Moreover, the single-salary schedule too often pays teachers for earning additional units that are unrelated to their teaching assignments, such as earning degrees in educational administration that prepare them to leave the classroom. Research also shows that on average, after the first few years of teaching, greater experience is not associated with more expertise and success in the classroom (Murnane, 1983).

Most organizations outside of education also base annual salary increases on years of experience or seniority. But as these organizations restructure into higher-performing entities, they often also change their pay structure towards a system that pays directly for the knowledge and skills needed in the work environment. Researchers have shown that such compensation changes also fit with current education initiatives: teachers need better content knowledge, more curriculum and instructional strategies, and the skills to engage productively in broader school-based management actions (Conley and Odden, 1995; Kelley, 1997; Odden and Conley, 1992; Odden, 1996). As the above section argued, engaging in opportunities to learn these new knowledge and skills is intrinsically motivating for teachers because they enjoy doing it and feel more professional when they have expanded their professional repertoire. Adding salary increments for the development of such knowledge and skills would simply provide an extrinsic reward—additional pay—to the intrinsic incentive of expanding one's knowledge and skills.

If teacher salary expenditures could be altered or augmented to provide more direct incentives for teachers to develop and use the knowledge and skills needed to restructure all schools into high-performance educational organizations and teach students to high academic standards, half of all education expenditures would then be reinforcing actions that directly impact the primary purpose of schools: student academic achievement. Chapter 11 discusses how this could be accomplished.

Incentives to Improve Student Performance

An additional extrinsic incentive would be a salary bonus provided to all individuals in a school that met or exceeded specific student performance improvement targets; this is what many refer to as a school-based performance award. While knowledge- and skill-based incentives provide rewards to develop the expertise needed to teach students to higher standards, a school-based performance award would be provided when student academic achievement actually rose.

Such programs are somewhat controversial in education, and many commentaries on them are based on opinion rather than fact. Studies of the programs in Charlotte-Mecklenburg, North Carolina, and in the states of Kentucky and Maryland generally show that such programs can function as strong incentives for teachers. The data suggest that by being school- (rather than individually) based, these incentives stimulate collaborative work in schools, which, as argued above, is intrinsically motivating. Results also show that such programs make system goals for student academic achievement very clear, which also, as argued above, is intrinsically motivating; where these programs exist, schools know their student achievement improvement goals and basically agree that they are attainable. As a result, teachers do not necessarily work harder, but they work more efficiently by channeling their energies to activities focused on improving the curriculum and instructional program in areas where student achievement is weak. The research also shows that teachers value the monetary bonuses that they receive. Although teachers report that they are not solely motivated by the money but rather that they are more strongly motivated by the goals and the expectation of improving student achievement, they nevertheless appreciate receiving a monetary bonus (Heneman, 1998; Kelley, 1998a).

In sum, research shows that these programs hold considerable promise and should be considered by all states and districts. Perhaps the greatest effect has been to solidify the priority of student achievement in the core academic subjects. This alone might be well worth the modest costs. Chapter 11 outlines in more detail how such programs can be designed and implemented in education.

3. INCENTIVES FOR SCHOOLS

The work of education occurs in classrooms and schools, because schools are the place where teaching and learning occur. Although students and teachers represent the primary individuals who work in schools and who can respond to individually targeted incentives, the school as a social organization operates in several important ways, each of which could be the focus of a school-based incentive. Although individual student and teacher incentives overlap to some degree with school-based incentives, the school itself, along with the locale around which many aspects of children's lives are structured, could also be the focus of a set of incentives. The following are suggested as a set of school-based incentives:

- Incentives for schools to restructure towards higher-performance visions,
- Incentives for reallocating education resources to more productive uses, and
- Incentives for producing increases in student achievement.

Incentives for Restructuring toward Higher-Performance Visions

The major task for schools under standards- and school-based reform is to determine the at-the-site strategy for dramatically improving student achievement. Although many schools can improve student performance in the short term by doing what they now do better (by emphasizing certain elements of their current instructional program), schools likely will need to take more dramatic efforts to double or triple results, as we argued in Chapter 8. Other organizations in the broader economy that have had to increase results by quantum levels generally undergo a thorough restructuring, rebuilding themselves from the ground up (Mohrman, Galbraith, and Lawler, 1996). Thus, after making some short-term, modest improvements, schools might have to design or adopt a higher-performance school vision and restructure themselves according to this vision over a three- to five-year time period. At least three types of incentives can help propel schools onto this path:

Grant schools more authority.   The first is to provide schools with the autonomy they need to engage in the basic restructuring described above. This can be done by devolving power, authority, and other responsibilities from the central office to the school site, which will free them to devise or adopt a vision that will allow them to teach their students to high standards in a more rigorous curriculum program. To be sure, states and districts will continue to set directions, goals, and standards, measure performance, and administer an accountability system. But whether through school- or site-based management, schools need more authority so they can determine how best to accomplish those goals.

Although many districts now argue that they provide schools with such authority, that is not usually the case. The most recent study of school decentralization in Charlotte-Mecklenburg, Chicago, Cincinnati, Denver, Los Angeles, and Seattle found that although these efforts represented some of the most robust devolution initiatives in the country, districts provided schools with quite unclear authority concerning budgets and personnel rights, little training, few if any ideas about how schools could restructure themselves, and mounted only weak accountability systems (Bryk, Hill, and Shipps, 1997). As a result, the rhetoric about their changes vastly exceed the reality, and only modest improvements were produced. We have outlined the key elements that make school-based management work in the third section of Chapter 7, and we will not repeat those items here.

A decentralized management approach does not mean that schools would decide their own goals, curriculum standards, and results for which they would be held accountable. Determining goals, standards, and core results are state and district responsibilities for ensuring that a school-based management approach focuses on curriculum, instruction, and student achievement. As stated above, states and districts should set mission, goals, standards, measure results, and administer a real accountability system largely focused on student academic achievement. If they did so, all schools would be working to accomplish similar goals, but within these parameters decentralization would free each school to determine how best to boost student performance with *their* students and *their* faculty.

Public school choice.   Public school choice can be viewed as a correlate to school decentralization. With choice programs, parents can select the school their child attends. In general, choice programs allow students to attend schools within their district or in a nearby district as long as space is available. With public school choice, parents and students vote with their feet and find a school that meets their needs (Education Commission of the States, 1996).

Unlike the present system—in which public schools share common approaches to curriculum, organization, and focus—an expansion of choice programs under a decentralized management approach could result in schools that differ dramatically from each other. For example, schools collaborating with the New American Schools can select eight very different school designs, giving parents and students a wide selection of school strategies.

Public school choice encourages schools to offer unique visions and programs. Students who choose to attend these schools, as well as faculty who choose to teach there, can be more motivated as a result (Hill, Pierce, and Guthrie, 1997). Research shows that student achievement also can be higher (Gamoran, 1996; Hill, Foster, and Gendler, 1990).

The fiscal incentive that can be embodied in public school choice has to do with the budget. If schools were funded by a needs-based funding formula, as discussed in Chapter 9, the school budget would increase as the number of students enrolled increased. Thus, as the school became more attractive, its budget also would rise. Most state public school–choice-funding mechanisms could be improved to make this fiscal incentive more transparent and easier to operate (Odden and Kotowski, 1992; Odden and Busch, 1998). As long as the system were confined to public schools, this strategy would be close to cost-free. The same dollars would be spent; only the location where the dollars are spent would change: they would be spent in the school of choice.

Expand charter school programs. Charter schools represent the most robust form of school flexibility and autonomy. Charter school programs enable teachers (as well as parents and others) to design the schools to which they are committed, including the curriculum, organization, and management of that school (Education Commission of the States, 1995; Finn, Manno, and Bierlein, 1996).

Though charter schools are only accountable for results, they often are granted waivers from programmatic, budgetary, personnel, and collective bargaining requirements. Theoretically, at their strongest, charter schools can be free from virtually all regulations except those governing civil rights, safety, and students with disabilities.

At the same time, many current charters fail to specify the results, the measures that would be used, or the improvements that would be required for their accountability. Further, many charter school teachers and administrators believe they are accountable primarily to the parents in terms of whether they continue to enroll their students (Wohlstetter and Griffin, 1997). Such a perspective is not sufficient. Charter schools should be held to the same student performance standards as their more traditional public counterparts. Annual and five-year performance targets should be written into their charter.

Just as with public school choice, the fiscal incentive that is part of charter school programs concerns the budget of these schools. The greater the number of students, the larger the budget. Though as Odden and Busch (1998) showed, state funding mechanisms for charter schools were quite cumbersome at the beginning of the 1990s, they began changing towards the end of the 1990s, largely according to the proposals outlined by Odden and Busch. Several states now treat charter schools as a district with no local property tax base and fund them according to their regular state school finance formulas.

Incentives for Reallocating Education Resources
to More Productive Uses

The largest reservoir of funds for school restructuring are the dollars already provided to each school site for their instructional program, student support, and site
administration. Providing schools their budget in a lump sum is a large incentive
that requires no additional funding and generally results in better use of current
dollars. Research in nearly every country, state, or district that has implemented a
real school-based funding system has found it to be highly motivational for school
administrators and faculty. Further, research shows that schools with control over
their budget almost immediately begin to reallocate at least a small portion of
funds to site priorities, whereas schools without lump sum budgets have great difficulty envisioning alternative ways to use their resources (Cooperative Research
Project, 1996; Odden and Odden, 1996a, 1996b; Thomas and Martin, 1996).

The incentive power of providing schools the authority over the major portion of their budget cannot be understated. Giving schools control of their budgets quickly and significantly increases staff and faculty support for the new policies. Such support can last for several years. Even though it takes more work,
faculties simply prefer to make their own decisions on how to spend school resources, rather than cede that power to district or state officials.

Despite the positive aspects, there have been three basic problems with implementing a school-based financing system in the United States. First, many
states or districts claim they already are implementing such a system, when in ac-
tuality they are not. Second, few states understand that such budget decentralization is best structured from the state level so that all districts would follow a set of
common procedures, which still could result in quite different specific decisions
about how much money to decentralize and how to construct the formula to determine each school's budget. Third, school-based formula funding requires districts (and states) to decide very concretely and publicly which functions remain
at the center (as well as their budgets) and which functions (and their budgets)
are devolved to schools. The more explicit these decisions are, the better the
school-based financing policy.

In an analysis of school-based financing in England, Victoria (Australia),
and the United States, Odden and Busch (1997) concluded that at least 75 percent of a district's operating budget should be budgeted in a lump sum to school
sites. This requires devolving the instructional, instructional and student support,
and site administration budgets. We provide additional details about how to design such a strategy in Chapter 10.

It should be clear that a school-based funding system would produce a system that would have all dollars follow the child, including dollars for the regular
instructional program as well as dollars for any specific educational need. Since
the system proposed would be based largely on the number of students, and
since each school would be funded on the basis of the number and characteristics
of students enrolled in the school, the system would have dollars follow the child
in reality, thus matching the rhetoric that surrounds many discussions today.
School-based funding strategies would fiscally support school-based management, public school choice, or charter school programs as well.

Incentives for Producing Increases in Student Achievement

The previous section on teacher incentives described a school-based performance award (i.e., a program that would provide monetary bonuses to schools that met or exceeded specified improvements in student academic achievement). Such a program also fits in this section on school incentives, both because it is school-based, serving as a vehicle that motivates collegial action within a school to improve the most valued results, and because it first sends any financial award or bonus money to the school site. The previous section made the argument for why this type of program is motivating to teachers; essentially the same arguments hold for their motivational impact at the site level.

At the site level, it would be wise to specify how such monies could be used. In Kentucky, the funds were provided to the school site, and each school's teachers (and only the teachers) decided how the money was to be used, whether for school improvement, for salary bonuses (and for whom), or some combination. While such a strategy has a rationale—teachers at the site know best who should be rewarded and how much—it produced significant controversy, none of which reinforced the primary goal of improving student achievement. Therefore, this type of practice is not recommended.

States and districts will have to make their own decisions about how large a financial bonus to include in a school-based performance bonus program and how such funds should be used. Salary bonuses for all individuals in a school is one option. Individual school improvement accounts would be another option. Use for schoolwide improvement could be a third use. A fourth use could be for additions to the student body fund that could be used to provide an incentive for students to work hard to produce results as well. Districts or states could specify which combination of these uses would be allowed. They also could provide some choice. For example, they could allow faculties to determine how to divide an amount of money between school improvement and the student body fund.

In sum, the school-based incentive that can be most directly tied to improvements in student achievement results is a school-based performance award. Such programs are relatively new in education, but they are rapidly evolving across the country, and early research shows that they hold significant promise. States and districts should be encouraged to continue to develop such programs. They should be encouraged just as strongly to evaluate them and to assess how they affect teacher and student motivation to teach and learn to higher standards, in order to determine over time the best design features.

SUMMARY

This chapter has discussed a series of incentives for students, teachers, and schools that could help motivate all key actors in the education system to focus their efforts on producing high levels of student achievement. The incentives discussed are in addition to those imbedded in state-to-district school finance formulas as discussed in Chapter 3. The incentives discussed in this chapter have more to do with people and actions at the subdistrict level. Again, we would encourage states, districts, and schools to consider adopting all of the incentives we discuss because they have all been proven to positively impact student achievement. We also note that many of the incentives we discuss have low or no-cost implications, and many others entail only alternative uses of existing resources. Though school finance policymakers might focus only on the incentives that have a cost, the education system would be wise to consider all of these incentives.°

° This chapter draws heavily from a background paper on incentives for students, teachers, and schools written for the Education Commission of the States (ECS) in 1997 and published by ECS as *A Policymakers Guide to Incentives for Students, Teachers and Schools:* Denver, CO: ECS.

—Chapter 10—————————————————————

School-Based Financing: Formula Funding of School Sites*

In the United States, the issue of school-based financing is just beginning to emerge. The 1999 annual yearbook of the American Education Finance Association was devoted to this subject (Goertz and Odden, 1999). The issue also is rising in international contexts. The International Institute for Educational Planning of the United Nations Education, Social and Cultural Organization published a book on the topic in early 1999 that reviewed the school based financing strategies already being implemented in England, Australia, New Zealand, and North America (Ross and Levacic, 1999) and provided suggestions for how this technology could be used in developing countries.

As discussed in this book, school finance in the United States during most of the twentieth century concerned state-to-district funding structures. The formula portion of state school finance laws as well as school finance texts (e.g., see Chapter 4) addressed such funding systems. But school-based financing concerns district formula funding of schools, or as Ross and Levacic put it, needs-based formula funding of schools. The general idea is to provide schools with a lump-sum budget based on the number of students, the educational needs of students, and other objective needs of the school site.

School-based financing differs from current practice largely in providing schools with an unallocated lump sum of dollars rather than a specified set of staff. Most districts in the United States provide schools with tangible resources such as teachers, instructional aides, counselors, administrators, books, materials, and supplies, rather than just a lump sum of money (Guthrie, 1988). In such situations, districts have made most of the decisions about how the education dollars

---

* This chapter draws from but changes the recommendations in Odden and Busch (1998), Chapter 6.

will be spent. Under school-based financing, districts would provide each school with a lump sum of dollars on a fair and equitable basis, and then schools would be responsible for deciding how to spend those dollars.

The rationale for school-based financing is at least fourfold. First, it is a key element of an effective and complete school-based management strategy, as discussed in the latter half of Chapter 7. Second, spending dollars differently at the school site is important for improving the productivity of the education dollar, as shown in the first part of Chapter 7. Third, it constitutes a fiscal incentive for schools, as argued in Chapter 9. And fourth, it aligns the direction of education policy, which has recently targeted school-level issues, such as public school choice and charter schools, with the focus of education funding: the site rather than the district (Odden and Clune, 1998).

We would encourage readers to learn more about the school-based financing systems now being implemented in other countries by reading Odden and Busch (1998), which includes chapters on England and Victoria, Australia. The aforementioned Ross and Levacic (1999) book would also prove useful. The ideas developed in this chapter draw from these strategies and seek to tailor them to the U.S. education finance context.

Section 1 describes the key elements of the overall structure. Section 2 discusses the rationale for a series of functions that districts should or could retain at the district level. Section 3 discusses the district process for devolving budgetary and functional authority to schools and describes how the formula for determining each school's budget should be designed. This section also describes five school-based financing systems that existed in North America in December 1997. The last section suggests possible categories for the school-site budget.

1. THE OVERALL STRUCTURE OF A SCHOOL SITE-BASED FINANCING SYSTEM

A school site-based financing system is one in which the state requires school districts to provide the bulk of operating revenues from all government sources—local, state, and federal—to school sites in a lump sum. Such a requirement could simply be mandated by the state (i.e., the state could require that each district devise a mechanism for devolving the bulk of its fiscal resources to each school site). But no country or state in the world that has enacted a school-based financing system has done so without also creating an overall policy framework within which such a major change in education finance can be implemented.

Nevertheless, the first task for the state is to decide whether it will allow each local school district to devise its own system for budgeting dollars to the school without any structure or guidelines from the state. This has been the approach taken for the funding of many states' charter school programs, which is at least in part school-based financing. But as Odden and Busch (1998) show, the result has been confusion and inequity, and is not the approach that we recommend for constructing a school-based financing system (see also Bierlein and Fulton, 1996;

Wells, 1996). Instead, we recommend that states construct an overall school-based financing framework within which each district would design its specific site-funding formula, as England has done. The framework proposed here includes funds for just the operating budgets (i.e., the general fund and categorical program funds) and is thus a simplified version of the one suggested by Odden and Busch (1998). States also could decide to exempt small districts from such budget decentralization, particularly when there are only one to three schools in the district.

It also should be clear that we are not advocating direct funding of schools by the state. School districts are an integral part of the American education system and will remain at least into the twenty-first century. Our model assumes that states will continue to fund school districts, but then structures how school districts would provide school sites with lump-sum dollar budgets.

In the framework proposed here, states would require districts to construct their school-based financing system in four steps. The four steps include:

1. Specifying the minimum percentage of the operating budget that would be devolved to schools sites, termed the "minimum school percentage," and discussing how that percentage could rise over time.
2. Identifying key district roles and functions in a decentralized system, giving them a budget, and calling the remaining funds the "school budget."
3. Structuring the formula each district would develop to calculate the school budget for each school site.
4. Describing the general type of program budget each school site would be required to develop from their lump-sum budget allocation.

It is important to note at the outset that steps one and two do not require that a district moving to a school-based reform strategy strip away all district roles and responsibilities. In fact, the assumption in education that school-based management eviscerates the role of the central office is simply wrong. When a district or any large system adopts a decentralized management strategy to improve system results, the district or central office must redesign the entire system, including the roles and functions of the central office; Chapter 8 of Odden and Busch (1998) outlines these roles and functions.

Taking a closer look at the actions involved with carrying out each of these steps, step one would require setting some minimum school percentage of the operating budget that would be devolved to school sites. This step would also entail specifying whether this minimum would be increased over time, and how much it would rise.

Step two would involve two important decisions. The first would identify the key roles and functions of the district, as well as specifying their funding amounts. The second would identify those functions that initially could be administered by the district, but which over time could be decentralized to the school site. In making these decisions, there are a couple of points to consider. On the one hand, it may be wise to be as parsimonious as possible in delineating key roles and functions of the district for the first part of this step. Policymakers and education leaders must be clear that there are very important responsibilities and functions that are best provided by the district, even in a decentralized, site-based managed education system.

On the other hand, identifying those functions that eventually could be administered by the site is also important. This step allows the many different districts in a state to tailor a decentralization strategy to their specific context. Though it might be wise to decentralize a certain function in a large district, it might not be efficient to do so in a small district, or vice versa. We would expect that there would be significant differences in the decisions that city, suburban, rural, small, and large districts make about these functions. In short, there needs to be flexibility in the system so it can be crafted at the district level to work to maximum efficiency and effectiveness.

Although this approach would work quite well for schools that remain within the governing structure of the district, it would not function well for charter schools, which would be administering more functions than regular public schools. Thus, we suggest that states either fund charter schools directly by considering them as a school district with no local property wealth, as they are now doing in states such as Minnesota, or providing them with their proportion of the budget for all discretionary district functions identified above.

Step three would specify how districts would construct the formula for determining each school's budget. This step would identify the degree to which the formula would need to be based on pupil units, the definition of those pupil units, the weights that could be provided for grade-level differences, the weights that could be provided for extra students needs, and other relevant but objective factors. This step would also stipulate whether variables other than pupil-related factors could be used to determine the school budget, such as the size of the physical building or the land area of the school.

Finally, step four would require that sites create program budgets and specify a minimum number of budget program categories that must be included. The state could also require that site-based managed schools clearly link their budget to their school-improvement plan.

Figure 10.1 identifies the major elements of the proposed school-based financing framework. Recall that this framework should cover revenues from the major operating funds and budget categories, including the general fund, the special-purpose funds for student-related categorical program services, the pupil transportation fund, food services, and the community services fund. The remainder of the chapter discusses the rationales for the major decisions regarding school-based budgeting that have been presented here.

2. THE MINIMUM SCHOOL PERCENTAGE

Odden and Busch's (1998) framework drew from the practice in England and adapted it to the United States. England had identified six functions that would

FIGURE 10.1   A School-Based Financing Framework

*Overall Framework: Key District Roles and Responsibilities
in a Decentralized System*

I. **The School Budget**
  A. Minimum school percentage:
     Year 1: 70 percent
     Years 2–8: 2 percent more each year, so by year 10, a minimum of 84 percent of the district operating budget is devolved to sites

II. **The District Budget**
  A. Key district roles and functions: Administration, planning, evaluation, accountability, change management, transportation, assuring IEP programs, etc.
  B. Discretionary district roles and functions: Operation and maintenance, food services, etc.

III. **The School-Based Funding Formula**
  A. 85 percent minimum budgeted to school on a weighted per-pupil basis
  B. Weights for:
     • education level—elementary, middle, high school
     • student need— low income, disabled, limited English proficient, gifted and talented, etc.
  C. Other factors for budgeting the remaining maximum of 15 percent:
     • characteristics of buildings and lands
     • school size in terms of number of pupils, such as a lump sum
     • provisions for the severely disabled or other categories of additional educational needs
     • other measurable factors

be mandated district functions, and identified a series of other functions as discretionary district functions. Once those were funded, the remaining budget constituted the potential school budget. England then required districts to provide schools only a percentage of the potential school budget. Although Odden and Busch recommended a similar approach for a U.S. state, when discussing this approach with many education leaders in the United States, they found that the general response was that the English approach was more complicated than necessary. Practitioners suggested it would be better to identify a core portion of the operating budget that should be devolved to school sites, and gradually increase that percentage as districts and schools became comfortable with the decentralized approach to budgeting. Although this strategy identifies core district functions only indirectly, it still requires districts to identify each district and site function, so the approach can work quite similarly to the English approach.

   The first decision, then, is to identify the minimum proportion of the operating budget that will be devolved to school sites. This should not be an arbitrary decision. We provide benchmarks for this decision, the details of which would need to be made individually by each state. We generally suggest that the minimum school percentage be about 70 percent. As documented in Chapter 6, about 60 percent of the operating budget of the average school district is spent on instruction, the bulk of which can be devolved to the school site. About 6 percent of the budget is expended on site administration: principals, assistant principals, and site office classified support. About 10 percent of the budget is spent on pupil and instructional support, split in various ways between the site and the central office. These comprise a rough approximation of core site functions, and constitute an average maximum of 76 percent of the operating budget. But because some portions of the instructional, and instructional support and pupil support functions might still be provided by the central office, we suggest rounding down when initially specifying the minimum school percentage. This substantial portion of the budget to be decentralized to the site is also supported by the discussion in Chapter 8, which showed that instructional, instructional support, and pupil support professionals are the key staff involved in resource reallocation activities; thus, schools need control over these budget items in order to engage substantively in such productivity-enhancing actions.

Another reason to devolve only about 70 percent of the budget to sites initially is not to force an overly hasty implementation of school-based financing. Requiring that such a portion of funds be devolved to the schools allows a state and its local districts to phase in a school-based financing system, thereby providing for a smoother transition to a decentralized, school-based management and finance structure.

At the same time, this small percentage makes the proposed system somewhat inadequate for financing charter schools. Charter schools should be provided this 70 percent, plus their proportion of the funds in the district optional functions, because those functions would be performed at the site level for charter schools.

3. DISTRICT ROLES AND FUNCTIONS

As Odden and Busch (1998) wrote, there are several district responsibilities even in a decentralized system. They include:

- Orchestrating a change process to implement standards-based education reform and to decentralize the district,
- Developing curriculum content and student performance standards, and an aligned assessment system, and
- Creating the conditions that support decentralized school management, such as a school-based funding formula, a school-based information system, ample professional development, and a site-based accountability

system that could include a school-based performance award and new ways of compensating teachers (see Chapter 11).

Odden and Busch (1998) elaborate these functions. In addition, districts may engage in new roles in a decentralized system, such as evaluation, reviewing school performance, and ensuring that each school has an effective instructional vision. Some of these are elaborated below where we specify core district functions. As is made clear below, moreover, there are other functions that remain at the district level, in addition to the new ones required by a decentralization strategy; all need to be considered as each LEA designs its unique school-based financing system.

Identifying district roles and functions proceeds in two stages: the first identifies core roles and functions, and the second identifies optional roles and functions. Core roles and functions are those that have strong rationales for being performed by the district rather than the site, either new roles essential to make a decentralization strategy work, legal responsibilities, or traditional tasks more efficiently performed by the district.

We suggest that states identify 10 mandatory district functions and 22 optional district functions. This framework simply identifies a set of functions that must be retained by the district and a set of functions that could be retained by the district, and then requires each district to identify which optional functions they will retain and the amounts of money that will be budgeted for each district function.

Core District Functions

The chapter recommends that states *require* districts to retain 10 functions at the central office level (Figure 10.2). Several of these functions may need only small budgets, and several reflect important new roles that districts must provide to make decentralization successful.

FIGURE 10.2　Core District Functions

Mandatory Functions	Budget Amount
1. Board of Education	
2. Office of the Superintendent	
3. Information systems, quality benchmarks	
4. Accountability system	
5. Developing IEPs	
6. Monitoring federal/state categorical programs	
7. Home-to-school transportation	
8. Legal services	
9. LEA education initiatives	
10. Federal program services not devolved	

Board of education. Few if any states are proposing any type of radical school district reorganization that would involve either eliminating or reconstituting school boards. One of the strengths of school-site–based financing is that it can be implemented within the current board and district structure; indeed, it could be argued that the existence of many districts and boards enhances the ability of a state to effectively implement any decentralized management strategies by allowing boards and districts to tailor specific designs to local contexts. Although decentralization will likely change some of the roles and responsibilities of school boards and central offices (Hill, Pierce, and Guthrie, 1997), school boards will continue to exist and will continue to play important policy- and decision-making roles. Therefore, just as is done today, this function should be retained at the district level.

Office of the superintendent. In addition to the board function, the office of the superintendent must also be included as a core district function with a specific budget.

However, this function should be limited to the roles and the office of the superintendent only. It should not include any other district offices, such as those for curriculum and instruction, categorical programs, business and administration, personnel administration, or professional development, etc. Each of these other offices and their functions should be addressed separately and independently.

The superintendent's office can vary in size and staffing, but it should be limited to the superintendent and his or her direct roles and functions. The superintendent's office could include a policy function and a public relations and communication function, but it would not include any operational functional tasks.

Information services and quality benchmarks. This is suggested as a new, core district function; it is now often a weakly implemented function that is embedded within general administrative support. This function would have two specific emphases. First, it would have the responsibility for creating and administering an Internet-based *school*-based information system that would include:

1. Fiscal data, such as revenues, expenditures, and expenditures relative to budget,
2. An electronic purchasing and invoicing system,
3. Data on student achievement, including longitudinal data, and data that could be disaggregated by subject area, topic within subject area, and by characteristics of students,
4. An instructional management system that teachers could use to monitor individual student performance relative to performance standards,
5. Descriptions of best practices, for example, curriculum programs or units, instructional strategies, professional development strategies, and whole-school, high-performance designs such as those from the New

American Schools, the Edison Project, and other school reform networks (Education Commission of the States, 1997c), and

6. A personnel records system for teaching, professional, and classified staff.

This system should, in the medium term, be an online, interactive, relational database, easily usable by each school site within the state. Thus, the system we recommend would be similar to the emerging Seattle fiscal system (http://sps.gspa.washington.edu/sps/), with the Northwest Education Laboratory's system on best practices (http://www.nwrel.org), and with other systems including achievement and personnel data. Oregon hoped to begin implementing such a system in late 1999.

The system should incorporate and build upon any state's current management information systems. But changes in how these systems are used and changes in-state–required data reporting are needed to produce accurate school-level fiscal, student, and teacher information (Cohen, 1997; Farland, 1997). First, districts and schools need to code all appropriate expenditures to school sites or administrative units. This means the state must develop a *common* mechanism for districts to allocate all central-office expenditures on behalf of schools (e.g., operations and maintenance) to the appropriate school sites. Second, districts and schools need training to code all expenditures in comparable ways. Third, states would need to require reporting by school site or administrative unit. Fourth, the entire system needs to be automated statewide, most efficiently through the World Wide Web, and not just housed in various large district and regional computer systems. Fifth, teacher data would need to be fully automated and incorporated into the overall, relational data set. Finally, longitudinal student data would need to be included.

The second focus of the information and best practices function would be for the district to provide quality benchmarks for various curriculum programs and units, instructional strategies, professional development programs and opportunities, and whole-school, high-performance designs that it puts on the information system. This district function should be designed to help school sites select effective school designs, curriculum, and professional development strategies, while leaving major decisions up to schools. The Northwest Regional Education Laboratory's review of effective curriculum programs and school designs is a good example.

Developing and monitoring an accountability system. This is suggested as a separately identified district function as well. Creating and administering an accountability system is a critical district function under site-based management. It entails:

1. Developing curriculum content and student performance standards consistent with state standards,

2. Selecting and administering a testing system that would be used for public accountability purposes,
3. Creating a database of results for each school,
4. Negotiating a set of specific, annual performance-improvement targets for each school, to be called the school-site performance agreement (see also Chapter 11),
5. Designing types of awards that would be provided to schools for meeting or exceeding performance-improvement targets including, for example, a new compensation system that provides base pay increases for skills and competencies rather than education units and years of experience, and school-based performance awards that could be used either for salary bonuses or school-improvement purposes (see Chapter 11 and Odden and Kelley, 1997), and
6. Creating sanctions that could be used for schools that consistently fail to meet performance targets or whose performance consistently drops.

Although the specific nature of each district's accountability system could vary, the state could require that it include at least the above six components. But for the purpose of the finance system, this important district function would need to be recognized and funded in the budget development process.

Developing individual education plans for disabled students.   Under current federal law, the development of an Individual Education Plan (IEP) for disabled students is the responsibility of each school district. There is no reason to change the placement of this responsibility. A school-based financing system can operate with this assessment and program development function technically remaining with the district, since in nearly all instances both site professionals and parents will be involved. Further, this responsibility has remained at the district level in England for the last eight years and has worked quite well.

Monitoring state and federal categorical programs.   This required district function, largely a legal requirement of federal and state categorical programs, is to monitor state and federal categorical programs, such as Title I, special education, programs for limited English proficient students, gifted and talented students, desegregation, etc. This function, which is often a part of instructional administration, should be minimal and should focus on conducting compliance monitoring that focuses only on state and federal requirements, leaving as much discretion as possible to the site for designing and implementing programs. If not restructured by the state, the district should seek to monitor categorical programs in the most efficient way by consolidating monitoring activities for all or nearly all categorical programs into one process that is conducted at each site at only one point in time during the year or over some multiple-year time period (Odden, 1988).

Home-to-school transportation.   This would generally be expenditures from the pupil transportation fund. In nearly all cases, home-to-school transportation is more efficiently provided by a central authority, in this case, the school district. Devolving responsibility for organizing and administering home-to-school transportation would preclude most schools from being able to take advantage of the economies of scale that many districts enjoy by operating a transportation system for a larger geographic area. Further, a districtwide transportation system is also best designed to help transport students who choose to attend a school different from the school within which attendance boundary they reside.

In small districts, where there is little need for home-to-school transportation, transportation responsibilities could be devolved to school sites, but many of those districts could be excluded from decentralization altogether, as their smallness substitutes for decentralization. But the vast majority of districts probably can provide transportation services more efficiently from a districtwide perspective than the school. Most districts would retain transportation for disabled students at the district level.

This function does not include transportation required at the school level for school trips and other types of school-initiated excursions. These funds and the arrangements for transportation services, which could include purchase of the service from the district transportation office, should be made a site responsibility.

It should be noted that in the most recent state charter school laws, home-to-school transportation is often specifically identified as a function that would be provided by the district. We generally agree with that trend.

Legal advice and counseling. Superintendents and school boards will continue to be legally responsible for school districts' compliance with laws affecting public sector entities, as well as with laws, regulations, and court orders specifically pertaining to public schools. But in an era of changing school contexts including site-managed schools, charter schools, and even contract schools, school boards could begin to offer free or fee-based legal assistance to schools. As the degree of decentralization progresses, and schools become more independent organizations (as they are in England and Victoria, Australia), they will need legal advice and representation on contracts, labor law, and liability.

Further, the laws pertaining to individual schools are evolving rapidly as charter and contract schools, privately managed but publicly accountable, are established. For the foreseeable future, schools will face uncertainties about their legal rights and obligations. Central offices will likely need to offer legal advice and occasional representation for at least the short to medium term, until the legal responsibilities of districts and schools are resolved. The volume of legal work to be done also would depend on whether state and federal laws affecting school districts can be simplified.

LEA-wide education initiatives. This is a proposed new function. England allows districts to retain a maximum proportion of their total budget for districtwide education initiatives. Some districts with low reading scores have created a districtwide literacy initiative; others have started science initiatives to enhance the science program across the district. Today, many districts create technology initiatives, or even professional development initiatives. Such dis-trictwide initiatives tend to be very focused and short- to medium-term rather than long term. We recommend that the option for districts to create some type of district-wide educational initiative be included in the funding structure, but with the condition that such initiatives be limited to a maximum of two percent of the district's overall budget.

Federal program services (that cannot legally be devolved to schools).   There are some federal, and perhaps even state categorical program service responsibilities that cannot legally be devolved to school sites. In addition, for those that can, particularly under the federal law that allows districts to consolidate Title I, Eisenhower, Bilingual Education and several other programs at the school level, states must seek permission for schools to merge such funds to provide more co-herent services at the site level. Currently, funds and services under the Federal Individuals with Disabilities Education Act are not part of the aforementioned consolidation program, but could be consolidated as long as IEPs were modified to reflect that services are being provided in a more inclusive and coherent school environment. In any case, this budget category would cover all remaining federal and state categorical programs that cannot be devolved to school sites.

Optional District Functions

The chapter also recommends that 22 additional functions be identified as op-tional district functions (Figure 10.3). These are functions that could be adminis-tered by the central office but which also could be devolved over time.

Student meals and food services.   Providing meals and other food services, both for students eligible for free or reduced lunches and for students who purchase their meals, often can be provided more efficiently by districts. Districts tend to have the ability to negotiate lower prices by purchasing food in larger quantities. Districts might also be able to negotiate better prices with companies if they de-cide to outsource the food services function to a private firm.

On the other hand, school meals are not known for their high quality. Fur-ther, many districts operate their own food services program even though they lack quality management expertise for this activity. Many schools in Victoria, Aus-tralia, where the education system was decentralized four years ago, lost money when they ran their own food services function but made money when they sub-contracted the function to a private contractor (Odden and Odden, 1996b). There are anecdotal examples of similar practices in schools in the United States, particularly charter schools. For example, the Vaughn Street Charter School in Los Angeles claimed to have saved tens of thousands of dollars the first year they operated their own food program, outside of the district program, by adopting the management techniques recommended by a food services consultant.

In short, although food services and school meals often can be provided most efficiently to all schools by the district, scenarios can be constructed that

FIGURE 10.3   Optional District Functions

Function	Budget
1. Food services	
2. Insurance and workers compensation	
3. Business support services—fiscal, accounting, payroll	
4. Business support services—personnel records and administration	
5. Business support services—purchasing, invoicing, audit	
6. Instructional administration: categorical programs	
7. Specialist staff—if they travel across buildings	
8. Substitute teachers—long term and/or short term	
9. Services for the severely disabled	
10. Community services	
11. Instructional support, curriculum development, and supervision	
12. Instructional support—professional development for administrators and leaders	
13. Instructional support—professional development for teachers	
14. Instructional support—media: computer, printer and software purchase, and support	
15. Pupil support services: counseling, psychologists, social workers, attendance, other	
16. Pupil support services: health services, nurses, etc.	
17. Major facilities renovation	
18. Minor facilities renovation	
19. School operations costs	
20. School maintenance costs	
21. Salary transition	
22. Extracurricular sports	

would have schools providing better and cheaper meals. Thus this function is recommended as an optional district function.

Liability and comprehensive insurance and workers compensation.   This function covers both liability insurance for teachers, administrators, and school council members and comprehensive insurance for fire, theft, vandalism, or other damage to school property. In many if not most cases, districts should be able to negotiate more cost-effective insurance rates for all their schools, as compared to having each school individually negotiate for insurance needs. An insurance company can usually lower the price to a district since the insurance package would be larger and the risk for any one school would be spread over a larger number of schools. Thus, in many cases it would be cost-effective to have insurance remain a district function.

However, in many instances, it would be to the advantage of schools to negotiate their own insurance coverage. First, specific insurance needs vary by school site; a districtwide contract would require each school essentially to have the same insurance package. Second, individual schools could produce a school-specific record through their own effort that would qualify it for a lower insurance rate. For example, vandalism and theft are generally high in urban districts thus triggering higher-than-average insurance rates. But individual schools, even in high-crime neighborhoods, could create programs or community involvement strategies that dramatically reduce vandalism and theft and should be allowed to enjoy the fiscal benefits of such efforts through lower insurance costs.

For these reasons, the chapter recommends that districts be given the option of devolving insurance responsibility to sites. Of course, an intermediate strategy would be for the district to negotiate prices and to devolve insurance funds to each school site, allowing each site to purchase the insurance package it desires based on the needs of the specific school.

The argument for workers compensation is generally the same: that such costs could be lower if provided on a district-wide basis by spreading risk over all schools. But individual schools could reduce the need for workers compensation, and there are many examples across the country of individual schools actually doing so. This, too, is a function that districts could choose to retain or devolve, depending on the context of the district and its individual schools, and perhaps the desires of the different schools.

Business support services.   Given the powers and capabilities provided by today's computer technologies, it would be wise for districts—indeed, it would be wise for the state—to create a computer software system that could automate the processing elements of business services: purchasing, invoicing, maintaining personnel records, payroll, etc. This still leaves many elements of the business office, such as negotiating contracts, purchasing in bulk, etc., which could remain a central office function. On the other hand, many schools believe for reasons of timeliness, quality, and choice that they can purchase materials more inexpensively on their own. Thus, aside from creating and operating the information system and the processing functions that accompany it, reasonable arguments could be made to either devolve or to retain central office business functions.

Instructional administration: categorical program monitoring.   Districts legally will retain the responsibility for monitoring categorical program implementation, but they do not have to retain any role in categorical program implementation, such as working on categorical program quality or even writing proposals for, or reports about, the district's or school's categorical programs. Other than providing categorical funds to schools as part of the formula for distributing the school budget, the district role in categorical program administration has a weaker rationale and, just as with the role for curriculum supervision, could well be a function fully devolved to schools over a relatively short time frame.

Traveling specialist staff. These costs are expended within the regular instruction budget. Many districts provide art, music, physical education, and even librarian staff to small schools on a part-time basis; often, these staff travel from school to school to provide their specialist services. The dollars for these staff, and the functions they perform, could simply become part of the school-based funding formula, or the staff could be retained at the district level and the services could be provided to schools under the authority of the central office.

Substitute teachers. Many would argue that substitute teacher costs, generally part of regular instruction, should be borne by the district, especially the need for long-term substitute teachers. But again, most places that have implemented a decentralized education system have quickly devolved the responsibility for substitute teachers and the revenue streams for substitutes to school sites. In England, districts often purchase insurance to protect themselves against the need for long-term substitutes. Districts can negotiate the insurance rates for such coverage, devolve the funds to schools, and encourage schools to purchase the insurance. Further, when schools have the responsibility for providing substitute teachers, they often become quite clever in providing it, and generally the need for substitute teachers is reduced. Schools that are successful in reducing the money spent on substitute teachers and who have control over that revenue stream have thus created for themselves a new revenue source that they can allocate towards some other more pressing school priority.

Special education for the more severely disabled. Although the district would retain the financial responsibility for the services required by all disabled students, including severely disabled students, they could devise a variety of structures for providing the services. Indeed, districts could develop special programs in selected schools to serve these students or provide these services through other special mechanisms. As both Victoria, Australia, and England implemented their school-based management and financing strategies, districts (LEAs) adopted the full range of possibilities for this function and the revenues supporting it, including full retention at the center, partial devolution to schools, and full devolution to schools. Each state should determine the type of service provision for severely disabled students that best meets the needs of its districts' unique contexts.

Community services. Both schools and districts provide services that are expended in the community services budget area. The funds for the school portion, which tends to comprise the bulk of these expenditures, should be sent to schools, but the funds for district provided community services activities, such as perhaps adult education, could be retained at the central office.

Instructional support: curriculum development and supervision. Districts clearly have a role to play in creating clear and high-quality curriculum content and student performance standards. But, their role in actually developing curriculum units or other elements of curriculum is less clear. A school-based reform strategy, particularly one that involves each school implementing its version of a high-performance school vision with a high-standards curriculum at its core, assumes that schools have the concomitant responsibility to decide on the specific instructional and curriculum approaches that they will use. This was a finding of a five-year study of school restructuring (Newmann and Wehlage, 1995) and is a key feature of each high-performance school design of the New American Schools (New American Schools, 1995; Stringfield, Ross, and Smith, 1996). To be sure, districts could provide ideas, advice, and even materials to schools, but they could simply devolve those tasks to schools. Thus, some or all of this function could be retained, or some or all of this function could be devolved to school sites.

Because school sites have more curriculum responsibility in a school-based reform strategy and can adopt different strategies for their curriculum approach, the rationale for a district role in curriculum *supervision* is called into question even more strongly. This function could well be one that would be retained at the district in the early years of a decentralization strategy and then devolved to schools over a fairly short time period.

Instructional support: professional development. In most districts, the large bulk of professional development is controlled by the district. But as argued in Chapter 7, there are clear divisions in professional development roles and responsibilities in a site-managed system. There are appropriate central office roles (e.g., training principals and leaders in management and fiscal skills), and there are roles that should be under the control of the school (e.g., training in specific instructional strategies). Further, schools should be given the authority to purchase the professional development they need from any appropriate source; for example, if they are implementing a high-performance school design such as those that are part of the New American Schools, they could hire experts from a design team, or from a variety of other national school reform networks. Schools could also purchase training from the central office on a fee-for-service basis if the central professional development unit provided desired training programs. These are some of the reasons why neither the professional development function nor professional development financing should be predetermined by the state as a district or school activity. Decisions about how this function should be handled could vary quite dramatically across the diverse districts in most states, and there likely would be differences linked to school district size, geographical location, and nature of education improvement strategy selected.

Instructional support: media, technology purchase, and support.   Many districts believe that it is a district responsibility not only to create the technology infrastructure to support school use of computer technologies, but also to purchase computers, printers, video, software, and other computer-based courseware for each school. However, research is fairly strong in concluding that schools should choose their own computer and software in order to increase the probability that it will be strongly linked to the school's instructional program and used by teachers. Again, this is a function that could remain at the district or could be decentralized to school sites, depending on the desires of different districts in the state.

Whether it's a district or site responsibility, the education system will need to invest in computer technologies, software, upgrades for each, and maintenance of the overall system on an annual basis for many years into the future. Therefore, the budget system at both the district and the school sites should be structured to identify the degree to which this need will receive resource attention.

Pupil support services: counselors, social workers, psychologists, nurses, etc. This chapter generally recommends that the budgets for these individuals and services be decentralized to schools. Sometimes school districts provide the services of these categories of pupil support professionals to schools on a formula basis; under this structure, the professionals are considered site-staff and are managed at the site. In other districts, these staffing positions remain central office positions, and the individuals in those positions provide services to school on a hourly or daily basis. In many high-performance school designs, these functional responsibilities are integrated into broader teacher roles, and the funds used to support these positions are used for other purposes (Odden, 1997a). Thus, districts could make many different decisions about these staffing positions and how these functions could be provided in a site-managed system.

Major and minor facilities renovation.   The conventional wisdom would retain facilities repair at the district level. But here, too, the practice in places that have adopted a school-based financing policy tends to be devolution of this function to school sites. To be sure, the responsibility for completely renovating a school in significant disrepair should remain with the district. But short of that drastic scenario, arguments could be made for devolving both major and minor facilities repair or allowing districts to determine how much of this function could be devolved. For example, many districts in England devolve facilities repair or enhancements under a certain dollar amount (or certain pound amount in the British context); others fix up all buildings in the short term and then completely devolve future facilities repairs to the schools. Further, many school sites invest considerable funds in upgrading the school building, including adding classrooms. Thus, both major and minor facility repair is another function that could be addressed at either the site or district level; thus, the decision for doing so should be left to each local district.

Operations and maintenance costs.   These are the costs for electricity, heating, telephones, cleaning, and other necessities to operate and maintain school buildings on an ongoing basis. Most districts manage these operations from the central office, although most operations staff are located at school sites. However, districts often do not keep school-specific records for utility costs, so they do not know the actual costs for each building. Further, if a building requires less than the average operations and maintenance services, and thus spends below the average, districts rarely return the saved funds to schools and allow them to use the funds for other purposes.

Although it takes some new expertise to manage these site operations and maintenance activities, they can be taught and learned in a relatively short time. The practice in Edmonton, Victoria, and England has been to devolve these functions and the revenues supporting them to school sites, and that is the recommendation made by this chapter. Nevertheless, this function is placed in this category of potentially retained functions within the potential school budget to let each district decide for itself to what degree they will devolve this function to their school sites and phase it in over time.

Salary transition funding.   A critically important issue in designing and implementing a school-based financing system involves expensing staff salaries. The question is whether to charge schools for the actual salary of each person in a school or the district-average salary for the position that each individual holds. The fact is that individual teacher salaries differ depending upon the years of experience and the number of education units the teacher has earned. Further, the average mix of years of experience and education units varies quite dramatically across schools, and these differences lead to differences in resources provided to schools. When most districts resource schools by a staffing formula, giving schools with equivalent students the same number of staff, they actually provide more dollars to schools whose staff have above-average years of experience and education units and provide fewer dollars to schools with less senior or less-educated staff.

Each state will need to decide whether to continue this inequitable distribution of resources, by charging each school for the average rather than the actual teacher salary, or over some time period, change to charging the actual teacher salary. While schools would not get the same amount of money under the latter approach, that strategy would reflect a policy of more fairly distributing resources. However, it would need to be phased-in over a multiple-year time period in order to let schools with above-average salaries manage their staff costs. The fact that some sites might choose to save money by hiring lower-priced, inexperienced teachers reinforces the need to have a strong accountability system that provides rewards and sanctions based on results to help ensure that schools select the strategies that produce the largest impacts on system results and the school performance agreement.

This recommendation flows from the experience of others. Although Edmonton, Canada, and Victoria, Australia, have charged for the average teacher salary, they are reconsidering this policy. From the beginning, England has charged schools for the actual teacher salary, but provided for transition to this policy. Initially, England thought it would take five years to implement a policy of charging for the actual teacher salary, but it actually took seven years. In the United States, Los Angeles is under a court decree to charge each school for the actual salary; the court allowed the district seven years to transition from their previous system of resourcing schools via a staffing formula to resourcing via a per-pupil formula and requiring each school to manage their salary costs within their equal per-pupil base budgets.

This chapter recommends that states adopt a policy of having each district charge schools for actual teacher salary costs, and allow them to transition into this system over a seven-year time period. This budget category simply includes the funds districts would need to augment the budgets of schools with above-average salary costs, which should phase to zero over the seven-year transition period, and should be a relatively small amount within as few as three to four years.

This chapter also recommends that the employee benefits charges, now often included as a component of a separate expenditure item called fixed charges, be tracked to individual staff and that charges reflect actual salaries and benefits for each individual. Compensation costs are the sum of salary and benefits and should not be completely separated, but they should follow each individual and be charged as a pair.

Extracurricular sports. This is a complicated function, generally included in regular instruction. Some might be concerned that if these dollars are devolved to schools, then some schools might decide to deemphasize competitive sports. On the other hand, most team sports are school-specific, so it would make sense to give the budget for this activity to each site. Although the state could mandate how this function should be handled, it would make better sense to let each community and thus each school district debate and discuss this issue, and decide which portion, if not all, would be retained by the district and which portion, if not all, would be decentralized to the school site.

Summary. There could well be other types of functions that districts could decide to retain and finance. But the above represent the major categories that are likely to be retained, based on the experiences of other places that have implemented a school-based budgeting system. Further, if states adopt a policy of requiring 70 percent devolution initially and ultimately a minimum of 84 percent over an eight-year time period, then districts would need to incrementally devolve more and more functions and their supporting revenues over that implementation period. Since most states have literally hundreds of diverse districts, each with different community desires and different district and school contexts, the proposed framework would permit each district to choose which functions and services to retain or to devolve and would require that a maximum of 16 percent of the operating budget be retained after the eight-year phase-in period.

4. THE SCHOOL BUDGET

In this context, the school budget is the amount of money actually provided to school sites in a lump sum. This section first discusses the major types of functions that would accompany the school budget and then describes how we recommend that districts design the formula they would use to determine each site's school budget.

Functions Devolved to School Sites

The above identification of both core and optional district functions may appear to include a significant number of functions. But given the experience in other places, over time this will reflect only a small portion of the overall district budget, and the rest of the budget will be devolved to schools. Further, because the largest two functions, instruction and school administration, actually comprise an average of 65 percent of the education budget in most districts, a number of functions that remain at the district reflect only small dollar amounts. Therefore, it is useful to have an understanding of the types of functions and services that most likely would be devolved to schools in most districts. The following is one such listing. It should be considered representative of those areas that have changed to school-based budgeting, but should not be construed as an exhaustive list of functions that could be devolved to schools:

- School administration,
- Regular instruction (i.e., regular-classroom teaching staff),
- Categorical program teaching, such as those in vocational education, compensatory education (Title I), special education for the mild to moderately disabled, bilingual education, desegregation, gifted and talented, etc.,
- Instructional aides from both the general fund and other funds,
- Curriculum development and supervision, and teacher supervision,
- Instructional materials including textbooks, workbooks, paper, supplies, etc.,
- Professional development determined by the site,
- Technology including computers, software, printers, video, etc.,
- Guidance counselors, social workers, and psychologists,
- Clerical and other administrative staff,
- Staff travel,
- Transportation for school activities, and
- School-improvement planning and implementation.

Again, these are the functions that have the highest probability for being devolved to school sites. Certainly the first three, school administration, regular instruction, and categorical program instruction, would very likely be devolved in most districts. Most districts would probably devolve the other functions in the list as well. But the strength of the proposed framework is that all of the above specific decisions would be made by each district, within the constraints proposed, which include determining the mandatory and optional district functions and devolving a minimum percentage of the overall operating district budget. This flexibility allows the state school-based financing framework to structure the process of devolution for all districts, while providing each district considerable autonomy to tailor the specifics to their unique community context.

The School Budget

Once districts determine the proportion of the budget that they will distribute to school sites, they still need a process and formula for determining each school's specific dollar amount. States also should structure this step for each district.

First, we recommend that states require each district to budget a minimum of 85 percent of the school budget to schools through a weighted-pupil formula. Districts should be able to set weights for pupils according to school level (e.g., elementary, middle or high school) and educational need (e.g., low-income, limited English proficient, mild disabilities such as learning disabled and mildly mentally handicapped, gifted and talented, vocational education, etc.). The remaining funds could be provided to schools on the basis of a variety of different but measurable factors such as size, square footage of buildings or school lands, historical utilities costs, other special circumstances and conditions, or even a lump sum to each school to cover the basic costs of a principal for very small school sites.

This approach requires that the bulk of school dollars be determined on the basis of a weighted-student count, but again allows districts the discretion to consider the unique needs and requirements of their schools, which could vary dramatically across both districts and schools. Districts know very well that no single formula is sufficient to ensure that each school has the funds it needs, particularly very small schools. By providing districts the authority to budget a percentage of site funds on a basis other than the number of weighted students, states would allow each district to address the unique and sometimes idiosyncratic needs of particular schools.

Odden (1999) shows how this general procedure has been used by four localities in the United States (Broward County, Florida; Cincinnati, Ohio; Pittsburgh, Pennsylvania; and Seattle, Washington) and one city in Canada (Edmonton [Alberta, Canada]). These districts made very different decisions about the portion of the district budget that would be devolved to schools, ranging from 49.2 percent in Seattle to 80.9 percent in Edmonton, figures substantially below the nearly 90 percent of the budget that is devolved to school sites in England.

Drawing on the formulas in the five districts, Odden (1999) shows that once the amount that would be budgeted to school sites had been determined, the formulas for doing so had five general elements:

- a base allocation for the "norm" student,
- adjustments for grade-level differences,
- enhancements for curriculum purposes,
- adjustments for different student needs, and
- adjustments for different and unique school needs.

Overall, these elements mirror the general categories of state-to-district funding formulas; the interesting fact is that each of the districts discussed had all of these elements and often times several adjustments for each element. For example, under the curriculum enhancement category, districts provided extra funds for magnet schools, vocational education, dropout prevention, foreign language, and numerous small, targeted curriculum enhancements. In the different student-need categories, each district had multiple, elaborate, and extensive adjustments for students from low socioeconomic backgrounds, low-achieving students, students with disabilities, students with limited proficiency in English, and dropouts. Under the special school needs, each district had some type of or multiple augmentations for small school size; the most common approach was to provide each school, regardless of size, a flat lump sum that was sufficient to provide a principal, office secretary, and perhaps even core staffing. In short, these districts created relatively comprehensive and sophisticated mechanisms for formula funding their school sites, and the formulas addressed not only core educational needs but also additional educational needs related to curriculum, students, and school sites.

Perhaps the most surprising finding for the formulas were the adjustments for different grade levels. The common practice across the world is to provide more funds for secondary than for primary schools (OECD, 1997), and the typical pattern in the United States is to provide about 25–30 percent more for high schools as compared to elementary schools (see Chapter 4). Indeed, one of the primary contentions that has emerged as government funding has been shifted to the school site has been the higher funding of secondary students (Odden and Busch, 1998, Chapters 4 and 5). The formulas in these five districts took very different approaches to this issue (Table 10.1). Pittsburgh was the only district to provide such differential funding to secondary students. The other districts either provided no or very small distinctions between elementary and secondary students (Edmonton and Broward County), or actually weighted the system in favor of elementary school students (Seattle). In this sense, the grade-level weights in the five school districts studied represented quite different resource allocation decisions.

Although the grade-level weights adopted by these five jurisdictions cannot be taken as indicative of practice across North America, they nevertheless reflect a major fiscal value shift in the basic allocation of resources for these districts, away from the traditional bias of funding secondary students at higher levels toward a new bias of greater funding for elementary students, particularly elementary students in grades K–3. The rationale for this shift in resource allocation is

TABLE 10.1 Weight 1.0 Allocation and Grade-Level Weights in Five North American Districts

	Broward County	Cincinnati	Edmonton	Pittsburgh	Seattle
Allocation for Students with Weight of 1.0	Elementary: $1,868 Middle: $1,931 High: $1,802 Applied to Weighted FTE	Elementary: $3,051 Middle: $3,488 K–8: $3,334 High: $3,011	K–12: $3,127 Applied to Weighted FTE	K–12: $4,632 Applied to Weighted Pupils	K–12: $2,441 Applied to Weighted Pupils
	Pupil Weight	Pupil Weight	Pupil Weight	Pupil Weight	Pupil Weight
Grade K	1.234 (1.00)	1.01	1.0	1.0	1.0
Grade 1	1.234 (1.00)	1.01	1.0	1.0	1.0
Grade 2	1.234 (1.00)	1.01	1.0	1.0	1.0
Grade 3	1.234 (1.00)	1.01	1.0	1.0	1.0
Grade 4	1.0 (0.83)	1.01	1.0	1.0	0.94
Grade 5	1.0 (0.83)	1.01	1.0	1.0	0.94
Grade 6	1.0 (0.83)	1.01	1.0	1.384	0.87
Grade 7	1.0 (0.83)	1.15	1.0	1.384	0.87
Grade 8	1.0 (0.83)	1.16	1.0	1.384	0.87
Grade 9	1.179 (0.96)	1.0	1.03	1.505	0.88
Grade 10	1.179 (0.96)	1.0	1.03	1.505	0.88
Grade 11	1.179 (0.96)	1.0	1.03	1.505	0.88
Grade 12	1.179 (0.96)	1.0	1.03	1.505	0.88

Source: Odden, 1999.

that it is most important to develop basic skills early in the elementary career of a child, under the assumption that if students can read, write, and do mathematics proficiently by grade three, teachers at higher grades will have a much greater chance of reaching student achievement expectations. Of course, this also reflects a shift away from late intervention for secondary students who have not developed good literacy and numeracy skills, as it is not only inefficient but also very difficult to make effective. We should note that these practices also reveal the regional differences in staffing discussed in Chapter 8.

The five districts also had elaborate adjustments for special-pupil needs (Table 10.2). Although all four U.S. districts received substantial funds for low-achieving students in low-income communities from the federal Title I program and provided those funds to each school site, both Pittsburgh and Seattle supplemented this provision with budget augmentations based on sociodemographic condition. Seattle provided extra weights for students eligible for the federal free and reduced-price lunch program, a program that provides free lunches to students from a family with an income below the poverty level (about $16,000 for a family of four) and reduced-price lunches for students from families with an income up to 150 percent of the poverty level (about $24,000), recognizing that poverty is a general indicator of the need for additional services. For grade levels, the weights were 0.087, 0.109, and 0.18 providing $212, $266, and $439 for elementary, middle, and high school students, respectively. The Pittsburgh program averaged the percent of students in a school eligible for free or reduced-price lunch with the percentage of students not living with both parents, multiplied that percentage times the school enrollment, and provided an extra $400 for each such student. Both of these amounts were in addition to the Title I school allocation, which is provided according to a different formula, and can reach $900 per pupil in high-poverty schools. Neither Broward County, Cincinnati, nor Edmonton provided an additional amount based on these factors, though Cincinnati was considering adding such an adjustment.

Broward County and Pittsburgh also provided extra resources for students scoring below certain levels on the district's test of student achievement. Broward County provided this enhancement only for middle and high schools, and splits the district's approximately $2 million among the numbers of students scoring below the 18th percentile on the reading and math portions of the Stanford Achievement Test. Pittsburgh provided a small extra weight for students scoring at or below the 30th percentile. The weight was larger the lower the percentile (i.e., the lower the achievement), and the weight was larger for students in grades 9–12 than it is for students in grades K–8. The dilemma in providing funding adjustments based on actual student achievement is that the funding is lost when achievement is improved. So unless the achievement score is based on performance from another level of schooling, the workings of such a funding augmentation can sometimes be awkward.

In sum, as districts have adopted school-based funding formulas, they have created comprehensive and sophisticated structures. Many of these share commonalities with current state-to-district school finance formulas, suggesting that

TABLE 10.2   Pupil-Specific Factors for Economic or Education Disadvantage in Five North American Districts

	Broward County	Cincinnati	Edmonton	Pittsburgh	Seattle
Local funding of high needs based on socio-demographic condition	NA	Title I funds %Pov / $/Pupil <50 / 210 50–60 / 325 60–70 / 375 70–80 / 420 80–85 / 500 85–90 / 590 >90 / 640	NA	Average of percent of students (1) eligible for free/reduced lunch and (2) not residing with both parents, times enrollment, times $400 per pupil	Extra weight of 0.087 for grades K–5, 0.18 for grades 6–8, and 0.109 for grades 9–12, based on number of students eligible for free and reduced lunch.
Test Scores	Total district allocation of $1.938 million for non-Title I middle and high schools: *Middle schools:* 75% of number of students scoring below 18th percentile on reading and math portion of Stanford Achievement Test. *High Schools:* 75% of the number of 10th grade pupils scoring below 18th percentile on math and/or reading portion of 9th grade Stanford Achievement Test.	NA	NA	NA	0–10 percentile: extra weight of 0.05 for grades 1–8, and 0.12 for grades 9–12. 11–20 percentile: extra weight of 0.03 for grades 1–8, and 0.08 for grades 9–12. 21–30 percentile: extra weight of 0.02 for grades 1–8, and 0.04 for grades 9–12.

Source: Odden, 1999.

NA = not applicable.

while it is a very involved process, it is not entirely foreign to the U.S. education system. Rather, it is a matter of devolving authority even further.

Example of a School Formula

The proposed framework provides districts wide freedom in designing the specific formula they would use to calculate each school's budget. Districts should be encouraged to construct as simple a formula as possible so that it may be easily understood, while still providing a fair and equitable amount to each school site. The initial experience in places around the world that have moved to a school-based financing structure is that districts create quite complex overall allocation formulas, often using multiple formulas even for small portions of the budget. Over time, districts learn that simpler formulas can be designed to produce about the same distribution of revenues, and begin to redesign their formulas according to these simpler structures.

The following is one example of a simple yet comprehensive version of a school-site formula. The proposed grade-level weights reflect those currently used in many states: 0.5 for a kindergarten half-day student, 1.0 for each full-day kindergarten and grades 4–5 student, 1.2 for students in grades 1–3 and grades 6–8, and 1.3 for each grade 9–12 student.

A. Lump sum: $100,000 for elementary schools
                 $150,000 for middle schools
                 $200,000 for high schools
B. Base allocation and pupil weights:
                 Base allocation = $2,800
                 1.0 for grades K, 4–5
                 1.2 for grades 1–3
                 1.2 for grades 6–8
                 1.3 for grades 9–12
   Extra weights for special need:
                 0.4 for compensatory education
                 1.3 for all categories combined of disabled students
                 0.2 for limited English proficient students
C. Special factors:
                 square footage of buildings or land
                 unique school needs
                 special programs for the severely disabled

The base allocation could be determined as follows. Assume before designing the formula, the district provided one teacher for every 25 students, plus an extra 20 percent for planning and preparation time. For a school with 625 pupils, this would require 25 teachers for the school; at a cost of $50,000 in salaries and benefits for each teacher, this would total about $1 million, or $2,000 per student.

Assume the district also provides one principal ($80,000), two secretaries ($50,000), and $20,000 in materials and supplies; this would total $150,000 or $300 per student. Assume the district provided a guidance counselor, family outreach counselor, nurse, one reading tutor, and $50,000 in instructional aides; this would total another $250,000 or $500 per student. Adding this amount together would total $2,800 for the base allocation per pupil.

The 0.4 weight for low-income students would produce $1,120 extra (0.4 times $2,800) for each low-income student, and the bilingual weight of 0.2 would provide an extra $560 for each limited English proficient student. These weights applied against the base allocation would provide dollar amounts that are sufficient for schools to deploy program strategies that are effective for helping such students learn to standards, as we discussed in Chapter 4.

For a K–5 elementary school with 500 students (about 83 students in each grade), 50 percent of them low-income and 10 percent disabled, this formula would provide a lump-sum budget as follows:

$$\$100,000 + \$2,800[84(1.0) + 250(1.2) + 166(1.0) + (0.50)(500)(0.4) + 500(0.10)(1.3)]$$
$$+ \text{ unique factors,}$$

or, $100,000 + $2,800 (84 + 300 + 166 + 100 + 65) + unique factors,
or, $100,000 + $2,800 (715) + unique factors,
or $100,000 + $2,002,000 + unique factors,
or $2,102,000 + any unique budget factors.

In short, this formula shows that the school would receive a lump sum of about $2.102 million plus any budgets for unique factors.

Of course, the above is just one example. Formulas could be more or less elaborate, and the weights and base allocation amounts could be different across districts. The weights and base allocation levels also would be constrained by the size of the total budget, the functions, and their revenues that are retained at the district, and the size of the actual school budget.

CONCLUSION

Each state's school-based financing framework should require each district to develop and make public its specific responses to the requirements previously discussed in this chapter. Further, the state should require each district to provide an annual budget and expenditure report for all of the above functions, for both the district and for each school. It should be noted that in the combined list of functions in Figure 10.4, school sites could have expenditures for all functional categories below those identified as required district functions. Such annual fiscal reporting would provide detailed information on both school-level spending and district-level spending, and the amounts spent at each level of different functions.

FIGURE 10.4   Budget Functions/Categories for Both Districts and School Sites

Required District Functions	Budget Amount
1. Board of Education	
2. Office of the Superintendent	
3. Information systems, quality benchmarks	
4. Accountability system	
5. Developing IEPs	
6. Monitoring federal/state categorical programs	
7. Home-to-school transportation	
8. Legal services	
9. LEA education initiatives	
10. Federal program services not devolved	

Optional District/Site Functions	Budget
1. Food services	
2. Insurance and workers compensation	
3. Business support services—fiscal, accounting, payroll	
4. Business support services—personnel records and administration	
5. Business support services—purchasing, invoicing, audit	
6. Instructional administration: categorical programs	
7. Specialist staff—if they travel across buildings	
8. Substitute teachers—long term and/or short term	
9. Services for the severely disabled	
10. Community services	
11. Instructional support, curriculum development, and supervision	
12. Instructional support—professional development for administrators and leaders	
13. Instructional support—professional development for teachers	
14. Instructional support—media: computer, printer and software purchase, and support	
15. Pupil support services: counseling, psychologists, social workers, attendance, other	

FIGURE 10.4   Budget Functions/Categories for Both Districts and School Sites *(continued)*

Optional District/Site Functions	Budget
16. Pupil support services: health services, nurses, etc.	
17. Major facilities renovation	
18. Minor facilities renovation	
19. School operations costs	
20. School maintenance costs	
21. Salary transition	
22. Extracurricular sports	

Site Functions	Budget
1. School administration	
2. Regular instruction	
a. Regular-classroom teachers	
b. Regular-education specialists, such as art, music, etc.	
3. Categorical programs	
a. Compensatory education	
b. Programs for the disabled	
c. Programs for limited english proficient students	
d. Gifted and talented	
e. Other	
4. Instructional aides	
5. Tutors	
6. Instructional facilitators	
7. Curriculum development/supervision	
8. Teacher supervision	
9. Professional development determined by site	
10. Technology including computers, printers, etc.	
11. Guidance counselors, psychologists, social workers, etc.	
12. Family outreach and support	
13. Clerical and other administrative staff	
14. Transportation for school-provided services	
15. School-improvement planning, implementation, evaluation	

Figure 10.4 summarizes the three lists of functions discussed in previous sections. It indicates the full range of decisions districts must make in determining the total amount of money that would be devolved to schools, the likely functions that would be devolved to schools in that process, and both district and site expenditures by function.

— *Chapter 11* ———————————————————

Changing Teacher Salary Structures*

The major external reward in most education systems around the country is the salary paid to each individual teacher and administrator. Salary and benefit expenditures comprise about 85 percent of the average district's operating budget, and teacher salaries and benefits alone comprise about 50 percent of the education budget (National Commission on Teaching and America's Future, 1996; Wood, Thompson, Picus, and Tharpe, 1995). Put a different way, 50 cents of every dollar expended on public education is spent on teacher salaries and benefits, making it all the more important to spend that money wisely. Therefore, the question for this chapter is whether the current teacher salary structure, which provides pay increases on the basis of education units, degrees, and years of experience, could be altered to function more as a direct incentive to enhance the productivity of the education system.

Recall that the management portion of Chapter 7 identified rewards—largely salaries—as a key ingredient for making school-based management work. This suggests that redesigning the current structure of teacher salaries could be part of an effort to make school-based management work better. Further, as identified in Chapter 9, new approaches to teacher salaries could function as a major external incentive that would reinforce current education reform strategies. Bolstering this claim, Kelley (1997) argued that the current single-salary structure, which provides salary increases on the basis of the number of steps (years of experience) and the number of lanes (education units and/or degrees), though appropriate for the time in which it was created, is not supportive of current

° This chapter draws from the following: Odden and Kelley (1997); Milanowski, Odden, and Youngs (1998); and Odden (1998).

403

education reform, and that it has not been supportive of education reforms for the past two or three decades. She further showed how the salary structure in any organization, but particularly for schools, can be made to align more with the goals, management, worker roles, and other elements of an organization's overall strategy, and suggested quite strongly that it may be time to rethink how teachers are paid.

Outside of education, many organizations have found that providing pay on the basis of entry-level skills and years of experience, basically the way teachers (and administrators) have been paid, is inappropriate for a fast-paced environment when results matter and the knowledge and skills of workers need to change rapidly over time (Lawler, 1990; Schuster and Zingheim, 1992). Indeed, many high-performance organizations across America that are restructuring to produce higher levels of results are changing their compensation systems in two ways:

- First, they are replacing or modifying pay increments based on seniority or years of experience (and education units within education) to pay increments based on new knowledge, skills, and abilities. In this way, the pay system rewards individuals for developing and using the array of new expertise needed to produce greater results.
- Second, they are adding group-based performance bonuses for all individuals in a work organization that meets or exceeds annual improvement targets; such awards can be salary bonuses for improving performance or bonuses for maintaining quality but reducing costs, or both. These bonuses allow the pay system to, at least in part, reward people for improving the performance of the system.

School systems also are beginning to launch these new types of pay innovations. Several states and districts now provide bonuses to everyone in a school that meets or exceeds performance-improvement targets, and the notion of increased pay for knowledge and skills is also catching on quickly within education (see www.wcer.wisc.edu/cpre/). In short, high-performance organizations, including some school systems, are beginning to pay individuals for their knowledge, skills, and professional expertise, and to pay groups of individuals for improving system-wide performance.

1. LINK TO STANDARDS- AND SCHOOL-BASED EDUCATION REFORM

These kinds of changes in teacher compensation can be directly linked to the goals and strategies of standards- and school-based education reform, which as we have argued at several points in the book, is the dominant education reform strategy across the country. Odden and Conley (1992) and Mohrman, Mohrman, and Odden (1996) discuss how compensation can be restructured to reinforce this goal of boosting student performance and improving the education system.

The standards- and school-based education reform strategy has three strategic elements: (1) a focus on school performance and student achievement; (2) an emphasis on new curricula and the professional skills that they require for effective implementation; and (3) implementation at the school level and an understanding that schools need to be restructured to provide this type of teaching and thus produce the new level of student achievement. Each of these strategic elements could be reinforced by new teacher compensation elements.

First, focusing on results reminds teachers and educational organizations what needs to be achieved: higher levels of student achievement in core academic subjects. Student achievement is the complex result of individual differences and learning styles and educational experiences. In turn, educational experiences are a function of the overall organizational capabilities and the knowledge and skills of the teachers in the schools. By having the system focus on results, teachers know they need to work on developing the knowledge, skills, and abilities that allow them to improve student achievement.

Compensation practices can focus attention on results by tying them to rewards that are based on school-wide performance. Since the most effective schools are characterized by cooperative and collegial work, appropriate rewards would be based on school results, not individual performance (see also Lawler, 1990). One purpose of this chapter is to outline how such a school-based performance award program might work.

Second, research shows that while there is strong, positive teacher response to new ambitious curriculum standards, teachers generally do not have all of the knowledge, skills, and expertise needed to effectively teach this new curriculum (Goertz, Floden, and O'Day, 1995; Little, 1992). The new curriculum requires deeper and more conceptual understandings of curricula content; an array of new pedagogical strategies that focus on concept development and problem solving tailored to the developmental needs of each individual child; understanding of how these can be incorporated into curriculum units that can be aggregated into a schoolwide curriculum program; and a set of new assessment strategies that measure what students have achieved. Indeed, many teachers must engage in a "paradigm shift" from what and how they are now teaching to an entirely different mode of pedagogy (Cohen, McLaughlin, and Talbert, 1993). This will require new knowledge and expertise; some of this expertise will be common across all teachers, and some of this new expertise will vary by school context.

Creating this new professional expertise will require substantial investment of time and energy on the part of teachers and substantial investment of funds by the education system in ongoing professional development. Although enhancement of professional expertise provides an intrinsic reward to teachers, a change in the compensation structure to reward teachers who develop and use such new knowledge would also provide an extrinsic reward. Such a compensation structure could directly link funds spent on compensation to the expertise teachers need to effectively teach the new curriculum and increase student achievement.

A little later, this chapter addresses how knowledge and skills-based pay systems could be designed.

Third, the standards- and school-based education reform strategies require teachers to become much more involved in the management of the school, including how the school organizes the teaching and learning process, how the faculty develops a schoolwide instructional program that works with its students, and how the school redeploys resources for the specific school strategy. To engage in these leadership, management, and restructuring activities, teachers need an additional set of knowledge, skills, and expertise, which could be bolstered by knowledge and skill elements in a new compensation structure.

In short, the standards- and school-based education reform strategy suggests at least the following new elements for compensation: (1) knowledge and skills-based pay to develop the wide array of skills needed both to teach a rigorous high-standards curriculum and to engage in effective school-based management and (2) group performance awards for meeting specified improvements and results in school.

2. CHANGE TEACHER COMPENSATION TO INCLUDE PAY FOR KNOWLEDGE AND SKILLS

As currently designed, however, the typical single-salary schedule for teachers is either neutral to or only mildly supportive of the need for teachers to fundamentally change, enhance, and broaden their professional knowledge and skills. The current single salary pays teachers for earning additional units, but it does not ensure that these courses are related to their teaching or other school assignments. For example, teachers can increase their salary by earning a degree in educational administration that actually prepares teachers to leave the classroom. Research also shows that, on average, after the first few years of teaching, greater experience is not associated with more expertise and success in the classroom (Murnane, 1983).

A New Form of the Single-Salary Schedule

Most organizations outside of education also base annual salary increases on years of experience or seniority. But as these organizations restructure into higher-performing entities, they often also change their pay structure towards a system that pays directly for knowledge and skills needed in the work environment. These systems reward employees for developing demonstrable knowledge, skills, and abilities that enable organizational performance. As a result, these systems create a path for employees to the goal of higher performance by defining the skills needed for that performance and providing a structure of skill development via the knowledge and skills that are rewarded in the salary schedule. These skill-development strategies compliment group-based performance awards (see next section) by providing employees with the expertise needed to achieve organizational performance goals.

Such a knowledge- and skill-based pay system could similarly compliment standards- and school-based education reform: as discussed above, teachers need better content knowledge, more curriculum and instructional strategies, and new skills to engage productively in broader school-based management actions in order to accomplish ambitious education reform goals. If schools are likely to have difficulty in meeting student achievement standards because teachers lack the needed skills, a human resources strategy that included a pay system based on the knowledge and skills needed to improve student achievement could have a synergistic effect on performance (i.e., provide a pathway to higher performance). As previously argued in this book, engaging in opportunities to learn these new knowledge and skills is intrinsically motivating for teachers because they enjoy doing it and feel they are better professionals when they have expanded their professional repertoire (see Chapter 9 and Odden and Kelley, 1997). Adding salary increments for the development of such knowledge and skills would simply provide an extrinsic reward—more pay—to the intrinsic incentive of expanding one's knowledge and skills.

A Knowledge and Skill Pay Structure

A knowledge- and skill-based pay system requires two key elements: (1) clear descriptions of and standards for the knowledge and skills desired and (2) valid and reliable assessments that determine whether individual teacher's practice meets those standards. The Educational Testing Service (ETS) through its PRAXIS assessments (Dwyer, 1998), the Council of Chief State School Officers through its INTASC assessments (Moss, Schutz, and Collins, 1998), and the National Board for Professional Teaching Standards (Bond, 1998; Jaeger, 1998) are all developing such teaching standards and assessments (see also, Porter, Youngs and Odden, forthcoming).

Each has developed rich, detailed descriptions of teaching practice that indicated in comprehensive ways what teachers need to know and be able to do to show that their professional performance meets the standards. The PRAXIS III system outlines more general teaching strategies that would be required for beginning teachers (Dwyer, 1998). Its accompanying assessment system is based on classroom observations of teachers. ETS also has a two-part PRAXIS II system, one part of which includes over 50 tests of teacher content knowledge and the second part of which includes tests of teacher professional knowledge, such as how students learn complex content and pedagogical strategies to teach the content. Though initially the PRAXIS materials were meant to be used for licensing beginning teachers directly after university training, states are also using these instruments during the one- to three-year induction and mentoring period for new teachers.

The INTASC instruments include written descriptions of teaching practice in 11 different areas: mathematics, science, language arts, and history/social science at both the high school and middle school levels; general standards for elementary teachers; one for bilingual education; and one for special education. Each also has an assessment system based on a teacher-prepared portfolio of practice, which assesses the professional expertise of teachers to the written standards. INTASC also is developing content tests as well as tests of professional teaching knowledge; ETS is the contractor for the latter. Although INTASC too was designed originally as a way to license beginning teachers, it is now being sequenced in some states after some type of initial PRAXIS-type review procedure. The INTASC standards and assessments move beyond just general teaching strategies and probe content-specific pedagogical strategies.

Finally, the National Board for Professional Teaching Standards (NBPTS) (http://www.nbpts.org) has prepared standards and assessments in about 32 different areas, covering all the major content areas at all levels of teaching. Their goal was to identify accomplished practice of experienced teachers. The standards are lengthy: 30–50 pages of detailed descriptions of the professional practice of accomplished, experienced teachers. Their assessments include a rich portfolio of 10 individual exercises, including videotapes of the teachers teaching curriculum units, simulated exercises, and examples of schoolwide collegial work.

All three standards and assessments were designed for "high-stakes" purposes, either licensure or as a basis for higher pay or a gateway into leadership positions. These descriptions and assessments were also meant largely to be used on a national basis (i.e., they reflect a core set of instructional expertise that all teachers, regardless of state or district, should acquire). This is important because the cost and complexity of developing knowledge- and skill-based pay systems is high due to the effort needed to define the needed knowledge and skills and developing ways to assess them. Initial research also showed that the assessments had to meet standards for validity and reliability (Dwyer, 1998; Jaeger, 1998; Moss, et al., 1998; Porter, Youngs, and Odden, forthcoming).

The developmental processes for the PRAXIS III, INTASC, and NBPTS assessments included the significant amount time and effort needed to do it right. Thus it would make sense for states or districts to use the instruments throughout their human resource management system, such as staffing, training and development, and performance evaluation, even before pay is linked with knowledge and skills. Making compensation the last element to be linked provides development time and operational experience with the model before it becomes associated with high stakes. The link to pay then serves as a reinforcement, rather than the sole driver, of knowledge and skill development.

Indeed, the three sets of standards and assessments mentioned above were developed not with pay in mind, but in order to support staffing, performance evaluation, and professional development programs (PRAXIS III, INTASC) or to recognize and promote accomplished teaching practice (NBPTS). The next step is to link them to pay.

Recently, Charlotte Danielson, who was an ETS researcher, published a book that provides an additional needed element for crafting a knowledge- and skills-based pay system. Danielson (1998) has outlined a framework for instruction that bridges the entire career of a teacher, from novice to accomplished. This framework describes the elements of good instruction in four domains, 22 components, and several elements under each component. Because Danielson had worked on both the PRAXIS III assessment and several National Board assessments (as ETS is now the sole contractor that produces National Board assessments), her framework was designed to incorporate the best elements of both. The framework can serve as a district or state "core" structure to describe quality instruction. ETS also provides materials and training that can be used by districts to assess teacher practice to different levels of quality—basic, proficient, and advanced. Embellished by the PRAXIS and INTASC external assessments for beginning teachers and the National Board's external assessments for more experienced teachers, the combination provides a district or state with all core elements for constructing a knowledge- and skills-based pay system.

Table 11.1 shows how such a new system could be conceptualized; Odden and Kelly (1997) identify several other models. As in Table 11.1, initial licensure could be provided after graduation from college or university. Then there could be an extensive period for new teacher induction, training, and mentoring, during which all new teachers would be expected to enhance their professional expertise beyond its status at college graduation. States and districts would need to accompany this approach with substantial investments in new teacher professional development. During this time period, which could be one to two years for some teachers and much longer for others, there could be a series of knowledge and skills assessments—PRAXIS II content, PRAXIS II professional knowledge, Danielson Basic, PRAXIS III, Danielson Proficient, and INTASC—each of which could be used as the rationale for a salary increase based on acquisition of new knowledge and skills. The Danielson assessments would be internal to the district, and the others would be external. One or more of these assessments could be used for granting the full professional licensure; this step could then be accompanied with a more substantial salary increase, such as 10 percent.

TABLE 11.1   A Sequence of Knowledge and Skills for a New Teacher Salary Structure

Year	Assessment
0	Graduation from college, initial licensure
1–2	PRAXIS II Content Test
1–2	PRAXIS II Test of Professional Teaching Knowledge
2–3	Danielson Basic; PRAXIS III Assessment
2–4	Danielson Proficient; INTASC Assessment
3–5	Content Masters
5+	Danielson Advanced; state board certification; Second content minor; Second licensure in related field
6+	National Board certification
7+	Post-board-certification leadership

A state or district could decide that it wanted all teachers to advance their professional expertise to one of these levels, perhaps to the Danielson Proficient or the INTASC level. Meeting one or the other could even replace the tenure process in some places. Accomplishing this goal would also lead to a substantial salary rise.

Beyond this level, teachers could take many different approaches to continually improving their professional expertise. One would be earning a master's degree in their content area; another could be earning the equivalent of a minor in a second content area; a third would be to become licensed in a second and related content field and thus become more valuable to a school or district, which could recognize this value with another pay increase.

There is growing recognition that there is considerable distance between the performance required to meet the Danielson Proficient INTASC standards and the performance required to meet the National Board's standards. The Danielson Advanced level would provide one step. In addition, states could create a step, which could be called state board certification. In late 1998, teacher compensation commissions in both Delaware and Iowa were considering this option, which would be accompanied by another substantial pay increase.

Further, this is a time period during which peer review and assistance programs could be used. Indeed, in most organizations outside of education, assessment for salary increments is usually done via peer assessment (Heneman and Ledford, 1998), and several districts now use the Danielson framework for both of these purposes. This time period also could include skills needed for specific school designs or for local programs such as lead teacher, as found in the Cincinnati district, or outstanding teacher, as found in Douglas County, Colorado. Demonstrating acquisition of these skills would lead to a pay increase between that associated with a strong command of the basics and mastery of the teaching profession. Another possibility is to provide a pay increase for passing some, but not all, of the NBPTS assessments, or for achieving a score below the level currently required for certification but above some minimum.

Next would come board certification, which again could produce a large pay increase. For example, Iowa provides all board-certified teachers with a $10,000 pay increase for each of five years, and teachers in Los Angeles Unified School district earn a 15 percent pay increase when they earn board certification.

These national or state knowledge and skill "anchors" could be augmented with locally specified knowledge and skills as well. Districts like San Antonio, Texas, and New York City Community District #2, which provide years of reading training for all elementary teachers, could add acquisition of this expertise to a knowledge and skills pay structure. Further, there would be some knowledge and skills required due to the choice of a specific educational program or organizational form at the site level. Schools that choose to use national school reform designs, such as Roots and Wings or Modern Red Schoolhouse designs of the New American Schools Development Corporation (Stringfield, Ross, and Smith, 1996), may want teachers to develop skills particular to that school and curriculum approach. These skills could also be specified and assessed and be the basis for additional knowledge- and skill-based pay increases. A district also might want teachers to engage in broader roles including leadership, training, participation in financial management, and curriculum development. These skills could be identified and assessed at the local level.

Examples of Knowledge- and Skills-Based Pay Structures

All of the above represent opportunities for creating knowledge- and skill-based pay increases in a salary schedule. Douglas County, Colorado, has tried variations of these ideas for several years; two evaluation reports suggest the effort met with considerable success (Hall and Caffarella, 1996, 1998). In late 1997, Robbinsdale, Minnesota, approved a knowledge and skill pay structure for new teachers, which puts $15,000 of pay at stake for developing a broad array of knowledge and skills that range from locally identified needs to national skills embodied in the National Board. The National Board for Professional Teaching Standards offered the first opportunity to pay teachers for knowledge and skills. The following describes these innovations in more detail.

Douglas County, Colorado implemented a new pay plan in 1994–95, with several knowledge and skill elements, as well as performance elements.

First, the district offered a competitive base pay plan, designed to allow this growing district to attract new teachers.

Second, the district gave a knowledge credit for a specified number of hours of study after the teaching certificate had been acquired. This is similar to the lane element of current salary schedules (i.e., the degree credits portion).

Third, Douglas County teachers must annually receive a satisfactory evaluation. Annual experiential increases linked to length of service are no longer provided. Teachers must satisfy all criteria on new annual evaluations in order to receive the annual experience or step increase.

The other five elements of Douglas County's pay plan are voluntary incentives on top of the base salary structure, all designed to encourage and recognize teacher performance and development of knowledge and skills.

The fourth element invites teachers to apply each year to be designated as an outstanding teacher, which entitles them to a one-time-only $1,000 bonus. There are no quotas on the number of teachers who qualify; in 1995–96, 252 teachers (28 percent) submitted portfolios, and 246 were awarded the outstanding designation. The criteria Douglas County used was borrowed from the National Board for Professional Teaching Standards and focused on three areas: assessment and instruction, knowledge of content and pedagogy, and degree of collaboration and partnership.

The fifth component provides additional pay bonuses ($250–$350) for demonstrating mastery in specified skill blocks (for example, ClarisWorks spreadsheet training, authentic assessment, and gender and ethnic expectations).

While not yet fully implemented, the sixth component is a Master

Teacher designation. It was intended to mesh with the state changes in teacher licensure mandated in 1991. However, as of 1997, the state still had not established requirements for a master teacher.

The seventh component recognizes teachers for their extra duties through responsibility pay. Schools receive a pool of cash, $5.50 per student, and a teacher committee decides how the stipends are distributed.

Finally, a group incentive is available for outstanding performance. It is meant to encourage teacher groups to work cooperatively on common goals designed to improve student performance. A group submits its plan to the Group Incentive Board (GIB), which recommends revisions and grants final approval. At the end of the school year, the group must compile a final report on how the plan was enacted, its effect on students, and reflection on why certain goals may not have been met. The GIB then determines whether a bonus should be awarded.

The amount of money budgeted for group awards is small. Overall, the funding for these elements comprises less than 1 percent of teacher salary expenditures, but they have stimulated widespread activities focused on district and teacher priorities, and the program is quite popular among teachers.

Robbinsdale, Minnesota approved a new salary schedule in late 1997 that allows new teachers to earn up to an additional $15,000 based on a performance portfolio that is submitted to a six-person review committee. This knowledge- and skill-based pay element would be added to the teacher's base salary for a five-year time period, when it would be reviewed via portfolio for another five years. Teachers can choose from the following eight categories to compile their portfolio; a score of 100 points would qualify a teacher for the full $15,000:

	Points
1. Certification by the National Board for Professional Teaching Standards	100
2. Evaluation by principal or supervisor	20
3. Record of past accomplishments	20
4. Participation in district priority projects	20
5. Contribution to teams	20
6. Knowledge of the content of their teaching license	10
7. Recognition by professional organizations	10
8. Customer-satisfaction information	10

Over the next two years, Robbinsdale developed the standards and benchmarks to assess how an individual earns the points in the above areas.

Certification from the National Board for Professional Teaching Standards. The most robust salary element that pays teachers for knowledge and skills comes when districts and states provide teachers with either a salary bonus or a permanent salary increase for earning certification from the national board. Hammond, Indiana, negotiated a contract change that made board certification equivalent to the Ph.D. salary lane. Kentucky has made board certification equivalent to the masters degree plus 30 units. Other states and localities either subsidize the board assessment (which costs $2,000 per teacher) and/or offer salary increases, up to 10 percent of salary in North Carolina, and $10,000 per year in Iowa. The Los Angeles school district provides a 15 percent salary increase for board certification.

There are many other ways a state or district could modify its teacher salary schedules to include knowledge and skill pay elements. Most districts essentially retain the current single-salary structure and either add or replace certain elements with knowledge and skill elements (see the Consortium for Policy Research in Education's teacher compensation web site [www.wcer.wisc.edu/cpre/] for additional descriptions of teacher compensation innovations).

Odden and Kelley (1997) discuss four generic models of possible knowledge and skill-based teacher salary structures. It is important to note that each model incorporates to at least some degree additional pay for earning certification from the National Board for Professional Teaching Standards. Model 1 essentially retains the current single-salary schedule and adds some knowledge and skill elements. Model 2 is similar but requires a successful annual review in order to earn any annual increases. Model 3 places significant value on National Board certification, providing experience increments only for teachers who have earned such certification. Finally, Model 4 is one example of a more fully developed knowledge and skill salary schedule, one that could completely replace the current salary schedule.

Implementation Issues

One implementation issue is the form of pay tied to demonstration of knowledge and skills. Most private sector systems provide permanent base pay increases for mastering higher levels of knowledge and skill. Base pay increases for acquiring additional educational credits are, of course, nearly universal in current teacher pay systems. But some private sector organizations have provided bonuses, rather than base pay increases. This strategy may be appropriate where the nature of the knowledge and skills change frequently. It may make sense to reward knowledge and skills related to specific local programs or those that are more narrowly applicable with bonuses, while rewarding more portable or broadly applicable competencies with base pay increases. The system in Douglas County, Colorado, makes some but not exclusive use of bonuses to reward the acquisition of specific, locally defined skills.

In terms of funding, knowledge- and skill-based pay elements could be used as a rationale for new money for education or teacher compensation. For example, nearly all state and local support for National Board certification is new money. Thus, proposals for adding knowledge and skill elements to a teacher salary schedule could also be accompanied with requests for new pots of salary money for experimental innovations; such requests might make these approaches more attractive to teachers and teacher unions in the short term. Though new money is usually folded into base funding over time, initially it can be an add-on.

Odden and Kelley (1997) provide a lengthy and detailed overview of the process for designing a knowledge- and skill-based pay system. A critical element is to involve teachers and teacher unions heavily in the development process. Because this is a cutting-edge issue in education, there is no one right way to add knowledge- and skill-based elements to a teacher salary schedule, and methods that might initially seem promising may not work out perfectly in practice. Still, involvement of all key people and groups affected develops the trust needed to modify and improve new structures over time.

To date, there has not been much research on how knowledge and skill pay elements would work in education. Though a few experiments have been attempted and evaluated, more innovations need to be developed, implemented, and researched. In organizations outside of education, these types of pay innovations have been shown to be relatively effective at enhancing individual expertise, raising worker morale, and improving organizational productivity, but much additional research is needed (Heneman and Ledford, 1998).

Finally, these uses of teacher assessments could be augmented with compensation elements that directly measure improvements in student achievement. In most organizations outside of education, knowledge- and skill-based pay systems are used in conjunction with group performance awards (Lawler, Mohrman, and Ledford, 1995), which are addressed in the next section.

3. PROVIDE SCHOOL-BASED PERFORMANCE INCENTIVES

School-based performance incentives could also appropriately be part of a revised teacher compensation and school finance system (Odden and Clune, 1998). Such programs are controversial in education, largely because they were designed poorly in the past, provided individual rather than group awards, and because states and districts usually eliminated their funding after a year or two (Murnane and Cohen, 1986). But school-based performance awards could be formal, extrinsic elements that function as incentives (as proposed in both Chapters 7 and 9) for boosting organizational, in this case, schoolwide, student achievement performance. For schools as well as most organizations in the private and public sectors today, performance awards are most appropriately provided to groups of all individuals within an organization, since the work is best conducted in collegial, team-based settings (Mohrman, Lawler, and Mohrman, 1992; Richards, Fishbein, and Melville, 1993).

Particularly if schools receive a base level of funds that has been determined to be adequate for teaching the average student to state/district standards, the extra funds needed to teach special-needs students to that level (the school finance structure suggested in Chapter 4), it would seem reasonable, over time, to hold schools accountable for producing that level of results. At a minimum, it would seem appropriate to provide incentives to schools to continually show progress towards that goal. School-based performance awards are one strategy for implementing that objective.

Designing the specifics of a school-based performance award is complex and requires careful attention to the following six technical issue areas:

1. *The dimensions of performance to include student achievement (mathematics, science, language arts, writing, history/social science, etc.), graduation rates, drop-out rates, attendance, etc., and the weights assigned to each dimension.* Nearly all plans around the country at the end of 1998 included both academic achievement and other student performance factors. Most decided to have academic achievement account for 75–80 percent of the performance measure, usually equally weighting achievement in the different content areas that were included. But by having elements other than academic achievement, the plans were able to recognize that the education system produces valued results beyond just academic achievement.

2. *How performance is measured, including the specific tests that are used to measure student achievement, and how improved performance is calculated.* Plans designed and implemented by a state have used the state tests or assessments that were already in place to measure performance, particularly student academic achievement. Local plans have also used state assessments if there was a state test. Many state and local assessment programs used versions of the following three commercial tests: Terra Nova (McGraw-Hill), The Stanford 9 (Harcourt Brace), and the New Standards (Harcourt Brace). After much discussion, most state and local policymakers tended to decide that current psychometric expertise can provide acceptable measures of student academic performance (Hamilton and Klein, 1998).

   Improved performance was measured in three different ways by the districts that have developed such measures. The first was merely some percentage improvement or a simple number of points improvement, such as three points on a scale of 100. The second was improvement toward a standard. This has been done by following a two-step process. First, the gap between performance in the base year and desired performance was identified. Then a period of time was identified for the school to improve performance to the standard; this period ranged from 12 to 20 years. The gap was then divided by this number of years, and the result was the increase required annually (see Kelley [1998a] for how Kentucky made such a calculation). The third procedure was "value-added," where the idea was to reward schools that produced more than an expected level of improvement on an annual basis; Dallas and North

Carolina each had different approaches to calculating value added. In all instances, schools competed against themselves (i.e., had improvement targets based on performance in the previous or a base year).

3. *How the "rules of the game" are made fair in terms of adjustments for student mobility, disability, initial low achievement, limited English proficiency, and other special issues.* Clearly, this was an important area for those that have been through this process. Many programs required that students had to be in a school for a minimum number of days in order for their score to count; others required a score for a high percentage of all enrolled students to encourage high levels of attendance on test-taking day. Some gave tests in the native language for LEP students; others simply required scores of LEP students even for tests in English. Many required movement of students at all ranges of achievement to ensure that schools focused attention on those in the bottom as well as those in the top half; put differently, rarely were simple average scores used. As yet there still is no science that clearly defines how to make the adjustments needed to recognize the special conditions of students and schools. But, during the development of each state's or district's program, these issues were placed on the agenda and led to extensive discussions of how they would make adjustments to ensure that the system measures performance change in a fair way (Kellor and Odden, 1998).

4. *The size of the bonuses, and whether there will be different levels of awards, based on different amounts of improvement produced.* This is turning out to be a major issue as the new century dawns. Until 1998, most programs provided a maximum of a $1,000–$1,200 teacher salary bonus on an annual basis. A few programs provided a second-level award, usually half of the above, for schools that almost met their improvement target. Some programs provided only school-improvement funds to the site, with no salary bonuses. But as discussed below, these small levels of bonuses were not that motivating to teachers, and school-improvement grants seemed to be even less motivating. So states and districts began to consider larger bonuses. For example, when North Carolina created a statewide program that provided up to $1,500 bonuses in the 1998–99 school year, Charlotte-Mecklenburg, which had had a bonus program providing $1,000 to teachers in qualifying schools, decided to align their local program with the state program and provide their bonus on top of the state bonus. This was done in part as a response to research that showed their previous bonus had a low motivating force (Heneman, 1998).

5. *Who is eligible for the awards, such as professional staff, administrators, paraprofessional and classified staff, as well as how to adjust reward amounts for resignations, terminations, long-term absences, etc.* The trend thus far has been to include both professional and classified staff in schools, with the latter at a lower bonus level. But each state and district needs to address eligibility issues or there likely will be challenges

once the awards are distributed. We also would suggest that states and districts specify in advance who is eligible and the level of the award. Kentucky allowed teachers at each school to make these decisions, a process that produced mainly controversy and confusion (Elmore, Ableman, and Fuhrman, 1996; Kelley, 1998a).

6. *How the awards are financed.* Most of the programs studied were financed with new money, most often public money but sometimes private money for the first year or two. At the $1,000 per-teacher level, they require about 1 percent of the operating budget; at a higher level they might require about 2 percent of the operating budget. Once rolled into the budget in this way, however, the funds will always be there if they are provided each year as a bonus.

The following discusses the typical elements that make up a School-Based Performance Award program (Heneman, 1998; Kelley, 1998b; Kelley, Heneman, and Milanowski, 1999; Odden, Heneman, Wakelyn, and Protsik, 1996):

1. Student achievement in the core academics—reading, writing, mathematics, science, history/social science—forms the core of the performance measure. Student achievement on state tests in these subjects typically constitutes 75–80 percent of the performance measure.

    For illustrative purposes, assume last year's composite performance measure for a school was that 40 percent of students were achieving at or above proficiency.

2. Each school competes with itself, and specific targets are set for annual improvement. The most straightforward way to set a target is to specify that the performance measure to qualify for an award must be a certain percentage greater than the previous year, or so many percentile points higher. Sometimes the performance measure is linked to be a proficiency standard, and the target is linked to closing the gap between the actual score and the proficiency standard.

    Again, for illustrative purposes, assume the proficiency standard is 85 percent. Then the state or district might set a target of improving the gap between actual performance (40 percent) and proficient performance (85 percent), which is 45 percentage points, by 5 percent each year, or 2.25 percentage points (45 point gap divided by 20). So the target for this year would be 40 + 2.25, or 42.25 percent. This approach has all schools performing at proficiency over a 20-year time period, but allows them to make improvements gradually, one year at a time.

    Performance measures have to be calculated carefully, capturing improvements of students at the bottom end as well as the top end, including students with at least mild disabilities as well as students who speak a language other than English, and making appropriate adjustments for student mobility among schools.

3. Schools are eligible for incentive awards if they meet or exceed their improvement targets. Typically, the award is a $1,000 bonus for each professional staff member in the school, and about half that for each classified staff member. A second-tier award is often also provided at half the above amounts for schools that meet or exceed 75 percent of their improvement targets. We might suggest that states and districts try somewhat higher award levels, closer to the $2,000 level, because current bonus levels are somewhat but not dramatically motivating (Kelley, Milanowski, and Heneman, 1998).

4. Schools that consistently do not improve are first put on a "watch" list and then subject to intervention and sometimes takeover and reconstitution. The Distinguished Educator program in Kentucky is an exemplar. Schools put on "watch," called "schools in decline" in Kentucky, are provided a full-time distinguished educator for one year; the role of that individual is to help the school identify strengths and weaknesses and to design a dramatic improvement plan. Though schools do not want to be declared "in decline," those that have report superb experiences with their distinguished educator; in the first cycle of awards, three-fourths of the schools in decline qualified for an incentive award in the next cycle, showing that the distinguished educators were quite successful in turning schools around toward improvement (Kelley and Protsik, 1997).

5. The costs of a typical school-based incentive programs is approximately 1 percent of a district's operating budget, but could be higher if the award levels were higher, as we suggest above.

Examples of School-Based Performance Awards

We describe three of the most well-known and longest-lasting school-based performance award programs below:

> **Charlotte-Mecklenburg, North Carolina,** implemented a school-based performance program in 1992–93. The foundations for the program are improvement goals in: (1) primary grade readiness, (2) absenteeism, (3) social studies and science, (4) mathematics and reading, (5) writing, (6) prealgebra, (7) dropouts, (8) higher-level course enrollment, and (9) end-of-course subject matter mastery. There are specific subgoals, tailored to specific grade levels, within each content area. Across grade levels, there are between 14 and 44 subgoals.
>
> Each year an overall district-improvement goal is set in each area (e.g., the percentage of students who score below the competent range on the writing test will decrease by 5 percent). Improvement goals for each school are then set by the district, based on the performance level of the previous year's students in each grade. Maintenance goals are also established for schools already performing at a high level, such as having 95 percent of its students prepared for prealgebra. There are separate improvement goals for white, African American, and other students.

To calculate a school's level of goal attainment, 100 bonus points are divided evenly among the school's subgoals (e.g., if a school has 25 subgoals, each subgoal is worth 4 points). A fully met subgoal receives 100 percent of the assigned bonus points, a partially met goal receives 75 percent of the bonus points, and an unmet goal receives no bonus points. Points earned on subgoals are summed to form a school's total score. Schools that receive 75+ points fall into the 100 percent bonus category; schools earning between 60 to 74 points are in the 75 percent bonus category; and schools receiving fewer than 60 points are in the no-bonus category (there is no special designation). The maximum bonus has been $1,000 per teacher and principal.

As noted above, this program was modified in 1998–99 to align with the state's program. The state provides bonuses of $1,000 to teachers in schools that meet expected improvements, and $1,500 to teachers in schools that exceed expectations; in those schools, classified staff receive $375 and $500, respectively. On top of this, Charlotte-Mecklenburg adds $725 and $544 for teachers and $290 and $217 for classified staff in the "exceeded" and "meets improvement" school categories, respectively.

Kentucky's Bonus Program was established in 1991–92. It rewards schools that show improvements toward performance over time. Every two years, schools that exceed their improvement goals receive funds that teachers in each school distribute as they see fit. Funds may be used for many purposes, including salary bonuses, professional development, and school improvement funds.

An accountability index is used to measure improvements in school performance. The index is based on the results of reading, math, social studies, science, writing, arts and humanities, and vocational/practical living scores. Student performance is rated from lowest to highest as novice, apprentice, proficient, or distinguished. An additional noncognitive component is based on attendance, retention, dropout rates, and transition to adult life. Students are assessed in grades 4–5, 7–8, and 11–12; accountability is measured across cohorts rather than as longitudinal performance of a particular group of students.

The improvement goal is school-specific, and is equal to one-tenth of the difference between the baseline composite score and a "proficient" rating. The baseline is taken from the previous cycle's performance.

Schools fall into one of five general categories based on their performance on the accountability index compared to their performance goal:

1. Eligible for Rewards: These are the schools that receive the bonus. They must exceed their improvement goal by at least one point and move at least 10 percent of "novices" to the "apprentice" level or higher.
2. Successful: These schools receive neither rewards nor sanctions for their performance. These schools meet their performance goal or exceed it by less than one point.
3. Not Meeting Threshold: These schools are required to develop a school-improvement plan. Their scores are between baseline and goal.

4. In Decline: These schools must develop an improvement plan, are eligible for school-improvement funds, and may have a "distinguished educator" assigned to them to help them improve. This category includes schools whose scores are less than five points below baseline.

5. In Crisis: Schools identified as in crisis are subject to possible takeover or closure. These schools must develop an improvement plan, are eligible for school-improvement funds, and are assigned a "distinguished educator" who can make binding recommendations for termination of employees, and can override school-site council decisions. This category includes those schools that score five points or more below baseline.

For 1996, the awards amounted to about $2,000 per teacher in eligible schools, or a total appropriation of $27 million. In 1998, the legislature required a redesign of the program, the details of which were not known as of the publication of this book.

Indiana created a program that provides improving schools with monetary bonuses and confers special "Four Star" recognition to schools that continue to be high-performing. Under Indiana's accountability system, monetary awards are provided to schools that show improvement in two of four performance areas (student attendance, mathematics proficiency scores, language arts proficiency scores, and scores on Indiana's statewide testing program). Sixty percent of public schools have qualified for this award.

Schools that already have high scores in these four areas, and thus experience difficulty in producing improvements, are not eligible for monetary awards. To recognize these schools, a "Four Star School" status is conferred to schools scoring in the top 25 percent in all four areas. In 1993–94, 21 percent of Indiana's schools qualified for this distinctive "Four Star" recognition.

Research on School-Based Performance Awards

The CPRE Teacher Compensation Group has been conducting considerable research on school-based performance award programs. Research to date has studied the program in Kentucky and Charlotte-Mecklenburg. The research includes interviews with teachers in dozens of schools as well as surveys of large, representative samples of thousand of teachers in both places. The research used a combined expectancy/goal-setting model of teacher motivation to guide data collection and analysis, focusing on how a school-based performance award motivates teachers to reach student achievement goals (Heneman, 1998; Heneman and Milanowski, 1999; Kelley, 1998a, 1998b; Kelley and Protsik, 1997; Kelley, Milanowski, and Heneman, 1998; Milanowski, 1999). Briefly, the model indicates that a teacher will be motivated to try to reach the school's student achievement goals to the extent that s/he: (1) perceives a high probability that teacher effort will lead to reaching the student achievement goals (expectancy perception);

(2) perceives a high probability that goal attainment will lead to certain consequences or outcomes such as a bonus award (instrumentality perception); and (3) places value, either positive or negative, on these outcomes. The model indicates that the teacher's expectancy perception depends on the perception of one's own knowledge and skills and on the presence of "system enablers" such as principal leadership.

Some of the major findings about teacher motivation under school-based performance award programs are as follows:

1. Student achievement goals for a school help to provide teachers a focus for their work, efforts, and energy. They help channel teacher's work to the most important goals of the system, mainly those included in the performance measure, which, in the cases being studied, were largely student achievement in the core academic subjects. To be sure, performance awards did not eliminate all other "noise" in the system, as there were other competing goals. But the research nevertheless found that the programs studied helped teachers understand that greater student achievement in the core academic subjects was the most important goal.

2. On average, teachers believed with about 50–60 percent probability that increased effort on their part would lead to attaining their school's student achievement goals. There were wide variations among teachers in this probability. Several factors accounted for that variation, including:

   a. whether the school had previously received an award, in which case the positive outcomes of the overall program helped enhance motivation to work harder, and whether the school was in a nonimproving mode, in which case the negative outcomes, or sanctions part of the program, helped enhance motivation to improve.

   b. the perceived presence of several "system enablers," including principal leadership, alignment of curriculum with testing, professional development focused on the curriculum, achievement feedback and the ability to analyze the feedback for instructional change, control over school resources, the ability to create a cohesive staff through recruitment and training of site staff, and creation of a professional community.

3. Teachers placed value on many outcomes of the program, and those outcomes helped motivate teachers to work in more focused ways to produce improved student achievement. The general conclusion is that an array of outcomes motivates teachers, some positive and some negative, with the implications that all of these outcomes had an impact.

Positive outcomes most highly valued included:

- personal satisfaction from increasing student achievement,
- student achievement improvements,

- professional recognition for doing a good job, and
- receiving a monetary bonus.

Negative outcomes that had an equal motivating force included:

- increased pressure and stress to improve results,
- school labeled as a "school in decline" and the accompanying professional embarrassment,
- loss of freedom through some state-directed assistance or takeover, and
- increased work hours.

Additional findings about the bonus part of the program were that teachers who reported they were most motivated by the program and wished to see it continue were those who:

- were most dissatisfied with their current level of pay,
- felt it was fair to receive a bonus for improving student achievement, and
- felt that administration of the bonus process was fair.

The general conclusion is that, contrary to the ideas of some, monetary bonuses are valued and can be motivating, and that sanctions such as school reconstitution or identification as a school in decline are also valued (though negatively) and can function to motivate teachers to improve results.

4. Teachers perceive that their knowledge, skills, and school conditions are critical elements that help them accomplish accountability goals, or to continuously improve student achievement. Teacher perceptions of helpful principal leadership, getting feedback on results, and the ability to access their implications for new instructional strategies, curriculum alignment, professional development, and creation of a professional community at the school are generally more strongly associated with schools that accomplish their goals for improving student achievement than schools that did not.

In short, research to date on school-based performance award programs has found that from the teachers' perspective, a school-based performance award program is much more than just a bonus system; it includes all the key elements that comprise a comprehensive education improvement strategy. The same researchers also suspect that when they research knowledge- and skill-based pay systems and how they affect teacher motivation, they will find the same thing. The knowledge and skills must be those that comprise the capacity that is needed, there must be strategies in place to develop these knowledge and skills, and teachers and others in schools must have the authority and power to organize and run schools so they can use this knowledge and skill to teach a more rigorous curriculum program designed to have students learn to higher levels.

4. AN EXAMPLE OF A COMPREHENSIVE NEW TEACHER COMPENSATION SYSTEM

Table 11.2 displays the core features of a full-fledged, comprehensive, new salary schedule implemented in Fall 1998 at the Vaughn Next Century Learning Center, a charter school that is the former Vaughn Street School in Los Angeles. This school enrolls about 1,200 students, nearly all of whom have limited English proficiency and are eligible for free and reduced-price lunch. The new salary schedule includes both knowledge- and skills-based pay elements as well as school-based performance award elements. The school has developed similar new pay schedules for the principal and the classified staff (see Kellor, Milanowski, and Odden, 1999). There are eight aspects of the new pay plan in Table 11.2 that should be noted.

First, it includes some pay increments for years of experience. For the first five years, teachers have an extra $1,000 added each year to their starting salary of $30,000 if they pass an annual performance review.

Second, there are three categories of pay increases for teacher credentials. A full professional California teaching credential improves base pay by $1,000, a master's degree by another $1,000, and certification from the National Board for Professional Teaching Standards by an additional $4,000.

Third, the school pays for several specific skills and knowledge needed for the instructional program in the school: $1,300 for literacy expertise, $1,300 for ESL or language development skills for their multilingual student body, $400 for computer technology skills, and $300 for special-education inclusion.

Fourth, the school is investigating additional skill areas that would be added to this list in the future. In particular, the school will be incorporating a new mathematics and science curriculum program and will pay increments to teachers for learning the knowledge and skills required to implement this curriculum program. Other skill areas will also be identified over time.

Fifth, the school has four contingency pay elements (i.e., pay increments provided contingent upon some task or activity occurring). The current schedule includes $250 for each of certain levels of student attendance and student discipline, and $150 for each of a level of parent partnerships and teaming efforts. The point of this pay element is to provide an incentive for teachers to engage in certain activities or to help cause certain behaviors.

Sixth, the school has several outcome-related pay elements. Each teacher will receive an additional $1,500 if the school increases schoolwide performance. Currently, the school teaches 44 percent of students to proficiency on the test used; the school will need to increase that by 5 percentage points to 49 percent to

TABLE 11.2   Key Elements of the New Teacher Salary Schedule for the Vaughn Next Century Learning Center, Los Angeles

Base salary	
Year 1	$30,000
Experience increments	
Year 2	$1,000, subject to satisfactory evaluation
Year 3	$1,000, subject to satisfactory evaluation
Year 4	$1,000, subject to satisfactory evaluation
Year 5	$1,000, subject to satisfactory evaluation
Credential increments	
California teaching credential	$1,000
Master's degree	$1,000
National Board certification	$4,000
Knowledge and skills	
Literacy (reading/writing)	$1,300
ESL, sheltered english, language development	$1,300
Technology	$ 400
Special-education inclusion	$ 300
Contingency-based	
Student attendance	$ 250
Student discipline	$ 250
Parent partnership	$ 150
Teaming efforts	$ 150
Outcome-based	
Schoolwide achievement	$1,500
Schoolwide bilingual redesignation	$ 250
Grade-level achievement	$ 500
Individual classroom achievement	$ 500
Management/leadership-expertise-based	
Committee chair	$ 500
Clan leader	$ 500
Faculty chair	$ 500
Mentor	$ 500
Afterschool	$ 500
Extended year	Extra month's pay
Staff development leaders	Fixed amount per session
Gain-sharing	
Substitute teacher costs	$ 250

qualify for this bonus next year. There also are $500 bonuses for grade-level achievement goals and individual classroom achievement goals, as well as a $250 bonus for having a specified number of bilingual students reclassified for enrollment in a regular classroom where English is the language of instruction.

Seventh, the schedule includes several additions for what it calls expertise-based skills and what we have called managerial or leadership skills. For example, pay increases of $500 are provided for each of being a school committee chair, a school "clan" leader (which is leader of a small team within the school), a faculty chair, and a teacher mentor.

Finally, there is a gain-sharing program, under which each teacher will share in any cost reductions produced. The current schedule includes a bonus of $250 for each teacher if as a whole they reduce expenditures for substitute teachers. In the future, the school hopes to have gain-sharing plans to reduce costs for other areas, such as building insurance and workers compensation.

Since this is a school within the boundaries of the Los Angeles school district and possesses many of the education challenges that many Los Angeles and other large, urban schools also face, it serves as an excellent example of the type of comprehensive, teacher compensation change that a state or district could consider. It not only identifies several areas of new expertise that it would like teachers to develop, but also identifies the most important school results it wants teachers to produce.

CONCLUSION

Comprehensive education reform and school-finance change strategies today should include new forms of rewards for individuals and groups, rewards that are linked both to the knowledge and skills needed to improve results and to the accomplishment of actually improving results. Such new forms of rewards can be incorporated into new forms of teacher compensation through two major innovations:

- **pay for knowledge and skills** (i.e., base pay increases provided to individual teachers when they gain the knowledge, skills, and expertise that are needed to teach a more rigorous, high-standards curriculum more successfully to all students) and
- **school-based performance awards** (i.e., bonus payments provided to all individuals in a school when targets for improving student achievement are met or exceeded).

These compensation innovations would not only reinforce nearly all elements of the standards- and school-based education reform strategy that is being deployed around the country, but also would add extrinsic rewards to what teachers already consider intrinsically satisfying: adding to their professional repertoire and improving student achievement.

Appendix

This appendix provides initial documentation for the use of the simulation that accompanies this book. Students are encouraged to download the simulation from McGraw-Hill's web site (http://www.mhhe.com/schoolfinance) and use it in conjunction with the material in Chapters 4 and 5. The simulation requires that you have Microsoft Excel for Office 97 available and running on your computer. Students do not need to be familiar with Excel to run the simulation, but the program itself must be installed for the simulation to operate correctly.

Additionally, the state-level simulations can be used to estimate the impact of school finance proposals in your own state in the future. *Because we view the simulation as a dynamic product that will continue to change as school finance in the 50 states change, it is important that you carefully read the documentation pages provided at the web site before using the simulation.* These pages will contain information documenting the status of each state simulation. This will include information as to the date and source of the finance data available, as well as information on any updates that have been made to state simulations and to the 20-district simulation. The balance of this appendix describes the system requirements for using the simulation and provides an introduction to its use.

SYSTEM REQUIREMENTS

At the time of publication, the simulation was only available in Windows format. We intend to make it available on the Macintosh platform before the end of 1999. The documentation on the web site will indicate its availability. In the meantime, operation of the simulation requires that you have Microsoft Excel for Office 97 (or a higher version) running on your computer. To get the most out of this simulation, we recommend you have a Pentium-based computer with at least 32 megabytes of RAM. The simulation will run on smaller configurations, but the calculation time for the state simulations will be quite lengthy.

As documented on the web site, the files you download will be Microsoft Excel for Office 97 files. The program relies on the Visual Basic application language that is part of Excel; therefore, the simulation will not operate without the Excel software.

RUNNING THE SIMULATION THE FIRST TIME

Before you run the simulation the first time, you will need to install two of Excel's built-in add-ins. These two add-ins provide Excel with substantial data-analysis capabilities that the simulation uses to calculate the equity statistics displayed in the printouts.

To install the add-ins, start Excel on your computer. When you have a blank worksheet, do the following:

1. Click on the **Tools** menu.
2. From the menu that appears below the word **Tools,** select the **Add-Ins** option.
3. You will see a dialogue box with the title "Add-Ins" in the blue bar across the top. The dialogue box contains a list of add-ins available to Excel. Place a check mark in the first two—**Analysis ToolPak** and **Analysis ToolPak—VBA.** You can place these check marks simply by clicking in the box to the left of each title.
4. Click on the box marked **OK.**

This will install the **Analysis ToolPak** on your version of Excel. You only need to do this the first time you run the simulation. After that, Excel will automatically include these functions when it starts. *Remember that if you are using the simulation from a computer on a network installation at your institution, you will have to make sure the **Analysis ToolPak** is installed on each computer you use.*

Once the Analysis ToolPak is installed, you can start the simulation. Follow the instructions on the web site to download the simulation you want to run. Once the file has been downloaded, double-click on the file's icon, and it will start.

RUNNING THE SIMULATION

Once you have started the simulation, its operation is very easy. You will see a welcome screen describing the simulation. The typical Excel menus across the top of the program have been replaced with one option called **Simulation.** Click on the word "Simulation," and a menu of options will appear. (Please note that the menu may change over time. This will be noted in the documentation on the web site.) Take the following actions to see the simulation results you want to consider in your analysis.

View Base Data

Select the **View Base Data** option from the drop-down menu to see the base data for the simulation you are running. To print this out, select the **Print** option from the **Simulation** menu and check the appropriate option in the dialogue box that appears.

Run a Simulation

Select the **Run Simulation** option from the **Simulation** drop-down menu. You will see a dialogue box with four tabs across the top. Select the type of simulation you wish to run from the tabs and then fill in the simulation parameters. The simulation will then make a number of calculations, which could take some time if you have an old computer. When the calculations are complete, the computer will display the output from the simulation option you selected.

Print the Results

From the **Simulation** menu, select the **Print** option and select the option you want to print. It will print the results of your most-recent simulation.

View a Graph of Your Results

To view a graph of revenue versus wealth for the simulation you just ran, select **Graphs** from the **Simulation** pull-down menu and select the appropriate option from the dialogue box that appears.

WEIGHTED PUPILS

The 20-district simulation allows you to create a weighted-pupil scenario using weights for children with disabilities, children from low-income families, and children who have limited English proficiency. To include pupil weights in your 20-district simulation, select the **Weighted pupils** option from the **Simulation** drop-down menu. You will find a dialogue box that asks if you want to use pupils weights, asks what weights should be used for each student category, and asks you to determine the percentage of students in each district who meet the requirements of the three weighting options. *Note that if you select the "do not use pupil weights" option, no weights will be used, regardless of what is filled in on this dialogue box.* When you return to the simulation and choose a simulation option, pupil weights will be used. This will be reflected in the column headings that appear in the printouts.

For individual states, pupil weightings will vary. Check the documentation that accompanies each state simulation to get updated information about individual state options.

EXITING FROM THE SIMULATION

To exit from the simulation, choose the **Exit** option from the **Simulation** pull-down menu. It is essential that you exit in this manner. If you fail to do so, Excel may not display the standard menu items across the top the next time you start Excel. If this happens, simply restart the simulation and exit correctly. That will fix the problem.

Summary of Steps for Operating the Simulation

1. Make sure Microsoft Excel for Office 97 or higher is installed on your computer.
2. Be sure that the Analysis ToolPak add-ins have been installed on Excel.
3. Log into the McGraw-Hill web site (http://www.mhhe.com/school-finance).
4. **Read the documentation update available on the web site.**
5. Download the simulation you want to run. We suggest you start with the 20-district simulation to become familiar with the operation of this program.
6. Run the simulations you want to analyze.
7. Exit from the program using the **Exit** command on the **Simulation** pull-down menu.

Enjoy the simulation. If you have comments or suggestions, please send an e-mail to the address listed at the web site.

Glossary

This glossary contains a number of tax, education, and statistical terms that are used in school finance research and policy analysis. In order to make comparisons of tax and expenditure data among school districts, adjustments must be made in many measures. The purpose of these adjustments is to create a set of comparable numbers and a set of common terms. Standard procedures are used to make these adjustments, and the glossary indicates how some of the adjustments are made.

ADA, ADM ADA is an abbreviation for student average daily attendance, and ADM is an abbreviation for student average daily membership. ADA and ADM are the official measures that most states use to represent the number of students in a school district for the purpose of calculating state aid. ADA is always less than ADM.

adequacy Adequacy entered the educational arena primarily in the 1990s. For school finance, it means providing sufficient funds for the average district/school to teach the average child to state standards, plus sufficient additional revenues for students with special needs to allow them to meet performance standards as well. Many school finance court cases have shifted from challenging fiscal disparities to challenging the adequacy of the funding system.

assessment ratios The assessed valuation of property in most states is usually less than the market value of the property. In other words, owners are able to sell property for a price higher than the assessed valuation of that property. Although most states have a legal standard at which all property should be assessed, assessed valuations are usually below even the legal level and may vary widely among jurisdictions in a state. The actual assessment level or assessment ratio is determined by comparing actual assessed valuations to market values.

assessed valuation The assessed valuation is the total value of property subject to the property tax in a school district. Usually, it is established by a local government officer and is only a percentage of the market value of the property.

assessed valuation, adjusted or equalized Because local assessing jurisdictions in a state usually have different actual assessment ratios, the reported assessed valuations need to be adjusted or equalized in order to compare them among school districts. The best way to make such adjustments is to convert the assessed valuations to what they would be if all counties were assessed at 100 percent of market value and then adjust them to the legal standard (for example, 33 1/3 percent). The mathematical way to make the adjustment is to divide the assessed valuation by the assessment ratio and multiply the result by 0.333. The result is called the adjusted or equalized assessed valuation. The following is an example:

Consider two school districts, A and B.

District A has an assessed valuation of $200,000.
District B has an assessed valuation of $250,000.

Focusing just on assessed valuations, district A would appear to be poorer in property wealth than district B. However, assume that the actual assessment ratio in district A is 20 percent, while it is 25 percent in district B.

Assuming that the legal ratio is 33 1/3 percent, the computation of the adjusted assessed valuation for district A is as follows:

$$\text{adjusted assessed valuation} = \$200,000 \times 0.333 = \$333,333 \ 0.20$$

The computation of the adjusted assessed valuation for district B is:

$$\text{adjusted assessed valuation} = \$250,000 \times 0.333 = \$333,333 \ 0.25$$

Both school districts have the same adjusted assessed valuation. That is, both school districts effectively have the same total tax base, despite the differences in the reported assessed valuation.

Adjusted assessed valuations must be used to compare property wealth among school districts and should be the basis on which state equalization aid is calculated.

assessed valuation per pupil, adjusted The adjusted or equalized assessed valuation per pupil is the adjusted assessed valuation for a school district divided by the district's total ADA or ADM.

categorical programs Categorical programs refer to state aid that is designated for specific programs. Examples would be transportation aid, special-education aid, and aid for vocational education. Equalization formula aid is not an example of categorical aid. Formula funds provide general aid that can be used for any purpose.

correlation Correlation is a statistical term indicating the relationship between two variables. When two variables are said to be positively correlated, as one variable increases the other variable also tends to increase. When two variables are said to be negatively correlated, as one variable increases, the other variable tends to decrease.

correlation coefficient The correlation coefficient is a number indicating the degree of relationship between two variables. Because of the way a correlation coefficient is calculated, it always will have a value between -1.0 and $+1.0$. When the correlation coefficient is around $+0.5$ to $+1.0$, the two variables have a positive relationship or are positively correlated—when one variable gets larger, the other tends to get larger. When the correlation coefficient is around zero, the two variables do not appear to have any relationship. When the correlation coefficient is around -0.5 to -1.0, the variables have a negative relationship or are negatively correlated—as one gets larger, the other tends to get smaller.

current operating expenditures Current operating expenditures include education expenditures for the daily operation of the school program, such as expenditures for administration, instruction, attendance and health services, transportation, operation and maintenance of plant, and fixed charges.

district power equalization (DPE) See *guaranteed tax base program.*

elasticity of tax revenues The elasticity of tax revenues refers to the responsiveness of the revenues from a tax to changes in various economic factors in the state or nation. In particular, policymakers may want to know whether tax revenues will increase more rapidly, as rapidly, or less rapidly than changes in personal income. The revenues from an elastic tax will increase by more than 1 percent for each 1 percent change in personal income. Income taxes are usually elastic tax sources. In general, elastic tax sources have progressive patterns of incidence, and inelastic tax sources have regressive patterns of incidence. Expenditure elasticity may be defined similarly.

equalization formula aid Equalization formula aid is financial assistance given by a higher-level government—the state—to a lower-level government—school districts—to equalize the fiscal situation of the lower-level government. Because school districts vary in their abilities to raise property tax dollars, equalization formula aid is allocated to make the ability to raise such local funds more nearly equal. In general, equalization formula aid increases as the property wealth per pupil of a school district decreases.

expenditure uniformity Expenditure uniformity is part of the horizontal equity standard in school finance requiring equal expenditures per pupil or per weighted pupil for all students in the state. (See *fiscal neutrality.*)

fiscal capacity Fiscal capacity is the ability of a local governmental entity, such as a school district, to raise tax revenues. It is usually measured by the size of the local tax base, usually property wealth per pupil in education.

fiscal neutrality Fiscal neutrality is a court-defined equity standard in school finance. It is a negative standard stating that current operating expenditures per pupil, or some object, cannot be related to a school district's adjusted assessed valuation per pupil, or some fiscal capacity measure. It simply means that differences in expenditures per pupil cannot be related to local school district wealth. (See *expenditure uniformity.*)

flat grant program A flat grant program simply allocates an equal sum of dollars to each public school pupil in the state. A flat grant is not an equalization aid program because it allocates the same dollars per pupil regardless of the property or income wealth of the local school districts. However, if *no local* dollars are raised for education and all school dollars come from the state, a flat grant program becomes equivalent to full-state assumption.

foundation program A foundation program is a state equalization aid program that typically guarantees a certain foundation level of expenditure for each student, together with a minimum tax rate that each school district must levy for education purposes. The difference between what a local school district raises at the minimum tax rate and the foundation expenditure is made up in state aid. In the past, foundation programs were referred to as minimum foundation programs, and the foundation level of expenditure was quite low. Today, most newly enacted foundation programs usually require an expenditure per pupil at or above the previous year's state average. Foundation programs focus on the per-pupil expenditure level and thus enhance the state government's fiscal role in education.

full-state assumption Full-state assumption (FSA) is a school finance program in which the state pays for all education costs and sets equal per-pupil expenditures in all school districts. FSA would satisfy the expenditure per-pupil "uniformity" standard of equity. Only in Hawaii has the state government fully assumed most of the costs of public education.

guaranteed tax base program (GTB) Guaranteed tax base (GTB) refers to a state equalization aid program that "equalizes" the ability of each school district to raise dollars for education. In a pure GTB program, the state guarantees to both property-poor and property-rich school districts the same dollar yield for the same property tax rate. In short, equal tax rates produce equal per-pupil expenditures. In the property-poor school districts, the state makes up the difference between what is raised locally and what the state guarantees. In property-rich school districts, excess funds may or may not be "recaptured" by the state and distributed to the property-poor districts. Most GTB state laws do not include recapture provisions. However, Montana and Utah included recapture mechanisms in their school finance laws. GTB programs are given different names in many states, including district power equalizing programs (DPE), guaranteed yield programs, and percentage equalizing programs. GTB programs focus on the ability to support education and, thus, enhance the local fiscal role in education decision making. GTB would satisfy the "fiscal neutrality" standard without achieving "uniformity" of expenditures among school districts.

guaranteed yield program See *guaranteed tax base.*

median family income Median family income usually is that reported in the decennial U.S. census. It reflects income for the year before the census was taken (i.e., 1989 income for the 1990 census, or 1999 income for the 2000 census). If the income of all families in a school district were rank ordered, the median income would be the income of the family midway between the lowest- and the highest-income families.

municipal overburden Municipal overburden refers to the fiscal position of large cities. Municipal overburden includes the large burden of noneducation services that central cities must provide and that most other jurisdictions do not have to provide (or at least do not have to provide in the same quantity). These noneducation services may include above-average welfare costs, health and hospitalization, public housing, police, fire, and sanitation services. These high noneducation fiscal burdens mean that education must compete with many other functional areas for each local tax dollar raised, thus reducing the ability of large-city school districts to raise education dollars. The fiscal squeeze caused by the service overburden, together with the concentration of the educationally disadvantaged and children in need of special-education services in city schools, puts central-city school districts at a fiscal disadvantage in supporting school services.

percentage equalizing programs See *guaranteed tax base.*

progressive tax A progressive tax is a tax that increases proportionately more than income as the income level of the taxpayer increases. Under a progressive tax, high-income taxpayers will pay a larger percent of their income toward this tax than low-income taxpayers.

property tax circuit breaker program A property tax circuit breaker program is a tax relief program, usually financed by the state, that focuses property tax relief on particular households presumed to be overburdened by property taxes. That is, it is intended to reduce the presumed regressivity of the property tax. A typical circuit breaker attempts to limit the property tax burden to a percent of household income and applies only to residential property taxes. The percent usually rises as income rises in an attempt to make the overall burden progressive. Initially most states enacted circuit breaker programs just for senior citizens, but a few states have extended circuit breaker benefits to all low-income households, regardless of the age of the head of the household. The circuit breaker is based on actual or estimated taxes paid on residential property and generally takes the form of a credit on state income taxes.

property tax incidence or burden-traditional and new views   The traditional view of property tax incidence divided the tax into two components: that which fell on land and that which fell on improvements (i.e., structures). Property taxes on land were assumed to fall on landowners. The part on improvements was assumed to fall on homeowners in the case of owned homes, to be shifted forward to tenants in the case of rented residences and to be shifted forward to consumers in the case of taxes on business property. Nearly all empirical studies based on the traditional view found the incidence pattern to result in a regressive burden distribution, markedly regressive in lower income ranges. The new view of property tax incidence considers the tax to be, basically, a uniform tax on all property in the country. Such a tax is borne by owners of capital and, thus, the burden distribution pattern is progressive. Although the new view allows for modifications caused by admitted tax-rate differentials across the country, adherents of the new view hold that even with the modifications, the tax would exhibit a progressive pattern of incidence over much of the range of family incomes.

proportional tax   A proportional tax is a tax that consumes the same percent of family income at all income levels.

pupil-weighted system or weighted-pupil programs   A pupil-weighted system is a state-aid system in which pupils are given different weights based on the estimated or assumed costs of their education program; aid is allocated on the basis of the total number of weighted students. Usually, the cost of the education program for grades 4–6 is considered the standard program and weighted 1.0. For states such as Florida that choose to invest more dollars in the early school years, pupils in grades K–3 are given a weight greater than 1.0, typically around 1.3. In other states, high school students are weighted about 1.25, although these secondary weightings are slowly being eliminated. The two major programmatic areas where numerous weightings have been used are special and vocational education. Weighted-pupil programs, therefore, recognize that it costs more to provide an education program for some students than for others and includes the extra costs via a higher weighting. State aid is then calculated and distributed on the basis of the total number of weighted students in each school district. Determining the appropriate weight is a difficult matter.

regressive tax   A regressive tax is a tax that increases proportionately less than income as the income level of the taxpayer increases. Under a regressive tax, low-income taxpayers will pay a larger percent of their income toward this tax than high-income taxpayers.

revenue gap   A revenue gap exists when projected expenditures exceed projected tax revenues. Although revenue gaps usually are not allowed to exist in fact for current fiscal years, of importance are the projected values. If revenue gaps are projected, tax-rate increases or expenditure cuts, both politically difficult, will be required. Revenue gaps usually occur when the elasticity of expenditures exceeds the elasticity of revenues. This often happens at the state and local level because state and local taxes are, in most instances, less elastic than expenditures. If states want to eliminate the occurrence of revenue gaps and the constant need to increase tax rates or decrease projected expenditure levels, attention must be given to ways to increase the elasticity of state tax systems, usually by increasing reliance on income taxes. (See *elasticity of tax revenues*.)

school district tax rate   School district tax rate is the term states use to indicate the local school property tax rate. The tax rate often is slated as the amount of property tax dollars to be paid for each $100 of assessed valuation or, if given in mills, the rate indicates how much is raised for each $1,000 of assessed valuation. For example, a tax rate of $1.60 per hundred dollars of assessed valuation means that taxpayers pay $1.60 for each $100 of their total assessed valuation: a tax rate of 16 mills indicates that $16 must be paid for each $1,000 of assessed valuation. The tax rate can also be expressed as a percent, so a tax rate of 1.6 percent would be the same as a tax rate of 16 mills or $1.60 per hundred dollars of assessed valuation.

state aid for current operating expenses   State aid for current operating expenses is the sum of the equalization formula aid and categorical aid for vocational education, special education, bilingual education, transportation, and other categorical aid programs. (See *categorical programs.*)

tax burden (or sometimes tax incidence)   Tax burden typically refers to the percent of an individual's or family's income that is consumed by a tax or by a tax system. Usually, one wants to know whether a tax or tax system's burden is distributed in a progressive, proportional, or regressive manner. In the United States, a tax system that is progressive overall seems to be the most acceptable to a majority of people. Tax burden analysis takes into account the extent of tax shifting.

tax incidence   See *tax shifting* and *tax burden.*

tax price   The tax price generally is the tax rate a district must levy to purchase a given level and quality of school services. Poor districts generally have to levy a higher tax rate, and thus pay a higher tax price, to purchase such a given bundle of school services than a wealthy district, because, at a given tax rate, the poor district would raise less dollars per pupil than the wealthy district.

tax shifting or tax incidence   Tax shifting refers to the phenomenon wherein the party that must legally pay a tax (for example, a store owner) does not in fact bear the burden of the tax but shifts the tax to another party (for example, the consumer of an item that is sold in the store). Taxes can be shifted either forward or backward. For example, landlords might be able to shift their property taxes forward to tenants in the form of higher rents, and a business might be able to shift property or corporate income taxes backward to employees in the form of lower salaries. The ability to shift taxes depends on a variety of economic factors, and there is great debate among economists over the extent to which some taxes are shifted. It is usually agreed, however, that individual income taxes are not shifted and rest on the individual taxpayer. It also generally is agreed that sales taxes are shifted to the consumer. There is argument over the extent to which corporate income taxes are shifted to consumers in the form of higher prices or to employees in the form of lower wages, versus falling on the stockholders in the form of lower dividends. There is also debate about who effectively pays the property tax. Tax incidence analysis examines how various taxes may or may not be shifted.

References

Aaron, Henry J. (1975). *Who Pays the Property Tax? A New View.* Washington, D.C.: The Brookings Institution.

Adams, E. Kathleen. (December 1980). *Fiscal Response and School Finance Simulations: A Policy Perspective* (Report No. F80-3). Denver, CO: Education Commission of the States.

Adams, E. Kathleen, and Allan Odden. (1981). Alternative Wealth Measures. In K. Forbis Jordan and Nelda H. Cambron-McCabe, eds., *Perspectives in State School Support Programs.* Cambridge, MA: Ballinger, pp. 143–165.

Adams, Jacob E. (1994). "Spending School Reform Dollars in Kentucky: Familiar Patterns and New Programs, But Is This Reform?" *Educational Evaluation and Policy Analysis.* 16(4), 375–390.

Adams, Jacob E. (1997). "School Finance Policy and Students' Opportunities to Learn: Kentucky's Experience." *The Future of Children: Financing Schools,* 7(3), 79–95.

Advisory Commission on Intergovernmental Relations. (1984). *Significant Features of Fiscal Federalism: 1982–83 Edition.* Washington, D.C.: U.S. Government Printing Office.

Advisory Commission on Intergovernmental Relations. (1989a). *Local Property Taxes Called Worst Tax.* News release of 18th annual ACIR poll, Washington, D.C.: Advisory Commission on Intergovernmental Relations.

Advisory Commission on Intergovernmental Relations. (1989b). *Significant Features of Fiscal Federalism, 1989 Edition* (vol. 1), (Report M-163). Washington, D.C.: Advisory Commission on Intergovernmental Relations.

Advisory Commission on Intergovernmental Relations (ACIR). (1995). *Tax and Expenditure Limits on Local Governments.* Washington, D.C.: Author. Advisory Commission on Intergovernmental Relations.

Alexander, Arthur J. (1974). *Teachers, Salaries and School District Expenditures.* Santa Monica, CA: The RAND Corporation.

Alexander, Kern. (1982). "Concepts of Equity." In Walter McMahon and Terry Geske, eds., *Financing Education.* Urbana, IL: University of Illinois Press.

Alexander, Kern, John Augenblick, William Driscoll, James Guthrie, and R. Levin. (1995). *Proposals for the Elimination of Wealth-Based Disparities in Public Education.* Columbus, OH: Department of Public Instruction.

Alexander, Kern, and Richard Salmon. (1995). *Public School Finance.* Boston: Allyn and Bacon.

Allington, Richard L., and Peter Johnston. (1989). "Coordination, Collaboration, and Consistency: The Redesign of Compensatory and Special Education Interventions." In Robert E. Slavin, Nancy L. Karweit, and Nancy A. Madden, eds., *Effective Programs for Students At Risk.* Needham Heights, MA: Allyn & Bacon, pp. 320–354.

Anderson, David M. (1996). "Stretching the Tax Dollar: Increasing Efficiency in Urban and Rural Schools." In Picus, Lawrence and J. Wattenbarger, eds. *Where Does the Money Go? Resource Allocation in Elementary and Secondary Schools.* Thousand Oaks, CA: Corwin Press, 156–177.

Anderson, Lascelles, Herbert J. Walberg, and Thomas Weinstein. (1998). "Efficiency and Effectiveness Analysis of Chicago Public Elementary Schools: 1989, 1991, 1993." *Educational Administration Quarterly,* 34(4), 484–504.

Augenblick, John. (1997). *Recommendations for a Base Figure and Pupil-Weighted Adjustments to the Base Figure for Use in a New School Finance System in Ohio.* Columbus, OH: Ohio Department of Education.

Augenblick, John, and E. Kathleen Adams. (1979). *An Analysis of the Impact of Changes in the Funding of Elementary/Secondary Education in Texas: 1974/75 to 1977/78.* Denver, CO: Education Commission of the States.

Bailey, Stephen, and Edith Mosher. (1968). *ESEA—The Office of Education Administers a Law.* Syracuse, NY: Syracuse University Press.

Barro, Stephen M. (1972). *Theoretical Models of School District Expenditure Determination and the Impact of Grants-In-Aid.* Santa Monica, CA: The RAND Corporation.

Barro, Stephen. (1989). "Fund Distribution Issues in School Finance: Priorities for the Next Round of Research." *Journal of Education Finance,* 11(1), 17–30.

Barro, Stephen M. (1992). *What Does the Education Dollar Buy? Relationships of Staffing, Staff Characteristics, and Staff Salaries to State Per-Pupil Spending.* Los Angeles, CA: The Finance Center of CPRE, Working Paper.

Barro, Stephen M., and Stephen J. Carroll. (1975). *Budget Allocation by School Districts: An Analysis of Spending for Teachers and Other Resources.* Santa Monica, CA: The Rand Corporation.

Barzelay, Michael. (1992). *Breaking through Bureaucracy: A New Way for Managing in Government.* Berkeley, CA: University of California Press.

Beck, Lynn, and Joseph Murphy. (1996). *The Four Imperatives of a Successful School.* Thousand Oaks, CA: Corwin Press.

Bell, Earl J. (June 1984). "Administrative Inequity and Property Assessment: The Case for the Traditional Approach." *Property Tax Journal,* 3, 123–131.

Bell, Julie D. (June 1998). "Smaller = Better?" *State Legislatures.* http://www.ncsl.org/programs/educ/class.htm

Bell, Michael E., and John H. Bowan. (1986). "Direct Property Tax Relief." In *Final Report of the Minnesota Tax Study Commission,* vol. 1. St. Paul and Boston: Butterworth's, 291–326.

Berke, Joel. (1974). *Answers to Inequity: An Analysis of the New School Finance.* New York: Russell Sage Foundation.

Berne, Robert. (1988). "Equity Issues in School Finance." *Journal of Education Finance,* 14(2), 159–180.

Berne, Robert, and Leanna Stiefel. (1979). "Taxpayer Equity in School Finance Reform: The School Finance and Public Finance Perspective." *Journal of Education Finance,* 5(1), 36–54.

Berne, Robert, and Leanna Stiefel. (1984). *The Measurement of Equity in School Finance.* Baltimore, MD: Johns Hopkins University Press.

Berne, Robert, and Leanna Stiefel. (1999). "Concepts of School Finance Equity: 1970 to Present." In Helen Ladd, Rosemary Chalk and Janet Hansen, eds., *Equity and Adequacy in Education Finance: Issues and Perspectives.* Washington, D.C.: National Academy Press.

Berne, Robert, Leanna Stiefel, and Michelle Moser (1997). "The Coming of Age of School-Level Finance Data." *Journal of Education Finance,* 22(3), 246–254.

Bernstein, Charles D., William T. Hartman, and Rudolph S. Marshall. (1976). "Major Policy Issues in Financing Special Education." *Journal of Education Finance,* 1(3), 299–317.

Berrueta-Clement, J.R., Lawrence Schweinhart, Steve Barnett, A. Epstein, and David Weikart. (1984). *Changed Lives: The Effects of the Perry Pre-School Program on Youths through Age 19.* Ypsilanti, MI: High Scope.

Betts, J.R. (1996). "Is There a Link between School Inputs and Earnings? Fresh Scrutiny of an Old Literature." In Gary Burtless, *Does Money Matter? The Effect of School Resources on Student Achievement and Adult Success.* Washington, D.C.: The Brookings Institution, pp. 141–191.

Bierlein, Louann A., and Mary F. Fulton. (May 1996). *Emerging Issues in Charter School Financing: Policy Brief.* Denver, CO: Education Commission of the States.

Bishop, John. (1998a). *Do Curriculum-Based External Exit Exam Systems Enhance Student Achievement?* (CPRE Research Report Series, RR-40). Philadelphia: University of Pennsylvania, Graduate School of Education, Consortium for Policy Research in Education.

Bishop, John. (1998b). "The Effect of Curriculum-Based External Exit Exam Systems on Student Achievement." *Journal of Economic Education,* 29(2), 171–182.

Blank, Rolf K., Roger E. Levine, and Lauri Steel. (1996). "After 15 Years: Magnet Schools in Urban Education." In Bruce Fuller and Richard F. Elmore (with Gary Orfield), eds., *Who Chooses? Who Loses? Culture, Institutions, and the Unequal Effects of School Choice.* New York: Teachers College Press.

Bobbitt, Sharon A., and Marilyn Miles McMillen. (1990). *Teacher Training, Certification and Assignment.* Paper presented to the annual meeting of the American Educational Research Association, Boston, MA.

Bodilly, Susan. (1996). *Lessons from New American Schools Development Corporation's Demonstration Phase.* Santa Monica, CA: The RAND Corporation.

Bodilly, Sue. (1998). *Lessons from New American Schools' Scale-Up Phase: Prospects for Bringing Designs to Multiple Sites.* Santa Monica, CA: The RAND Corporation.

Bond, Lloyd. (1998). "Disparate Impact and Teacher Certification." *Journal for Personnel Evaluation in Education,* 12(2), 211–220.

Borg, Mary O., Paul M. Mason, and Stephen L. Schapiro. (1991). *The Economic Consequences of State Lotteries.* New York: NY Praeger.

Bowman, John H. (1974). "Tax Exportability, Intergovernmental Aid, and School Finance Reform." *National Tax Journal,* 27(2), 163–173.

Brazer, Harvey E. (1974). "Adjusting for Differences among School Districts in the Costs of Educational Inputs: A Feasibility Report." In Ester Tron, ed., *Selected Papers in School Finance: 1974.* Washington, D.C.: U.S. Office of Education.

Break, George F. (1980). *Financing Government in a Federal System.* Washington, D.C.: Brookings Institution.

Brown, Lawrence L., et al. (1977). *School Finance Reform in the Seventies: Achievements and Failures.* Washington, D.C.: U.S. Department of Health, Education and Welfare, Office of the Assistant Secretary for Planning and Evaluation and Killalea Associates, Incorporated.

Brown, Patricia, and Richard Elmore. (1982). "Analyzing the Impact of School Finance Reform." In Nelda Cambron-McCabe and Allan Odden, eds., *The Changing Politics of School Finance.* Cambridge, MA: Ballinger, 107–138.

Browning, E. (1985). "Tax Incidence, Indirect Taxes, and Transfers." *National Tax Journal,* 38, 525–534.

Brownlee, O.H. (1960). *Estimated Distribution of Minnesota Taxes and Public Expenditure Benefits.* Minneapolis, MN: University of Minnesota Press.

Bruer, John. (1993). *Schools for Thought.* Cambridge, MA: MIT Press.

Bryk, Anthony, John Q. Easton, David W. Kerbow, Sharon G. Rollow, and Penny B. Sebring. (1997). *Charting Chicago School Reform: Democratic Localism as a Lever for Change.* Boulder, CO: Westview Press.

Bryk, Anthony S., Paul Hill, and Dorothy Shipps. (1997). *Decentralization in Practice: Toward a System of Schools.* Chicago: Consortium on Chicago School Reform.

Bryk, Anthony, Valerie E. Lee, and P. Holland. (1993). *Catholic Schools and the Common Good.* Cambridge, MA: Harvard University Press.

Buday, Mary, and James Kelley. (November 1996). National Board Certification and the Teaching Profession's Commitment to Quality Assurance. *Phi Delta Kappan,* 78(3), 215–219.

Bureau of Economic Analysis (1998). Survey of Current Business. Washington, D.C.: U.S. Department of Commerce. http://www.bea.doc.gov/bea/ARTICLES/NATIONAL/NIPA/1998/0898nip3.pdf/Table 1, p. 147.

Burtless, Gary, ed. (1996). *Does Money Matter?* Washington, D.C.: Brookings Institution.

Busch, Carolyn, and Allan Odden. (1997a). "Collection of School-Level Finance Data." *Journal of Education Finance,* 22(3).

Busch, Carolyn, and Allan Odden. (1997b). "Introduction to the Special Issue-Improving Educational Policy with School Level Data: A Synthesis of Multiple Perspectives." *Journal of Education Finance,* 22(3), 225–245.

Busch, Carolyn, Karen Kucharz, and Allan Odden. (1996). "Recognizing Additional Student Need in Wisconsin: A Re-Examination of Equity and Equity Analysis." In Barbara LaCost, ed., *School Finance Policy Issues in the States and Provinces.* Lincoln, NE: University of Nebraska and American Education Finance Association, pp. 109–126.

Card, David, and Alan B. Krueger. (1996). "The Economic Return to School Quality." In William J. Baumol and William E. Becker, eds., *Assessing Educational Practices: The Contribution of Economics.* Cambridge, MA: The MIT Press, pp. 161–182.

Cardenas, Jose, J.J. Bernal, and N. Kean. (1976). *Bilingual Education Cost Analysis: Texas.* San Antonio, TX: Intercultural Development Research Association.

Carpenter-Huffman, P., and S. M. Samulon. (1981). *Case Studies of Delivery and Cost of Bilingual Education Programs.* Santa Monica, CA: The RAND Corporation.

Carroll, Stephen J., and Rolla Edward Park. (1983). *The Search for Equity in School Finance.* Cambridge, MA: Ballinger.

Chaikind, Steve, Louis C. Danielson, and Marsha L. Braven. (1993). "What Do We Know about the Costs of Special Education? A Selected Review." *Journal of Special Education,* 26(4), 344–370.

Chambers, Jay G. (1978). *Educational Cost Differentials across School Districts in California.* Denver, CO: Education Commission of the States.

Chambers, Jay G. (1980). *The Development of a Cost of Education Index for the State of California.* Final reports, Parts 1 and 2, prepared for the California State Department of Education.

Chambers, Jay G. (1981). "Cost and Price Level Adjustments to State Aid for Education: A Theoretical and Empirical View." In K. Forbis Jordan and Nelda Cambron-McCabe, eds., *Perspectives in State School Support Programs.* Cambridge, MA: Ballinger.

Chambers, Jay G. (1995). "Public School Teacher Cost Differences across the United States: Introduction to a Teacher Cost Index (TCI)." In *Developments in School Finance* [on-line]. Available: http://www.ed.gov/NCES/pubs/96344cha.html.

Chambers, Jay G. (1998). *Report on $ and Personnel by Site in Ohio.* Washington, D.C.: National Center for Education Statistics.

Chambers, Jay G. (1999). "The Patterns of Expenditures on Students with Disabilities: A Methodological and Empirical Analysis." In Jay Chambers, Thomas Parrish, and Cassandra Guarino, eds., *Funding Special Education.* Thousand Oaks, CA: Corwin Press, pp. 89–123.

Chambers, Jay G, and William T. Hartman, eds. (1983). *Special Education Policies: Their History, Implementation and Finance.* Philadelphia: Temple University Press.

Chambers, Jay G., Allan Odden, and Phillip E. Vincent. (1976). *Cost of Education Indices Among School Districts.* Denver, CO: Education Commission of the States.

Chambers, Jay G, and Thomas Parrish. (1983). *The Development of a Resource Cost Model Funding Base for Education Finance in Illinois.* Stanford, CA: Associates for Education Finance and Planning.

Chambers, Jay G, and Thomas Parrish. (1994). "State-Level Education Finance." In *Advances in Educational Productivity.* Greenwich, CT: JAI Press, pp. 45–74.

Chambers, Jay G, Thomas Parrish, and Cassandra Guarino, eds. (1999). *Funding Special Education.* Thousand Oaks, CA: Corwin Press.

Clark, Catherine. (1998). "Using School-Level Data to Explore Resources and Outcomes in Texas." *Journal of Education Finance,* 23(3), 374–389.

Clune, William. (1994a). "The Shift from Equity to Adequacy in School Finance." *Educational Policy,* 8(4), 376–394.

Clune, William. (1994b). "The Cost and Management of Program Adequacy: An Emerging Issue in Education Policy and Finance." *Educational Policy,* 8(4).

Clune, William. (1995). "Adequacy Litigation in School Finance Symposium." *University of Michigan Journal of Law Reform,* 28(3).

Clune, William, and Paula White. (1988). *School-Based Management: Institutional Variation, Implementation and Issues for Further Research.* New Brunswick, NJ: Rutgers University, Center for Policy Research in Education.

Clune, William, and Paula White. (1992). "Education Reform in the Trenches: Increased Academic Course Taking in High Schools with Lower Achieving Students in States with Higher Graduation Requirements." *Educational Evaluation & Policy Analysis,* 14(1), 2–20.

Coeyman, Marjorie. (November 24, 1998). "Small-Town Schools: Changing Times and Budgets Put the Squeeze On." *Christian Science Monitor,* 90(252), 15.

Cohen, David K., and Heather Hill. (1997). *Instructional Policy and Classroom Performance: The Mathematics Reform in California.* Philadelphia: University of Pennsylvania, Graduate School of Education, Consortium for Policy Research in Education.

Cohen, David K., and Heather Hill. (1998). *State Policy and Classroom Performance: Mathematics Reform in California* (Policy Brief RB-23). Philadelphia: University of Pennsylvania, Graduate School of Education, Consortium for Policy Research in Education.

Cohen, David K., Milbrey McLaughlin, and Joan Talbert. (1993). *Teaching for Understanding.* San Francisco: Jossey-Bass.

Cohen, Matthew C. (1997). "Issues in School-Level Analysis of Education Expenditure Data." *Journal of Education Finance,* 22(3), 255–279.

Cohn, Elchanan. (1974). *Economics of State Aid to Education.* Lexington, MA: Heath Lexington Books.

Cohn, Elchanan and Terry G. Geske. (1990). *The Economics of Education,* 3d ed. Oxford, England: Pergamon Press.

Comer, James P. (1993–94). *A Brief History and Summary of the School Development Program: Summary of School Development Program (SDP) Effects.* New Haven, CT: Yale University, Yale Child Study Center.

Comer, James P., Norris M. Haynes, Edward T. Joyner, and Michael Ben-Avie. (1996). *Rallying the Whole Village: The Comer Process for Reforming Education.* New York: Teachers College Press.

Conley, Sharon C. (1991). "Review of Research on Teacher Participation in School Decision Making." In Gerald Grant, ed., *Review of Research in Education,* 17, Washington, D.C.: American Educational Research Association, pp. 225–266.

Conley, Sharon, and Allan Odden. (1995). "Linking Teacher Compensation to Teacher Career Development." *Educational Evaluation and Policy Analysis,* 17(2), 219–238.

Coons, John, William Clune, and Stephen Sugarman. (1970). *Private Wealth and Public Education.* Cambridge, MA: Belknap Press of Harvard University Press.

Cooper, Bruce. (March 1993). *School Site Cost Allocations: Testing a Microfinancial Model in 23 Districts in Ten States.* Paper presented at the annual meeting of the American Education Finance Association, Albuquerque, NM.

Cooper, Bruce S., and Associates. (1994). "Making Money Matter in Education: A Micro-Financial Model for Determining School-Level Allocations, Efficiency, and Productivity." *Journal of Education Finance,* 20(1), 66–87.

Cooperative Research Project. (1996). *A Three-Year Report Card: Leading Victoria's Schools of the Future.* Melbourne, Australia: Directorate of School Education.

Corcoran, Thomas B. (1995). *Helping Teachers Teach Well: Transforming Professional Development.* New Brunswick, NJ: Consortium for Policy Research in Education Policy Briefs.

Corcoran, Thomas B., and Margaret Goertz. (1995). "Instructional Capacity and High Performance Schools." *Educational Researcher,* 24(9), 27–31.

Consortium on Renewing Education. (1998). *20/20 Vision: A Strategy for Doubling America's Academic Achievement by the Year 2020.* Vanderbilt University: Peabody Center for Education Policy.

Cubberly, Elwood Patterson. (1905). *School Funds and Their Apportionment.* New York: Teachers College Press.

Cubberly, Elwood Patterson. (1906). *School Funds and Their Apportionment.* New York: Teachers College, Columbia University.

Cummins, James. (1980). "The Exit and Entry Fallacy in Bilingual Education," *NABE Journal,* 4, 25–60.

Danielson, Charlotte. (1998). *Enhancing Professional Practice: A Framework for Teaching.* Arlington, VA: Association for Supervision and Curriculum Development.

Darling-Hammond, Linda. (1996). "Beyond Bureaucracy: Restructuring Schools for High Performance." In Susan Fuhrman and Jennifer O'Day, eds., *Rewards and Reform: Creating Educational Incentives That Work.* San Francisco: Jossey-Bass.

Darling-Hammond, Linda. (1997). *The Right to Learn.* San Francisco: Jossey Bass.

Darling-Hammond, Linda, and Deborah Ball. (1998). *Teaching for High Standards: What Policymakers Need to Know and Be Able to Do* (JRE-04). Philadelphia: University of Pennsylvania, Graduate School of Education, Consortium for Policy Research in Education.

Darling-Hammond, Linda, and Milbrey McLaughlin. (1995). "Policies that Support Professional Development in an Era of Reform." *Phi Delta Kappan,* 76(8), 597–604.

Deal, Terrance, and Kent Peterson. (1994). *The Leadership Paradox: Balancing Logic and Artistry in Schools.* San Francisco: Jossey-Bass.

DeLeeuw, Frank, and Nkanta Ekanem. (1971). The Supply of Rental Housing. *American Economic Review,* 62, 806–817.

Demographics.com. (1996). *Decreasing Profits for State Lotteries.* http://www.demographics.com/publications/fc/96_FC/9611_FC/9611F03.HTM

Downes, Thomas, and Thomas Pogue. (1994). "Adjusting School Aid Formulas for the Higher Cost of Educating Disadvantaged Students." *National Tax Journal,* 47(1), 89–110.

Doyle, Denis, and Terry Hartle. (1985). *Excellence in Education: The States Take Charge.* Washington, D.C.: American Enterprise Institute.

Due, John F., and John L. Mikesell. (1994). *Sales Taxation: State and Local Structure and Administration,* 2d ed. Washington, D.C.: The Urban Institute.

Duncombe, William, John Ruggiero, and John Yinger. (1996). "Alternative Approaches to Measuring the Cost of Education." In Helen F. Ladd, ed., *Holding Schools Accountable: Performance-based Reform in Education.* Washington, D.C.: The Brookings Institution, pp. 327–356.

Duncombe, William, and John Yinger. (1999). "Performance Standards and Educational Cost Indices: You Can't Have One without the Other." In Helen Ladd, Rosemary Chalk, and Janet S. Hansen, eds., *Equity and Adequacy in Education Finance: Issues and Perspectives.* Washington, D.C.: National Academy Press.

Dwyer, Carol Anne. (1998). "Psychometrics of Praxis III: Classroom Performance Assessments Certification." *Journal for Personnel Evaluation in Education,* 12(2), 163–187.

Dye, Robert F., and Teresa I. McGuire. (1991). "Growth and Variability of State Individual Income and Sales Taxes." *National Tax Journal,* 44, 55–66.

Ebel, Robert D., and James Ortbal. (1989). "Direct Residential Property Tax Relief." *Intergovernmental Perspective,* 16, 9–14.

Edison Project. (1994). *An Invitation to Public School Partnership.* New York: The Edison Project.

Edison Project. (1996a). *Boston Renaissance Charter School End-of-year Report: Follow-up Data on Student Achievement and Customer Satisfaction.* New York: The Edison Project.

Edison Project. (1996b). *Dodge-Edison Partnership School End-of-year Report: Follow-up Data on Student Achievement and Customer Satisfaction.* New York: The Edison Project.

Edison Project. (1996c). *Dr. Martin Luther King, Jr., Academy End-of-year Report: Follow-up Data on Student Achievement and Customer Satisfaction.* New York: The Edison Project.

Edison Project. (1996d). *Washington Elementary School End-of-year Report: Follow-up Data on Student Achievement and Customer Satisfaction.* New York: The Edison Project.

Edison Project. (1997). *Annual Report on School Performance.* New York: The Edison Project.

Edison Project. (1998). *Annual Report on School Performance.* New York: The Edison Project.

Education Commission of the States. (1995). *Charter Schools: What Are They Up To?* Denver, CO: Education Commission of the States.

Education Commission of the States. (1996). *Bending without Breaking—Improving Edu-*

cation through Flexibility and Choice. Denver, CO: Education Commission of the States.

Education Commission of the States. (1997a). *A Policymaker's Guide to Standards-Led Assessment.* Denver, CO: Education Commission of the States.

Education Commission of the States. (1997b). *So You Have Standards: Now What?* Denver, CO: Education Commission of the States.

Education Commission of the States. (1997c). *State Policymaker's Guide to Reform Networks.* Denver, CO: Education Commission of the States.

Education Commission of the States. (1998). "Class Size Reduction Measures." Education Commission of the States, Information Clearinghouse: http://www.ecs.org/ecs/ecsweb.nsf.

Elmore, Richard. (1990). *School Restructuring: The Next Generation of Educational Reform.* San Francisco: Jossey-Bass.

Elmore, Richard, Charles Abelman, and Susan Fuhrman. (1996). "The New Accountability in State Education Policy." In Helen Ladd, ed., *Performance Based Strategies for Improving Schools.* Washington, D.C.: The Brookings Institution, pp. 65–98.

Elmore, Richard, and Deanna Burney. (1996). *Professional Development and Instructional Improvement in Community School District #2, New York City.* Philadelphia: University of Pennsylvania, Consortium for Policy Research in Education.

Enrich, Paul. (1995). "Leaving Equality Behind: New Directions in School Finance Reform." *Vanderbilt Law Review,* 48, 100–194.

Evans, William, Sheila Murray, and Robert Schwab. (1997). *State Education Finance Policy after Court Mandated Reform: The Legacy of Serrano. 1996 Proceedings of the Eighty-Ninth Annual Conference on Taxation.* Washington, D.C.: National Tax Association-Tax Institute of America.

Farland, Gary. (1997). "Collection of Fiscal and Staffing Data at the School Site Level." *Journal of Education Finance,* 22(3), 280–290.

Fashola, Olatokunbo, and Robert Slavin. (1997). "Promising Programs for Elementary and Middle Schools: Evidence of Effectiveness and Replicability." *Journal of Education for Students Placed at Risk,* 2(3), 251–307.

Federation of Tax Administrators. (1996). "FTA Surveys Sales Taxation of Services." *Tax Administrators News,* 60(12). http://sso.org/fta/services.html.

Feldman, Sandra. (October 5, 1997). "Two Wrong Solutions (Social Promotion and Retention)." *The New York Times.*

Feldstein, Martin. (1975). "Wealth Neutrality and Local Choice in Public Education." *American Economic Review,* 64, 75–89.

Ferguson, Ronald F. (Summer 1991). "Paying for Public Education: New Evidence on How and Why Money Matters." *Harvard Journal on Legislation,* 28, 465–497.

Ferguson, Ronald F., and Helen Ladd. (1996). "How and Why Money Matters: An Analysis of Alabama Schools." In Helen Ladd, ed., *Holding Schools Accountable.* Washington, D.C.: Brookings, pp. 265–298.

Finn, Chester E., LouAnn A. Bierlein, and Brunno V. Manno. (1996). "Finding the Right Fit." *Brookings Review,* 14(3), 18–21.

Finn, Jeremy. (1996). *Class Size and Students At Risk: What Is Known? What Next?* Paper prepared for the National Institute on the Education of At-Risk Students, Office of Educational Research and Improvement, U.S. Department of Education.

Finn, Jeremy, and Charles Achilles. (1990). "Answers and Questions About Class Size: A Statewide Experiment." *American Educational Research Journal,* 27(3), 557–577.

Finnan, Christine, Edward St. John, Jane McCarthy, and Simeon Slovacek. (1996). *Accelerated Schools in Action*. Thousand Oaks, CA: Corwin Press.

Firestone, William A., Margaret E. Goertz, Brianna Nagle, and Marcy F. Smelkinson. (1994). "Where Did the $800 Million Go? The First Years of New Jersey's Quality Education Act." *Educational Evaluation and Policy Analysis*, 16(4), 359–374.

Florida Department of Revenue. (n.d.). *Outstanding Research and Analysis in the Florida Department of Revenue*. Application to the Federation of Tax Administrators. Mimeo.

Folger, John. (1990). *The Cost-Effectiveness of Adding Aides or Reducing Class Size*. Paper presented at the annual meeting of the American Educational Research Association, Boston, MA.

Folger, John, ed. (1992). "Project STAR and Class Size Policy." *Peabody Journal of Education*, 67(1).

Fox, James. (1987). "An Analysis of Classroom Spending." *Planning and Changing*, 18(3), 154–162.

Fox, William F. (1981). "Reviewing Economies of Size in Education." *Journal of Education Finance*, 6(3), 273–296.

Fuhrman, Susan H., ed. (1993). *Designing Coherent Education Policy: Improving the System*. San Francisco: Jossey-Bass.

Fuhrman, Susan F., and Richard F. Elmore (1992). *Takeover and Deregulation: Working Models of New State and Local Regulatory Relationships*. New Brunswick, NJ: Rutgers University, Consortium for Policy Research in Education.

Fullerton, Don, and Diane Lim Rogers. (1993). *Who Bears the Lifetime Tax Burden?* Washington, D.C.: The Brookings Institution.

Gamoran, Adam. (1996). "Student Achievement in Public Magnet, Public Comprehensive and Private City High Schools." *Educational Evaluation and Policy Analysis*, 18(1), 1–18.

Gandal, Matt. (1996). *Making Standards Matter*. Washington, D.C.: American Federation of Teachers.

Garcia, O. (1977). "Analyzing Bilingual Education Costs." In G. Banco, et al., eds., *Bilingual Education: Current Perspectives*. Arlington, VA: Education Center for Applied Linguistics.

Garms, Walter I. (1979). "Measuring the Equity of School Finance Systems." *Journal of Education Finance*, 4(4), 415–435.

General Accounting Office. (1988). *Legislative Mandates: State Experiences Offer Insights for Federal Action*. Washington, D.C.: General Accounting Office.

General Accounting Office. (1997). *School Finance: State Efforts to Reduce Funding Gaps between Poor and Wealthy Districts*. Washington, D.C.: General Accounting Office.

Glass, Gene V., B. McGaw, and M.L. Smith. (1981). *Meta-Analysis in Social Research*. Beverly Hills, CA: Sage.

Glass, Gene V., and M.L. Smith. (1979). "Meta-Analysis of Research on Class Size and Achievement." *Educational Evaluation and Policy Analysis*, 1(1), 2–16.

Glidden, Heidi. (1998). *Making Standards Matter 1998*. Washington, D.C.: American Federation of Teachers.

Goertz, Margaret. (1983). "School Finance in New Jersey: A Decade after Robinson v. Cahill." *Journal of Education Finance*, 8(4), 475–489.

Goertz, Margaret. (1988). *School District's Allocation of Chapter 1 Resources*, Princeton, NJ: Educational Testing Service.

Goertz, Margaret. (1997). "The Challenges of Collecting School-Based Data." *Journal of Education Finance*, 22(3), 291–302.

Goertz, Margaret, Robert Floden, and Jennifer O'Day. (1995). *Studies of Education Reform: Systemic Reform. Volume I: Findings and Conclusions.* Philadelphia: University of Pennsylvania, Graduate School of Education, Consortium for Policy Research in Education.

Goertz, Margaret, Margaret McLauglin, Virginia Roach, and Suzanne Raber. (1999). "What Will It Take: Including Students with Disabilities in Standards-Based Education Reform." In Jay Chambers, Thomas Parrish, and Cassandra Guarino, eds., *Funding Special Education.* Thousand Oaks, CA: Corwin Press, pp. 41–62.

Goertz, Margaret, and Allan Odden, eds. (1999). *School-Based Financing.* Thousand Oaks, CA: Corwin Press.

Goertz, Margaret, and Leanna Stiefel. (1998). "Introduction to the Special Issue." *Journal of Education Finance,* 23(4), 435–446.

Gold, Stephen D., David M. Smith, Stephen B. Lawton and Andrea C. Hyary, eds. (1992). *Public School Finance Programs in the United States and Canada, 1990–1991.* Albany: State University of New York, Center for the Study of the States.

Gold, Steven D. (1986). *Reforming State Tax Systems.* Denver, CO: National Conference of State Legislatures, pp. 11–30.

Gold, Steven D.. (1994). *Tax Options for States Needing More School Revenue.* Washington, D.C.: National Education Association

Gold, Steven D., David M. Smith, and Stephen B. Lawton. (1995). *Public School Finance Programs of the United States and Canada: 1993–94.* New York: American Education Finance Association of Center for the Study of the States, The Nelson A. Rockefeller Institute of Government.

Gonzalez, Rosa Maria. (1996). *Bilingual/ESL Programs Evaluation, 1995–96* (Publication No. 95-01). Austin, TX: Austin Independent School District. (ERIC Document Reproduction Service No. ED 404877.)

Greene, Jay P., Paul E. Peterson, and Jiangtao Du. (1997). *The Effectiveness of School Choice: The Milwaukee Experiment* (Occasional Paper 97-1). Cambridge, MA: Harvard University, Educational Policy and Governance.

Greene, Jay P., William G. Howell, and Paul E. Peterson. (1997). *An Evaluation of the Cleveland Scholarship Program.* Mimeo prepared for the Program on Policy and Governance, Harvard University.

Greenwald, Rob, Larry V. Hedges, and Richard D. Laine. (1996a). "The Effect of School Resources on Student Achievement." *Review of Educational Research,* 66(3), 361–396.

Greenwald, Rob, Larry V. Hedges, and Richard D. Laine. (1996b). "Interpreting Research on School Resources and Student Achievement: A Rejoinder to Hanushek." *Review of Educational Research,* 66(3), 411–416.

Grieson, Ronald. (1973). "The Supply of Rental Housing: Comment." *American Economic Review,* 63: 303–307.

Guskey, T.R., and K.D. Peterson (1996). "The Road to Classroom Change." *Educational Leadership* 53(1), 10–14.

Guthrie, James W. (1979). "Organizational Scale and School Success." *Educational Evaluation and Policy Analysis,* 1(1), 17–27.

Guthrie, James W. (1988). *Understanding School Budgets.* Washington D.C.: U.S. Department of Education.

Guthrie, James W., and Richard Rothstein. (1999). "Enabling Adequacy to Achieve Reality: Translating Adequacy Into State School Finance Distribution Arrangements." In Ladd, Helen F., Rosemary Chalk and Janet S. Hansen, eds. *Equity and Adequacy in Education Finance.* Washington, D.C.: National Academy Press, 209–259.

Guthrie, James W., Walter Garms, and Lawrence Pierce. (1988). *School Finance and Education Policy.* Englewood Cliffs, NJ: Prentice Hall.

Guthrie, James W., Michael W. Kirst, and Allan R. Odden. (1990). *Conditions of Education in California, 1989.* Berkeley, CA: University of California, School of Education, Policy Analysis for California Education.

Hall, Eugene, and Edward Caffarella. (1996). *First Year Implementation of the Douglas County, Colorado School District Performance Pay Plan for Teachers (1994–95).* Greeley, CO: University of Northern Colorado, School of Education.

Hall, Eugene E., and Edward Caffarella. (1998). *Third Year Implementation Assessment of the Douglas County, Colorado School District Performance Pay Plan for Teachers (1996–97).* Greeley, CO: University of Northern Colorado, School of Education.

Haller, Emil, David H. Monk, Alyce Spotted Bear, Julie Griffith, and Pamela Moss. (1990). "School Size and Program Comprehensiveness: Evidence from *High School and Beyond.*" *Educational Evaluation and Policy Analysis,* 12(2), 109–120.

Hamilton, Laura, and Stephen Klein. (1998). *Large-Scale Measure of Student Achievement in the United States.* Paper prepared for the National Research Council Committee on School Finance Equity, Adequacy and Productivity.

Hamilton, Stephen F. (1983). "The Social Side of Schooling: Ecological Studies of Classrooms and Schools." *The Elementary School Journal,* 83(4), 313–334.

Hannaway, Jane. (1996). "Management Decentralization and Performance-Based Incentives: Theoretical Consideration for Schools." In Eric A. Hanushek and D. W. Jorgenson, eds., *Improving America's Schools: The Role of Incentives.* Washington, D.C.: National Academy Press, pp. 97–109.

Hanushek, Eric A. (1981). "Throwing Money at Schools." *Journal of Policy Analysis and Management,* 1(1), 19–41.

Hanushek, Eric A. (1986). "The Economics of Schooling: Production and Efficiency in Public Schools." *Journal of Economic Literature,* 24(3), 1141–1177.

Hanushek, Eric A. (1989). "The Impact of Differential Expenditures on Student Performance," *Educational Researcher,* 18(4), 45–52.

Hanushek, Eric A. (1994a). *Making Schools Work: Improving Performance and Controlling Costs.* Washington D.C.: The Brookings Institution.

Hanushek, Eric A. (1994b). "Money Might Matter Somewhere: A Response to Hedges, Laine, and Greenwald." *Educational Researcher,* 23(3), 5–8.

Hanushek, Eric A. (1997). "Assessing the Effects of School Resources on Student Performance: An Update." *Educational Evaluation and Policy Analysis,* 19(2), 141–164.

Harris, Russell. (1978). "Reforming School Finance in Pennsylvania." *Journal of Education Finance,* 3(4), 487–501.

Hart, Ann Weaver. (1994). "Work Feature Values of Today's and Tomorrow's Teachers: Work Redesign as an Incentive and School Improvement Policy." *Educational Evaluation and Policy Analysis,* 16, 458–473.

Hartman, William. (1980). "Policy Effects of Special Education Funding Formulas," *Journal of Education Finance.* 6(2), 135–139.

Hartman, William. (1988a). "District Spending: What Do the Dollars Buy?" *Journal of Education Finance,* 13(4), 436–459.

Hartman, William. (1988b). *School District Budgeting.* Englewood Cliffs, NJ: Prentice Hall.

Hartman, William. (1994). "District Spending Disparities Revisited." *Journal of Education Finance,* 20(1), 88–106.

Haynes, Norris, Christine Emmons, and Darren Woodruff. (1998). "School Development

Program Effects: Linking Implementation to Outcomes." *Journal of Education for Students Placed At Risk,* 3(1), 71–85.

Hayward, Gerald C. (1988). *The Two Million Dollar School.* Berkeley, CA: University of California, School of Education, Policy Analysis for California Education.

Hedges, Larry V., Richard D. Laine, and Rob Greenwald. (1994a). "Does Money Matter? A Meta-Analysis of Studies of the Effects of Differential School Inputs on Student Outcomes." *Educational Researcher,* 23(3), 5–14.

Hedges, Larry V., Richard D. Laine, and Rob Greenwald. (1994b). "Money Does Matter Somewhere: A Reply to Hanushek." *Educational Researcher,* 23(3), 9–10.

Heise, Michael. (1995). "State Constitutions, School Finance Litigation and the 'Third Wave': From Equity to Adequacy." *Temple Law Review,* 68(3), 1151–1176.

Heneman, Herbert G., III. (1998). "Assessment of the Motivational Reactions of Teachers to a School-Based Performance Award Program." *Journal of Personnel Evaluation in Education,* 12(1).

Heneman, Herbert G., III, and Anthony Milanowski. (1999). "Teacher Attitudes about Teacher Bonuses under School-Based Performance Award Programs." *Journal for Personnel Evaluation in Education,* 12(4), 327–342.

Heneman, Robert L., and Gerald E. Ledford, Jr. (1998). "Competency Pay for Professionals and Managers in Business: A Review and Implications for Teachers Certification." *Journal for Personnel Evaluation in Education,* 12(2).

Hentschke, Guilbert C. (1986). *School Business Administration: A Comparative Perspective,* Berkeley, CA: McCutchan Publishing Company.

Hertert, Linda. (1996). "Does Equal Funding for Districts Mean Equal Funding for Classroom Students? Evidence from California." In Lawrence O. Picus and James L. Wattenbarger, eds., *Where Does the Money Go? Resource Allocation in Elementary and Secondary Schools.* 1995 Yearbook of the American Education Finance Association, Newbury Park, CA: Corwin Press, pp. 71–84.

Hertert, Linda, Carolyn A. Busch, and Allan R. Odden. (1994). "School Financing Inequities among the States: The Problem from a National Perspective." *Journal of Education Finance,* 19(3), 231–255.

Hess, Fred. (1995). *Restructuring Urban Schools: A Chicago Perspective.* New York: Teachers College Press.

Hickrod, G. Alan, Ramesh B. Chaudhari, and Ben C. Hubbard. (1981). *Reformation and Counter-Reformation in Illinois School Finance: 1973–1981.* Normal, IL: Center for the Study of Education Finance.

Hill, Paul T., Gail E. Foster, and Tamar Gendler. (1990). *High Schools with Character.* Santa Monica, CA: The RAND Corporation.

Hill, Paul T., Lawrence Pierce, and James Guthrie. (1997). *Reinventing Public Education.* Chicago: University of Chicago Press.

Hinrichs, William L., and Richard D. Laine. (1996). *Adequacy: Building Quality and Efficiency into the Cost of Education.* Springfield, IL: Illinois Board of Education.

Hirsch, E. Donald. (1996). *The Schools We Need and Why We Don't Have Them.* New York: Doubleday.

Hirth, Marilyn. (1994). "A Multistate Analysis of School Finance Issues and Equity Trends in Indiana, Illinois, and Michigan, 1982–1992." *Journal of Education Finance,* 20(2), 163–190.

Hodge, Michael. (1981). "Improving Finance and Governance of Education for Special Populations." In K. Forbis Jordan and Nelda Cambron-McCabe, eds., *Perspectives in State School Support Programs.* Cambridge, MA: Ballinger.

Hovey, Hal. (1998). "Tax Revenue Growth in Individual States." *State Policy Reports,* 16(8), Hilton Head, SC: State Policy Research.

Hyman, D., and E. Pasour. (1973). Property Tax Differentials and Residential Rents in North Carolina. *National Tax Journal,* 26: 303–307.

Jaeger, Richard M. (1998). "Evaluating the Psychometric Qualities of the National Board for Professional Teaching Standards' Assessments: A Methodological Accounting." *Journal for Personnel Evaluation in Education,* 12(2), 189–210.

Johns, Roe, Kern Alexander, and K. Forbis Jordan, eds. (1971). *Planning to Finance Education, vol. 3.* Gainesville, FL: National Education Finance Project.

Johnson, Gary, and George Pillianayagam. (1991). "A Longitudinal Equity Study of Ohio's School Finance System: 1980–89." *Journal of Education Finance,* 17(1), 60–82.

Johnson, Susan Moore. (1986). "Incentives for Teachers: What Motivates, What Matters." *Educational Administration Quarterly,* 22(3), 54–79.

Johnston, Jocelyn, and William Duncombe. (1998). "Balancing Conflicting Policy Objectives: The Case of School Finance Reform." *Public Administration Review,* 58(2), 145–157.

Joyce, Bruce, and Emily Calhoun, eds. (1996). *Learning Experiences in School Renewal: An Exploration of Five Successful Programs.* Eugene, OR: ERIC Clearinghouse on Educational Management.

Kakalik, James. (1979). "Issues in the Cost and Finance of Special Education." *Review of Educational Research, vol. 7.* Washington, D.C.: American Educational Research Association.

Kakalik, James, W.S. Furry, M.A. Thomas, and M. F. Carney. (1981). *The Cost of Special Education.* Santa Monica, CA: The RAND Corporation.

Katzenbach, Jon R., and Douglas K. Smith. (1993). *The Wisdom of Teams: Creating the High-Performance Organization.* Boston: Harvard Business School Press.

Kaufman, Phillip, Marilyn McMillen, and Denise Bradby. (1992). *Dropout Rates in the Unites States: 1991.* Washington, D.C.: National Center for Education Statistics.

Kearney, Phillip, Li-Ju Chen, and Marjorie Checkoway. (1988). *Measuring Equity in Michigan School Finance: A Further Look.* Ann Arbor, MI: University of Michigan, School of Education.

Kelley, Carolyn. (1997). "Teacher Compensation and Organization." *Educational Evaluation & Policy Analysis,* 19(1), 15–28.

Kelley, Carolyn. (1998a). "The Kentucky School-Based Performance Award Program: School-Level Effects." *Educational Policy,* 12(3), 305–324.

Kelley, Carolyn. (April 1998b). *Schools That Succeed: The Role of Enabling Conditions in Facilitating Student Achievement in School-Based Performance Award Programs.* Paper presented at the American Educational Research Association annual conference held April 13–18, 1998, in San Diego, California. Available from the Consortium for Policy Research in Education, Wisconsin Center for Education Research, University of Wisconsin—Madison.

Kelley, Carolyn, Herbert Heneman, III, and Anthony Milanowski. (1999). *School-Based Performance Award Programs, Teacher Motivation and School Achievement.* Paper prepared for the University of Wisconsin—Madison, Wisconsin Center for Education Research, Consortium for Policy Research in Education.

Kelley, Carolyn, Anthony Milanowski, and Herbert G. Heneman, III. (April 1998). *Changing Teacher Compensation: Cross-Site Analysis of the Effects of School-Based Performance Award Programs.* Paper presented at the American Educational Research Association annual conference held April 13–18, 1998, in San Diego, California.

Available from the Consortium for Policy Research in Education, Wisconsin Center for Education Research, University of Wisconsin—Madison.

Kelley, Carolyn, and Jean Protsik. (1997). "Risk and Reward: Perspectives on the Implementation of Kentucky's School-Based Performance Award Program." *Educational Administration Quarterly,* 33(4), 474–505.

Kellor, Eileen, and Allan Odden. (1998). *Cincinnati: A Case Study of the Design of a School-Based Performance Award Program.* Madison, WI: University of Wisconsin, Wisconsin Center for Education Research, Consortium for Policy Research in Education.

Kellor, Eileen, Anthony Milanowski, and Allan Odden. (1998). A Case Study of the Next Century Learning Center's Knowledge and Skills Based Pay Program. Madison, WI: University of Wisconsin, Wisconsin Center for Education Research, Consortium for Policy Research in Education.

Kenny, L., D. Denslow, and Irving Goffman. (1975). "Determination of Teacher Cost Differentials among School Districts in the State of Florida." In Ester Tron, ed., *Selected Papers in School Finance.* Washington, D.C.: U.S. Office of Education.

King, Jennifer. (1994). "Meeting the Educational Needs of At-risk Students: A Cost Analysis of Three Models." *Educational Evaluation and Policy Analysis,* 16(1), 1–19.

King, M. Bruce, Karen Seashore Louis, Helen M. Marks, and Kent D. Peterson. (1996). "Participatory Decision Making." In Fred Newmann, ed., *Authentic Achievement: Restructuring Schools for Intellectual Quality.* San Francisco: Jossey-Bass, pp. 245–263.

King, M. Bruce, and Fred Newmann. (1998). *School Capacity as a Mission for Professional Development: Mapping the Terrain in Low Income Schools.* Paper prepared for the U.S. Department of Education and available from the University of Wisconsin—Madison.

King, Richard A. (1985). "Resource Allocation: From Macro- to Micro-Level Analyses." *Planning and Changing,* 226–233.

Kirst, Michael. (1977). "What Happens at the Local Level after School Finance Reform?" *Policy Analysts,* 3(1), 302–324.

Kirst, Michael. (1997). *Signals and Incentives Sent by Higher Education Admissions and Placement Policies to Students, Parents and Schools.* Stanford, CA: Stanford University, School of Education, National Center for Post Secondary Improvement.

Klein, Steven, and Robert M. Bell. (1995). "How Will the NCAAs New Standards Affect Minority Student Athletes?" *Change Magazine,* 8(3), 18–21.

KMPG Peat Marwick. (1993). *Report of the Study of the Iowa Tax System.* Washington, D.C.: KMPG Peat Marwick/Policy Economics Group.

Kochin, Lewis A., and Richard W. Parks. (March 1982). "Vertical Equity in Real Estate Assessment: A Fair Appraisal." *Economic Inquiry,* 20, 511–531.

Krashen, Steve, and Douglas Biber. (1988). *On Course: Bilingual Education's Success in California.* Sacramento, CA: California Association for Bilingual Education.

Krueger, Alan B. (March 1998). "Reassessing the View That American Schools Are Broken." *Federal Reserve Bank of New York Economic Policy Review,* 29–43.

Ladd, Helen. (1975). "Local Education Expenditures, Fiscal Capacity and the Composition of the Property Tax Base." *National Tax Journal,* 28(2), 145–158.

Ladd, Helen, and John Yinger. (1989). *America's Ailing Cities: Fiscal Health and the Design of Urban Policy.* Baltimore: Johns Hopkins University Press.

Ladd, Helen, and John Yinger. (1994). "The Case for Equalizing Aid." *National Tax Journal,* 47(1), 211–224.

Laine, Richard D., Rob Greenwald, and Larry V. Hedges. (1996). "Money Does Matter: A

Research Synthesis of a New Universe of Education Production Function Studies." In Lawrence O. Picus and James L. Wattenbarger, eds., *Where Does the Money Go? Resource Allocation in Elementary and Secondary Schools.* Thousand Oaks, CA: Corwin Press, pp. 44–70.

Lankford, Hamilton, and James H. Wyckoff. (1995). "Where Has the Money Gone? An Analysis of School Spending in New York." *Educational Evaluation and Policy Analysis,* 17(2), 195–218.

Lawler, Edward E., III. (1986). *High Involvement Management: Participative Strategies for Improving Organizational Performance.* San Francisco: Jossey Bass.

Lawler, Edward E., III. (1990). *Strategic Pay: Aligning Organizational Strategies and Pay Systems.* San Francisco: Jossey-Bass.

Lawler, Edward E., III. (1992). *The Ultimate Advantage: Creating the High Involvement Organization.* San Francisco: Jossey-Bass.

Lawler, Edward E., III. (1996). *From the Ground Up: Six Principles for Building the New Logic Organization.* San Francisco: Jossey-Bass.

Lawler, Edward E., III, Susan Mohrman, and Gerald Ledford. (1995). *Creating High Performance Organizations.* San Francisco: Jossey-Bass.

Le Tendre, Mary Jean. (1996). "The New Improving America's Schools Act and Title I." *Journal for Students Placed At Risk,* 1(1), 5–8.

Lee, Valerie, Robert Croninger, and Julia Smith. (1997). "Course Taking, Equity and Mathematics Learning: Testing the Constrained Curriculum Hypothesis in U.S. Secondary Schools." *Educational Evaluation and Policy Analysis,* 19(2), 99–122.

Leppert, Jack, and Dorothy Routh. (1979). *A Policy Guide to Weighted Pupil Education Finance Systems: Some Emerging Practical Advice.* Washington, D.C.: National Institute of Education.

Levacic, Rosalind. (1999). "Case Study 2: United Kingdom. In Kenneth Ross and Rosalind Levacic, eds., *Needs-Based Resource Allocation in Schools via Formula-Based Funding.* Paris: UNESCO, International Institute for Educational Planning.

Levin, Betsy. (1977). "New Legal Challenges in Educational Finance," *Journal of Education Finance,* 3(1), 54–69.

Little, Judith Warren. (1993). "Teachers' Professional Development in a Climate of Educational Reform." *Educational Analysis and Policy Analysis,* 15(2), 129–152.

Loucks-Horsley, Susan, Peter W. Hewson, Nancy Love, and Katherine E. Stiles. (1997). *Designing Professional Development for Teachers of Science and Mathematics.* Thousand Oaks, CA: Corwin Press.

Louis, K., H. Marks, and S.D. Kruse. (1996). "Teachers' Professional Community in Restructured Schools." *American Educational Research Journal,* 33(4).

Louis, Karen Seashore, Sharon D. Kruse, and Helen M. Marks. (1996). "Schoolwide Professional Community." In Fred Newmann and Associates, eds., *Authentic Achievement: Restructuring Schools for Intellectual Quality.* San Francisco: Jossey-Bass, pp. 179–203.

Madigan, Timothy. (1997). *Science Proficiency and Course Taking in High School: The Relationship of Science Course-Taking Patterns to Increases in Science Proficiency between 8th and 12th Grades.* Washington, D.C.: National Center for Education Statistics.

Malen, Betty, Rodney T. Ogawa, and Jennifer Kranz. (1990). "What Do We Know about School Based Management? A Case Study of the Literature—A Call for Research." In William H. Clune and John F. Witte, eds., *Choice and Control in American Education: Volume 2, The Practice of Choice, Decentralization and School Restructuring.* Bristol, PA: The Falmer Press, pp. 289–342.

Marks, Helen, and Karen Seashore Louis. (1997). "Does Teacher Empowerment Affect the Classroom? The Implications of Teacher Empowerment for Instructional Practice and Student Academic Performance." *Educational Evaluation and Policy Analysis,* 19(3), 245–275.

Massell, Diane. (1998). *State Strategies for Building Local Capacity: Addressing the Needs of Standards-Based Reform* (Policy Brief RB-25). Philadelphia: University of Pennsylvania, Graduate School of Education, Consortium for Policy Research in Education.

Massell, Diane, Margaret Hoppe, and Michael Kirst. (1997). *Persistence and Change: Standards-Based Reform in Nine States.* Philadelphia: University of Pennsylvania, Graduate School of Education, Consortium for Policy Research in Education.

McClure, William. (1976). "Pupil Weightings." *Journal of Education Finance,* 2(1), 72–82.

McDonnell, Lorraine M., Margaret J. McLauglin and P. Morison, eds. (1997). *Educating One and All: Students With Disabilities and Standards-Based Reform* (A report by the National Research Council Committee on Goals 2000 and the Inclusion of Students with Disabilities). Washington, D.C.: National Academy Press.

McGuire, C. Kent. (1982). *State and Federal Programs for Special Student Populations.* Denver, CO: Education Commission of the States.

McLauglin, Margaret. (1999). "Consolidating Categorical Educational Programs at the Local Level." In Jay Chambers, Thomas Parrish, and Cassandra Guarino, eds., *Funding Special Education.* Thousand Oaks, CA: Corwin Press, pp. 22–40.

McLaughlin, Milbrey W., and Sylvia Yee. (1988). "School as a Place to Have A Career." In Ann Lieberman, ed., *Building a Professional Culture in Schools,* New York: Teachers College Press.

McMahon, Walter W. (1994). "Intrastate Cost Adjustment." In *Selected Papers in School Finance* [On-line]. Available: http://www.ed.gov/NCES/pubs/96068ica.html.

McUsic, Molly. (1991). "The Use of Education Clauses in School Finance Reform Litigation." *Harvard Journal on Legislation,* 28(2), 307–340.

Mieszkowski, Peter. (1972). "The Property Tax: An Excise Tax or Profits Tax?" *Journal of Public Economics,* 1, 73–96.

Mikesell, John L. (1986) *Fiscal Administration: Analysis and Application for the Public Sector.* Homewood, IL: Dorsey.

Mikesell, John L. (1997). "The American Retail Sales Tax: Considerations on Their Structure, Operations and Potential as a Foundation for a Federal Sales Tax." *National Tax Journal,* 1(1), 149–166.

Milanowski, Anthony. (1999). "Measurement Error or Meaningful Change? The Consistency of School Achievement in Two School-Based Award Programs." *Journal of Personnel Evaluation in Education,* 12(4), 343–364.

Milanowski, Anthony, Allan Odden, and Peter Youngs. (1998). "Teacher Knowledge and Skill Assessments and Teacher Compensation: An Overview of Measurement and Linkage Issues." *Journal for Personnel Evaluation in Education,* 12(2), 83–102.

Miles, Karen Hawley. (1995). "Freeing Resources for Improving Schools: A Case Study of Teacher Allocation in Boston Public Schools." *Educational Evaluation and Policy Analysis,* 17(4), 476–493.

Miles, Karen Hawley, and Linda Darling-Hammond. (1997). *Rethinking the Allocation of Teaching Resources: Some Lessons from High Performing Schools* (CPRE Research Report Series RR-38). Philadelphia: University of Pennsylvania, Graduate School of Education, Consortium for Policy Research in Education.

Miles, Karen Hawley, and Linda Darling-Hammond. (1998). "Rethinking the Allocation of

Teaching Resources: Some Lessons from High-Performing Schools." *Educational Evaluation and Policy Analysis,* 20(1), 9–29.

Minnesota Department of Revenue, Tax Research Division. (1993). *Minnesota Tax Incidence Study.* St. Paul, MN: Minnesota Department of Revenue.

Minorini, Paul, and Stephen Sugarman. (1999a). "School Finance Litigation in the Name of Educational Equity: Its Evolution, Impact and Future." In Helen Ladd, Rosemary Chalk, and Janet Hansen, eds., *Equity and Adequacy in Education Finance: Issues and Perspectives.* Washington, D.C.: National Academy Press.

Minorini, Paul, and Stephen Sugarman. (1999b). "Educational Adequacy and the Courts: The Promise and Problems of Moving to a New Paradigm." In Helen Ladd, Rosemary Chalk, and Janet Hansen, eds., *Equity and Adequacy in Education Finance: Issues and Perspectives.* Washington, D.C.: National Academy Press.

Mohrman, Allan, Susan Albers Mohrman, and Allan Odden. (1996). "Aligning Teacher Compensation with Systemic School Reform: Skill-Based Pay and Group-Based Performance Rewards." *Educational Evaluation and Policy Analysis.* 18(1), 51–71.

Mohrman, Susan Albers. (1994a). "High Involvement Management in the Private Sector." In Susan Albers Mohrman and Priscilla Wohlstetter, eds., *School-Based Management: Organizing for High Performance.* San Francisco: Jossey-Bass, pp. 25–52.

Mohrman, Susan Albers. (1994b). "Large Scale Change." In Susan Mohrman and Priscilla Wohlstetter, eds., *School-Based Management: Organizing for High Performance.* San Francisco: Jossey-Bass.

Mohrman, Susan Albers, Jay R. Galbraith, Edward E. Lawler, III, and Associates. (1998). *Tomorrow's Organization: Crafting Winning Capabilities in a Dynamic World.* San Francisco: Jossey-Bass.

Mohrman, Susan Albers, and Edward E. Lawler. (1996). "Motivation for School Reform." In Susan Fuhrman and Jennifer O'Day, eds., *Rewards and Reform: Creating Educational Incentives That Work.* San Francisco: Jossey-Bass, pp. 115–143.

Mohrman, Susan Albers, Edward E. Lawler, III, and Allan M. Mohrman, Jr. (1992). "Applying Employee Involvement in Schools." *Education Evaluation and Policy Analysis,* 14(4), 347–360.

Mohrman, Susan Albers, and Priscilla Wohlstetter, eds. (1994). *School-Based Management: Organizing for High Performance.* San Francisco: Jossey-Bass.

Monk, David. (1987). "Secondary School Size and Curriculum Comprehensiveness," *Economics of Education Review,* 6(2), 137–150.

Monk, David. (1990). *Educational Finance: An Economic Approach.* New York: McGraw-Hill.

Monk, David. (1992). "Educational Productivity Research: An Update and Assessment of Its Role in Education Finance Reform." *Educational Evaluation and Policy Analysis,* 14(4), 307–332.

Monk, David. (1997). "Challenges Surrounding the Collection and Use of Data for the Study of Finance and Productivity." *Journal of Education Finance,* 22(3), 303–316.

Monk, David, and Brian O. Brent. (1997). *Raising Money for Schools: A Guide to the Property Tax.* Thousand Oaks, CA: Corwin Press.

Monk, David, Christopher F. Roellke, and Brian O. Brent. (1996). *What Education Dollars Buy: An Examination of Resource Allocation Patterns in New York State Public School Systems.* Madison, WI: University of Wisconsin, Wisconsin Center for Education Research, Consortium for Policy Research in Education.

Monk, David, and Billy Walker. (1991). "The Texas Cost of Education Index." *Journal of Education Finance,* 17(2), 172–192.

Moody, Scott, ed. (1998). *Facts and Figures on Government Finance,* 32nd ed. Washington, D.C.: Tax Foundation.

Moore, Mary, T. E. William Strang, Myron Schwartz, and Mark Braddock. (1988). *Patterns in Special Education Service Delivery and Cost.* Washington, D.C.: Decision Resources Corporation.

Moss, Pamela A., Aaron M. Schutz, and Kathleen Collins. (1998). An Integrative Approach to Portfolio Evaluation for Teacher Licensure Certification. *Journal for Personnel Evaluation in Education,* 12(2), 139–161.

Mosteller, Frederick. (Summer/Fall 1995). The Tennessee Study of Class Size in the Early School Grades. *The Future of Children: Critical Issues for Children and Youths,* 5, 113–27.

Murnane, Richard. (1983). "Quantitative Studies of Effective Schools: What Have We Learned?" In Allan Odden and L. Dean Webb, eds., *School Finance and School Improvement: Linkages for the 1983.* Cambridge, MA: Ballinger.

Murnane, Richard. (1991). "Interpreting the Evidence on 'Does Money Matter'?" *Harvard Journal on Legislation,* 28, 457–464.

Murnane, Richard, and David Cohen. (1986). "Merit Pay and the Evaluation Problem: Why Some Merit Pay Plans Fail and a Few Survive." *Harvard Educational Review,* 56(1), 1–17.

Murnane, Richard, and Frank Levy. (1996). *Teaching the New Basic Skills.* New York: The Free Press.

Murphy, John, and Lawrence O. Picus. (1996). "Special Program Encroachment on School District General Funds in California: Implications for Serrano Equalization." *Journal of Education Finance,* 21(3), 366–386.

Murphy, Joseph, and Lynn Beck. (1995). *School-Based Management as School Reform.* Thousand Oaks, CA: Corwin Press.

Murphy, Joseph, and Karen S. Louis. (1994). "Transformational Change and the Evolving Role of the Principal: Early Empirical Evidence." In Joseph Murphy and Karen S. Louis, eds., *Reshaping the Principalship.* Thousand Oaks, CA: Corwin Press.

Murray, Sheila, William Evans, and Robert Schwab. (1998). "Education Finance Reform and the Distribution of Education Resources." *American Economic Review,* 88(4), 789–812.

Musgrave, Richard, and Darwin Daicoff. (1958). "Who Pays the Michigan Taxes?" *Michigan Tax Study Papers.* Lansing, MI: Michigan Tax Study Committee.

Musgrave, Richard, and Peggy Musgrave. (1989). *Public Finance in Theory and Practice.* New York: McGraw-Hill.

Nakib, Yasser. (1995). "Beyond District-Level Expenditures: Schooling Resource Allocation and Use in Florida." In Lawrence Picus and James Wattenbarger, eds., *Where Does the Money Go?* Thousand Oaks, CA: Corwin Press, pp. 106–131.

National Center for Education Statistics. (1989). *Digest of Educational Statistics, 1989.* Washington, D.C.: National Center for Educational Statistics.

National Center for Education Statistics. (1993). *Digest of Education Statistics, 1992.* Washington, D.C.: U.S. Department of Education.

National Center for Education Statistics. (1994). *Schools and Staffing Survey, 1993–94.* Washington, D.C.: National Center for Education Statistics.

National Center for Education Statistics. (1996a). *Digest of Education Statistics, 1996.* Washington, D.C.: U.S. Department of Education.

National Center for Education Statistics. (December 1996b). "Public School Choice Programs, 1993–94: Availability and Student Participation." *Issues Brief.*

National Center for Education Statistics. (1997). *Time Spent Teaching Core Academic Subjects in Elementary Schools.* Washington, D.C.: U.S. Department of Education.

National Center for Education Statistics. (1998a). *Digest of Education Statistics, 1997.* Washington, D.C.: National Center for Education Statistics.

National Center for Education Statistics. (1998b). *Federal $upport for Education: Fiscal Years 1980–1998.* (NCES 98-155, p. 11). Washington, D.C.: U.S. Department of Education.

National Center for Education Statistics. (1998c). *State Comparisons of Education Statistics: 1969–70 to 1996–97.* Report Number 065-000-01207-3. Washington, D.C.: United States Department of Education, National Center for Education Statistics.

National Commission on Excellence and Equity in Education. (1983). *A Nation At-Risk: The Imperative of Educational Reform.* Washington, D.C.: United States Department of Education.

National Commission on Teaching and America's Future. (1996). *What Matters Most: Teaching in America.* New York: Teachers College Press.

National Commission on Time and Learning. (1994). *Prisoners of Time.* Washington, D.C.: U.S. Government Printing Office.

National Council of Teachers of Mathematics (NCTM). (1989). *Curriculum and Evaluation Standards for School Mathematics.* Reston, VA: NCTM.

National Education Association. (1998). *1996–97 Estimates of School Statistics.* Washington, D.C.: NEA.

National Research Council. (1996). *Improving America's Schools: The Role of Incentives.* Washington, D.C.: National Academy Press.

National Research Council. (1999). *Report of the Panel on Special Education.* Washington, D.C.: NRC.

National Conference of State Legislatures. (1998). *State Tax Actions, 1998.* Denver, CO: National Conference of State Legislatures. http://www.ncsl.org/programs/fiscal/sta98sum.htm/.

Nelson, F. Howard. (1984). "Factors Contributing to the Cost of Programs for Limited English Proficient Students." *Journal of Education Finance,* 10(1), 1–21.

Netzer, Dick. (1966). *Economics of the Property Tax.* Washington, D.C.: The Brookings Institution.

New American Schools. (1995). *An Introduction.* Arlington, VA: NAS.

New American Schools. (1996). *Working towards Excellence: Early Indicators from Schools Implementing New American School Designs.* Arlington, VA: NAS.

Newmann, Fred, and Associates. (1996). *Authentic Achievement: Restructuring Schools for Intellectual Quality.* San Francisco: Jossey-Bass.

Newmann, Fred, M. Bruce King, and Mark Ringdon. (1996). *Accountability and School Performance: Implications From Restructuring Schools.* Madison, WI: Wisconsin Center for Education Research.

Newmann, Fred, and Gary Wehlage. (1995). *Successful School Restructuring.* Madison, WI: Wisconsin Center for Education Research, University of Wisconsin—Madison.

O'Neill, G. Patrick. (1996) "Restructuring Education: Lessons from Chicago, Edmonton and Wellington." *House,* 70(1), 30–31.

Oates, Wallace E. (1972). *Fiscal Federalism.* New York: Harcourt, Brace, Jovanovich.

Odden, Allan. (1975). *The Incidence of the Property Tax under Alternative Assumptions: The Case in Minnesota, 1971.* Unpublished paper. Denver, CO: Education Commission of the States.

Odden, Allan. (1978). "Missouri's New School Finance Structure." *Journal of Education Finance,* 3(3), 465–475.

Odden, Allan. (1979). "Simulation Results: Third Round." Prepared for the New York State Task Force on Equity and Excellence in Education. Denver, CO: Education Commission of the States.

Odden, Allan. (1980). "Simulation Results: Fourth Round." Prepared for the New York State Task Force on Equity and Excellence in Education. Denver, CO: Education Commission of the States.

Odden, Allan. (1982). "School Finance Reform: Redistributive Policy at the State Level." In Joel Sherman, Mark Kutner, and Kimberly Small, eds., *New Dimensions of the State-Federal Partnership in Education.* Washington, D.C.: The Institute for Educational Leadership.

Odden, Allan. (1988). "How Fiscal Accountability and Program Quality Can Be Insured for Chapter I." In Denis Doyle and Bruce Cooper, eds., *Federal Aid to the Disadvantaged: What Future for Chapter I?* New York: Falmer Press.

Odden, Allan. (1990). "School Funding Changes in the 1980s." *Educational Policy,* 4(1), 33–47.

Odden, Allan, ed. (1991). *Education Policy Implementation.* Albany, NY: State University of New York Press.

Odden, Allan. (1995a). *Educational Leadership for America's Schools.* New York: McGraw-Hill.

Odden, Allan. (1995b). *Missouri School Finance System: Fiscal Equity after S.B. 380.* Paper prepared for the Missouri Performance Commission.

Odden, Allan. (1996). "Incentives, School Organization and Teacher Compensation." In Susan Fuhrman and Jennifer O'Day, eds., *Rewards and Reform: Creating Educational Incentives That Work.* San Francisco: Jossey-Bass, pp. 226–256.

Odden, Allan (1997a). *The Finance Side of Implementing New American Schools.* Paper prepared for the New American Schools, Alexandria, VA.

Odden, Allan. (1997b). "Having to Do More with Less: Stretching the School Budget Dollar." *School Business Affairs,* 63(6), 2–10.

Odden, Allan. (1998). *Improving State School Finance Systems: New Realities Create Need to Re-Engineer School Finance Structures* (CPRE Occasional Paper Series OP-04). Philadelphia: University of Pennsylvania, Graduate School of Education, Consortium for Policy Research in Education.

Odden, Allan. (1999). "Case Study 3: School-Based Formula Funding in North America." In Kenneth Ross and Rosalind Levacic, eds., *Needs-Based Resource Allocation in Schools via Formula-Based Funding.* Paris: UNESCO, International Institute for Educational Planning.

Odden, Allan, and William Massy. (1993). *Education Funding for Schools and Universities: Improving Productivity and Equity.* Madison: University of Wisconsin, Wisconsin Center for Education Research, Consortium for Policy Research in Education, Finance Center.

Odden, Allan, Sarah Archibald, and Anita Tychsen. (1998). *Can Wisconsin Schools Afford Comprehensive School Reform?* Madison, WI: University of Wisconsin, Wisconsin Center for Education Research, Consortium for Policy Research in Education.

Odden, Allan, and John Augenblick. (1981). *School Finance Reform in the States: 1981.* Denver, CO: Education Commission of the States.

Odden, Allan, Robert Berne, and Leanna Stiefel. (1979). *Equity in School Finance.* Denver, CO: Education Commission of the States.

Odden, Allan, and Carolyn Busch. (1995). "Costs and Impacts of Alternative Plans for Reforming Wisconsin School Finance and Providing Property Tax Relief." In Carla

Edlefson, ed., *School Finance Policy Issues in the States and Provinces.* Columbus, OH: The Ohio State University, Policy Research for Ohio Based Education and American Educational Research Association, pp. 192–203.

Odden, Allan, and Carolyn Busch, eds. (1997). Special Issue: Collection of School-Level Finance Data. *Journal of Education Finance,* 22(3).

Odden, Allan, and Carolyn Busch. (1998). *Financing Schools for High Performance: Strategies for Improving the Use of Educational Resources.* San Francisco: Jossey-Bass.

Odden, Allan, and William Clune. (1998). "School Finance Systems: Aging Structures in Need of Renovation." *Educational Evaluation and Policy Analysis,* 20(3), 157–177.

Odden, Allan, and Sharon Conley. (1992). "Restructuring Teacher Compensation Systems." In Allan Odden, ed., *Rethinking School Finance: An Agenda for the 1990s.* San Francisco: Jossey-Bass, pp. 41–96.

Odden, Allan, Herbert Heneman III, David Wakelyn, and Jean Protsik. (1996). *School-Based Performance Award Case.* Madison, WI: University of Wisconsin, Wisconsin Center for Education Research, Consortium for Policy Research in Education.

Odden, Allan, and Carolyn Kelley. (1997). *Paying Teachers for What They Know and Do: New and Smarter Compensation Strategies to Improve Schools.* Thousand Oaks, CA: Corwin Press.

Odden, Allan, and Nancy Kotowski. (1992). "Financing Public School Choice: Policy Issues and Options." In Allan Odden, ed., *Rethinking School Finance: An Agenda for the 1990s.* San Francisco: Jossey-Bass, pp. 225–259.

Odden, Allan, C. Kent McGuire, and Grace Belsches-Simmons. (1983). *School Finance Reform in the States: 1984.* Denver, CO: Education Commission of the States.

Odden, Allan, David Monk, Yasser Nakib, and Lawrence Picus. (1995). "The Story of the Education Dollar: No Academy Awards and No Fiscal Smoking Guns." *Phi Delta Kappan,* 77(2), 161–168.

Odden, Allan, and Eleanor Odden. (1996a). "Applying the High Involvement Framework to Local Management of Schools in Victoria, Australia." *Educational Research and Evaluation,* 2(2), 150–184.

Odden, Allan, and Eleanor Odden. (1996b). *The Victoria, Australia Approach to School-Site Management.* Madison, WI: University of Wisconsin, Wisconsin Center for Education Research, Consortium for Policy Research in Education.

Odden, Allan, Robert Palaich, and John Augenblick. (1979). *Analysis of the New York State School Finance System, 1977–78.* Denver, CO: Education Commission of the States.

Odden, Allan, and Lawrence O. Picus. (1992). *School Finance: A Policy Perspective.* New York: McGraw Hill.

Odden, Allan, and Phillip E. Vincent. (1976). *The Regressivity of the Property Tax* (Report No. F76-4). Denver, CO: Education Commission of the States.

Odden, Eleanor, and Priscilla Wohlstetter. (1995). "Strategies for Making School-Based Management Work." *Educational Leadership,* 52(5), 32–36.

Odden, Allan, Priscilla Wohlstetter, and Eleanor Odden. (1995). "Key Issues in Effective School-Based Management." *School Business Affairs,* 61(5), 4–16.

Odden, Allan, and Van Dougherty. (1984). *Education Finance in the States, 1984.* Denver, CO: Education Commission of the States.

Office of Bilingual Education, California State Department of Education. (1984). *Schooling and Language for Minority Students: A Theoretical Framework.* Los Angeles: California State University, Evaluation, Dissemination and Assessment Center.

Olson, Lynn. (June 4, 1997). "Power of the Purse." *Education Week,* 23–28.

Organization for Economic Cooperation and Development. (1997). *Education at a Glance: OECD Indicators.* Paris: Organization for Economic Cooperation and Development.

Ornstein, Allen C. (1990). "How Big Should Schools and Districts Be?" *Education Digest,* 56(2), 44–48.

Orr, Larry. (1968). "The Incidence of Differential Property Taxes on Urban Housing." *National Tax Journal,* 12, 253–262.

Osborne, David, and Peter Plastrik. (1997). *Banishing Bureaucracy: The Five Strategies for Reinventing Government.* Reading, MA: Addison-Wesley.

Owen, J. (1996). *Why Our Kids Don't Study.* Baltimore: Johns Hopkins University Press.

Pallas, Aaron, Gary Natriello, and Edward McDill. (1988). "The Changing Nature of the Disadvantaged Population: Current Dimensions and Future Trends." *Educational Researcher,* 18(5), 16–22.

Park, Rolla Edward, and Stephen J. Carroll. (1979). *The Search for Equity in School Finance: Michigan School District Response to a Guaranteed Tax Base.* Santa Monica, CA: The RAND Corporation, R-2393-NIE/HEW.

Parrish, Thomas B. (1994). "A Cost Analysis of Alternative Instructional Models for Limited English Proficient Students in California." *Journal of Education Finance,* 19(3), 256–278.

Parrish, Thomas. (1996). "Special Education Finance: Past, Present and Future." *Journal of Education Finance,* 21(4), 451–476.

Parrish, Thomas B. (1997). *Special Education in an Era of School Reform.* (Product of the Federal Resource Center.) Palo Alto, CA: Center for Special Education Finance.

Parrish, Thomas, and Jean Wolman. (1999). "Trends and New Developments in Special Education Funding: What the States Report." In Jay Chambers, Thomas Parrish, and Cassandra Guarino, eds., *Funding Special Education.* Thousand Oaks, CA: Corwin Press, pp. 203–229.

Peat Marwick, Mitchell and Company. (1982). *Report to the American Retail Federation on Costs to Retailers of Sales Use Tax Compliance.* New York: Peat Marwick, Mitchell, and Company.

Pechman, Joseph A. (1985). *Who Paid the Taxes, 1966–85.* Washington, D.C.: The Brookings Institution.

Pechman, Joseph A. (1986). *Who Paid the Taxes, 1966–85, Revised Tables.* Washington, D.C.: The Brookings Institution.

Pechman, Joseph A., and Benjamin A. Okner. (1974). *Who Bears the Tax Burden?* Washington, D.C.: The Brookings Institution.

Phares, Donald. (1980). *Who Pays State and Local Taxes?* Cambridge, MA: Oelgeschlager, Gunn and Hain, Publishers, Inc.

Phillips, Robyn. (1988). "Restoring Property Tax Equity." *California Policy Choices,* 4, pp. 143–169. Los Angeles: University of Southern California, School of Public Administration.

Picus, Lawrence O. (1988). *The Effect of State Grant-In-Aid Policies on Local Government Decision Making: The Case of California School Finance.* Santa Monica, CA: The RAND Corporation.

Picus, Lawrence O. (1992). "Using Incentives to Promote School Improvement." In Allan Odden, ed., *Restructuring School Finance for the 1990s.* New York: Jossey-Bass, Inc. pp. 166–200.

Picus, Lawrence O. (1993a). *The Allocation and Use of Educational Resources: School Level Evidence from the Schools and Staffing Survey.* Los Angeles: USC Center for Research in Education Finance, Working Paper No. 37.

Picus, Lawrence O. (1993b). *The Allocation and Use of Educational Resources: District Level Evidence from the Schools and Staffing Survey.* Paper prepared for the Consortium for Policy Research in Education Finance Center, University of Wisconsin—Madison.

Picus, Lawrence O. (1994a). "Achieving Program Equity: Are Markets the Answer?" *Educational Policy,* 8(4), 568–581.

Picus, Lawrence O. (1994b). "Estimating the Determinants of Pupil/Teacher Ratios: Evidence from the Schools and Staffing Survey." *Educational Considerations,* 21(2), 44–52.

Picus, Lawrence O. (1994c). "The Local Impact of School Finance Reform in Texas." *Educational Evaluation and Policy Analysis,* 16(4), 391–404.

Picus, Lawrence O. (1997a). "Does Money Matter in Education? A Policymaker's Guide." In William Fowler, ed., *Selected Papers in School Finance, 1995.* Washington D.C.: National Center for Education Statistics.

Picus, Lawrence O. (1997b). "Using School-Level Finance Data: Endless Opportunity or Bottomless Pit?" *Journal of Education Finance,* 22(3), 317–330.

Picus, Lawrence O. (February 1999a). "Defining Adequacy: Implications for School Business Officials." *School Business Affairs.* 65.

Picus, Lawrence O. (1999b). "Site-Based Management: A Nuts and Bolts Approach for School Administrators." In Margaret Goertz and Allan Odden, eds., *School-Based Financing.* Thousand Oaks, CA: Corwin Press.

Picus, Lawrence O., and Minaz Bhimani. (August 1993). "Estimating the Impact of District Characteristics on Pupil/Teacher Ratios." *Journal of the American Statistical Association.* Proceedings of the annual conference of the American Statistical Association, San Francisco.

Picus, Lawrence O., and M. Fazal. (1996). "Why Do We Need to Know What Money Buys? Research on Resource Allocation Patterns in Elementary and Secondary Schools." In Lawrence O. Picus and James L. Wattenbarger, eds., *Where Does the Money Go? Resource Allocation in Elementary and Secondary Schools* (1995 Yearbook of the American Education Finance Association). Newbury Park, CA: Corwin Press, pp. 1–19.

Picus, Lawrence O., and Linda Hertert. (1993a). "A School Finance Dilemma for Texas: Achieving Equity in a Time of Fiscal Constraint." *Texas Researcher,* 4, 1–28.

Picus, Lawrence O., and Linda Hertert. (1993b). "Three Strikes and You're Out: Texas School Finance after Edgewood III." *Journal of Education Finance,* 18(3), 366–389.

Picus, Lawrence O., Donald R. Tetreault, and John Murphy. (1996). *What Money Buys: Understanding the Allocation and Use of Educational Resources in California.* Madison, WI: University of Wisconsin, Wisconsin Center for Education Research, Consortium for Policy Research in Education.

Picus, Lawrence O., and Laurence Toenjes. (1994). "Texas School Finance: Assessing the Impact of Multiple Reforms." *Journal of Texas Public Education.* 2(3), 39–62.

Pompa, Delia. (March 26, 1998). *Testimony on the Fiscal Year 1999 Budget Requests for Bilingual and Immigrant Education.* [On-line]. Available: http://www.ed.gov/speeches.

Popovich, Mark, ed. (1998). *Creating High Performance Government Organizations.* San Francisco: Jossey-Bass.

Porter, Andrew. (1991). "Creating a System of School Process Indicators." *Educational Evaluation and Policy Analysis,* 13(1), 13–30.

Porter, Andrew, and Jere Brophy. (1988). "Good Teaching: Insights from the Work of the Institute for Research on Teaching," *Educational Leadership,* 45(8), 75–84.

Porter, Andrew, Michael W. Kirst, Eric J. Osthoff, John S. Smithson, and Steve A. Schneider. (1993). *Reform Up Close: A Classroom Analysis* (Final Report to the National Science Foundation on Grant No. SPA-8953446 to the Consortium for Policy Research in Education). Madison, WI: University of Wisconsin—Madison, Wisconsin Center for Education Research.

Porter, Andrew, and John Smithson. (1997). *Enacted Curriculum Survey Items Catalogue: Middle School and High School Mathematics and Science,* 2d ed. Philadelphia: University of Pennsylvania, Graduate School of Education, Consortium for Policy Research in Education.

Porter, Andrew, Peter Youngs, and Allan Odden. (forthcoming). "Advances in Teacher Assessment and Their Uses." In Virginia Richardson, ed., *Handbook of Research on Teaching.* New York: Macmillan.

Porter, Tod S. (1991). "Equity and Changes in the Tax Base of Ohio's Public Schools: 1980–89." *Journal of Education Finance,* 16(4), 515–530.

Prince, Henry. (1997). "Michigan's School Finance Reform: Initial Pupil-Equity Results." *Journal of Education Finance,* 22(4), 394–409.

Public Agenda. (1997). *Getting By: What American Teenagers Really Think about Their Schools.* New York: Public Agenda.

Puelo, V. T. (1988). "A Review and Critique of Research on Full-Day Kindergarten," *Elementary School Journal,* 88(4), 425–439.

Pulliam, John D. (1987). *History of Education in America,* 4th ed. Columbus, OH: Merrill Publishing Company.

Purkey, Stewart C., and Marshall S. Smith. (1985). "The District Policy Implications of the Effective Schools Literature." *Elementary School Journal,* 85, 353–389.

Ravitch, Diane. (1983). *The Troubled Crusade.* New York: Basic Books.

Reschovsky, Andrew. (1994). Fiscal Equalization and School Finance. *National Tax Journal,* 47(1), 185–197.

Reschovsky, Andrew, and Jennifer Imazeki. (1998). "The Development of School Finance Formulas to Guarantee the Provision of Adequate Education to Low-Income Students." In William J. Fowler, ed., *Developments in School Finance 1997.* Washington, D.C.: National Center for Education Statistics. NCES 98-212.

Richards, Craig E., Daniel Fishbein and Paula Melville. (1993). "Cooperative Performance Incentives in Education." In Jacobson, Stephen L. and Robert Berne, eds., *Reforming Education: The Emerging Systemic Approach.* Thousand Oaks, CA: Corwin Press, 28–42.

Richardson, Virginia, ed. (forthcoming). *Handbook of Research on Teaching.* New York: Macmillan.

Riew, John. (1986). "Scale Economies, Capacity Utilization and School Costs: A Comparative Analysis of Secondary and Elementary Schools." *Journal of Education Finance,* 11(4), 433–446.

Robertson, Peter J., Priscilla Wohlstetter, and Susan Albers Mohrman. (1995). "Generating Curriculum and Instructional Changes through School-Based Management." *Educational Administration Quarterly,* 31(3), 375–404.

Robledo, M., M. Zarate, M. Guss-Zamora, and Jose Cardenas. (1978). *Bilingual Education Cost Analysis: Colorado.* San Antonio, TX: Intercultural Development Research Association.

Rosen, Harvey S. (1992). *Public Finance,* 3d ed. Homewood, IL: Irwin.

Rosenholtz, Susan. (1989). *Teachers' Workplace: The Social Organization of Schools*. New York: Longman.

Rosenshine, Barak, and Robert Stevens. (1986). "Teaching Functions." In Witrick, Merlin C., ed., *Handbook of Research on Teaching*. New York: Macmillan, 376–391.

Ross, Kenneth, and Rosalind Levacic, eds. (1999). *Needs Based Resource Allocation in Education via Formula Funding of Schools*. Paris: UNESCO, International Institute for Educational Planning.

Ross, Steven M., William Sanders, and Samuel Stringfield. (1998). *The Memphis Restructuring Initiative: Achievement Results for Years 1 and 2 on the Tennessee Value-Added Assessment System*. A Special Report Prepared for the Memphis City Schools. Memphis, TN: Memphis City Schools.

Rossmiller, Richard, and Lloyd E. Frohreich. (1979). *Expenditures and Funding Patterns in Idaho's Programs for Exceptional Children*. Madison, WI: University of Wisconsin.

Rossmiller, Richard, et al. (1970). *Educational Programs for Exceptional Children: Resource Configurations and Costs*. Madison, WI.: Department of Educational Administration, University of Wisconsin.

Rotberg, Iris, Mary Futrell, and Joyce Lieberman. (1998). "National Board Certification: Increasing Participation and Assessing Impacts." *Phi Delta Kappan,* 79(6), 462–466.

Rothstein, Richard, and Karen Hawley Miles. (1995). *Where's the Money Gone?* Washington, D.C.: Economic Policy Institute.

Rouse, Cecilia Elena, and Michele McLaughlin. (1999). *Can the Invisible Hand Improve Education? A Review of Competition and School Efficiency*. Paper prepared for the National Research Council, National Academy of Sciences, Commission on Behavioral and Social Sciences and Education.

Rowan, Brian. (1994). "Comparing Teachers' Work with Work in Other Occupations: Notes on the Professional Status of Teaching." *Educational Researcher,* 23(6), 4, 17–21.

Rubenstein, Ross H. (1997). *School-Level Budgeting and Resource Allocation in the Chicago Public Schools: Processes and Results*. Unpublished doctoral dissertation, New York University.

Ruggiero, John. (1996). "Efficiency of Educational Production: An Analysis of New York School Districts." *Review of Economics and Statistics,* 78(3), 499–509.

Salmon, Richard, Christina Dawson, Steven Lawton, and Thomas Johns. (1988). *Public School Finance Programs of the United States and Canada: 1986–87*. Sarasota, FL: American Education Finance Association.

Sample, Patricia Ritchey, and William Hartman. (1990). "An Equity Simulation of Pennsylvania's School Finance Simulation." *Journal of Education Finance,* 16(1), 49–69.

Schmidt, William, Doris Jorde, Leland Cogan, Emilie Barrier, Ignacio Gonzalo, Urs Moser, Katsuhiko Shimizu, Toshio Sawada, Gilbert Valverde, Curtis McKnight, Richard Prawat, David Wiley, Senta Raizen, Edward Britton, and Richard Wolfe. (1997). *Characterizing Pedagogical Flow*. Norwell, MA: Kluwer Academic Publishers.

Schmidt, William, Curtis McKnight, and Senta Raizen. (1997). *A Splintered Vision: An Investigation of U.S. Science and Mathematics Education*. Norwell, MA: Kluwer Academic Publishers.

Schuster, Jay, and Patricia Zingheim. (1992). *The New Pay*. Lexington. MA: Lexington Books.

Schwartz, Myron, and Jay Moskowitz. (1988). *Fiscal Equity in the United States: 1984–85*. Washington, D.C.: Decision Resources Corporation.

Seal, Kenna R., and Hobart L. Harmon. (1995). "Realities of Rural School Reform." *Phi Delta Kappan,* 77(2), 119–124.

Shepard, Lori, and Mary Smith. (1989). *Flunking Grades: Research and Policies on Retention.* New York: Falmer.

Sher, Jonathan, and Rachel B. Tompkins. (1977). "Economy, Efficiency and Equality: The Myths of Rural School and District Consolidation." In Jonathan P. Sher, ed., *Education in Rural America.* Boulder, CO: Westview Press.

Sherman, J., C. Best, and L. Luskin. (1996). *Assessment and Analysis of School-Level Expenditures.* Washington, D.C.: U.S. Department of Education, Office of Educational Research and Improvement. Working Paper 96-19.

Sherman, Joel. (1992). "Review of School Finance Equalization Under Section 5(d) of P.L. 81-874, The Impact Aid Program." *Journal of Education Finance,* 18(1).

Siegler, Robert. (1998). *Children's Thinking.* Upper Saddle River, NJ: Prentice Hall.

Sizer, Theodore. (1996). *Horace's Hope.* Boston: Houghton Mifflin.

Slavin, Robert. (1984). "Meta-Analysis in Education: How Has It Been Used?" *Educational Researcher,* 13(8), 24–27.

Slavin, Robert. (1989). "Achievement Effects of Substantial Reductions in Class Size." In Robert Slavin, ed., *School and Classroom Organization.* Hillsdale, NJ: Erlbaum, pp. 247–257.

Slavin, Robert, and Olatokunbo Fashola. (1998). *Show Me the Evidence! Proven and Promising Programs for America's Schools.* Thousand Oaks, CA: Corwin Press.

Slavin, Robert, Nancy Karweit, and Nancy Madden, eds. (1989a). *Effective Programs for Students at Risk.* Boston: Allyn and Bacon.

Slavin, Robert, Nancy Karweit, and Barbara Wasik. (1994). *Preventing Early School Failure: Research Policy and Practice.* Boston: Allyn & Bacon.

Slavin, Robert, Nancy Madden, Lawrence Dolan, and Barbara Wasik. (1996). *Every Child, Every School.* Thousand Oaks, CA: Corwin Press.

Smith, Julia. (1996). "Does An Extra Year Make Any Difference: The Impact of Early Access to Algebra on Long Term Gains in Mathematics Attainment." *Educational Evaluation and Policy Analysis,* 18(2), 141–154.

Smith, Marshall S., and Jennifer O'Day. (1991). "Systemic Reform." In Susan Fuhrman and Betty Malen, eds., *The Politics of Curriculum and Testing.* Philadelphia: Falmer Press, pp. 233–267.

Smylie, Mark A., Virginia Lazarus, and Jean Brownlee-Conyers. (1996). "Instructional Outcomes of School-Based Participative Decision-making." *Educational Evaluation & Policy Analysis,* 18(3), 181–198.

Sparkman, William. (1990). "School Finance Challenges in State Courts." In Julie Underwood and Deborah Verstegen, eds., *The Impacts of Litigation and Legislation on Public School Finance.* Cambridge, MA: Ballinger, pp. 193–224.

Sparkman, William. (1994). "The Legal Foundations of Public School Finance," *Boston College Law Review,* 35(3), 569–595.

Speakman, Sheree, Bruce Cooper, Hunt Holsomback, Jay May, Robert Sampieri, and Larry Maloney. (1997). "The Three Rs of Education Finance Reform: Re-Thinking, Re-Tooling and Re-Evaluating School-Site Information." *Journal of Education Finance,* 22(4), 337–367.

Speakman, Sheree, Bruce Cooper, Robert Sampieri, Jay May, Hunt Holsomback, and Brian Glass. (1996). "Bringing Money to the Classroom: A Systemic Resource Allocations Model Applied to the New York City Public Schools." In Lawrence Picus and

James Wattenbarger, eds., *Where Does the Money Go?* Thousand Oaks, CA: Corwin Press, pp. 106–131.

Steinberg, Lawrence. (1996). *Beyond the Classroom: Why School Reform Has Failed and What Parents Need to Do.* New York: Simon and Schuster.

Steinberg, Lawrence. (1997). "Standards outside the Classroom." In Diane Ravitch, ed., *The State of Student Performance in American Schools: Brookings Papers on Education Policy, Volume 1.* Washington, D.C.: Brookings Institution.

Strayer, George, and Robert Haig. (1923). *Financing of Education in the State of New York.* New York: MacMillan.

Stringfield, Samuel, Steven Ross, and Lana Smith. (1996). *Bold Plans for School Restructuring: The New American School Designs.* Mahwah, NJ: Lawrence Erlbaum.

Summers, Anita A., and Amy W. Johnson. (1996). "The Effects of School Based Management Plans." In Eric Hanushek and Dale Jorgenson, eds., *Improving America's Schools: The Role of Incentives.* Washington, D.C.: National Research Council, pp. 75–96.

Swanson, Austin, and Richard King. (1997). *School Finance: Its Economics and Politics.* New York: Longman.

Talbert, Joan, and Milbrey McLaughlin. (1994). "Teacher Professionalism in Local School Contexts." *American Journal of Education,* 102(2), 123–153.

Tax Foundation. (1998a). *Latest Income Tax Data Shows Top 1% Paying over 30% of Total Federal Individual Income Tax Collections.* Washington, D.C.: Tax Foundation. http://www.taxfoundation.org/prtopincome.html/.

Tax Foundation. (1998b). *Bottom Line on the Taxpayer Relief Act of 1997.* Washington, D.C.: Tax Foundation. http://www.taxfoundation.org/prfy987taxbill.html/.

Texas State Board of Education. (1986). *1985–96 Accountable Cost Study.* Austin, TX: Texas Education Agency.

Thomas, Hywell, and Jane Martin. (1996). *Managing Resources for School Improvement: Creating a Cost-Effective School.* London: Routledge.

Tiebout, Charles M. (1956). "A Pure Theory of Local Expenditures." *Journal of Political Economy,* 54, 416–424.

Tsang, Mun C., and Henry R. Levin. (1983). "The Impacts of Intergovernmental Grants on Education Spending." *Review of Educational Research,* 53(3), 329–367.

Tucker, Marc S., and Judy B. Codding. (1998). *Standards for Our Schools: How to Set Them, Measure Them and Reach Them.* San Francisco: Jossey-Bass.

Tyack, David, and Larry Cuban. (1996). *Tinkering toward Utopia.* Cambridge, MA: Harvard University Press.

Tyack, David, and Elizabeth Hansot. (1982). *Managers of Virtue.* New York: Basic Books.

Tychsen, Anita. (1999). *The Power of the Purse: An Examination of How Schools Reallocated Resources to Implement Reform Strategies.* Unpublished Ph.D. dissertation.

Underwood, Julie. (1995a). "School Finance Litigation: Legal Theories, Judicial Activism, and Social Neglect." *Journal of Education Finance,* 20(2), 143–162.

Underwood, Julie. (1995b). "School Finance as Vertical Equity." *University of Michigan Journal of Law Reform,* 28(3), 493–520.

Underwood, Julie, and William Sparkman. (1991). "School Finance Litigation: A New Wave of Reform." *Harvard Journal on Law and Public Policy,* 14(2), 517–544.

U.S. Bureau of the Census. (1998). *State and Local Government Finance Estimates, by State: 1994–95.* Washington, D.C.: U.S. Bureau of the Census. http://www.census.gov/ftp/pub/govs/www/esti95.html/.

Verstegen, Deborah. (1996). "Concepts and Measures of Fiscal Inequality: A New Approach and Effects for Five States." *Journal of Education Finance,* 22(2), 145–160.

Verstegen, Deborah. (1999). "Civil Rights and Disability Policy: An Historical Perspective." In Jay Chambers, Thomas Parrish, and Cassandra Guarino, eds., *Funding Special Education.* Thousand Oaks, CA: Corwin Press, pp. 3–21.

Verstegen, Deborah, Thomas Parrish, and Jean Wolman. (Winter 1997–1998). "A Look at Changes in the Finance Provisions for Grants to States under the IDEA Amendments of 1997." *The CSEF Resource.* Palo Alto, CA: Center for Special Education Finance.

Verstegen, Deborah, and Richard Salmon. (1991). "Assessing Fiscal Equity in Virginia: Cross-Time Comparisons." *Journal of Education Finance,* 16(4), 417–430.

Vincent, Phillip E., and Kathleen Adams. (1978). *Fiscal Response of School Districts: A Study of Two States—Colorado and Minnesota.* Report No. F78-3. Denver, CO: Education Finance Center, Education Commission of the States.

Wehlage, Gary, Eric Osthoff, and Andrew Porter. (1996). "Support from External Agencies." In Fred Newmann, ed., *Authentic Achievement: Restructuring Schools for Intellectual Quality.* San Francisco: Jossey-Bass, pp. 264–285.

Wells, Amy Stuart. (1996). *Charter Schools.* Presentation to the National Academy of Sciences/National Research Council Committee on Education Finance: Equity, Adequacy, and Productivity, Washington, D.C.

Wendling, Wayne. (1981a). "Capitalization: Considerations for School Finance," *Educational Evaluation and Policy Analysis,* 3(2), 57–66.

Wendling, Wayne. (1981b). "The Cost of Education Index: Measurement of Price Differences of Education Personnel among New York State School Districts," *Journal of Education Finance,* 6(4), 485–504.

Wenglinsky, Harold. (1997). *When Money Matters.* Princeton, NJ: Education Testing Service.

White, Paula, Adam Gamoran, John Smithson, and Andrew Porter. (1996). "Upgrading the High School Math Curriculum: Math Course-Taking Patterns in Seven High Schools in California and New York." *Educational Evaluation and Policy Analysis,* 18(4), 285–308.

Wildavsky, Aaron. (1975). *Budgeting: A Comparative Theory of Budgetary Processes,* Boston, MA: Little, Brown and Company.

Wildavsky, Aaron. (1988). *The New Politics of the Budgetary Process.* Glenview, IL: Scott Foresman.

Wilde, James A. (1968). "The Expenditure Effect of Grant-In-Aid Programs." *National Tax Journal,* 21(3), 340–361.

Wilde, James A. (1971). "The Analytics of Grant Design and Response." *National Tax Journal,* 24(2), 143–155.

Wise, Arthur. (1968). *Rich Schools—Poor Schools: A Study of Equal Educational Opportunity.* Chicago: University of Chicago Press.

Wise, Arthur. (1983). "Educational Adequacy: A Concept in Search of Meaning." *Journal of Education Finance,* 8(3), 300–315.

Witte, John F. (Winter 1998). "The Milwaukee Voucher Experiment." *Educational Evaluation and Policy Analysis,* 20(4), 229–251.

Witte, John F., Troy D. Sterr, and Christopher A. Thorn. (1995). *Fifth-Year Report: Milwaukee Parental Choice Program.* Paper available from the University of Wisconsin—Madison.

Wohlstetter, Priscilla. (1995). "Getting School Based Management Right: What Works and What Doesn't." *Phi Delta Kappan,* 77(1), 22–26.

Wohlstetter, Priscilla, and Kerri L. Briggs. (1994). "The Principal's Role in School-based Management." *Principal,* 74(2), 14–17.

Wohlstetter, Priscilla, Kerri Briggs, and Amy Van Kirk. (1997). "School-Based Management: What It Is and Does It Make a Difference." In D.L. Levinson, A.R. Sadovnik, and Peter W. Cookson, Jr., eds., *Education and Sociology: An Encyclopedia.* New York: Garland Publishing.

Wohlstetter, Priscilla, and Noel Griffin. (1997). *First Lessons: Charter Schools as Learning Communities.* Philadelphia: University of Pennsylvania, Graduate School of Education, Consortium for Policy Research in Education.

Wohlstetter, Priscilla, and Susan Albers Mohrman. (1996). *Assessment of School-Based Management.* Washington, D.C.: U.S. Department of Education, Office of Educational Research and Improvement.

Wohlstetter, Priscilla, Susan Mohrman, and Peter Robertson. (1997). "Successful School-Based Management: Lessons for Restructuring Urban Schools." In Diane Ravitch and Joseph Viteritti, eds., *New Schools for a New Century: The Redesign of Urban Education.* New Haven, CT: Yale University Press.

Wohlstetter, Priscilla, and Allan R. Odden. (1992). "Rethinking School-Based Management Policy and Research." *Educational Administration Quarterly,* 28(4), 529–549.

Wohlstetter, Priscilla, Roxane Smyer, and Susan Albers Mohrman (1994). "New Boundaries for School-Based Management: The High Involvement Model." *Educational Evaluation and Policy Analysis,* 16(3), 268–286.

Wohlstetter, Priscilla, Amy Van Kirk, Peter Robertson, and Susan Mohrman. (1997). *Organizing for Successful School-Based Management.* Alexandria, VA: Association for Supervision and Curriculum Development.

Wood, R. Craig, David Honeyman, and Verne Bryers. (1990). "Equity in Indiana School Finance: A Decade of Local Levy Property Tax Restrictions." *Journal of Education Finance,* 16(1), 83–92.

Wood, R. Craig., David Thompson, Lawrence O. Picus, and Don I. Tharpe. (1995). *Principles of School Business Administration,* 2d ed. Reston, VA: Association of School Business Officials International.

Wyckoff, J. H. (1992). "The Interstate Equality of Public Primary and Secondary Education Resources in the U.S., 1980–1987." *Economics of Education Review.* 11(1), 19–30.

Yee, Sylvia. (1984). *Careers in the Classroom: When Teaching Is More Than a Job.* New York: Teachers College Press.

Author Index

Subject Index